MW01621082

About the authors

Wolfgang Wild is the creator of Retronaut: 'hit records for archives' (*Financial Times*), 'enlightenment and wonder' (*Guardian*), 'literally rocks your brain' (*Fast Company*). Fired for the last time in 2009, Wild started a blog of seemingly anachronistic photographs after his wife told him he was fundamentally unemployable. The blog took off, and he and his helpers published more than 40,000 images on Retronaut.com.

In 2014, Wild licensed Retronaut to the US-based site Mashable, and he continues to oversee the weekly curation and publication of strange and startling archive images, each chosen to show you 'the past like you wouldn't believe'. With 250K Facebook fans and named #20 on *The Times* list of 'The 50 People You Should Follow on Twitter', Wild has written three Retronaut books, the first with National Geographic, and curated two Retronaut shows, including a four-month exhibition in 2016 of New York historic panoramas, on 5th Avenue, New York City.

He lives near Oxford, UK, in an almost painfully quaint Cotswold village with his wife, Annie, and their two children.

Jordan J. Lloyd does colouring in for a living: 'stunning' (*Daily Mail*), 'incredible and beautiful' (*Evening Standard*), 'the past brought to life' (*Guardian*). His work has been commissioned by brands like Jim Beam, Indian Motorcycles and *Surfer Magazine*, and by a range of publishers including *Time Life*. He has been a guest speaker for Apple, Adobe and the British Film Institute. Lloyd collaborates with many archives and museums across the world, and his work has been exhibited in London, Dresden and New York. Hailing from Hong Kong and living in London, Lloyd studied architecture at the University of Sheffield. He also plays bass in punk band Black Radio and competes in roller derby.

THE PAPER TIME MACHINE

COLOURING THE PAST

WOLFGANG WILD & JORDAN LLOYD

A Retronaut Book | The Past Like You Wouldn't Believe

This edition first published in 2017

Unbound
6th Floor Mutual House, 70 Conduit Street, London W1S 2GF
www.unbound.com

Editor: Jo Keeling
Art director: Tina Smith
Designer: Johnathan Montelongo

A CIP record for this book is available from the British Library

ISBN 978-1-78352-373-3 (trade hbk)
ISBN 978-1-78352-375-7 (ebook)
ISBN 978-1-78352-374-0 (limited edition)

Printed in Italy by L.E.G.O. S.p.A.

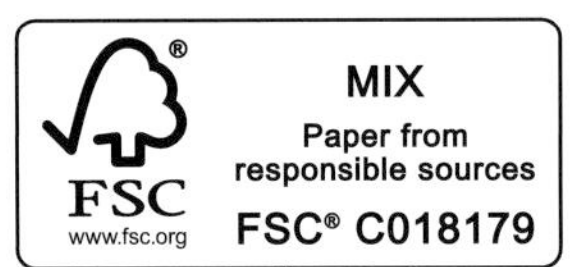

Wolfgang:
This book is dedicated to Charles Shaar Murray, David Jones and Bodger. Charles Shaar Murray introduced me to David, David introduced me to myself, and Bodger stuck around for the ride. Real cool traders.

Jordan:
To Gloria and Paul, who have given me the opportunity to follow the rabbit hole into Wonderland.

Dear Reader,

The book you are holding came about in a rather different way to most others. It was funded directly by readers through a new website: Unbound. Unbound is the creation of three writers. We started the company because we believed there had to be a better deal for both writers and readers. On the Unbound website, authors share the ideas for the books they want to write directly with readers. If enough of you support the book by pledging for it in advance, we produce a beautifully bound special subscribers' edition and distribute a regular edition and e-book wherever books are sold, in shops and online.

This new way of publishing is actually a very old idea (Samuel Johnson funded his dictionary this way). We're just using the internet to build each writer a network of patrons. Here, at the back of this book, you'll find the names of all the people who made it happen.

Publishing in this way means readers are no longer just passive consumers of the books they buy, and authors are free to write the books they really want. They get a much fairer return too – half the profits their books generate, rather than a tiny percentage of the cover price.

If you're not yet a subscriber, we hope that you'll want to join our publishing revolution and have your name listed in one of our books in the future. To get you started, here is a £5 discount on your first pledge. Just visit unbound.com, make your pledge and type TIMEMACHINE in the promo code box when you check out.

Thank you for your support,

Dan, Justin and John
Founders, Unbound

Contents

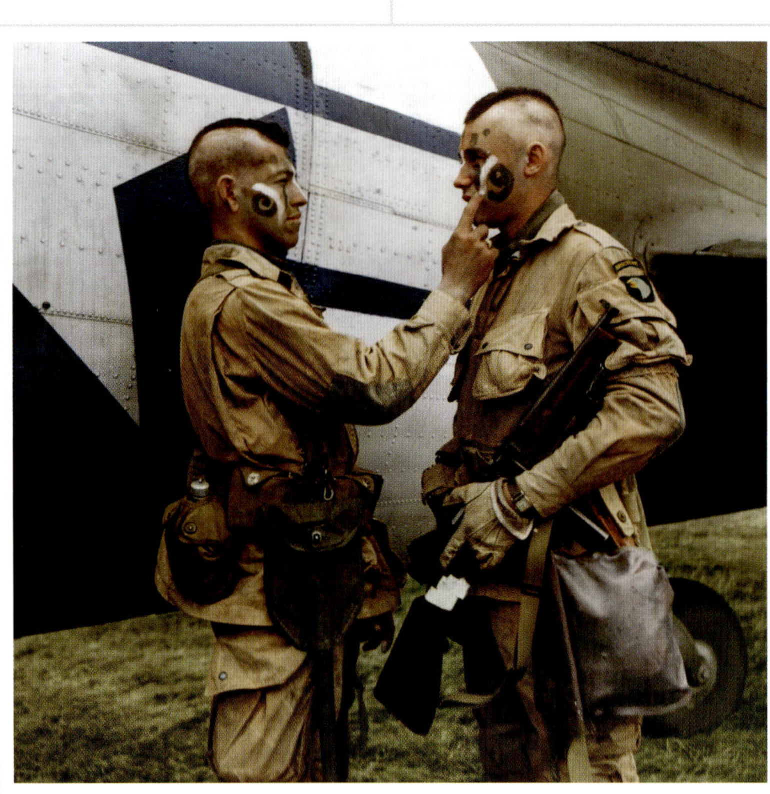

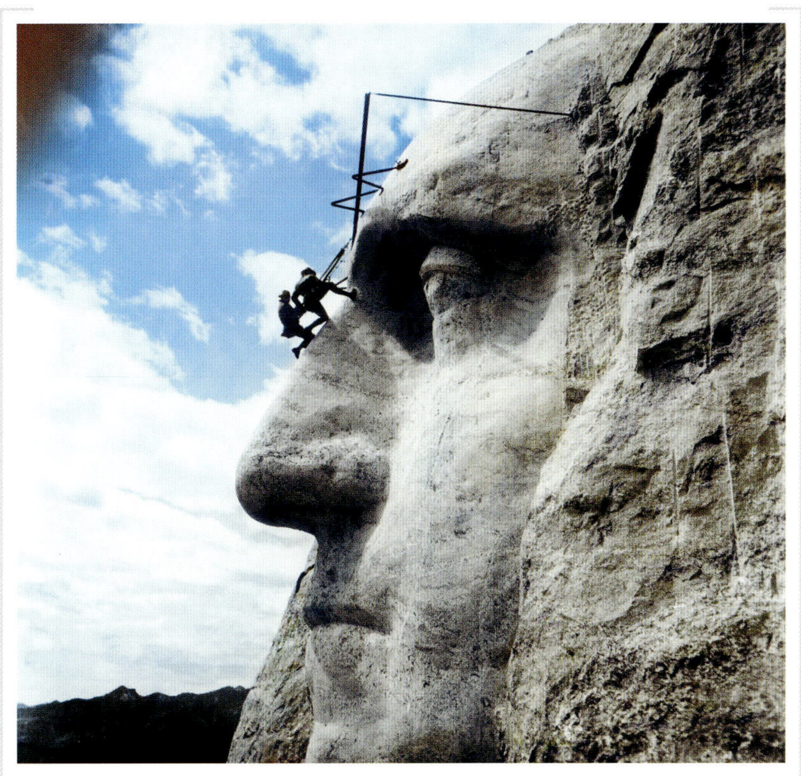

pp. 38–39 | **31 May 1932**
At Mount Rushmore, Gutzon Borglum and another sculptor hang from the forehead of George Washington

pp. 40–41 | ***c.* 1930**
An overhead view of people on 36th Street between 8th and 9th Avenues, in the heart of the Garment District, New York

pp. 42–43 | **1930s**
A Confederate and a Union veteran play cards at a Civil War reunion

pp. 44–45 | **19 October 1929**
Passengers surveying the scene from the verandah deck of the British Airship R100

pp. 46–47 | **1929**
The Airship R100 nears completion at the Royal Naval Air Service Air Station near Howden in Yorkshire

pp. 48–49 | **1928**
Looking down Glasshouse Street to the junction with Sherwood Street and towards the lights of Piccadilly Circus in London

pp. 50–51 | **28 December 1928**
A cameraman and a sound technician record the roar of Leo the Lion for MGM's famous movie ident

pp. 52–53 | **1926**
A flock of sheep walking along the Kingsway in London

pp. 54–55 | **28 March 1925**
Sakura cherry blossom, Potomac Park, Washington DC

pp. 56–57 | **26 June 1925**
A female Native American telephone switchboard operator

pp. 58–59 | **1924**
The 'Hollywoodland' sign in Los Angeles, later changed to read 'Hollywood'

pp. 60–61 | **July 1923**
A punt gun, used to shoot flocks of waterbirds from a punt

pp. 62–63 | **1922**
The contents of the central coffin of Tutankhamun's tomb

pp. 64–65 | **7 September 1921**
Margaret Gorman, the newly crowned Miss America, awaits the arrival of Neptune in her royal robes at the opening of the Atlantic City Beauty Pageant

pp. 66–67 | **1921**
Sound amplifiers at Bolling Field Air Force Base, Washington DC

pp. 68–69 | ***c.* 1920**
A view of a trilithon being re-erected at Stonehenge

pp. 70–71 | **1920**
Power house mechanic working on steam pump

pp. 72–73 | **1919**
Soldiers of the 369th 'Harlem Hellfighters' wearing the Cross of War medal pose for a photo on their trip back to New York

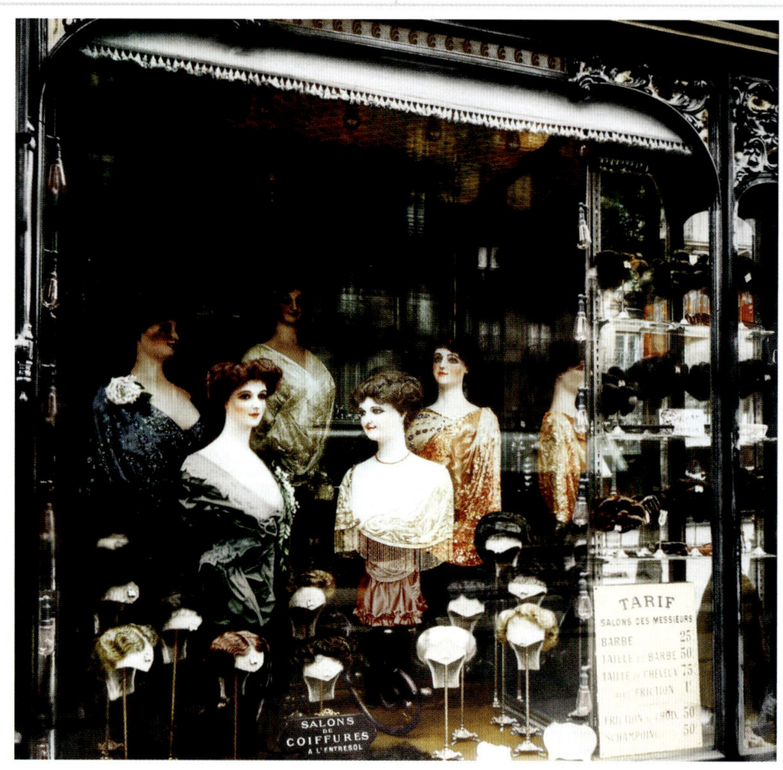
SALONS DE COIFFURES
TARIF

'The Broadway crowds proved that my rapid-fire picture machine was a gold mine'

Anatol Josepho, *Modern Mechanics*, November 1928

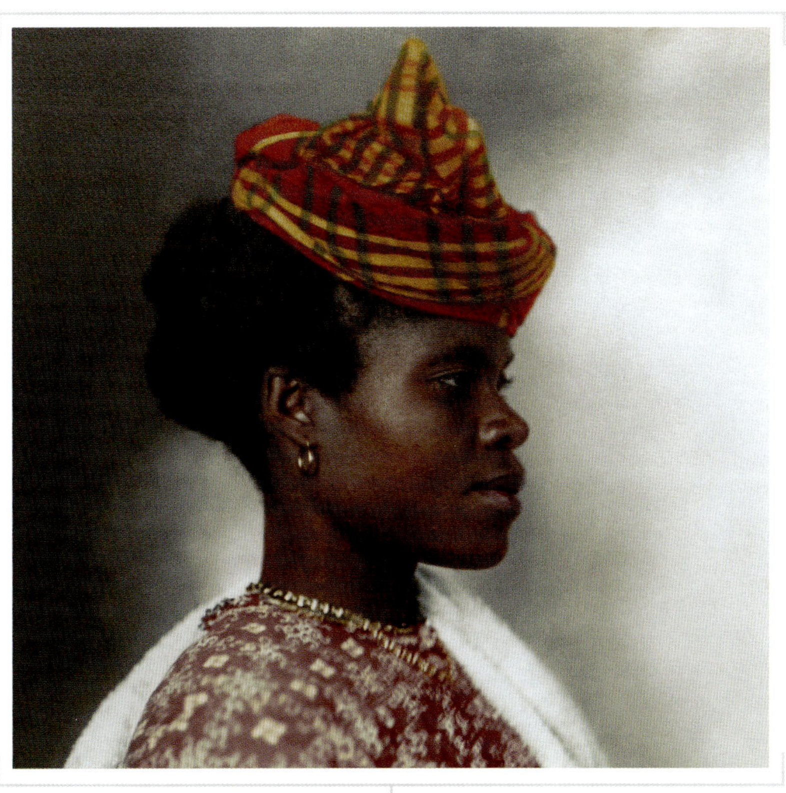

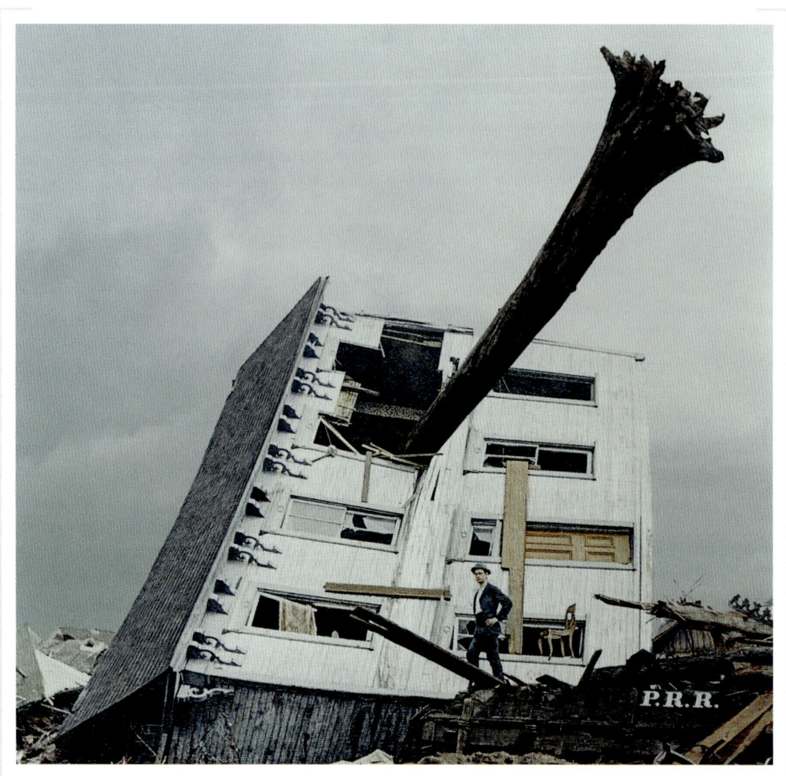

'The soldier's long term of service, and the restrictions upon his marriage, act as a direct encouragement to drunkenness and debauchery'

The British Army in 1868, Sir Charles E. Trevelyan

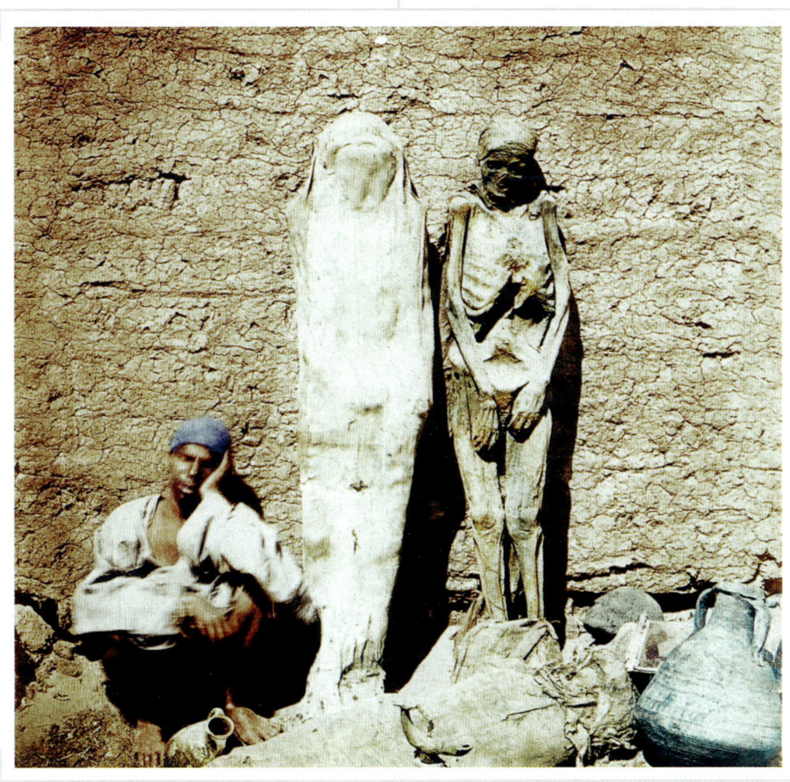

THE PAPER TIME MACHINE

COLOURING THE PAST

Step into the time machine

For many of us, the past was in black and white.

Logically, of course, we know that wasn't the case, just as we know that the people we see walking very fast in films at the turn of the twentieth century didn't actually walk as if speeded-up. But still, when we see an old black-and-white photograph, it tends to fit with the way we think the past was.

One reason for this is that we've all seen so many black-and-white pictures – online and also in the albums and shoeboxes of our family collections. We assume, perhaps subconsciously, that what we are looking at is the past, rather than simply a photographic impression of the past. The older a photograph is, the more likely it is to be in black and white – and, also, the more likely it is to be small, faded, scratched, even torn. The photographic record of the past often has those qualities, but we map those qualities onto the past itself.

But we're wrong. The past wasn't small, faded, scratched, torn – or in black and white. It was – as the 'never-ending now' always is – big, clear, sharp, complete and saturated in colour. The past and the present were the same, are the same, and what has changed is not the nature of the present moment, but rather the technical recording capabilities of our cameras.

Ever since I can remember, the idea of going back in time has captivated me. In 2010, I started Retronaut to share the archive photographs I had discovered that, for me, disrupted the way I imagined the past. When I saw a picture like this, it tore a hole in my internal map of time. My mind did a double take: a sort of temporal vertigo, if you like. This experience, this Retronautic hit, was the closest I could get to fulfilling my childhood dream of travelling back in time.

One of the most powerful ways a photograph could disrupt my idea of the past was for it to be in colour. A handful of inventors had experimented with colour in the late 1800s and, in 1907, the Lumière brothers brought the first commercial photographic process to the market: the Autochrome. Even so, colour photography remained very much the exception before the Second World War. The number of glimpses we have into the colour of the past is tantalisingly few.

In June 2015, I saw the colourisation work of Jordan J. Lloyd. Since starting Retronaut, I had seen many examples of photo colourisation – photographs that were originally monochrome, which had colour added to them digitally. The process is incredibly painstaking yet, in nearly every instance, these colourised photographs left me cold. One element or another of the colour would just feel ever so slightly off, and the illusion would be over before it had begun.

In Jordan's work, however, I encountered something curious – or, rather, two things. The first was that, in many of Jordan's pieces, I simply couldn't tell whether I was looking at an original colour photograph or a colourised image, so well-executed were the results.

The second curious thing was this – after a while, I ceased to notice the colour at all. For me, Jordan's colourisation was so good that the colour was rendered invisible, and all I saw was the extreme reality of the past, presented to me in a new, visceral way. Jordan's work propelled me into the past like you wouldn't believe.

It then occurred to me: what if we were to take photographs that already had a Retronautic quality – photographs that, in monochrome, already disrupted the way I imagined the past – and then apply Jordan's techniques? Would we get even closer to my childhood dream of time travel?

The Paper Time Machine is the result.

A number of people object to all image colourisation. Some comment that a photograph is a work of art, created by an artist, and it is at the very least presumptive, if not immoral, to tamper with a piece that the artist regarded as complete. Others see the addition of colour as an act of 'dumbing down', as though the viewer is regarded as incapable of appreciating photographs unless they are in colour, or as not having the imagination to know that the past was a colourful place. Still others say that the monochrome images are simply visually stronger and more beautiful, and that adding colour is a form of cultural vandalism.

We certainly understand these points of view. Jordan recognises the integrity of the original photographs, and of the intent of their creators. We do not suggest that these versions of the original photographs are equal to the original, let alone substitutes. We also know that people are perfectly able to enjoy monochrome images, visually, historically and artistically.

Visual cover versions

Alongside this, as Jordan mentions at the end of the book, photographic colourisation dates back to the very beginning of photography. The daguerreotype – the first publicly presented process for photography – was introduced to the world in 1839 by Louis Daguerre. Less than a year later, Johann Baptist Isenring created the first colourised daguerreotypes. Vast numbers of photographs were hand-coloured across the nineteenth century and, perhaps surprisingly, the practice was at its height between 1900 and 1940.

Our own approach is perhaps best explained by the fact that Jordan and I are both musicians. We are familiar with the fact that when an artist records a song – for example, 'Yesterday' by The Beatles – other artists will often regularly re-record the same song. 'Yesterday', with 1,600 versions, is currently the most covered song of all time. We don't believe those cover versions detract from the original – quite the opposite, in fact. Each version shows a new facet of the song and will almost certainly prompt you to listen to The Beatles' original version again. For us, these photographs are visual cover versions.

The photographs I chose with Jordan reflect something of the sweep of photographic history from the 1830s until just after the Second World War. The earliest, surviving known photograph in the world dates from either 1826 or 1827, and *The Paper Time Machine* goes

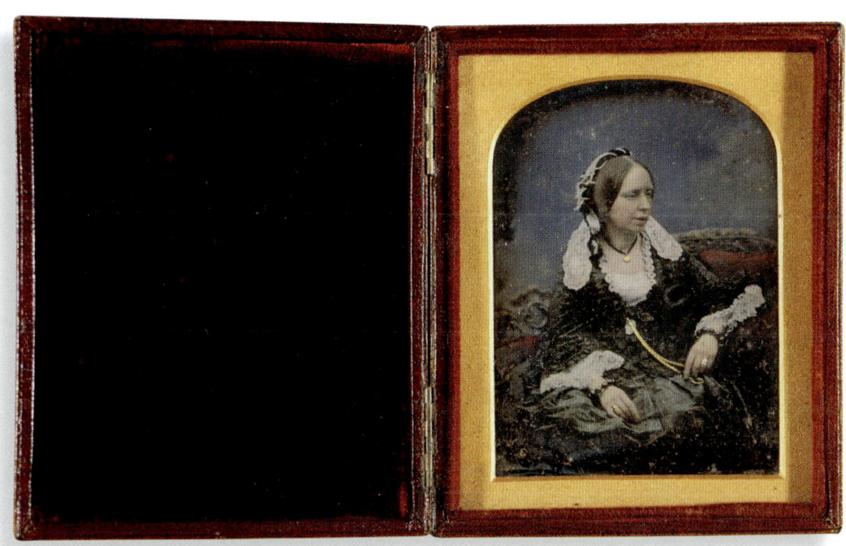

▲ **c. 1850** - Hand-coloured daguerreotype portrait of a woman (Antoine Claudet / The Finnish Museum of Photography)

back to within almost a decade of that date, with the Robert Cornelius self-portrait of 1839 (p. 208).

A handful of the photographs in this book are extremely well known, such as Lewis Hine's Power house mechanic (p. 70) and The train wreck at Montparnasse (p. 144). Others are taken by celebrated photographers, such as Margaret Bourke-White (p. 40), Roger Fenton (p. 200), Dorothea Lange (pp. 16, 18, 20, 24) and Henry Fox Talbot (p. 206).

Some photographs are of well-known people such as blues singer Robert Johnson (p. 28), suffragette Emmeline Pankhurst (p. 94), aviator Louis Blériot (p. 112), Alexander Graham Bell (p. 122), Jesse James (p. 186) and Abraham Lincoln (p. 204). Also of famous events: the discovery of Tutankhamen's tomb (p. 62), the Armistice (p. 76), the sinking of the *Titanic* (p. 102), the American Civil War (pp. 188, 190, 192). Most of the pictures in *The Paper Time Machine*, however, are not of famous subjects, and are (as far as we can determine) by unknown photographers. Whatever the subject and whoever the photographer, our one goal has been to find photographic material capable of disrupting our collective sense of time.

We chose to start *The Paper Time Machine* just after the end of the Second World War; the most recent photograph is Stanley Kubrick's photograph of the Chicago Theatre in 1949 (p. 4). This is because, as colour photography became more widely available after the war, we have a tendency to imagine the post-war world in increasing amounts of colour. The effect of *The Paper Time Machine* is at its strongest when we are not expecting to see any colour at all.

In order to make *The Paper Time Machine* an even more powerful vehicle, we have also drawn on original comments, speeches, reports and other documentary material to bring the photographs into the now.

Having worked with Jordan on this book for eighteen months, I now know what it is about his approach that caused it to have such a strong impact on me, and what it is about his craft that, in my view, sets him apart as a colouriser. It is his research. Jordan uses exhaustive – and exhausting – levels of research concerning every single detail in a photograph. His goal is, wherever possible, to eliminate guesswork from his results, and even to eliminate his own subjective views and preferences, in order to create as accurate a reconstruction as possible. His goal is impossible to achieve, yet the fact that he reaches for it gives his images true depth.

You will notice that the overall feel of the colour is very different from one picture to another. This is a factor of the underlying black-and-white information in the original photograph and, in particular, the levels of contrast across the image. What this means in practice is that for some pictures, such as of the XB-35 (p. 8), the colour appears super-sharp and precise. For other pictures, such as of the construction of Nelson's Column (p. 206), the colour becomes much less distinct. Jordan allows the original photograph to dictate the way the colour sits, and the result is a wide-ranging array of treatments, each working in harmony with the photographic source.

Removing the black and white

In all but one case, Jordan has also restored any damage to the original photograph: the fading, the scratches and the tears. To do this without undermining the historic information within the photograph is a delicate task. Jordan seeks to use as little correction as possible and, as you will see in his notes at the end of this book, is very clear about where he has repaired damage. The delicacy of his approach is self-evident to me and can yield spectacular results – witness the original picture of Lincoln in comparison to the colourised result (p. 204).

The one exception to this approach is the last photograph of the book: Robert Cornelius's self-portrait (p. 208). Rather than attempt to digitally repair the extensive damage to the original plate, we decided to take a different route, and hinted at the colour lying behind the damage. The result is one of my favourite pictures in the book.

As we were finishing *The Paper Time Machine*, I realised something else about Jordan's work, and perhaps about the nature of the past itself. Although it may sound somewhat contrary, the pictures you see in this book are, in fact, not ones to which Jordan has added colour – or, at least, that is not his intention. For Jordan, and for me, the colour doesn't need to be 'added' to the past; the past was in colour already. Rather than adding colour, what Jordan does – and what we have both sought to do – is to remove the black and white, literally and also metaphorically. The black and white, the filters through which we see the past, belong to each of us. We imagine the past in black and white, but it never was.

Wolfgang Wild

1949: People arriving at the Chicago Theatre

North State Street, Chicago, USA (Stanley Kubrick / Look Magazine / Library of Congress)

Stanley Kubrick is a hugely significant figure in the history of cinema, directing thirteen major feature films, including *Spartacus*, *A Clockwork Orange*, *The Shining*, *Full Metal Jacket* and the groundbreaking *2001: A Space Odyssey*.

Prior to his film career, the young Kubrick was an apprentice photographer at *Look* magazine. Initially using a camera for his school publication, he was offered an apprenticeship at *Look* after he submitted a photograph.

This picture of people arriving at the Chicago Theatre in Chicago is drawn from a set of pictures the twenty-one-year-old Kubrick took for the *Look* series 'Chicago: City of Extremes'. The theatre production in question, starring Jack Carson, Marion Hutton and Robert Alda, was *John Loves Mary*, a farce.

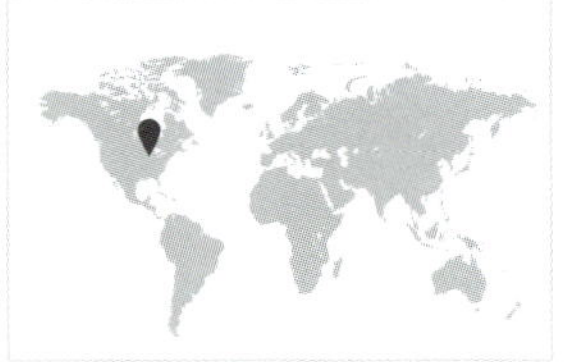

'Among the many plays that come to Broadway every season there may be one or two which have a long post-Broadway life ahead of them. The latest prospect for these happy ranks is *John Loves Mary*. Into his play, author Norman Krasna has packed all the ingredients for a good amateur show.'

LIFE magazine, 14 April 1947

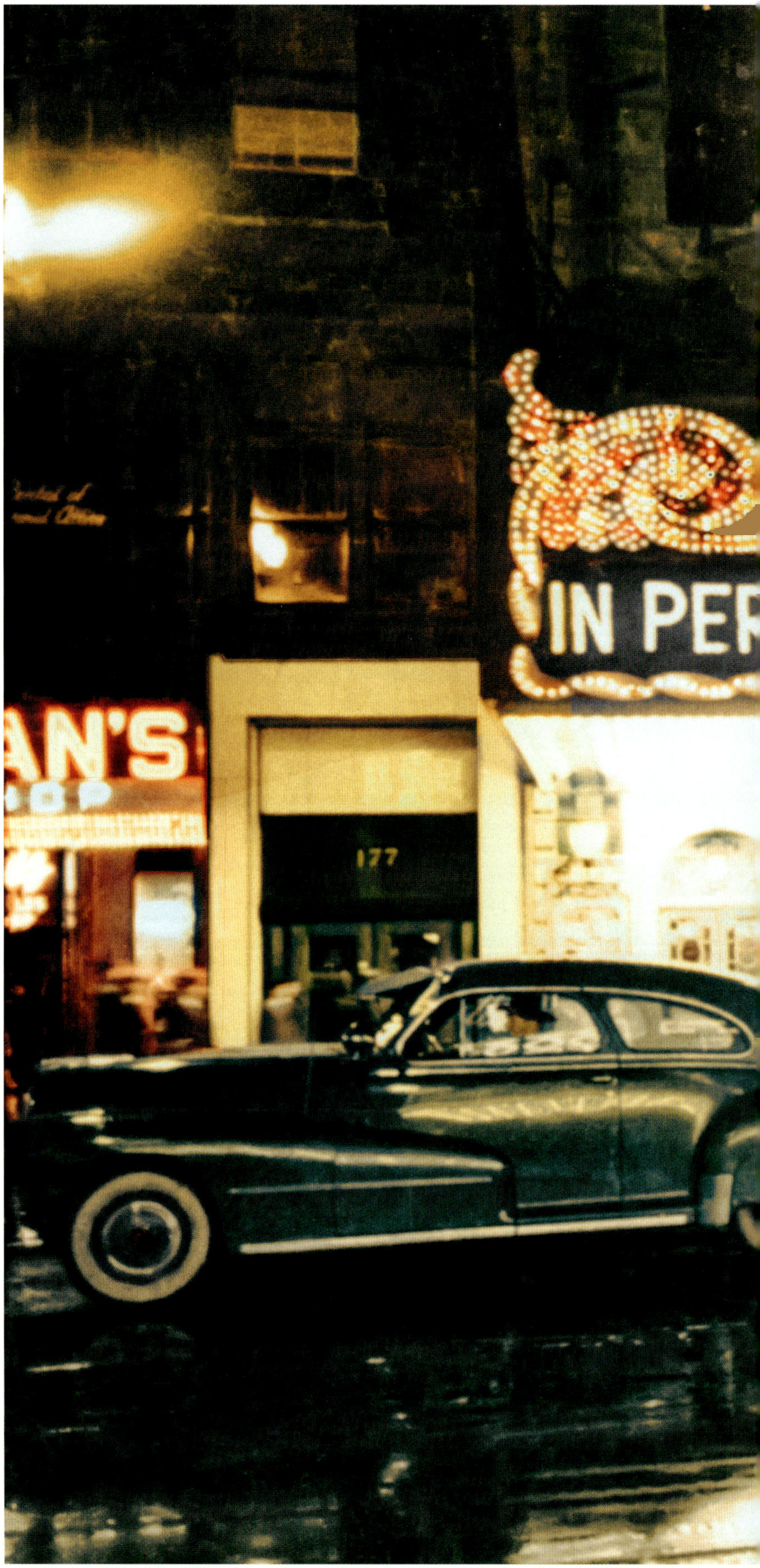

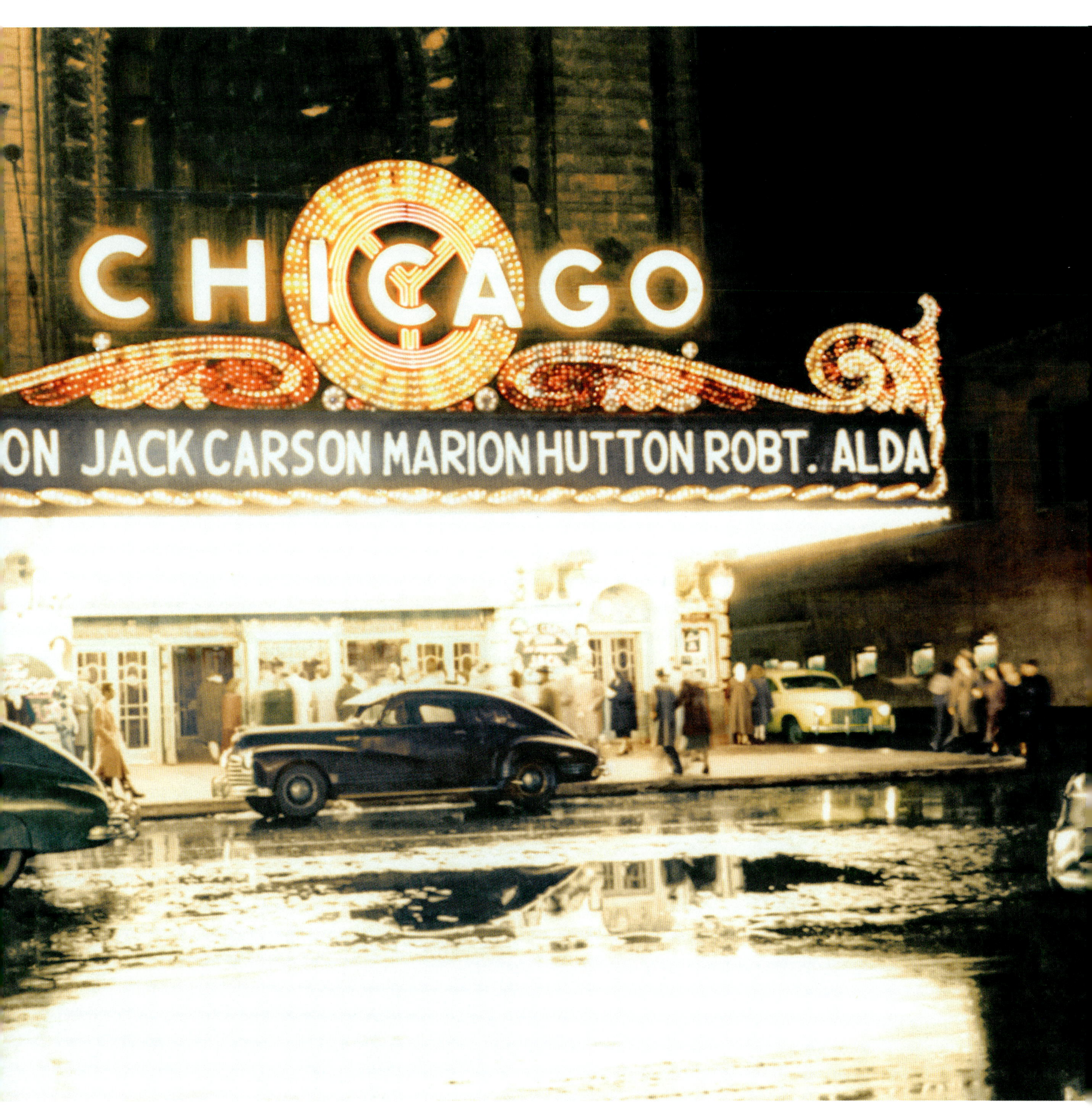
CHICAGO
ON JACK CARSON MARION HUTTON ROBT. ALDA

1940s

July 1947: **Portrait of Art Hodes, Kaiser Marshall, Henry (Clay) Goodwin, Sandy Williams and Cecil (Xavier) Scott**
Times Square, New York City, USA
(William Gottlieb / Library of Congress)

Although born in Ukraine, jazz pianist Art Hodes was brought up in Chicago and spent most of his career in 'The Windy City'. Hodes became known for the Chicago jazz style, but in order to find success, he had to move to New York in 1938.

Here, Hodes and his River Boat Jazz Band – Joseph 'Kaiser' Marshall on drums, Henry 'Clay' Goodwin on trumpet, Sandy Williams on trombone and Cecil 'Xavier' Scott on clarinet and tenor sax – are playing on a horse-drawn cart to promote their concert that night. They are accompanied by special guests Louis Armstrong and Jack Teagarden.

Writer and self-taught photographer William P. Gottlieb spent ten years between 1938 and 1948 interviewing and photographing the leading, largely New York-based jazz musicians of the time, including Duke Ellington, Ella Fitzgerald, Dizzy Gillespie and Billie Holiday. A columnist for the *Washington Post*, Gottlieb started to take his own pictures when the *Post* wouldn't pay a photographer.

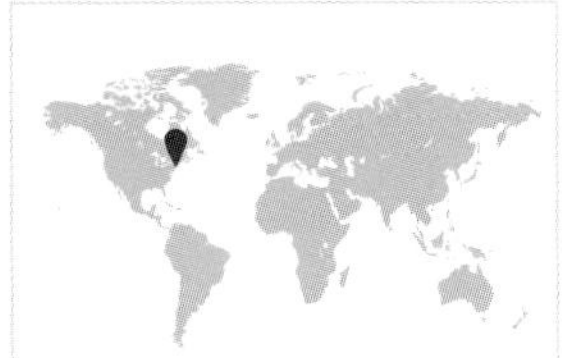

'Go back as far as you like – to the very beginnings of jazz. You'll find that the jazz people were making this music on any instrument they could lay their hands on. People were saying something on anything they could find; the lack of a lacquered horn didn't keep you from telling your story. That was the big thing – the story.'

Art Hodes, *Down Beat* magazine, 1964

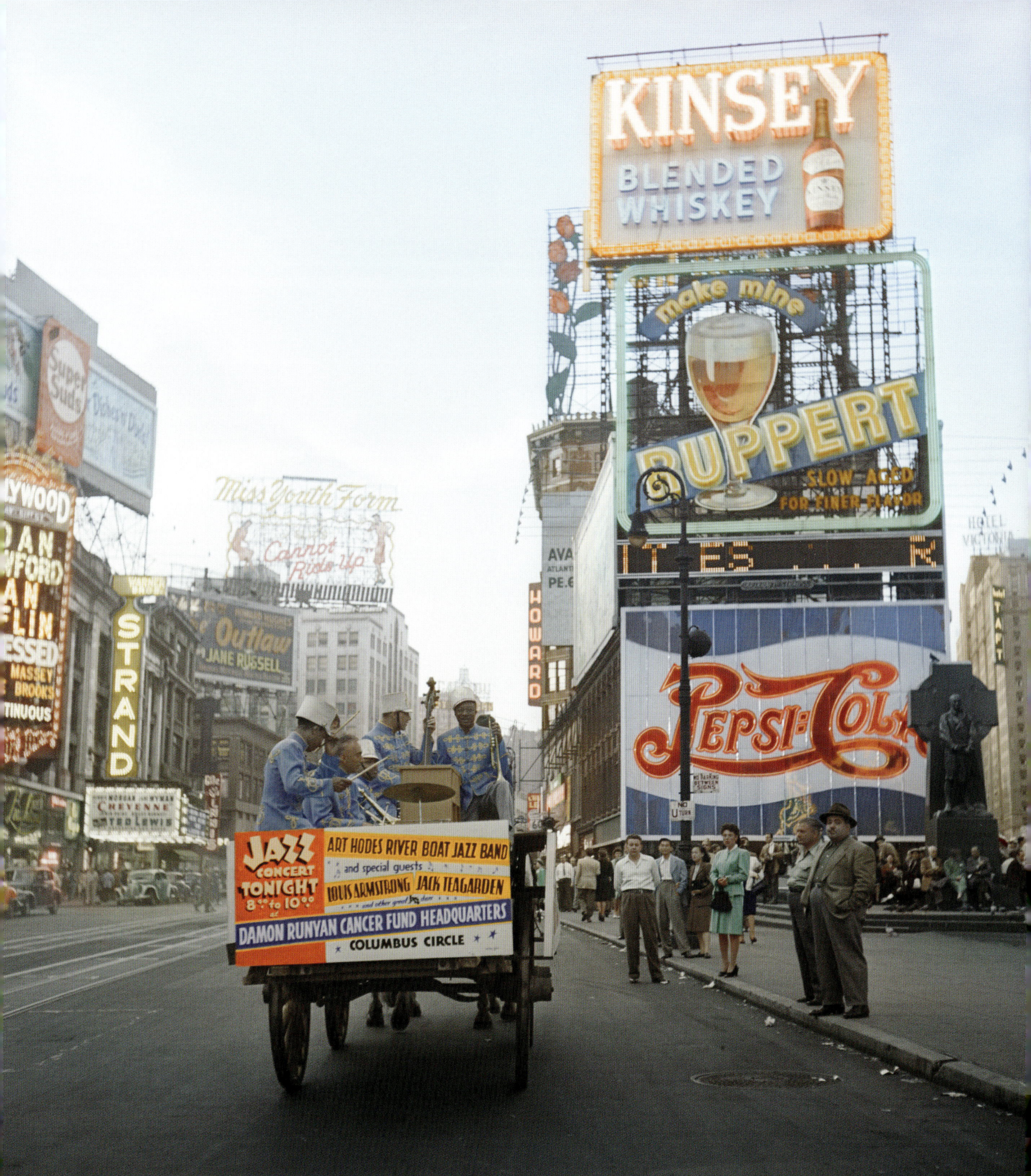
KINSEY
BLENDED WHISKEY
make mine
RUPPERT
SLOW AGED
FOR FINER FLAVOR
Miss Youth Form
Cannot Ride Up
Outlaw
JANE RUSSELL
STRAND
HOWARD
CHEYENNE
TED LEWIS
MASSEY
BROOKS
JAZZ
CONCERT
TONIGHT
8 to 10
ART HODES RIVER BOAT JAZZ BAND
and special guests
LOUIS ARMSTRONG
JACK TEAGARDEN
DAMON RUNYAN CANCER FUND HEADQUARTERS
COLUMBUS CIRCLE

1940s

25 May 1946: Northrop's XB-35 Flying Wing Bomber is wheeled onto the runway for its first taxi tests
Hawthorne, California, USA
(Unknown / Underwood Archive / Getty)

The Northrop XB-35 heavy bomber aircraft was an experimental craft created for the US Army towards the end of the Second World War, using a 'flying wing' design. The plane had a crew of nine, a maximum speed of 393 miles per hour, a range of 8,150 miles and the capacity to carry more than 51,000 pounds of bombs, supported by twenty machine guns in six turrets.

The initial impetus for the project was to create a strategic bomber, an American-based craft capable of bombing European enemy locations in the event that Britain fell to the Axis powers. However, the first flight by an XB-35 occurred after the war, in June 1946.

Ultimately, for reasons of stability, the craft did not reach full production, and the two prototype XB-35s in existence were scrapped in 1949. Its successor, the jet-powered YB-49, encountered similar problems and was axed as well.

'Initial Press Releases could certainly lead the average citizen to believe that the success of "this bat-like bomber, which can carry more bombs farther and faster than any aircraft in history" was already proven, and the statement that it can "get off the ground with sixty tons of bombs, and fly 10,000 miles with a 'substantial' bomb load..." should be enough to give any taxpayer a superiority complex for a week.'

Flight International magazine, 20 June 1946

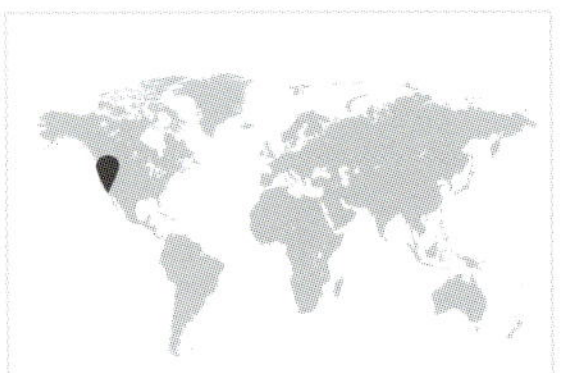

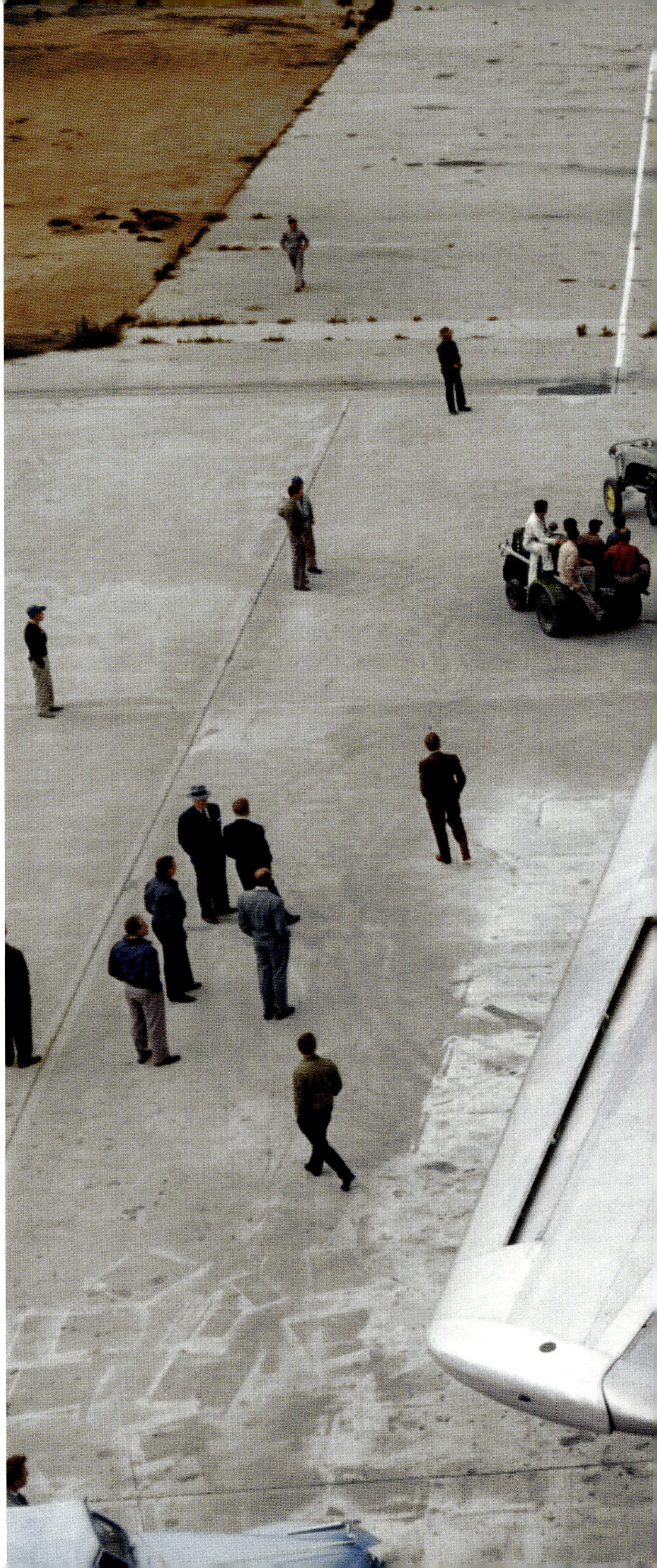

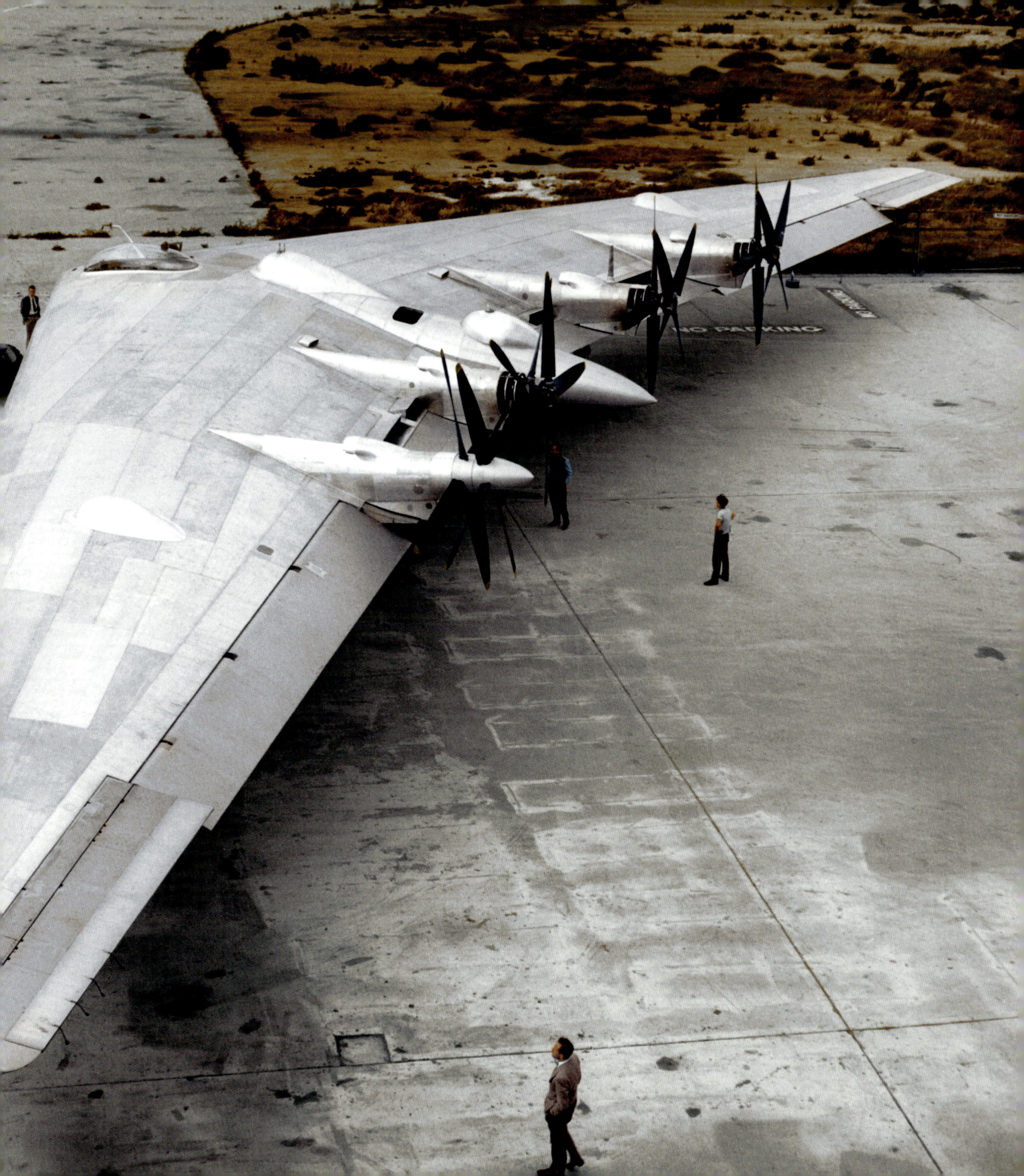
NO PARKING

1940s

June 1944: Private Ware applies last-second make-up to Private Plaudo

Exeter Airfield, Devon, UK
(US National Archives)

Private Clarence Ware and Private Charles 'Chuck' Plaudo were members of the 'Filthy Thirteen' or, to use the more prosaic name, the 1st Demolition Section of the Regimental Headquarters Company of the 506th Parachute Infantry Regiment, 101st Airborne Division. The work of the Demolition Section was to parachute behind enemy lines and demolish targets – arguably, suicide missions. The unit was unofficial.

A Demolition Section had thirteen men: two squads of six men each plus a section sergeant. Prior to D-Day, while stationed in Britain, the Section poached game – illegally – and cooked it in their water ration, rather than using the water to wash, shave and clean their uniforms, hence 'filthy'.

The mohawks and warpaint were inspired by Jake McNiece, the unit sergeant, who was part Choctaw Native American. McNiece would go on to make four combat jumps, an extremely high number for a paratrooper.

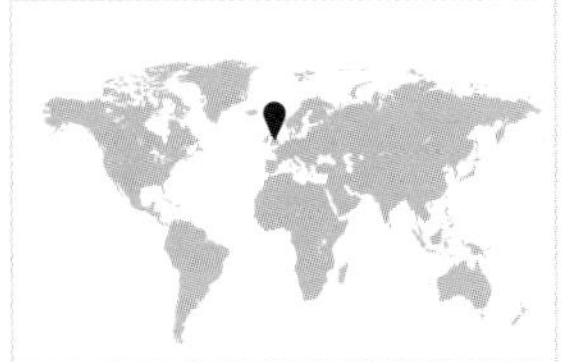

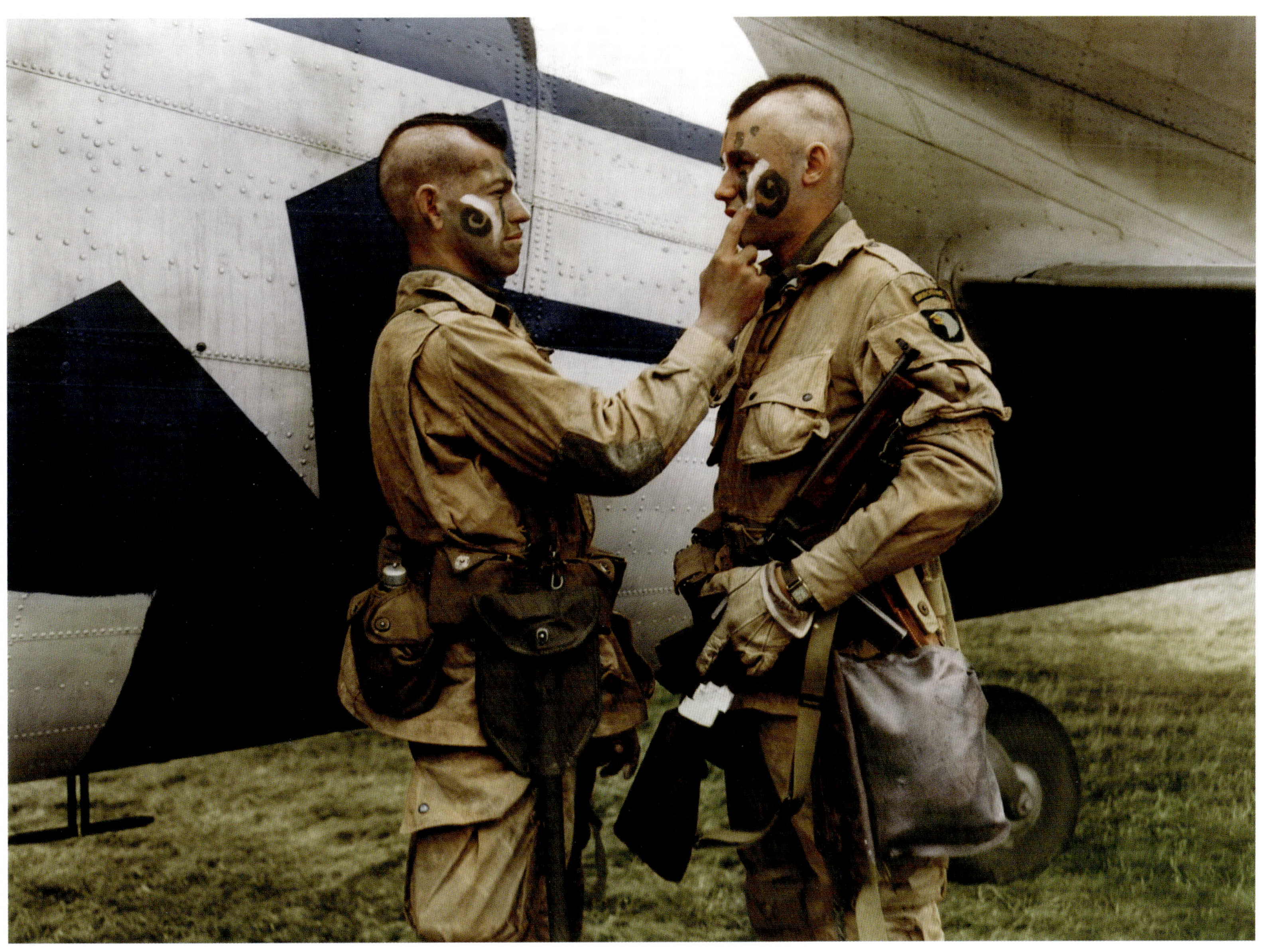

'We weren't murderers or nothing, we just didn't do everything we were supposed to do in some ways and did a whole lot more than they wanted us to do in other ways. We were always in trouble.'

Jack Agnew, member of the 'Filthy Thirteen'

1940s

1943: **A Douglas SBD 'Dauntless' dive bomber balanced on its nose after crash-landing on a carrier flight deck**
Pacific Theatre of War
(Library of Congress)

The Second World War US Navy Douglas SBD 'Dauntless' was a two-person scout craft and dive bomber – SBD stood for Scout Bomber Douglas. With a range of 1,115 miles, a maximum speed of 255 miles per hour and a bombing load of 2,250 pounds, it was an extremely successful aircraft in battle. First used at Pearl Harbour, and then across the Pacific Campaign and in Europe, in total almost 6,000 SBDs were built.

The SBD is best known for its role in the June 1942 Battle of Midway, when SBD squadrons attacked four Japanese fleet carriers, sinking or fatally damaging all four.

Towards the end of the war, the US Navy gradually replaced the SBD with the Curtiss SB2C Helldiver, an aircraft with more power.

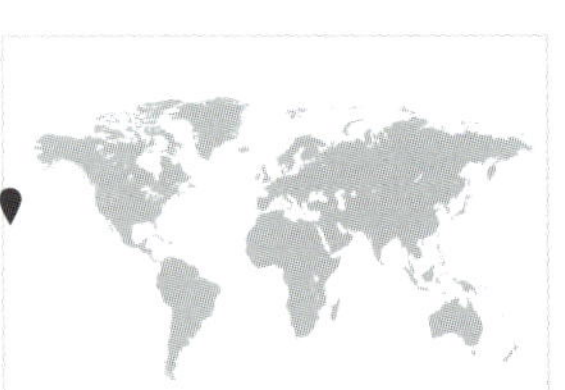

'The Japs know and have learned to fear the DOUGLAS SBD Dauntless dive bomber. In screaming plunges from 20,000 feet, these tough planes have ripped and torn the Nipponese fleet in the Pacific, dealing heavy, blasting, knock-out punches.'

Reed Kinert, *America's Fighting Planes in Action*, 1943

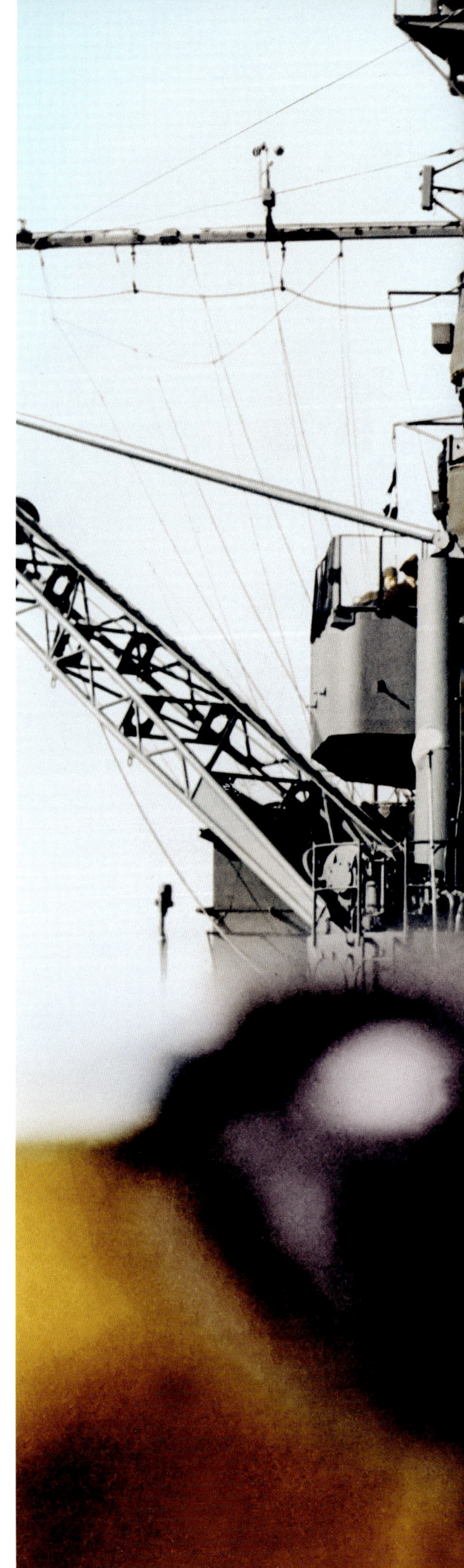

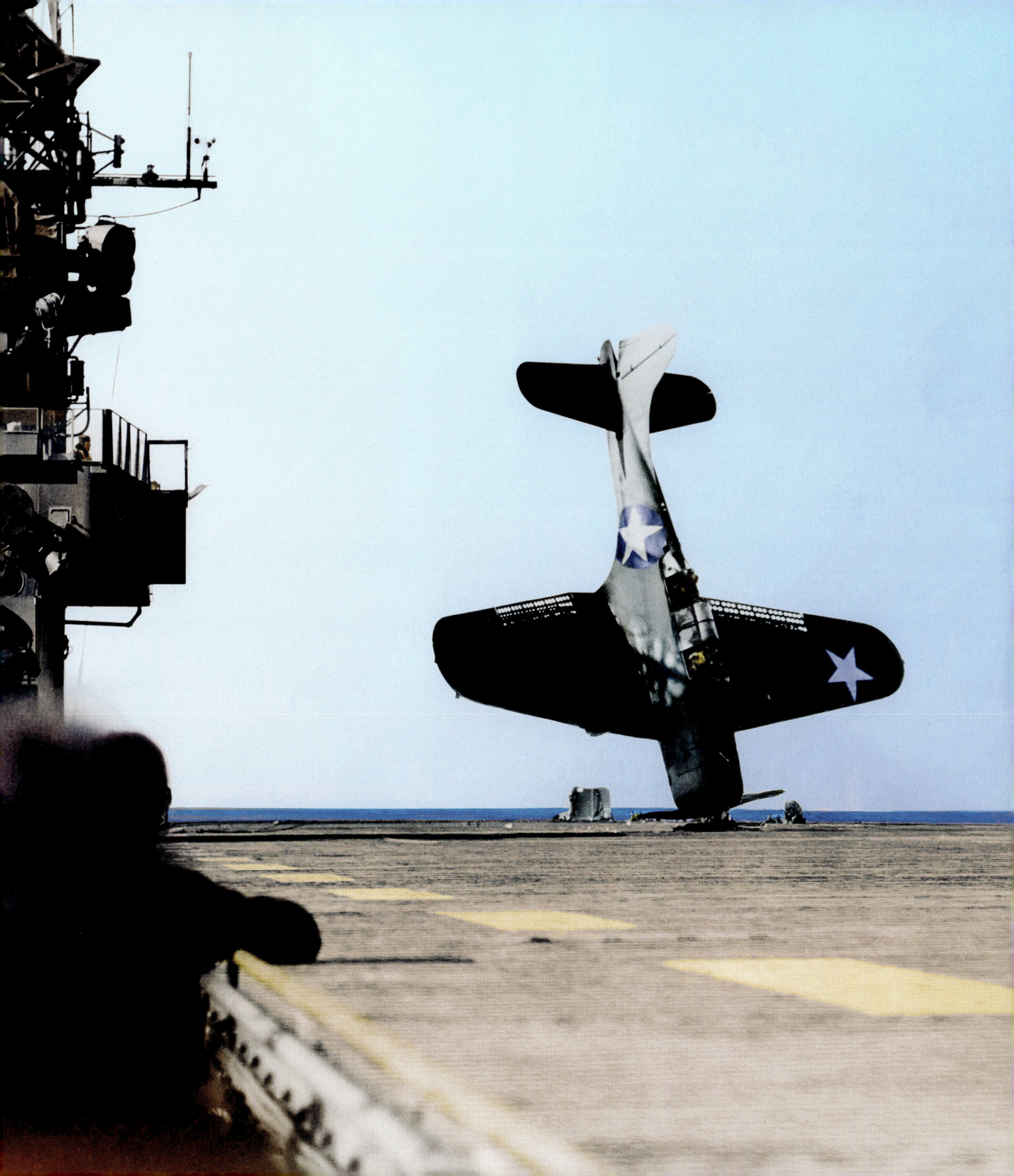

1940s

1942: Members of the US Signal Corps at the Taj Mahal in protective bamboo scaffolding
Agra, Uttar Pradesh, India
(Unknown / Library of Congress)

During the Second World War, the Taj Mahal was covered in a layer of bamboo scaffolding in an attempt to disguise it from Japanese and other Axis power fighter and bomber aircraft.

Signal Corps member Private First Class John C. Byrom Jr of Waco, Texas, appears to be trying to catch a goldfish in the marble-lined pool while Corporal Anthony J. Scopelliti and Private First Class Ray Cherry look on.

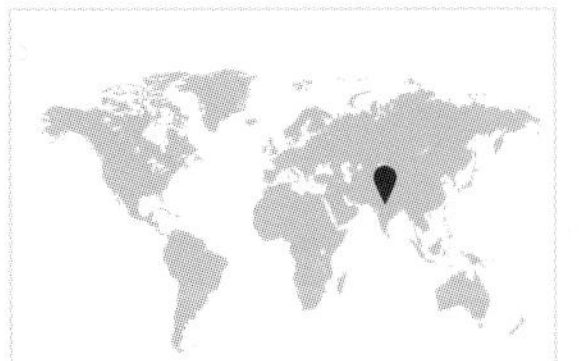

'The generals, the colonels, all the officers depend upon the Signal Corps to "get the message through". If we fall down, the general can't control his division. We are always working directly for the top people. Don't waste your time while you are here. The American Army is depending on the Signal Corps to deliver the goods.'

'Why You Are Here: A Message for the Signal Corps Soldier', 1943

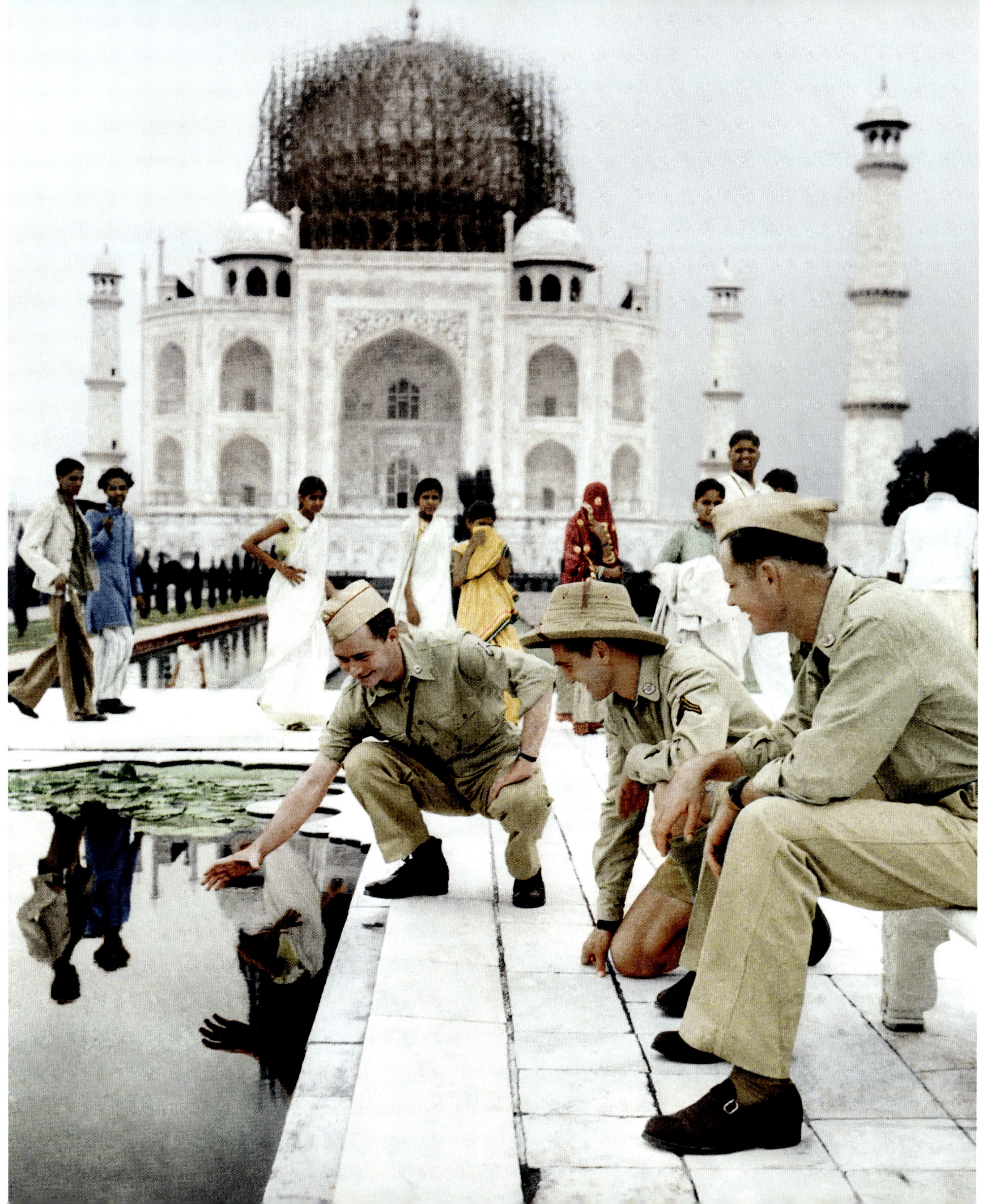

1940s

1942: Grandfather of Japanese ancestry teaching his grandson to walk at Manzanar War Relocation Authority Centre
Manzanar, California, USA
(Dorothea Lange / Library of Congress)

After the Japanese attack on Pearl Harbour in December 1941, around 120,000 Japanese Americans were forcibly removed from their homes. Leaving their businesses and goods behind, they were transferred to concentration camps, known as 'relocation centres'. Around 80,000 were native-born American citizens.

Documentary photographer Dorothea Lange took this image at the Manzanar camp, north-east of Los Angeles. More than 10,000 people were detained at the 500-acre camp. Like all such camps, Manzanar was treated as a military installation, with towers, barbed wire perimeters and armed guards. Before Manzanar closed at the end of 1945, 146 people had died as camp internees.

Lange created a significant body of work in the Depression era, working for the US Farm Security Administration. Born Dorothea Nutzhorn, her parents were second-generation immigrants from Germany. Awarded a Guggenheim Fellowship in 1941, she resigned in order to photograph the forced evacuation of Japanese Americans. Most of her images were seen as critical by the military, and were impounded for more than five decades.

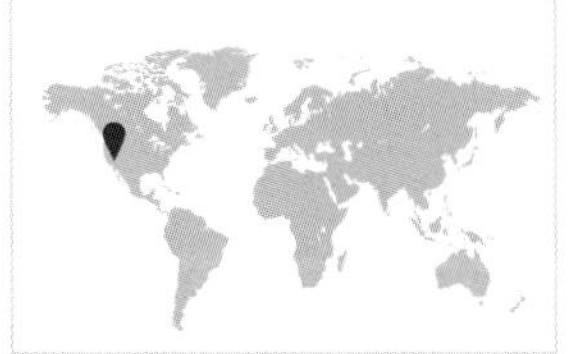

'The director of Manzanar has issued a detailed statement, showing that the food quotas there are no greater than elsewhere, and in some instances less. A good many reports have circulated as to the soft living, in the Jap camps, with intimation that our compulsory guests were being pampered with all the meat, sugar and butter they wanted, and that much of it was wasted. The rumour has been laid low at Manzanar.'

Madera Tribune, 4 February 1943

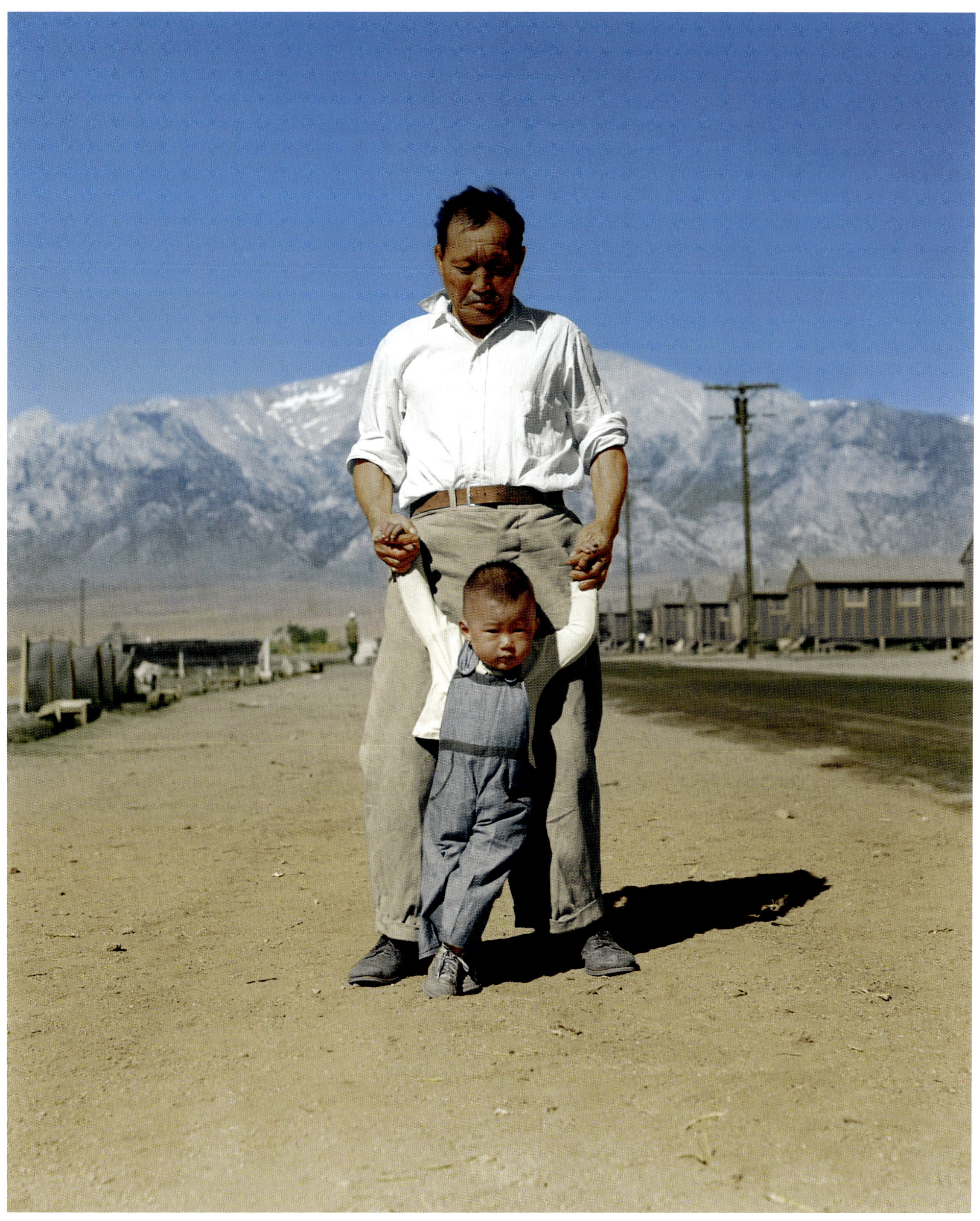

1930s

July 1939: Country store on dirt road, Sunday afternoon
Gordonton, North Carolina, USA
(Dorothea Lange / Library of Congress)

Dorothea Lange's photograph of a country store on a dirt road in Gordonton, North Carolina, was taken on a Sunday afternoon in July 1939, on behalf of the Farm Security Administration.

Lange's notes point out the gasoline pump on the right of the door, and a kerosene pump to the left. She also notes, 'Rough, unfinished timber posts have been used as supports for porch roof. The man standing in the doorway is the brother of the store owner.' While the pumps and signs no longer exist, the store still stands.

'My own approach is based upon three considerations: First – hands off! Whenever I photograph I do not molest or tamper with or arrange. Second – a sense of place. I try to picture as part of its surroundings, as having roots. Third – a sense of time. Whatever I photograph, I try to show as having its position in the past or in the present.'

Dorothea Lange

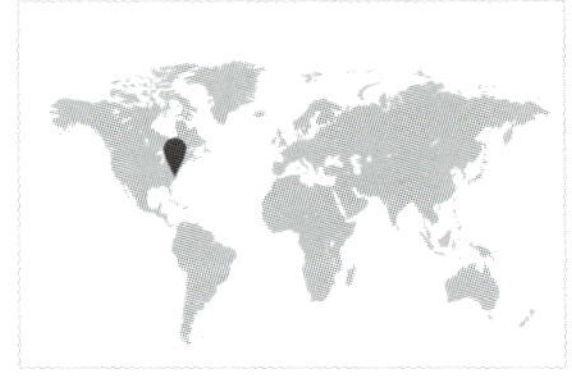

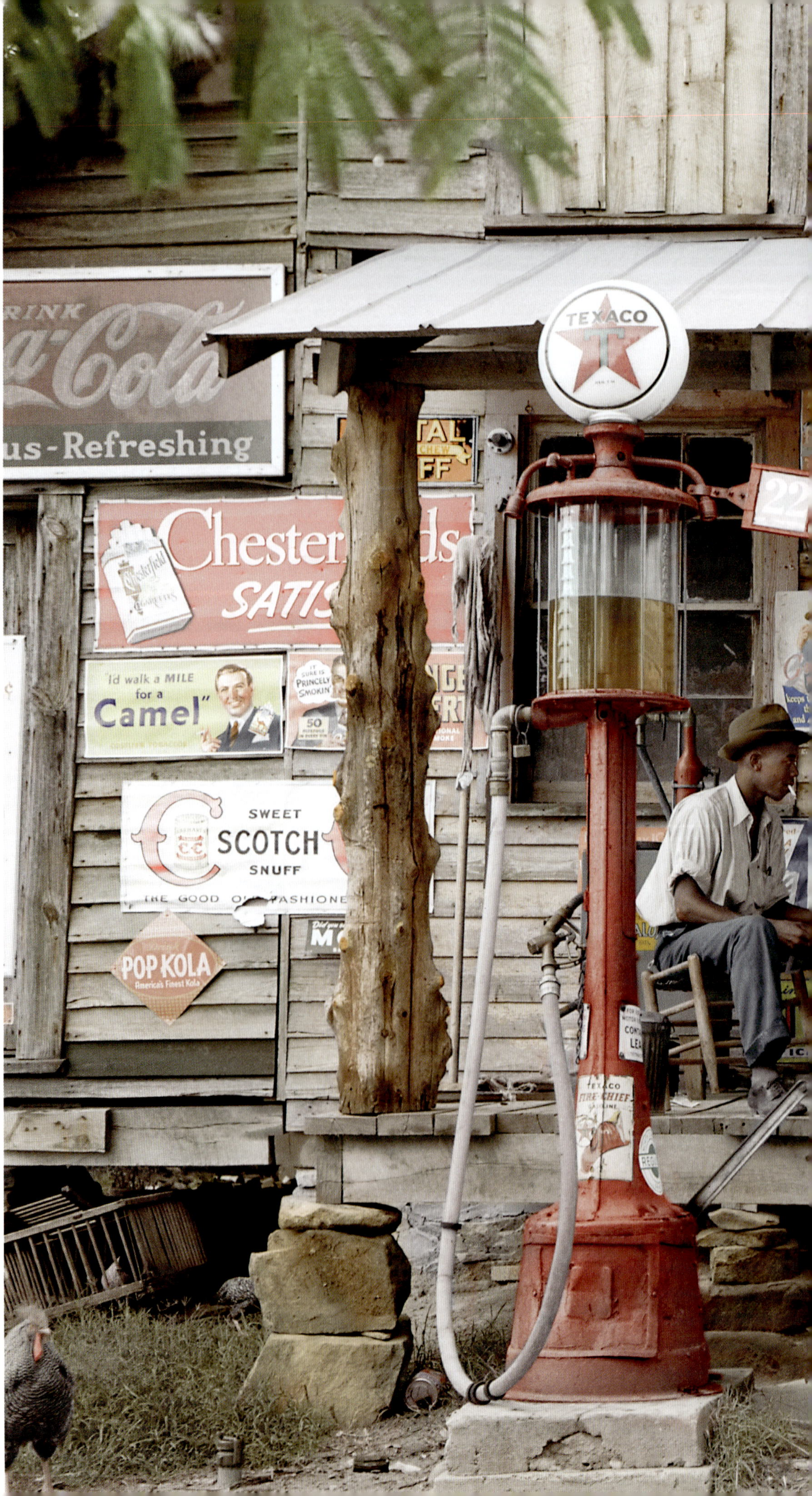

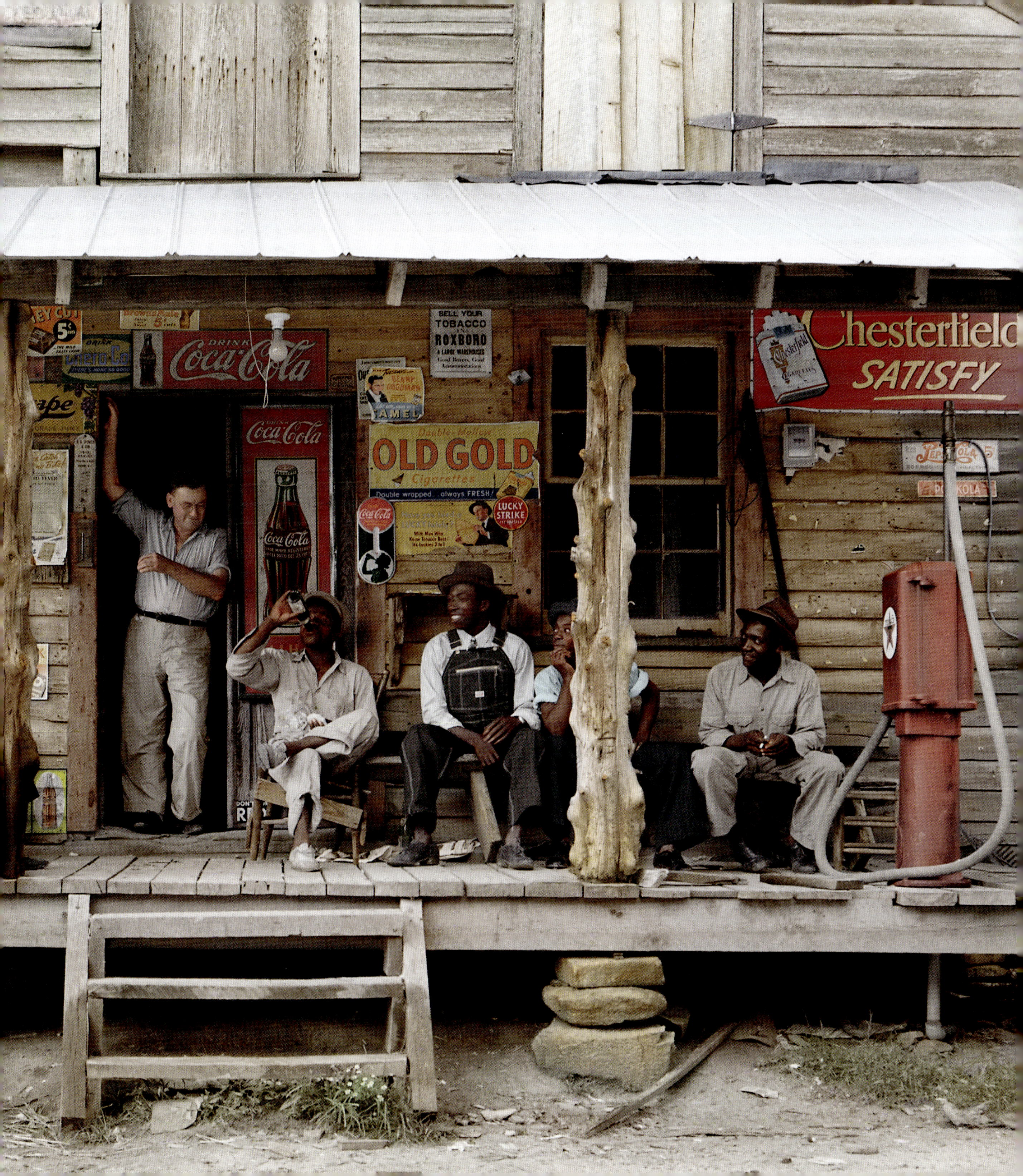
DRINK
Coca-Cola
Coca-Cola
SELL YOUR
TOBACCO
IN
ROXBORO
4 LARGE WAREHOUSES
Good Buyers, Good
Accommodations
BENNY
GOODMAN
CAMEL
Double-Mellow
OLD GOLD
Cigarettes
Double wrapped...always FRESH!
LUCKY
STRIKE
With Men Who
Know Tobacco Best
It's Luckies 2 to 1
Chesterfield
SATISFY

1930s

1938: Young boy in a Baltimore slum area, Maryland
Baltimore, Maryland, USA
(John Vachon / Library of Congress)

John Vachon, together with such names as Roy Stryker, Mary Post Wolcott, Jack Delano, Walker Evans, Gordon Parks and Dorothea Lange, was a key photographer for the Farm Security Administration (FSA). The FSA, part of Roosevelt's New Deal, was established to work towards alleviating the deep poverty experienced across rural America during the Great Depression.

Vachon never set out to be a photographer; the first job he took at the FSA was as an administrative assistant, doing the filing. A large proportion of the filing was photographs documenting the effects of the Depression on Americans' lives, which inspired Vachon to experiment with taking images himself. Encouraged by other FSA photographers, Vachon's first significant solo photographic assignment came at the end of 1938, in Nebraska.

Photography was to be his career: after the FSA with the Office of War Information, then in-house at Standard Oil. For two years from 1947, he was a staff photographer at *Life* magazine, followed by a quarter of a century at *Look* magazine. Vachon's images, and those of his colleagues, are perhaps the most significant legacy of the FSA.

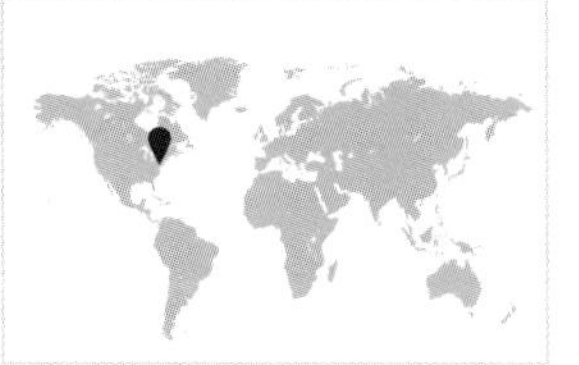

'When you do the filing, why don't you look at the pictures?'

Roy Stryker to John Vachon

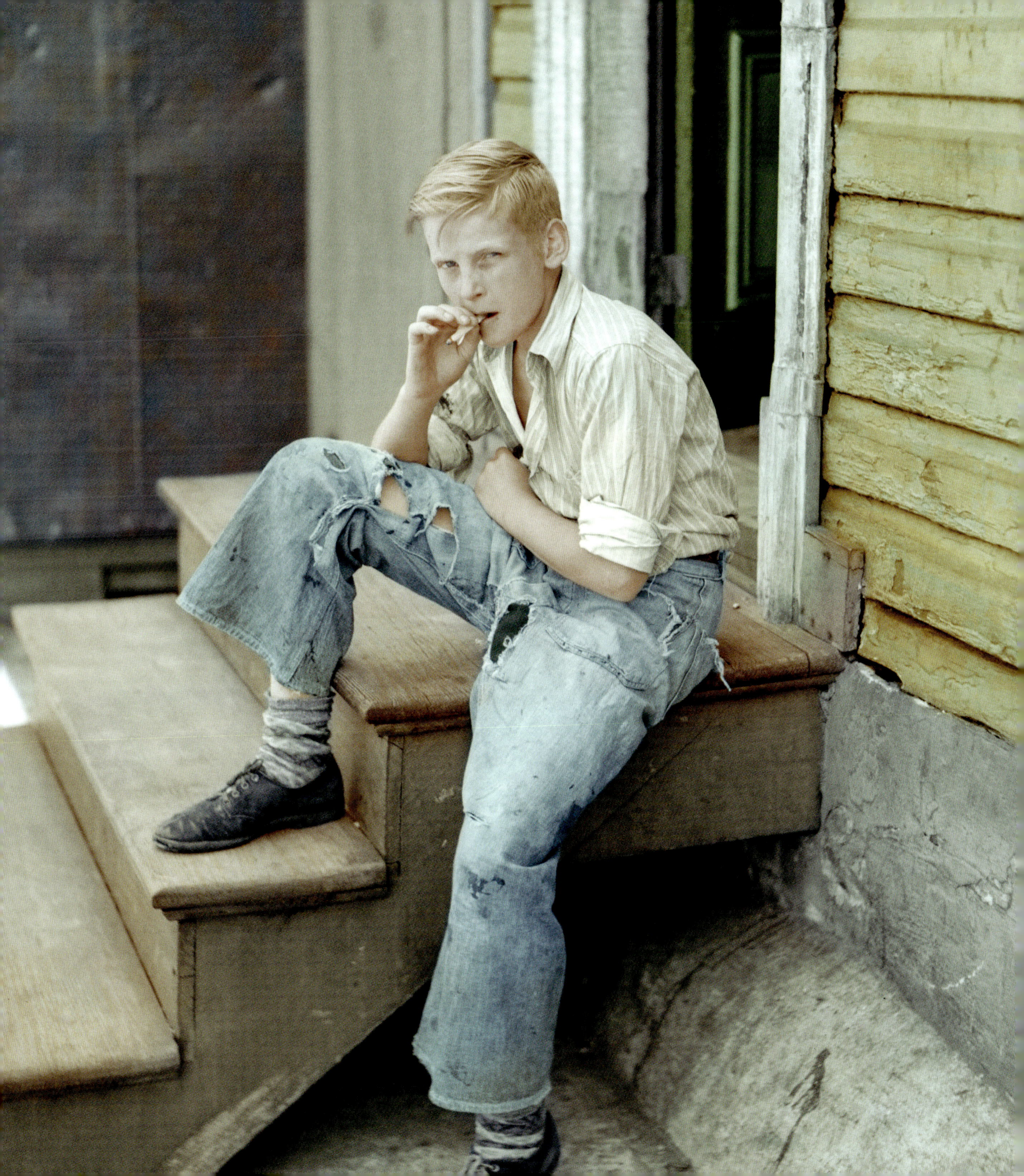

1930s

1937: Children's Pioneers defence drill, Leningrad

Leningrad, Soviet Union
(Viktor Bulla / Getty)

A year after this picture was taken, the photographer, Viktor Bulla, was either in exile or dead. A photographer like his father Karl, Viktor studied his craft in Germany before joining his father's business. He worked as a photojournalist for the Siberian Reserve Brigade during the Russo–Japanese War and went on to produce documentary films with his brother.

Viktor chronicled the 1917 Revolution in both stills and footage, and was an official portrait photographer to the Soviet Communist Party, photographing Lenin, Stalin and other leaders. But in the late 1930s, he was denounced by an employee of the family firm as an 'Enemy of the People'. A forced confession to charges of spying saw him placed in exile, in solitary confinement, though it is possible that he was simply shot.

This image shows a large group of children – a unit of 'Young Pioneers' – demonstrating their readiness for war in the case of a gas attack. The 'Young Pioneers', or 'Vladimir Lenin All-Union Pioneer Organisation', was a Soviet youth organisation for children between the ages of ten and fifteen.

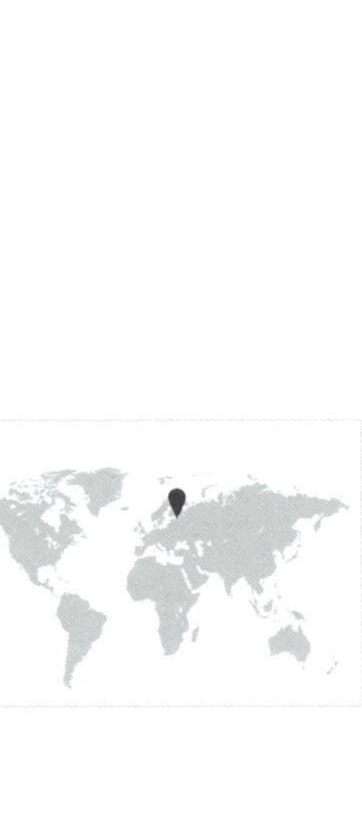

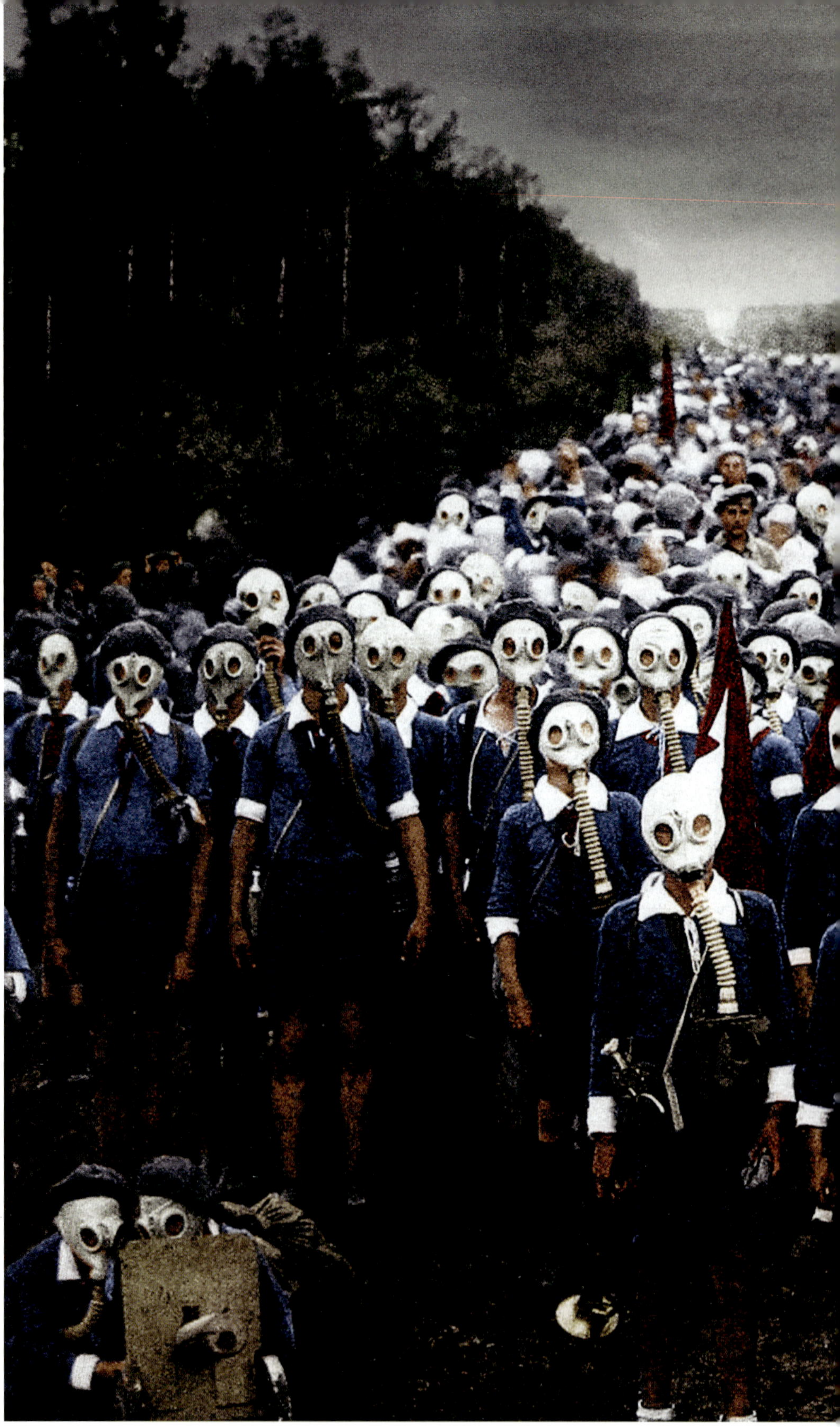

'High rise our campfires into the blue night,
We are pioneers – the children of the workers,
Near is the time of our best years
And the pioneers' motto is, "Always be ready!"'

'High Rise Our Campfires', Soviet Young Pioneers song

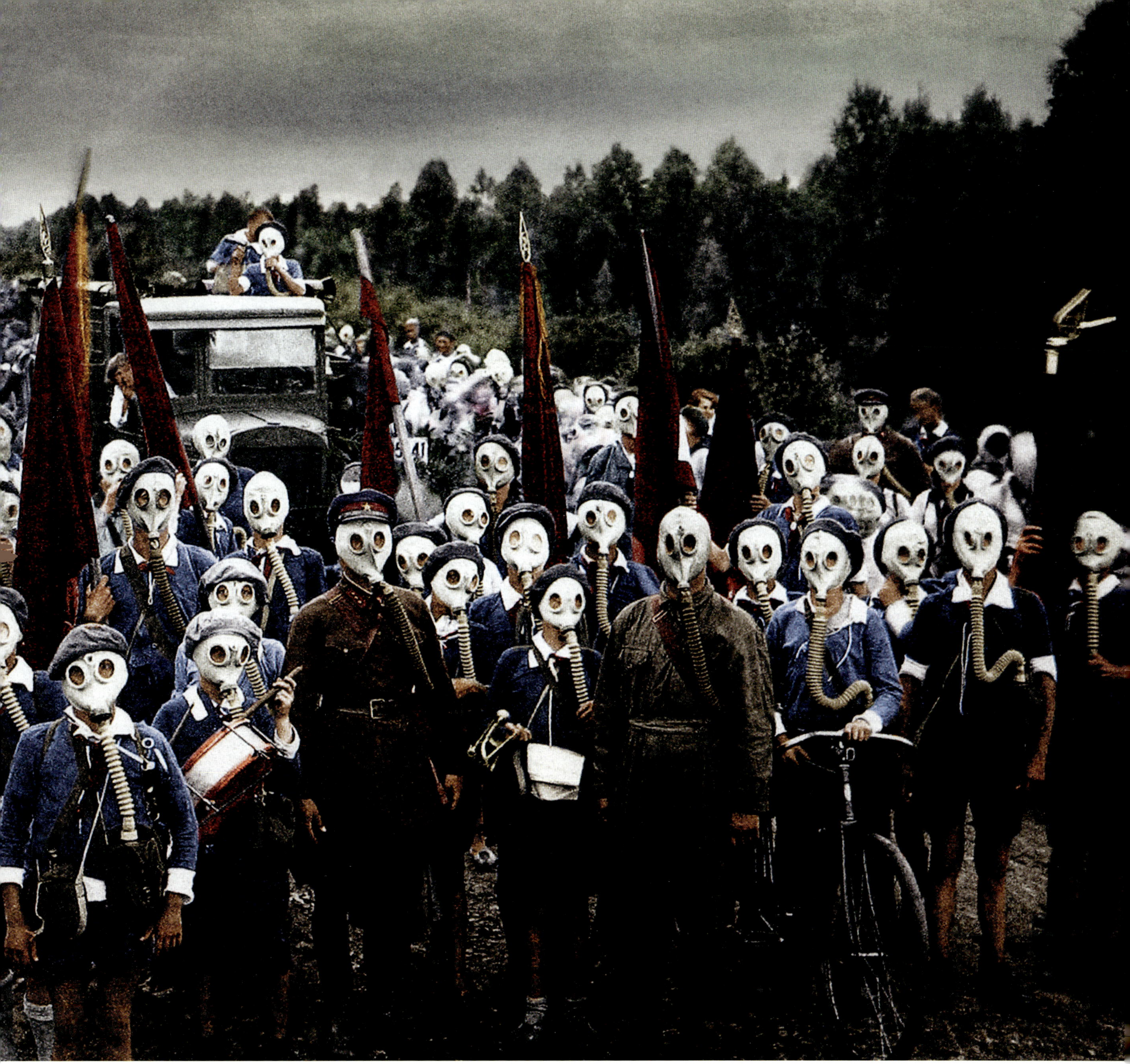

1930s

1936: **Florence Thompson with one of her children as part of Dorothea Lange's 'Migrant Mother' series**
Watsonville, California, USA
(Dorothea Lange / Library of Congress)

Florence Owens Thompson was only thirty-two in this picture, taken by Depression-era documentary photographer Dorothea Lange as an outtake from the session that generated the iconic 'Migrant Mother' collection.

Born in 1903 in what was then Indian Territory, now part of Oklahoma, Thompson's parents were displaced Native American Cherokees. Marrying at seventeen, she and her husband began a family in California. When her husband died, Florence was left with six children at the age of twenty-eight. She went on to have four more children, three with a Californian man, Jim Hill.

When Dorothea Lange encountered the family, their car had broken down while they were journeying to find crop-picking work. Hill and the boys in the family had walked into town to get parts for the car.

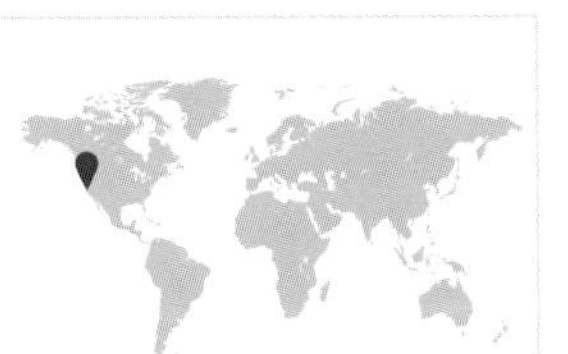

'She told me her age, that she was thirty-two. She said that they had been living on frozen vegetables from the surrounding fields, and birds that the children killed. She had just sold the tires from her car to buy food.'

Dorothea Lange

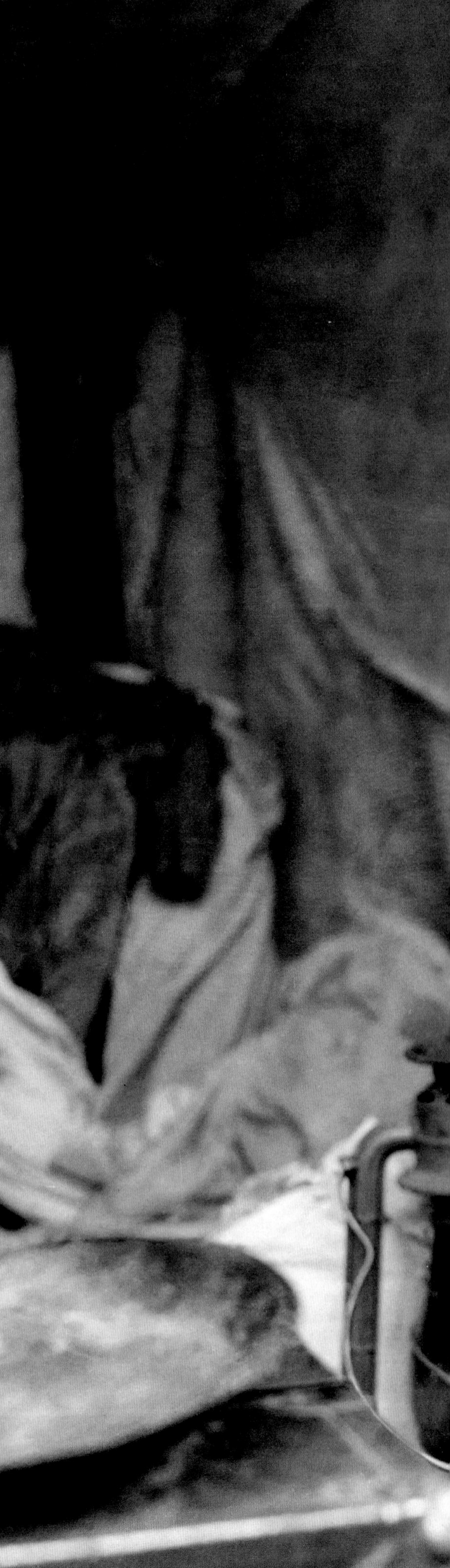

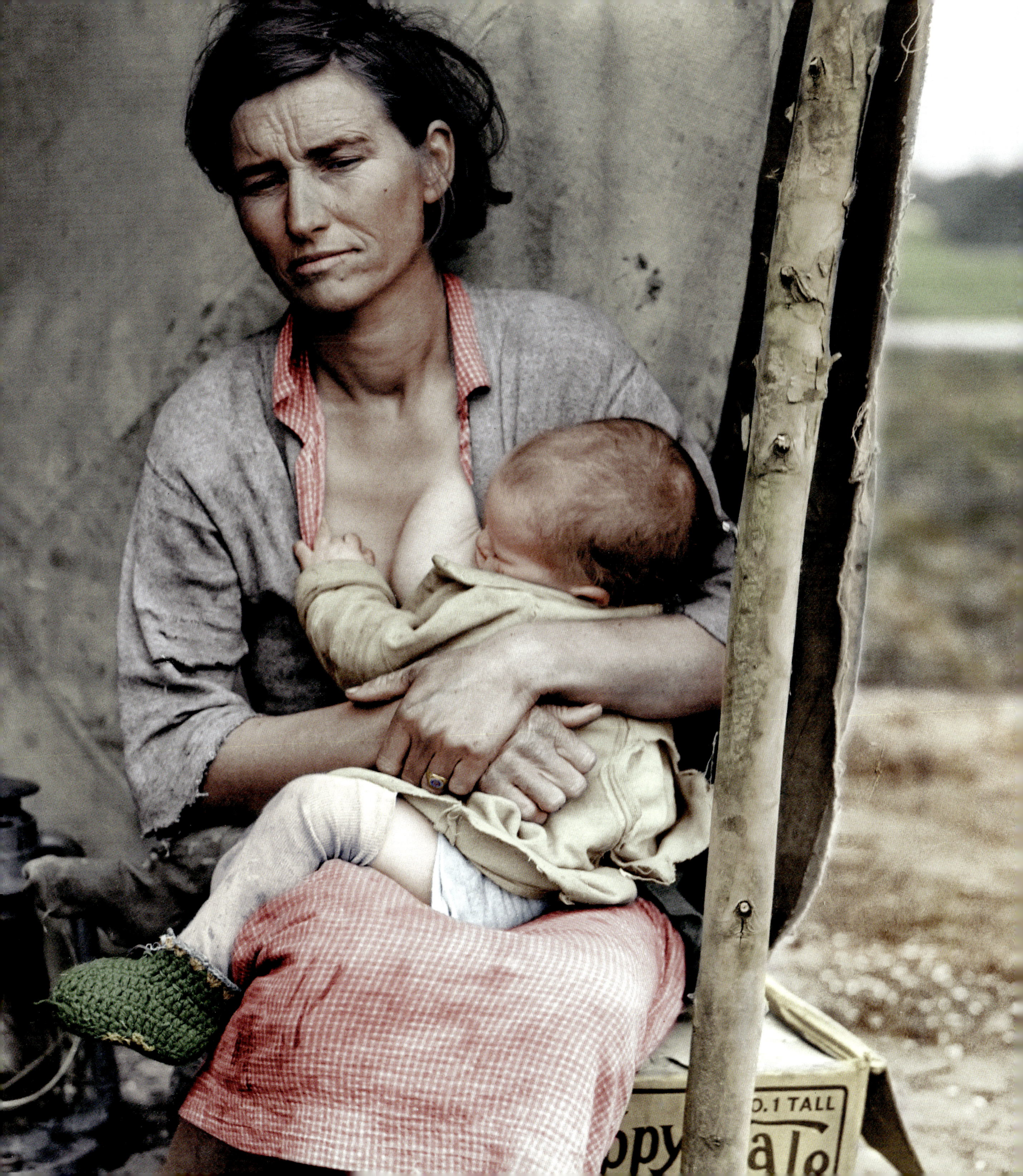
O.1 TALL

1930s

1936: August Landmesser refuses to salute at a Nazi rally, Germany

Hamburg, Germany
(Hulton Archive / Getty)

Twenty-six-year-old August Landmesser is shown here refusing to give the Nazi salute, at the end of a ceremony to launch the sailing ship *Horst Wessel*, on which he had worked. The event at a Hamburg shipyard had culminated in a speech by Rudolf Hess, standing alongside Adolf Hitler.

Landmesser had joined the Nazi party at the age of twenty-one on the assumption that it would increase his employment prospects. Four years later, he agreed to marry Irma Eckle, a Jew, and found he was expelled.

In 1937, August, Irma and their two-year-old daughter Ingrid attempted to flee to Denmark, but were arrested. Irma gave birth to their second daughter, Irene, in prison, and was later killed by the Nazis. After years in prison, August was drafted as a soldier, and died in action. Ingrid and Irene were placed in an orphanage and separated.

The *Horst Wessel* survived the war, was renamed *Eagle*, and is still in use as a training ship for the American military.

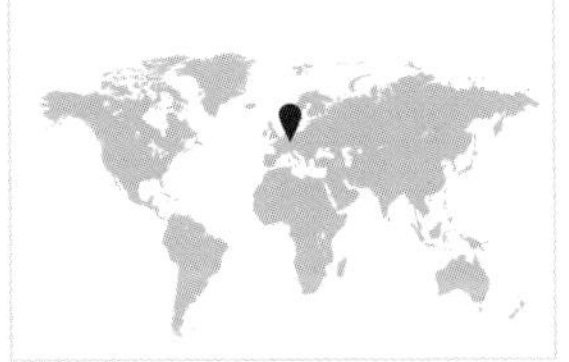

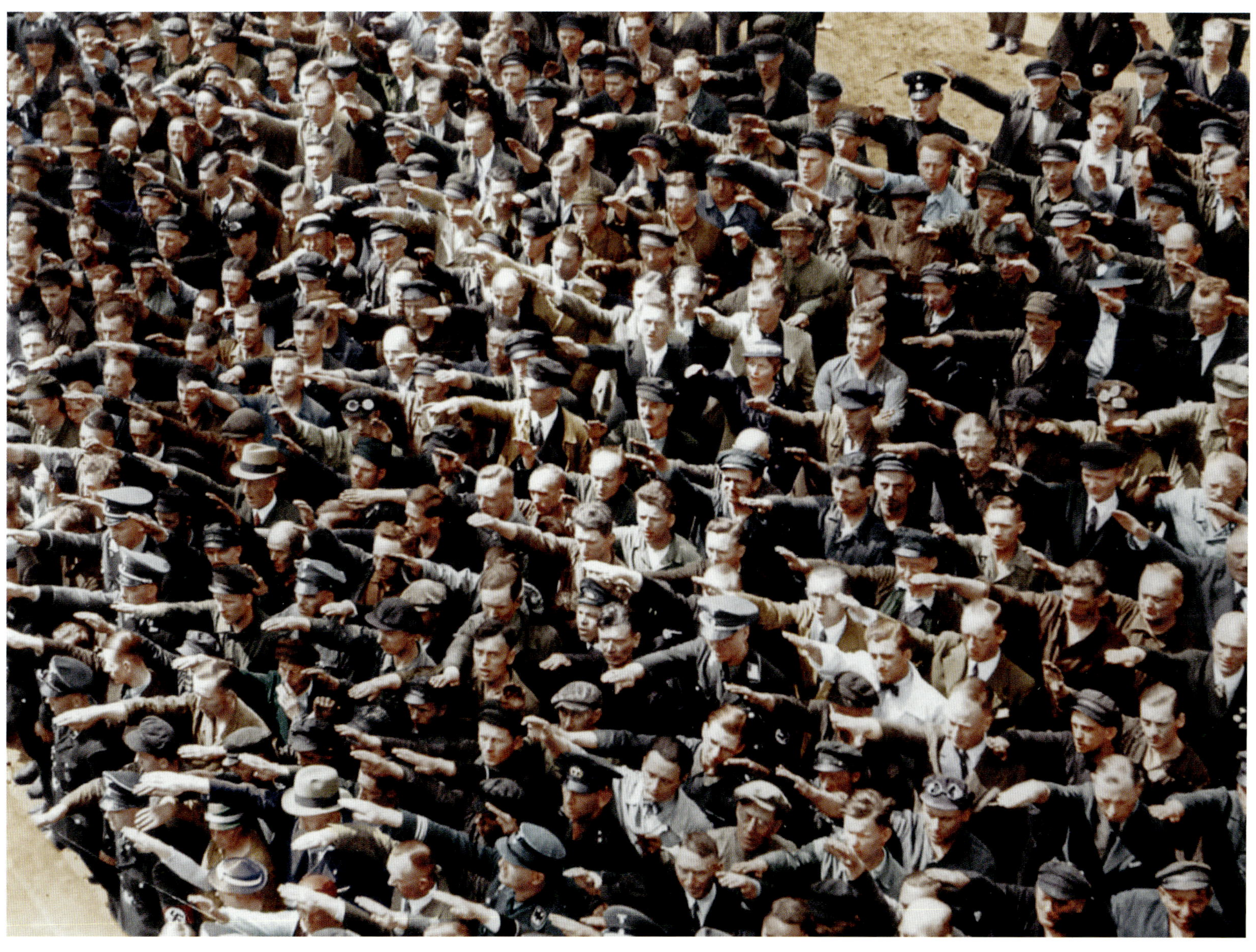

'In passing sentence on Landmesser, the Court maintained that if the purity of the German race is to be successfully maintained, such violations of the Race Protection Law (*Rassenschutzgesetze*) must be severely punished. However, in this case the Court did not totally ignore the human aspect of the case. The Court was concerned not so much with the relationship of the accused with the woman involved, who is hardly a very worthy character, but rather his relationship with his children, for which the Court has every sympathy. However, the situation was aggravated by the defendant resuming the forbidden relationship. This was also the reason for the Court's decision to impose a sentence of penal servitude. Dr Sch.'

German newspaper report, 26 October 1938

1930s

1935: Robert Johnson, blues singer and guitarist

USA
(Unknown)

Just twenty-seven when he died, Robert Leroy Johnson is arguably the most influential blues singer, songwriter and guitarist of all time – despite having recorded only twenty-nine songs. He was largely unknown until the posthumous release of his music in 1961.

Employing at least eight different surnames, and with three possible graves, lack of documentary evidence has given rise to seemingly endless myths about Johnson – most significantly, that he sold his soul to the devil at a Mississippi Delta crossroads in exchange for supernatural talent at the guitar.

This photo-booth picture is one of only two confirmed photographs of Johnson. The guitar he is holding is likely to be a Room 414 of the Gunter 1935-1936 Gibson L-00 model, with a capo on the second fret. Whatever the truth about the origin of his talent, the picture shows that Johnson had what appear to be remarkably long fingers.

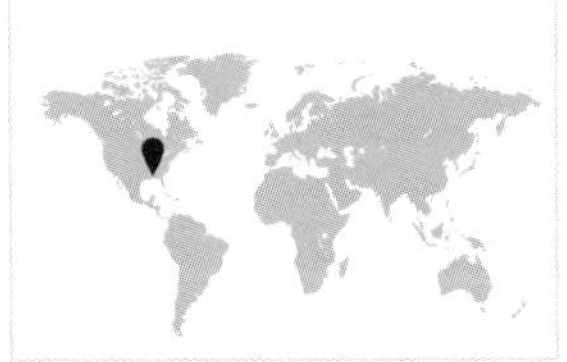

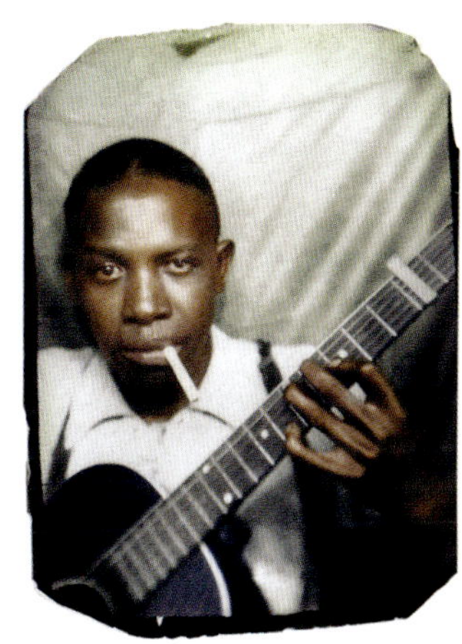

'He'd follow me and Willie around on Saturday night, me and Willie Brown, and every time we stopped to rest and set a guitar over on the corner or something, to go out and catch air, you know, he'd get the guitar and be tryin' to play it and be just noisin' the people.'

Son House

1930s

1935: Officials ride in one of the penstock pipes of the soon-to-be-completed Hoover Dam

Hoover Dam, Arizona, USA
(Unknown / Bureau of Reclamation)

In response to the rising demand for electricity across the southwestern US, and to curb the devastating floods to which the area was prone, a Federal decision was made to dam the Colorado River.

The building work commenced in 1930, and was a much-needed source of employment for more than 5,000 people during the Great Depression. The work required more than 3 million cubic yards of concrete and, when finished, became the world's largest man-made structure.

Its name was not without controversy. Initially known as Boulder Dam – after Boulder Canyon, a site later rejected – it was renamed Hoover Dam when work began. However, prior to opening in 1935, with President Roosevelt in office, the name was changed back to Boulder Dam. Twelve years later, President Truman approved an act of Congress to rename it once more, back to Hoover Dam.

It is possible that the penstock pipe in which the officials are standing is actually only twenty feet off the ground (over what is now a lay-by), and that the photographer has deliberately angled the camera to create the impression of a sheer drop.

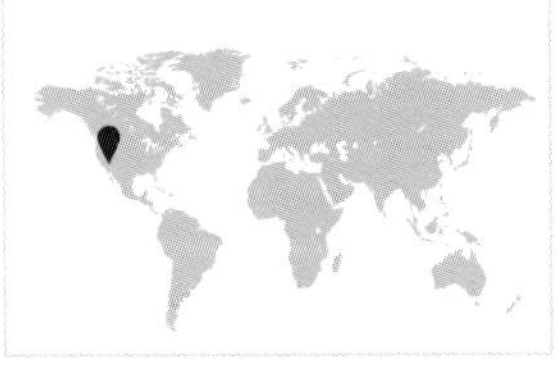

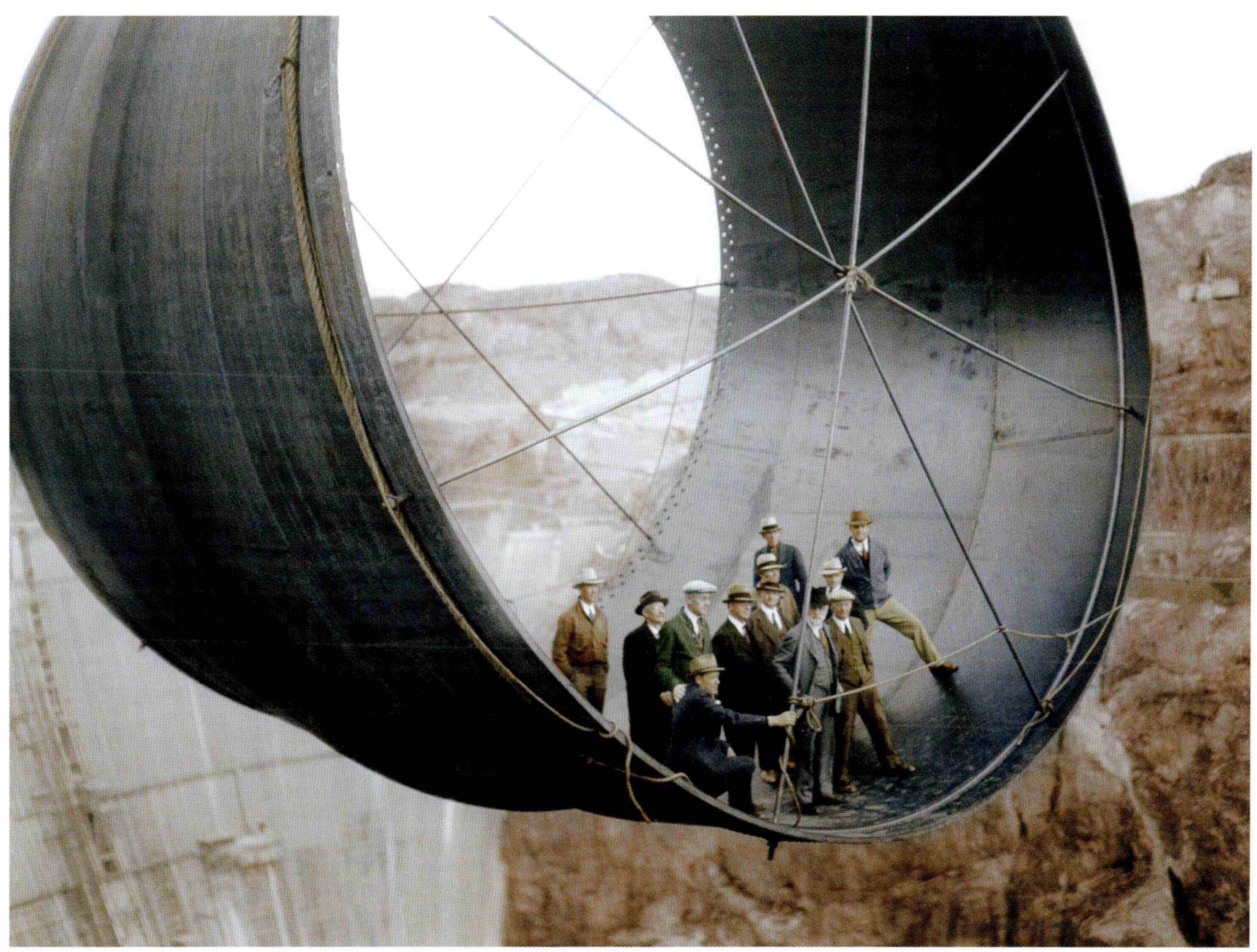

'The thing which every American, and especially every Californian, should understand is that Boulder Dam is a great monument of progress. It is a shield to protect the forward march of civilisation. It is proof that man can overcome obstacles which have buried other civilisations under desert sands, and that the time-worn saying, "history repeats" need not be true.

Indeed, Boulder Dam is a proof that there are two kinds of people in the world, those who meekly accept life as it is, and those who have the courage and will to change it for the better.'

'California Progress', 1936

1930s

16 July 1934: The Golden Gate Bridge under construction
San Francisco, California, USA
(Chas Hiller / Library of Congress)

The paint colour of the Golden Gate Bridge was a point of contention. The American Navy was eager to see the structure in yellow and black stripes to facilitate visibility in the region's fog, whereas the Army Air Corps rejected that scheme for stripes in red and white.

On arrival, the ironwork of the bridge had already been coated in a deep red anti-corrosion primer. For Irving Morrow, consulting architect to the design, this was indeed the perfect colour choice – International Orange. Not one to leave the result to chance, he wrote a report on the selection choice which ran to some twenty-nine pages. The bridge was officially opened on 27 May 1937.

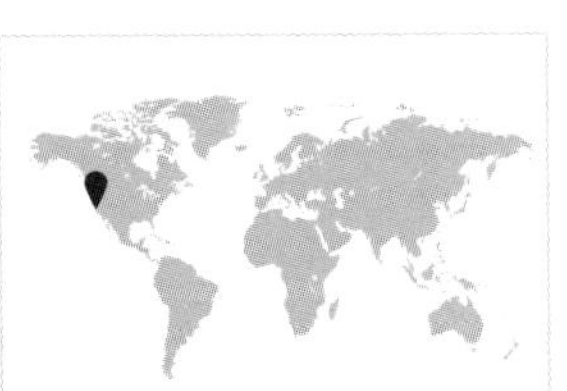

'The curtain rises. The pageant unrolls. Voices are lifted in song. Let us lift up our hearts with thanksgiving. Let us give honour to whom honour is due; to those who conceived this mighty project and to those who made its building possible; to the engineers who designed it and the directors and management that built it. Let us remember, in deep sorrow, those whose lives were sacrificed in the course of its construction.'

Angelo Rossi, Mayor of San Francisco, from the 'Official Program of the Golden Gate Bridge Fiesta', 27 May to 2 June 1937

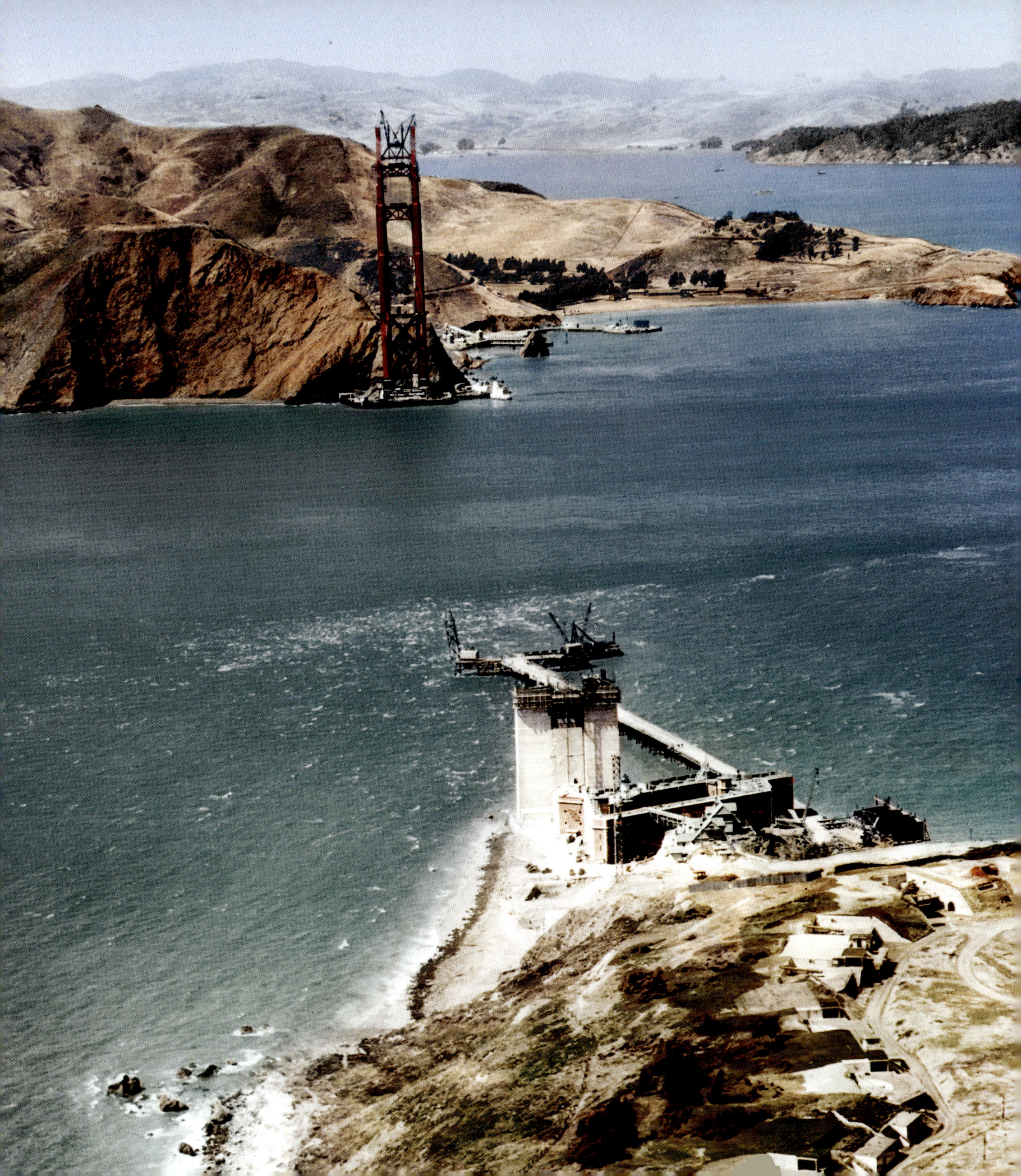

1930s

1933: A 'Hooverville' shanty town in Central Park, New York

Central Park, New York City, USA
(Unknown / Bettmann / Getty)

The Great Depression that followed the stock market crash of October 1929 saw massive rates of unemployment and homelessness across the United States. People without jobs were people without the means to pay rent. Suddenly, civic lodging houses built for the homeless were filling up to capacity. Shanty towns – some housing as many as 15,000 people – began to grow up in close proximity to soup kitchens and other sources of free food.

Such spontaneous towns were known colloquially as 'Hoovervilles', after Herbert Hoover. Hoover was the Republican President in 1929, and responsibility for the Depression was laid largely at his door.

The Hooverville in Central Park developed on the site of the park's lower reservoir. At one time drained and set aside to become a lawn, the reservoir project was derailed by the impact of the downturn. When it resumed in 1933, the Hooverville was gone, but not before it had gained notoriety, standing literally in the shadows of the opulent buildings that line the park – including The Beresford, opened mere months before the stock market crash.

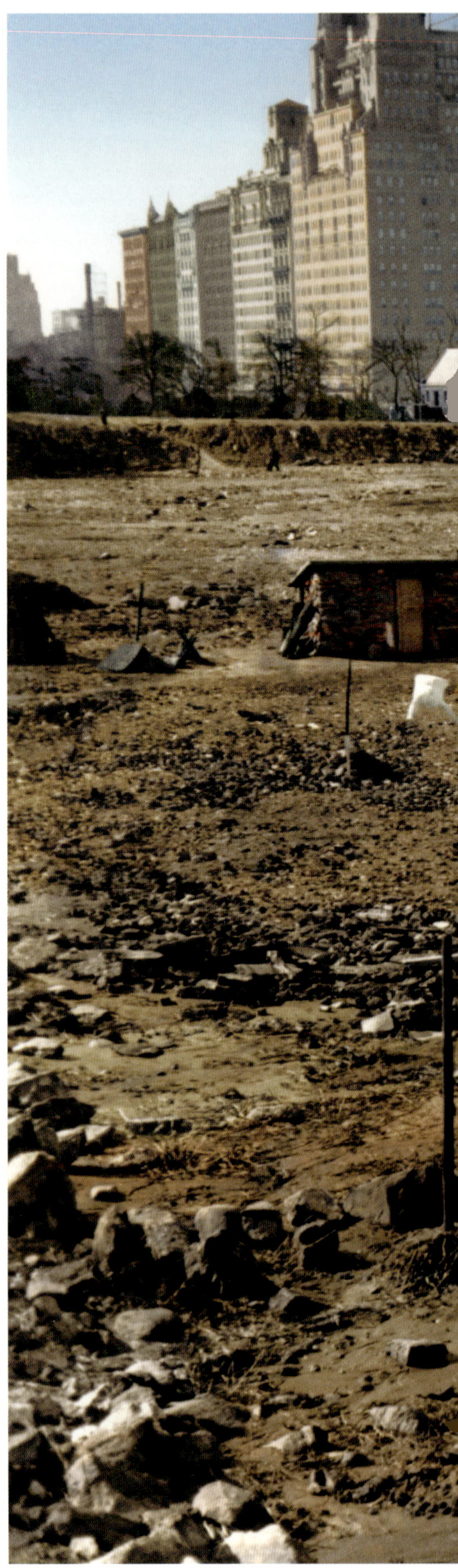

'Already the US Public Health Commissioner has testified before a Senate Committee that in more than seventeen farming states, as well as in the cities, there will be a tremendous death rate; all resulting from the terrible plight that the masses find themselves in today, many of whom are compelled to eat out of garbage cans, while the capitalist class is wallowing in luxury, holding forth at their banquets and balls and cynically laughing in the faces of the hunger corpses who are stalking throughout the country.'

'Petition to Seattle mayor and City Council', 13 February 1931

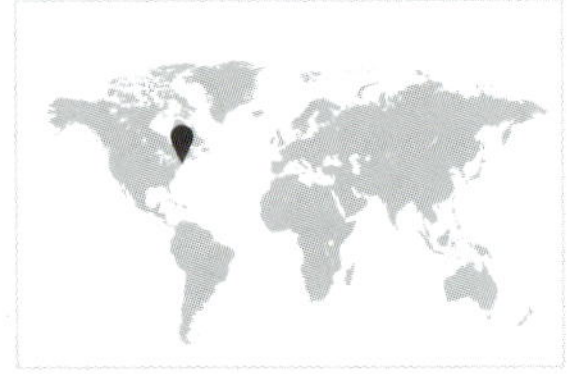

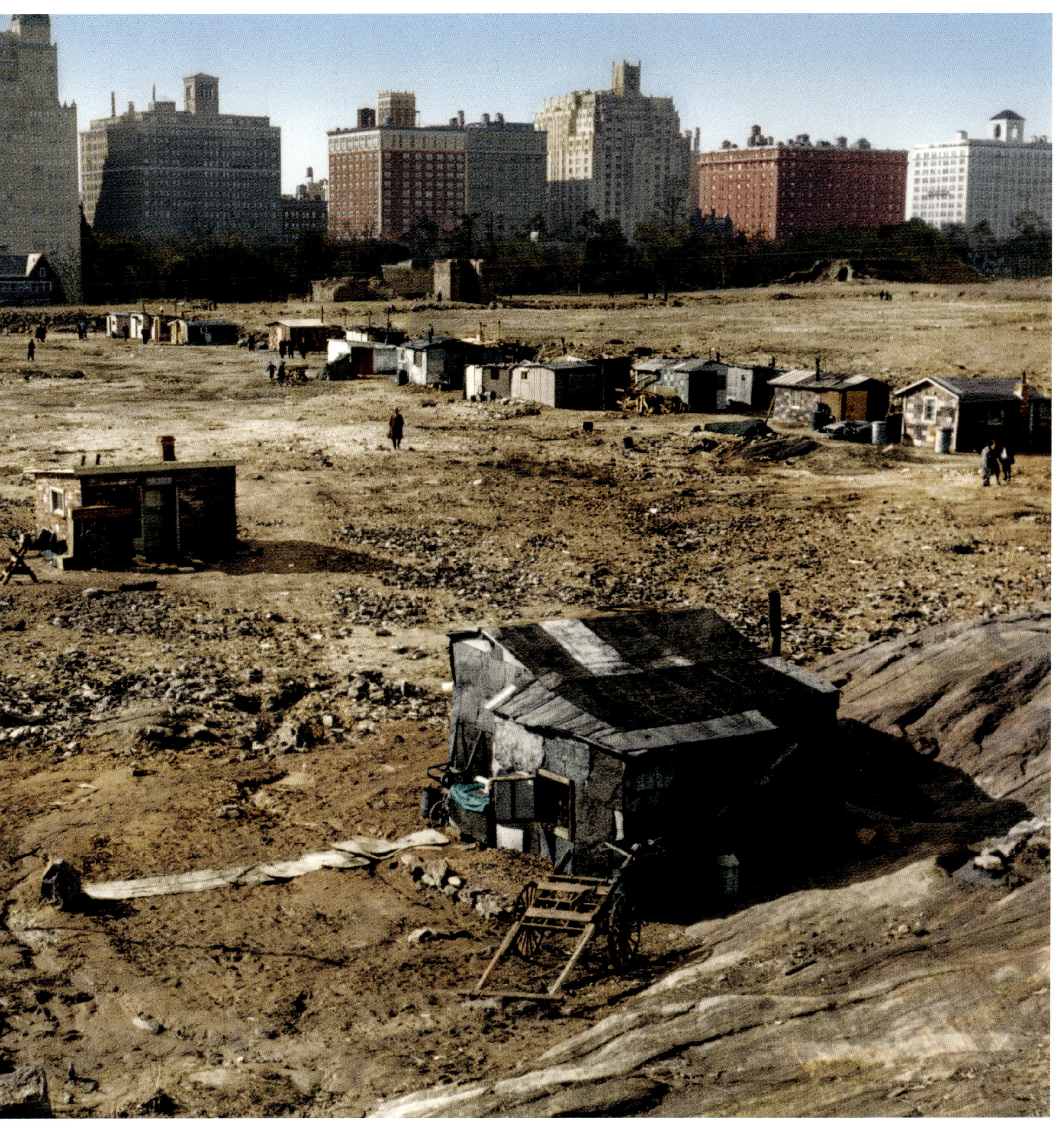

1932: **The Dynasphere being tested on the beach at Weston-super-Mare by Mr J. A. Purves of Taunton, who invented the machine with his son**
Weston-super-Mare, Somerset, UK
(Fox Photos / Getty)

1930s

With the first monowheel patent dating to 1869, the idea of a single-wheeled vehicle suggested several advantages over two-wheeled vehicles: less weight, less size and less resistance, all of which should theoretically equate to more efficiency.

A small stream of inventors pursued the concept, despite the not-insignificant problems that a single-wheel vehicle presented: reduced stability, reduced steerage and, self-evidently, a blocked view.

The monowheel shown here – the Dynasphere – was patented by sixty-year-old John Archibald Purves in 1930. Purves, from the town of Taunton in Somerset, UK, drew inspiration from an illustration by Leonardo da Vinci, and claimed he had created 'the high-speed vehicle of the future'. Reaching top speeds of thirty miles per hour, the ten-foot high, 1,000-pound wheel required Purves to lean out to either side in order to steer.

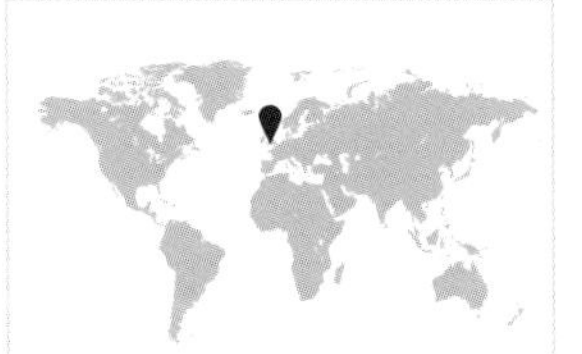

'This novel vehicle is capable of rolling along roads, or over fields and wild country, as easily as a ball runs along a smooth surface. It possesses so many advantages that we may eventually see gigantic wheels running along our highways in as many numbers as motor cars do today.'

Meccano magazine, February 1935

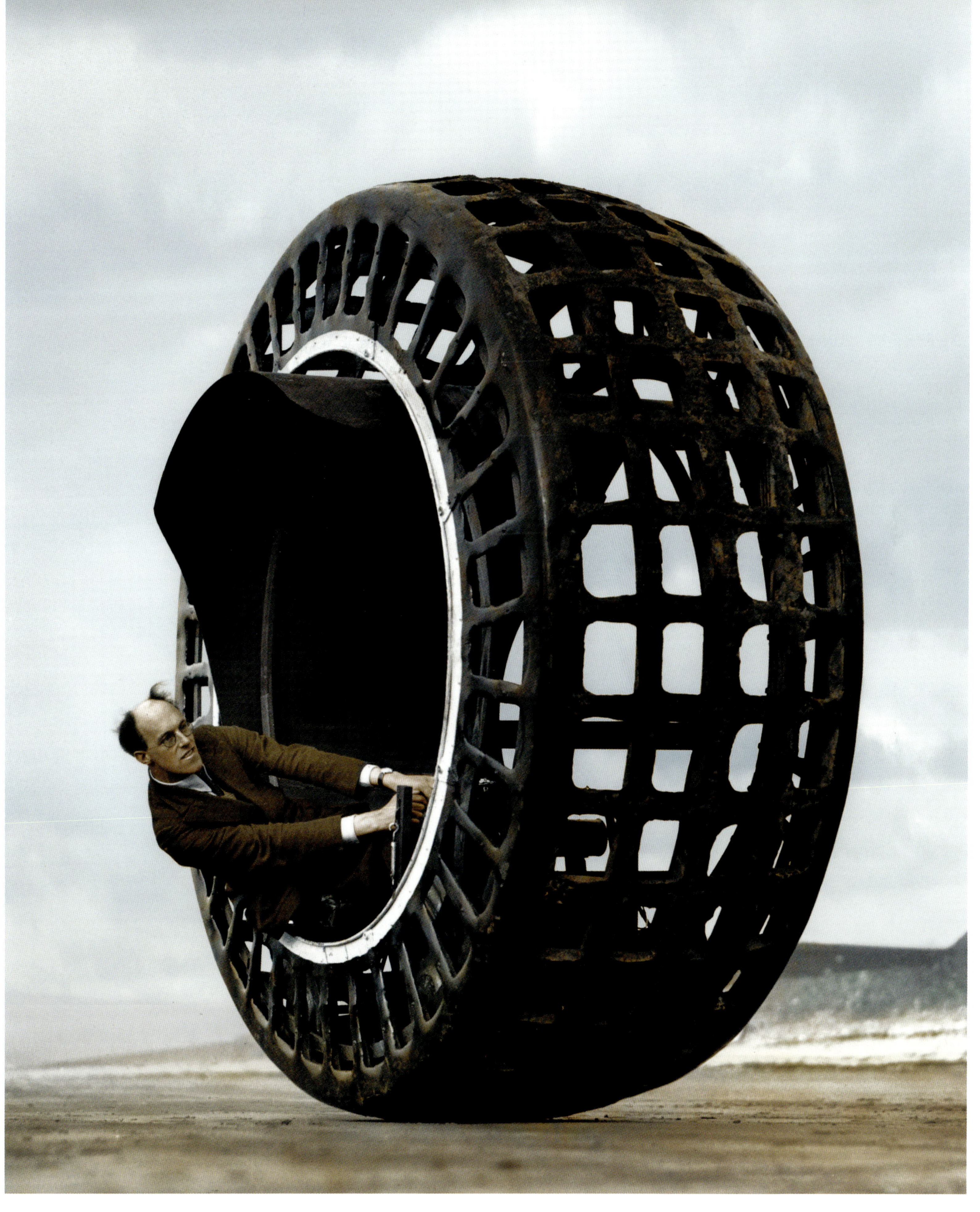

1930s

31 May 1932: At Mount Rushmore, Gutzon Borglum and another sculptor hang from the forehead of George Washington

Mount Rushmore, South Dakota, USA
(Unknown / Library of Congress)

Originally proposed in 1923 by State Historian Doane Robinson as a memorial to great heroes of the West, the design and carving of South Dakota's Mount Rushmore were executed by sculptor Gutzon Borglum. It was Borglum who persuaded Robinson to abandon the West theme – including Lakota Sioux leader Red Cloud – and instead to create a monument to American presidents. Work began in 1927, and was declared complete in October 1941. Borglum had died six months earlier.

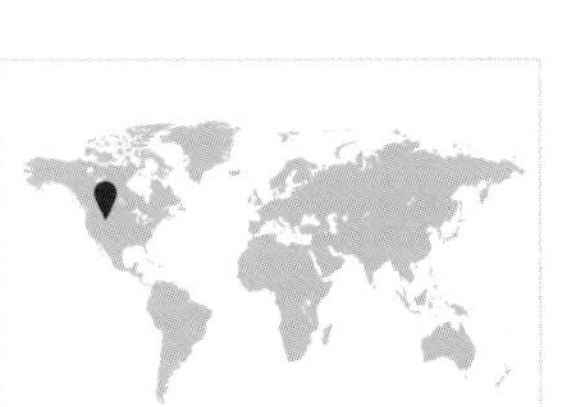

'On one occasion Borglum arranged for a meeting of senators. He wanted to carve a history of the United States on the mountainside, in English, Latin, Greek, and Sanskrit. Senator Tom Connally, of Texas, blurted out, "What in the world do you want to cut it in Sanskrit for? Nobody reads that."

Borglum turned on Tom with a withering look of scorn. Striking a dramatic pose, he said, as nearly as I can now recall: "Sir, Mount Rushmore is eternal. It will stand there until the end of time. This age will pass away and all its records will be destroyed; 10,000 years from now all our civilization will have passed without leaving a trace. A new race of people will come to inhabit the earth. They will come to Mount Rushmore and read there the record that we have made. If that record is written on that immortal mountain in four languages, those people will not have the difficulty in reading our record that we had in figuring out the hieroglyphics of Egypt."'

William J. Bulow, 'My Days with Gutzon Borglum', 1947

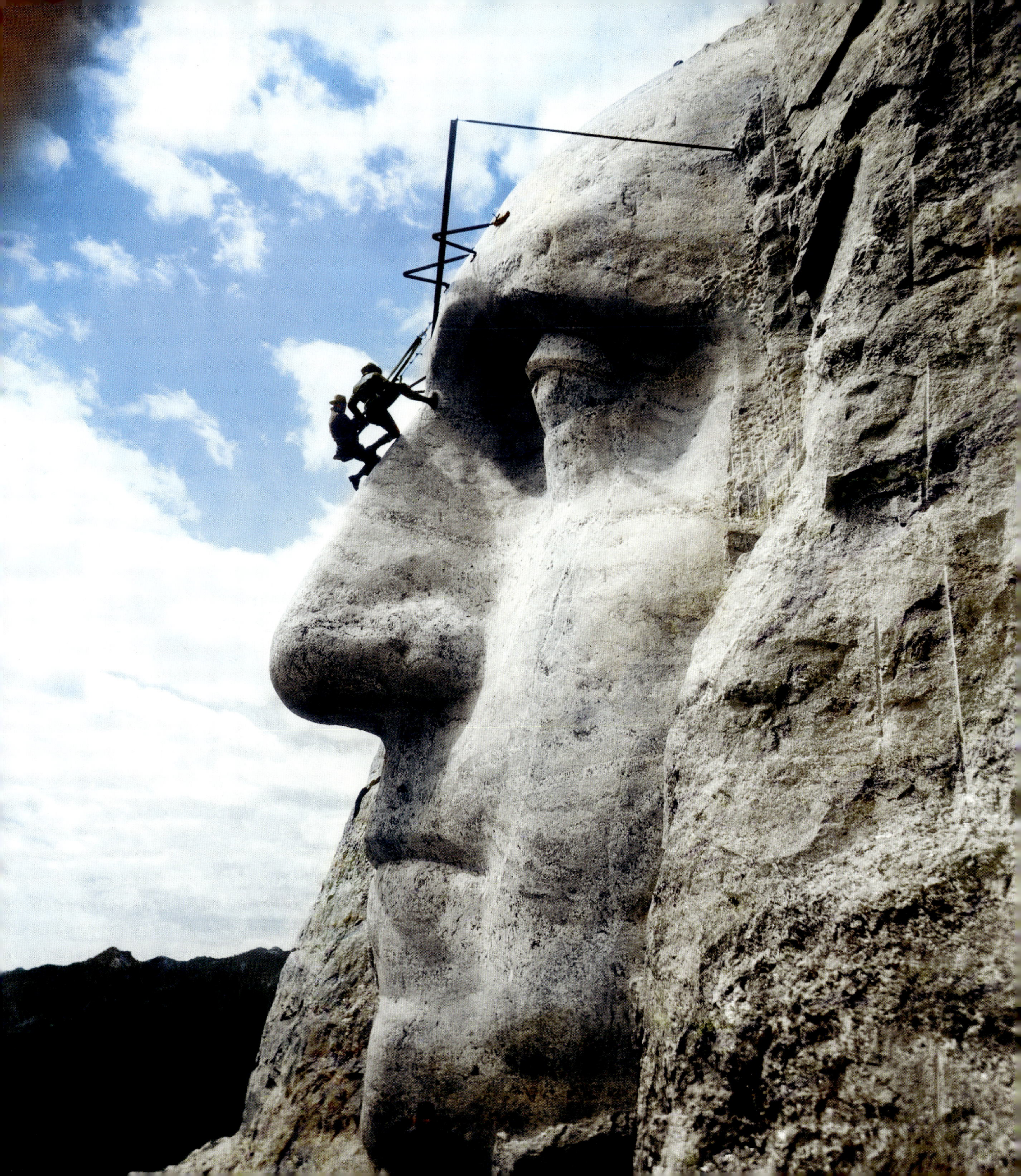

1930s

c. 1930: An overhead view of people on 36th Street between 8th and 9th Avenues, in the heart of the Garment District, New York

Garment District, New York City, USA (Margaret Bourke-White / Time & Life Pictures / Getty)

Manhattan's Garment District has been the centre of the American fashion industry since at least the turn of the twentieth century. In 1900, New York City's garment trade was its largest industry by a factor of three. The entire fashion ecosystem, from fabric suppliers to designer showrooms, existed within an area just under a square mile.

Native New Yorker Margaret Bourke-White was in her mid-twenties when she took this picture. She would later become *Life* magazine's first female photojournalist and, during the Second World War, the first female war correspondent.

The two cars shown are a 1930 Ford Model A 4-Door Sedan (*left*) and a Ford Model A Sports Coupe (*right*).

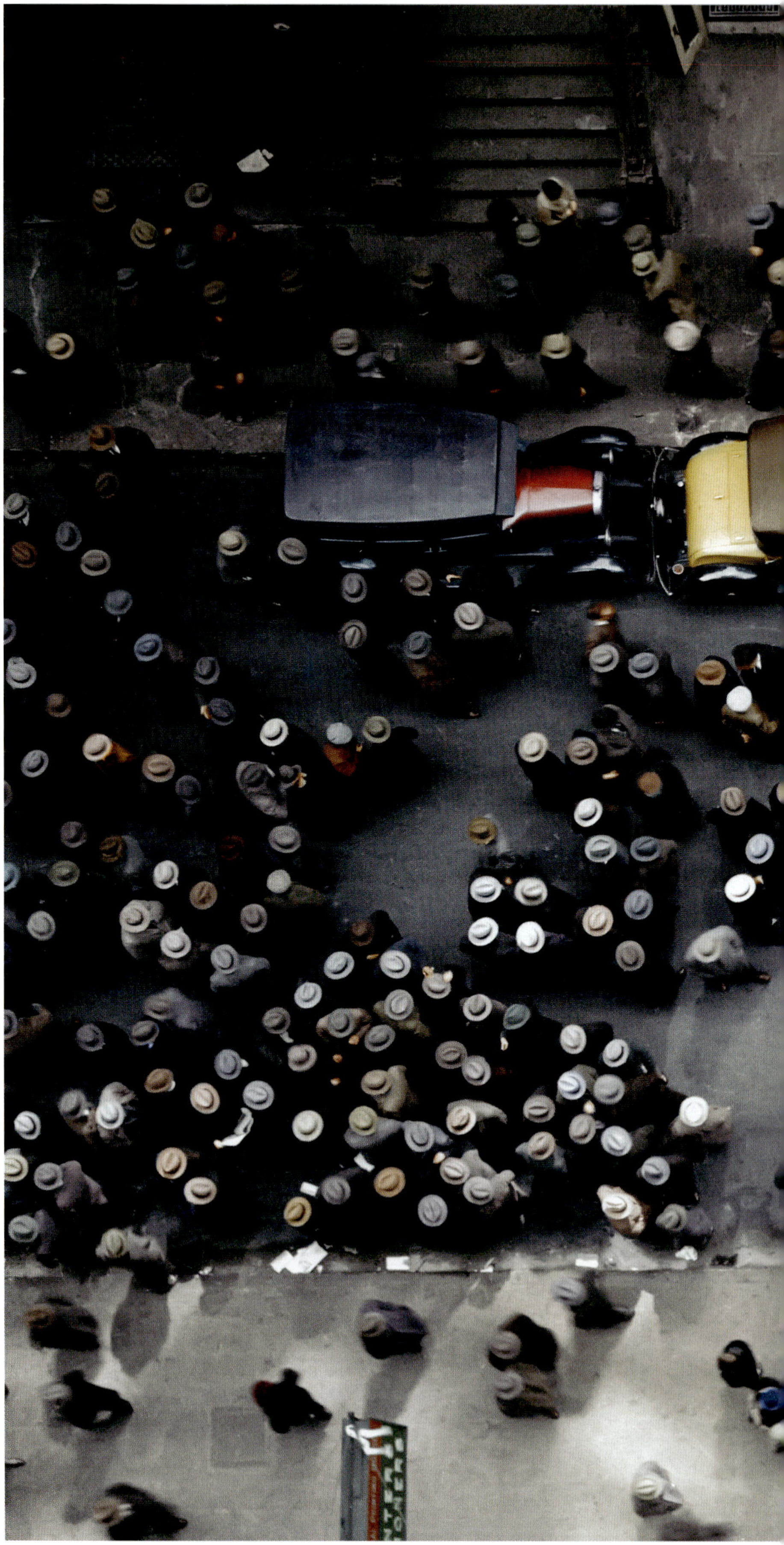

'New Ford Town Sedan. Luxurious transportation at low cost. Richly finished in every detail. The deep cushions are upholstered in Mohair or Bedford Cord according to choice. New Ford Convertible Cabriolet. Combines the Roadster's airy freedom and the snug comfort of a coupe. The convertible top may be easily raised or lowered.'

Ford Model A Full-Line Brochure, 1931

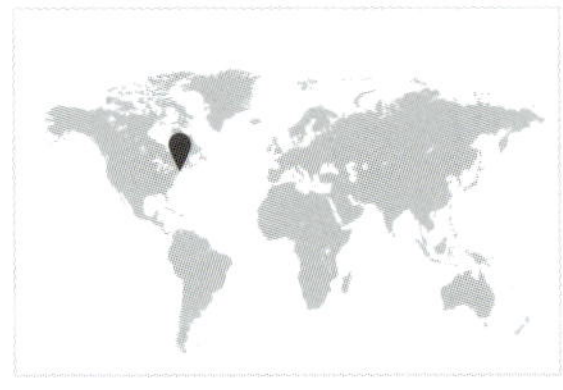

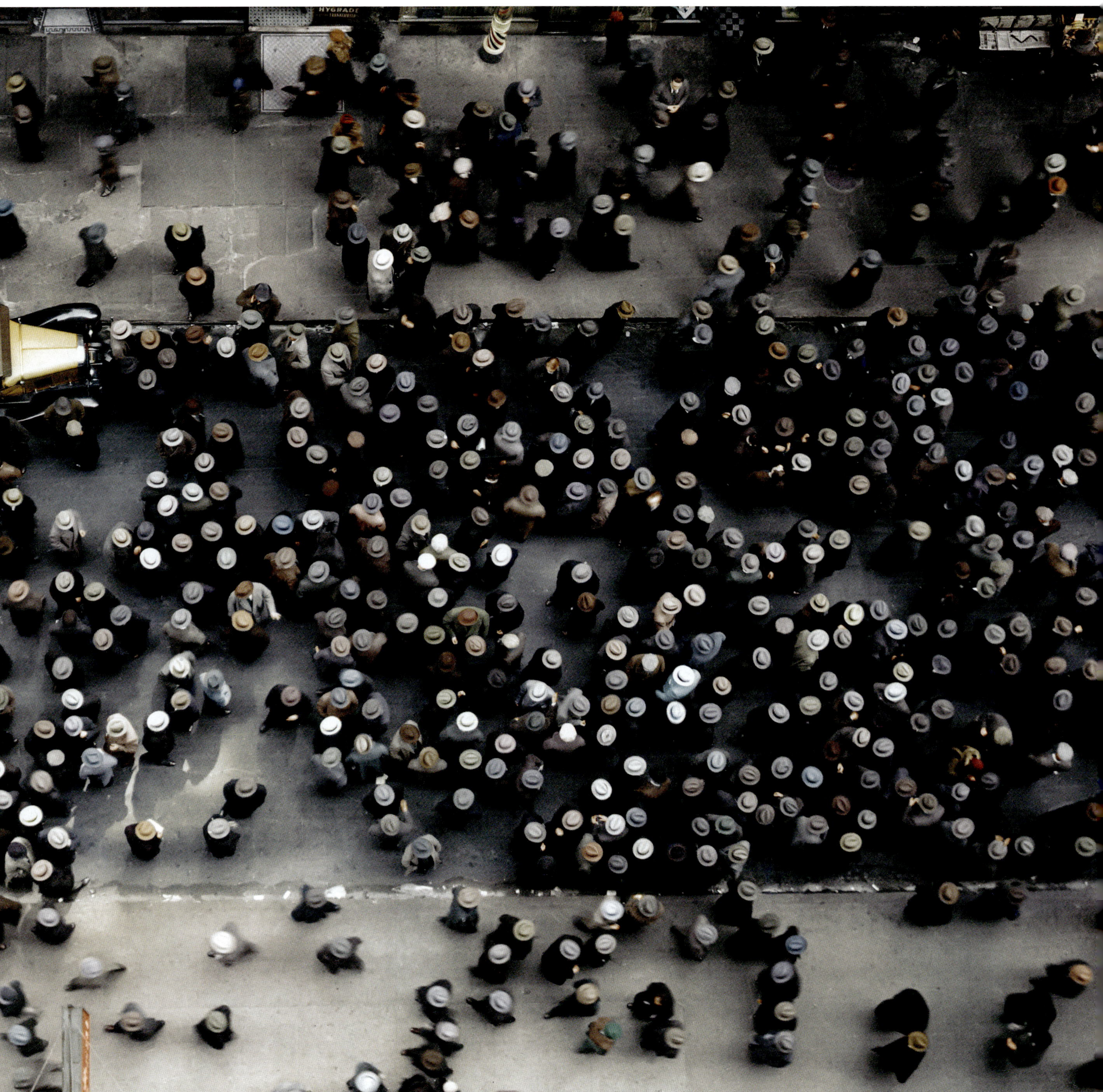
HYGRADE

1930s

1930s: A Confederate and a Union veteran play cards at a Civil War reunion

Gettysburg Battlefield, Pennsylvania, USA (Bettmann / Getty)

The most significant American Civil War reunion of the 1930s was held in July 1938. Seventy-five years after the event, a reunion of Confederate and Union troops took place at the American Civil War battlefield of Gettysburg. Of the 8,000 still living, just under 2,000 veterans of the war attended, taken to the battlefield in a dozen special trains. Out of that 2,000, twenty-five had fought at Gettysburg.

Echoing the events of the same reunion a quarter of a century before, in 1913, Confederate and Union veterans shook hands across the rock wall of The Angle area of the field. President Roosevelt gave an address to all attending and officially dedicated a new Peace Memorial of Eternal Light. More than a quarter of a million people came to hear the president speak.

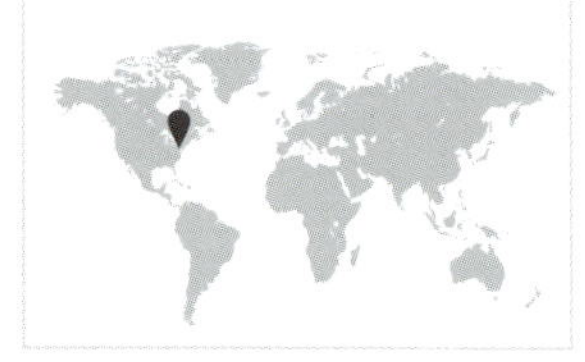

'Ladies and gentlemen, I feel highly honoured at the introduction of our worthy friend and comrade Captain, er, Doctor Lewis, and, er, I will do the best I know how to get that yell up for ya'. What few of us old corn-feds are left… we can't give you much but we'll give you what we got left. Ladies and gentlemen, I have the pleasure of announcing to you that we are going to make an effort to repeat the old Rebel Yell… one… two… THREE! (Charge 'em, boys, charge 'em!).'

Confederate Veteran introducing the Rebel Yell, 1930s

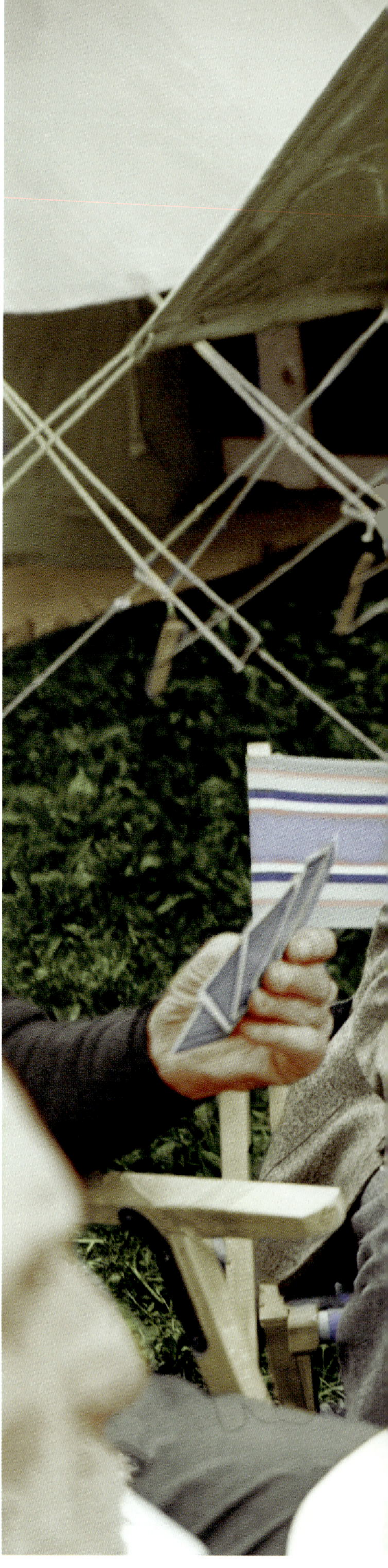

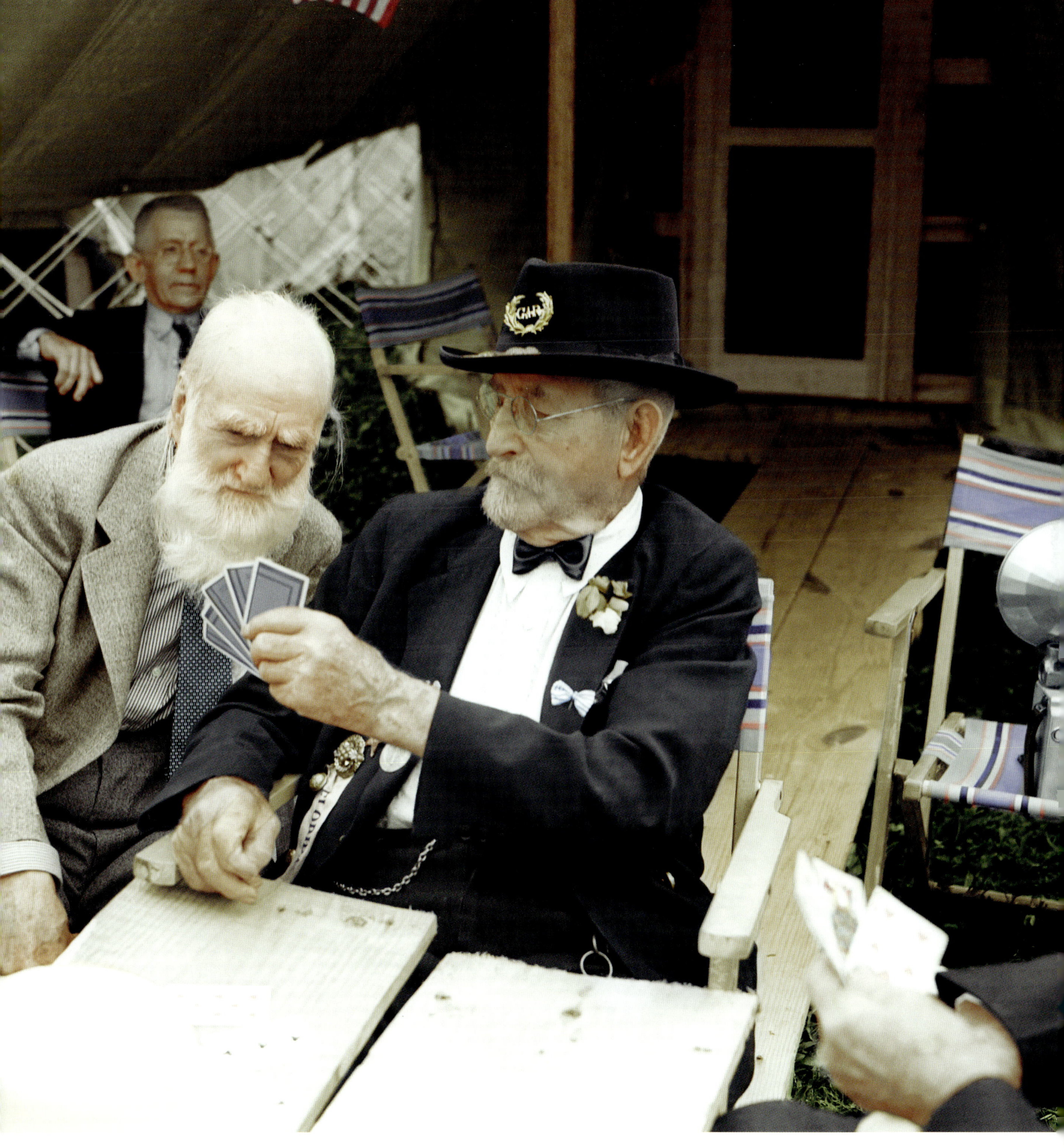

19 October 1929: Passengers surveying the scene from the verandah deck of the British Airship R100

Somewhere above the earth
(A. R. Coster / Getty)

1920s

The interior of the R100 airship was designed with luxury in mind, but also with weight or, rather, the lack of it. The craft could accommodate a hundred passengers, supported by thirty-seven staff. Passengers occupied the top two of three decks. Access to the salon-cum-dining-room from the cabins was via a double staircase. Two promenading decks ran either side of the salon, offering spectacular views to the guests, as shown here.

The mahogany detailing throughout the interior was a much lighter timber, stained to a darker hue. Privacy was also sacrificed for lightness; the cabins, which used bunk beds, were separated from each other only by cloth barriers.

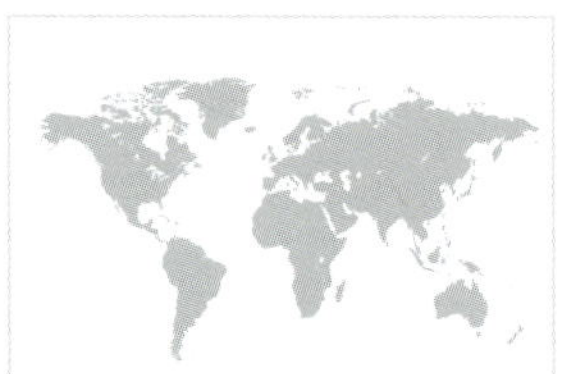

'The passengers enter the R100 through a door in the nose of the ship. The passenger saloon is slung from the main joints of the ship, and seats some fifty people comfortably. From the saloon, with its polished mahogany veneer pillars and 5-ply birch floor, which was polished and carpeted, staircases led up to the cabins and down to the control car.'

Flight International magazine, 27 December 1929

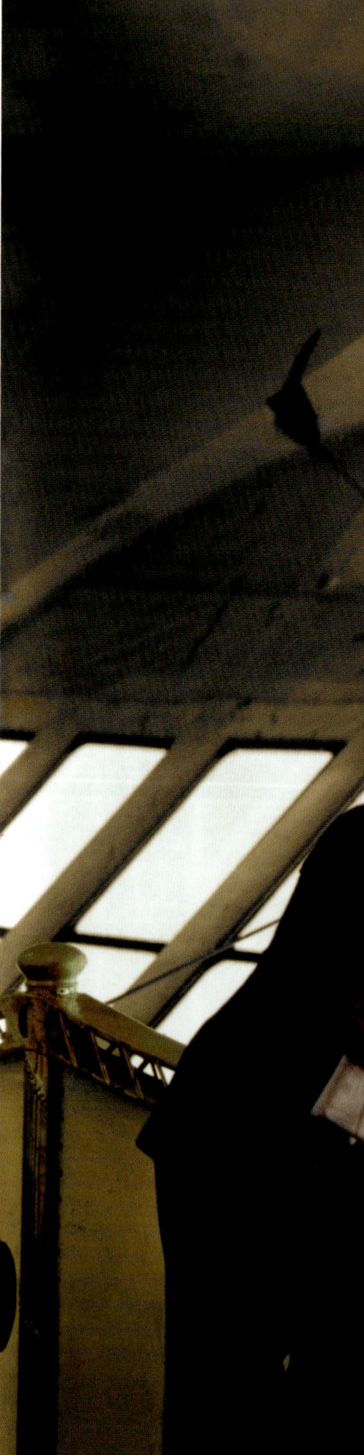

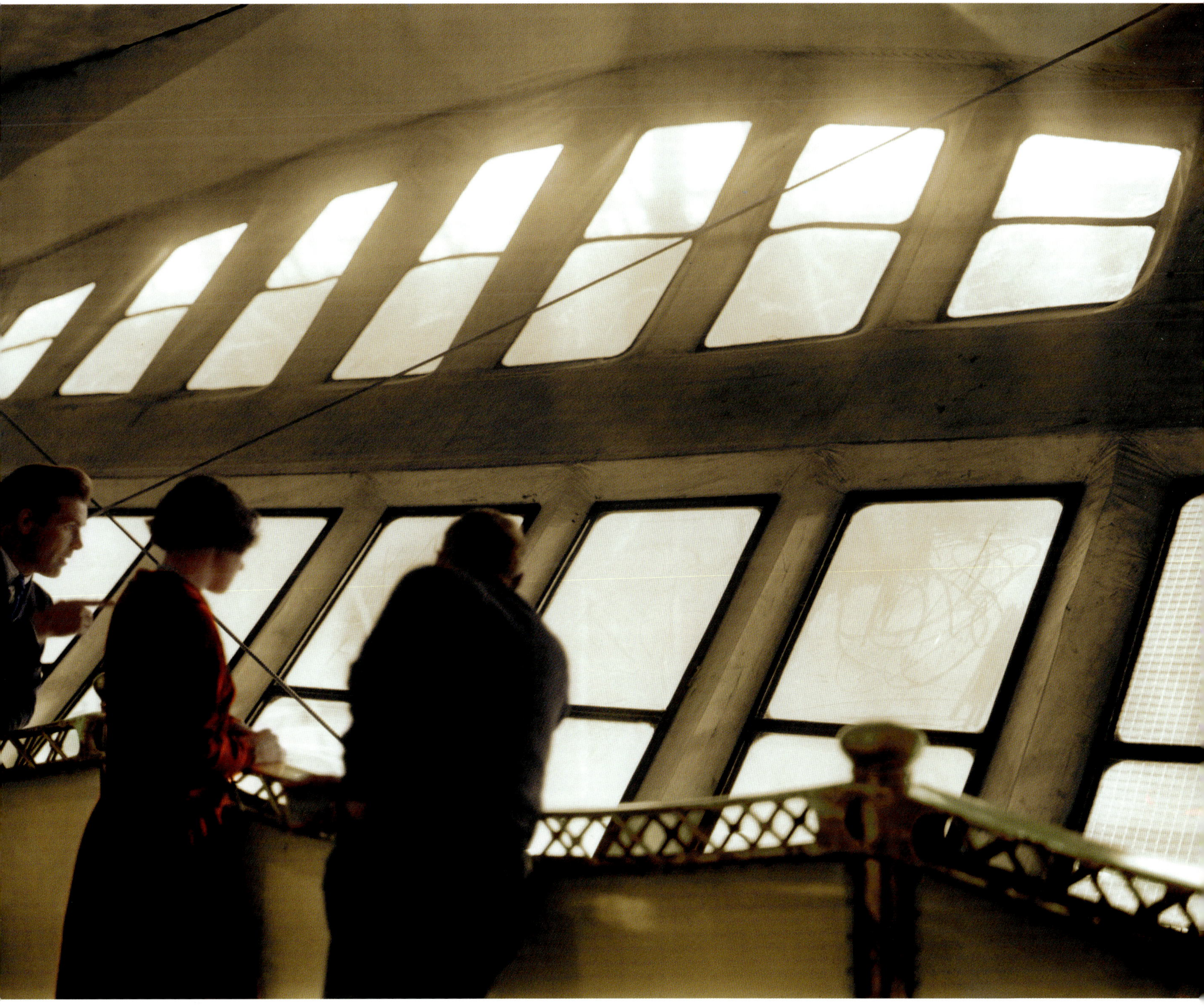

1929: **The Airship R100 nears completion at the Royal Naval Air Service Air Station near Howden in Yorkshire**

Howden, Yorkshire, UK
(Fox Photos / Hulton Archive)

The R100 was a response to the British Empire's requirement to manage its many and varied – and distant – colonial outposts. The ship's designer, Barnes Wallis, would go on to create the celebrated 'bouncing bomb' during the Second World War.

Commissioned in 1921, work commenced in 1925 at the No. 2 Double Rigid Shed, Royal Naval Air Service Air Station in Howden, Yorkshire. The shed, the largest in the world when it was built, had its doors heightened by another 10 feet to 140 feet in order to accommodate the R100. Rusting corrugated iron sheets made up the back wall. The workman was likely applying aluminium aircraft dope, a form of plasticised lacquer, onto the linen fabric envelope of the ship to make it weatherproof.

Four years later, the craft was launched, with space for 137 people – 37 crew and 100 paying passengers. Propulsion came from six petrol engines, and levitation by 5 million cubic feet of hydrogen.

The R100's first significant voyage, on 29 July 1930, was to Canada – a journey of some seventy-eight hours. But three short months later, its sister ship, the R101 was brought down by bad weather in France. Of the fifty-four people on board, only six survived. With that, the R100's flights were curtailed and the ship was crushed by a steamroller and sold for scrap.

1920s

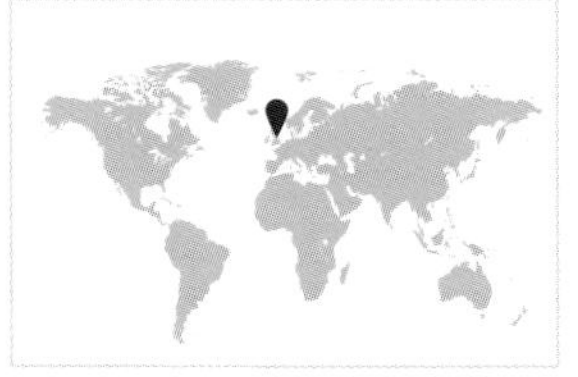

'On Thursday, 28 November, representatives of the press were invited to view R100 in her shed at Howden. It was a miserable, wet day, and everyone was glad when they got inside the huge shed, though as a matter of fact the rain was pouring freely through one section of the roof. Inside the shed it is impossible to get a complete view of the silver monster which fills it.'

Flight International magazine, 6 December 1929

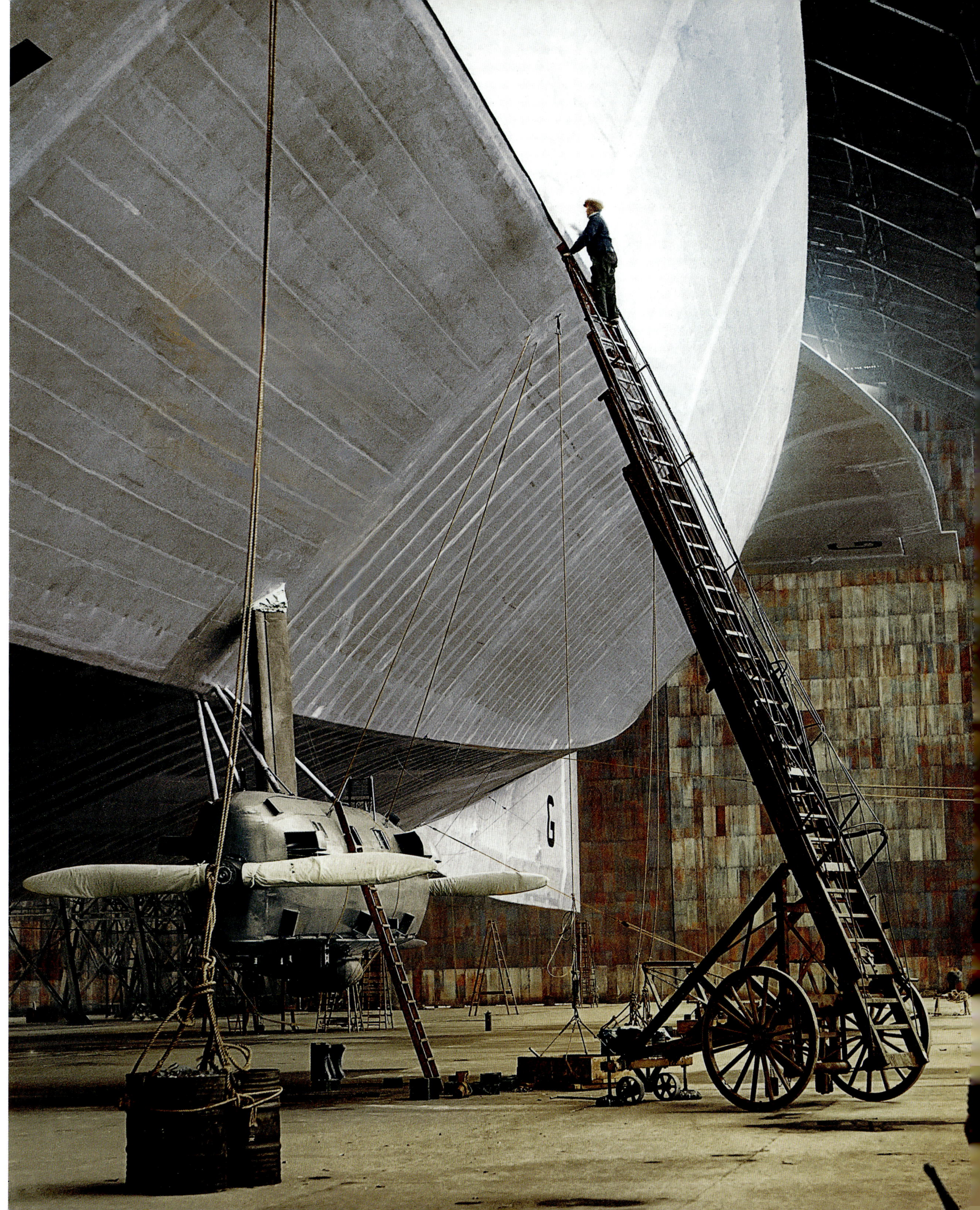
G

1920s

1928: Looking down Glasshouse Street to the junction with Sherwood Street and towards the lights of Piccadilly Circus in London
Piccadilly, London, UK
(Topical Press / Getty)

Piccadilly Circus hasn't been a circus – a circle – since 1886, when its shape was disrupted by the newly built Shaftesbury Avenue. In 1908, a sign for Perrier became the first illuminated advert in the plethora of signs for which Piccadilly Circus continues to be renowned. The first neon sign was an advert for Bovril, a meat extract.

This shot shows a multitude of signage, including 'Cannes: The Seaside of Flowers and Sports', 'Guinness is Good for You', Sandeman's Port, Army Club Cigarettes, Cafe Monico and Chop Suey Chinese Restaurant.

The sign for the London Pavilion gives the surnames of Pickford and Fairbanks, aka Mary Pickford and Douglas Fairbanks. Following their marriage in 1920, the pair produced their pictures at their co-owned Pickford-Fairbanks Hollywood studio.

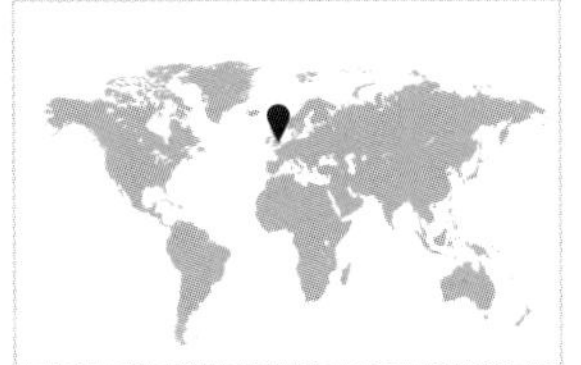

'You've smoked something worth smoking when you've smoked an ARMY CLUB. THE FRONT-LINE CIGARETTE. This is the cigarette for the fellow with the full-size man's job to do. When you're feeling all "hit up", it steadies the nerves.'

Army Club cigarette advert *c.* 1920

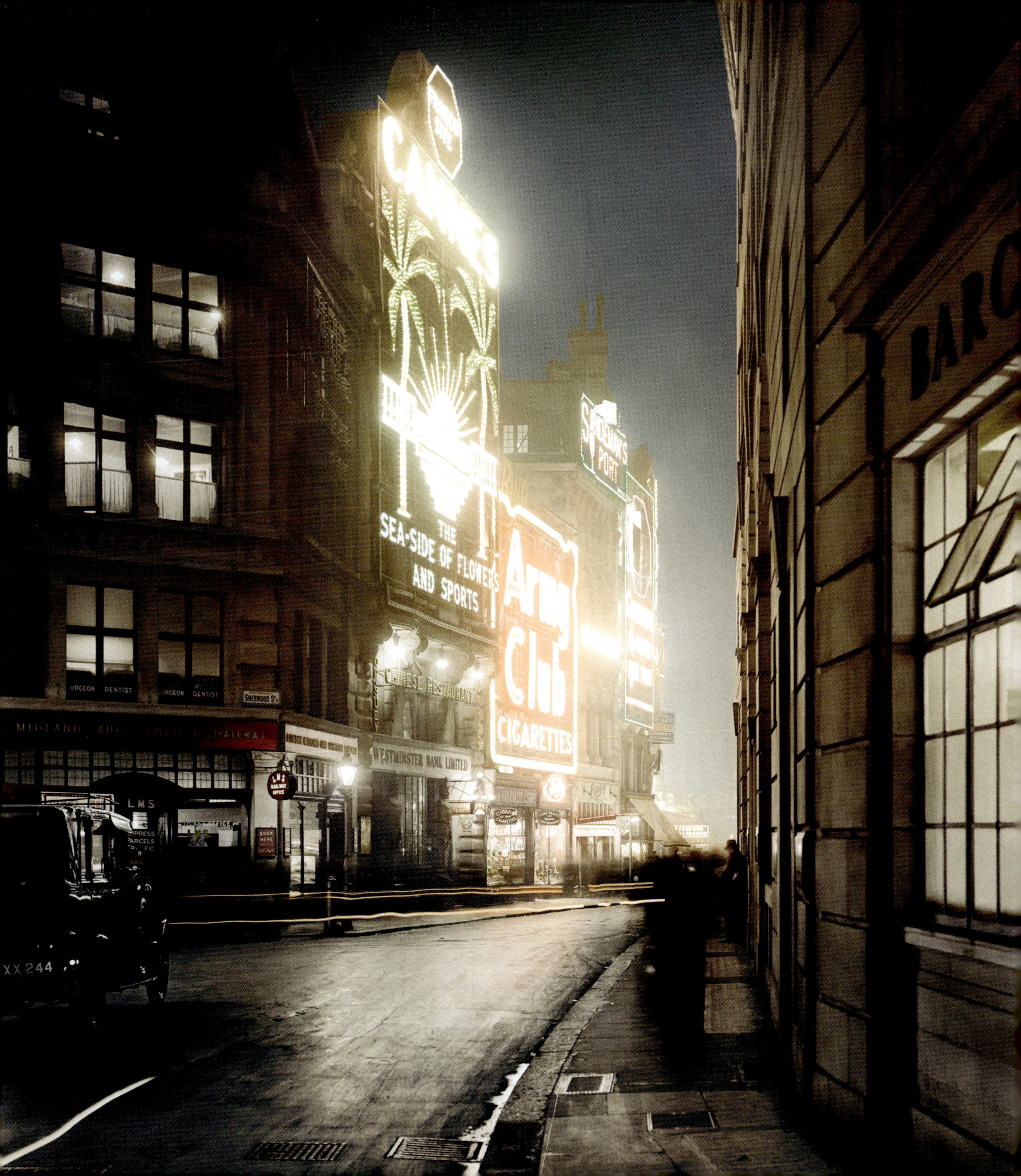

CANNES
THE
SEA-SIDE OF FLOWERS
AND SPORTS
Army Club
CIGARETTES
CHINESE RESTAURANT
WESTMINSTER BANK LIMITED
SHERWOOD St
LMS
XX 244

1920s

28 December 1928: A cameraman and a sound technician record the roar of Leo the Lion for MGM's famous movie ident

Hollywood, California, USA
(John Kobal Foundation / Getty)

Footage of a lion has been used by studio Metro-Goldwyn-Mayer's visual ident since 1924, but in the tradition of movie-making, 'Leo' was not exactly what he (or she) seemed. In fact, Leo did not exist per se but had, since 1916, been played by a total of seven different lions.

This picture, taken on 28 December 1928, shows Jackie the lion. A sound stage was especially built around Jackie's cage to make the recording. The second incarnation of Leo, Jackie was the first to be heard to roar, and a sepia-tinged Jackie appears at the beginning of 1939's *The Wizard of Oz*.

MGM went to the lengths of building Jackie a specially designed open-sided plane, housing Jackie's cage, flying the lion to different locations to generate publicity. In September 1927, en route from San Diego to New York, the plane crashed into the Arizona desert. Jackie and the pilot were unharmed. Four years later, she 'retired' to the Philadelphia Zoo.

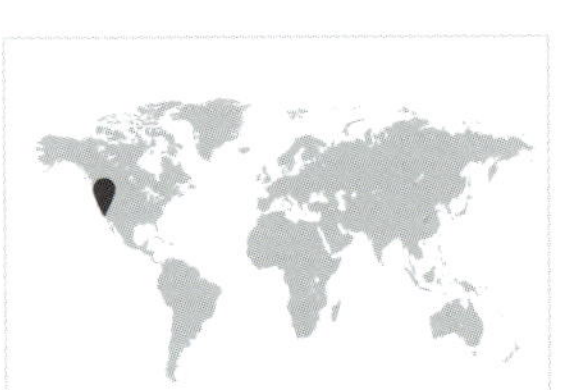

'She was the ugliest cat you had ever seen. Looking at her, you wouldn't think she had an ounce of brains. Yet, she was the smartest of all lions I ever worked.'

Melvin Koontz, *News Chronicle VISTA*, 1969

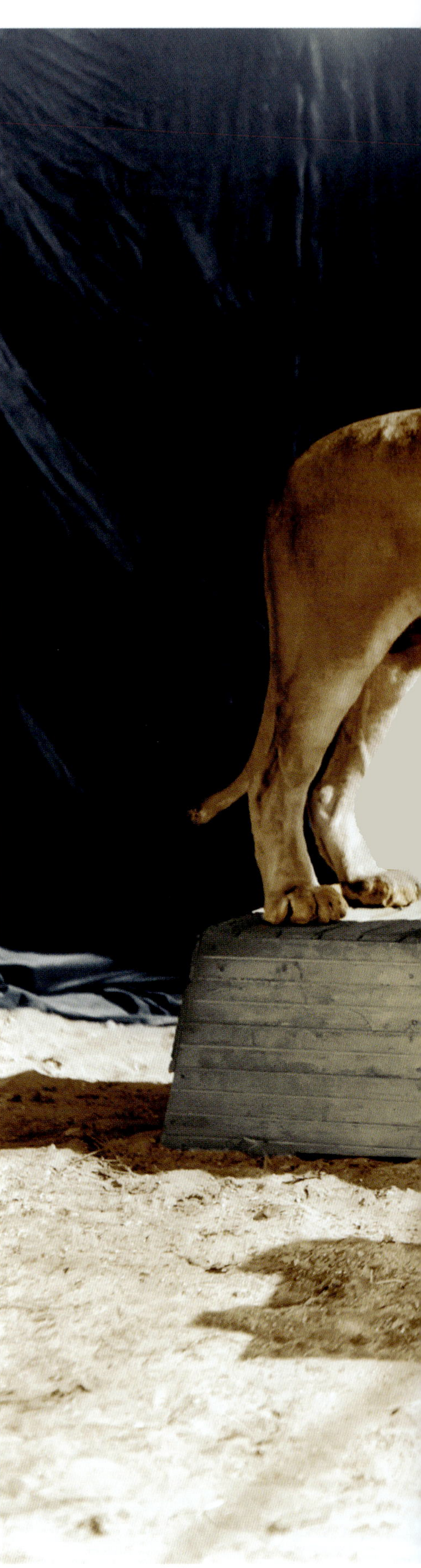

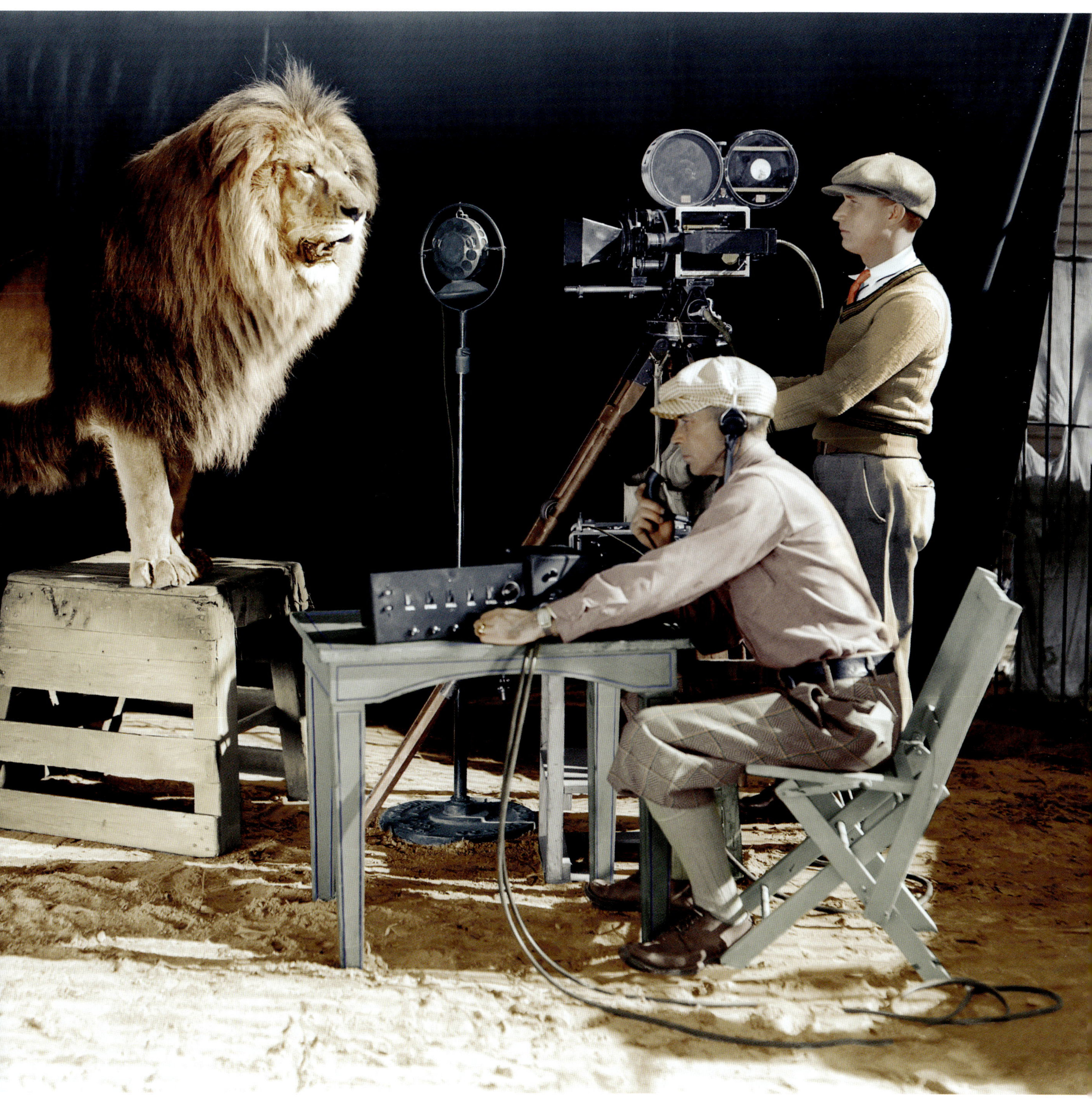

1920s

1926: A flock of sheep walking along the Kingsway in London

Kingsway, London, UK
(Unknown / Fox Photos / Getty)

Purely picturesque as this scene might seem, sheep were actually brought into central London for motives of efficiency. The cost of keeping the grass of the capital's many pastoral parks under control could be significantly reduced by outsourcing the task to flocks of sheep.

Competition existed within the shepherding community for the right to graze sheep on the pastures of London's parks. While sheep were barred, as it were, from the parks at the end of the 1950s, they have more recently been returning to their labours in the capital city, with flocks to be found on London's Hampstead Heath.

In this photograph, a flock is being driven down Kingsway from Aldwych towards Holborn.

'What else can show the eye a canvas such as this? A browsing flock, man's diligent friend, the sheepdog. Little wonder that passersby look on with contentment at such beauty.'

London shepherd, 1948

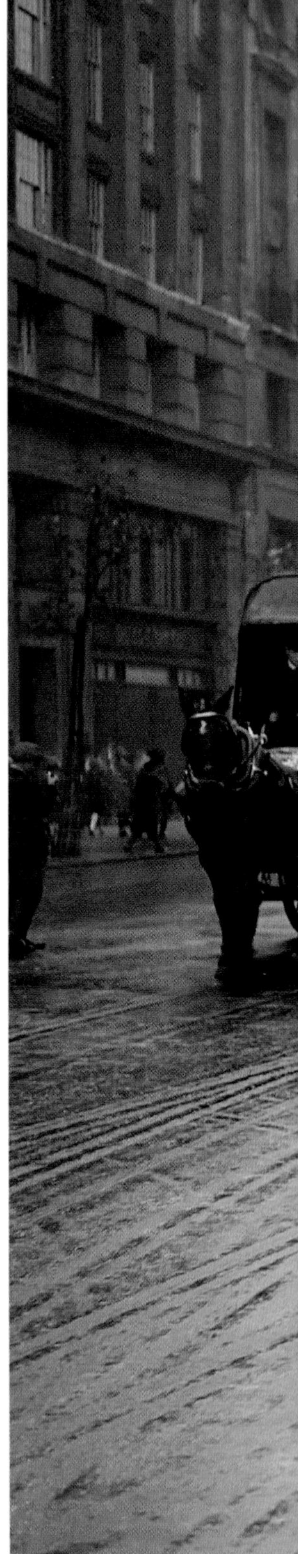

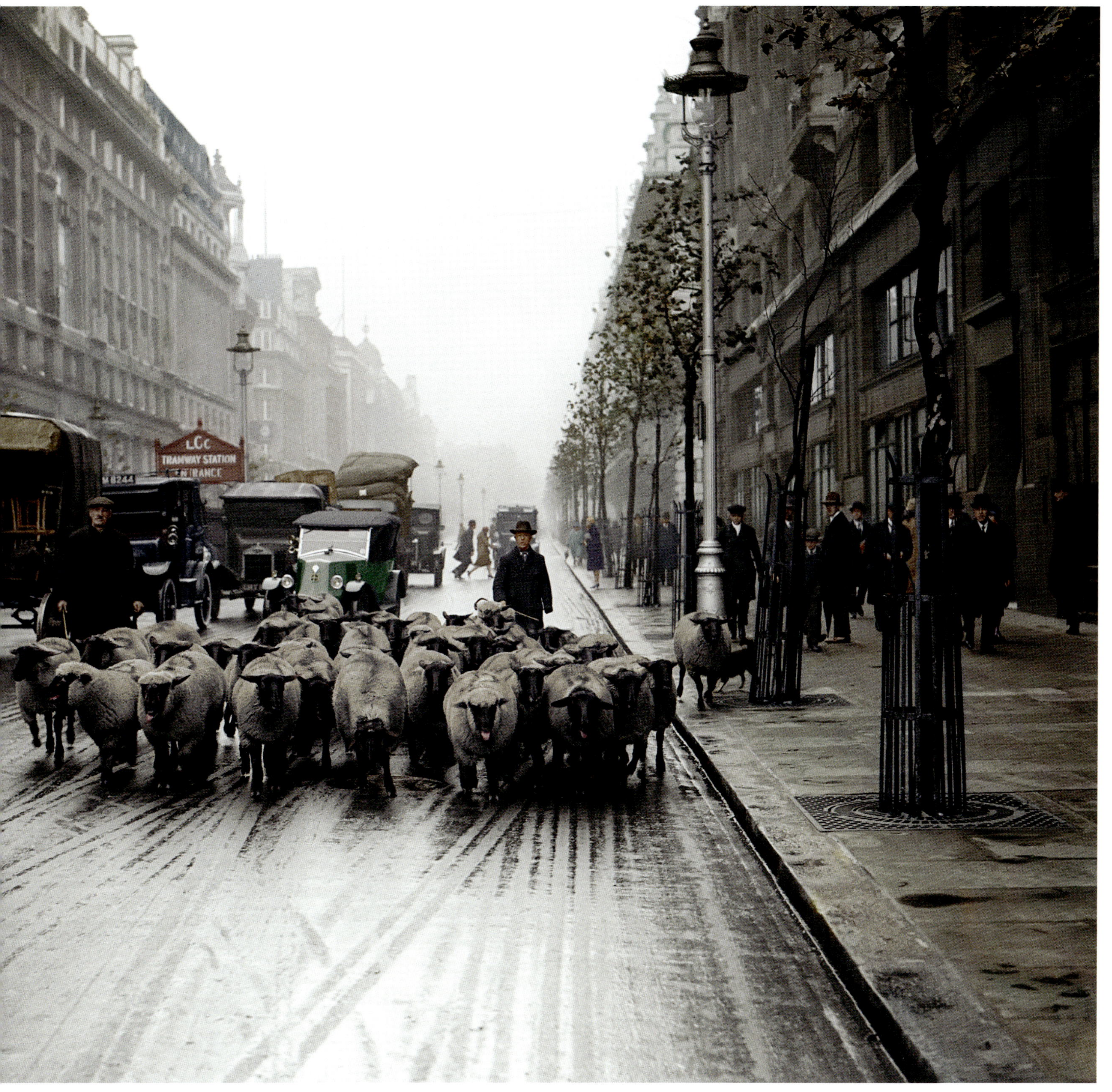
LCC
TRAMWAY STATION

1920s

28 March 1925: Sakura cherry blossom, Potomac Park, Washington DC

East Potomac Park, Washington DC, USA (Library of Congress)

The presence of sakura cherry trees in East Potomac Park, Washington DC, is a result of the passion of writer and traveller Eliza Ruhamah Scidmore, the first female board member of the National Geographic Society.

Scidmore, a frequent traveller to Japan, first suggested planting sakura to the park superintendent in 1885. The idea was rejected. Still determined, she spent the next twenty-four years bringing the same idea before every subsequent superintendent, still without success. Finally, in 1909, Scidmore pledged herself to raise the funds to buy the sakura and give them to the city by her own means.

She wrote to the new first lady, President Taft's wife Lady Helen Herron Taft, who had lived in Japan. Lady Taft took up the cause and suggested the trees form an avenue. Almost immediately, eminent Japanese chemist (and discoverer of adrenalin) Dr Jokichi Takamine donated 2,000 further sakura in the name of Tokyo. However, on arrival in Washington DC on 6 January 1910, the 2,000 trees were found to be irreparably diseased and were destroyed. Undeterred, Dr Takamine increased the number of trees he would donate to more than 3,000. In March 1912, Lady Taft and the wife of the Japanese Ambassador, Viscountess Chinda, planted two trees, and the remaining trees were placed in the park between 1913 and 1920. The original two still stand. Here we see Sumi and Sada Tamura, daughters of Mr Teijiro Tamura, former Third Secretary of the Japanese Embassy in the United States.

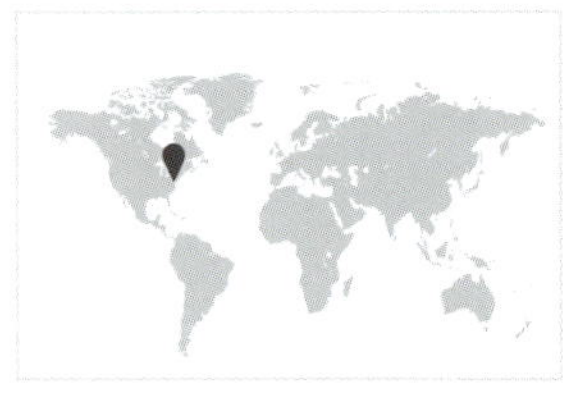

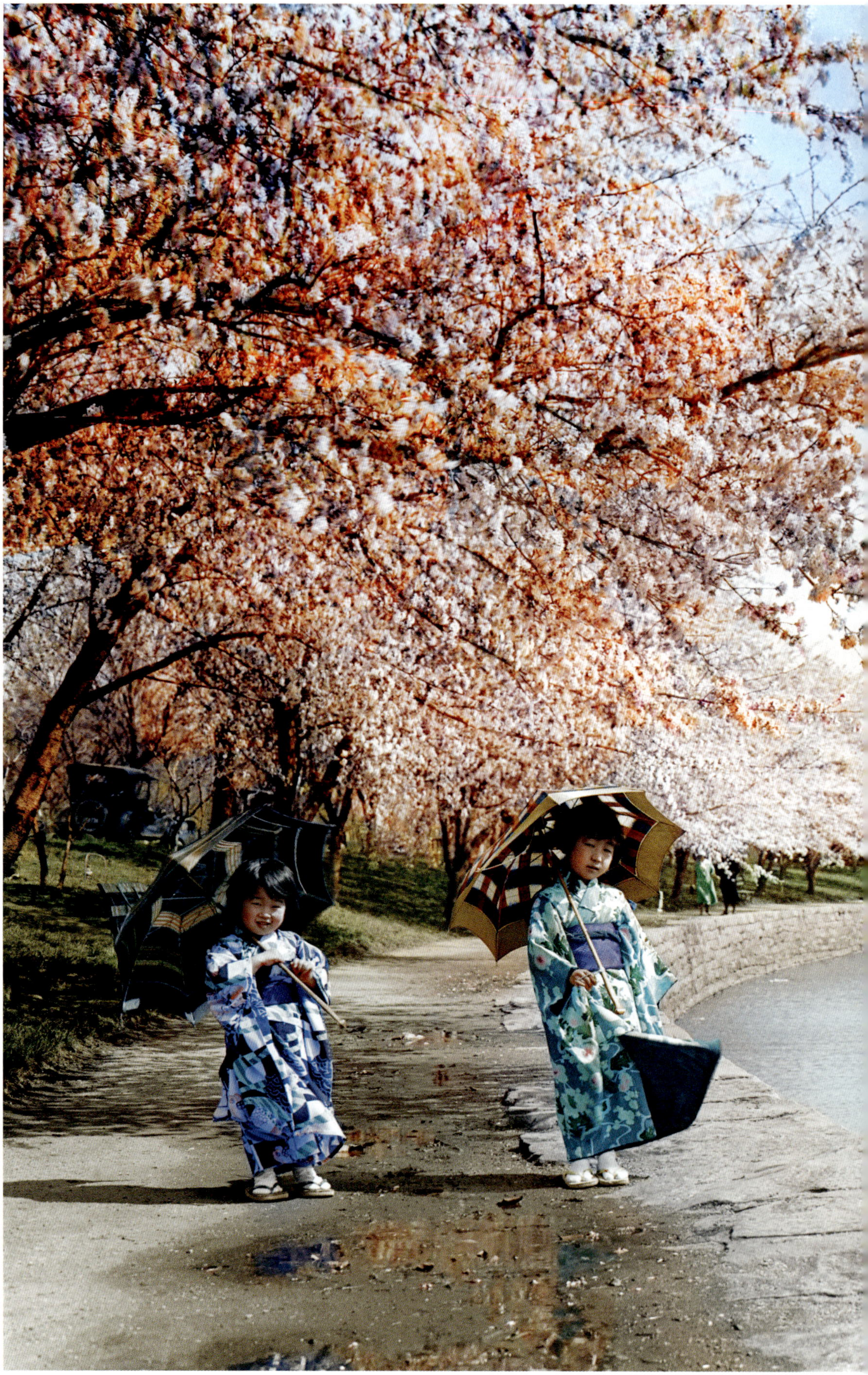

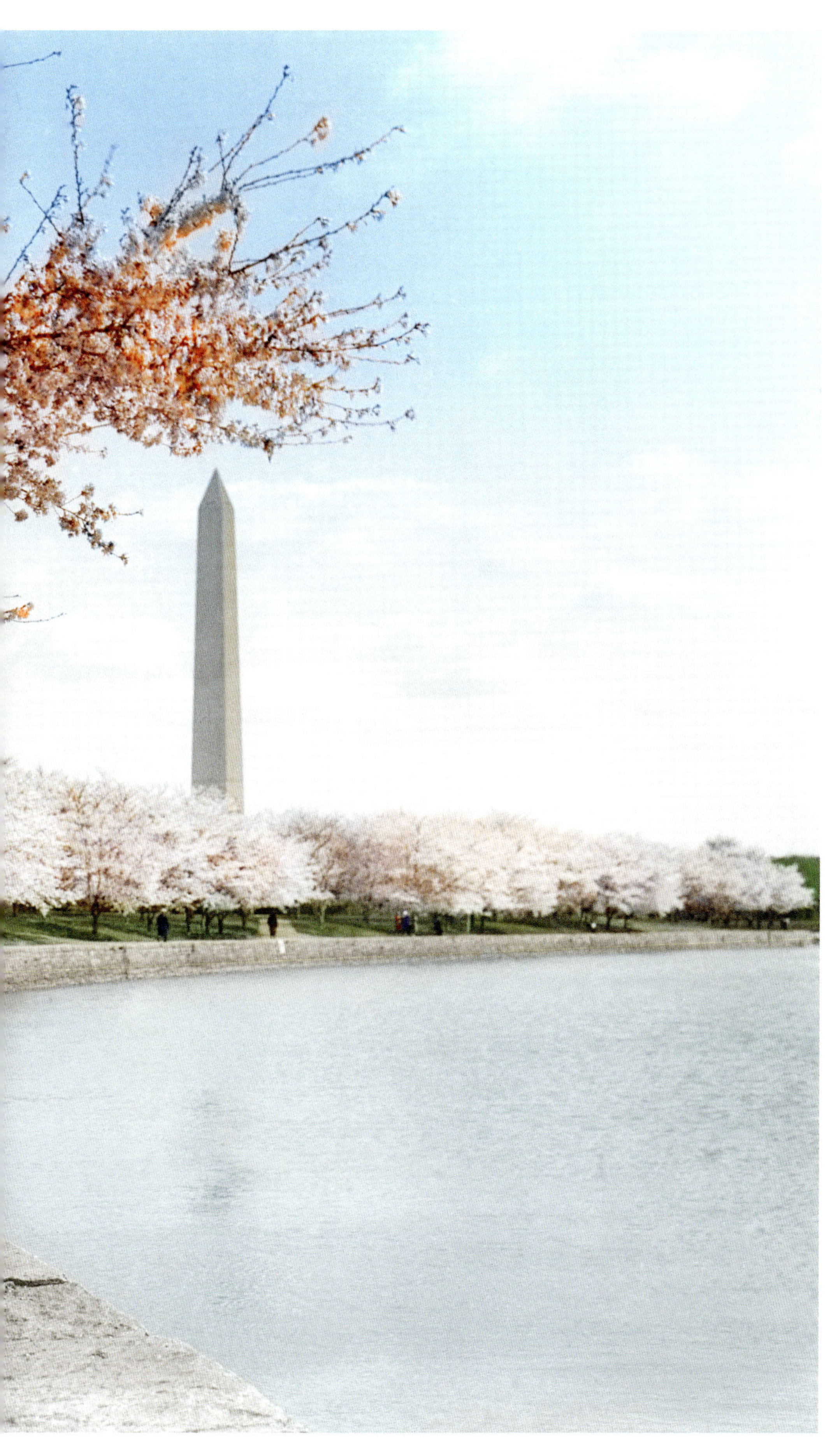

'The White House, Washington

7 April 1909

Thank you very much for your suggestion about the cherry trees. I have taken the matter up and am promised the trees, but I thought perhaps it would be best to make an avenue of them, extending down to the turn in the road. Of course, they could not reflect in the water, but the effect would be very lovely of the long avenue. Let me know what you think about this.

Sincerely yours,

Helen H. Taft'

Letter from Lady Taft to Eliza Scidmore, 1909

1920s

26 June 1925: A female Native American telephone switchboard operator

Glacier National Park, Montana
(Bain News Service / Library of Congress)

'Helen', a member of the Blackfeet Nation, is photographed here operating the switchboard at Many Glacier Hotel, in Glacier National Park, Montana. Telephone operators of the time worked at hotels as well as exchanges.

During this period, park concessionaires often required their Blackfeet employees, including bus drivers and telephone operators, to dress in 'traditional' clothing to appeal to eastern tourists. The hotel, the largest inside the park, was built by the Great Northern Railroad between 1914 and 1915 as accommodation for tourists to the National Park. The area in which the hotel sits is described as the 'Switzerland of North America' and the hotel is themed around a Swiss Chalet design.

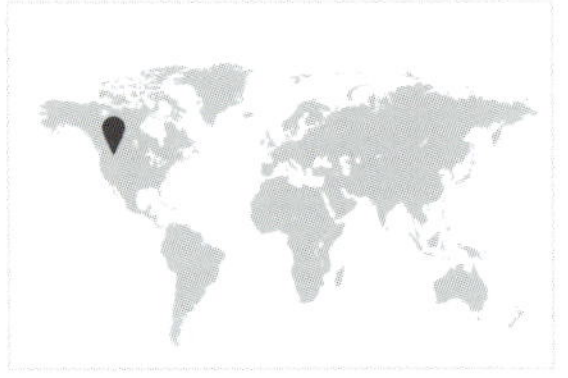

'Glacier National Park! Season June 15 to October 1. During the season of 1915 this tremendous mountain land may be enjoyed as never before. The accommodation and tours have been arranged to suit the most exacting tourist. A new mammoth mountain hotel, the "Many-Glacier", has been erected on Lake McDermott in the Park's heart – one of America's most notable tourist hotels.'

Advert for Glacier National Park, *The Glasgow Courier*, Montana, 14 May 1915

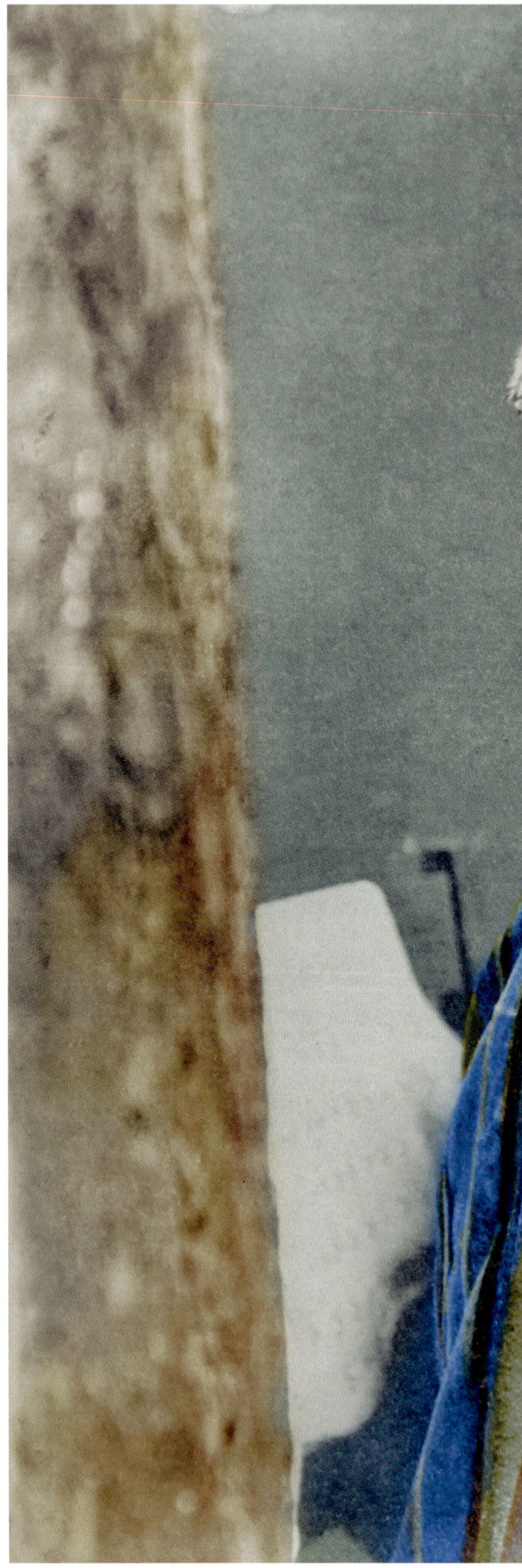

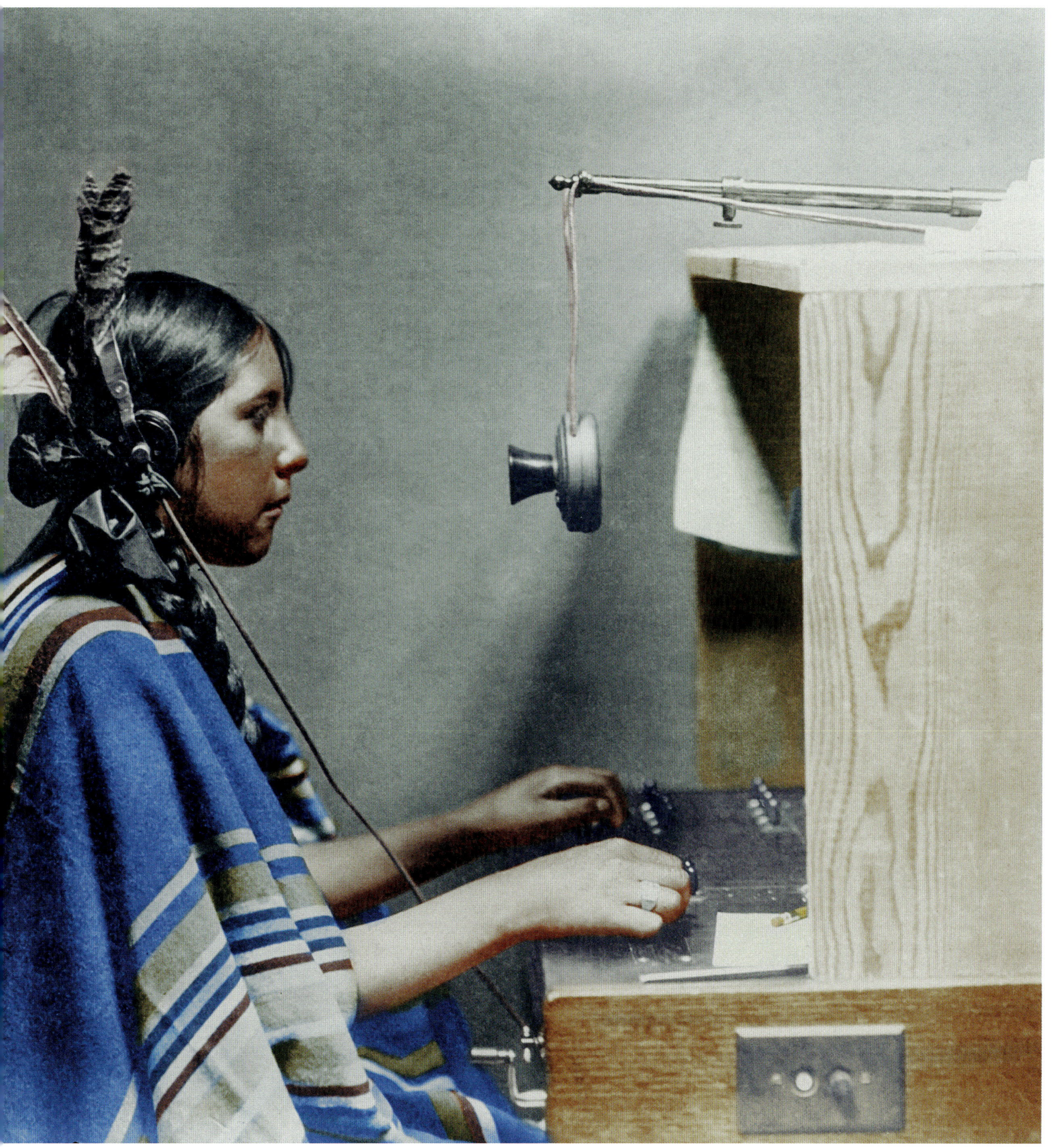

1920s

1924: **The 'Hollywoodland' sign in Los Angeles, later changed to read 'Hollywood'**
Hollywood, California, USA
(Underwood Archives / Getty)

Here, 'Hollywood' is an abbreviated form of reality – or, at least, of a real estate sign. The owner of the *Los Angeles Times*, Harry Chandler, erected the sign above a housing development he had created in the Hollywood Hills. The name of the development, and the word on the sign, was 'Hollywoodland'.

Originally intending the sign to be a temporary installation for eighteen months, Chandler paid $21,000 to have the fifty-foot high sign constructed. Each letter was illuminated with a multitude of electric light bulbs, and the three parts of the sign flashed in sequence before the entire name was lit, as well as being flooded by a searchlight.

In 1949, the 'land' element of the sign was removed by the Hollywood Chamber of Commerce.

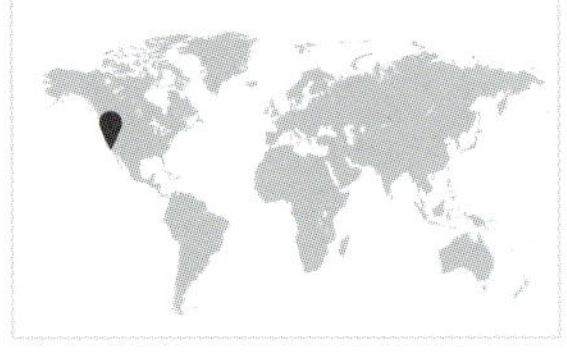

'Hollywoodland ABOVE THE TURMOIL OF THE CITY. "The Supreme Achievement in Community Building". Where Will You Live… When the second million has come? Will your family enjoy a delightful home in the clean pure mountain air of Hollywoodland, with its wonderful climate, broad open spaces, and plenty of "elbow room" – or – will you live in a "dwelling" in the flat, uninteresting houses-in-a-row solutions of the city, your family's freedom hampered by this madhouse of human existence?'

Advert for Hollywoodland, c.1924

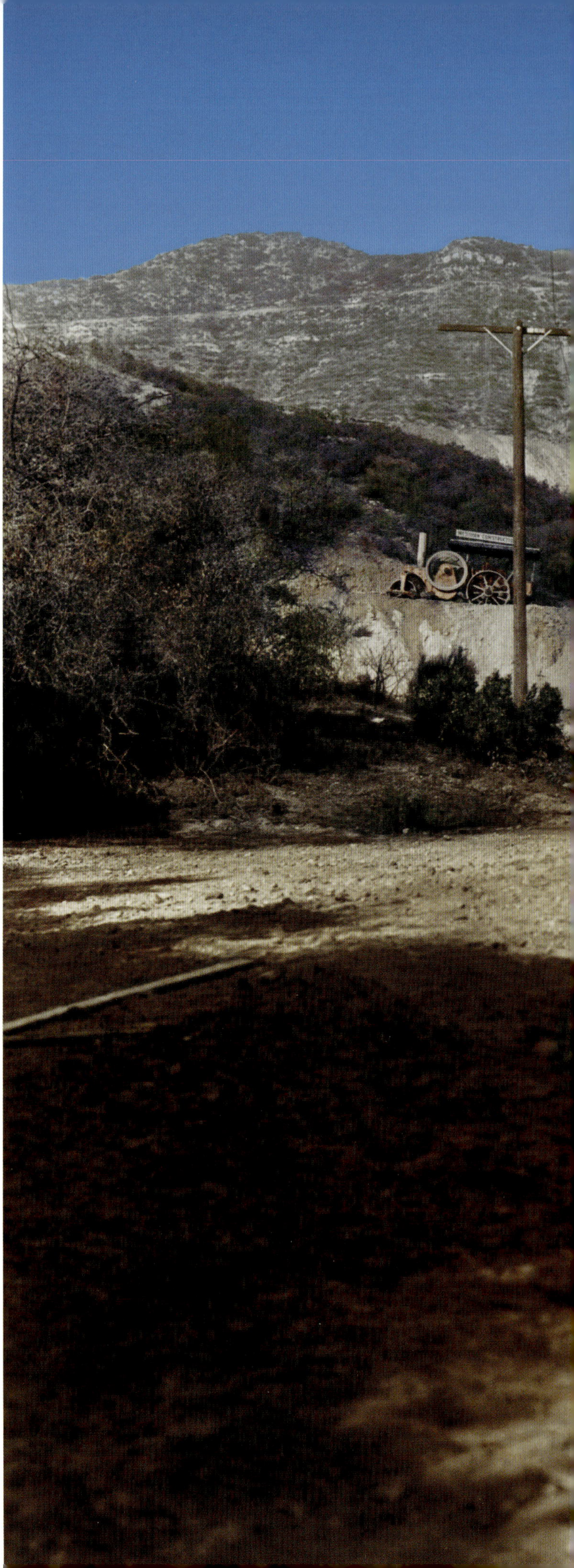

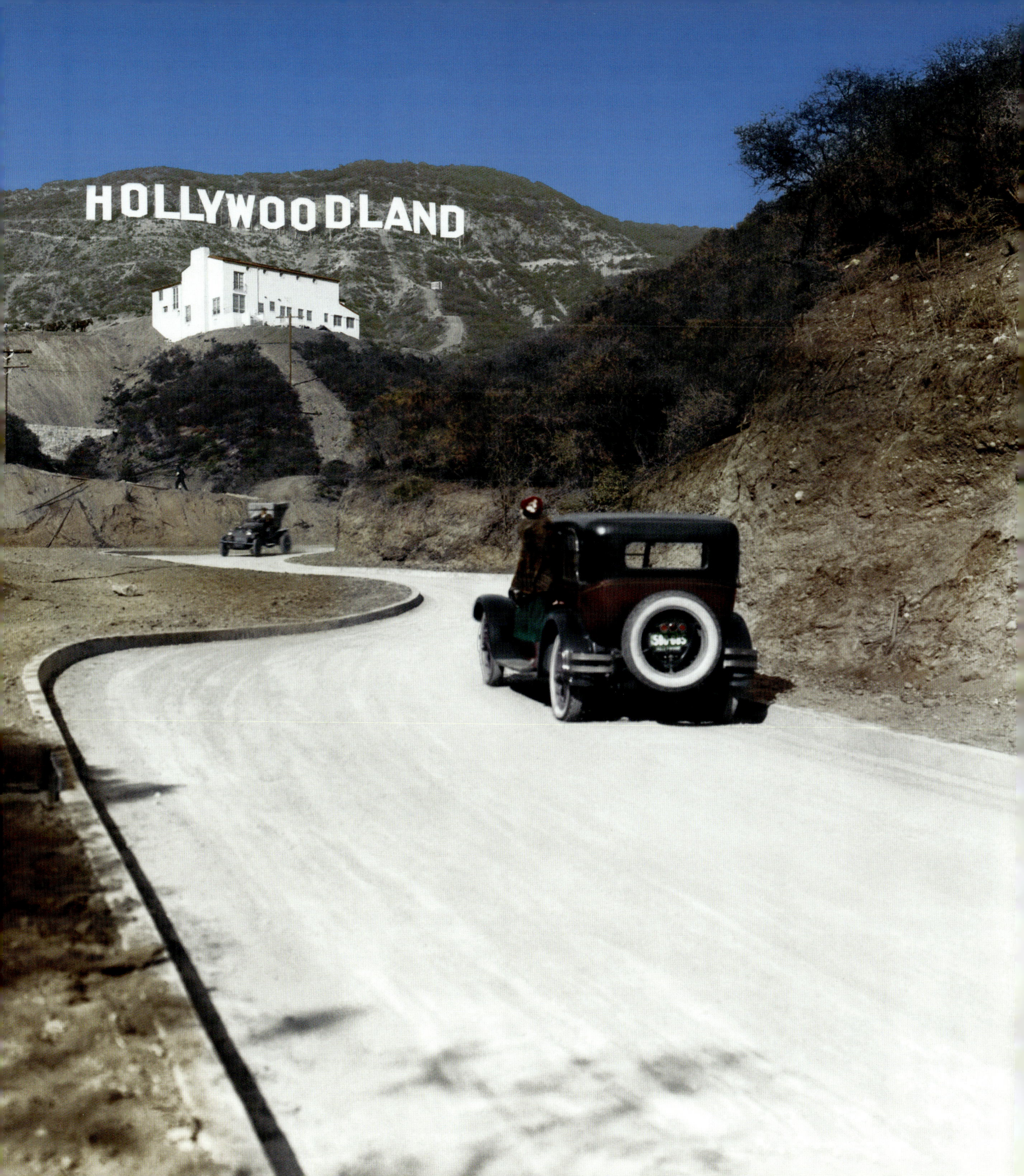
HOLLYWOODLAND

1920s

July 1923: A punt gun, used to shoot flocks of waterbirds from a punt
Washington DC, USA
(Library of Congress)

Punt guns were designed for punts – small boats – used to hunt waterbirds. With a bore often above two inches, and firing in excess of one pound of shot into a flock, punt guns are recorded as having killed almost 100 birds with a single blast.

The recoil of the gun, fixed to the punt, was sufficiently strong to propel the boat backwards across the water. Such was the level of destruction wreaked by punt guns that most American states banned their use by the mid 1800s. Punt guns continue to be used in the British Isles.

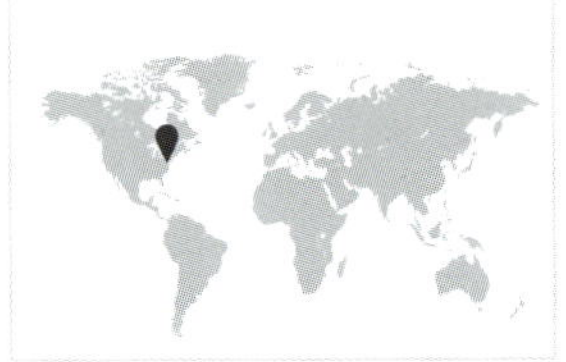

'The pursuers of the strange sport of punt-gunning have had remarkable experiences. Slipping along in their punts at dawn, they have come upon flocks so great that a single shot from the great swivel gun, which is almost a cannon, has bagged more than a longshore sportsman could get in a week.'

Washington Evening Star, 4 March 1911

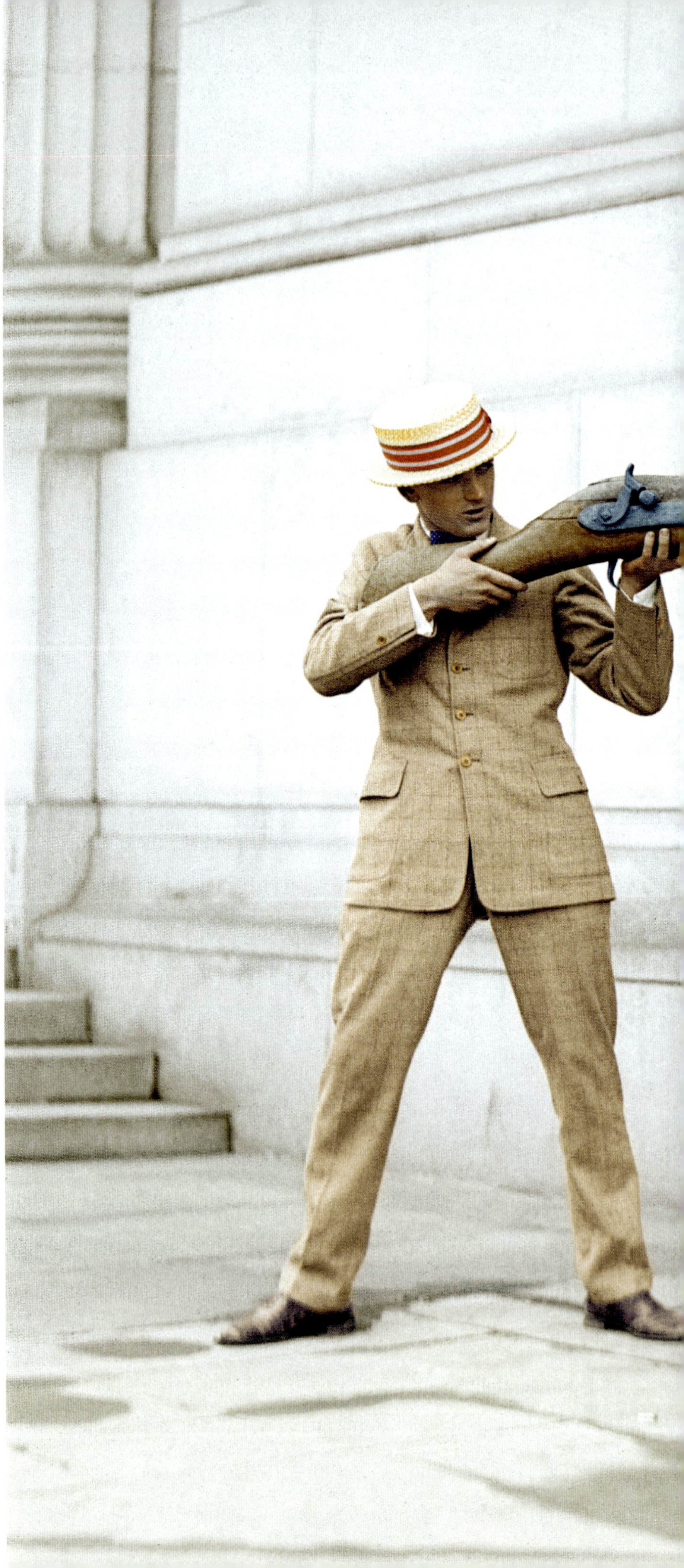

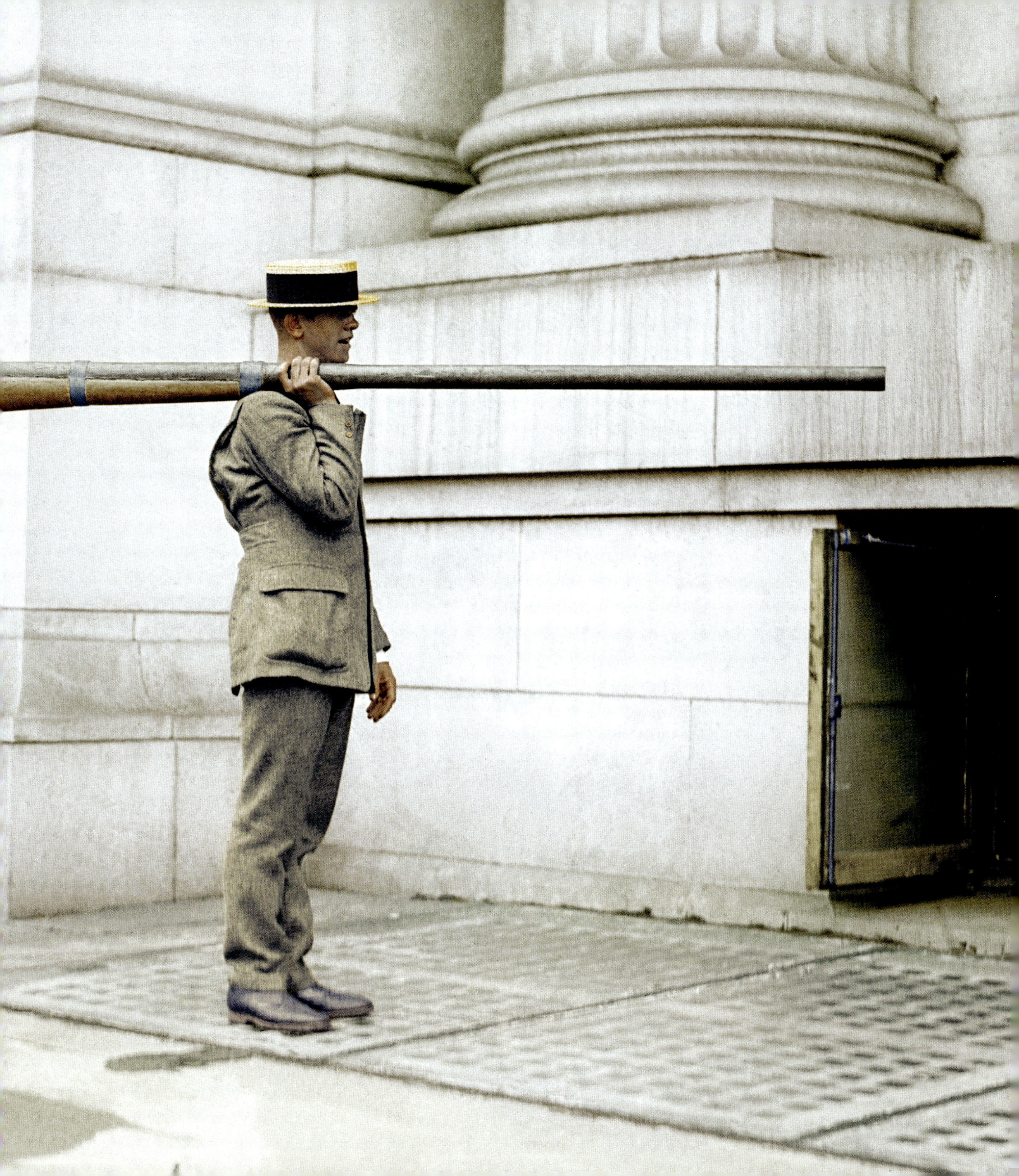

1920s

1922: The contents of the central coffin of Tutankhamun's tomb

East Valley of the Kings, Luxor, Egypt (Harry Burton / The Griffith Institute)

This sight was the culmination of many years of labour for archaeologist and Egyptologist Howard Carter and his backer George Herbert, 5th Earl of Carnarvon. After years of fruitless excavation, the discovery of the tomb of the boy pharaoh Tutankhamun came during the very last season of digging that Carnarvon was prepared to fund.

On 4 November, at the derelict site of an earlier dig, Carter's team stumbled upon a step. The following day, the step had become a stairway, leading to a door. Carter wired Carnarvon, and on 26 November, the two broke through the doorway. There then followed an eight-year-long process of deconstructing the tomb and its contents.

Opening the inner sarcophagus reveals the pharaoh's mummy, and its magnificent funerary mask of gold. The twenty-four-pound solid gold mask, inlaid with blue glass and semi-precious stones, was placed directly over the mummy. The eyes of the mask are made from lapis lazuli, quartz and obsidian. What you can't see here is the protection spell carved on the mask's back and shoulders.

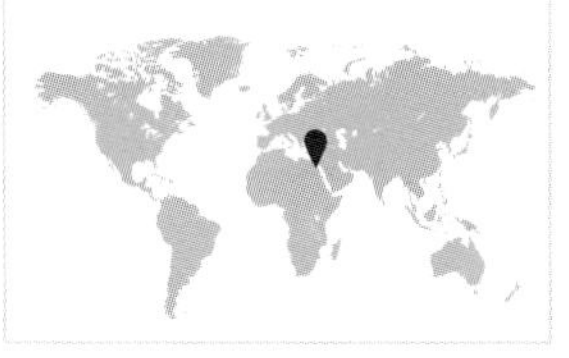

'The day following, 26 November, was the day of days, the most wonderful that I have ever lived through and certainly one whose like I can never hope to see again. The decisive moment had arrived. With trembling hands I made a tiny breach in the upper left-hand corner of the door. I inserted the candle and peered in. For a moment – an eternity it must have seemed to the others – I was struck dumb. When Carnarvon inquired, "Can you see anything?" all I could do was get out the words, "Yes, wonderful things."'

Howard Carter, 'The Tomb of Tutankhamun', 26 November 1922

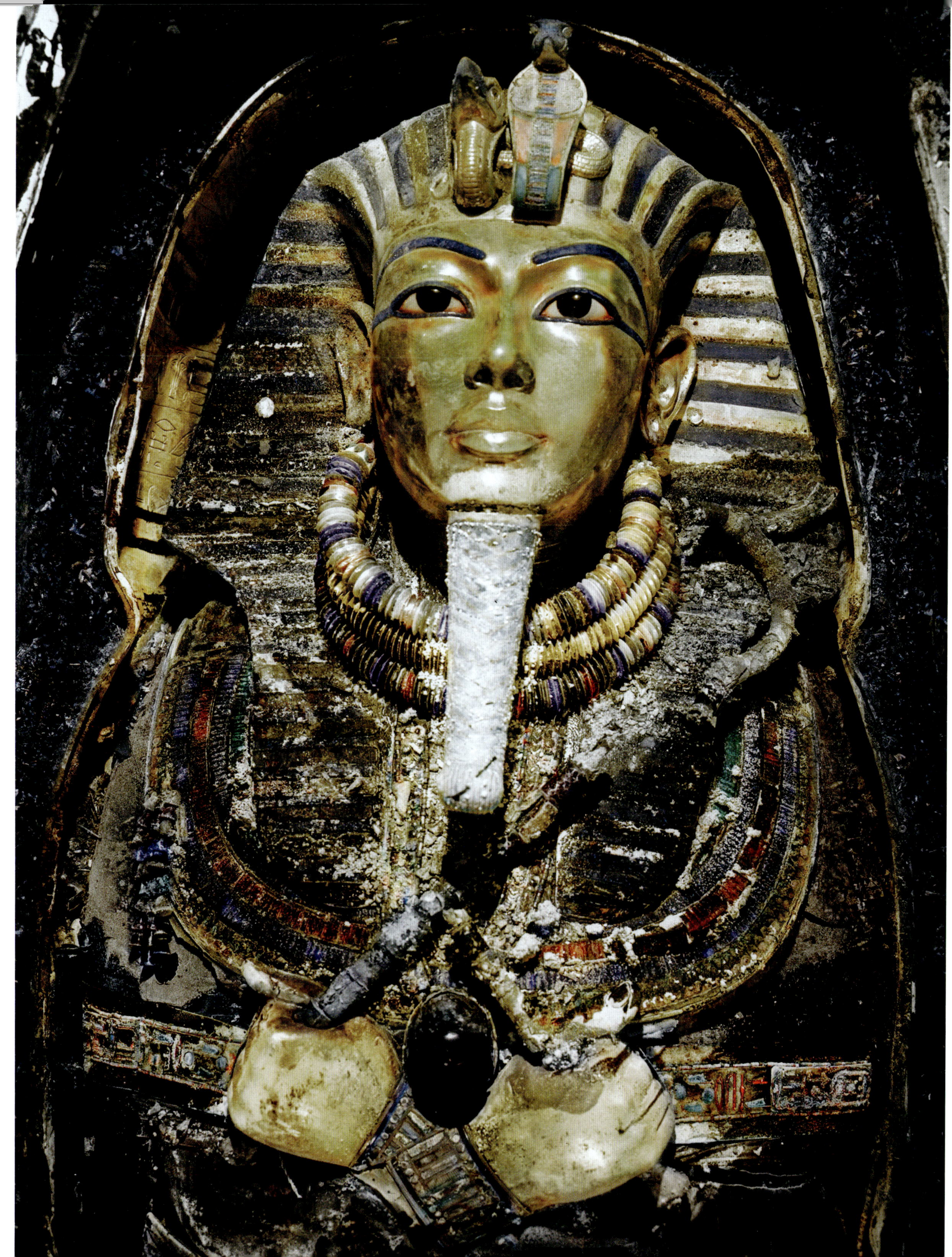

1920s

7 September 1921: **Margaret Gorman, the newly crowned Miss America, awaits the arrival of Neptune in her royal robes at the opening of the Atlantic City Beauty Pageant**
Atlantic City, New Jersey, USA
(Bettmann / Corbis / Getty)

Margaret Gorman was crowned 'Miss America' because no one knew what else to call her. Margaret had sent her photograph into a *Washington Herald* popularity contest at age sixteen, and still just a high-school junior. From around 1,000 entries, she and five other young women were selected as finalists. The six toured the city that summer, and Margaret was given the title 'Miss Washington, DC'.

Margaret was then entered into an 'Inter-City Beauty' contest in Atlantic City. She won, and was awarded the trophy of the 'Golden Mermaid'. The following year, by the time she returned to Atlantic City to defend her Golden Mermaid trophy, the *Washington Herald* had run a subsequent competition and given the title 'Miss Washington DC' to another woman. At a loss for a title for Margaret, the competition organisers alighted on 'Miss America', and thus created the Miss America pageant.

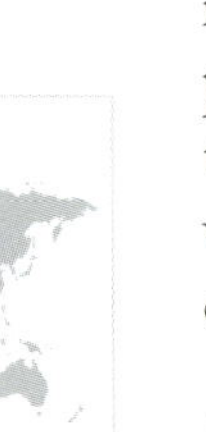

'Introducing "Miss America". Dedicated to Beautiful Miss Margaret Gorman. Who will be at our 7th St Store, in person – today from 2:30 to 5 p.m. Miss Gorman pronounced this new fall pump – the year's most beautiful shoe. So we have invited her to be present this afternoon, when we formally present it to Washington. The "Golden Mermaid" and other valuable trophies won by Miss Gorman – shown in our window. Hahn's Reliable Shoes.'

Washington Herald, 28 September 1921

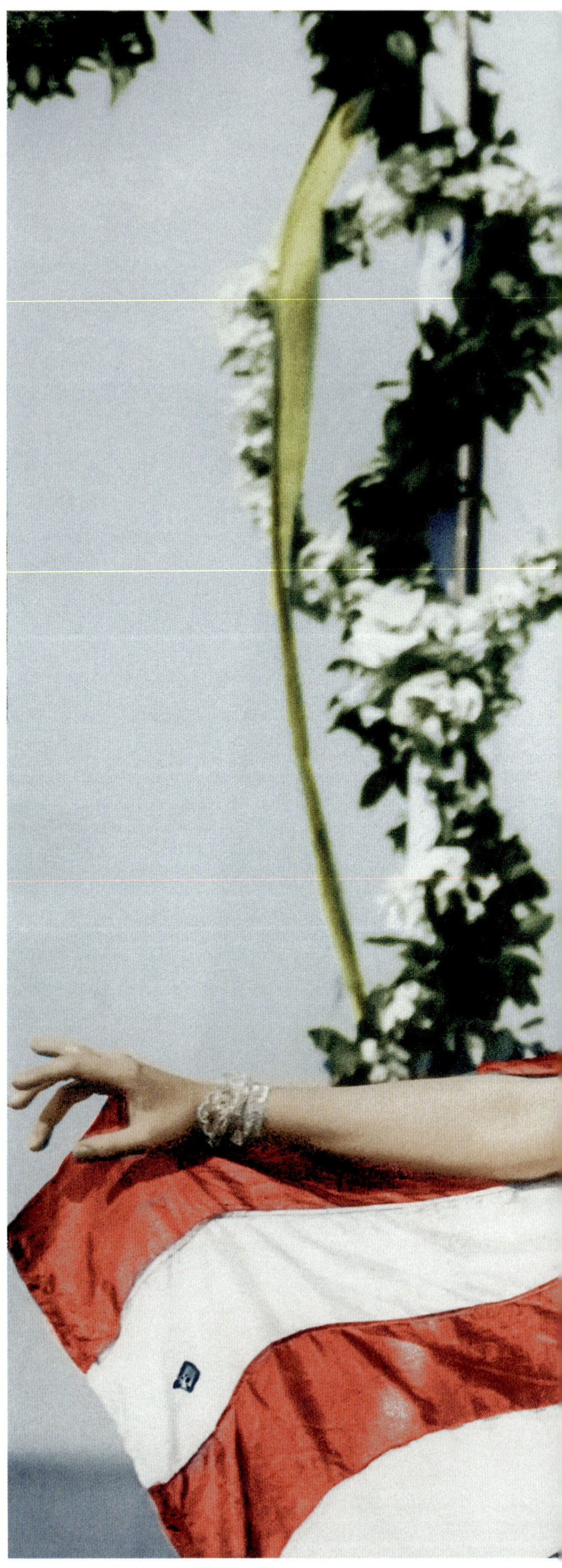

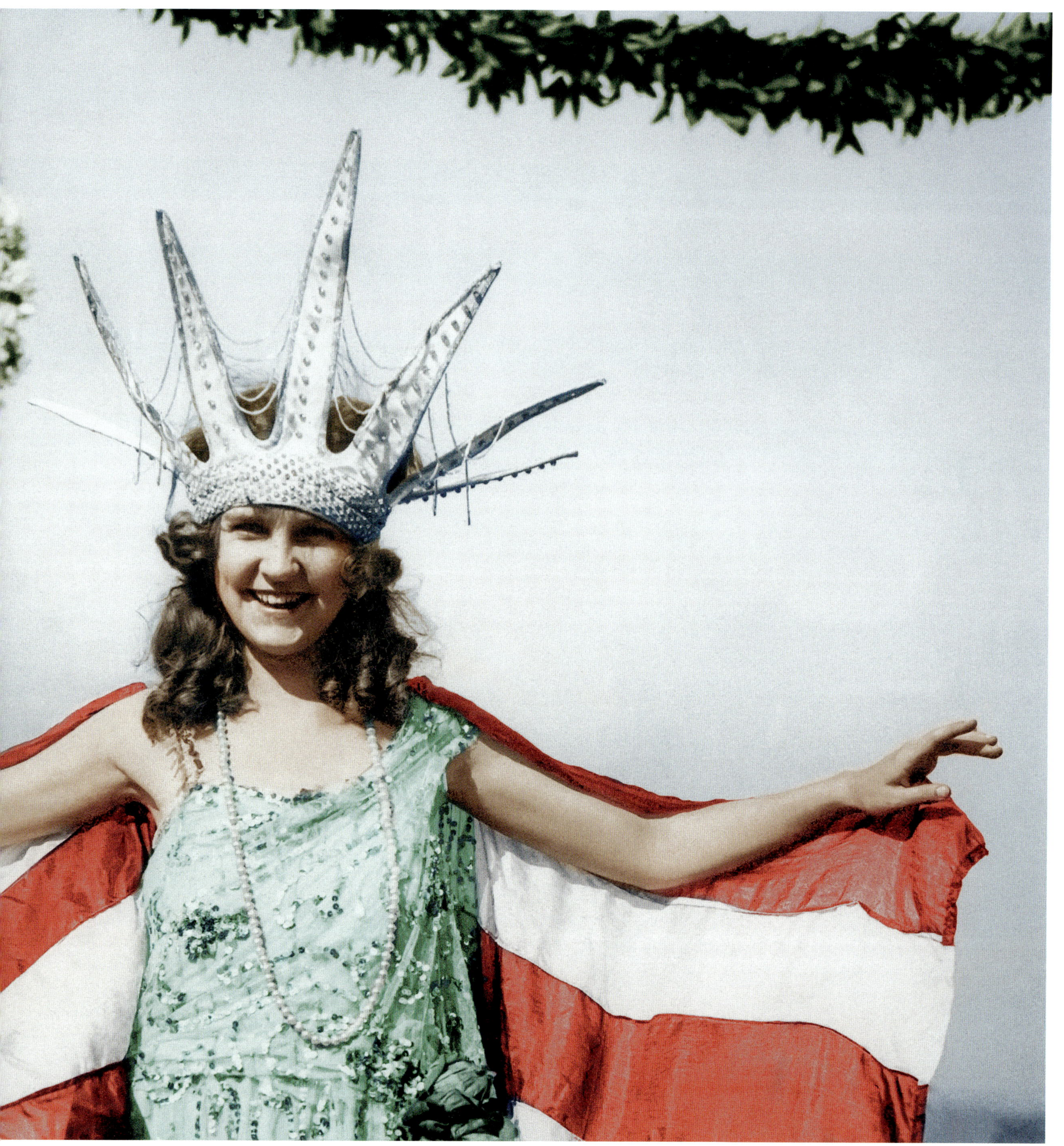

1920s

1921: Sound amplifiers at Bolling Field Air Force Base, Washington DC

Bolling Field Air Force Base,
Washington DC, USA
(Unknown / Getty)

These sound amplifiers, at Bolling Field Air Force Base, were a response to the increasing impact of aerial warfare. The sound volume of an aircraft was sufficient to be detected at large distances, providing, in theory, sufficient time for a defensive response.

With the advent of radar, devices such as these – essentially an elaborate equivalent of a cupped hand – became obsolete.

'In one day, recently, sixty-three German guns were located by this means, and destroyed by airplane bombs, although many of them had been so successfully camouflaged that probably they never would have been discovered by any other means.'

Popular Science, December 1918

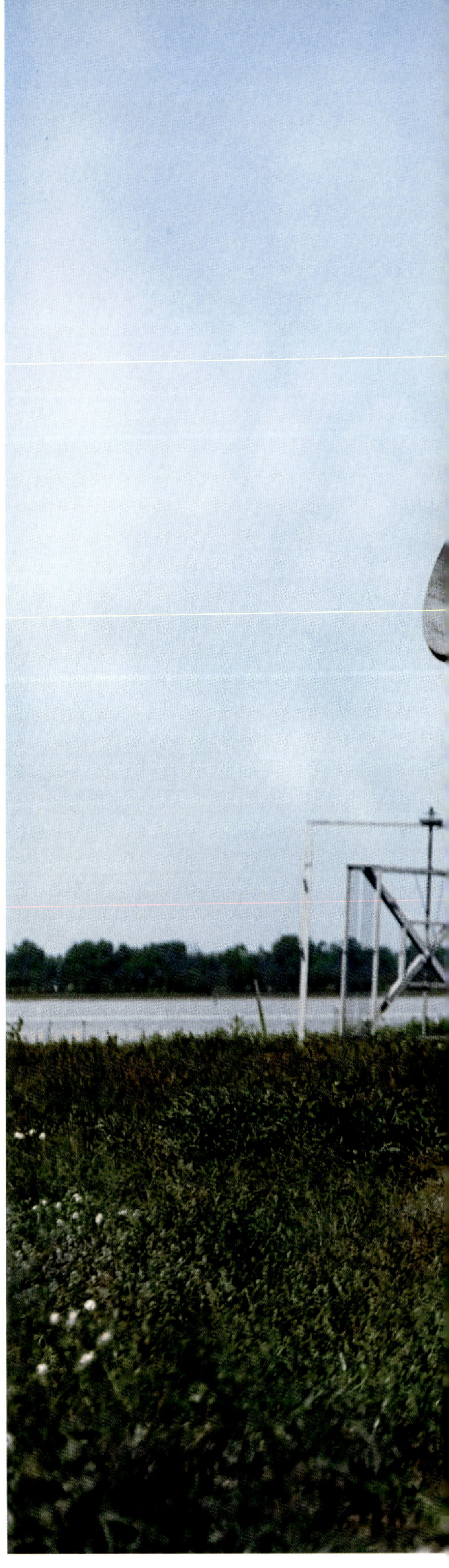

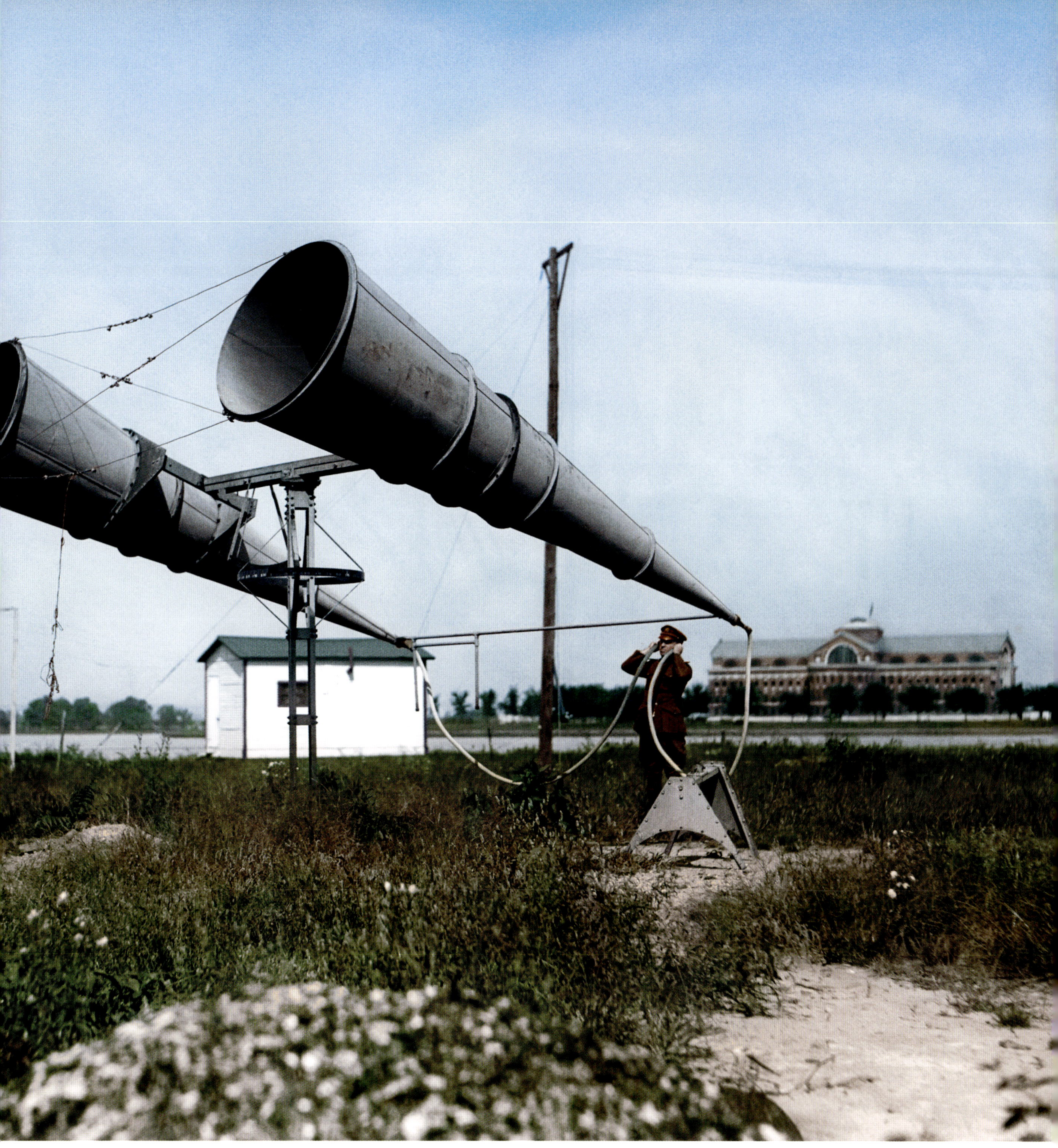

1920s

c. 1920: A view of a trilithon being re-erected at Stonehenge

Near Amesbury, Wiltshire, UK
(English Heritage / Hulton Archive)

The prehistoric monument Stonehenge in Wiltshire is a standing stone ring within earthworks. Currently believed to be between four and five thousand years old, while it appears to align with the position of the sun during the summer and winter solstices, its exact purpose remains a source of speculation.

Between 1919 and 1926, British archaeologist Lieutenant-Colonel William Hawley was employed by the Office of Work to conduct restoration work. Almost seventy years old when work began, Hawley carried out much of the work alone, though in this photograph a team are seen righting a fallen stone. During his work, Hawley discovered a bottle of port wine in the socket of a stone, left by earlier archaeologist William Cunnington in 1810.

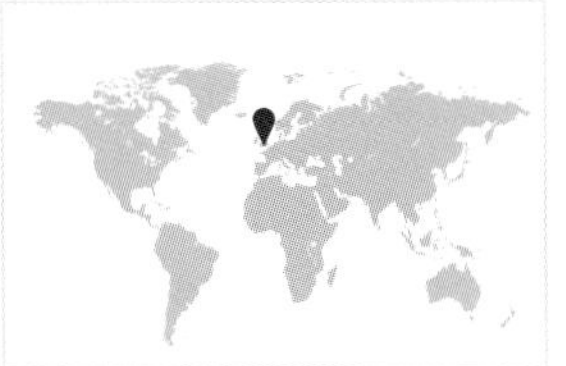

'In recording the finds made during the course of the exploration of the site, no account has been taken of the modern rubbish unless it has been of special interest or was found at an unusual depth, as it does not concern the ancient history of the monument. At one time, coursing meetings were annually held near Stonehenge, and, before each meeting glass and other noxious detritus likely to hurt the animals' feet were collected and buried, which will partly account for some of the modern materials found.'

Interim report on the exploration by Lt Col. W. Hawley, FSA, *The Antiquaries Journal,* 1921

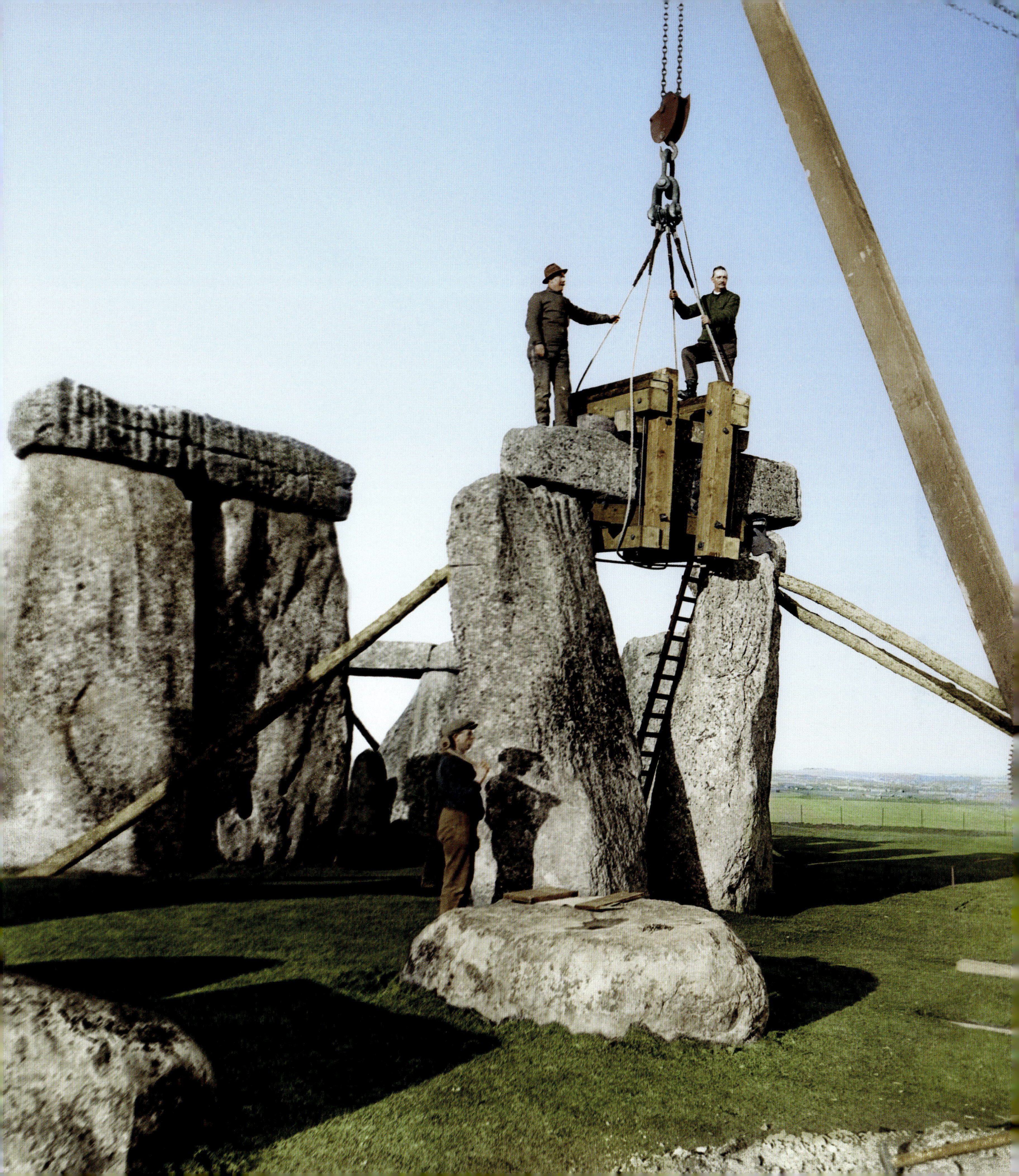

1920s

1920: Power house mechanic working on steam pump

Unknown location, USA
(Lewis Hine / US National Archives)

As well as creating a body of work documenting American child labour, sociologist and photographer Lewis Hine was also responsible for this now-iconic image – an example of Hine's photographic adjustment away from realist documents and towards a more compositional approach.

Hine's picture of a power house mechanic, one of his 'work portraits' series, had a deliberate intention behind it. Photographing for the US Work Progress Administration, Hine saw the significance of the human worker being overwhelmed by the proliferation of mechanisation. In this photograph, Hine attempts to redress the balance, placing the worker – and the machinery of his body – at the centre of the power house.

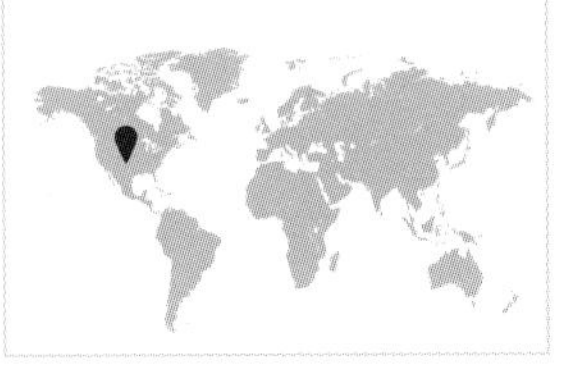

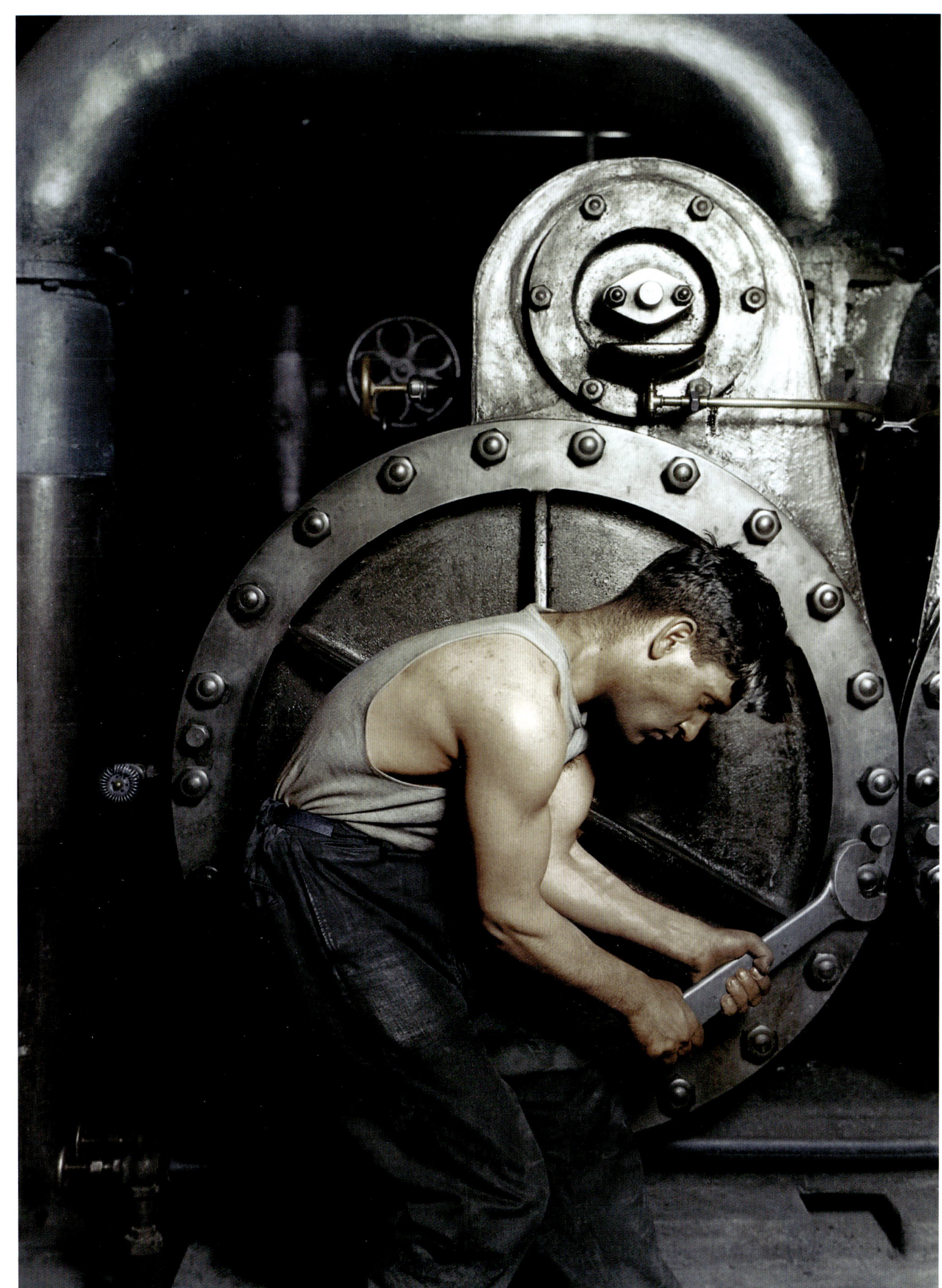

'I wanted to show the thing that had to be corrected: I wanted to show the things that had to be appreciated.'

Lewis Hine

1919: **Soldiers of the 369th 'Harlem Hellfighters' wearing the Cross of War medal pose for a photo on their trip back to New York**
Unknown location
(US National Archives)

1910s

Front row (*left to right*): Private Ed Williams, Herbert Taylor, Private Leon Fraitor, Private Ralph Hawkins. Back row (*left to right*): Sergeant H. D. Prinas, Sergeant Dan Storms, Private Joe Williams, Private Alfred Hanley and Corporal T. W. Taylor.

When America joined the Great War, the first African-American regiment to fight was the 369th Infantry, transported to France at the end of 1917. The racism and discrimination the soldiers encountered had begun during training in America, and continued in Europe, with many white US soldiers refusing to fight alongside the 369th. After April 1918, under the control of the French Army, such discrimination lessened.

Nicknamed the 'Harlem Hellfighters', members of the 369th were renowned for bravery, ability and ferocity. On their return to New York City after 1918, they received a euphoric welcome, marching up Fifth Avenue.

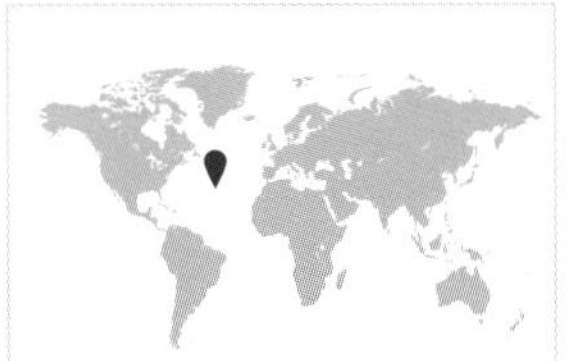

'When I was in conference with Frenchmen in Paris, I tried to explain as simply and temperately as I could the attitude of the whites in America towards the Negro, and when I had finished those Frenchmen said: "It is a kind of insanity, isn't it?" And when white American officers in France had decided it was necessary that the French should be told, lovingly and kindly, just how America treats Negroes in America, then the French war ministry collected every copy it could find of this circular and burned it.'

Professor W. E. B. Du Bois addressing a high-school crowd, *The Broad Ax*, Chicago, 24 May 1919

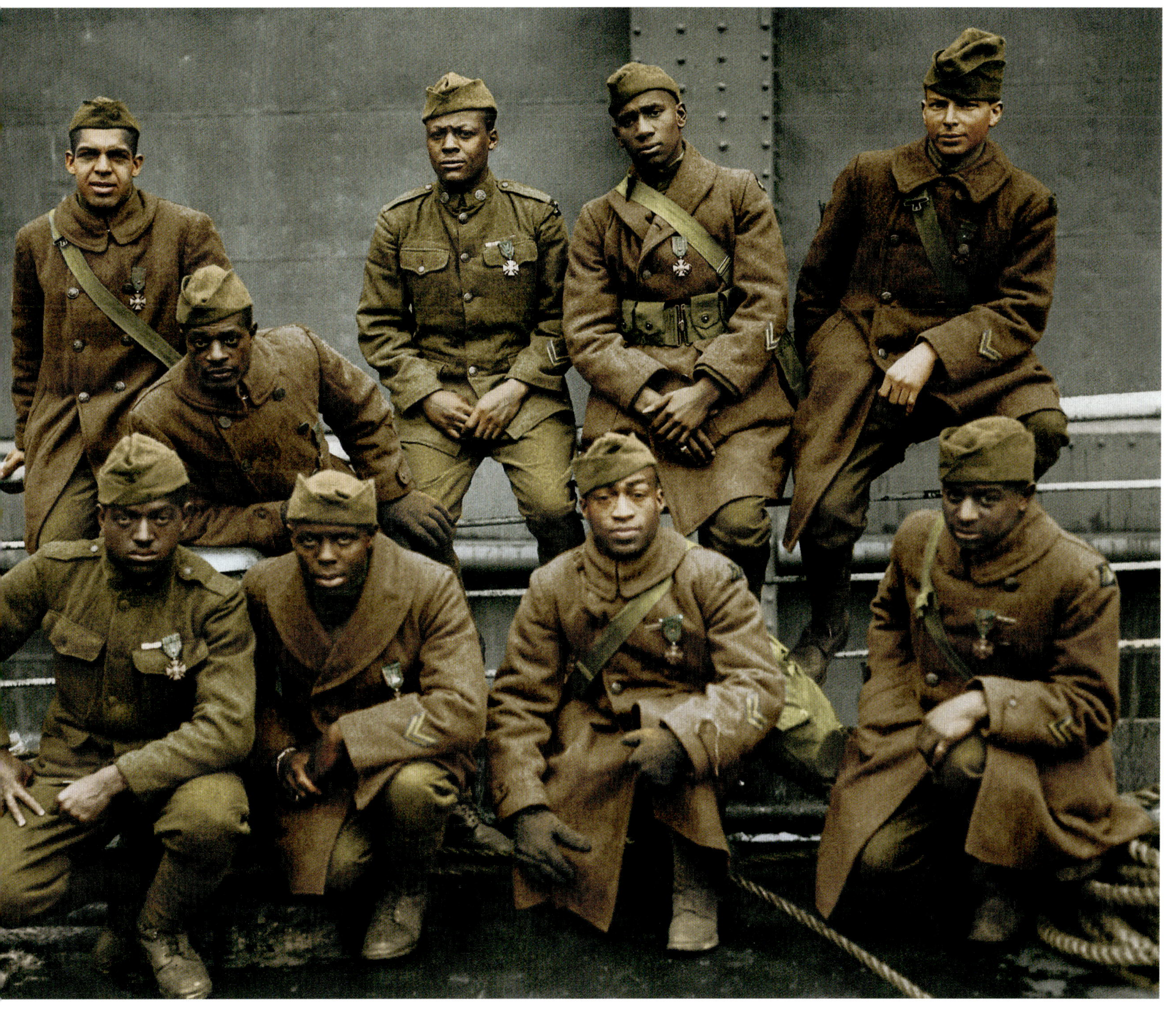

1910s

1919: The control room of a U-boat looking aft, starboard side

Wallsend, Tyne and Wear, UK
(Tyne and Wear Museums & Archives)

During the First World War, the German Navy possessed a fleet of approximately 350 submarines, known as *unterseeboote* or U-boats. The German U-boat campaign, begun in February 1915, undermined the British naval blockade in place around the British Isles.

For the German Navy, any ship in British waters was a target. Between October 1916 and January 1917 alone, U-boats sank almost 1.5 million tons of shipping.

This picture shows the interior of U-boat 110. The U-boat had been sunk in July 1918 in the North Sea, close to the town of Hartlepool, by HMS *Garry*. The controls include the air pressure gauges, hand wheels for pressure gear, the manhole to the periscope well and valve wheels for flooding and blowing.

Salvaged soon after, the boat is photographed here in Swan Hunter's Wallsend dry docks. After the Armistice, U-boat 110 was sold for scrap.

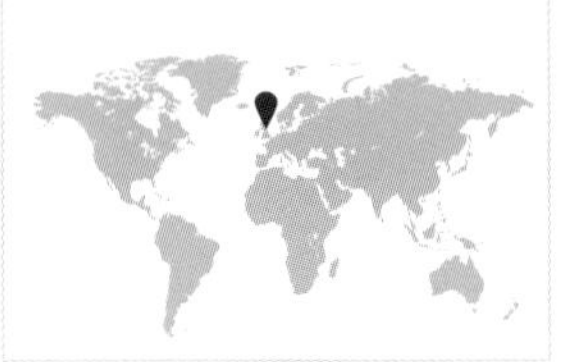

'Shall I risk another run at him, as he is still showing up on the surface? At all costs, he must not escape, so, once again we race through the water and settle the matter by hitting again and this time ripping her up completely and ourselves as well. Down went "U 110" where she belonged and down we went by the bows. I left the rescue work to the others, who picked up fifteen out of the water and then took stock of the damage we had sustained. No doubt it was serious and the vital question now was – should we chance it and try and get back to our base in the Humber?'

Charles Herbert Lightoller, Commander of the HMS *Garry* in *Titanic and Other Ships*, 1935

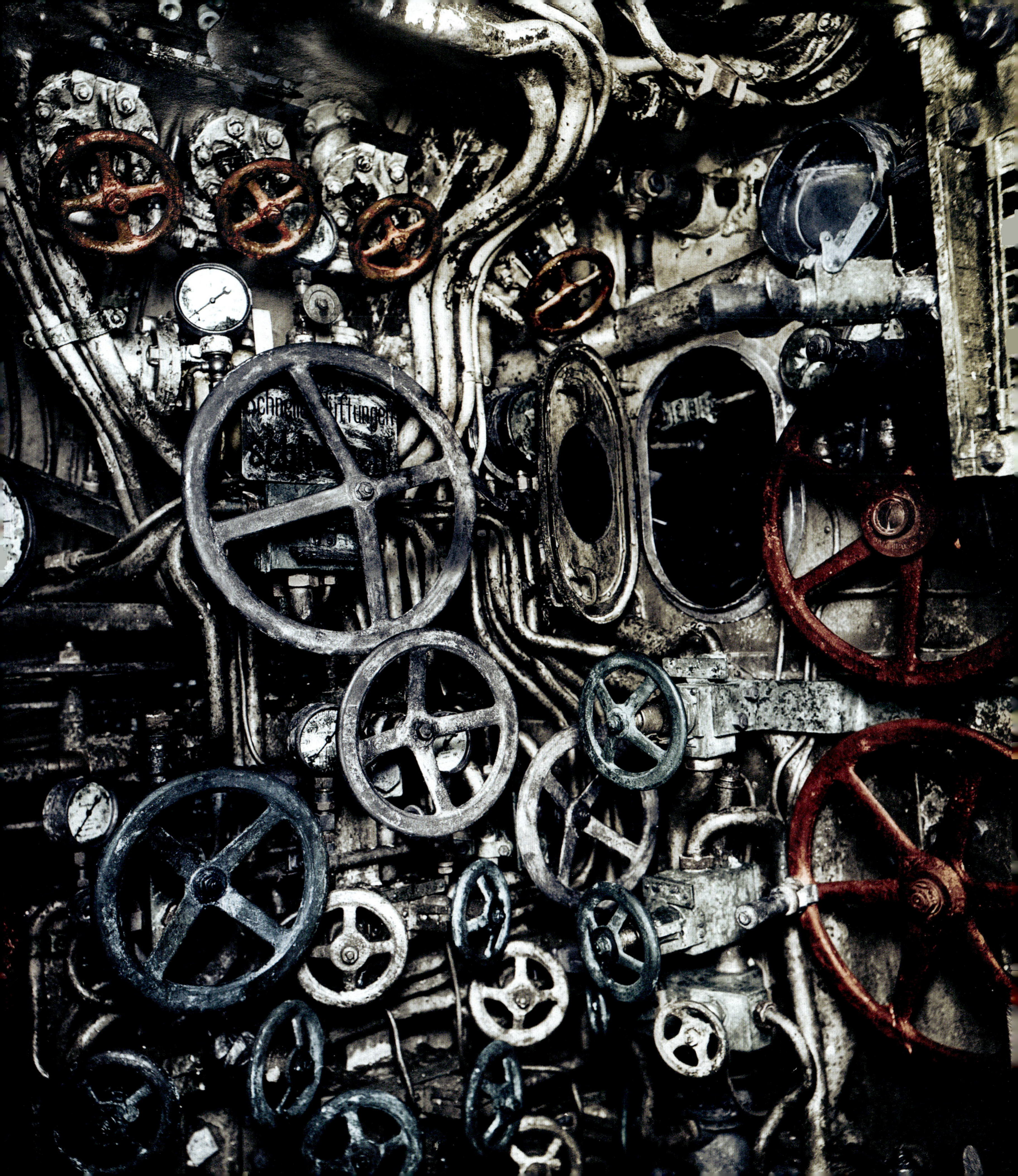

7 November 1918: Celebrations on Wall Street, New York, following the surrender of Germany

Wall Street, New York City, USA
(W. L. Drummond / Library of Congress)

1910s

This picture is almost what it seems, but not quite. We know the exact moment this picture was taken: 1:52 p.m. on Thursday, 7 November 1918, four days before the end of the First World War.

The premature report of the end of the Great War originated in a casual lunchtime conversation between Admiral Henry Wilson, commander of the American naval forces in French waters, and Roy Howard, President of United Press. Wilson passed on a report of a telephone call he had received from a friend employed in the American Embassy declaring an armistice had been signed.

Howard, believing he had just been handed the greatest news story of his career, circumnavigated the various systems of checks and censorship in place, going so far as to forge the signature of his foreign editor. He transmitted the story to New York unscrutinised, giving the time of cessation of hostilities as 2 p.m. – eight minutes after this picture was taken.

Traders on Wall Street were the first to be aware of the news, and trading ended at 1:00 p.m. As the news spread, the entire city was caught up in the celebrations. The next day, the *New York Times* described the United Press transmission as 'the most flagrant and culpable act of public deception'.

The Armistice treaty signed at the end of the First World War by the Allies and Germany at Compiègne, France, went into effect on the eleventh day of the eleventh month at the eleventh hour, 1918. Close to 3,000 men lost their lives on the final day of the war, as, despite the announcement of the Armistice, fighting did not actually cease until that specific moment.

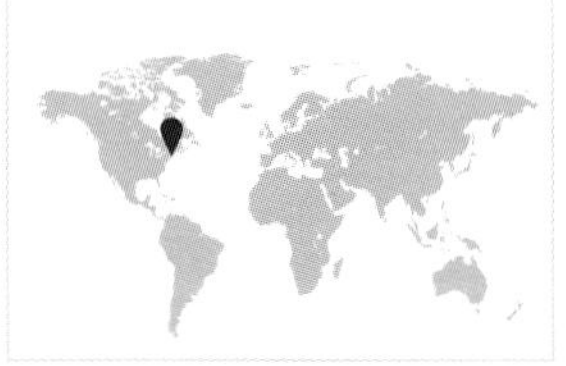

'All night long Broadway reverberated to to the crash of band music and the tooting of hundreds of thousands of horns, echoed to the clatter of exploding automobile exhausts firing volley after volley to the detriment of engines and the ears of passers-by, trembled to the footsteps of close to 1 million people who surged back and forth, screaming their exultation to the pale stars high above electric signs that blazed as though there had never been such a thing as the coal shortage.'

New York Tribune, 12 November 1918

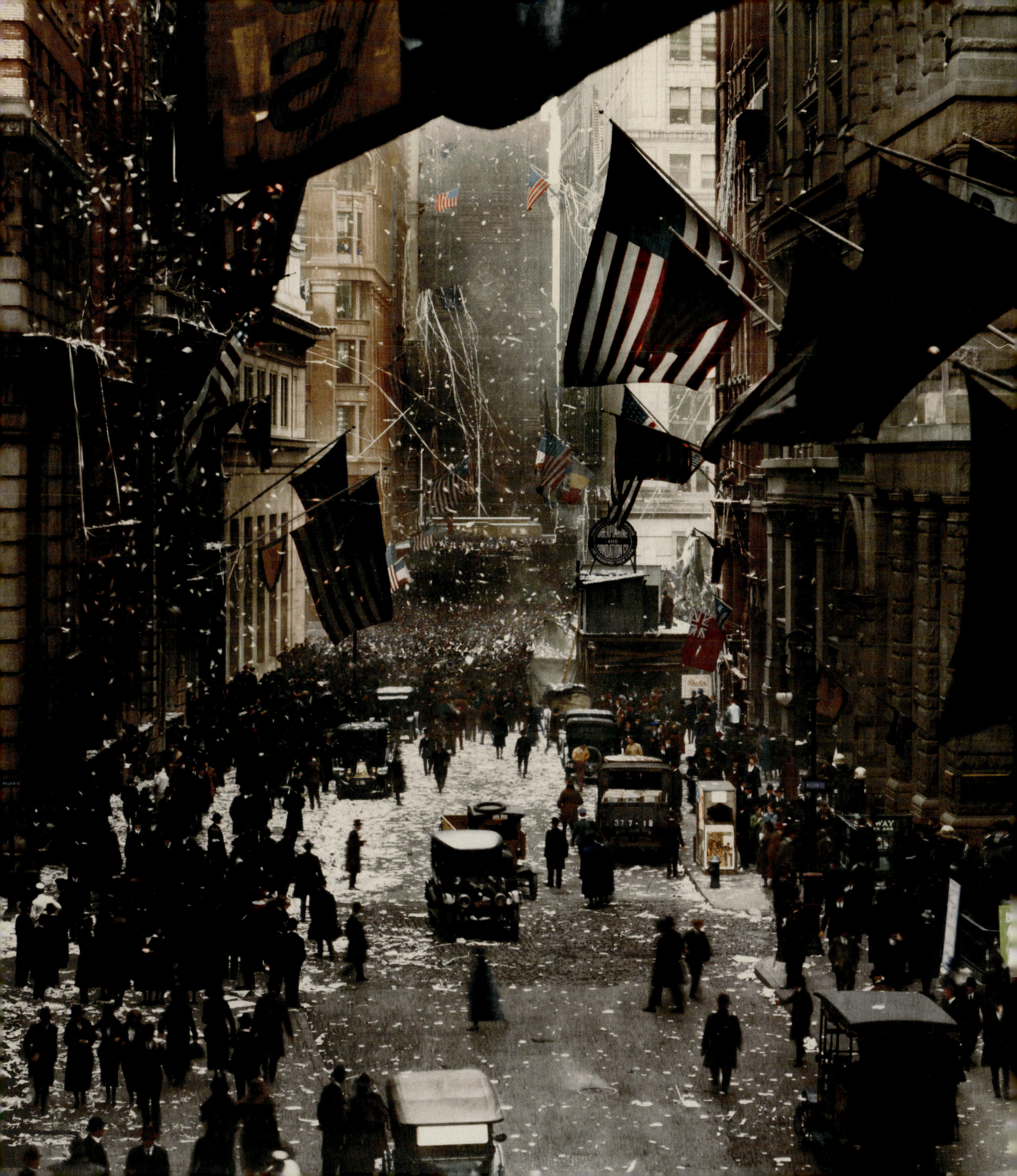
377-18

1910s

1918: **The interior of Amiens Cathedral with sandbag reinforcements against shell damage**
Amiens, France
(Unknown)

First World War shells were capable of inflicting widespread damage. As well as the threat – and reality – of aircraft attack, including raids by Zeppelin dirigibles, cannons and mortars could also launch enormous shells across vast distances – in some cases, up to seventy-five miles.

Historic and fragile buildings across northern France were at risk and, where supplies allowed, were protected with banks of sandbags. Art and artefacts were removed, as were whole windows of stained glass.

Amiens Cathedral was particularly vulnerable. More than 2,000 Allied heavy guns and 500 Germans heavy guns, as well as in excess of 2,000 planes, 500 tanks and some 100,000 men, fought the Battle of Amiens in August of 1918 and on into September of that year.

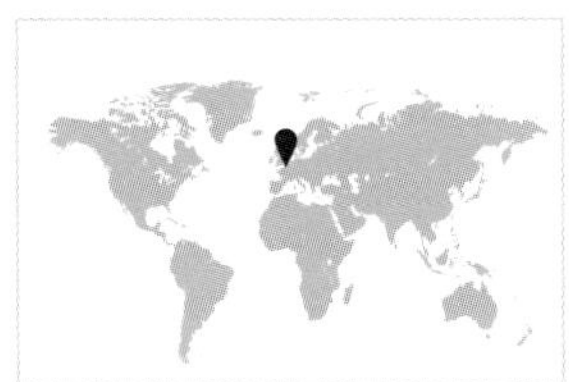

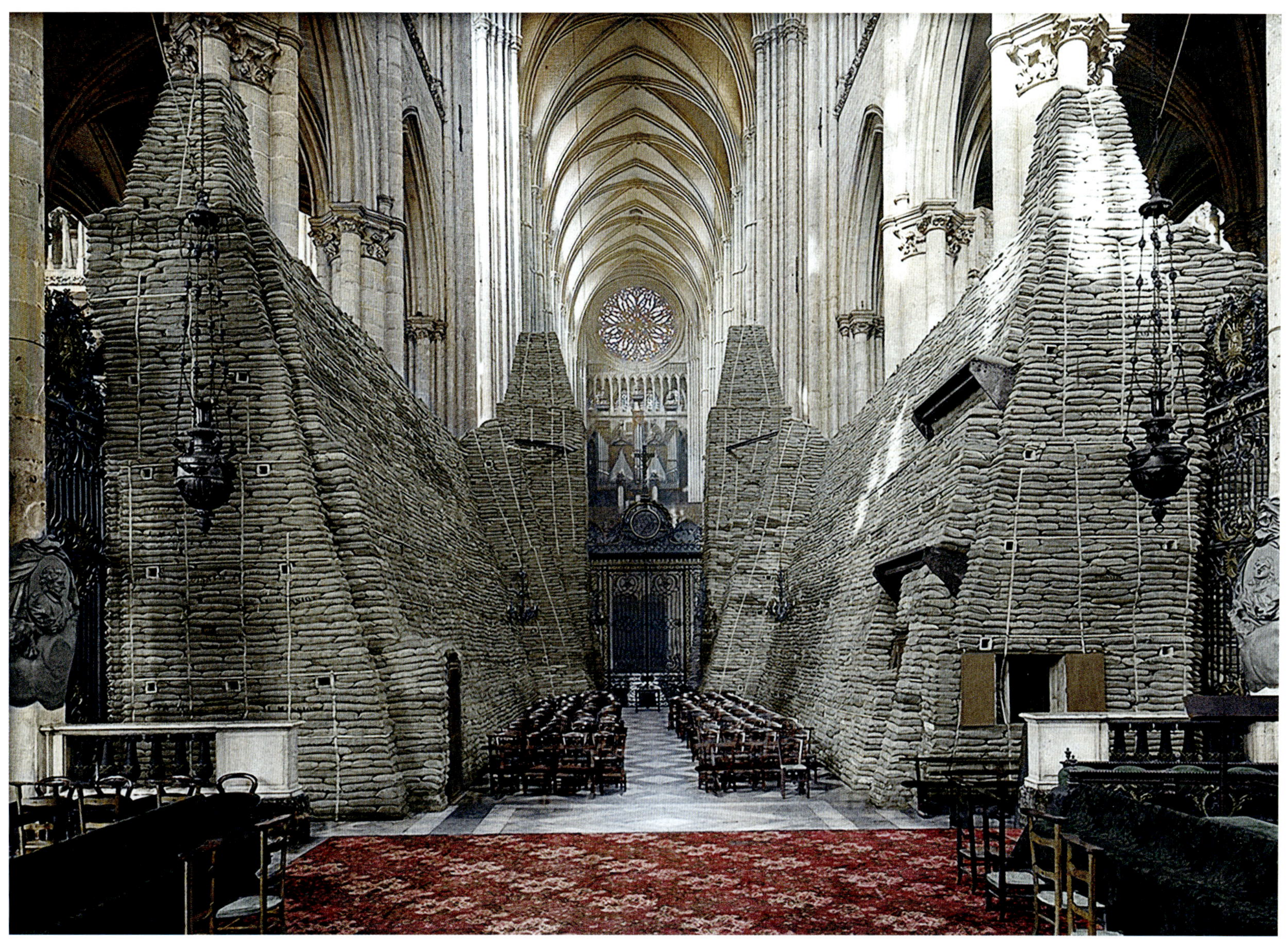

'Cathedrals and churches are favoured targets for German guns. This beautiful cathedral, ancient pride of Amiens, is now again their objective. It is built in the shape of a huge cross, and there, untold millions of French people have prayed to their God through the ages.'

Tacoma Times, 22 April 1918

1910s

1918: Airmen and sailors cheering the King from the aircraft carrier *Argus,* on his visit to the Fleet at Rosyth, Scotland. The carrier is painted in 'dazzle' camouflage
Rosyth, UK
(Topical Press / Getty)

Unlike conventional camouflage, dazzle ship camouflage was not intended to conceal. Dazzle was adopted after 1917 as a means of impeding an enemy's ability to track a ship's speed, distance and course – a form of misdirection, on a grand scale.

More than 4,000 of the Allied ships, both British and American, were painted with dazzle during the First World War. Each ship had its own unique 'fingerprint' of colour and shape, in order to avoid class of ship recognition by the enemy. Dazzle's implementation was triggered by the large ship losses experienced against German *unterseeboote* (U-boats), though its effectiveness is still open to debate.

At the outbreak of the First World War, HMS *Argus* existed as an ocean liner undergoing construction, the SS *Conte Rosso*. Bought by the British Admiralty in 1916, the ship was renamed *Argus* and became the first conventional aircraft carrier, from launch at the end of 1917. The ship's deck was of sufficient length to allow aircraft to both take off and to land. *Argus*'s flat appearance provided the nickname 'the hatbox'. Serving up to and across the the Second World War, the ship was sold for scrap in 1946.

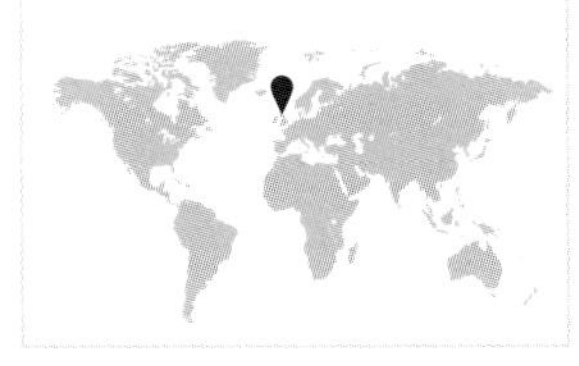

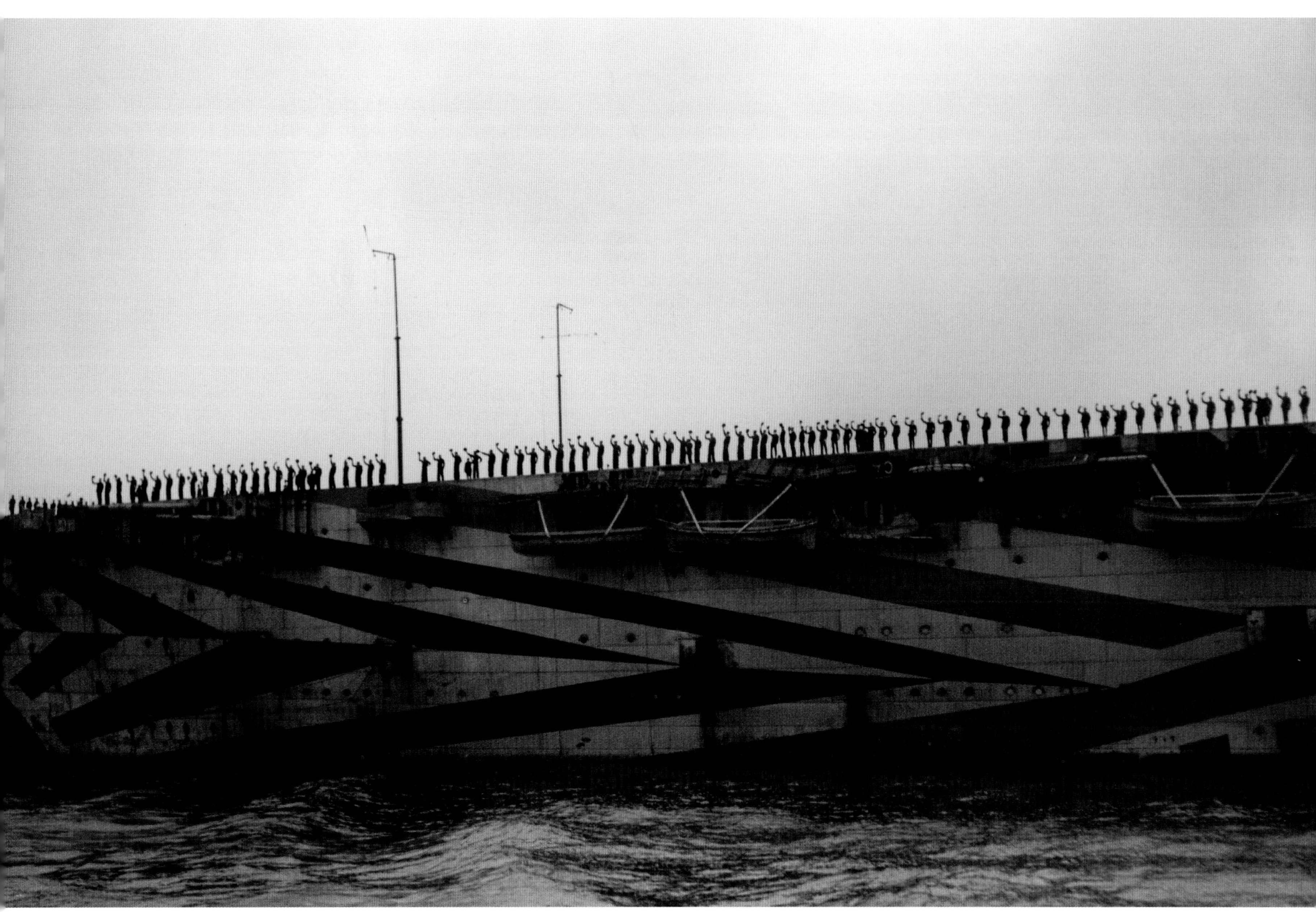

'Dodging the Kaiser's U-boats was the favourite sport of His Majesty's navy during the war and many schemes were resorted to in order to outwit the wiley foe. Chief among the successful ruses originated by officers and men of the fleet was the use of "dazzle" ships – ships camouflaged with fantastic patterns which bewildered the submarine commanders.'

Richmond Times, Virginia, 14 September 1919

1918: **A pilot smiles for the camera, Kelly Field, San Antonio**

Kelly Field, San Antonio, USA
(Paul Aldin Smith Kelly Field Album / San Diego Air & Space Museum)

The United States had entered the Great War the previous year, and this aviator is training the photographer to pilot a two-person biplane at Kelly Field. Biplanes, with two pairs of horizontal wings (one above the other), had by this point in aviation development found favour as the dominant craft. Two pairs of wings rather than one increased both the agility and the fortitude of the plane.

Before it was a centre for aeronautics, Kelly Field had been a cotton field. Following the US entry into the war, it became an Air Training Service Camp.

1910s

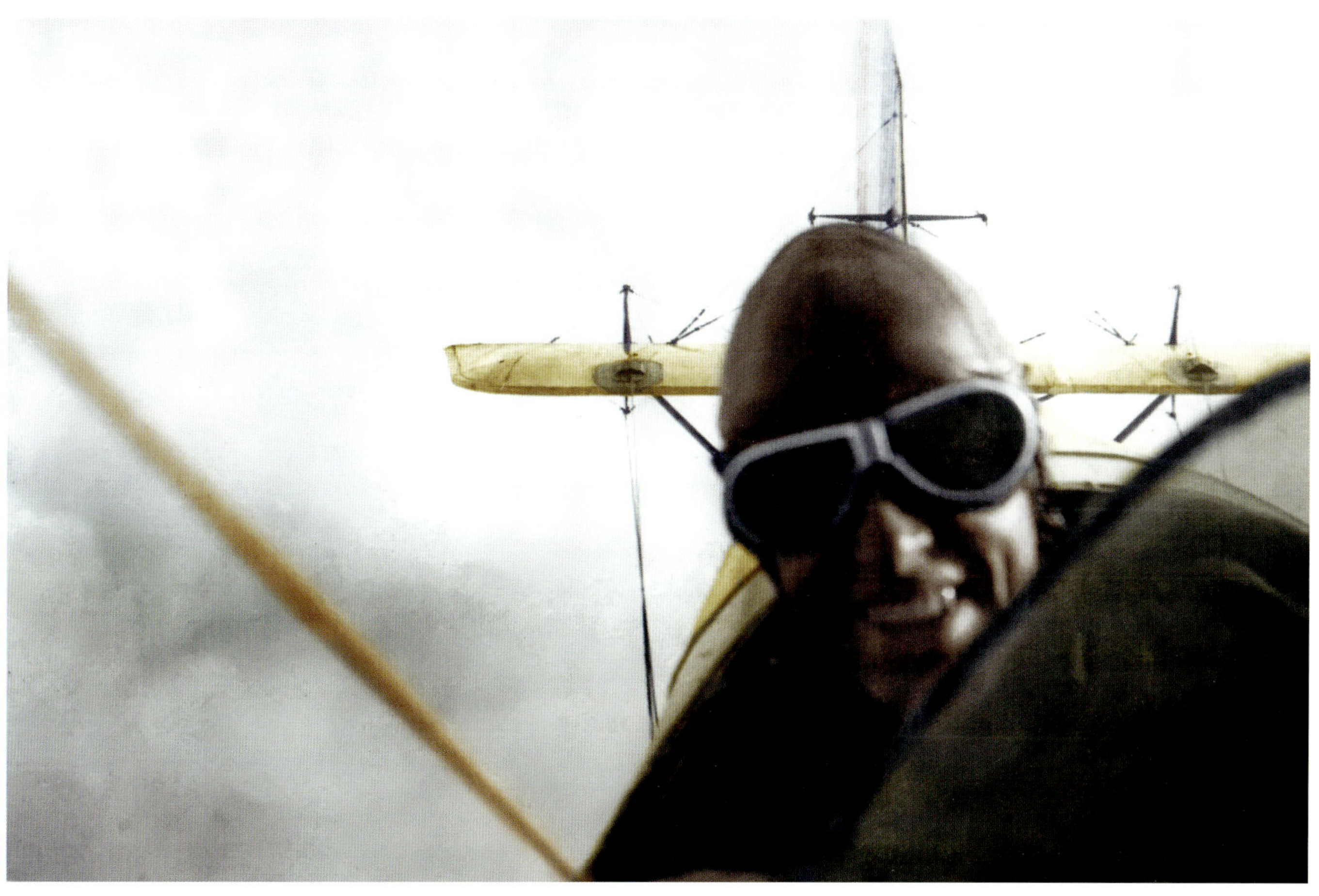

'It is assured that one of the attractions that winter tourists will find in San Antonio during the coming season will be that of flying men over and around the city. Already myriads of airplanes are often seen performing the various kinds of feats above Kelly Field. One day recently a great flock of buzzards was noticed to apparently join in the manoeuvres that were being conducted by the flying machine men. These birds went through evolutions that were being performed by the air-planes and their remarkable actions were viewed with interest by visitors.'

Rockingham Post-Dispatch, 7 March 1918

1918: A dirigible catches fire at Fort Sill, Oklahoma

Fort Sill, Oklahoma, USA (Library of Congress)

1910s

Oklahoma's Fort Sill – the burial place of the Native American, Geronimo – housed static kite balloons, inflated with hydrogen such as this one. The balloons were deployed for the observation of artillery attacks, and were secured with guiding cables by groups of ground staff.

Six troops were killed in the accident, captured here on camera at Henry Post Field at the Fort. The hydrogen in a balloon was ignited by a what is believed to have been a static electricity charge, created as the folds of the balloon fabric were rubbed together. Thirty more troops were injured.

'We just had a pretty bad accident. As they were bringing in the Observation Balloon about 5 p.m. the wind started to blow a pretty good gale and the men had a hard time handling it. It exploded. I saw one man's shirt burn right off him. The photographer's barracks was just 200 feet away and the hot gush was felt all through the barracks.'

Charles Moore, photographer at Fort Sill, in a letter to a friend, 2 April 1918

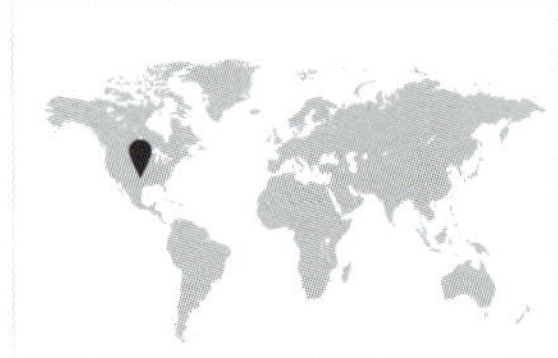

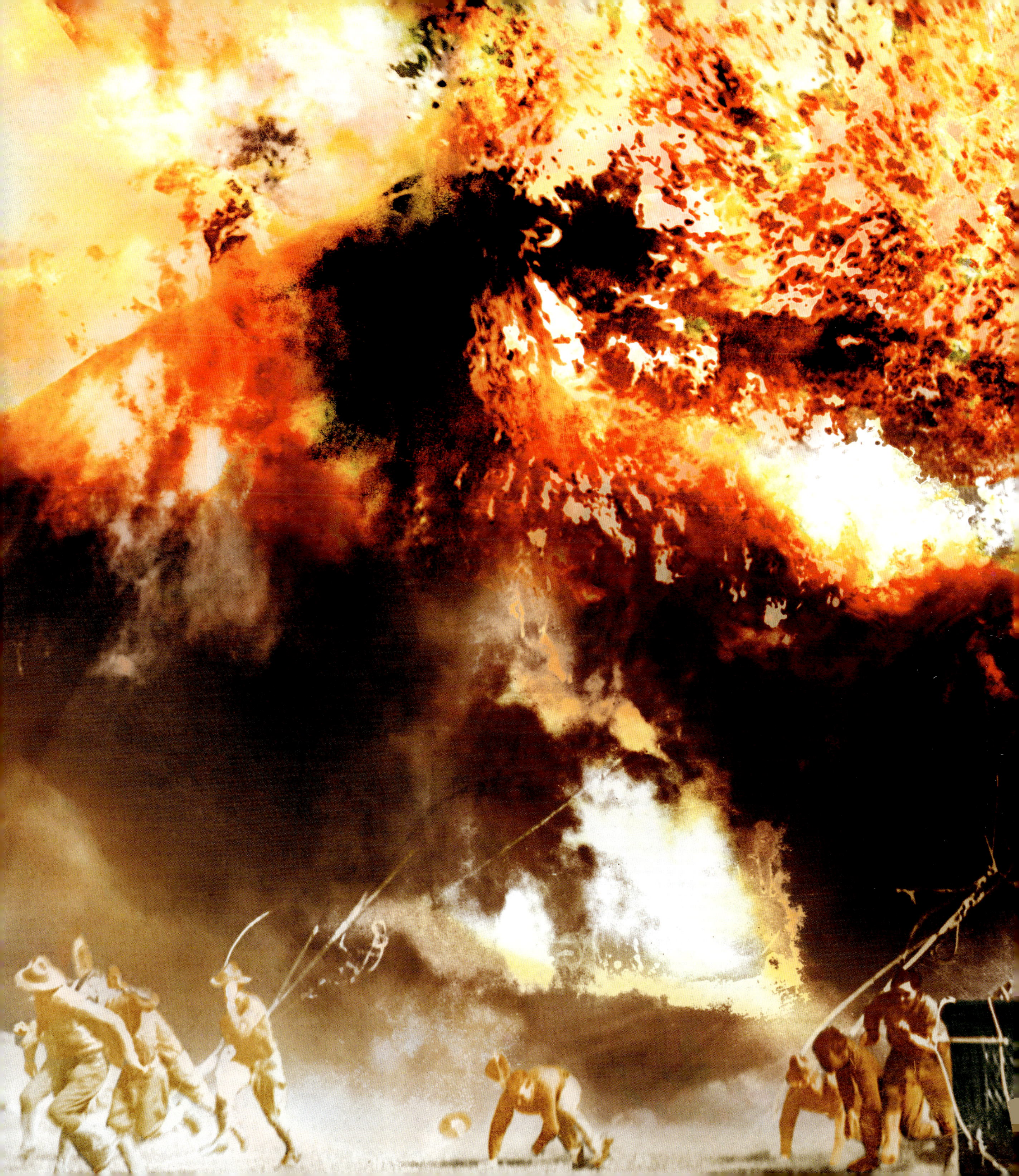

1910s

1917: The USS *Recruit*, a wooden battleship built by the navy in Union Square, New York City, to recruit seamen and sell Liberty Bonds from 1917 to 1920
Union Square, New York City, USA
(Bain News Service / Library of Congress)

In order to drive up recruitment to the navy – and to train those so recruited – the US military commissioned the construction of a full and sea-worthy battleship in the middle of Union Square, Manhattan. The ship was staffed, with a captain, and was equipped with wireless and quarters for officers and other crew. It also had searchlights, illuminated at night.

As well as functioning as a successful training and recruiting unit – more than 25,000 men joined the US Navy via *Recruit* – the ship was also deployed as an event and reception location, hosting, among other occasions, a visiting group of Native Americans and a christening.

The ship remained in Union Square for the duration of the war and beyond, finally being decommissioned and dismantled in 1920. The six guns it carried were replicas, made from wood.

The trees at the rear of the Square are Elm. At the base of the Frédéric Auguste Bartholdi's statue of the Marquis de Lafayette (*bottom right*) is a boot-black-boy. Bartholdi was also the sculptor of the Statue of Liberty. There appear to be no more than six women in the entire scene.

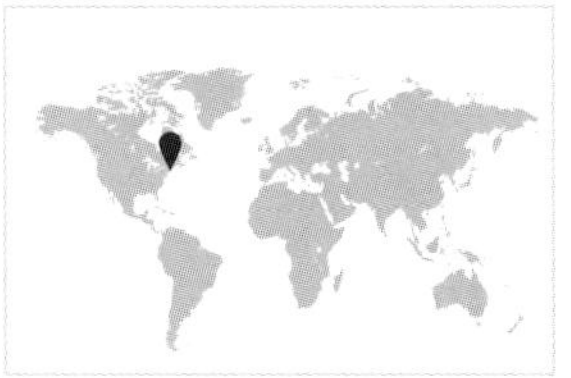

'A Reception on *Landship Recruit*. The United States *Landship Recruit*, in Union Square, is to have its first social function this afternoon, when a reception and entertainment will be held. The officers and crew of the ship are to act as hosts, and many invitations have been sent out to their friends. Tea is to be served, and the affair will last from 1 to 6 o'clock.'

New York Times, 8 September 1917

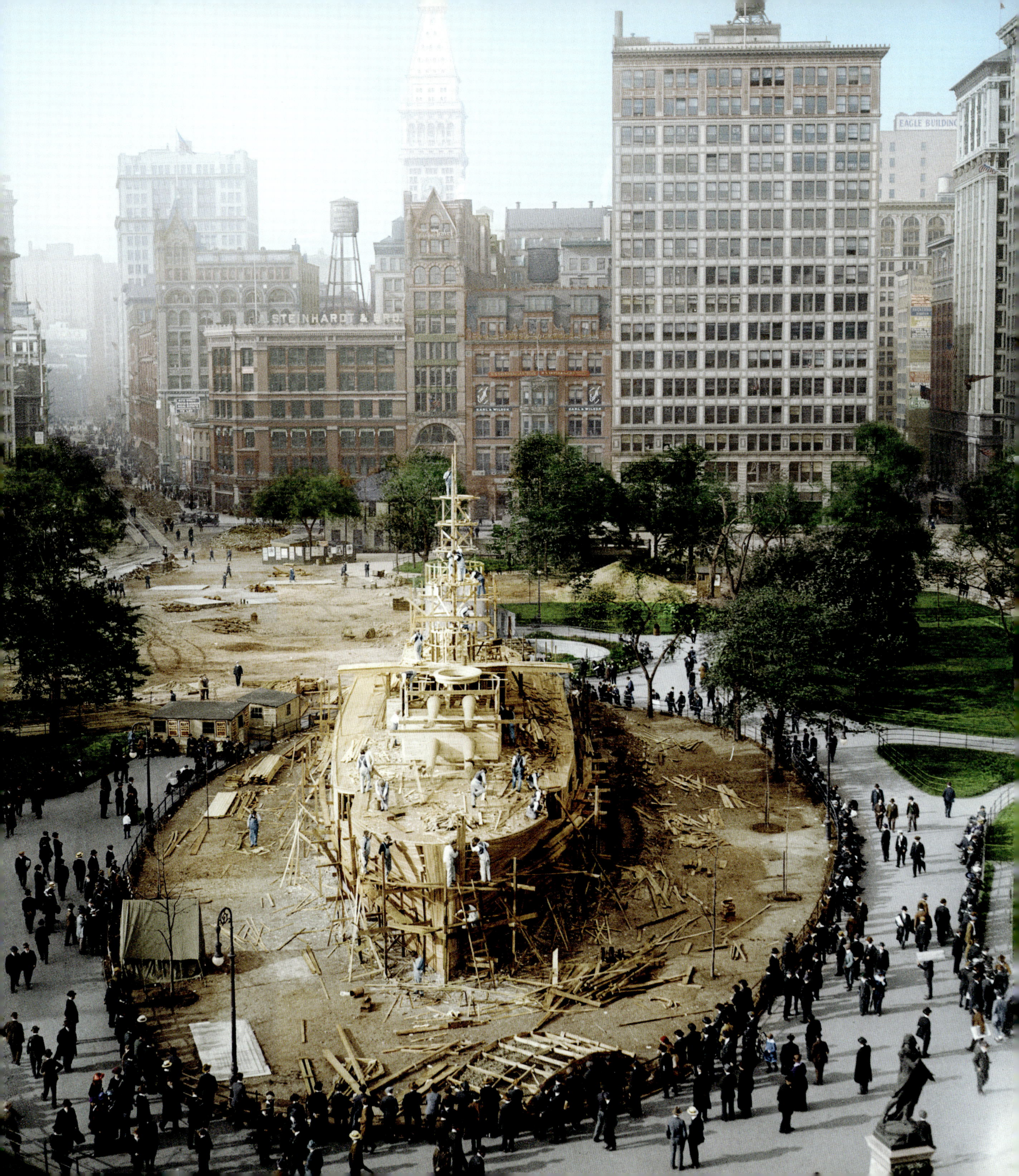
STEINHARDT &
EAGLE BUILDING

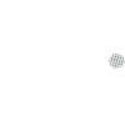

1910s

1917: 'Jammie' Reynolds, daredevil

Washington DC, USA
(Unknown / Library of Congress)

'Jammie' Reynolds went under a number of names: John Reynolds, Jack Reynolds, Jug Reynolds, 'The Human Fly','The Climbing Wonder' and 'The Lizard'. He began his vocation at the age of four, astonishing his parents and neighbours by balancing on the back of the furniture.

Jammie's first public appearance came two years later, aged six, balancing with his father – a steeplejack – on a fifty-foot high flagpole, on a ninety-foot high building in Buffalo. Aged twelve, Jammie ascended the side of Boston's Old South Building. He crowned this achievement by then balancing on four chairs on top of five tables, one on top of the other. He repeated the stunt at New York's Flatiron Building, in 1912, aged twenty-one.

Jammie was twenty-six when this picture was taken. He is balancing over the Lansburgh Furniture Building on 9th Street NW, Washington DC. Soon after, with America's entry into the Great War, Jammie was stationed at Kelly Field Air Base. After the war he developed a Vaudeville theatre balancing routine.

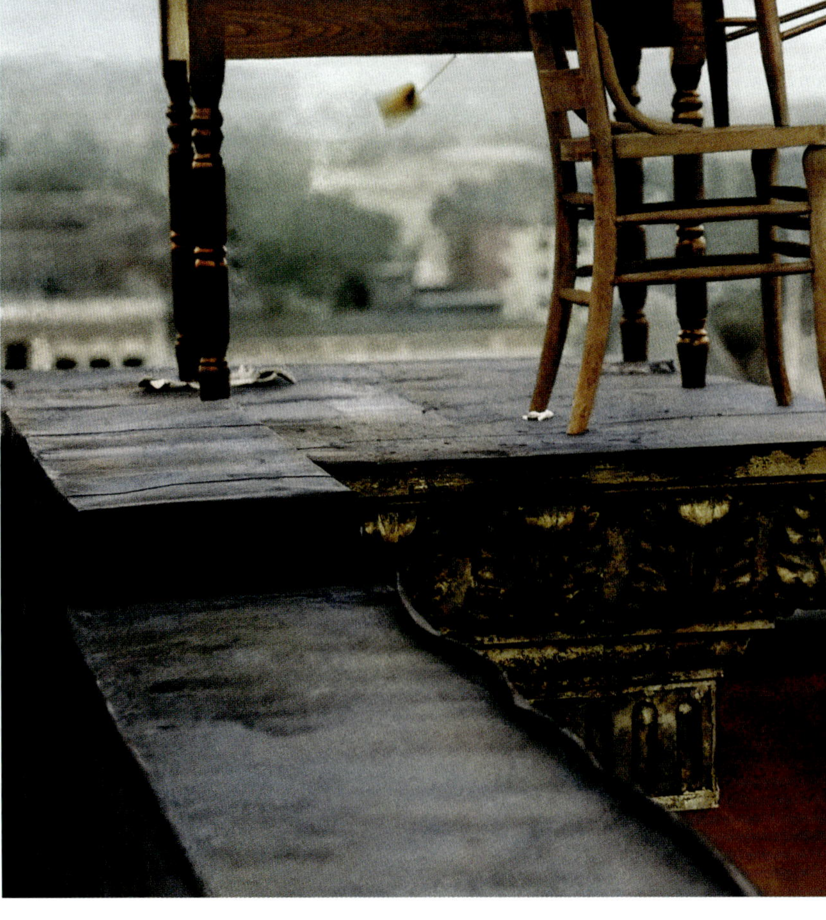

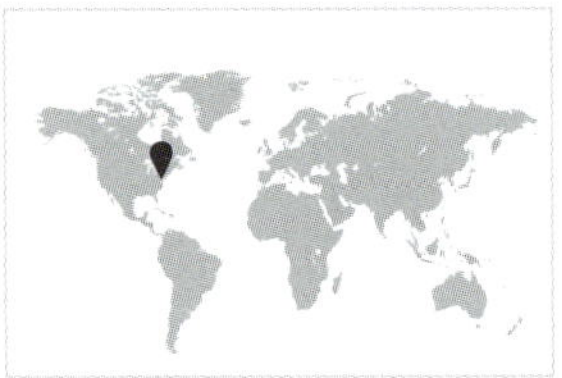

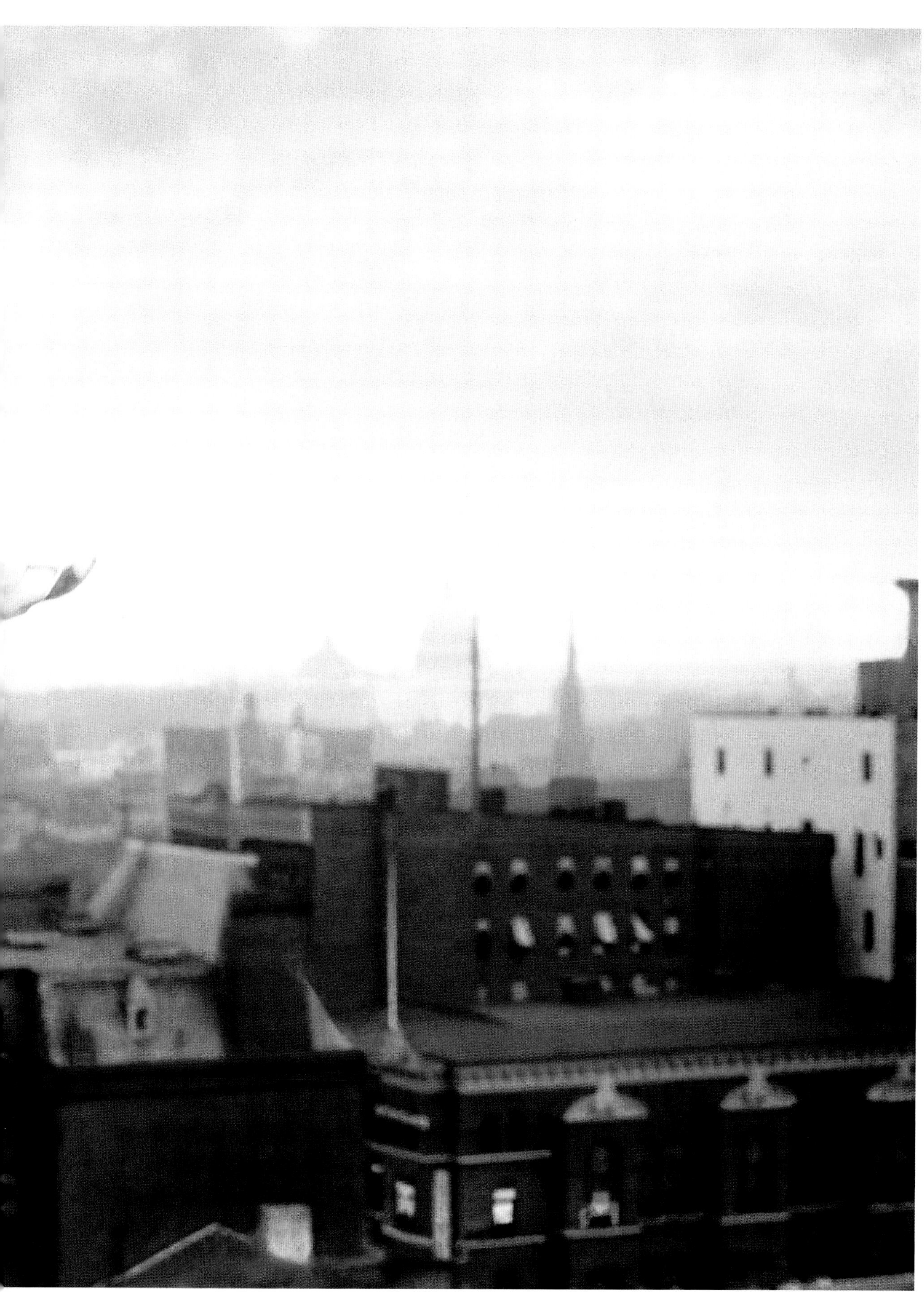

'If you can stand on your head in one place, you can do it in another.'

Jammie Reynolds, *Evening Public Ledger*, Philadelphia, 5 February 1915

1910s

1917: **Soldiers of the 164th Depot Brigade form a service flag at Fort Riley in Kansas**

Fort Riley, Kansas, USA
(Arthur Mole / Libray of Congress)

Arthur Mole achieved some renown as a photographer of patriotic American images, although, by birth, Mole was actually British. Still, he directed his photographic attention to US military bases and installations during the First World War, seeking to build up a sense of patriotic fervour and enthusiasm.

After composing and planning for a week, Mole and his associate brought an eighty-foot high platform to each military establishment, from whence, through a megaphone, Mole proceeded to direct vast numbers of serving troops and other staff into his enormous 'living insignia'. It would take several hours of moving and standing before the picture was laid out to Mole's satisfaction.

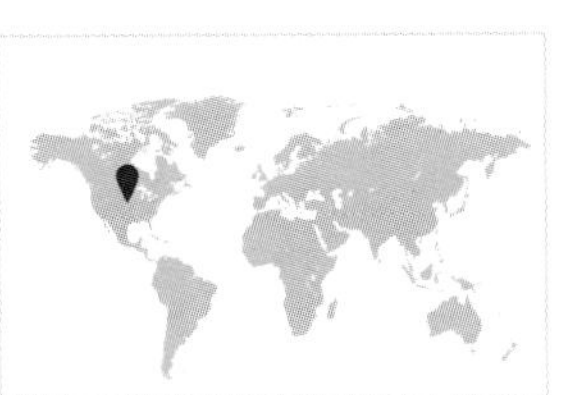

'Few have any conception of how the masses of men were arranged. The work was executed by Mr Arthur Mole, a young photographer of Zion City, Illinois, assisted by Mr John D. Thomas. Aside from its human interest and grandeur, the flag was an exceptional example of mathematical photography.'

Morgan City Daily Review,
15 January 1918

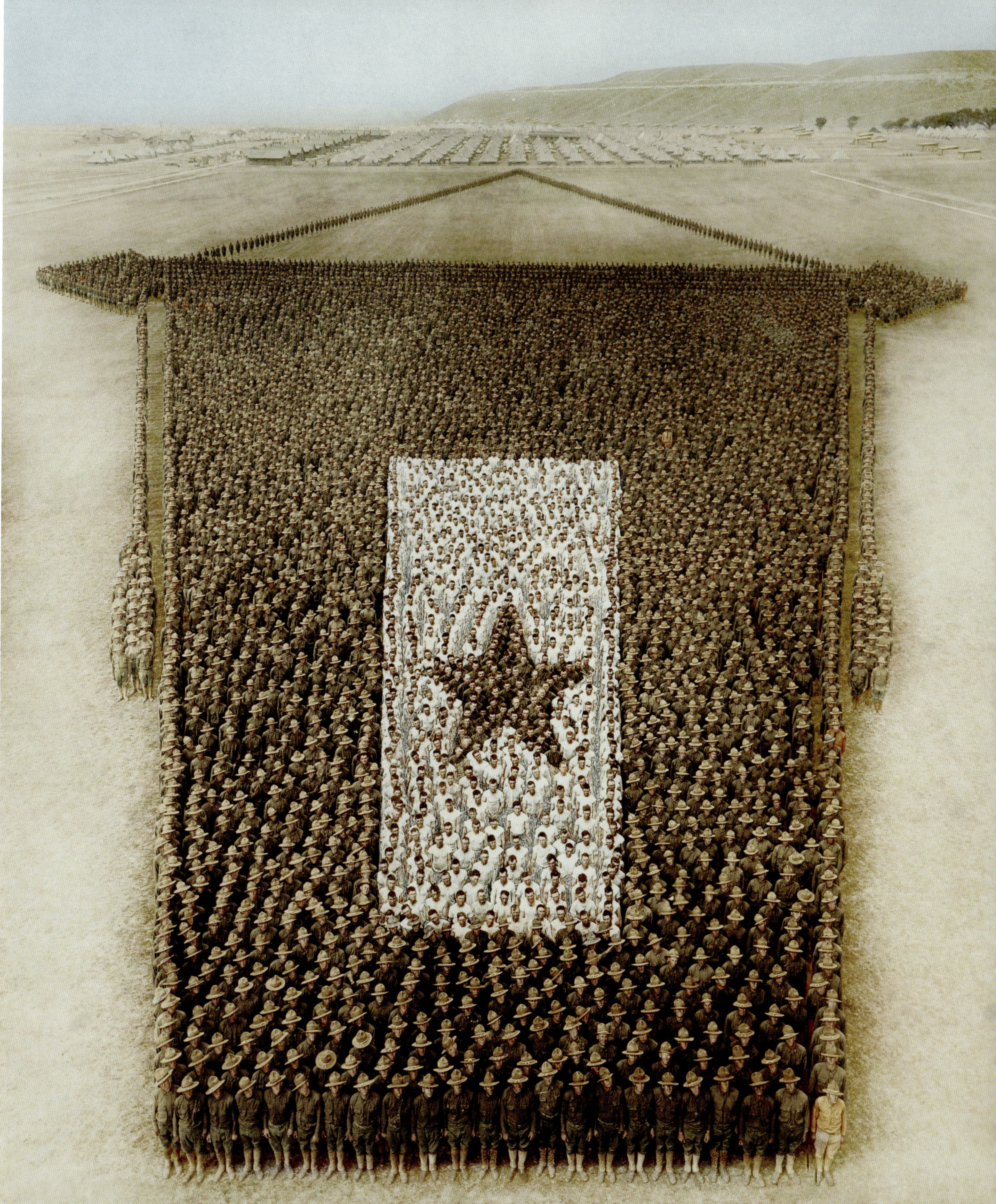

1910s

1916: A wounded British soldier holding his steel helmet, which has been pierced by a piece of shrapnel, during the advance on the Somme front near Hamel
Beaumont-Hamel, Somme, France
(Lt. Ernest Brooks / IWM / Getty)

The soldier in this photograph may have viewed his survival as a miraculous intervention. Tragically, seemingly miraculous occurrences were inevitable given the overwhelming number of casualties at the Somme.

He is clutching his MK I helmet, based on the design and patent of John Leopold Brodie. Brodie, born Leopold Janno Braude, was an entrepreneur who had made a fortune in gold and diamond mining. Such helmets were first used by the British Army in combat in the Spring of 1916. Before its introduction, British soldiers would charge at enemy machine guns wearing only cloth caps.

The Somme battle – the largest battle of the First World War – was essentially over by the time this picture was taken in December 1916. It had been fought on the River Somme from 1 July to 18 November, with over a million men killed or wounded. It was only with the onset of winter that the battle eventually came to a standstill.

'The Boche varied from place to place. Just near where we were he was very decent, and sent us in a list of the names of the prisoners he had taken. Afterwards we found that he'd buried our dead and put up crosses to them. "To a brave Englander. To brave English soldiers." This was a fine thing to have done. They were Bavarians who did this.'

A soldier quoted in *The Battle of the Somme*, John Masefield, 1919

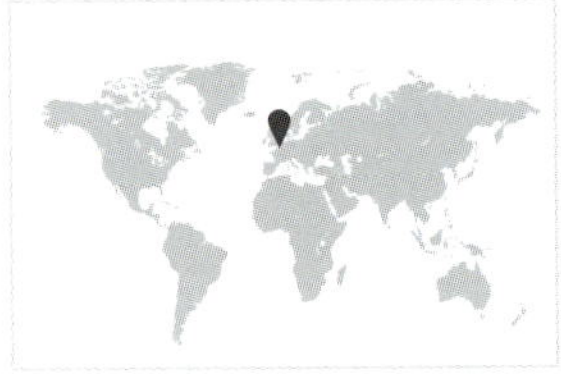

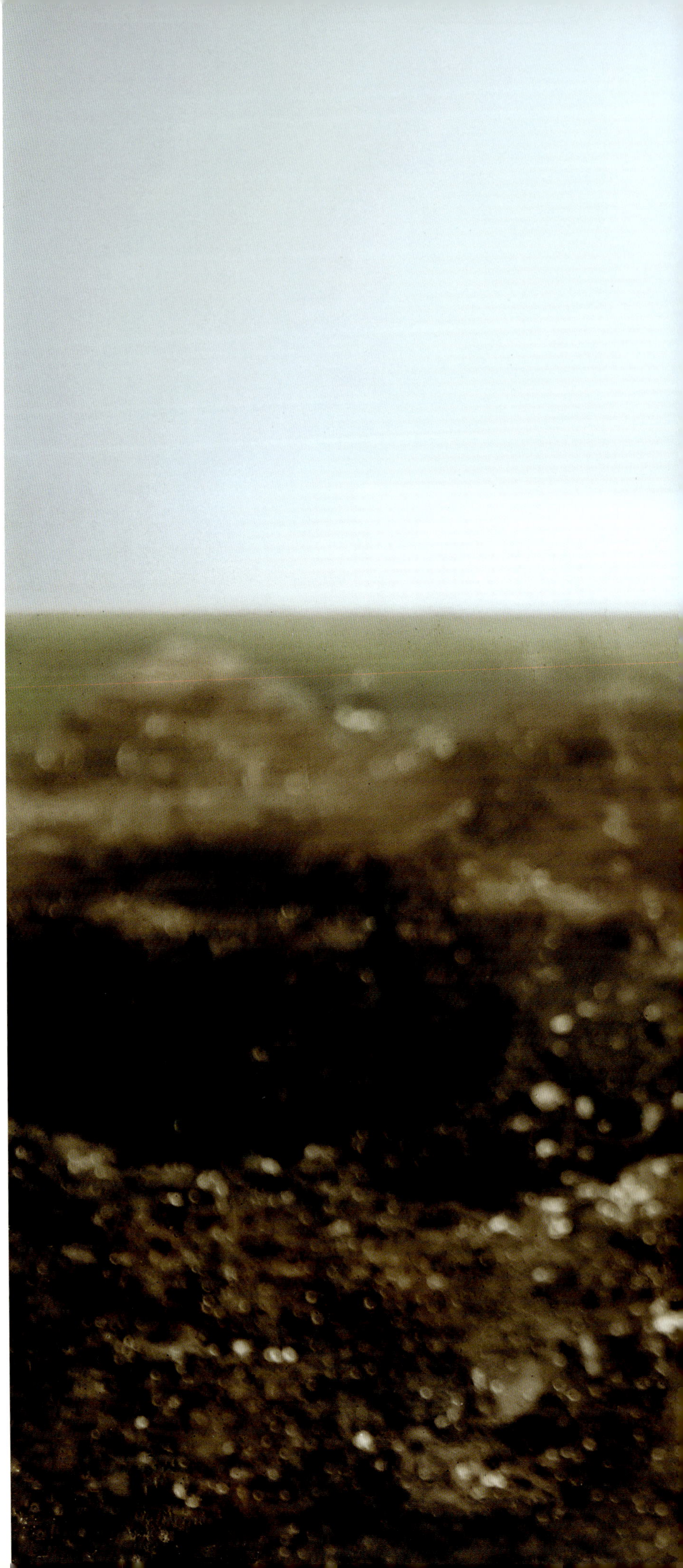

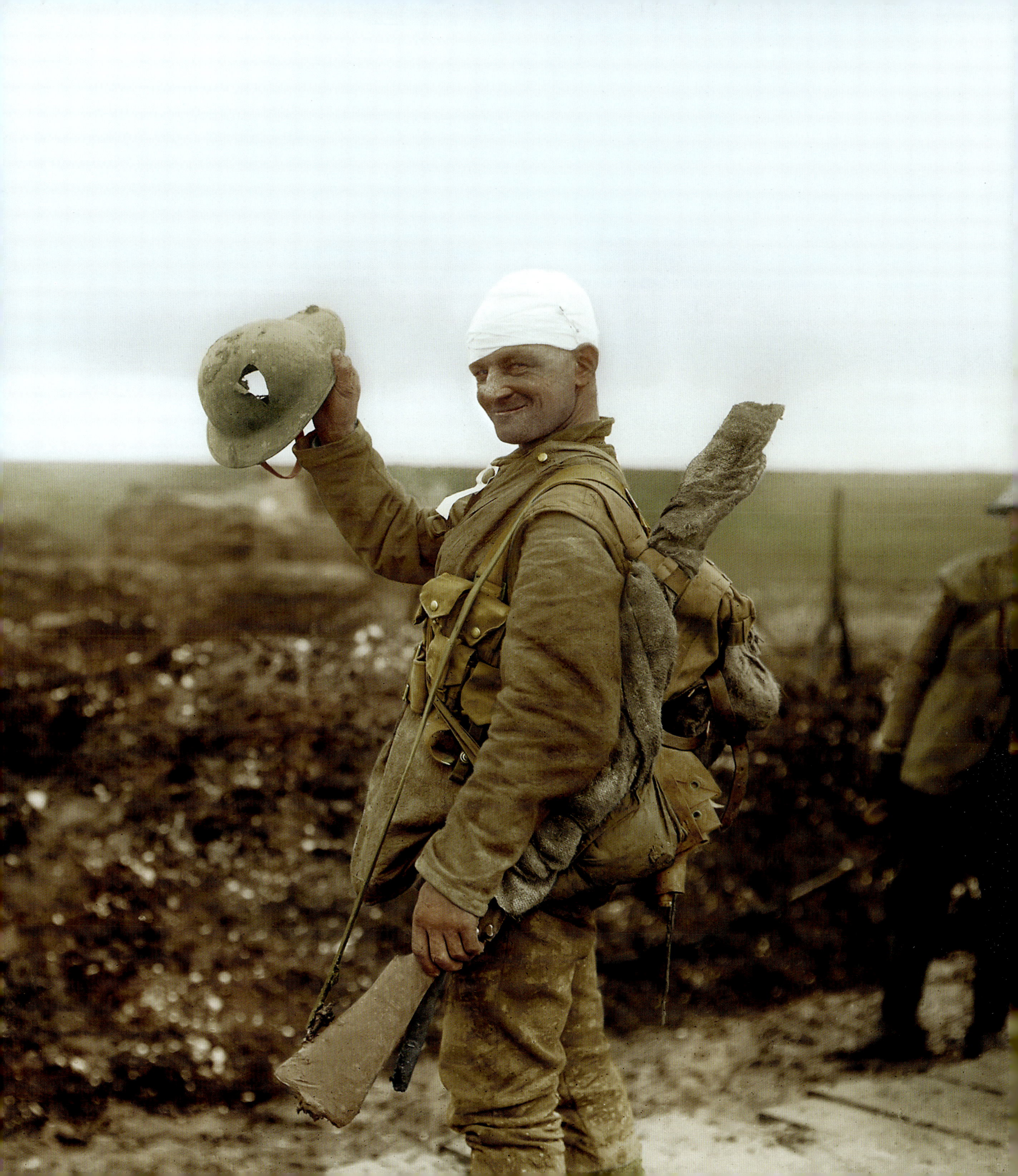

1910s

21 May 1914: Emmeline Pankhurst being removed from a suffragette protest by a policeman

Buckingham Palace, London, UK
(Topical Press / Getty)

Police officer Superintendent Rolfe arrests and physically removes Emmeline Pankhurst from outside the King's residence of Buckingham Palace, London, before being taken to Holloway gaol. Pankhurst's intention on this occasion was to submit a petition to the King. According to a report in *The Suffragette* newspaper, she cried out from her transport to the gaol, 'Arrested at the gates of the palace. Tell the King!'

This was neither the first nor last time that Pankhurst was jailed as part of the campaign to provide the vote to women. The first occasion was in February 1908, for attempting to submit a protest resolution to the prime minister in parliament. She was sentenced to six weeks imprisonment. In total, she was placed under arrest seven times before suffrage was approved in 1918.

While some women over thirty were given the vote in Britain in 1918, it would be another ten years before all British women were allowed to vote. A fortnight after this picture was taken, Superintendent Rolfe died of heart failure.

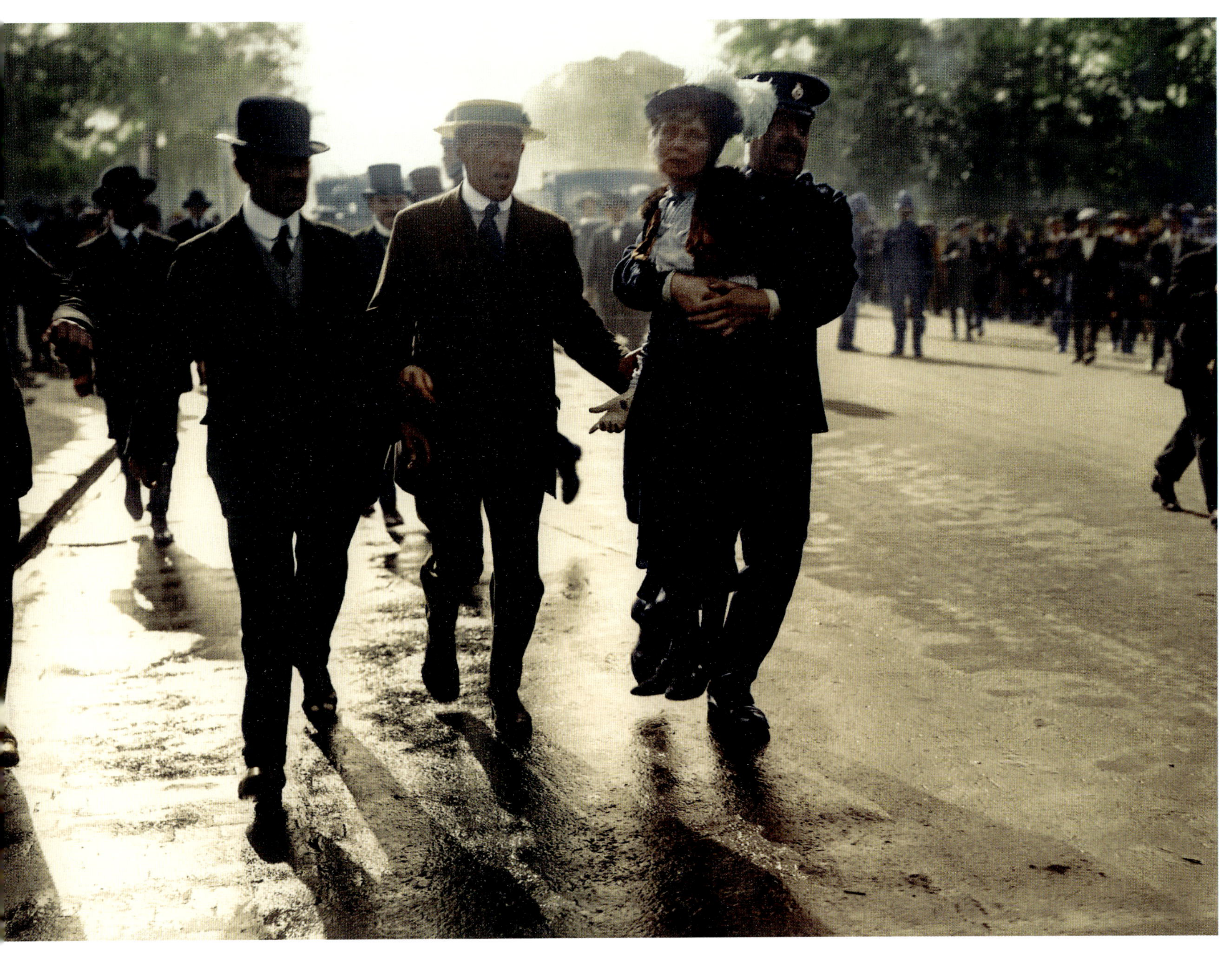

'When I was in my prison cell, I remembered how I had seen men laugh at the idea of women going to prison. A thought came to me in my cell and it was this: that to men, women are not human beings like themselves. Some men think we are superhuman. Other men think us subhuman. We are neither superhuman nor subhuman. We are just human beings like yourselves.'

'Why We Are Militant', a speech delivered by Mrs Pankhurst in New York City, 21 October 1913

1910s

15 April 1913: A zebra and trap and a London tram vie for business in Brixton

Brixton, London, UK
(Unknown / Hulton Archive / Getty)

A zebra pulls a carriage through Brixton, south London, towards Stockwell. Exotic animals were regularly deployed to advertise or promote products and events at the turn of the twentieth century. It is likely that the zebra and carriage were the property of music-hall artist, Gustav Grais, and were being used to promote his shows.

Grais, born Gustav Eichler, was skilled in juggling and the trapeze, and kept a circus of exotic animals, including the zebra and a number of baboons. He also secretly juggled at least two families in London, in close vicinity.

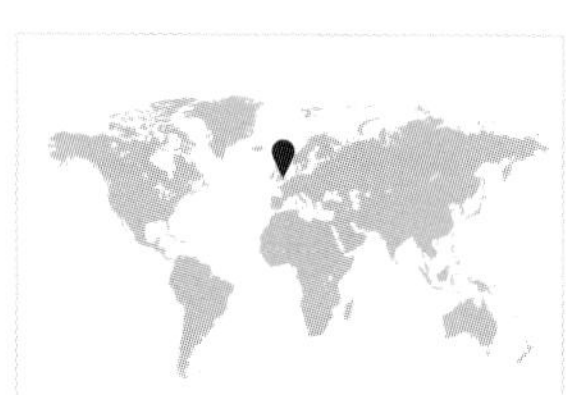

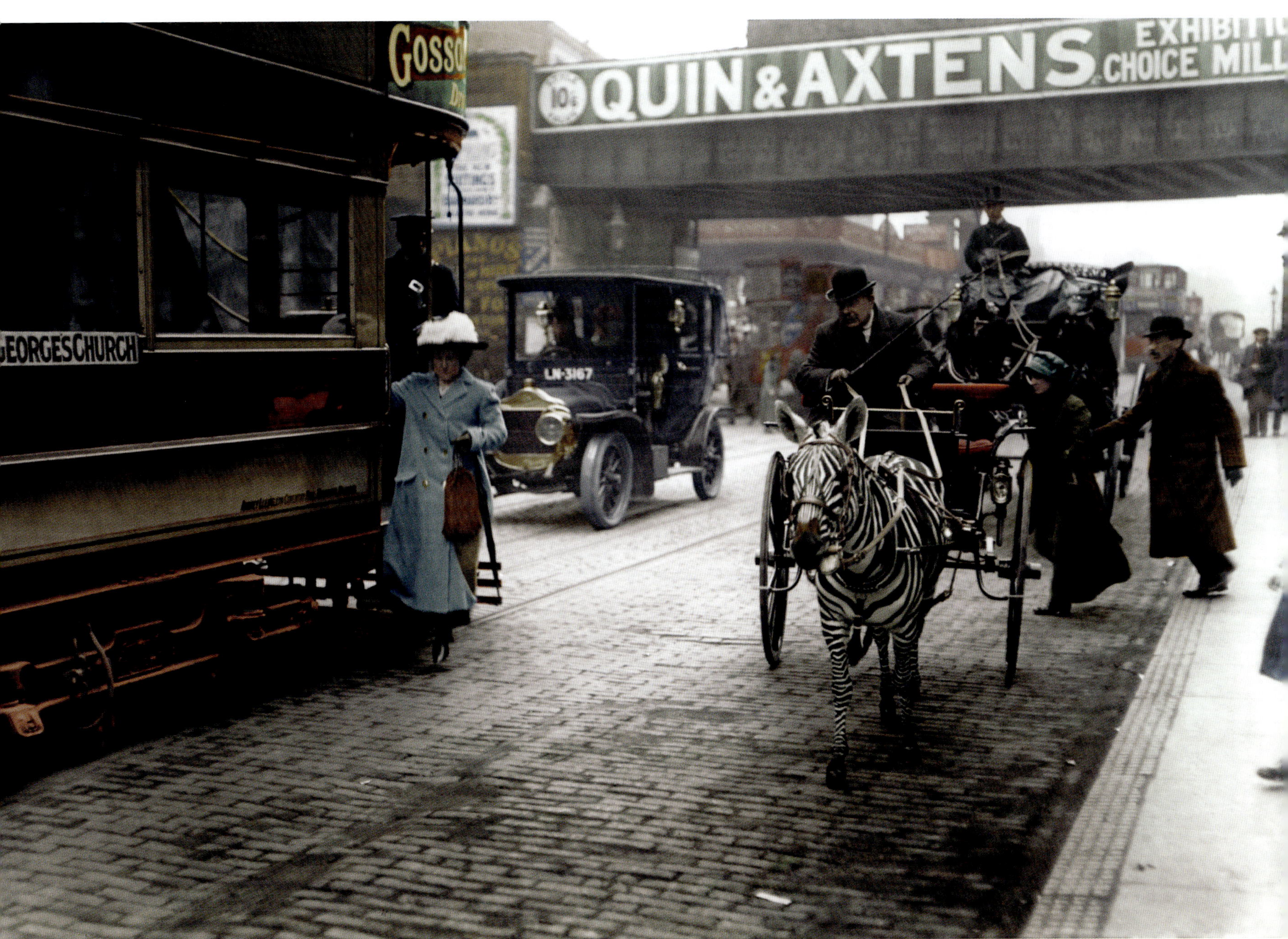

'A zebra harnessed to a pony-chaise. The zebra belongs to the music-hall artist, Mr Gustav-Grais. Having survived a fire it was stabled at Brixton and is seen here on its daily exercise route in south London.'

London Evening Standard, 13 August 1912

1910s

1912: Hairdresser's shop window, Boulevard de Strasbourg (Salon de Coiffures)

Boulevard de Strasbourg, Paris, France (Eugène Atget / George Eastman House)

French flâneur Eugène Atget turned to photography as a reaction to his self-perception as a failed artist. From 1898 onwards, he set himself the task of documenting the streets of old Paris before they were swept away in development.

The streets and buildings Atget captured on camera were indeed under threat. Georges-Eugène Haussmann's renovation of Paris saw the wholesale demolition of medieval districts and locales, even after Haussmann's dismissal from post by the Emperor in 1870. The implementation of Haussmann's plans would continue until 1927.

Atget's output was prodigious, much of it taken in the French capital's quiet streets at dawn – allowing him to use the long exposure times necessitated by his then-antiquated camera and equipment.

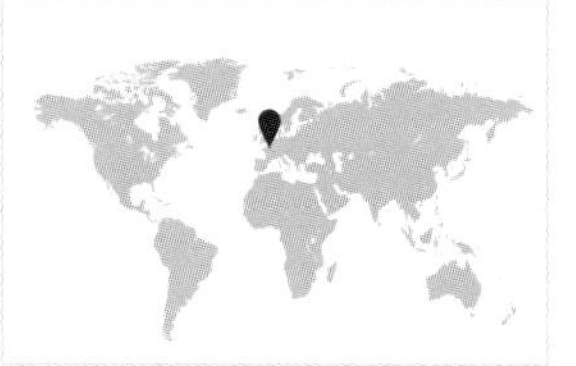

'Latest Paris Fashions. The fashion of framing the face in a halo of hair which is held up by artificial padding has now entirely disappeared. The tendency now is towards simple, natural effects, and if artificial additions to the hair are used it must be done with art and discretion so that the head is not enlarged out of all proportion to the body nor its natural lines of grace destroyed.'

Evening Standard, Ogden City, Utah, 23 March 1912

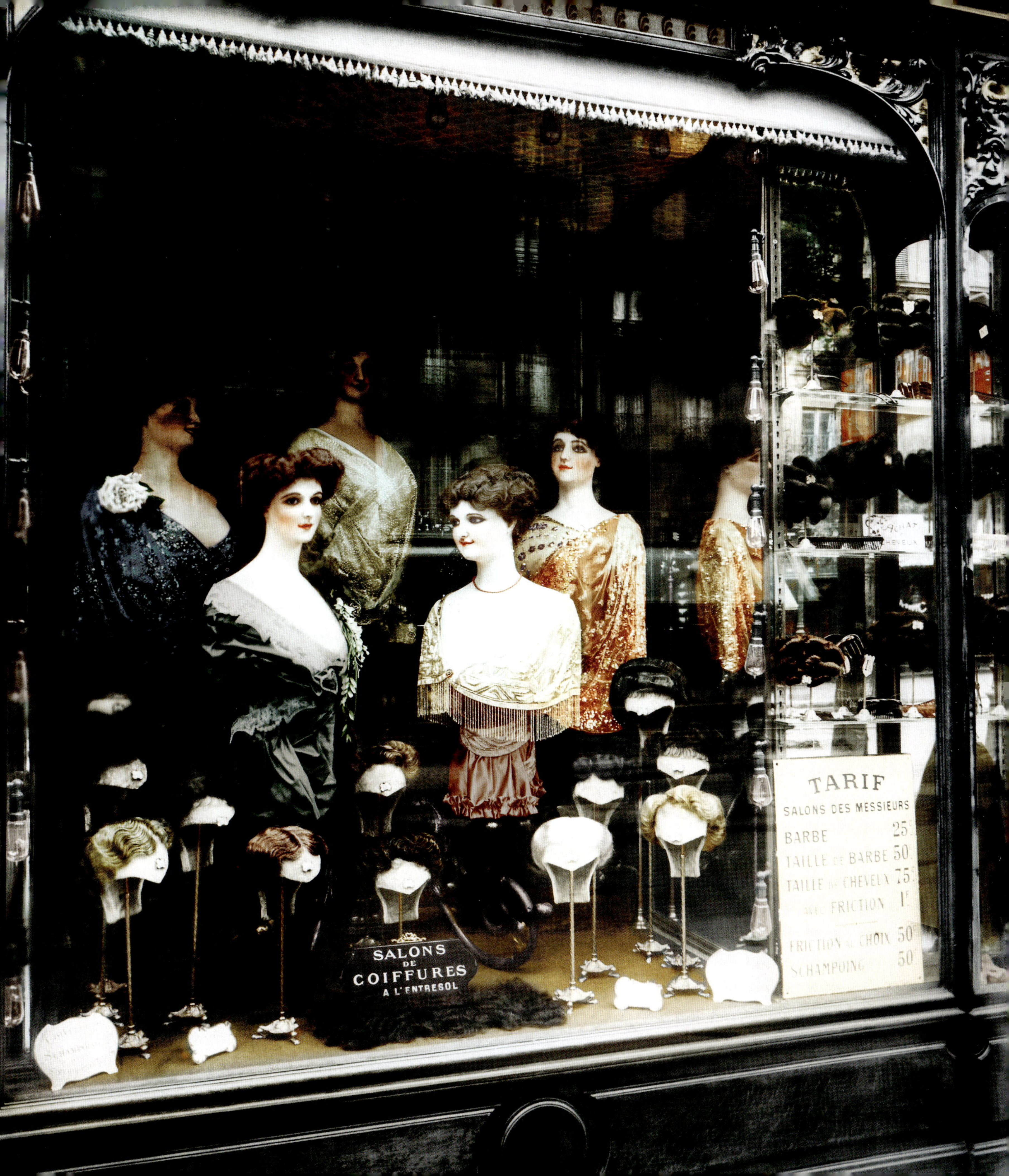

TARIF
SALONS DES MESSIEURS
BARBE 25
TAILLE BARBE 50
TAILLE CHEVEUX 75
FRICTION 1F
FRICTION CHOIX 50
SCHAMPOING 50
SALONS DE COIFFURES A L'ENTRESOL

1910s

c. 1912: A young woman uses a hand-cranked battery charger to power her electric Columbia Mark 68 Victoria automobile

USA

(Chenectady Museum; Hall of Electrical History Foundation / Getty)

The advantages of an electric car have always been obvious: easy to use, less noise, less pollution. Such vehicles have existed for just as long as the fossil-fuel-powered variety; the first electric cars were on the roads in the 1880s.

At the beginning of the 1910s, around 38 per cent of all cars in America were electric. Part of this wide adoption was due to the way the vehicles were marketed. Electric cars – quieter, cleaner, easier to start – were particularly aimed at women.

But this 38 per cent turned out to be the high-water mark. Despite some arguing that electric vehicles were deliberately suppressed to drive sales of fossil-fuel cars, at least one factor that led to their being overtaken is an element that's still a challenge to their success today – their limited range.

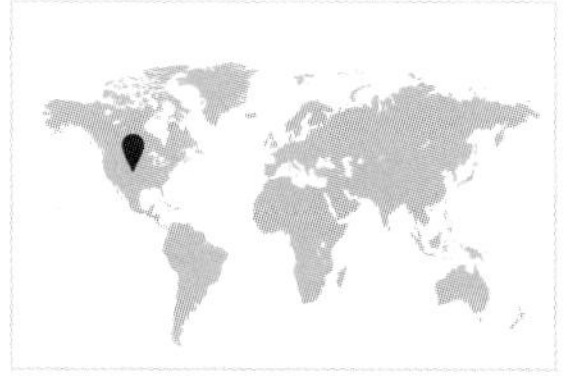

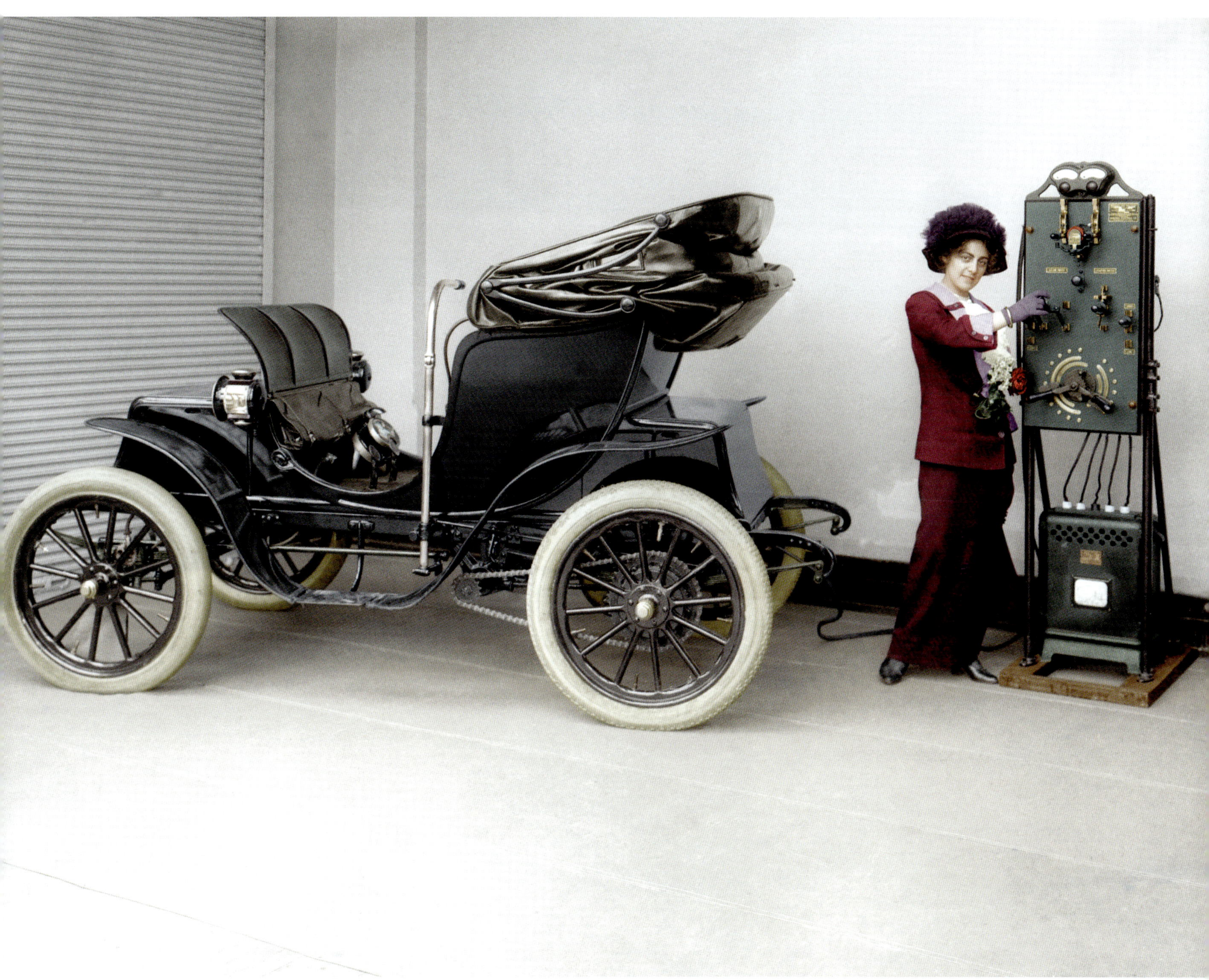

'The announcement is made that the United States Motor company of New Jersey has purchased the majority of the stock of the Columbia Motor Car company, making it evident to Wall Street that J. P. Morgan and his associates soon will control the automobile industry of the country, which has become one of its greatest industrial features.'

Omaha Daily Bee, 1 May 1910

1910s

1912: The iceberg that sank the *Titanic*

North Atlantic
(Universal Images Group / Getty)

On 12 April 1912, White Star Line's Olympic-class RMS *Titanic* sank on her maiden voyage from Liverpool to New York with the loss of over 1,500 lives.

This photograph was taken from the deck of the RMS *Carpathia*, answering the call to rescue survivors sometime between daybreak and 9 a.m. on Monday, 15 April 1912, and reportedly shows the iceberg in question. The *Carpathia* was en route to the Mediterranean when it was diverted.

Scientific research, using records of ocean drifts together with witness statements, suggests that the iceberg was around 100,000 years old and had originated to the south-west of Greenland. It is likely that at the point of impact with the *Titanic*, the iceberg was approximately 400 feet long.

'At a quarter to three I saw what we knew was an iceberg by the light from a star – I saw a streak of light right on the iceberg. From then on till four o'clock we were altering our course very often to avoid the bergs. In the meantime I had been firing rockets and the Company's signals every time we saw this green light. At five minutes past four I saw the light again, and I was going to pick the boat up on the port bow, but just as it showed the green light I saw an iceberg right ahead of me. It was very close, so I had to put round quick and pick up the boat on the starboard side.'

Testimony of Arthur H. Rostron, Master of the *Carpathia*, 21 June 1912

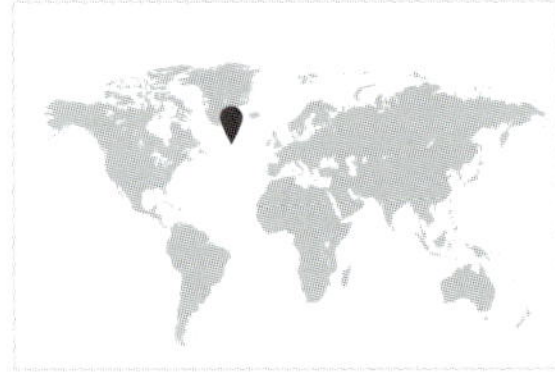

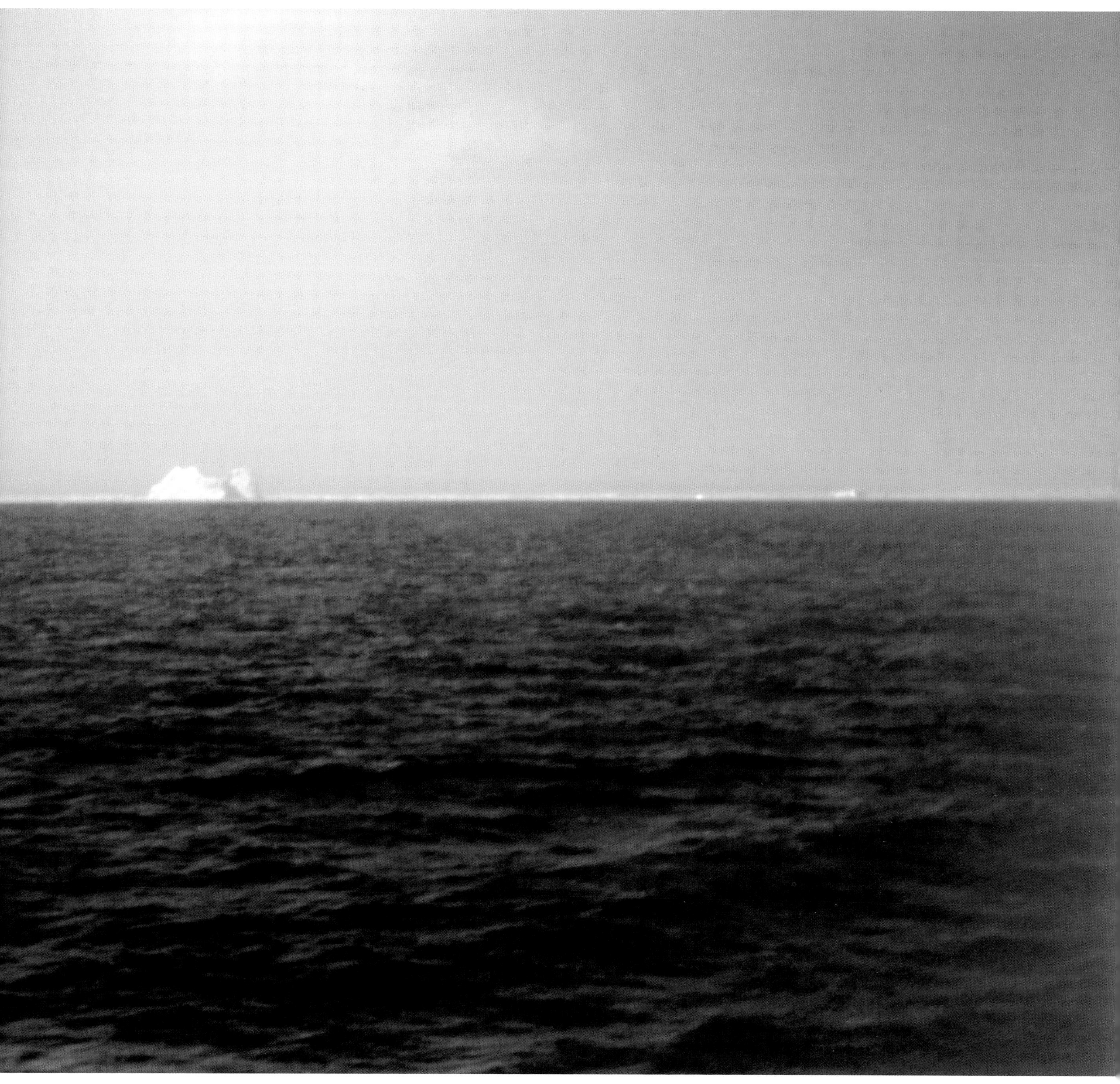

1911: Geologist Thomas Griffith Taylor and meteorologist Charles Wright in the entrance to an ice grotto during Captain Robert Falcon Scott's *Terra Nova* Expedition to the Antarctic. The *Terra Nova* is in the background.
Antarctica
(Herbert G. Ponting / Getty)

Scott's *Terra Nova* Expedition of 1910–1913 followed on from his *Discovery* Expedition of 1901–1904, which, by many measures, had been a success. Scott had set a new record for Southern exploration and had discovered the Polar Plateau.

Unlike the *Discovery* Expedition, the Terra Nova was at least 50 per cent privately financed, to the tune of £40,000. The cost of the ship alone was £12,500. Eight thousand men made an application to join the *Terra Nova*; sixty-five were selected, including seven veterans of *Discovery* and five of Shackleton's men.

Scott was spurred on to return to the Southern Hemisphere by rival Ernest Shackelton's narrow failure to reach the Pole in 1909, as well as reports of planned Japanese, Australian and Norwegian expeditions. En route to the Antarctic, Scott had communication from Norway's Roald Amundsen that he was also heading south. He was in a race.

Scott lost the race and ultimately his life, together with Dr Edward Wilson, Lawrence Oates, Henry 'Birdie' Bowers and Edgar Evans. More than twenty years later, in his acclaimed account *The Worst Journey in the World*, expedition member Apsley Cherry-Garrard felt: 'The whole business simply bristles with "ifs".'

1910s

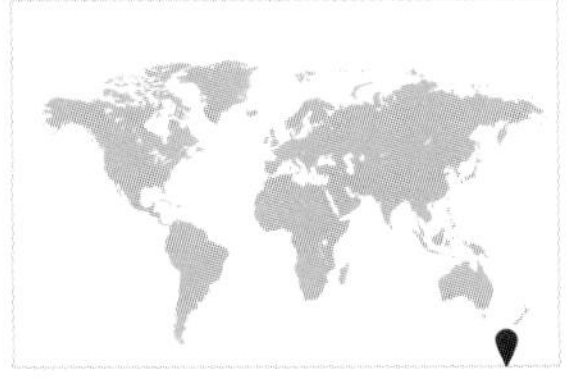

'The Pole. Yes, but under very different circumstances from those expected... Great God! This is an awful place and terrible enough for us to have labored to it without the reward of priority. Well, it is something to have got here.'

Diary of Robert Falcon Scott, 7 January 1912

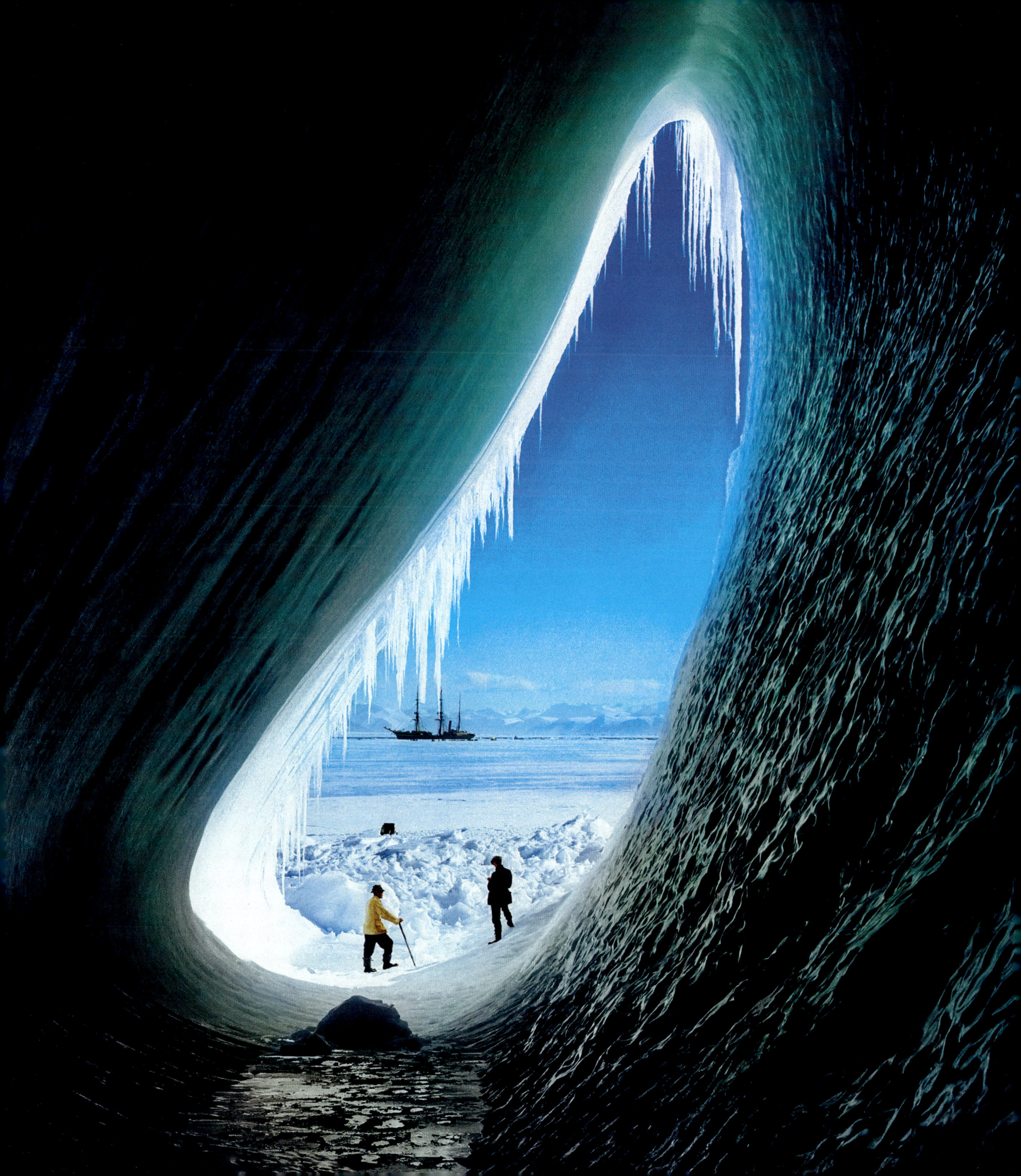

1910s

5 August 1910: The *Princess May*, wrecked in Alaska

Sentinel Island, Alaska, USA
(William Howard Case / Frank G. Carpenter / Library of Congress)

The steamship *Princess May* was a Canadian coastal liner, which ran the 800 miles from Vancouver to Skagway in Alaska from May 1901. Demand for travel to Skagway had escalated rapidly with the Klondike Gold Rush. As well as voyaging to Skagway, the ship also serviced the multitude of small industrial communities along the route.

This picture shows the *Princess May* stranded on Sentinel Island, Alaska, on 5 August 1910. Under Captain Macleod, the ship had left Skagway in thick fog. Running onto rocks, the ship's bulk provided enough momentum to force it up at a sharp angle. One hundred and forty-three people were on board; none were hurt. Also undamaged was the ship's cargo of Klondike gold. The photo became very popular and was bought a great many times.

'There was no panic when the *Princess May* struck the reef north of Sentinel Island this morning, but the women and children suffered much from cold in the small boats, the majority having left the sinking ship scantily clad.'

Los Angeles Herald, 6 August 1910

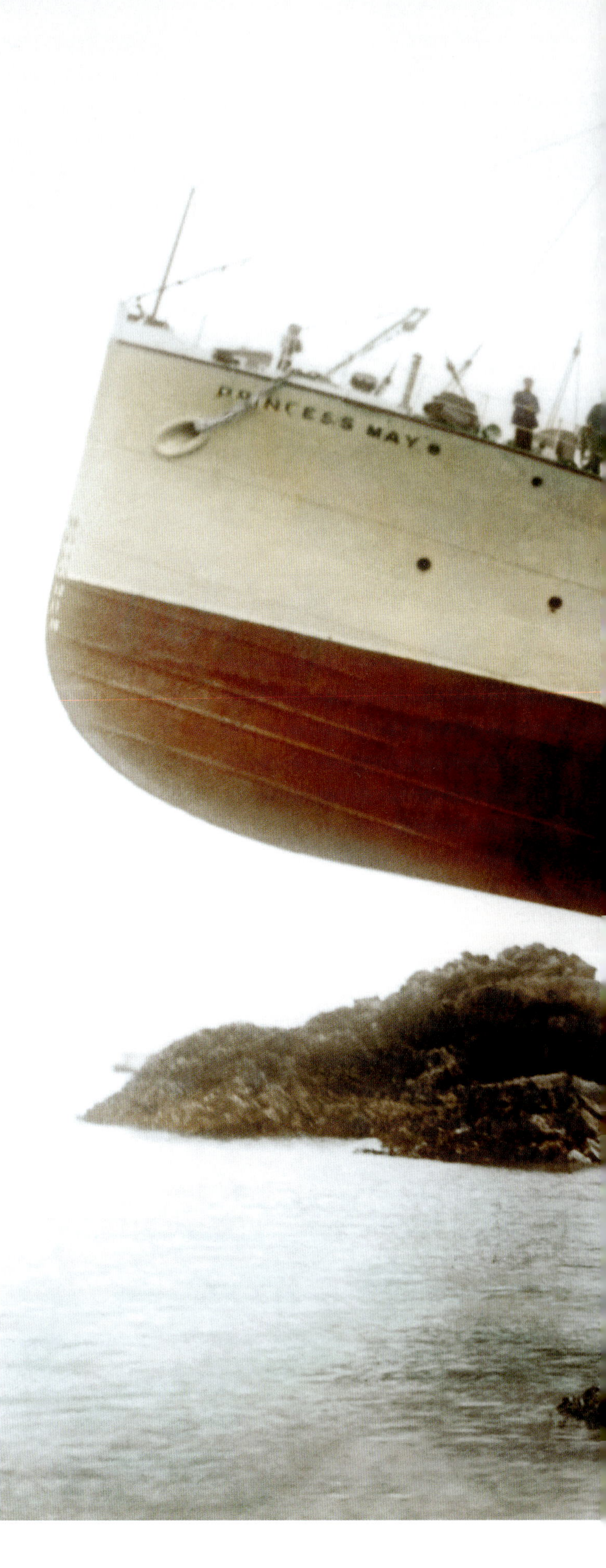

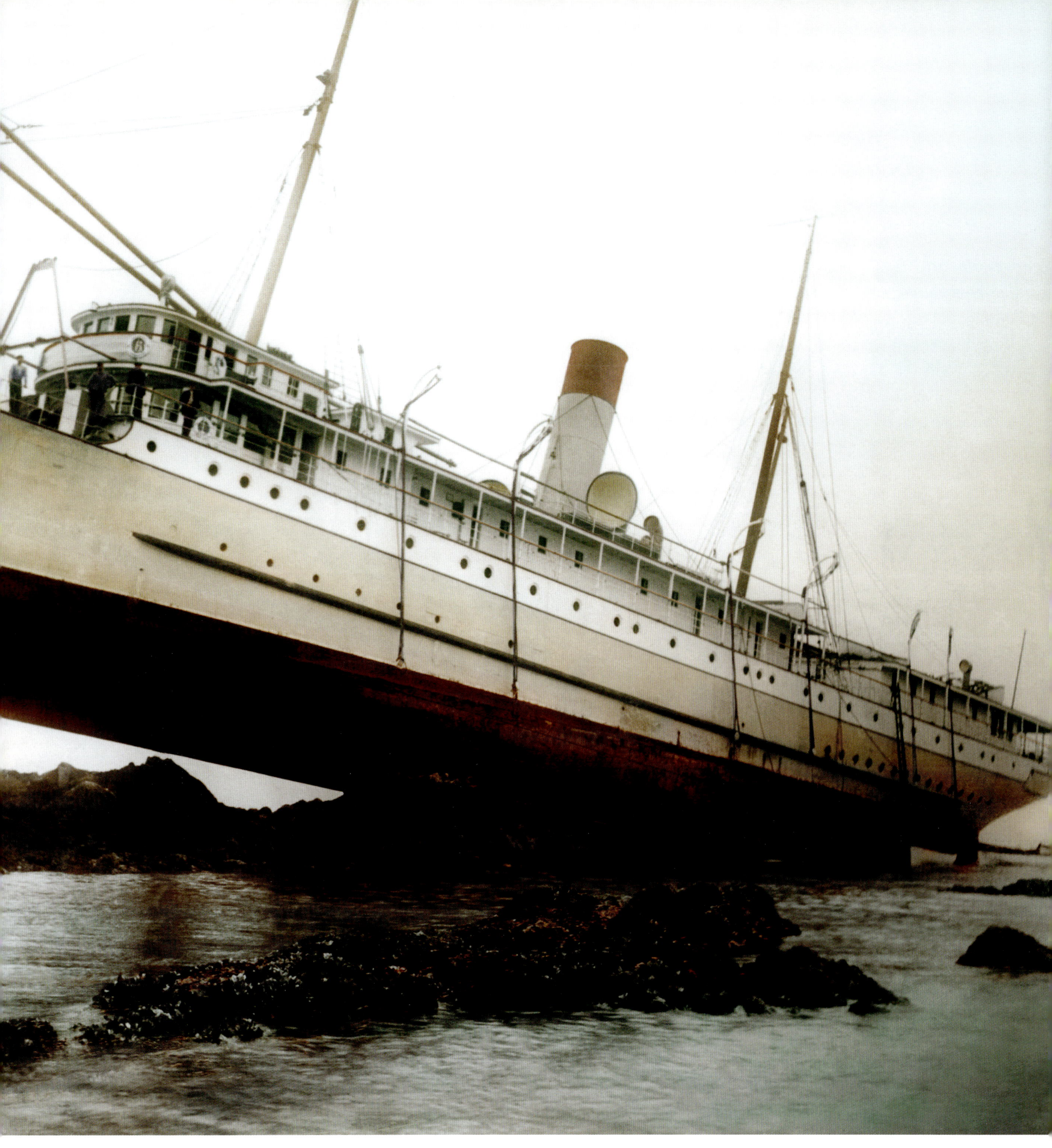

1910s

c. 1910: Father and son snapshots

Unknown

(Unknown / Simple Insomnia)

This set of four pictures, while likely to have been taken by a human photographer, appears to anticipate the strips of images taken in automatic photo booths – and such booths did exist in 1910.

Patented in America in 1888, the photo booth made its first real-world appearance in 1889 at the Paris World Fair. A year later, a German inventor created the 'Bosco' photo booth, the first to succeed commercially. Yet it wasn't until 1925 that the now-essential curtain arrived in a 'Photomaton' photo booth, brought to 1659 Broadway, New York, by Anatol Josepho. Twenty-five cents in Josepho's Photomaton bought you eight pictures, which took eight minutes to develop. 280,000 people used the booth in its first six months of existence.

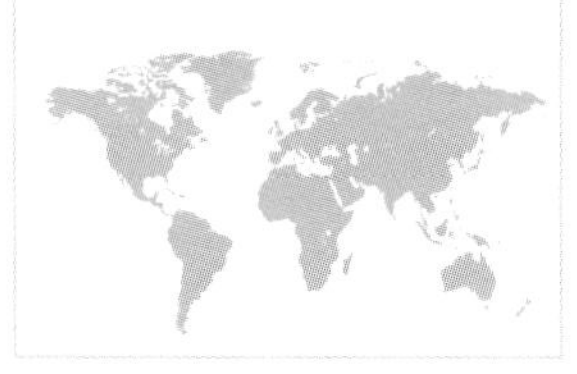

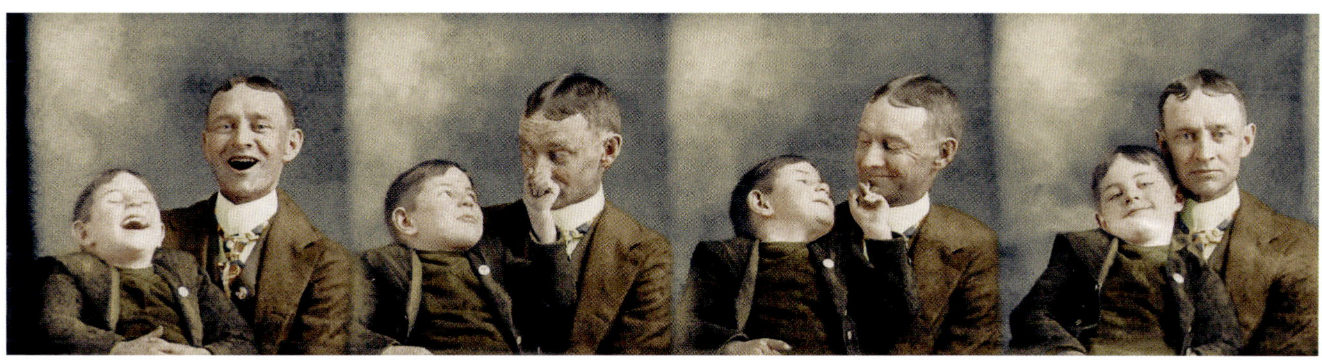

'Six months' trial was to prove whether the invention on which I had staked so much for fourteen years, was wanted by the public. We soon found out. Two thousand persons a day lined up at the studio and their quarters flowed into the slots. The Broadway crowds proved that my rapid-fire picture machine was a gold mine. I will never forget the meeting where Mr. Henry Morgenthau, who you know was once ambassador to Turkey, handed me a check for 1 million dollars for my interest in the Photomaton.'

Anatol Josepho, *Modern Mechanics*, November 1928

1910: **11 a.m. Newsies at Skeeter's Branch, Jefferson near Franklin. They were all smoking.**
St. Louis, Missouri, USA
(Lewis Hine / Library of Congress)

1910s

As a photographer working for social reform, Lewis Hine found a number of advantages in photographing 'newsies': boys who sold newspapers on the street. Unlike the work he did photographing child workers in mines, factories and mills, Hine could photograph the boys without seeking permission from employers or, more typically, by circumnavigating employers. The photographs could be achieved with more time, and with more focus and attention on the subjects he shot.

To achieve this sense of direct connection, Hine would bring his camera down to the eye level of his subjects. He didn't just take photographs of child workers, he also talked to them and sought to document their experience. In aggregate, he created a body of work that displayed an unacceptable standard of living for many thousands of children and which, ultimately, achieved a change in the law and in a cultural understanding of what it means to be a child.

'Attention. Newsboys. The record takes a great deal of pride in its street sales force, as the "little business men of the curb" each week dispose of up to 200 Records. To show our appreciation of the newsies and to encourage them to their best efforts, we are going to give ABSOLUTELY FREE A .22 CALIBER REPEATING RIFLE TO THE BOY SELLING THE MOST RECORDS BETWEEN 14 October 1910 and 1 January 1911.'

The Roundup Record, Montana, 7 October 1910

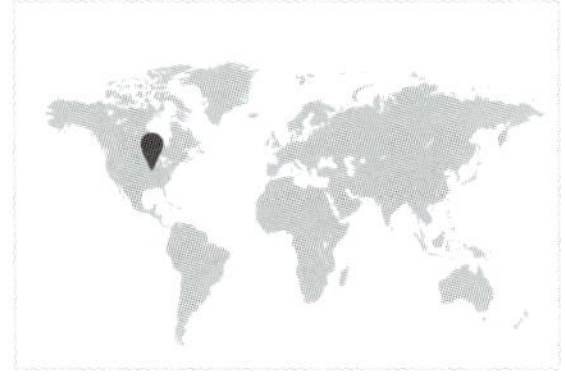

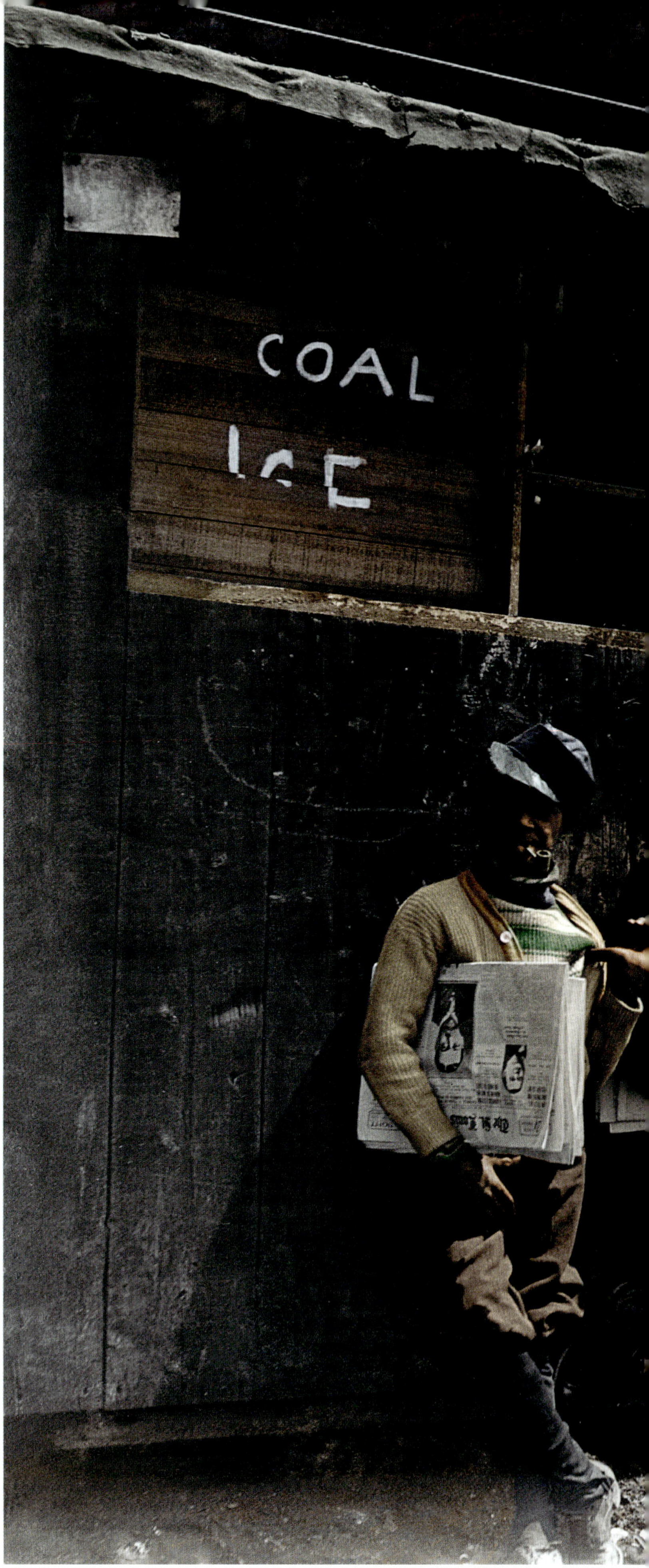

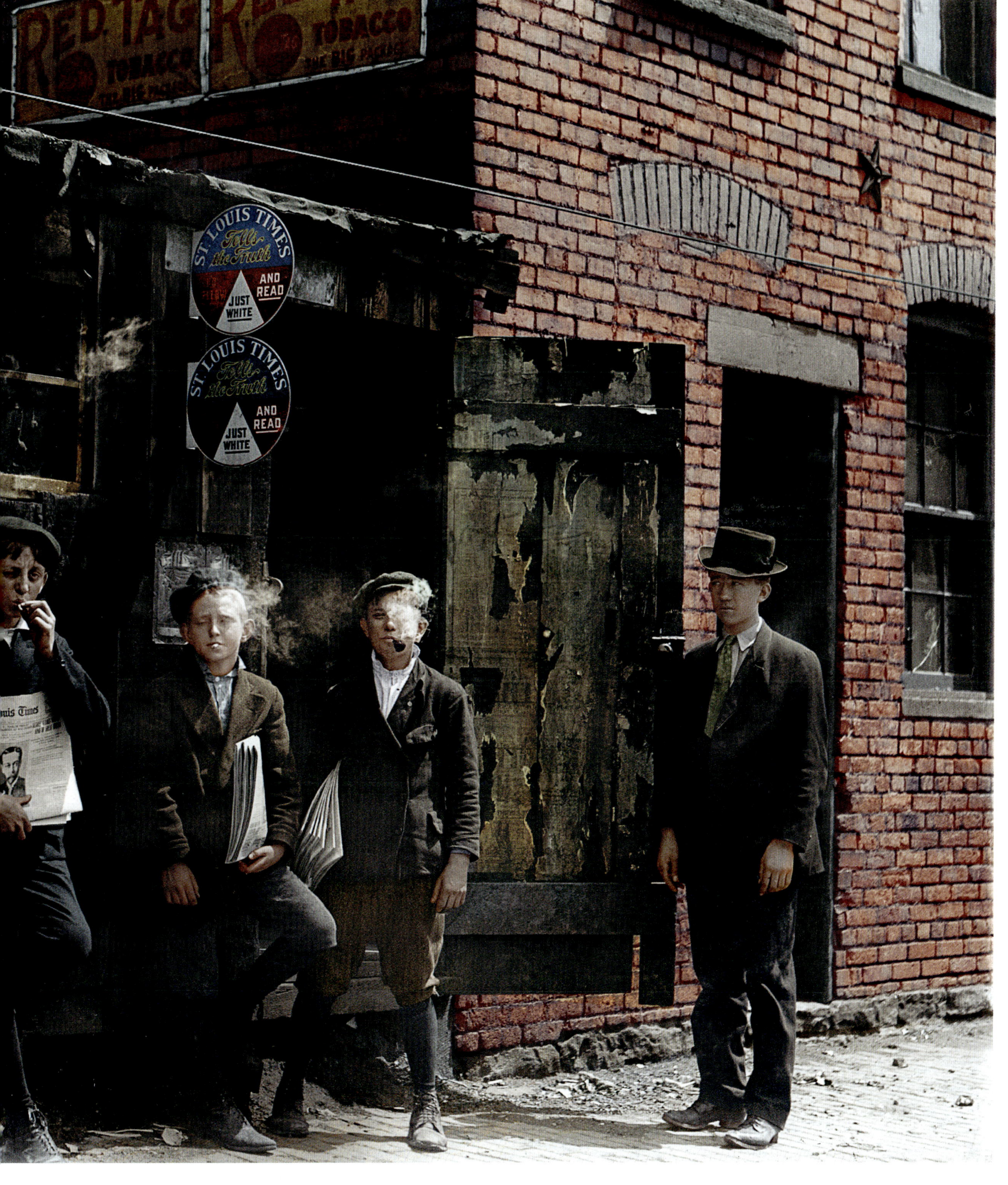
RED TAG
TOBACCO
ST. LOUIS TIMES
Tells the Truth
AND READ
JUST WHITE
ST. LOUIS TIMES
Tells the Truth
AND READ
JUST WHITE

1909: Louis Blériot leaving Calais, France

Calais, France
(Library of Congress)

French inventor Louis Blériot used the money he made from manufacturing truck headlamps to fund his work creating aircraft – in total, some 780,000 francs. The creator of the first modern monoplane, in 1909 Blériot achieved world fame making the first heavier-than-air-aircraft flight from France to the UK.

Around 20,000 people gathered at either Calais or Dover to witness the attempt. Blériot took off with the sunrise at 4:41 a.m. on 25 July. He had no compass and followed an escort ship, the *Escopette*, but then overtook it and lost sight of both the ship and land. Eventually arriving at the English cliffs, Blériot followed a course along the coast until he saw a man, a journalist from *Le Matin*, waving a large Tricolour.

The British *Daily Mail* newspaper awarded him a £1,000 prize for his trouble. This was double the prize they had offered in 1908.

1900s

'I got up at 2:30 in the morning in order to be ready, though I was not feeling well, my foot being painful.
I was dressed in a khaki jacket, lined with wool for warmth, over tweed clothes and beneath my engineer's suit of blue overalls. A close-fitting cap was fastened over my head and ears. I begin my flight towards the coast of England. I have no apprehension, no sensation.'

Louis Blériot, *Evening Star*, 26 July 1909

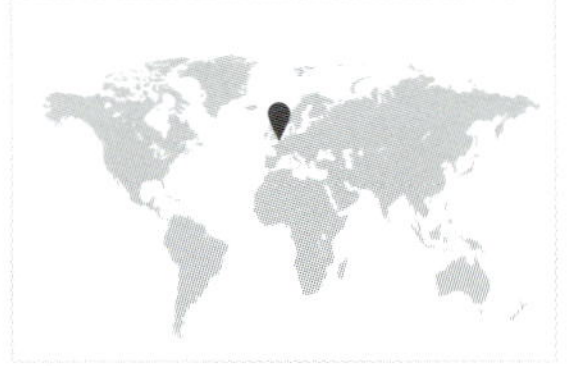

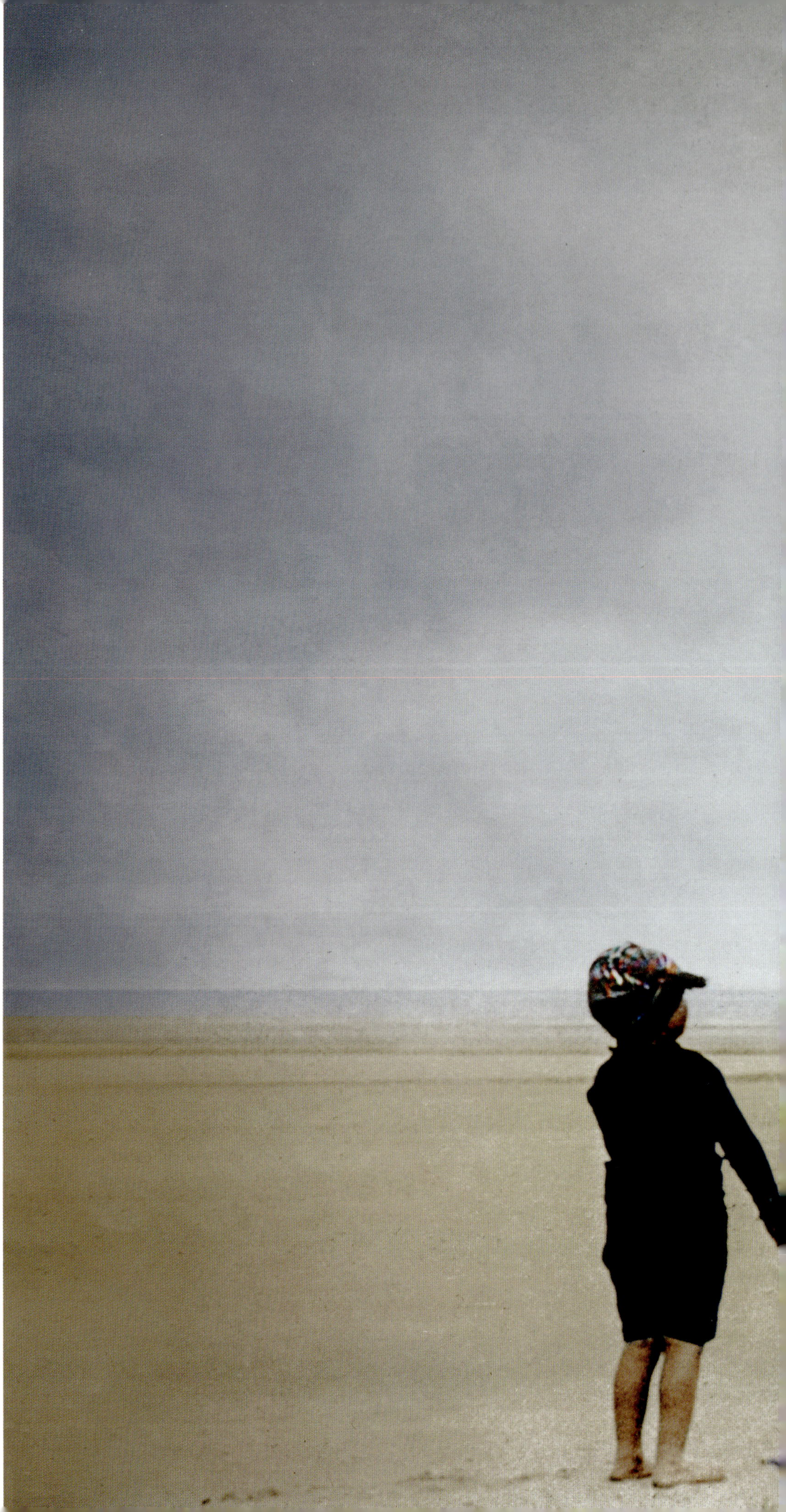

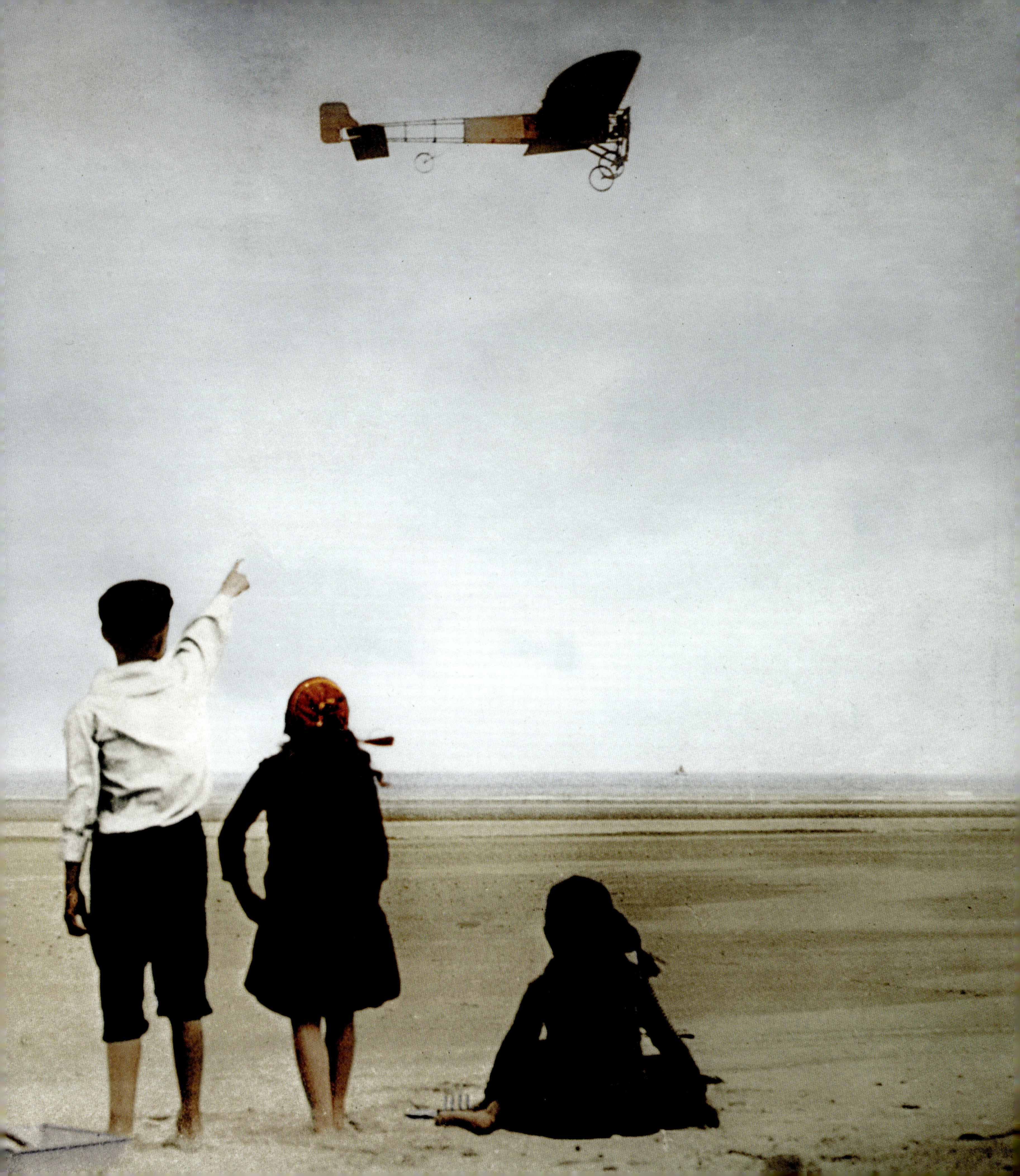

1908: Trapper boy, Turkey Knob Mine

Turkey Knob Mine, MacDonald, West Virginia, USA (Lewis Hine / Library of Congress)

Around 2 million children below the age of fifteen were working in industry in 1910. The benefits to employers were apparent: the ability of children to squeeze into small spaces, to manipulate fine tools, and to earn lower wages. For large families, those wages could mean the difference between getting by and destitution. Equally, the work undertaken was often beyond the capacity of a child. Accident rates were high, and compensation was negligible.

Teacher Lewis Hine acted as a photographer for the National Child Labor Committee, set up in 1904 to end child labour. Hine, with other photographers, was paid by the Committee to record the hardships experienced by children across America in mills, mines, yards and factories. Much of Hine's work was carried out without the knowledge of the children's employers.

1900s

The mining town of Turkey Knob, MacDonald, had grown up fifteen years before – its name derived from the wild turkeys hunted in the area. This boy's work was to wait in the darkness of the mine, and to open and close a door between two mining chambers. According to Hine's notes: 'Boy had to stoop on account of low roof, photo taken more than a mile inside the mine.'

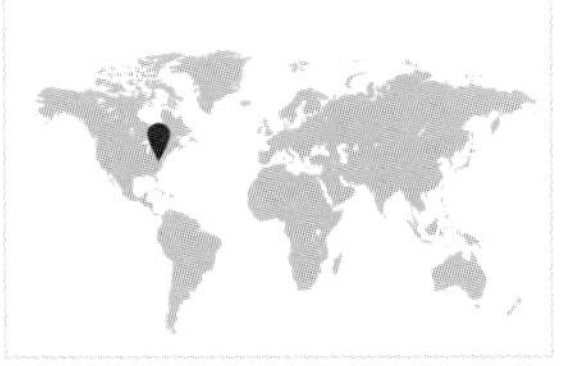

'In the bituminous mines of West Virginia, boys of nine or ten are frequently employed. Think of what it means to be a trap boy at ten years of age. It means to sit alone in a dark mine passage hour after hour, with no human soul near; to see no living creature except the mules as they pass with their loads, or a rat or two seeking to share one's meal; to stand in water or mud that covers the ankles, chilled to the marrow by the cold draughts that rush in when you open the trap door for the mules to pass through; to work for fourteen hours – waiting – opening and shutting a door – then waiting again for sixty cents; to reach the surface when all is wrapped in the mantle of night, and to fall to the earth exhausted and have to be carried away to the nearest "shack" to be revived before it is possible to walk to the farther shack called "home".'

John Spargo, *The Bitter Cry of the Children*, 1906

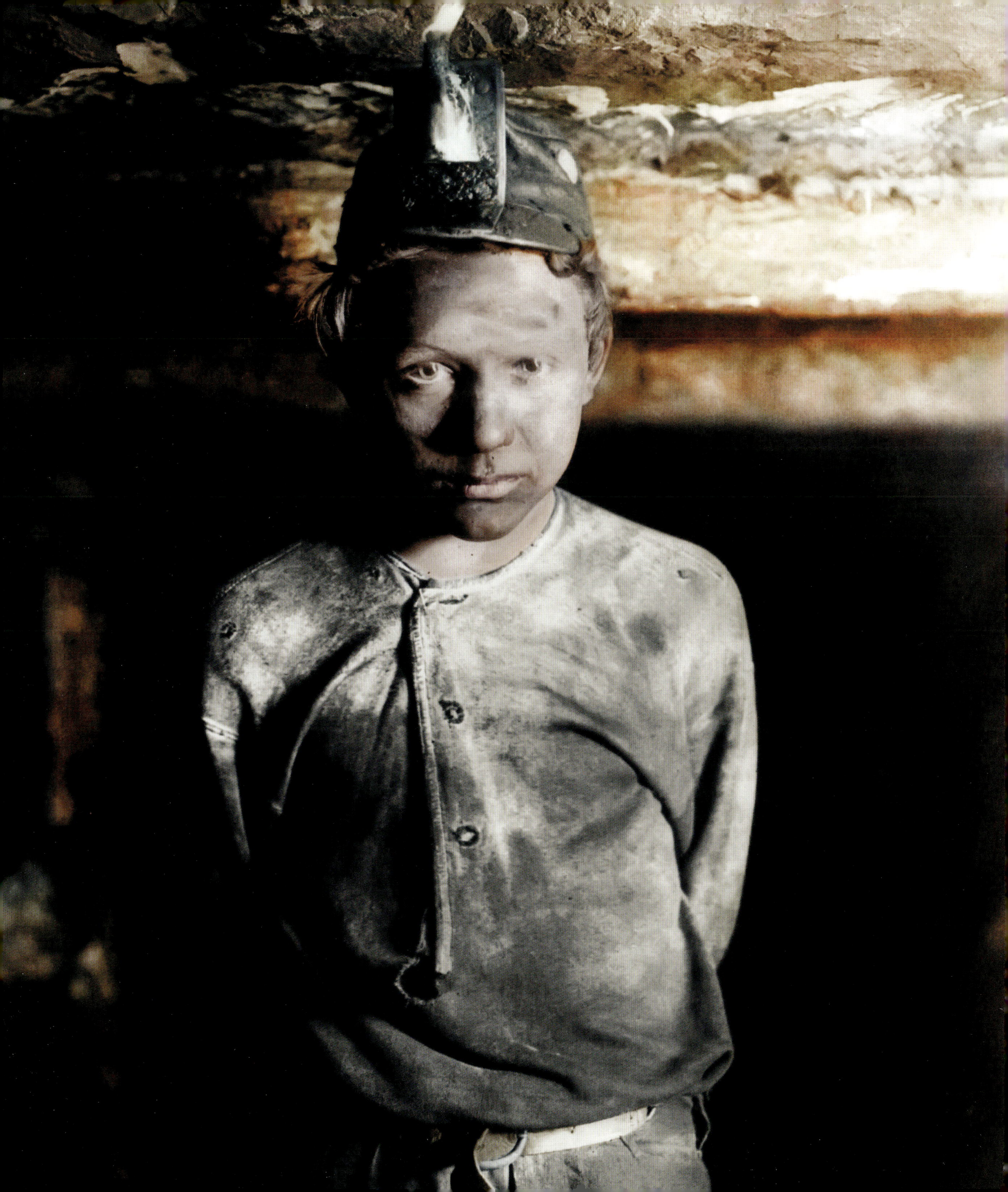

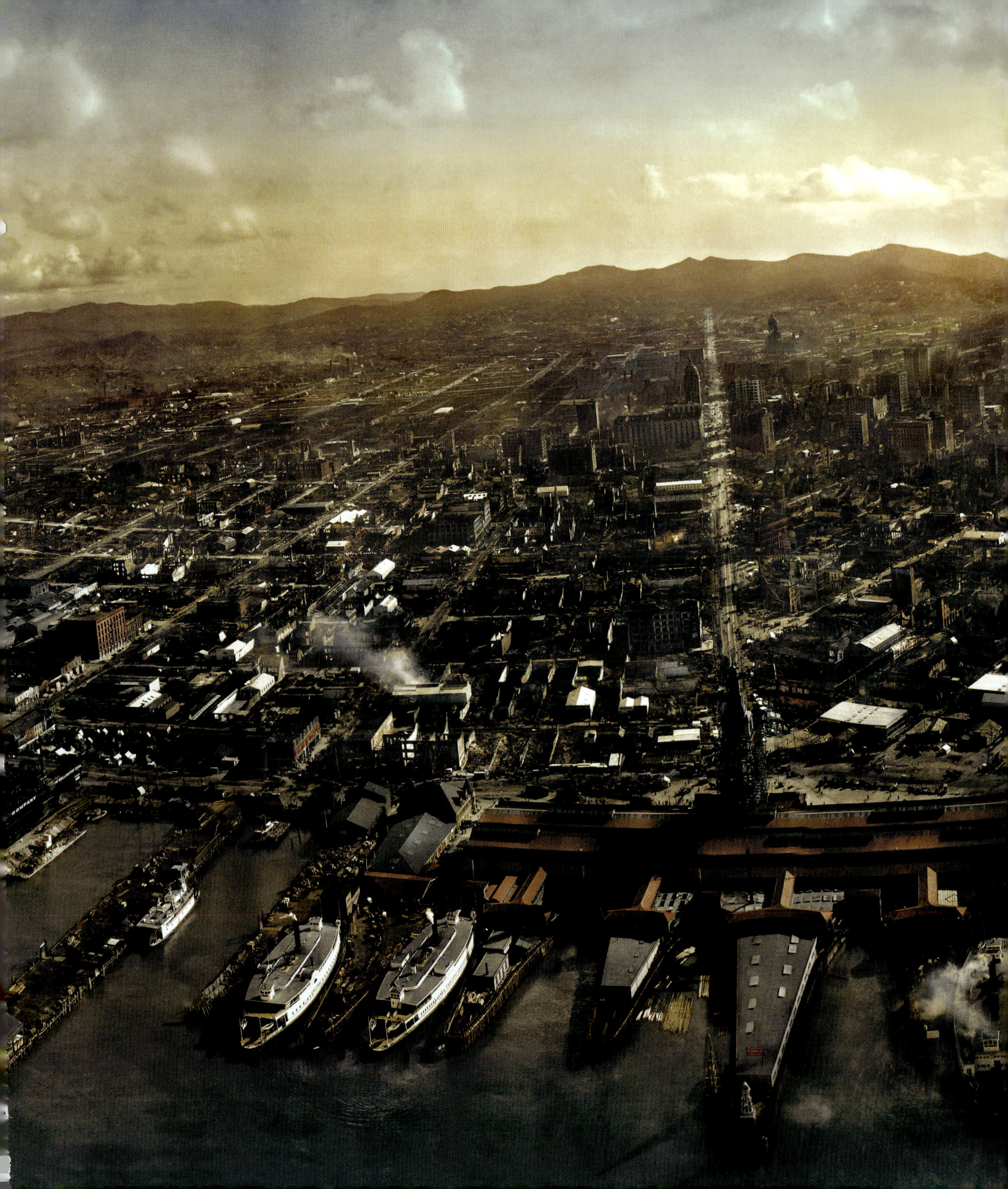

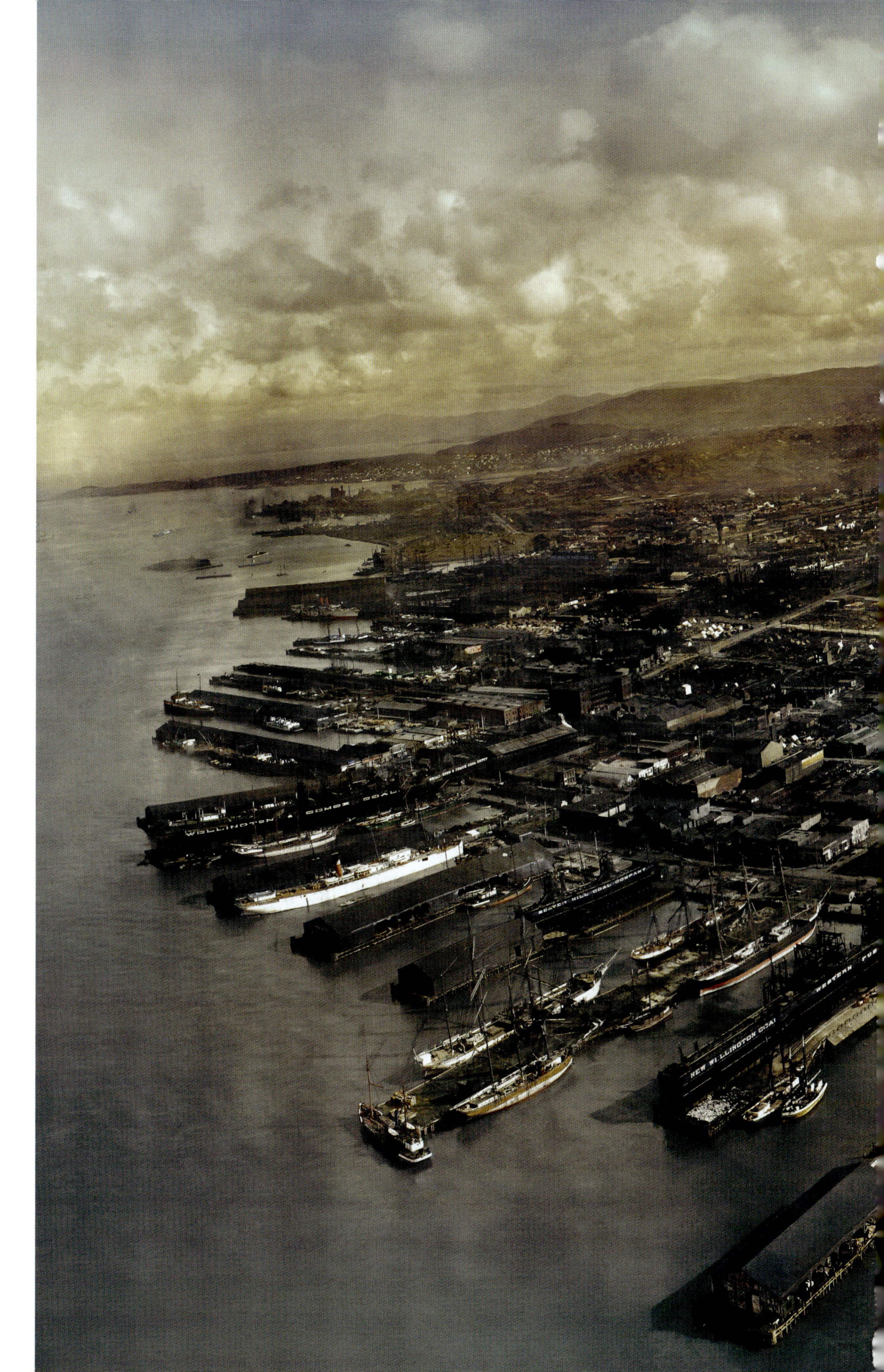
WELLINGTON & COMOX COAL
BEAVER HILL COAL COMPANY
NEW WELLINGTON
WESTERN

1900s

1906: San Francisco in ruins from Lawrence Captive Airship 2,000 feet (600 metres) above San Francisco Bay, overlooking waterfront. Sunset over Golden Gate.
San Francisco, California, USA
(George R. Lawrence / Library of Congress)

At 5:12 a.m. on Wednesday, 18 April 1906, San Francisco was hit by a magnitude 7.8 earthquake. By the end of the week, the city was in ruins. Eighty per cent of the buildings were destroyed not only by the earthquake but by the devastating fires that followed in its wake. Three thousand lives were lost and more than 200,000 people (from a total population of 410,000) were left without homes.

This incredible image was taken by George R. Lawrence using a kite flying at 2,000 feet (600 metres). Lawrence, whose Chicago studio used the tagline 'The hitherto impossible in photography is our specialty', sold prints of the image at $125 each. He generated at least $15,000 in sales.

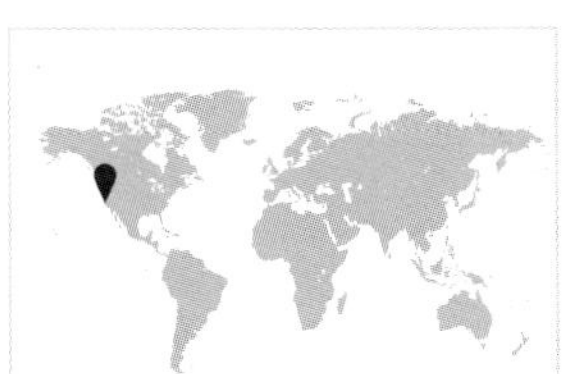

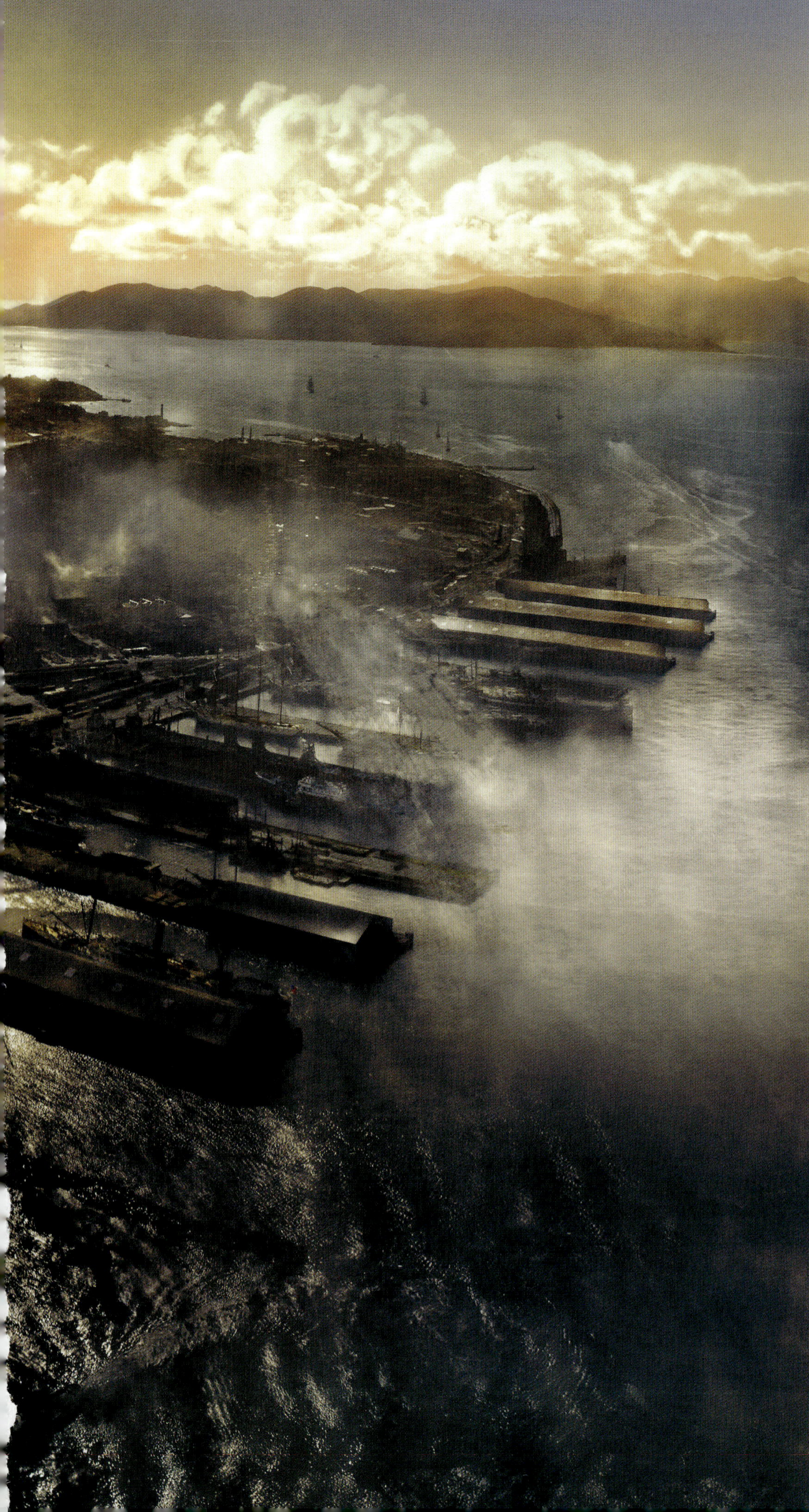

'Dear Mother,
The hills rolled like great billows and cracked open, houses sank between seven and eight feet in places. All the big cheap lodging houses collapsed with all the people in them. Then the fire which started in one hundred places – at once quickly burnt-up the dead and injured.

The flames spread like fury, jumping six and seven blocks at once, 450 blocks were burnt to the ground in all. The water mains were all broken, by the quake, so that the firemen had no water to fight the fire with. All they could was to blow up the buildings with dynamite, in spite of this the rapidly moving flames sped on their way . . . The fire was a beautiful sight – at night miles of skyscrapers being gutted or burnt to the ground.

The number of dead will never be known. Some big places fell with 400 to 500 people in them. Then the fire done the rest. Not an ash is left to tell the tale.

With love and best wishes to all,
Percy'

Percy H. Gregory, immigrant carpenter, 29 May 1906, nearly six weeks after the quake

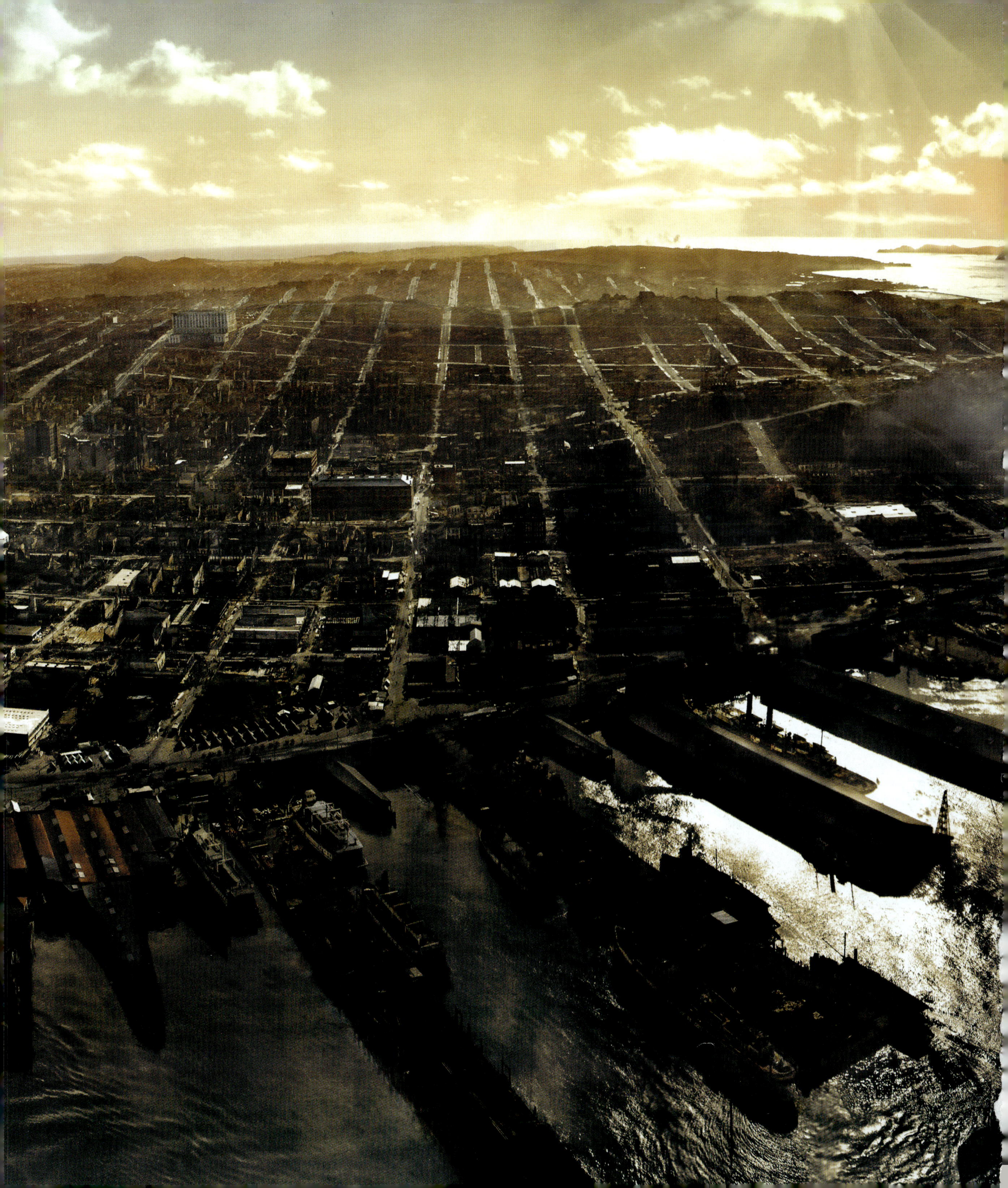

1900s

1905: **The Empire State Express (New York Central Railroad) passing through Washington Street, New York**

Syracuse, New York State, USA
(Detroit Publishing Company / Library of Congress)

The Empire State Express was the flagship train of the New York Central and Hudson River Railroad. It also had world renown as the first passenger train with a speed scheduled above fifty miles per hour as well as undertaking the longest scheduled non-stop run, between New York City and Albany, for 143 miles.

Trains have run on the roads of Syracuse, New York, since 1859, earning the city the sobriquet 'the city with the trains in the streets'. As well as the obvious safety concerns, the situation also brought noise, dirt and pollution to Syracuse citizens. At peak points, around sixty trains ran along Washington Street, though that era finally came to an end in 1936 with the arrival of an elevated railroad and a new station on Erie Boulevard East. The final train to run on Syracuse streets was the Empire State Express, eastbound.

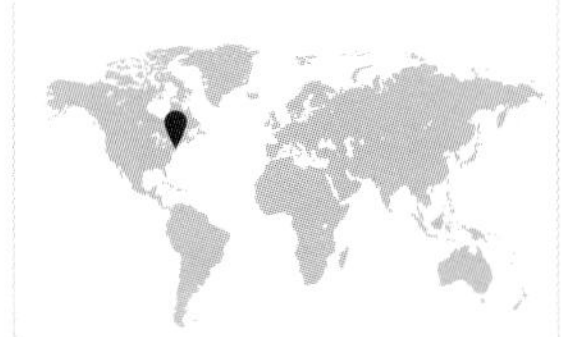

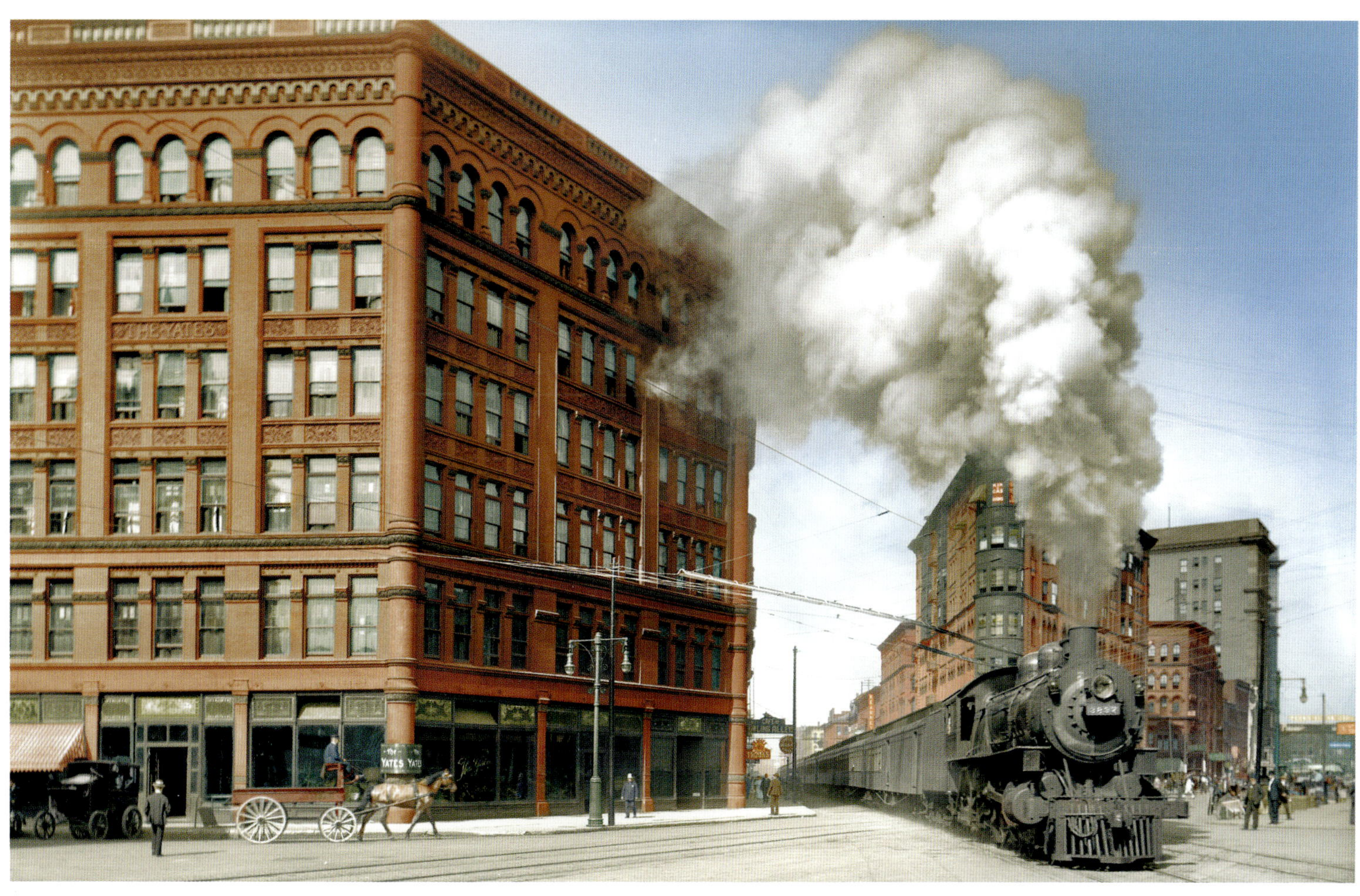

'The passengers on board said that the train flew along with the same steadiness that would have accompanied a slower rate of speed. There was no unusual swaying or jolting, and only persons who were looking out for manifestations of extraordinary speed would have noticed that the clickety-click of the rails sounded like the roar of musketry, and the telegraph poles along the track seemed like pickets in a fence.'

'Empire State Express Engine Travels at the Rate of 112 ½ Miles an Hour', *The New York Times*, 12 May 1893

c. 1905: Pulling out of the clearcut

Skagit County, Washington, USA
(Darius Kinsey / Getty)

Building a railroad across the United States was not an easy task, to say the least. In numerous places, the landscape to be traversed was deeply challenging, given the imperative to secure the rails to an entirely flat and smooth pathway. Not only did vast distances need to be spanned, so did deep canyons. Enter the trestle bridge. Rather than waiting for the delivery of permanent supplies to construct a bridge to last for decades, the onus was to build something that would work – fast – and which could be replaced later. More than 100 years later, original trestle bridges can still be found across the States and in Canada.

This train belongs to the Clear Lake Lumber Co. based in Skagit County, near the American–Canadian border. At its peak, the Clear Lake Lumber Co. employed 1,236 men.

Photographer Darius Kinsey worked across the west of Washington State between 1890 and 1940, directing his camera to the area's loggers and lumberjacks. His career came to an abrupt end in 1940 when he fell from a tree stump, aged seventy-one. He died in 1945.

1900s

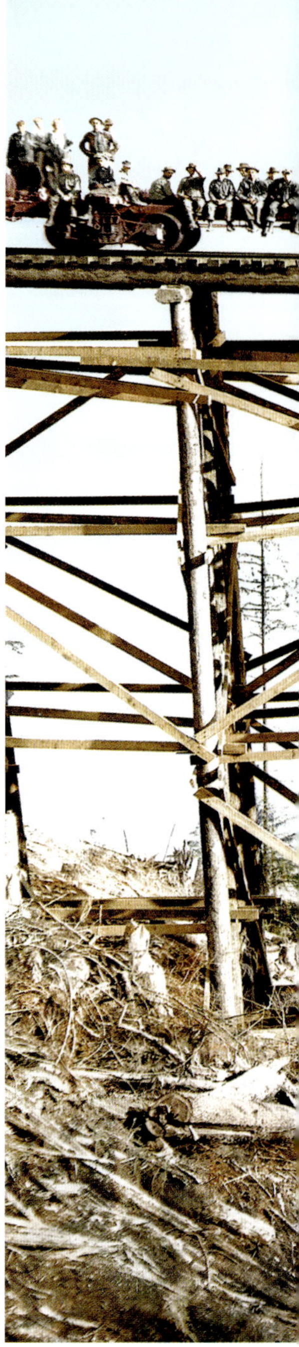

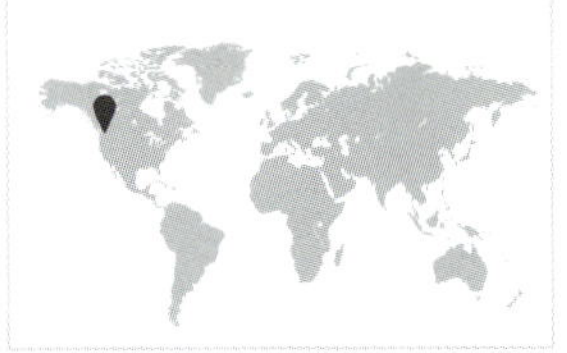

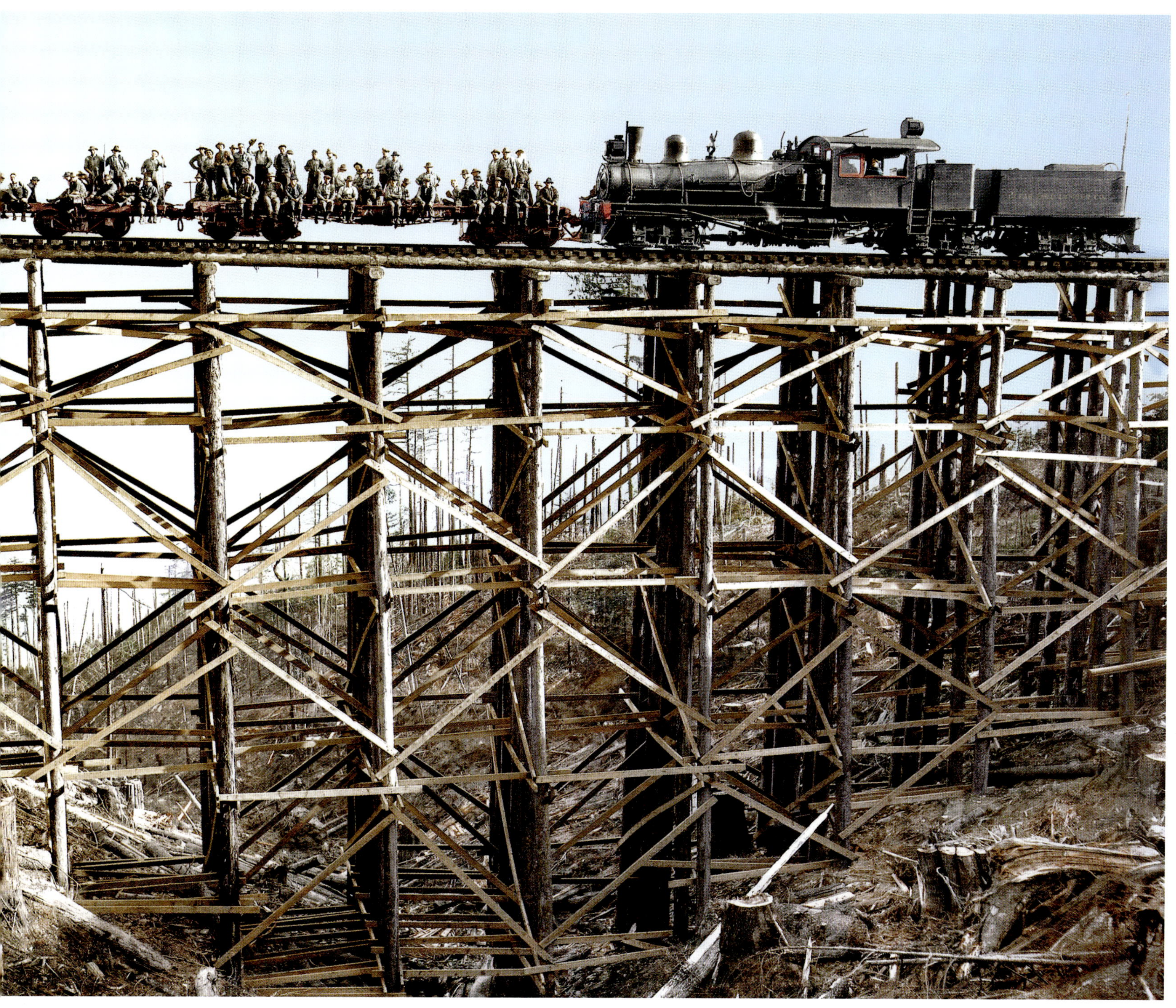

'Red Madden, known to the box car fraternity as "Cincy", last week in two minutes escaped from death by fire, from mangling under a railroad train, from destruction in a terrible fall, and from drowning. His clothes caught fire while he was cooking his dinner, he ran across a trestle bridge to get to the creek below, was caught by an express train, fell sixty feet from the trestle bridge, was swept over a forty-foot falls, and was dragged out by Sam Noradyke, fishing. "You came down fast," remarked Sam. "I was in a hurry," said Cincy.'

Omaha Daily Bee, 18 June 1905

1900s

***c.* 1905: On the springboards and in the undercut: a Washington lumberjack and his daughters, in the Cascade Mountains near Seattle, Washington**

Seattle, Washington, USA
(Darius Kinsey / Library of Congress)

The Pacific Northwest, and in particular Washington, was the heart of the American lumber industry, with land used for forestry stretching over 70 million acres. Stimulated by the Californian Gold Rush, the lumber industry supplied employment to two out of three of Washington State's men. In 1892 alone, almost 1.2 billion board feet of lumber were produced by Washington. The range of trees forested was wide, but centred around cedar, firs and spruce. When this photograph was taken, near Seattle, Washington, lumber work was almost entirely unmechanised.

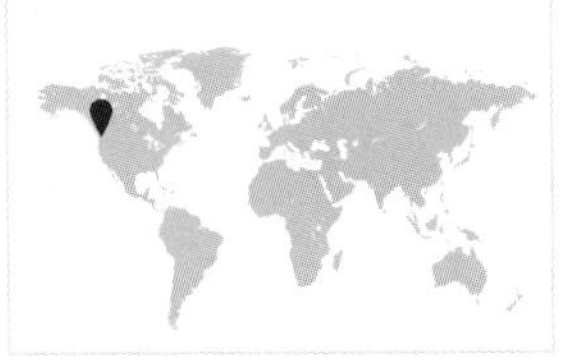

'"It's time that you were out, boys,"
the foreman he will say.
So they put on coats and mittens,
to the woods they haste away.
Another day in the pine woods,
all winter they'll remain.
Awaiting for the springtime, a-cutting
down the pine.'

'A-Cutting Down the Pine', traditional folk song

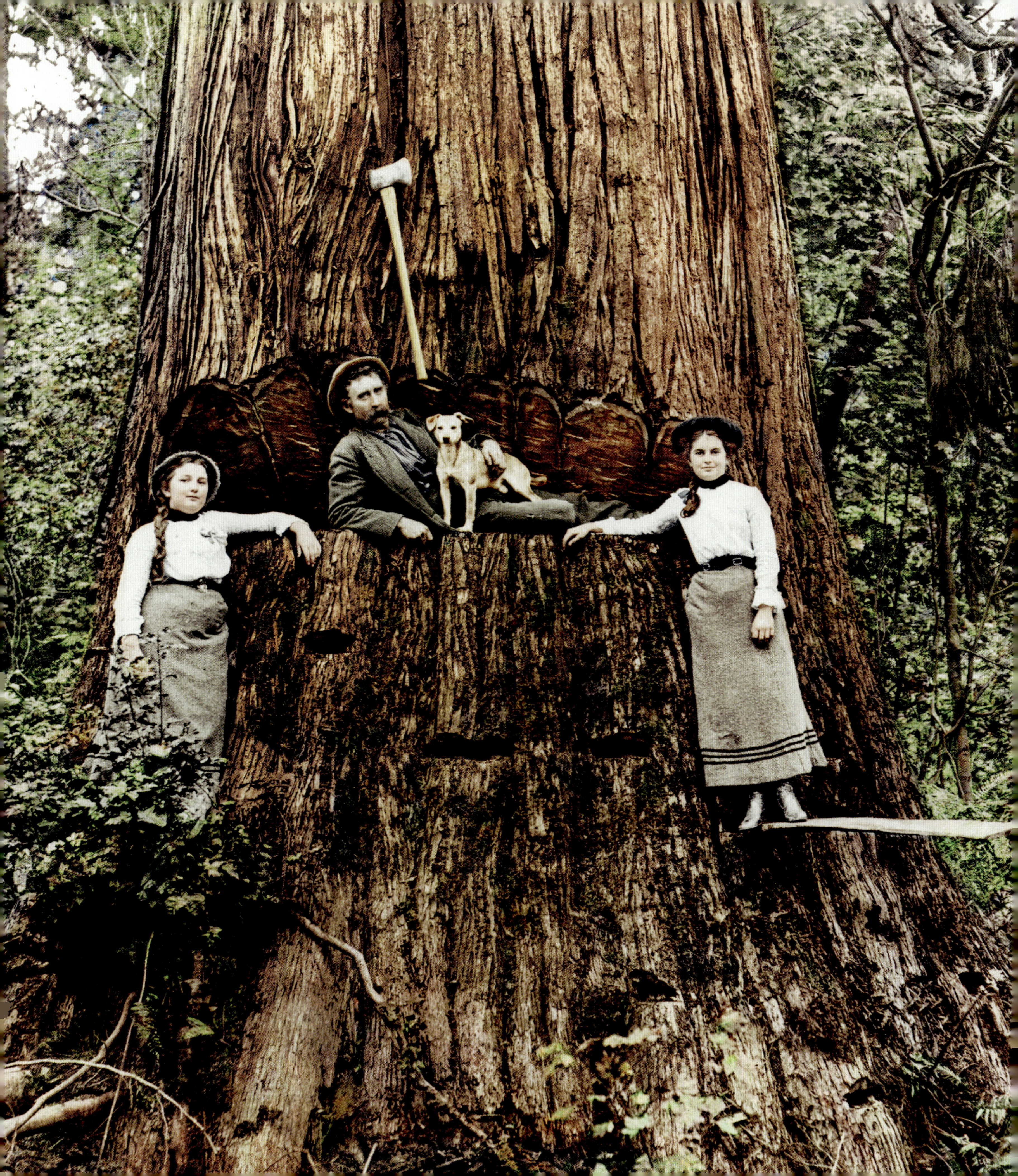

1900s

c. 1904: A ride at Coney Island's Luna Park

Coney Island, New York City, USA
(Geo. P. Hall & Son / New York Historical Society / Getty)

When Frederic Thompson and Elmer Dundy built their 'A Trip to the Moon' ride for an exposition in Buffalo, New York State, in 1901, they had a hit on their hands. The centrepiece of the ride was an airship named Luna, powered by wings which flapped.

Moving the ride to Coney Island's Steeplechase Park for 1902, Thompson and Dundy then leased more land and created Luna Park, using 1,000 spires, a quarter of a million lights, and $700,000. On its opening night, 60,000 people paid ten cents each to enter Luna Park; rides cost extra.

But in 1908, Luna Park was eclipsed by Dreamland, which had a million lights. Dundy died in 1907 and Thompson went bankrupt. Luna Park continued to exist, but successive owners struggled to realise any potential it possessed. In 1944, it was wiped out by fire.

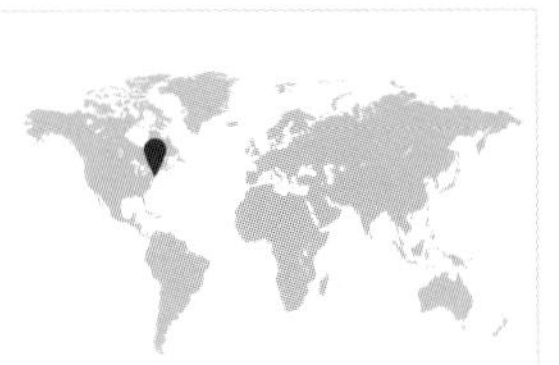

'Luna Park offers to the millions of pleasure seekers of this city and its environs a show place such as the ingenuity of the showman of the world has never devised before. World's fair, circus, hippodrome, menagerie, pleasure garden, swept with the salt breeze on which the spray of the ocean is hardly dry, a fairy land for man and child alike, it offers more to the eye and kindred senses than could be absorbed in a week of constant junketing.'

Advert for Luna Park, *The Evening World*, Saturday, 7 May 1904

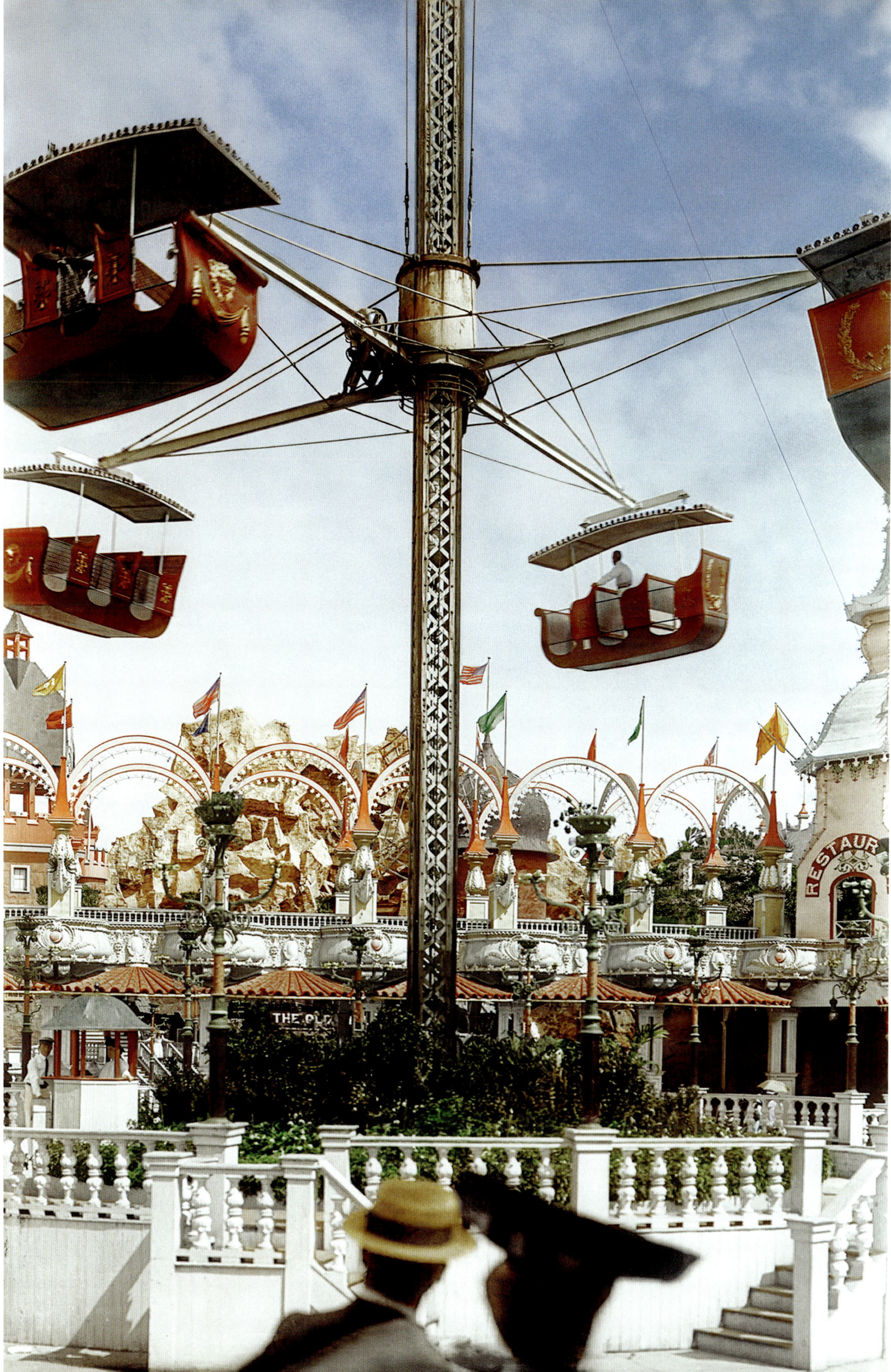
RESTAUR

1900s

16 October 1903: Alexander Graham Bell kissing his wife, Mabel Hubbard Gardiner Bell, who is standing in a tetrahedral kite
Baddeck, Nova Scotia, Canada
(Library of Congress)

Scottish inventor Alexander Graham Bell is well known for patenting the telephone. For Bell, however, the success of this invention was a mere distraction from his true calling to science, and his interests extended across a vast range of scientific fields.

Bell's experiments in the area of powered heavier-than-air flight began in earnest in 1891, and towards the end of the 1890s he turned his experiments to tetrahedral box kites; each cell in the compound structural kite provided lift to the whole. Bell's kits used crimson silk as a surface over spruce pine dowels. The kites were named Cygnet I, II and III. All flew with and without a passenger. Cygnet III, with more than 3,000 individual cells, flew successfully when towed by a steamship, though it was wrecked on landing. Its passenger, Lt. Thomas E. Selfridge, survived but became the first person to be killed in a powered flight as a passenger for the Wright Brothers.

Bell was fifty-six when this picture was taken and Mabel Bell was forty-six. Her father was first president of the Bell Telephone Company. Mabel's hearing had been destroyed by scarlet fever at the age of five – a significant factor in directing her husband's activity.

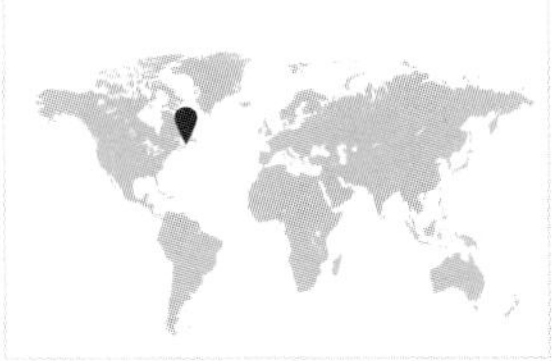

'In 1899, at the April meeting of the National Academy of Sciences in Washington DC, I made a communication on the subject of "kites with Radial Wings". Since then, I have been continuously at work upon experiments relating to kites. Why, I do not know, excepting perhaps because of the intimate connection of the subject with the flying machine problem.'

Alexander Graham Bell, *National Geographic* magazine, 1903

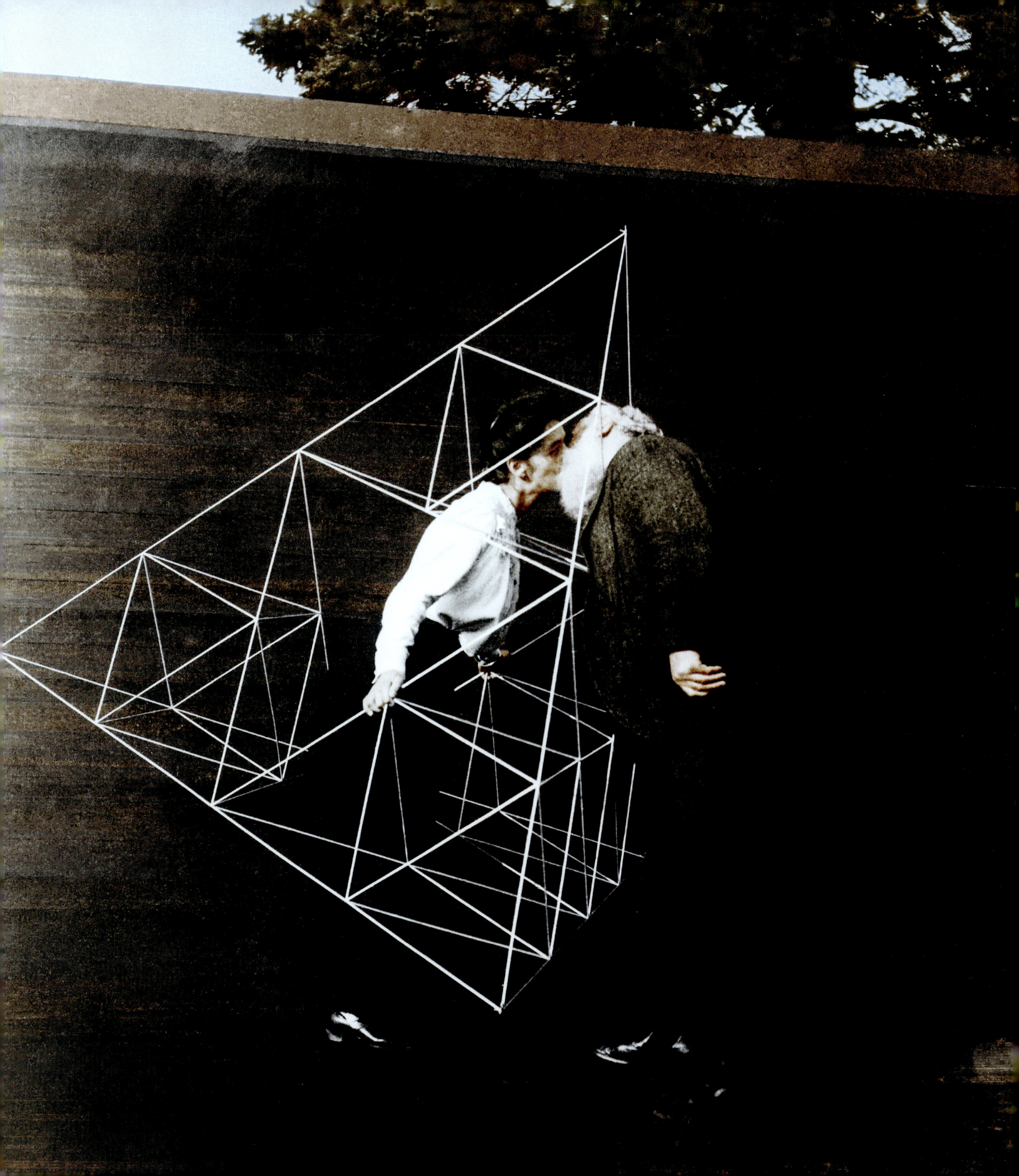

'Everybody is out of camp today but Will and myself. We went to the beach a number of times and have collected a whole bucketful of starfish besides a lot of shells and a couple of king crabs which we will bring home. Day before yesterday we had a wind of sixteen meters per second or about thirty miles per hour, and glided in it without any trouble. That was the highest wind a gliding machine was ever in, so that we now hold all the records! The largest machine, the longest time in the air, the smallest angle of descent and the highest wind!!! Well, I'll leave the rest of this "blow" till we get home.'

Orville Wright to his sister, Kitty Hawk, 28 October 1902

1902: Wilbur Wright gliding down the steep slope of Big Kill Devil Hill

1900s *Kitty Hawk, North Carolina, USA*
(Wright Brothers / Library of Congress)

In December 1903, the Wright brothers changed the nature of human movement forever with a powered flight over the sand dunes of Kitty Hawk, North Carolina. Prior to that, Orville and Wilbur had carried out hundreds upon hundreds – close to a thousand – of unpowered flights in gliders, such as this one, piloted by Wilbur.

Perhaps their most significant innovation was the control system the brothers developed to allow a flying machine to be steered; the lack of such controls had been partially responsible for the deaths of other flight innovators.

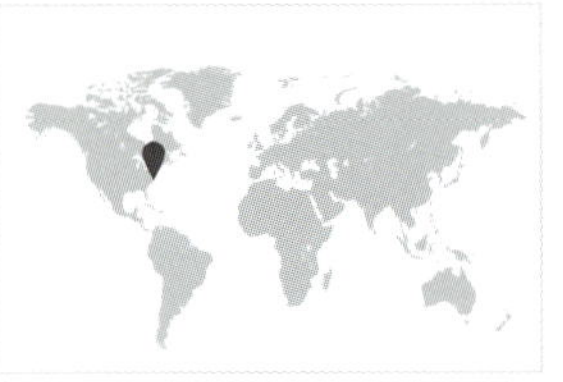

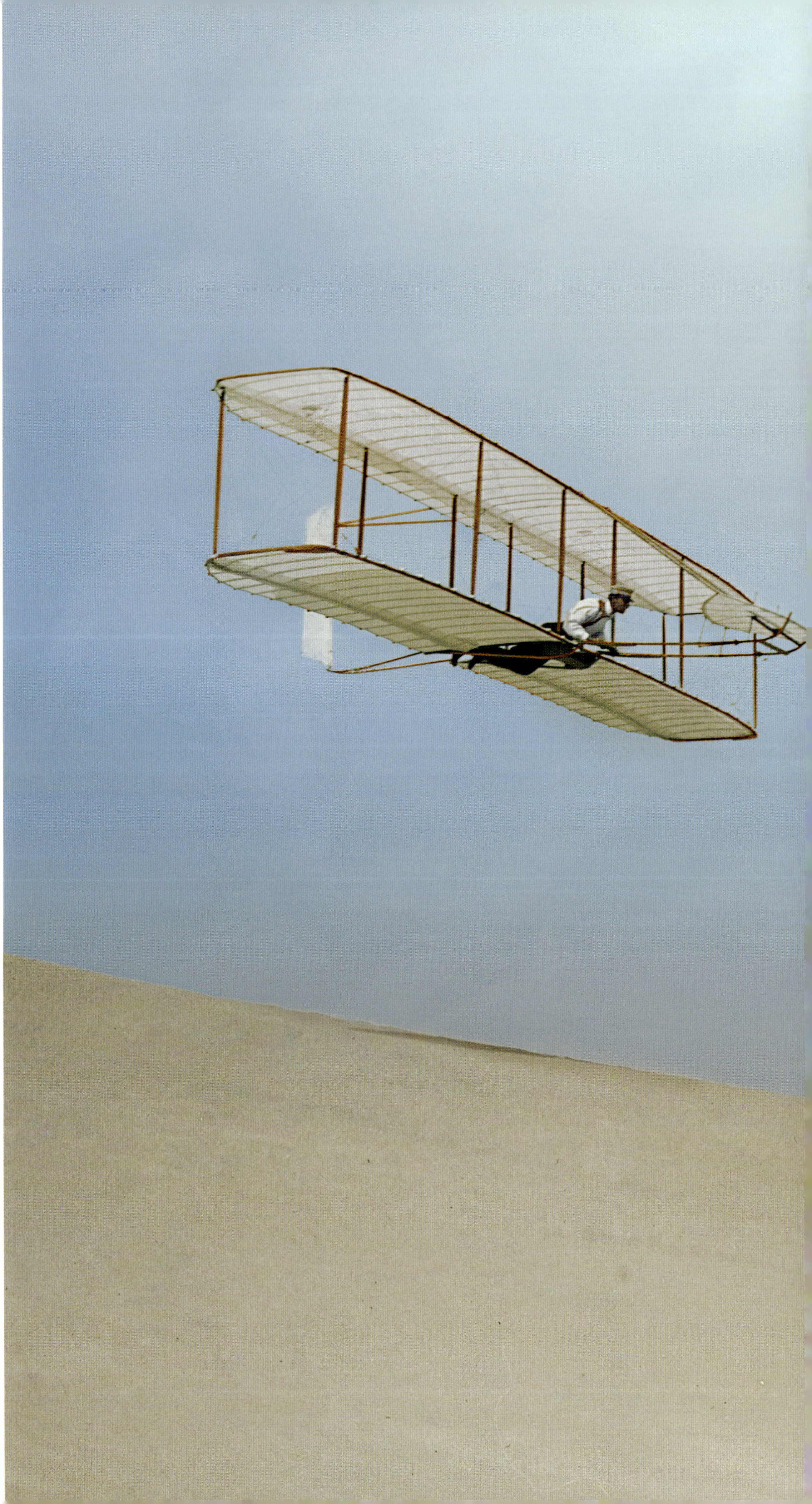

1900s

1902: The Cliff House Hotel, San Francisco

San Francisco, California, USA
(Unknown / Library of Congress)

This is the third incarnation of the Cliff House over Ocean Beach, in west San Francisco. The shore below the house has seen the wreck of more than thirty vessels. Built by engineer Adolph Sutro, the seven-storey structure survived the 1906 San Francisco earthquake with minimal damage but the following year it burnt to the ground. The current Cliff House Hotel is largely the same as the version built by Sutro's daughter, following the fire.

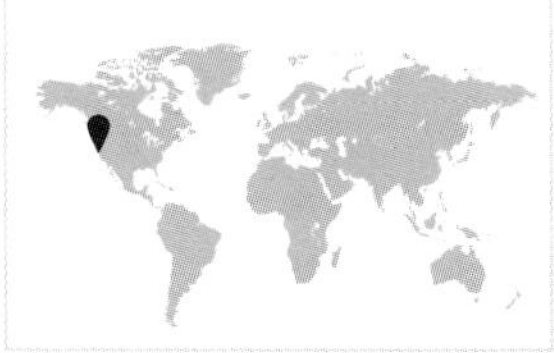

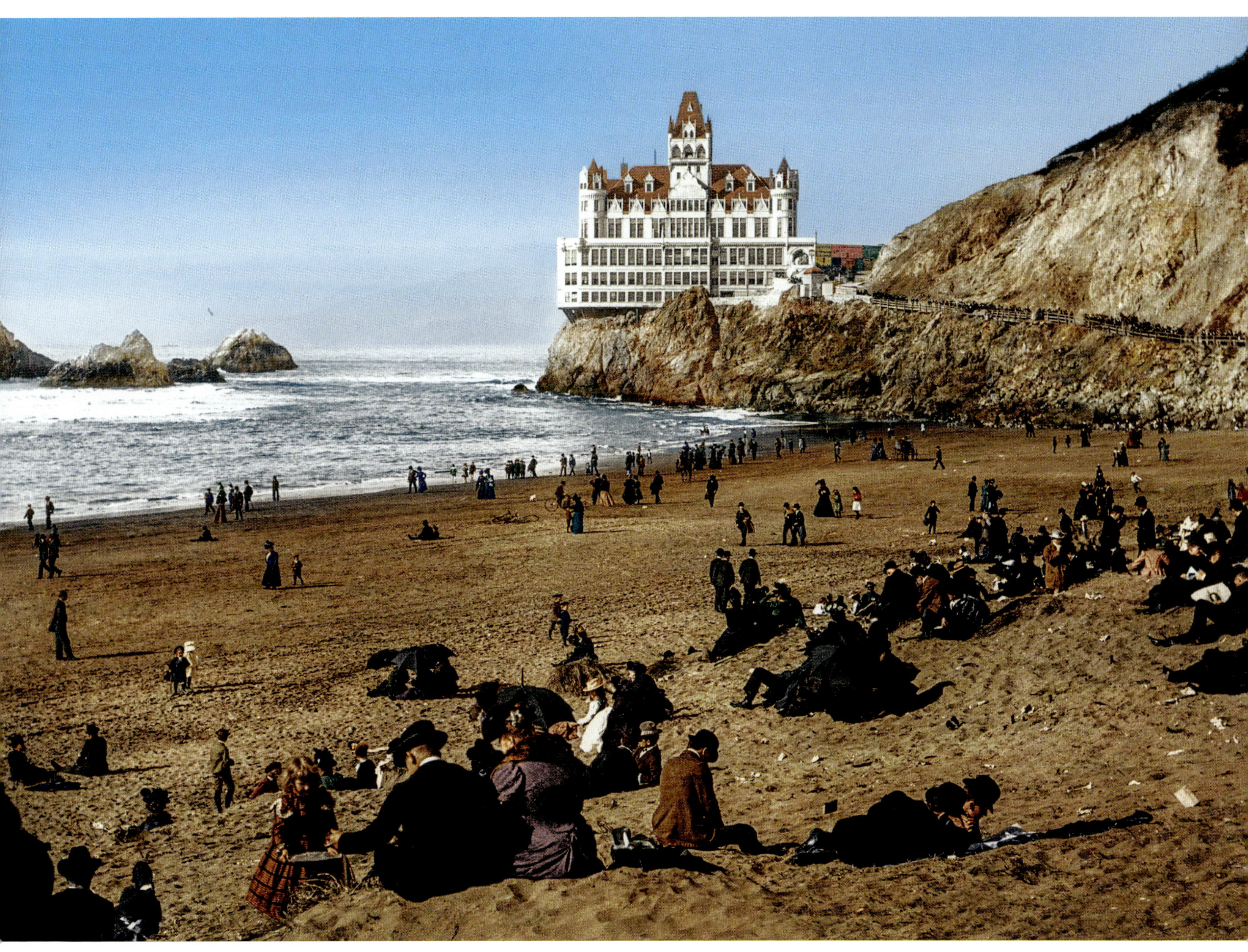

'There were great crowds at the opening of the new Cliff House yesterday. It is a magnificent building, handsomely proportioned and richly furnished. The reception-rooms, parlors, billiard-rooms and dining room and observatories all overlook the sea.'

San Francisco Call, 2 February 1896

1900s

c. 1902: The Flatiron Building under construction, New York

Broadway, New York City, USA
(Detroit Publishing Company / Getty)

Renowned for skyscraper designs, the Fuller Company bought a triangular plot in Manhattan. The prevailing opinion was that the oddly shaped building would be blown over by the wind, and it became known as 'Burnham's Folly' after its architect, Daniel Burnham. But it was the Flatiron name that stuck, after its resemblance to a (very tall) iron. When completed in June 1902, it was the tallest building in New York.

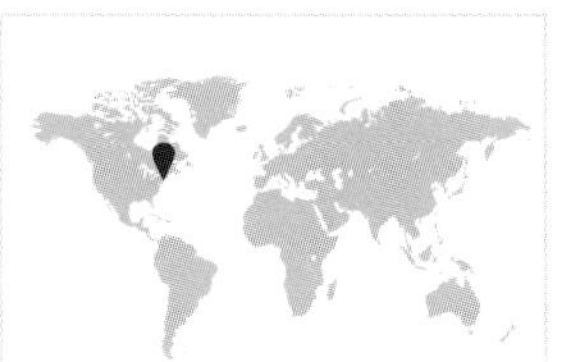

'Remarkable Feat of Steeplejack Astonished New Yorkers. The latest sensation in New York is the "Human Fly". Clinging like a fly to the surface of the famous Flatiron Building in Broadway, John Garrick, a thirty-year-old steeplejack, walked up and down the tall building while thousands below stood trembling at the daring feat.'

Western Kansas World, 25 November 1905

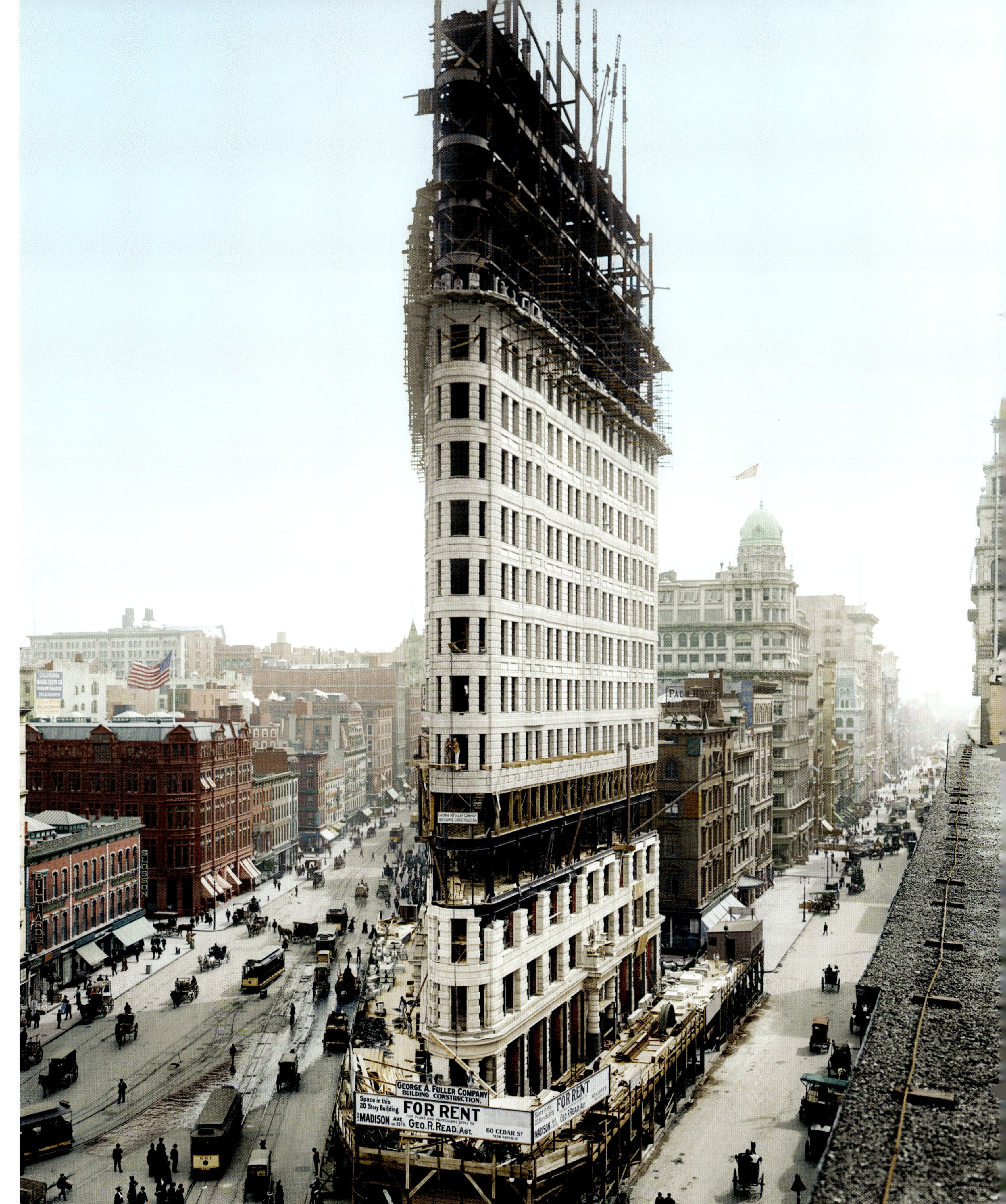
GEORGE A. FULLER COMPANY
BUILDING CONSTRUCTION.
Space in this
20 Story Building
FOR RENT
1 MADISON AVE. cor 23rd St
FOR PLANS AND PARTICULARS APPLY TO
GEO. R. READ. AGT.
60 CEDAR ST
FOR RENT
GEO. R READ. AGT
BILLIARDS
SLOSSON

1900s

1900s: Ellis Island immigrants

Ellis Island, New York City, USA
(Augustus Francis Sherman / New York Public Library)

These photographs show a tiny handful of the 12 million immigrants who entered the United States through the immigration station at New York's Ellis Island between 1892 and 1954. The men and women portrayed are wearing their finest clothes, often their national dress, brought with them from their homelands to America.

Around 5,000 immigrants entered the country every day at the height of Ellis Island's activity. The photographs were taken by Augustus Francis Sherman, the chief registry clerk at Ellis Island and an avid amateur photographer. They were captioned only with the subject's country of origin. In 1907, the portraits were published in *National Geographic*.

It is estimated that today more than a third of all Americans have an ancestor who came through Ellis Island.

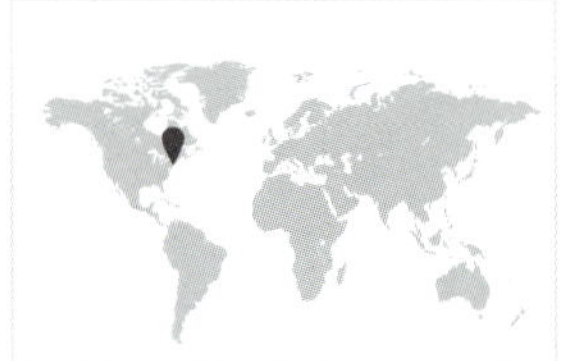

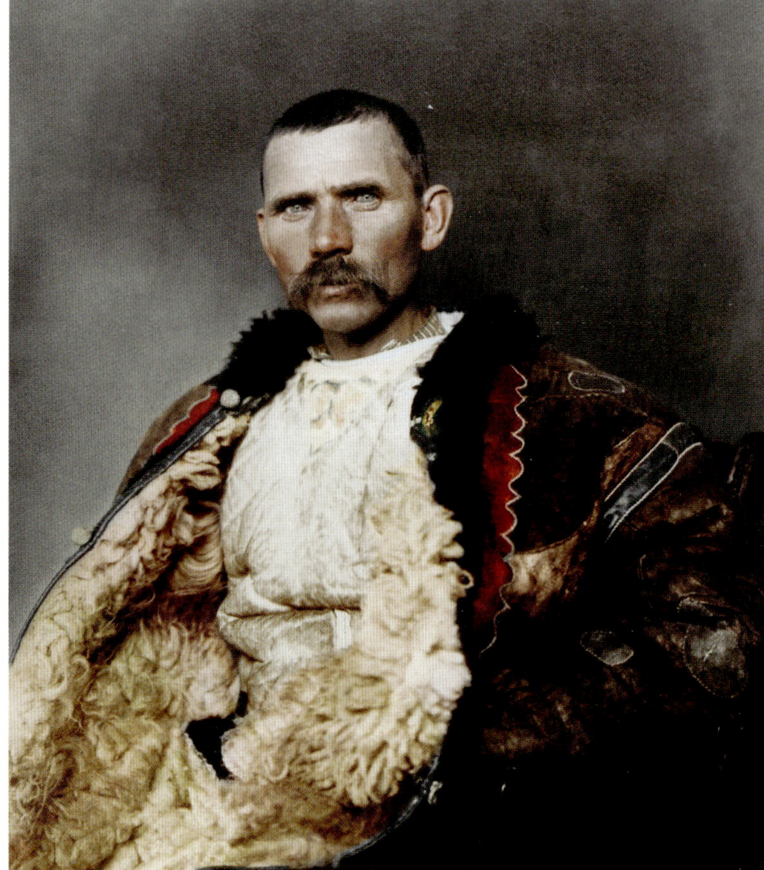

'We came by steerage on a steamship in a very dark place that smelt dreadfully. There were hundreds of other people packed in with us, men, women and children, and almost all of them were sick. It took us twelve days to cross the sea, and we thought we should die, but at last the voyage was over, and we came up and saw the beautiful bay and the big woman with the spikes on her head and the lamp that is lighted at night in her hand.'

Sadie Frowne, aged ten, immigrated from Poland in 1903, along with her mother following the death of Sadie's father and the failure of the small grocery store that provided them a living

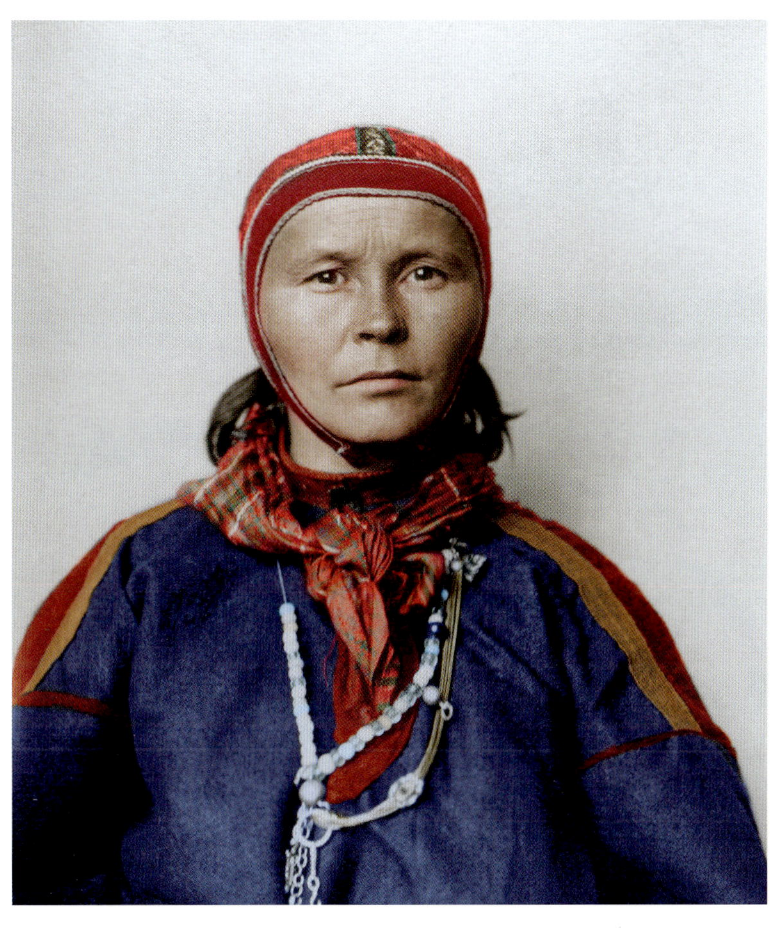
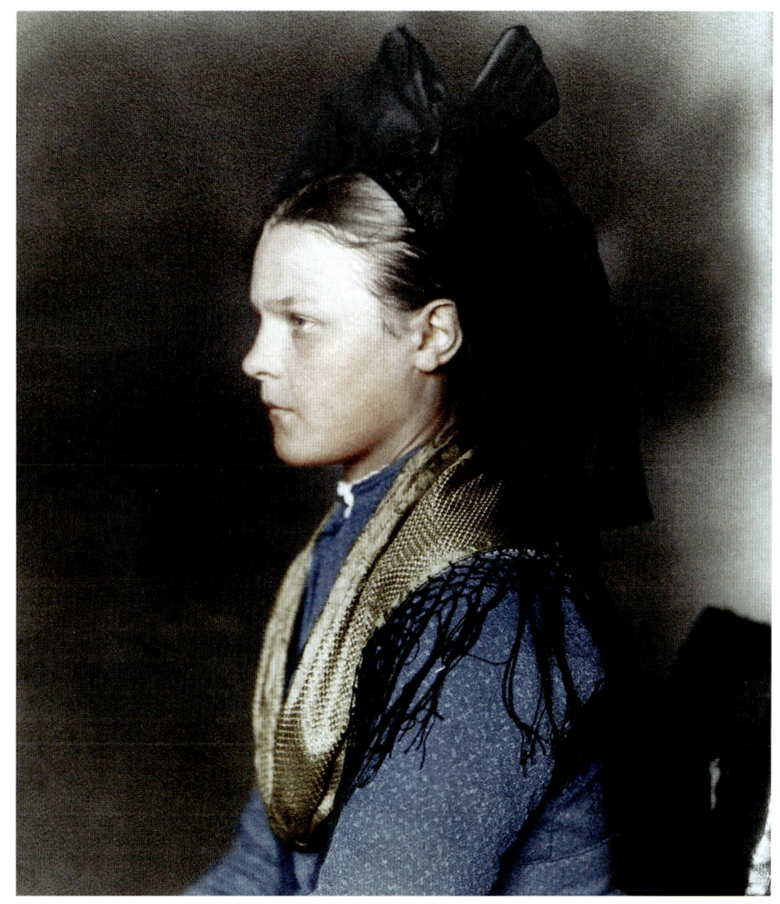
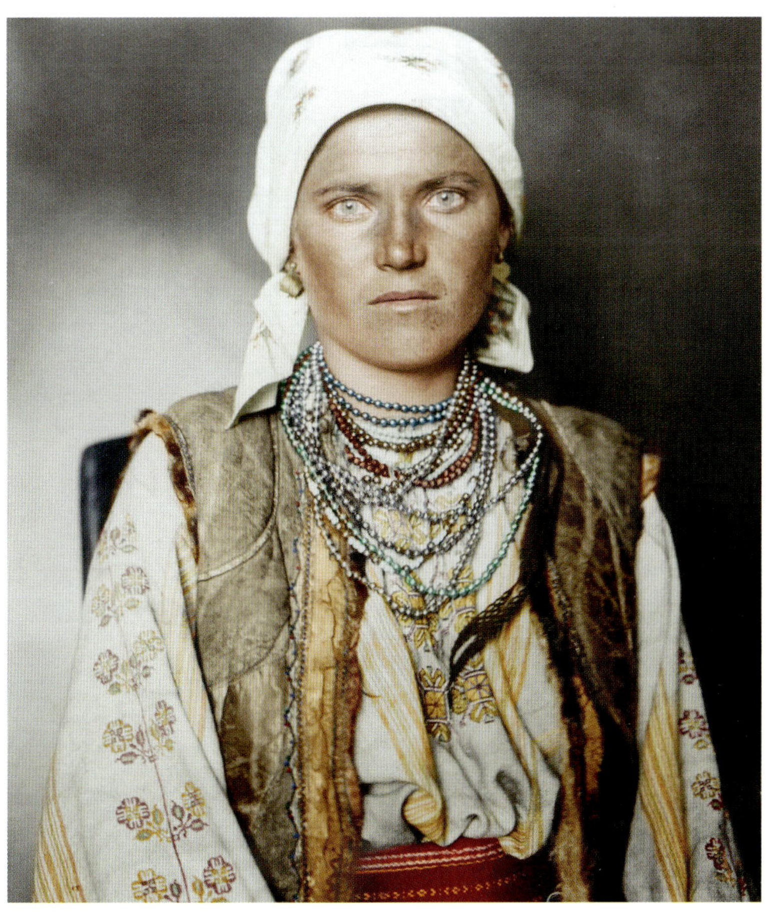
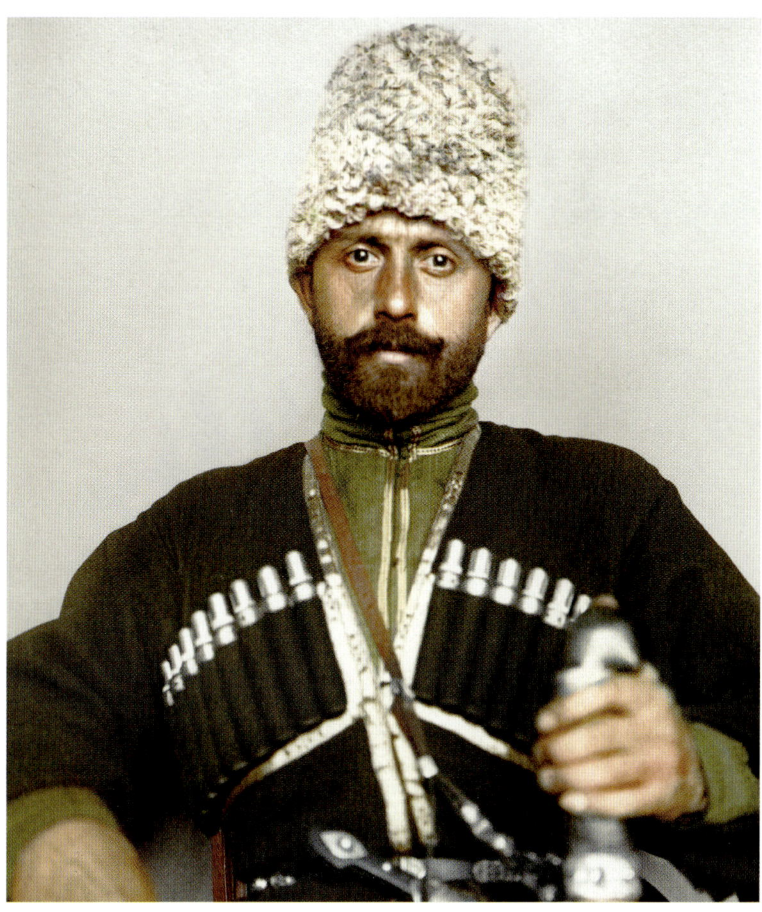

1900s

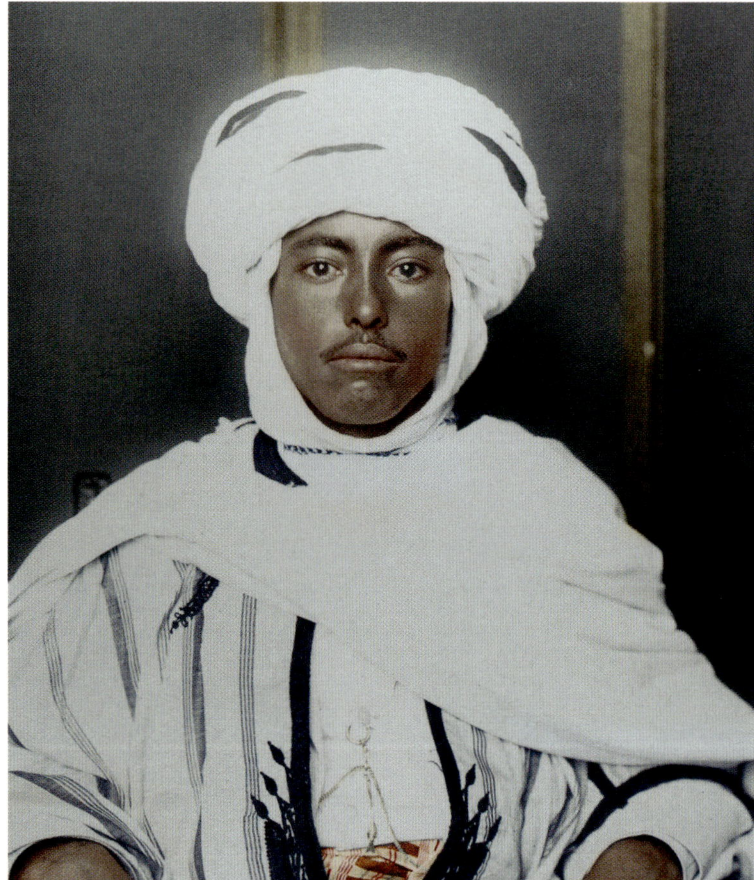

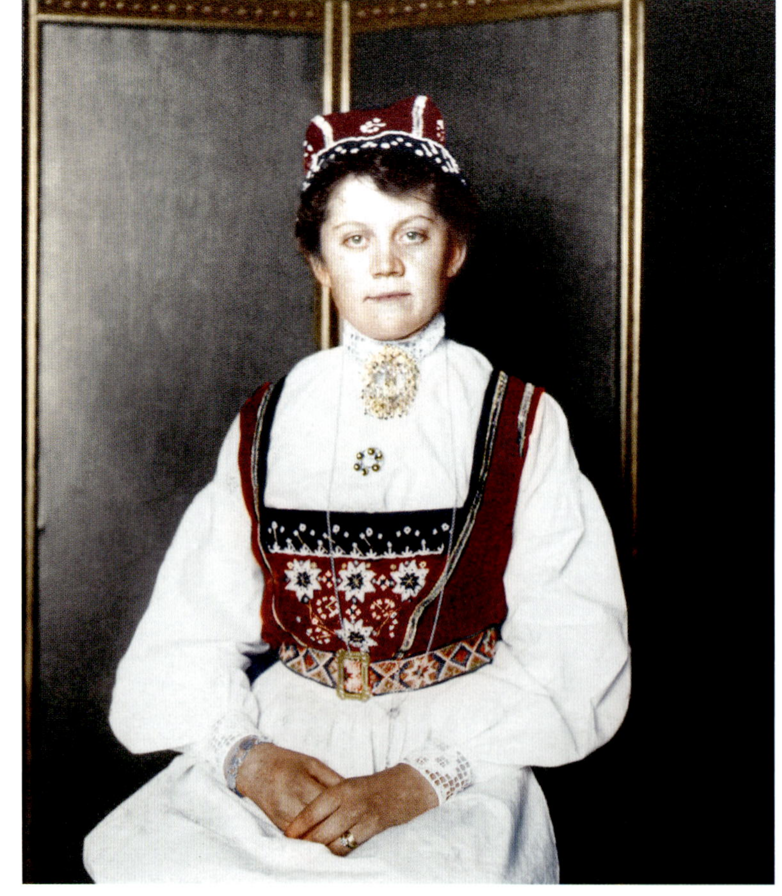

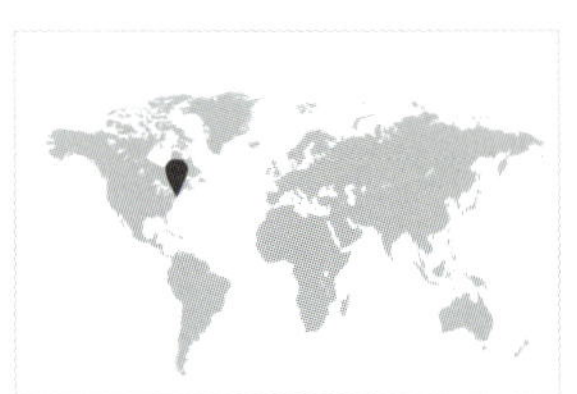

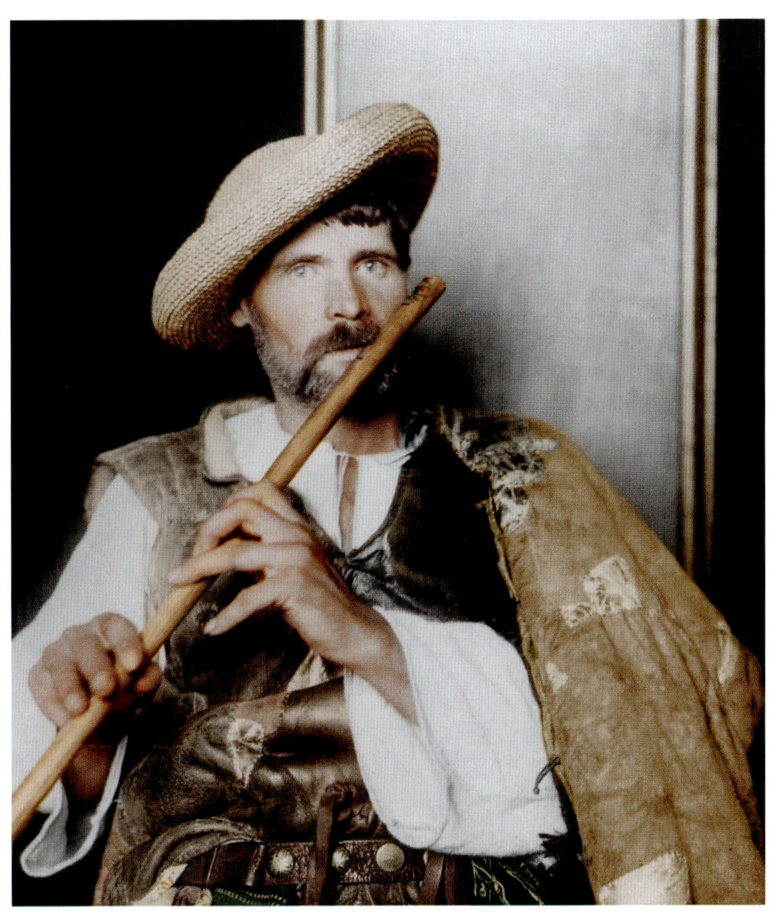
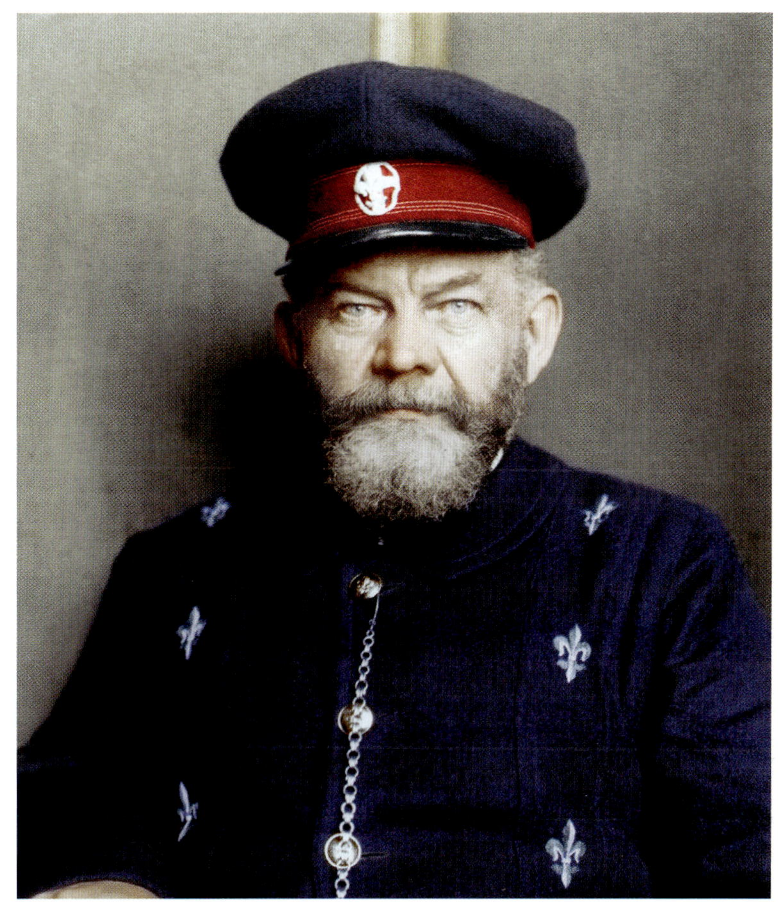
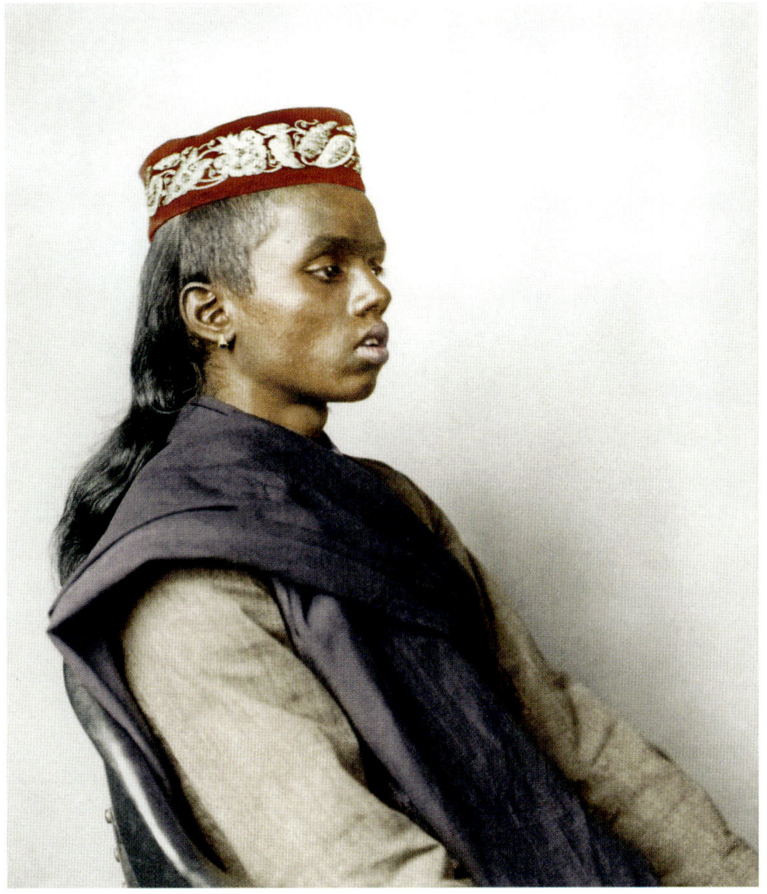
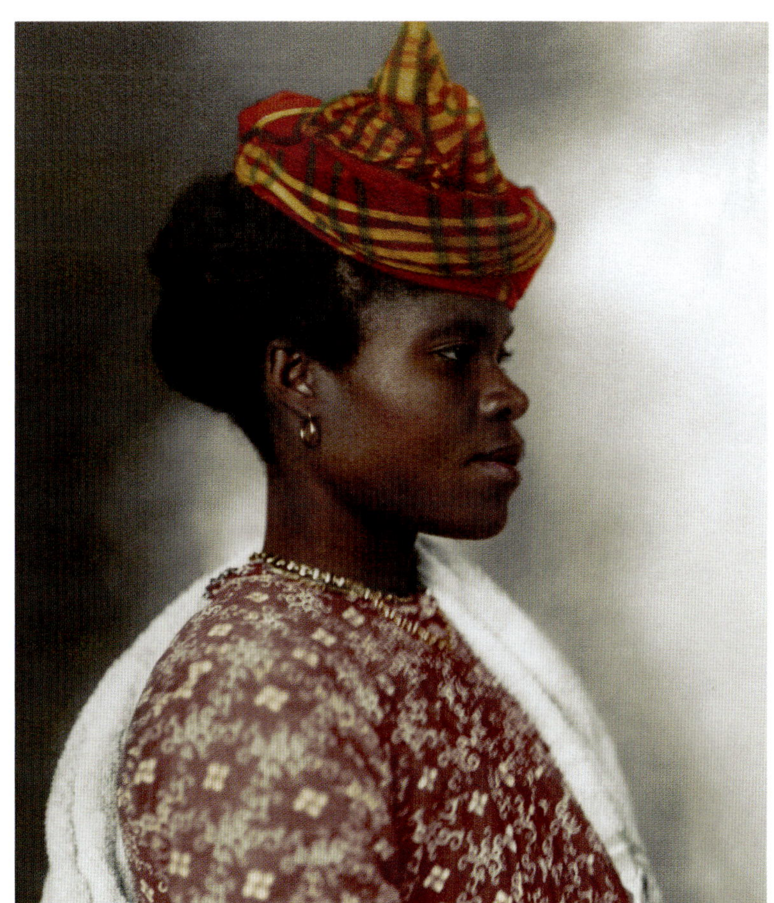

1900s

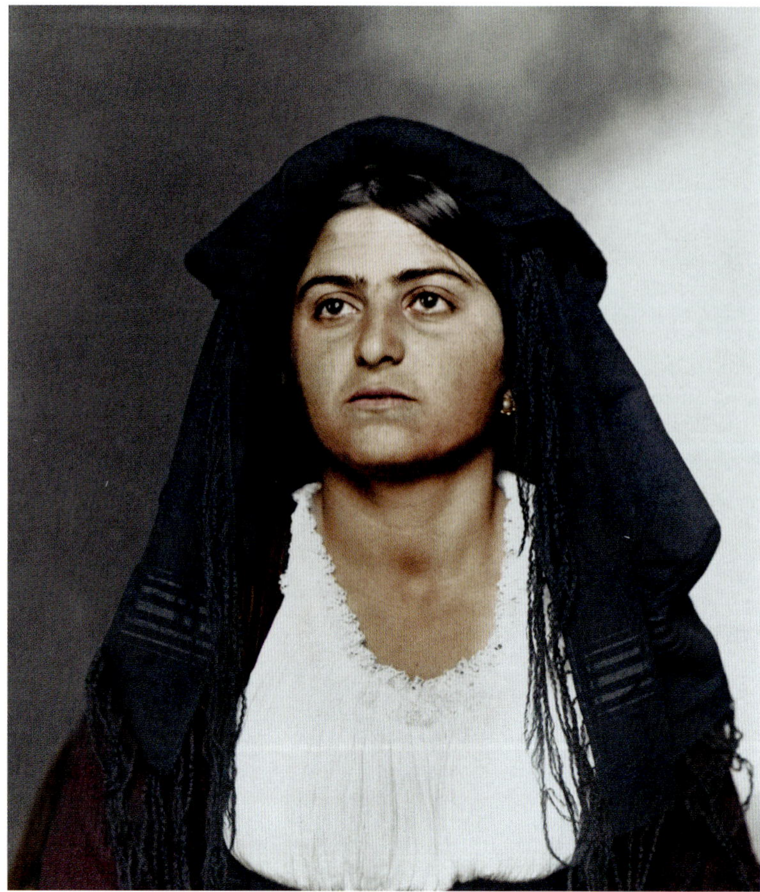

'When I got on the boat, I was only five and this little, this gentleman who had been back and forth several times, and well my mother took a liking to him because he was so knowledgeable about it. He spoke Italian. And he said, "You know what? When you get over to Ellis Island they're going to be examining your eyes with a hook," and he says, "Don't let them do it because you know what? They did it to me one eye fell in my pocket." So we get over there and everybody has to pass and I'm on the floor screaming. I passed without a physical, because the other seven passed.'

Elda Del Bino Willitts, immigrated from Lucca, Italy, in 1916, aged five

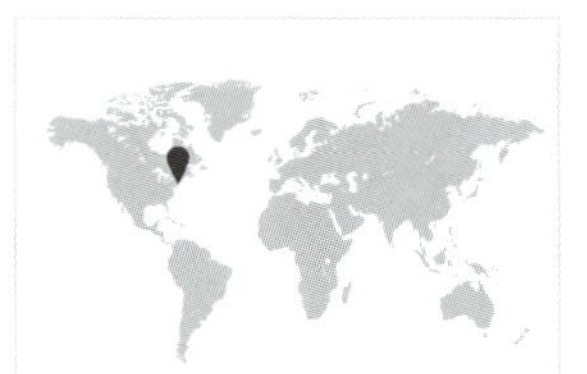

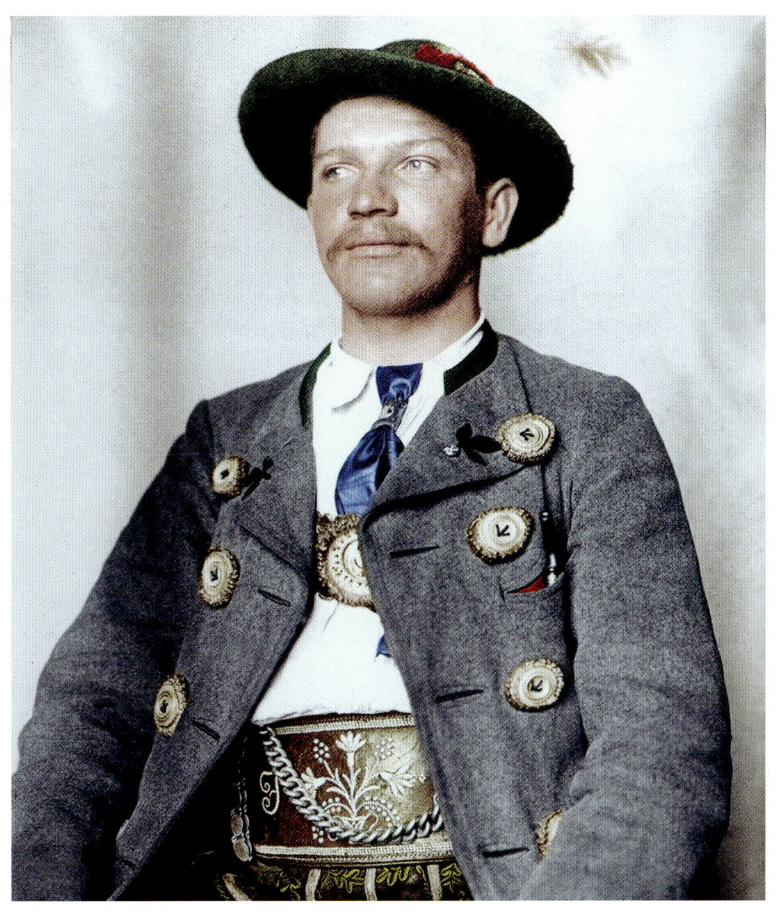

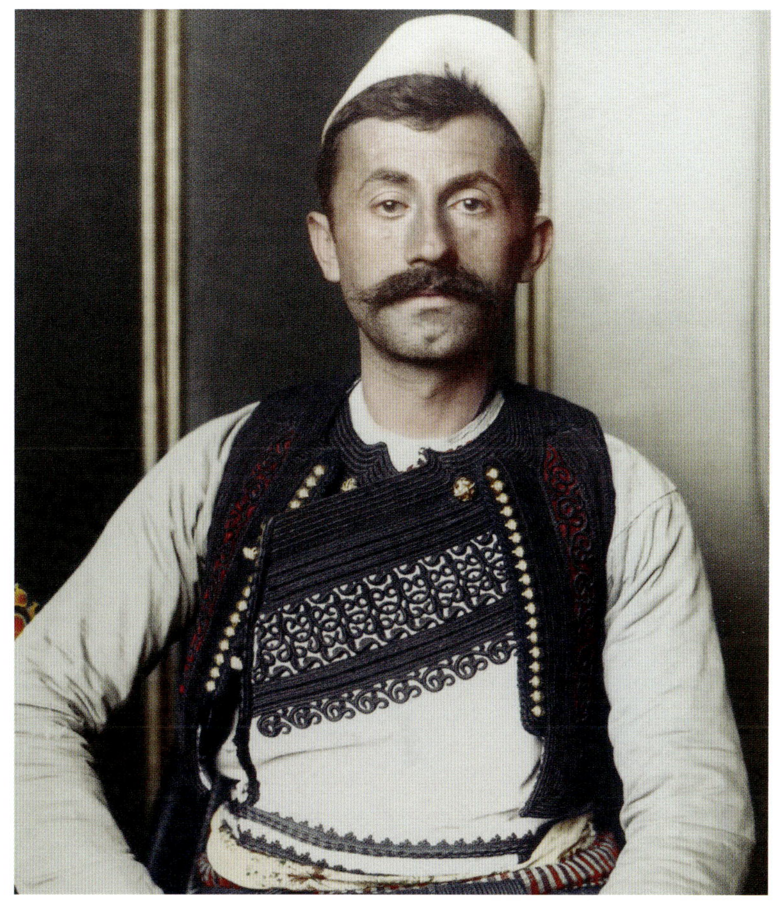

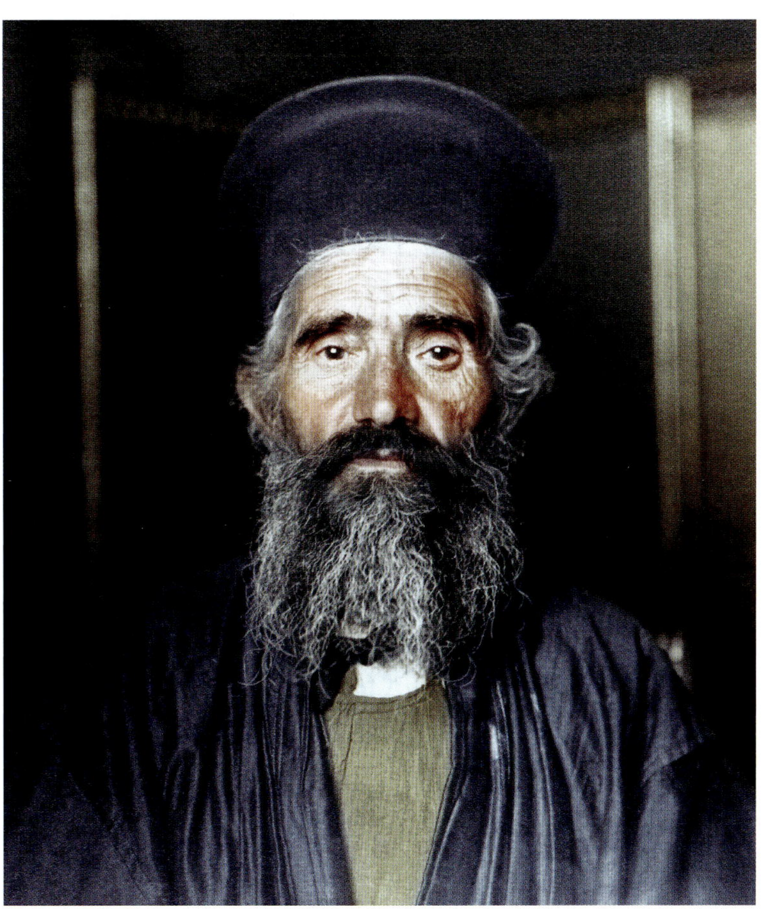

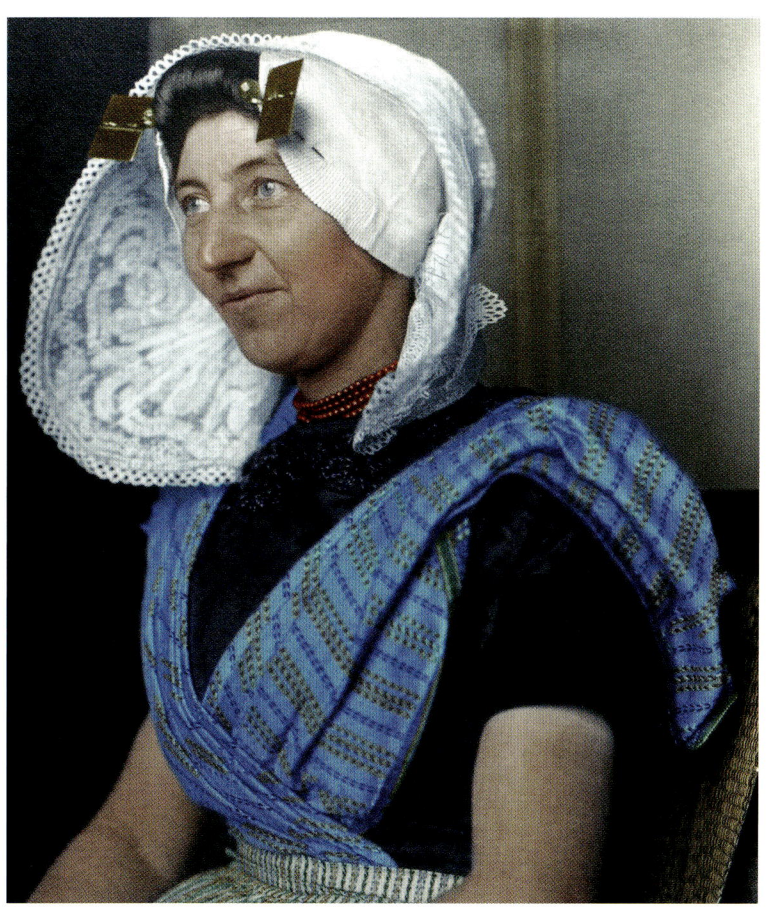

1900: **Patrons enjoying a ballet at the outdoor theatre of the Moulin Rouge, Paris**

Boulevard de Clichy, Paris, France
(Unknown / Hulton Archive / Getty)

Paris's Moulin Rouge nightclub was a new incarnation for the run-down White Queen Dance Hall. Bought in 1889 by businessmen Charles Zidler and Joseph Oller, the dance hall was renovated and relaunched with a red windmill on its roof – and so became the Moulin Rouge.

In 1900, Zidler and Oller installed a giant elephant made of plaster and wood in the garden of the club, taking inspiration from Coney Island's seven-storey Elephantine Colossus. Accessed by a spiral staircase, with an entrance fee of a franc, the interior of the elephant was the scene of intimate dances and 'other entertainments'.

1900s

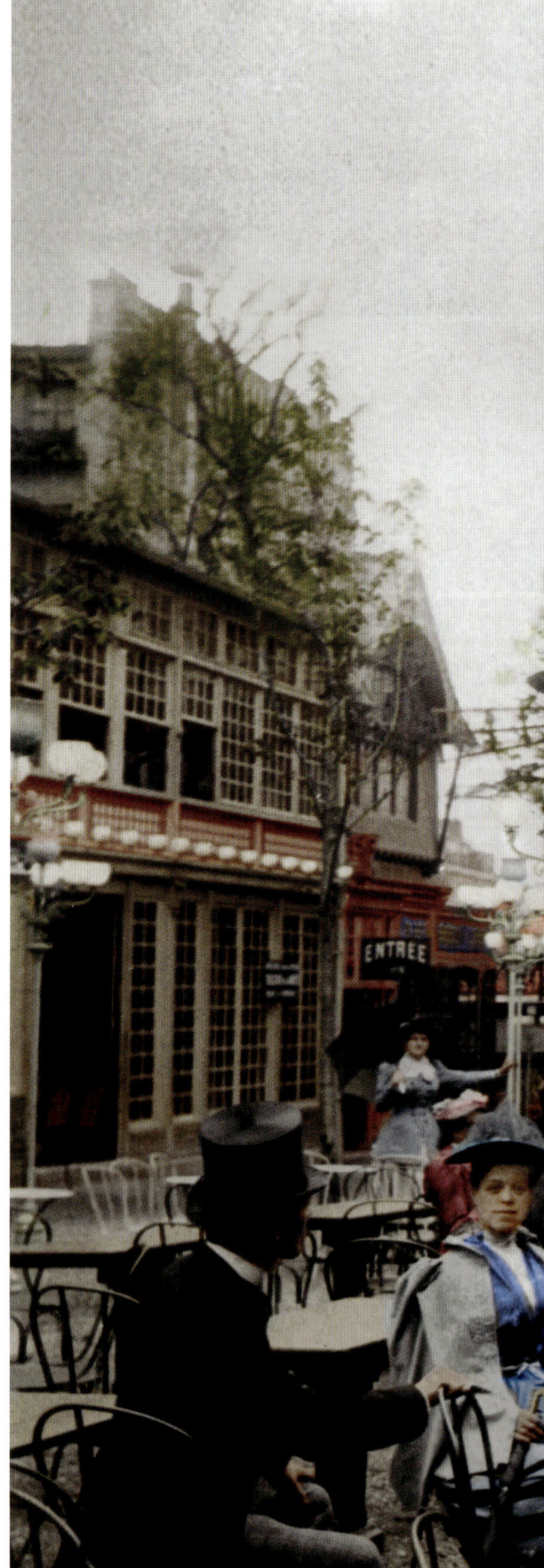

'Balls form one of the striking and popular amusements of Parisians, and curiosity leads a large number of visitors to attend. The Moulin Rouge, situated on the Boulevard Rochechouart, is certainly the most popular. It is essentially coarse and vulgar, and in our opinion this and similar entertainments are utterly unsuited to ladies, though large numbers attend out of curiosity.'

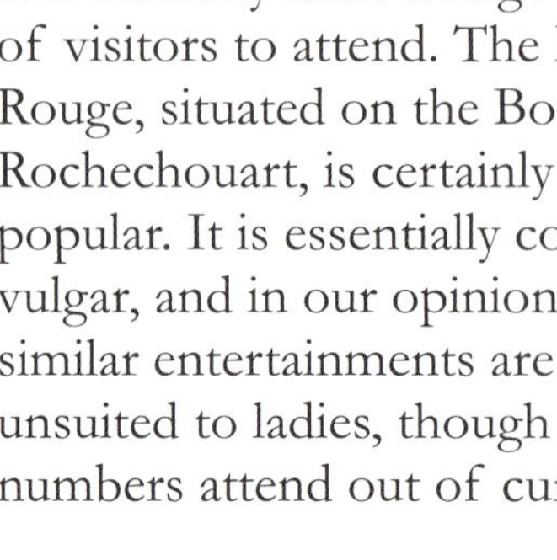

A Pictorial and Descriptive Guide to Paris and the Exhibition (second edition), 1900

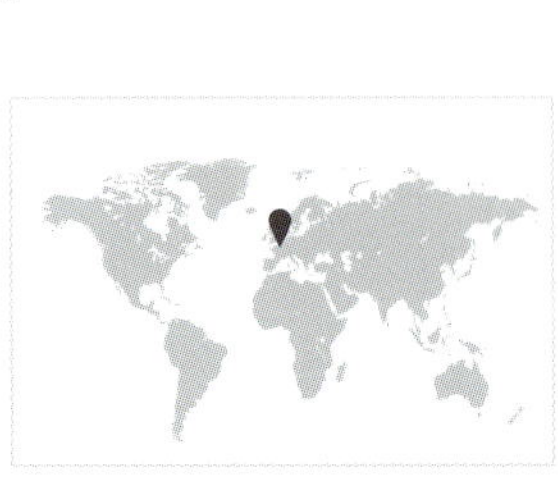

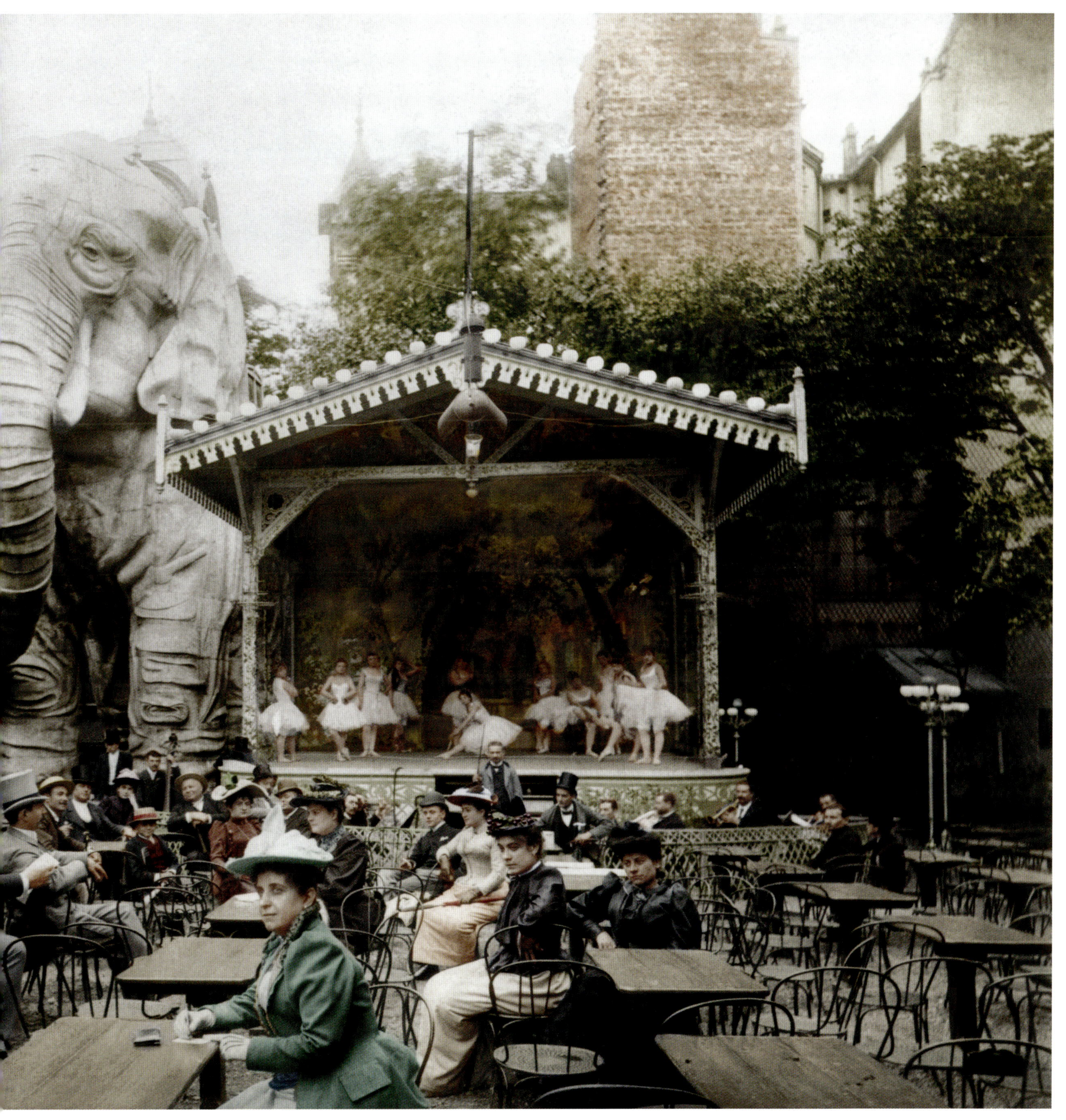

1900s

1900: Mulberry Street, Manhattan

Mulberry Street, New York City, USA
(Detroit Publishing Co. / Library of Congress)

Mulberry Street was at the very centre of Manhattan's Little Italy, an ethnic neighbourhood that followed from the mass immigration of Italians to New York after the 1880s. By the turn of the twentieth century, nine out of ten people in the Fourteenth Ward of Manhattan had an Italian background. Mulberry Street itself took its name from the Mulberry trees that grew around Mulberry Bend, the point in the street where it curved around what was then the Collect Pond.

This scene, shot in 1900, shows something of the breadth of activity of Little Italy: vegetable stalls; barefooted children; shoe, boot and clothing merchants; a wagon of barrels and sacks; furniture removal men and blankets, quilts and rugs left out to air (or to sell).

'Giocomo Santaniello, a butcher, of No. 6 Mulberry Street, was the victim of a vendetta which for weeks has raged through the Mulberry Bend colony of Italians, a colony where in the last year the police have collected a ton of stilettos and revolvers. But the weapon of this latest tragedy was a double-barrelled shotgun and its buckshot not only killed Santaniello, but wounded five others, three of whom were innocent bystanders.'

The World, 10 June 1903

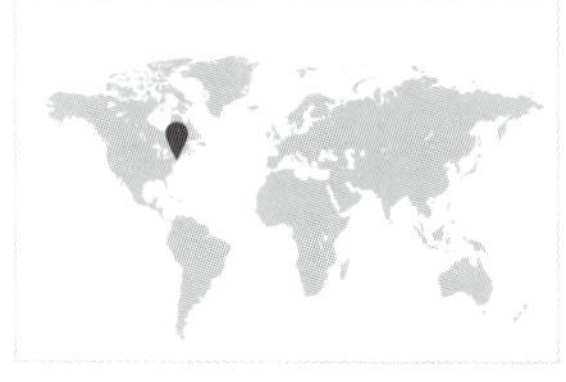

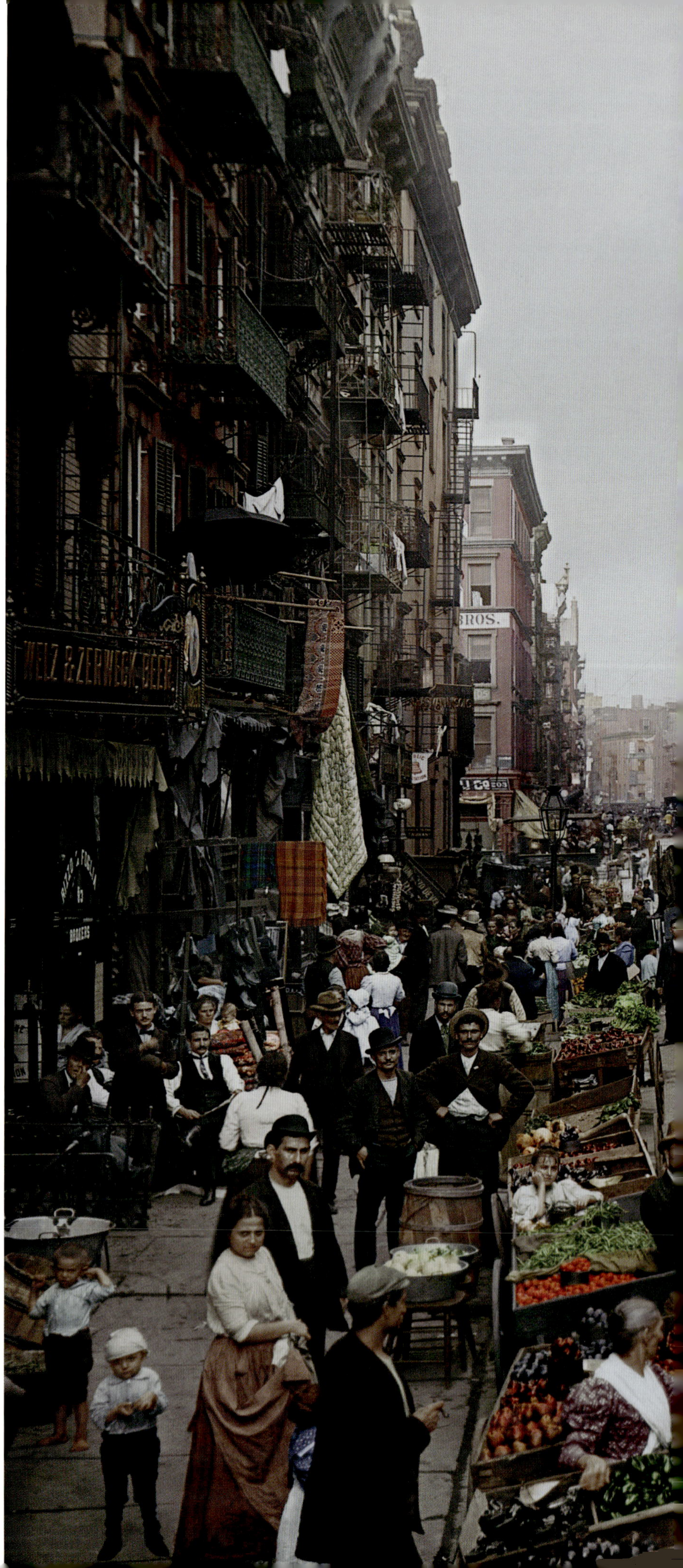

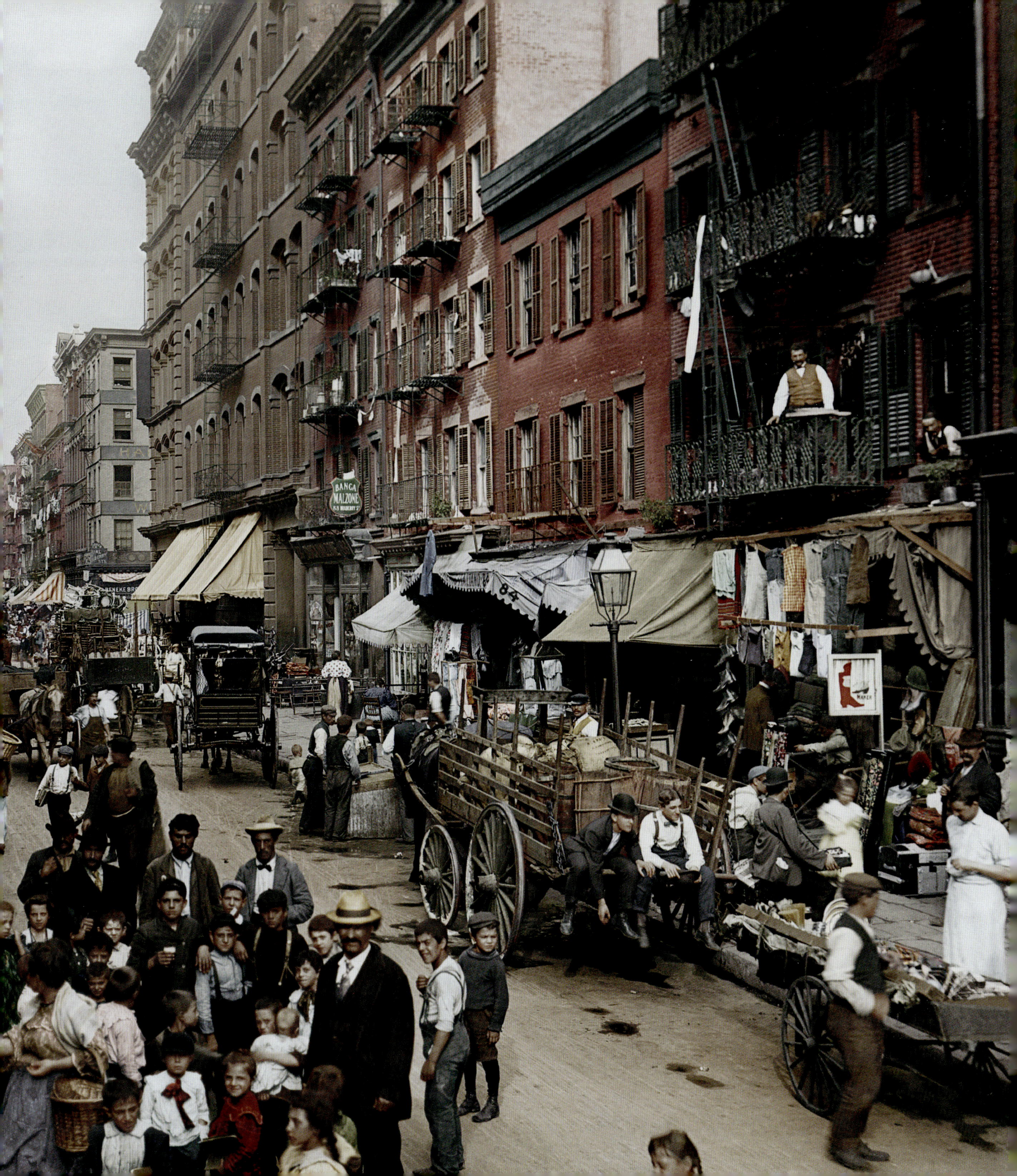
BANCA
MALZONE
84

1890s

c. 1897: Portrait of an unidentified man

USA

(Fred Holland Day / Science & Society Picture Library / Getty)

Fred Holland Day didn't have to work; his father was a wealthy merchant in Boston, USA. Using his financial means, Day co-founded publishing imprint Copeland and Day, releasing almost 100 titles in six years during the 1890s. Included on its list was *Salome* by Oscar Wilde, illustrated by Aubrey Beardsley, to whom Day was a significant patron.

While a large number of Day's photographs were, like this one, of young men, there is no evidence to suggest that he had any form of relationship with his models. Day regarded photography as a fine art and he tended towards images that exhibited strong mythological or allegorical themes. For his most renowned work, 'The Seven Last Words', showing the seven last words of Christ, Day was his own model, growing out his hair and starving his body to achieve the effect he sought.

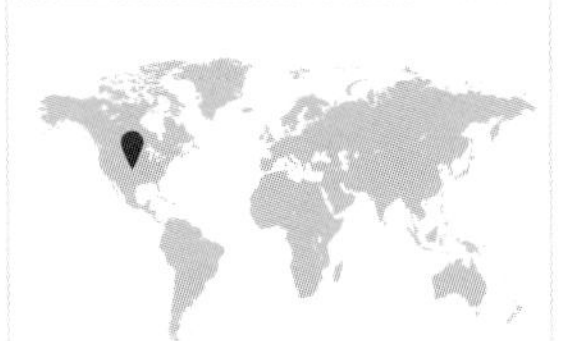

'No, let me repeat, that to produce art with a camera just as much serious thought, just as much hard study, just as much rigorous training, are necessary as to produce the same end, through any other medium, and perhaps a little more.'

F. Holland Day, 'The Virginia enterprise', 2 February 1900

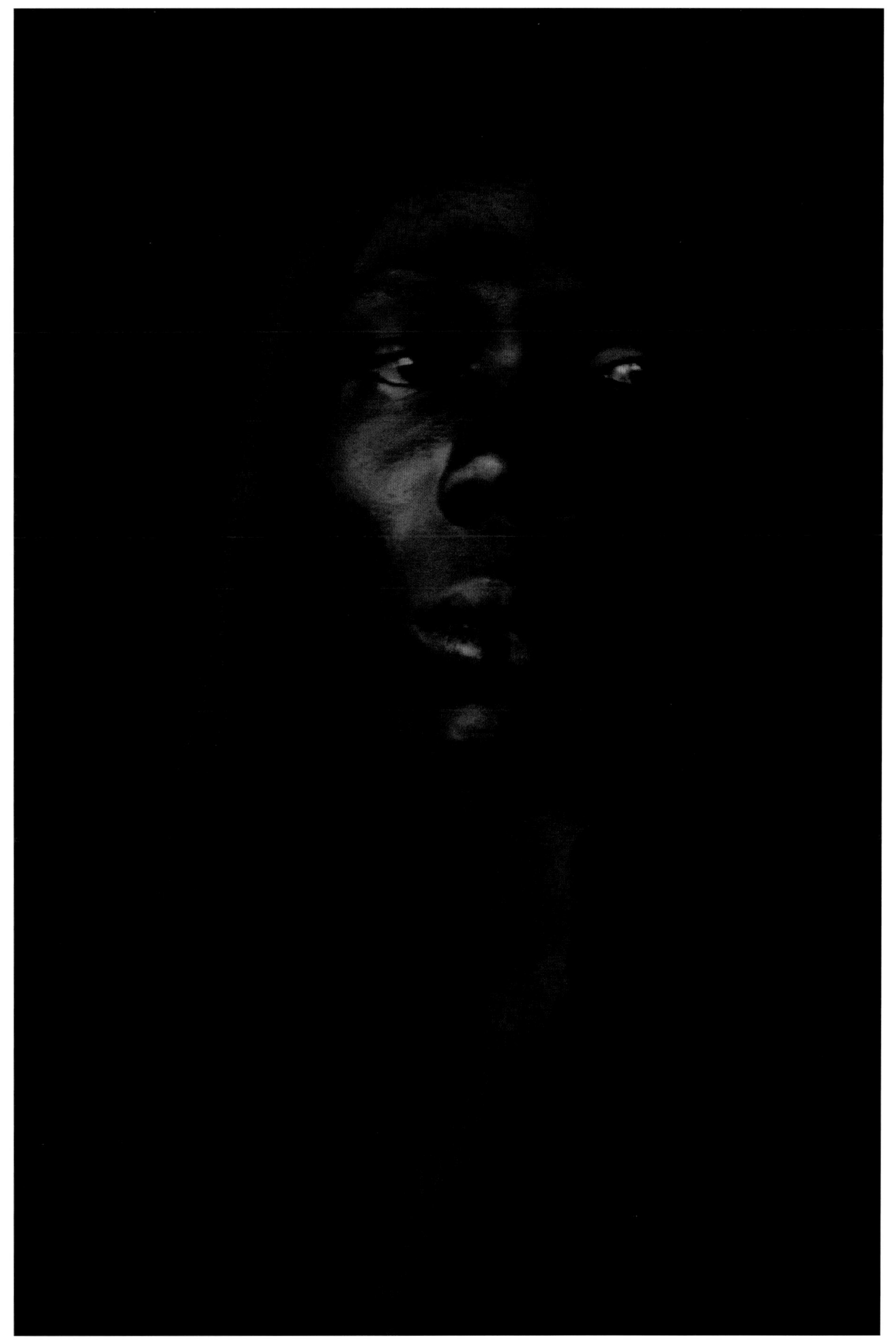

1896: The 'Street of Gamblers', Chinatown, San Francisco

Street of Gamblers, San Francisco, California, USA (Arnold Genthe / Library of Congress)

1890s

Two men and one woman on board the American brig *Eagle* were the very first Chinese immigrants to San Francisco. From 1849, Chinese people were drawn to the city by the labouring opportunities offered by the construction of the Transcontinental Railroad, as well as the California Gold Rush. However, racial discrimination was pronounced and enshrined in law, culminating in the Chinese Exclusion Act of 1892, which outlawed immigration from China for the next decade.

San Franciscan studio photographer Arnold Genthe was drawn to San Francisco's Chinatown, capturing many hundreds of photographs of its people, often without their knowledge. The pictures are true to the culture Genthe saw, although he also cropped out Western elements. Here, Genthe has captured the essence of a Chinese *hutong* market transposed into San Francisco, crowded with men wearing black *changshan* shirts and sporting the Manchu queue hairstyles, mandatory for all Chinese men until the 1910s.

Excepting Genthe's images, very few photographs remain of San Francisco's Chinatown prior to the earthquake and fires of 1906. Most photographic collections were lost, but Genthe's survived, stored in a bank vault.

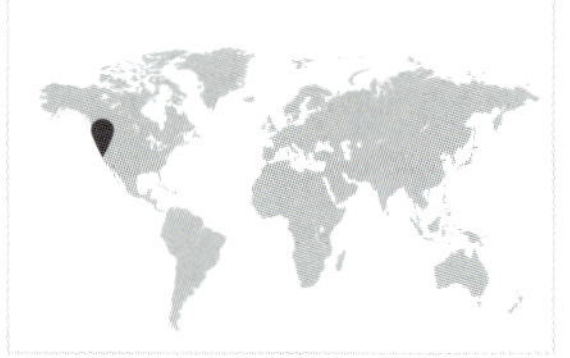

'Again and again I went to Chinatown until I became a familiar figure on its streets. Many days I stood for hours at a corner or sat in some wretched courtyard, immobile and apparently disinterested, as I waited, eager and alert, for the sun to filter through the shadows or for some picturesque group or character to appear.'

Arnold Genthe, *As I Remember*, 1936

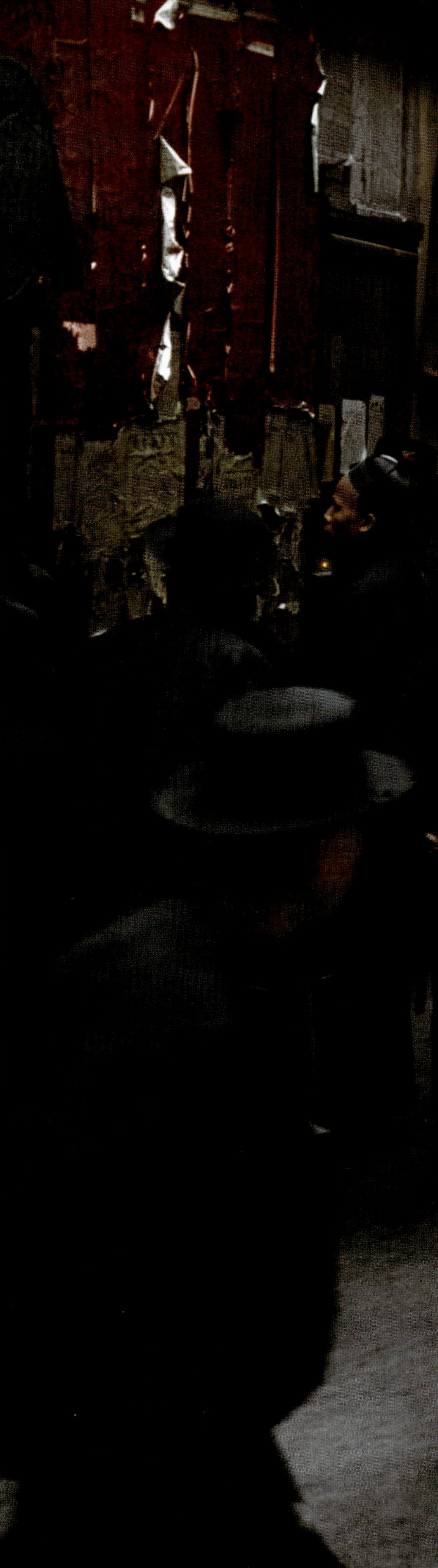

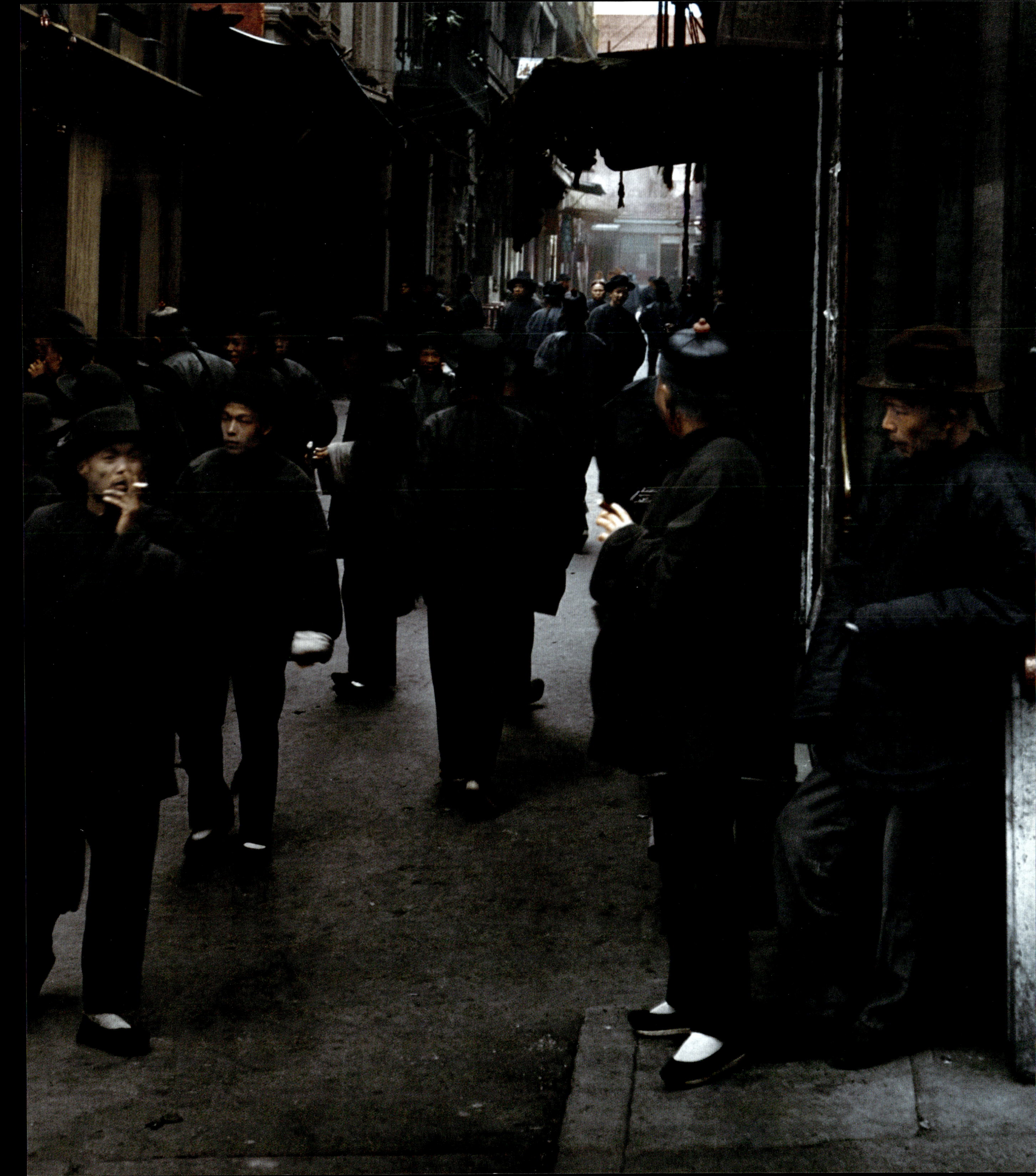

1890s

22 October 1895: Train wreck at Montparnasse, Paris

Montparnasse, Paris, France
(ND / Roger Viollet / Getty)

This extraordinary accident occurred on 22 October 1895 at Montparnasse, then known as Gare de l'Ouest. The driver of the express train from Granville to Paris, hoping to make up time for its 131 passengers, increased the train's speed and the air brake failed. Smashing through the track buffers, the express careered across the station concourse, broke through the station wall and crashed to the street below, where it remained for four days. A woman on the street was killed by falling masonry. Five passengers were injured, and the driver received a fifty franc fine.

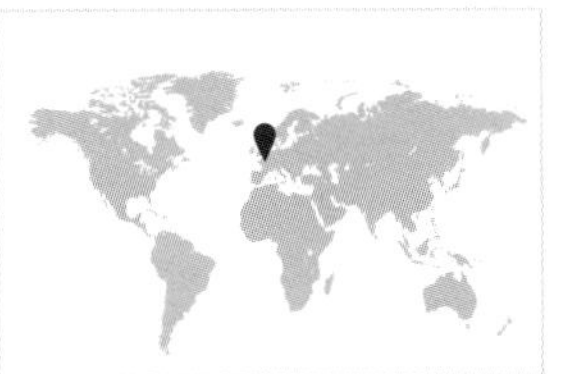

'Our readers will thus be able to readily take into account the results of this curious and singular accident which, by extraordinary chance, has only resulted in one victim, whereas the fall of the locomotive on the site where the tramways are stationed would have had terrible consequences.'

La Nature, Revue des Sciences, 1895

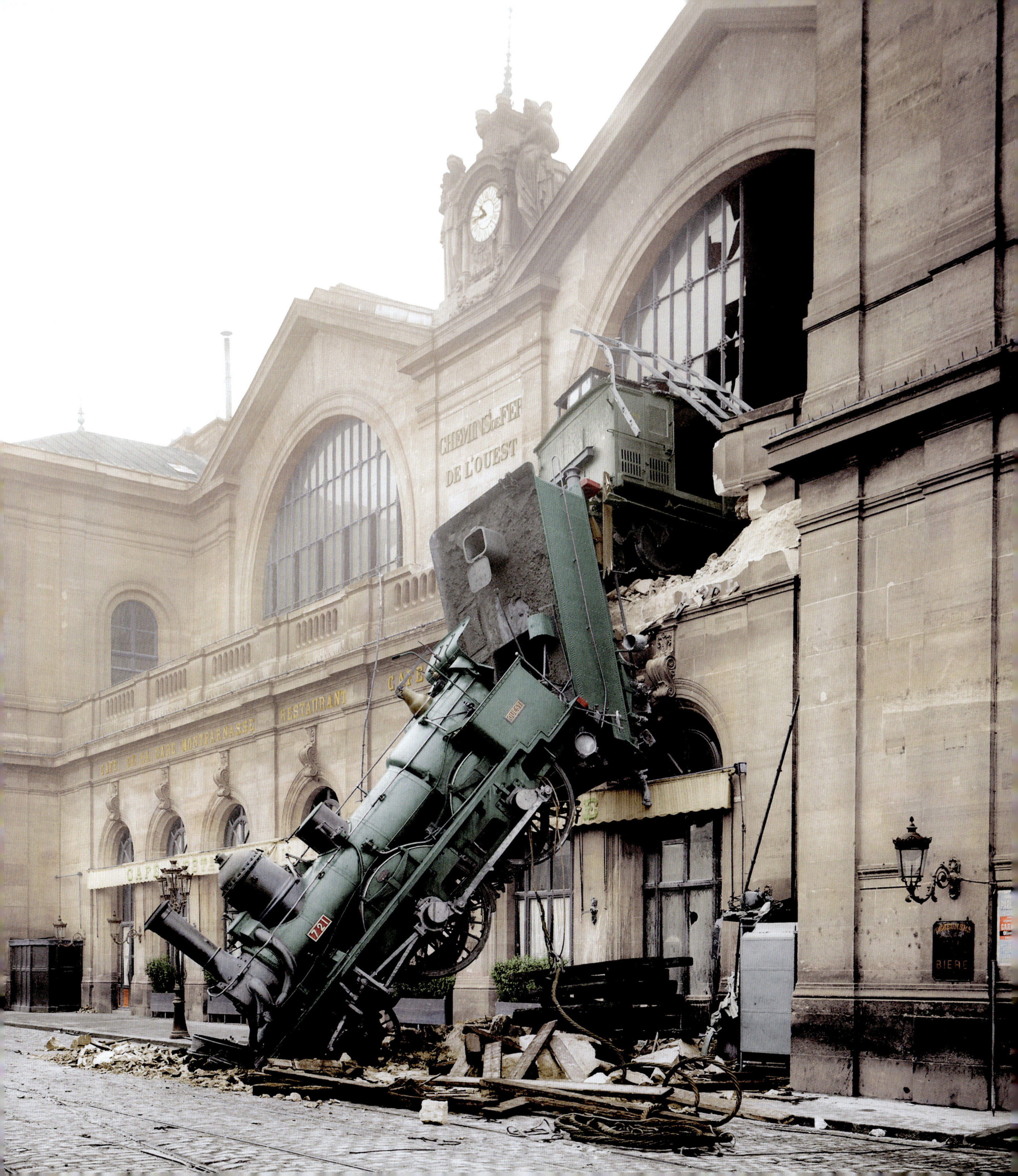
CHEMINS DE FER
DE L'OUEST
CAFE DE LA GARE MONTPARNASSE
RESTAURANT
OUEST
721

c. 1895: Man portraying Santa Claus in snowy scene
USA
(Unknown / Library of Congress)

With a heritage extending to the fourth-century bishop Saint Nicholas, the Dutch *Sinterklaas*, Germany's *Christkind* and even the Norse god *Wodan* – yes, reader, there is a Santa Claus. But Santa's appearance has not remained static. Clement Clarke Moore's hugely influential 1823 poem 'A Visit from St. Nicholas' locked down the jolly, white-bearded man in fur – but not, surprisingly, the colour of that fur. Some Victorian Santas had a red coat, after the cartoons of Thomas Nast; others had coats of green, after Charles Dickens' ghost of Christmas present; some were even blue.

Given the monochrome photography at the time, in this photograph it was of little concern what colour coat Santa wore in the studio. The coat was most likely tan, based on the black-and-white information but also the fact that it was much easier to find tan coats than red or green ones. The studio backdrop is grey because camera photography of the time could not render colour. However, it would have been hand-tinted for postcards with a red or a green coat, to taste.

1890s

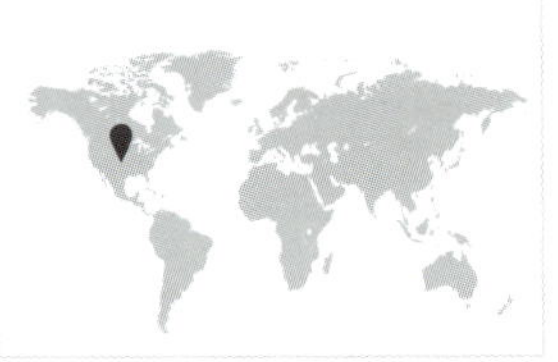

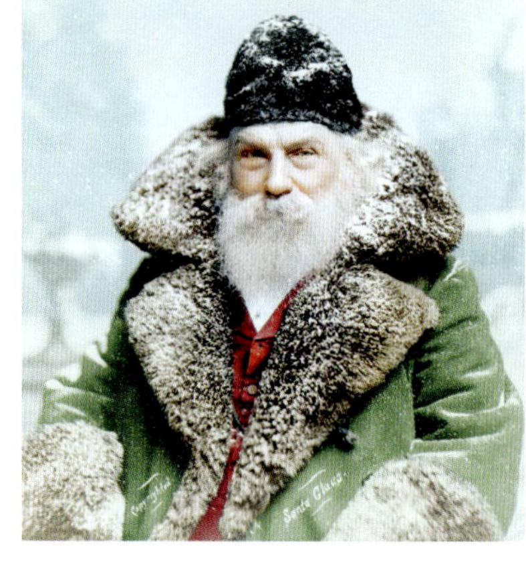

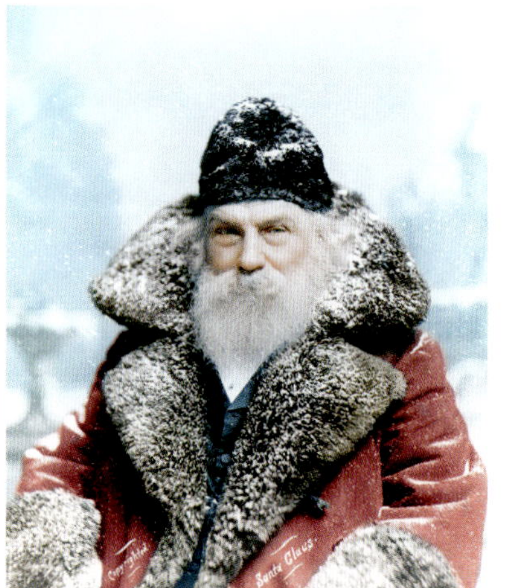

'DEAR EDITOR: I am 8 years old.
Papa says, "If you see it in THE SUN it's so."
Please tell me the truth; is there a Santa Claus?

VIRGINIA O'HANLON
115 WEST NINETY-FIFTH STREET'

'Yes, VIRGINIA, there is a Santa Claus. You might get your papa to hire men to watch in all the chimneys on Christmas Eve to catch Santa Claus, but even if they did not see Santa Claus coming down, what would that prove?

You may tear apart the baby's rattle and see what makes the noise inside, but there is a veil covering the unseen world which not the strongest man, nor even the united strength of all the strongest men that ever lived, could tear apart. Is it all real? Ah, VIRGINIA, in all this world there is nothing else real and abiding.'

The Sun (New York), 21 September 1897

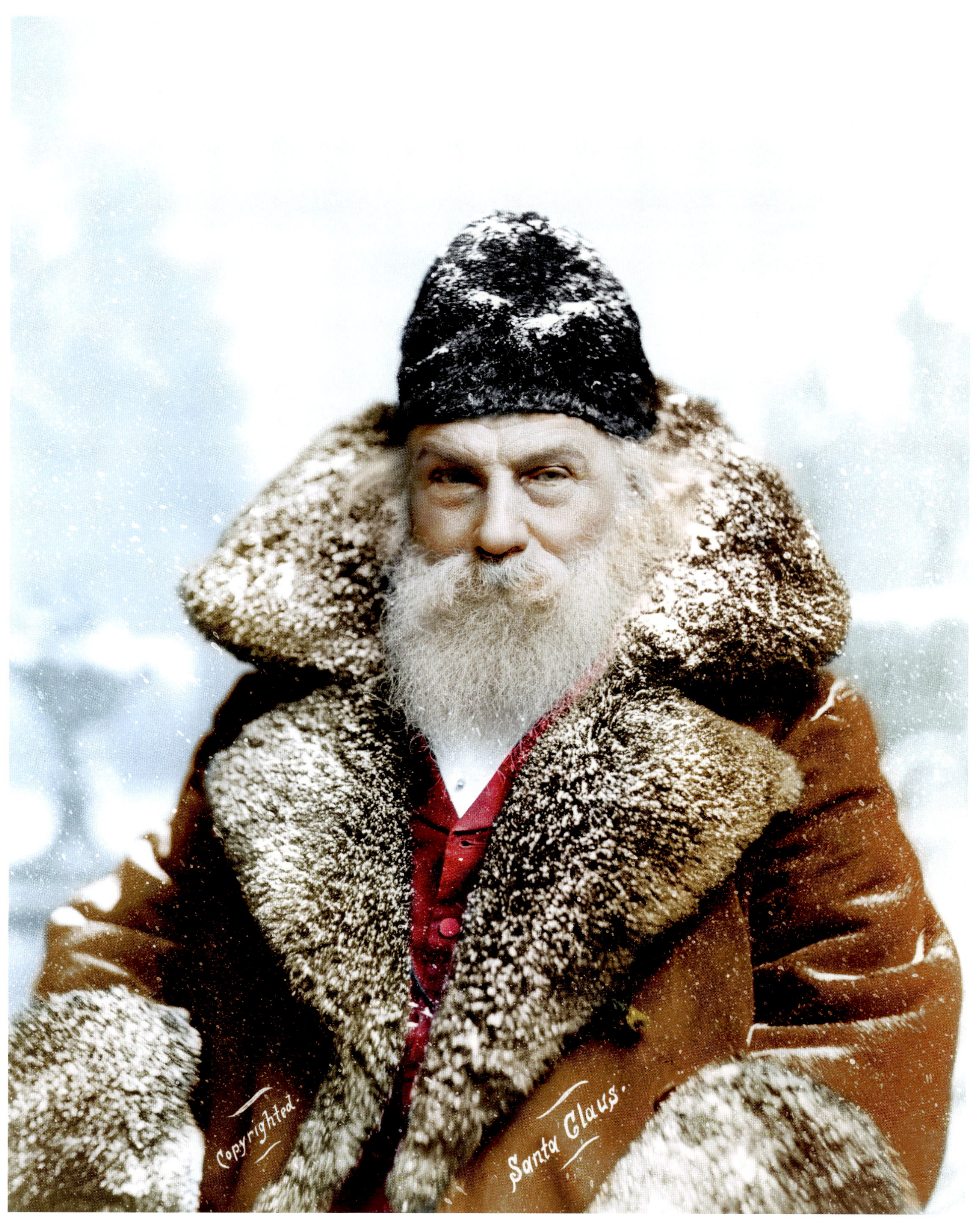
Copyrighted
Santa Claus.

1890s: A group of Victorian tourists visit the Temple of Olympian Zeus, Athens

Athens, Greece

(Unknown / School of Archaeology, University of Oxford)

Originally conceived by the sons of the tyrant Peisistratus to be the greatest temple in the known world, construction of the Temple of Olympian Zeus, at the centre of Athens, began in the sixth century BC. However, it was not completed until six centuries had elapsed. Just 100 years later, ransacked by barbarian hordes, it fell into disrepair, and began its path to ruin.

Aristotle, in his *Politics*, had used the temple as an example of the way tyrannical governments prevent rebellion by generating vast civic projects to engage – and exhaust – the people's time, energy and efforts.

On completion, the temple had 104 pillars. In this photograph, fifteen remain. One pillar was brought to the ground by gales in 1852. During the 1890s, when this picture was taken, the temple had been excavated by British archaeologist Francis Penrose, then in his late seventies.

1890s

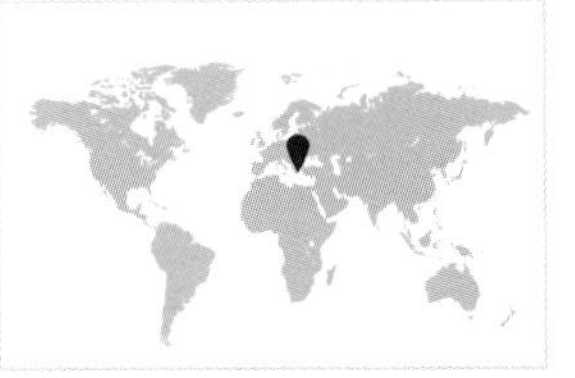

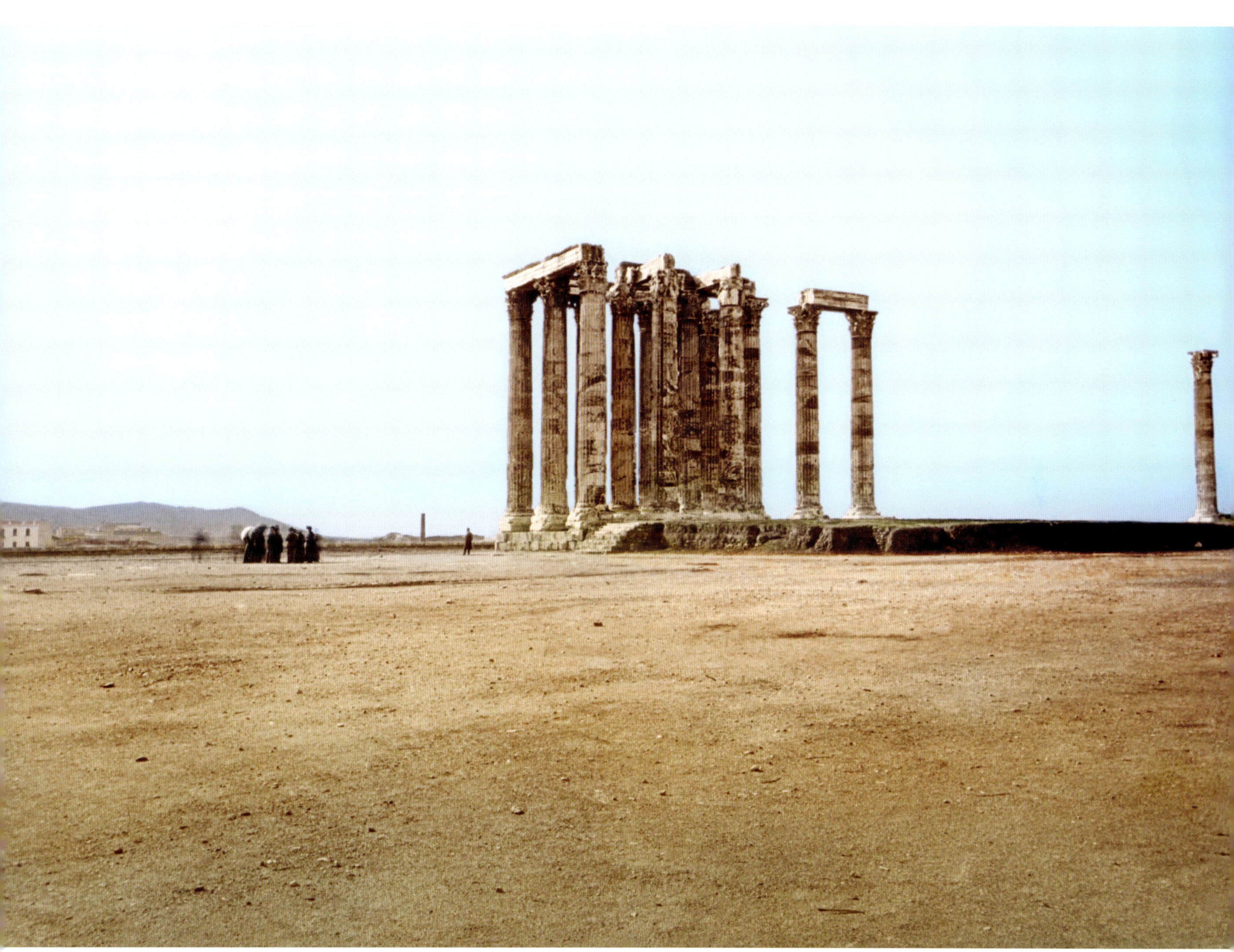

'There is perhaps nevertheless among all the remains of antiquity no ruin more impressive than that composed by the gigantic columns of the temple of Jupiter Olympius at Athens. The ruins stand quite alone.'

An Investigation of the Principles of Athenian Architecture, Francis Penrose, 1888

1880s

1889: Construction of Tower Bridge, London

Southwark, London, UK

(Unknown / English Heritage / Getty)

Construction of London's Tower Bridge began in 1881 to designs by Sir Horace Jones. Jones was the City Architect and also judge of the committee that selected the design. Officially opened for use in 1894, the Bridge incorporated a central twin 'bascule' bridge, which could be raised by steam-powered hydraulics to allow the passage of ships to and from the busy wharves of London. The 11,000 tonnes of steelwork would be eventually clad in Portland stone and Cheesewring granite from Cornwall, which can be seen at the base of the bridge.

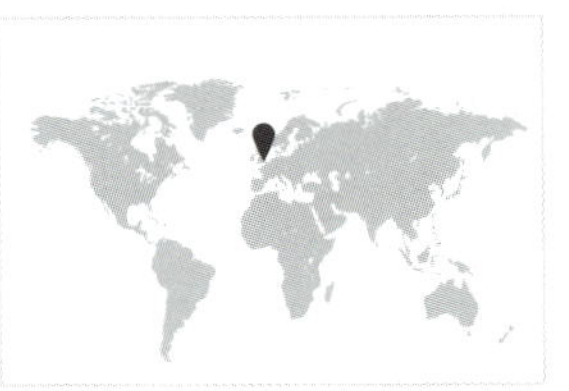

'A "bascule" or lifting bridge would perhaps save some small amount of time in the passage of vessels; it would render the alteration of the level of Tooley Street unnecessary, and would admit of a footway served by hydraulic lifts being practicable from shore to shore. I may perhaps be permitted to say that any of the three designs shown in the sketches would in my judgement be an ornament to the Port of London. My dear sir, yours very faithfully, J. Wolfe Barry, 17 October 1884.'

Letter to Mr Horace Jones, the City Architect, from engineer J. Wolfe Barry

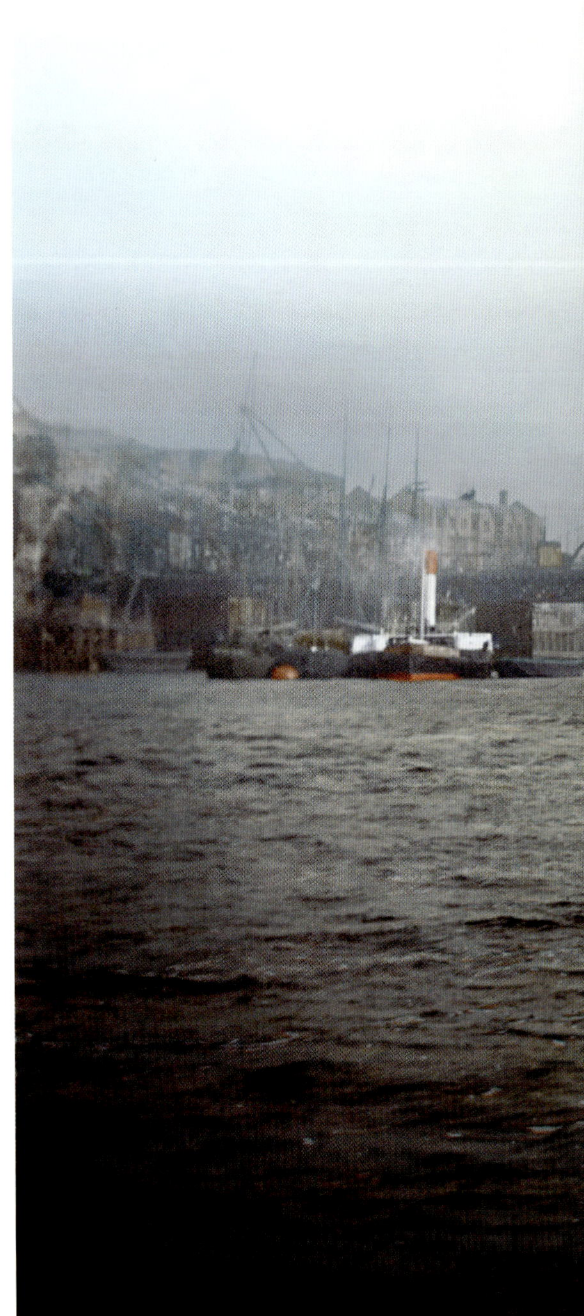

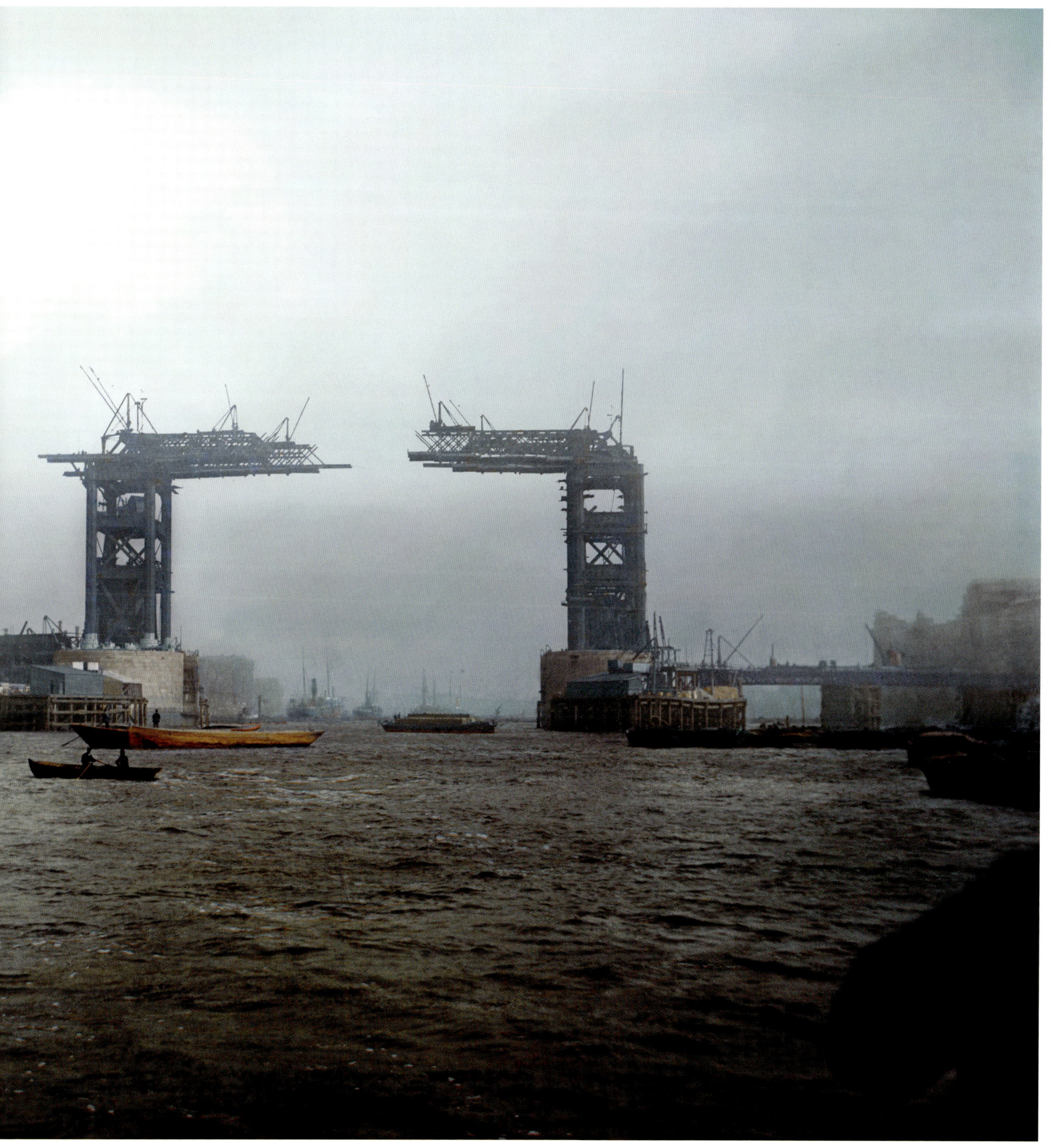

1880s

June 1889: A tree pierces a house in the Johnstown flood calamity, Pennsylvania

Johnstown, Pennsylvania, USA

(George Barker / Library of Congress)

The Johnstown calamity of 31 May 1889 annihilated the Pennsylvanian city of Johnstown. The city, located at the intersection of three rivers, was protected by the South Fork Dam, fourteen miles upstream. But, when six to ten inches of rain fell in twenty-four hours, the dam broke, releasing 20 million tons of water. A vast wave of water swept over the city. More than 2,200 people lost their lives – at the time, the single biggest loss of civilian life in the US.

This picture shows the impact of the flood on John Schultz's house. The entire building was swept to the end of Main Street from Union Street. Schultz and five other people were in the house and all survived.

'Of the dead, nearly sixty have been identified, among whom were James Macmillan, superintendent of Cambarian Iron company's store, wife and four children, and daughter-in-law; John P. Linton, leading lawyer, wife and five children; Mrs Thomas Kerlen and two children; John Nolan and seven of the family; Dr George Wagoner, wife and three children; Frank P. Bowman, wife and two children; Mrs Richard Worthington and seven children; Person Fisher, wife and six children.'

Butte Semi-Weekly Miner,
10:40 p.m., 1 June 1889

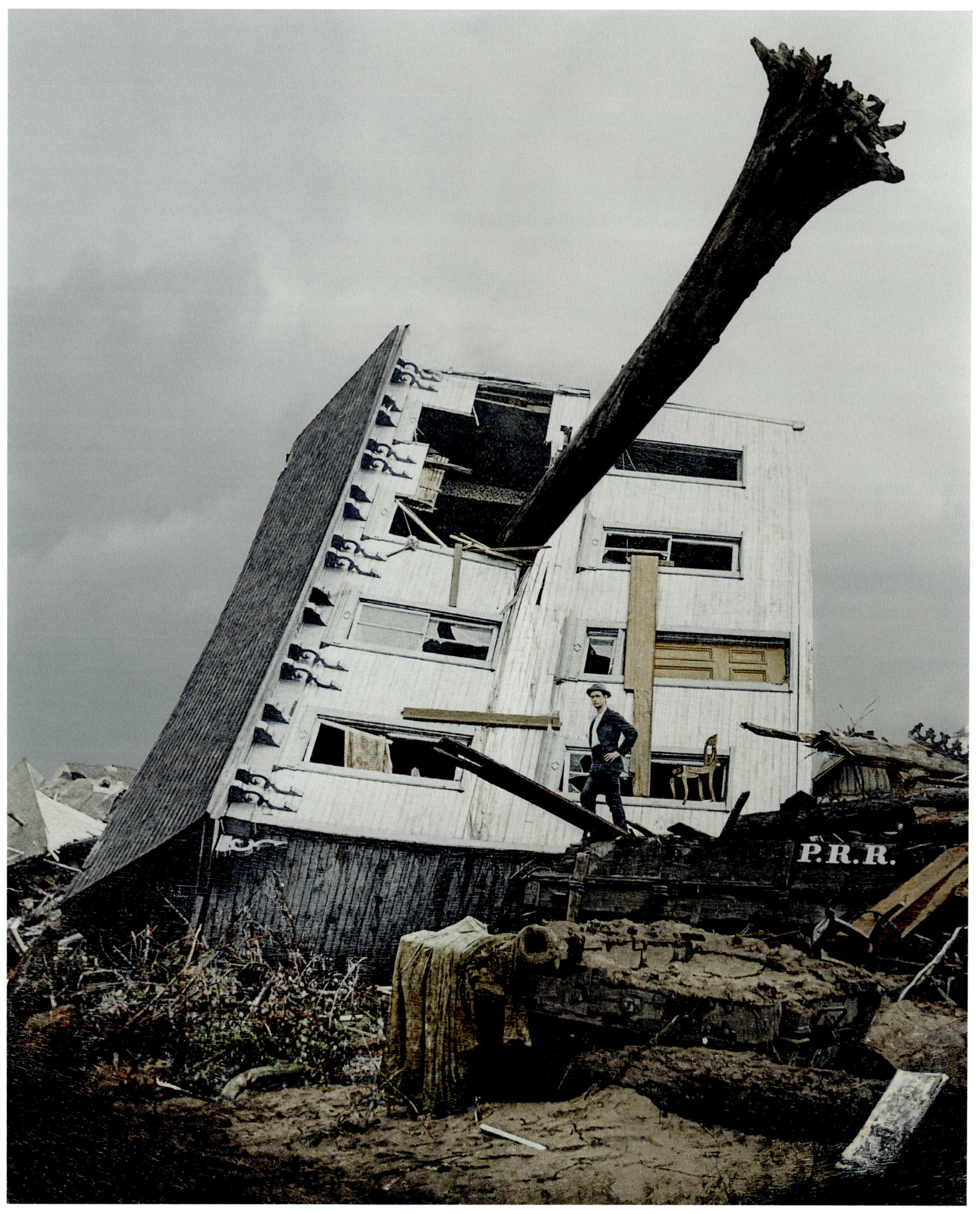
P.R.R.

1880s

July 1888: The Eiffel Tower under construction, Paris
Champs de Mars, Paris, France
(Roger Viollet / Getty)

The result of a competition to create a landmark building for the 1889 World's Fair, at nearly 1,000 feet the Eiffel Tower immediately became the world's tallest building. The structure was put together from more than 18,000 metal components, brought to the site in horse-drawn wagons and hoisted into place by cranes – both of which can be seen in this picture.

'Venetian Red' was the name of the original colour of the tower, applied to the metalwork in the workshop before being assembled on-site. The tower has since been repainted over a dozen times in shades ranging from a reddish-brown to bronze.

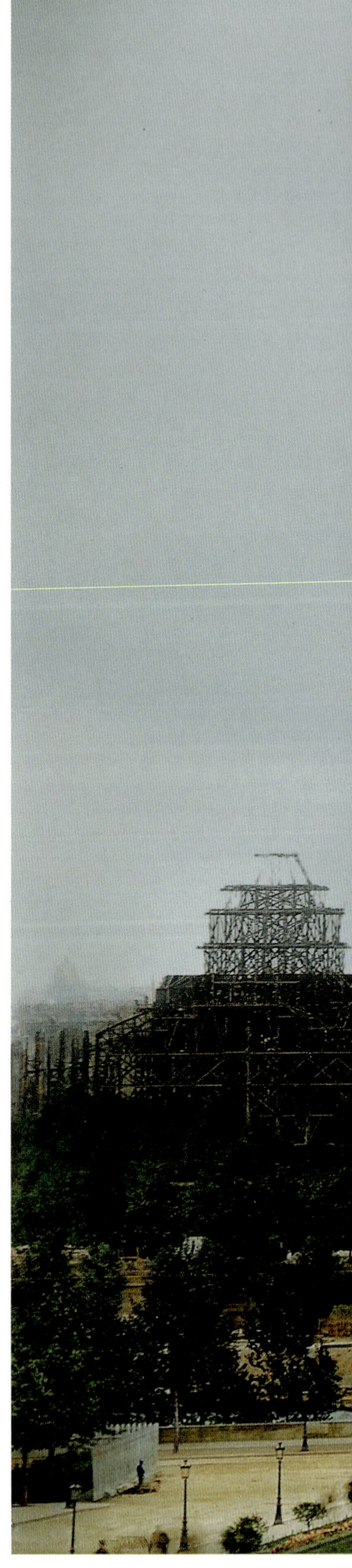

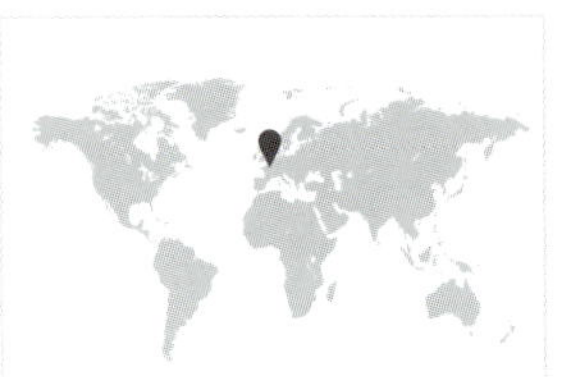

'It will be an observatory and a laboratory such as was never until now at the disposal of science; and from the first all our scientific men have encouraged me with their warmest sympathy.'

M. Eiffel, 1889

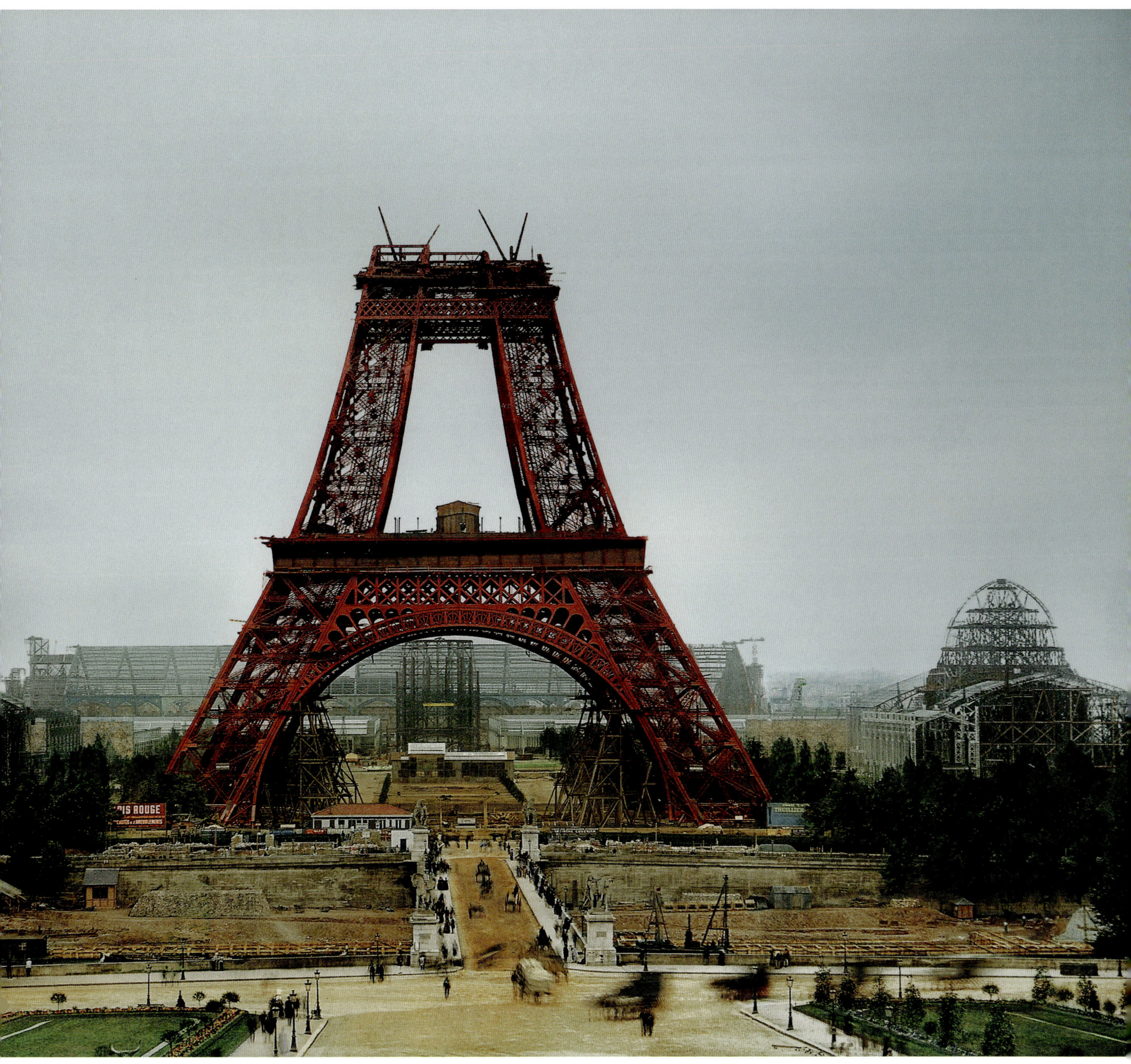
IS ROUGE

1880s

1887: A study in human locomotion

University of Pennsylvania, Pennsylvania, USA
(Eadweard Muybridge / Library of Congress)

When this sequence of photographs was taken, Eadweard Muybridge was already well known – a result of the large-scale images he took of California's Yosemite in 1868. Today, though, it is his studies in locomotion for which he is most widely famed. In total, he generated more than 100,000 stills of people and animals in motion.

The original trigger for this body of work was the idle question of race-horse owner Leland Stanford: did a horse raise all four hooves from the ground at once while trotting? Stanford hired Muybridge to answer the question, and in the process, Muybridge pioneered the photography of locomotion.

Muybridge was born with the slightly less enigmatic name of Edward Muggeridge – 'Eadweard Muybridge' was, he believed, its true Anglo-Saxon spelling. In 1874 he killed his wife Flora's lover with a gun at point-blank range, but the jury in his trial regarded the death as justifiable homicide, and Muybridge was acquitted.

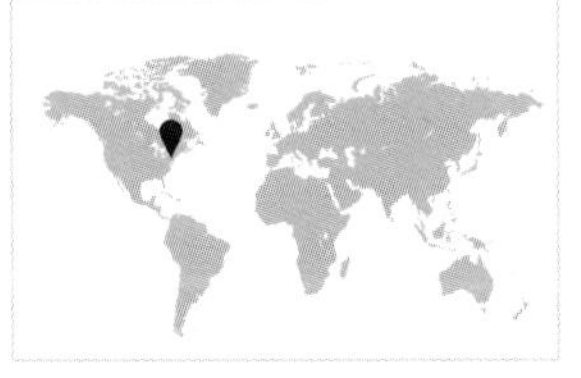

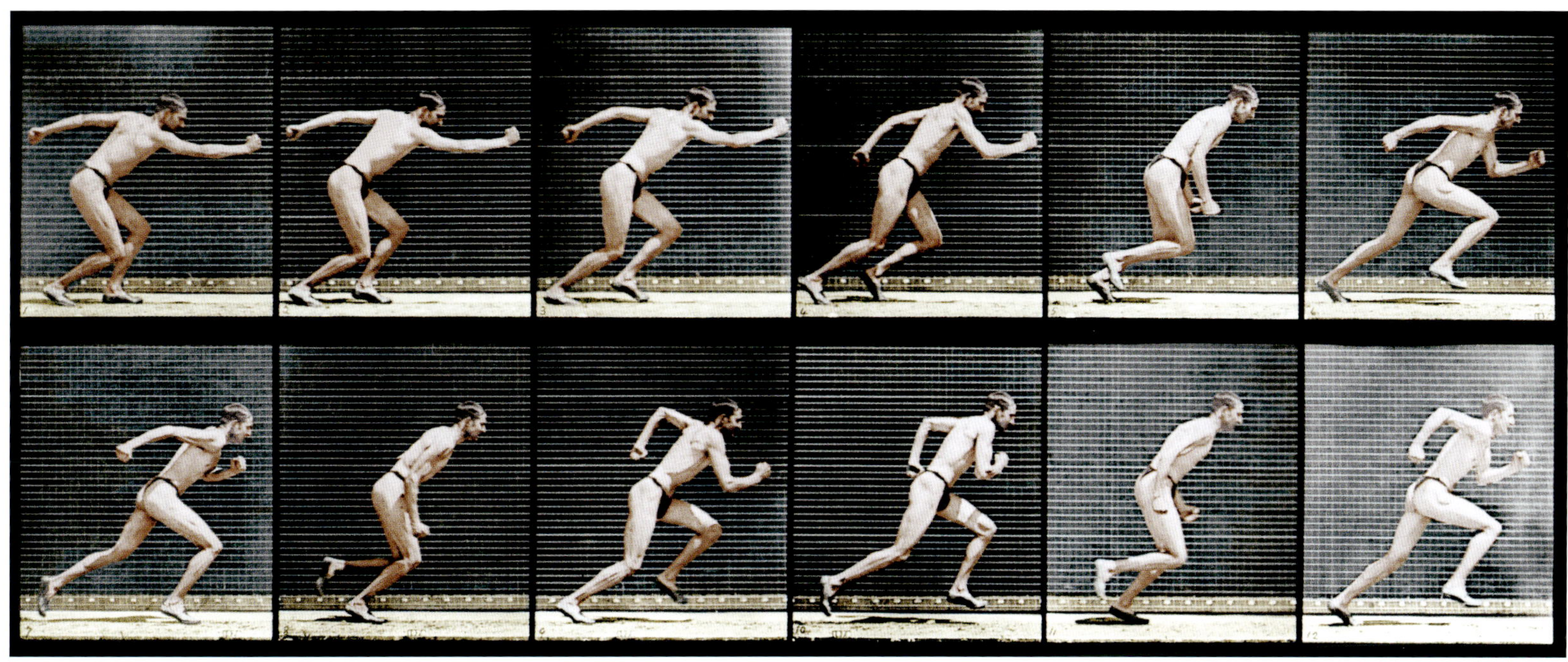

'Should certain phases of the movements be of sufficient naturally artistic value to permit their being copied without derogation to artistic effect, it is unnecessary to say it is not for that purpose they are published; their mission is simply to furnish a guide to the laws which control animal movements.'

Preface to *Animals in Motion: an electro-photographic investigation of consecutive phases of animal progressive movements*, Eadweard Muybridge, 1887

1887: A fisherman at home, Norfolk

Norfolk, UK
(Peter Henry Emerson / Royal Photographic Society / SSPL / Getty)

The Norfolk Broads are an area of interconnected rivers and lakes – 'broads' – in the east of England. Long thought to be natural features of the East Anglian landscape, the broads are now known to be the result of flooded medieval peat cutting.

This photograph of a Norfolk fisherman is taken from Peter Henry Emerson's limited edition book *Pictures From Life in Field and Fen*. The fisherman is chewing on the stem of a clay pipe while cleaning a telescope.

1880s

A very successful surgeon, Emerson bought his first camera in his late twenties to use on ornithological trips, though ultimately it would prove to be the key to his new profession. As a founding member of London's Camera Club, Emerson's subject was largely the people and places of East Anglia and the Norfolk Broads. He found himself in conflict with many of the photographic profession, passionately arguing for the need of a scientific and naturalistic approach in photographs.

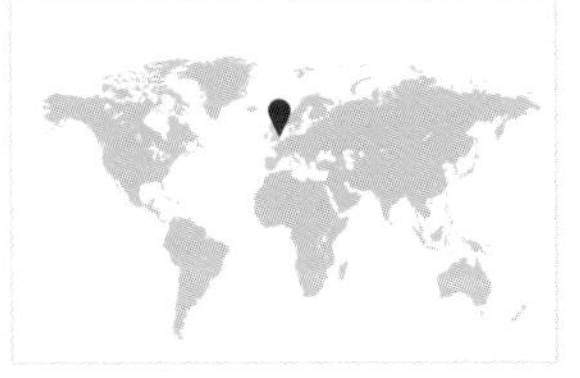

'The evidence is clear enough that had the artists and scientists who were the promoters of the first English Photographic Society held their own, photography would have been practised by artists and scientists alone – a noble and learned profession – instead of being practised, as is now too often the case, by illiterate and ignorant tradesmen.'

Peter Henry Emerson, Introduction to *Pictures from Life in Field and Fen*, 1887

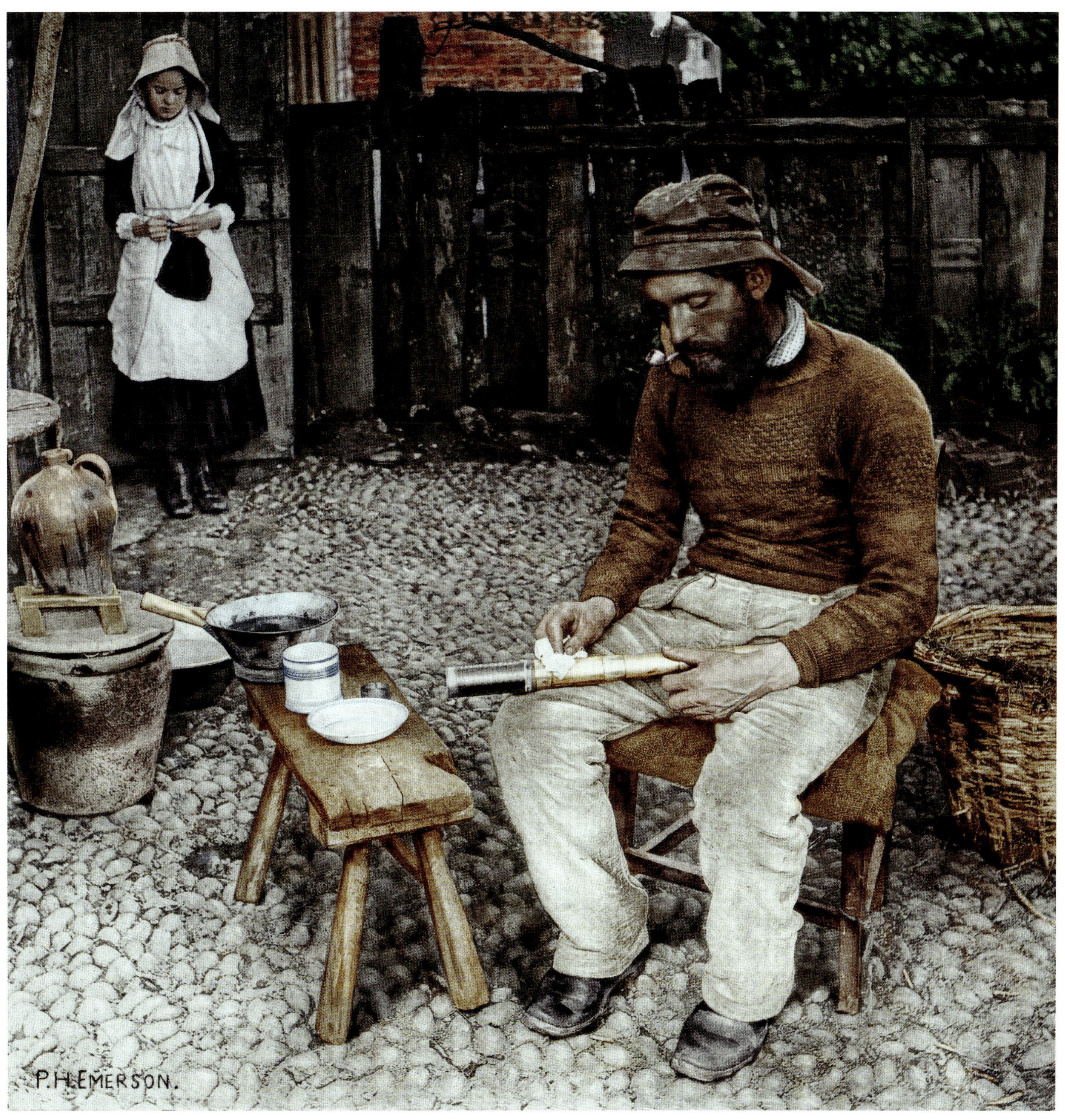
P.H.EMERSON.

1880s

1885: Sitting Bull and Buffalo Bill

Montreal, Quebec, Canada
(William Notman / David Francis Barry / Library of Congress)

Taken at William Notman's studios, Montreal, during 'Buffalo Bill's Wild West Show' in 1885, this photograph bore the title 'Foes in '76 – Friends in '85.'

Sitting Bull was fifty four when he agreed to join William Cody's 'Buffalo Bill's Wild West' in 1885. Paid a signing bonus of $125 and $50 a week, his role in what was essentially an American circus was to ride round the arena once per show, in the opening procession. Sitting Bull was the star attraction, but after four months he decided that he'd had enough and returned to the Standing Rock Reservation.

It was a far cry from 1876 when, as spiritual leader to the Lakota Sioux, Sitting Bull had inspired his tribe in the defeat of Custer's 7th Cavalry at the Battle of Little Big Horn. Following the battle, Sitting Bull was driven into exile in Canada, until the starvation forced him to surrender to the US government. Transferred onto Standing Rock, Sitting Bull was shot and killed by a Reservation police officer in 1890.

'Have much pleasure and much fatigue. Great difference between prairie travel on horse and foot and on the wagons drawn by the vapor horse. Major Burke very kind, all persons very kind. Think all the pale faces feel kind to the Sioux soldier. Believe they know why he held all his braves and all his people to starve rather than submit to what was wrong. Believe the pale faces respect him for his hard fights and do not wish to hurt him because he had to kill the pale faces when he was fighting. No wish to fight now. Always spoken truth to the pale faces and always been deceived.'

Sitting Bull to reporter at the *Buffalo Courier*, 1885

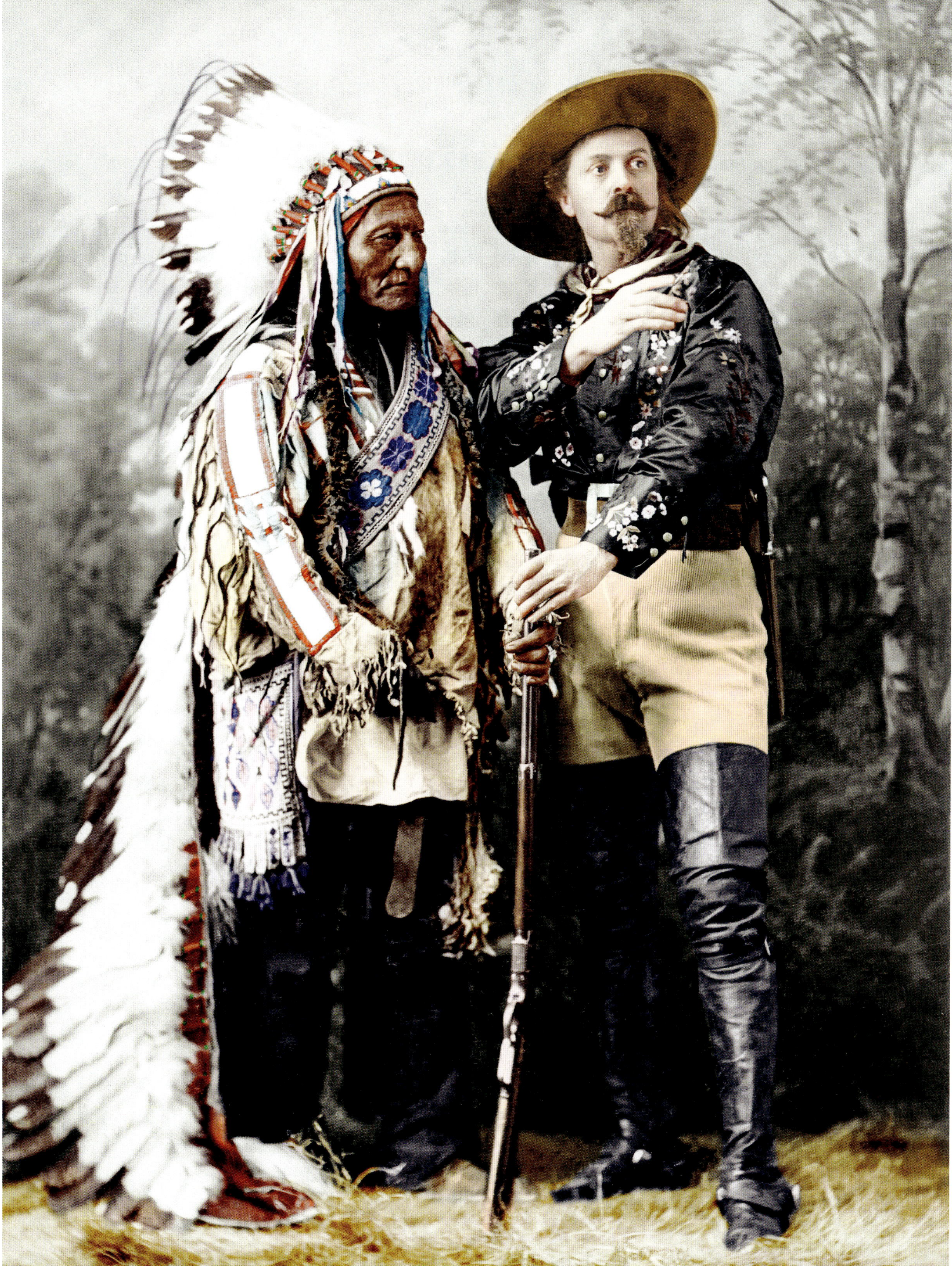

1880s

1885: A 'Mrs Frampton' combing her long hair with the help of a mirror

London, UK
(Unknown / London Stereoscopic Company / Getty)

The Victorian era placed huge aesthetic value on a Western woman's hair, as an indicator of both inherent femininity and of social standing. For girls, the transition to womanhood was at least partly marked by wearing one's hair up. Hair could be worn up in a range of styles, from simple coils to elaborate accessorised coiffures, but the hair remained uncut.

'Letting one's hair down' was seen not only as childish but also as immodest, and counter to the tradition of the church. Pictures such as this one, therefore, held an element of displaying what was otherwise forbidden.

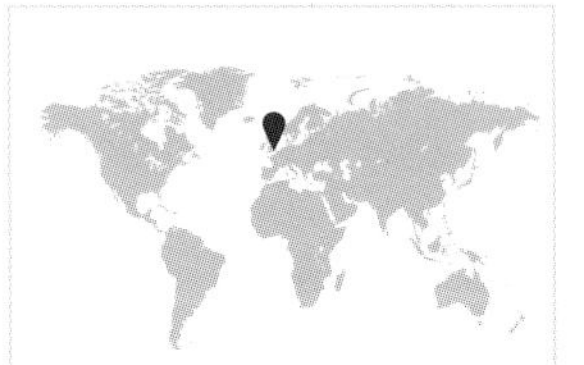

'Now as to the question of cutting. Women still have the privilege of wearing their hair its natural length, and what is more beautiful in woman than long hair? But the hair is apt to split at its ends, and requires, for health's sake, occasional cutting, and in certain instances much improves its growth. I know I am opposed in this view by many, but I am convinced all the same it is beneficial. The operation in women is really one of trimming.'

A lecture delivered by James Startin to the Hairdresser's Guild in St James's Hall, London, March 1885

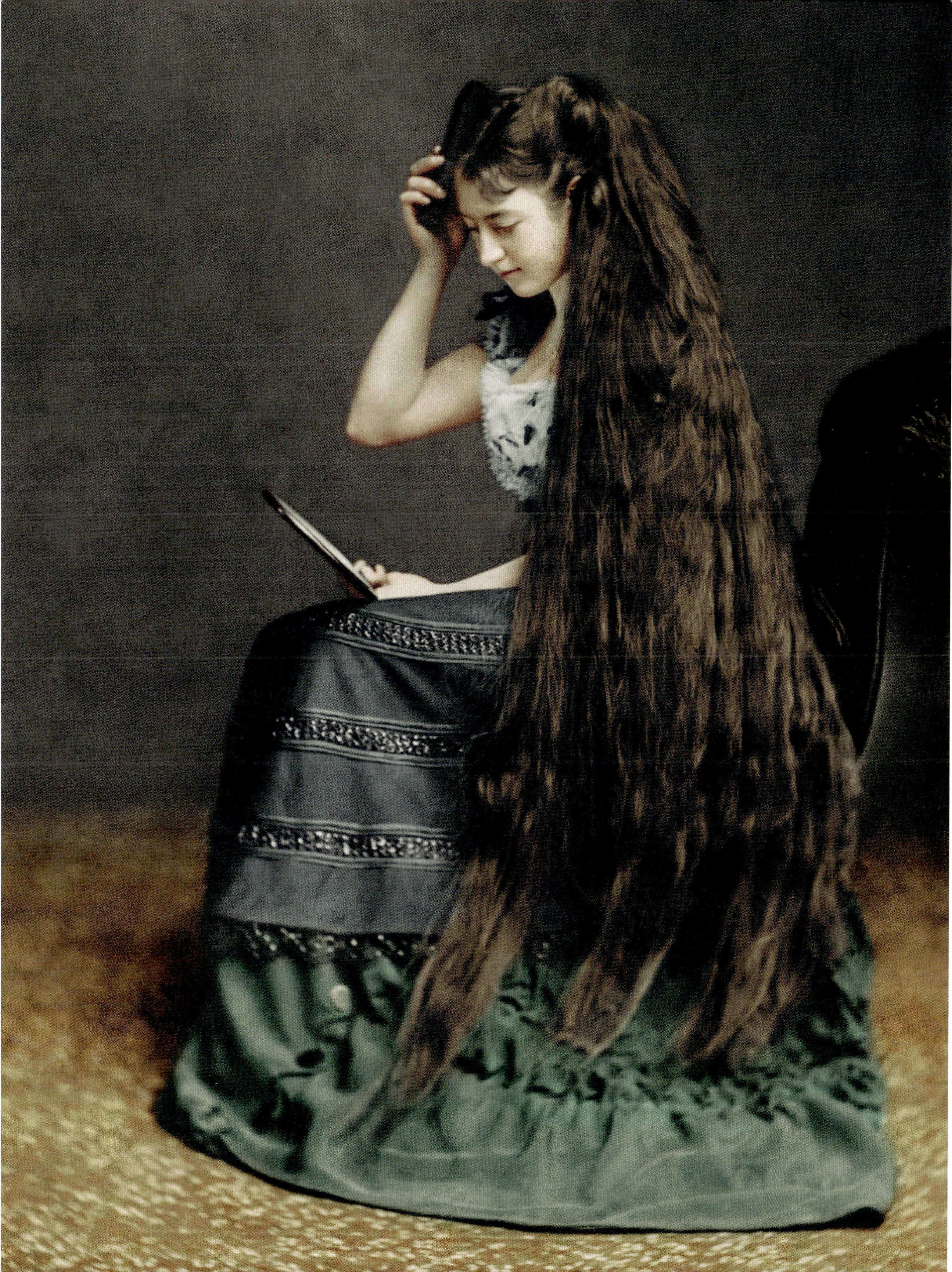

'A model was made just one-sixteenth the size of the contemplated statue. It was enlarged to one-fourth the size. After this came the full-size model. After this came wooden frames, upon which plaster was put. After this came the work of the French carpenters. After this came the sheets of copper, beaten on the inside with wooden mallets.'

Bartholdi souvenir: a sketch of the colossal statue presented by France to the United States, 1886

1882: Workers build the Statue of Liberty inside French sculptor Frédéric Auguste Bartholdi's workshop, Paris
Paris, France
(Albert Fernique / Library of Congress)

1880s

The idea for the Statue of Liberty was Frédéric Auguste Bartholdi's. The Parisian sculptor wanted to create a gift for the US nation in the wake of the abolition of slavery, referenced in the broken chain at the feet of the statue.

Construction commenced in 1877, and Bartholdi brought in engineer Gustave Eiffel to help with the statue's inner framework. In 1885, the completed statue was shipped to America, assembled and dedicated the following year.

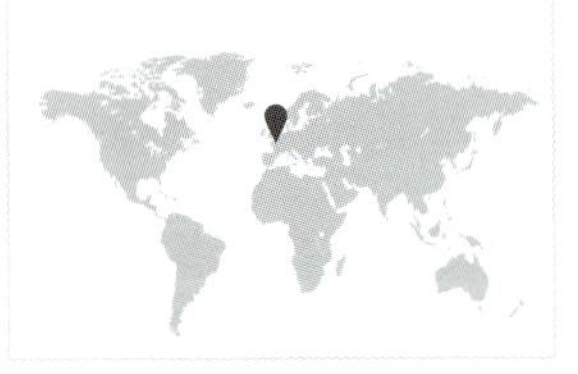

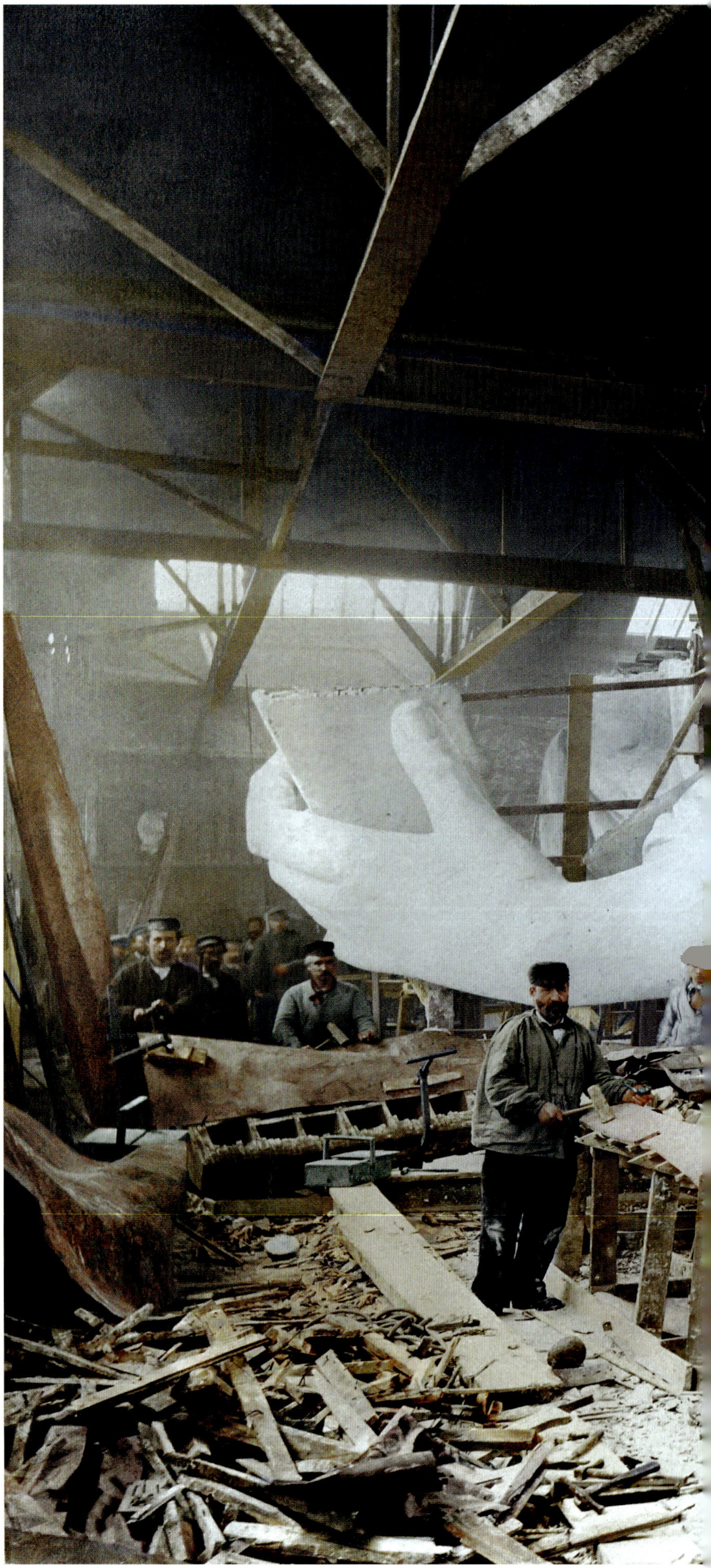

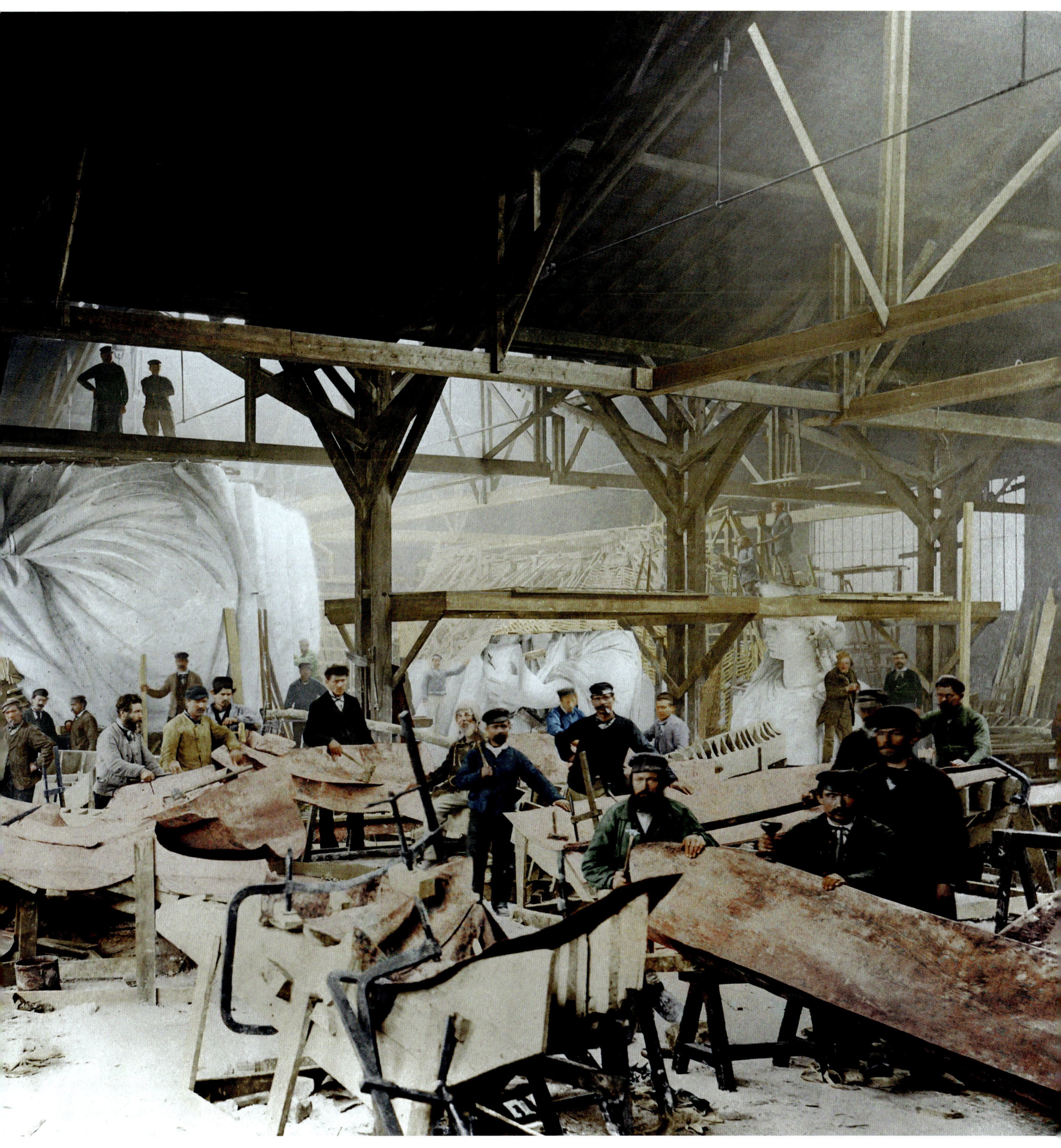

1880s: The bell tower of the Sacré-Cœur Basilica under construction on the Montmartre Hill, Paris

Montmartre, Paris, France
(Unknown / Keystone France / Getty)

The Parisian Roman Catholic church of Sacré-Cœur – in full, 'The Basilica of the Sacred Heart of Paris' (Basilique du Sacré-Cœur) – sits at the summit of Montmartre, the highest point in the French capital. Construction of the Basilica began in 1875 and was finished almost forty years later, in 1914.

The impetus for the work was the church's interpretation of France's defeat in the 1871 Franco–Prussian War, and of the Socialist Commune of the same year. Both were seen as forms of divine retribution for the nation's moral degeneracy since the Revolution, which had culminated in the execution of the Parisian Archbishop Georges Darboy at Montmartre by the Communards.

Visiting the scene in 1872, Derby's successor was possessed by a vision to construct the Basilica and so restore the Church's divine purpose to the city and French nation.

1880s

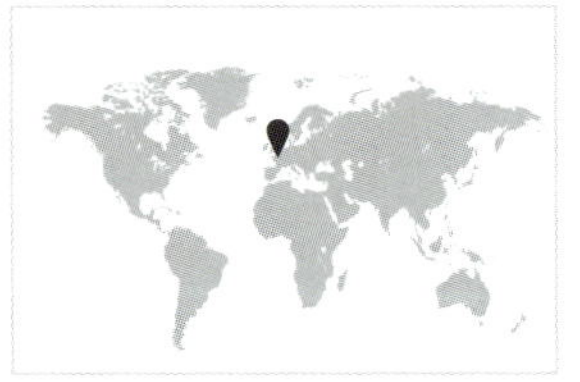

'A monster church is now in process of construction on the summit of the Butte Montmartre (Elise Sacré Cœur) and will be, when completed, the most conspicuous edifice in Paris; a good view of the works can be obtained from the Calvaire, or Jardin des Oliviers, to which pilgrimages are frequently made.'

Paris in Four Days: a complete and practical guide to all the sights and objects of interest in and around the metropolis (40th year of publication), C. Moonen, 1886–7

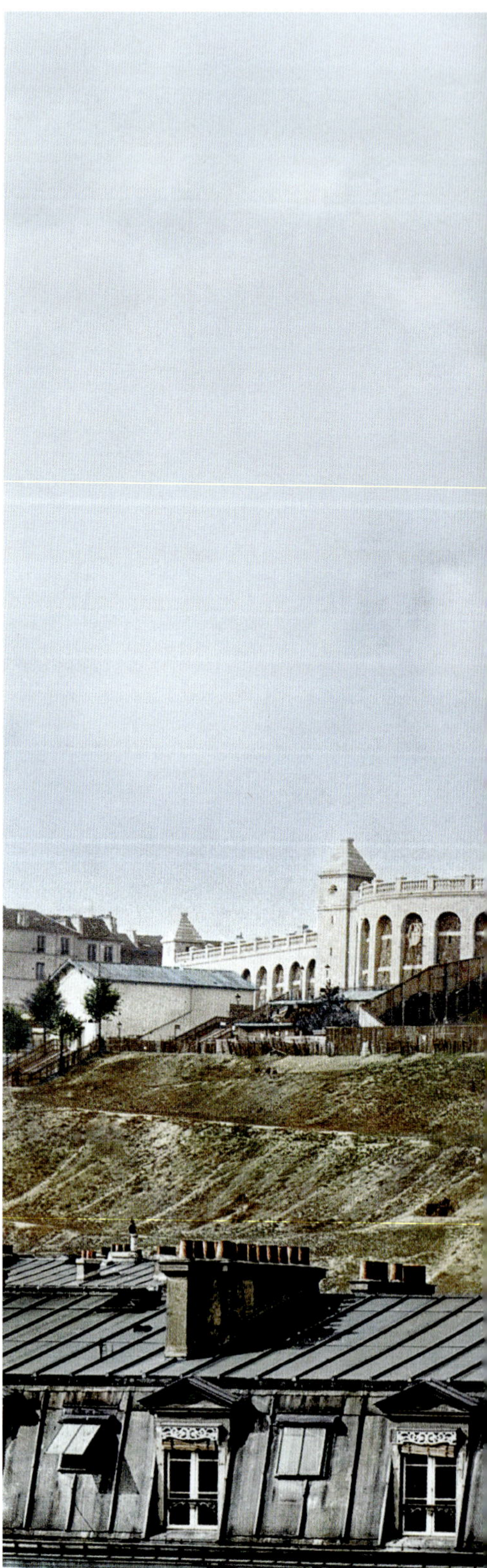

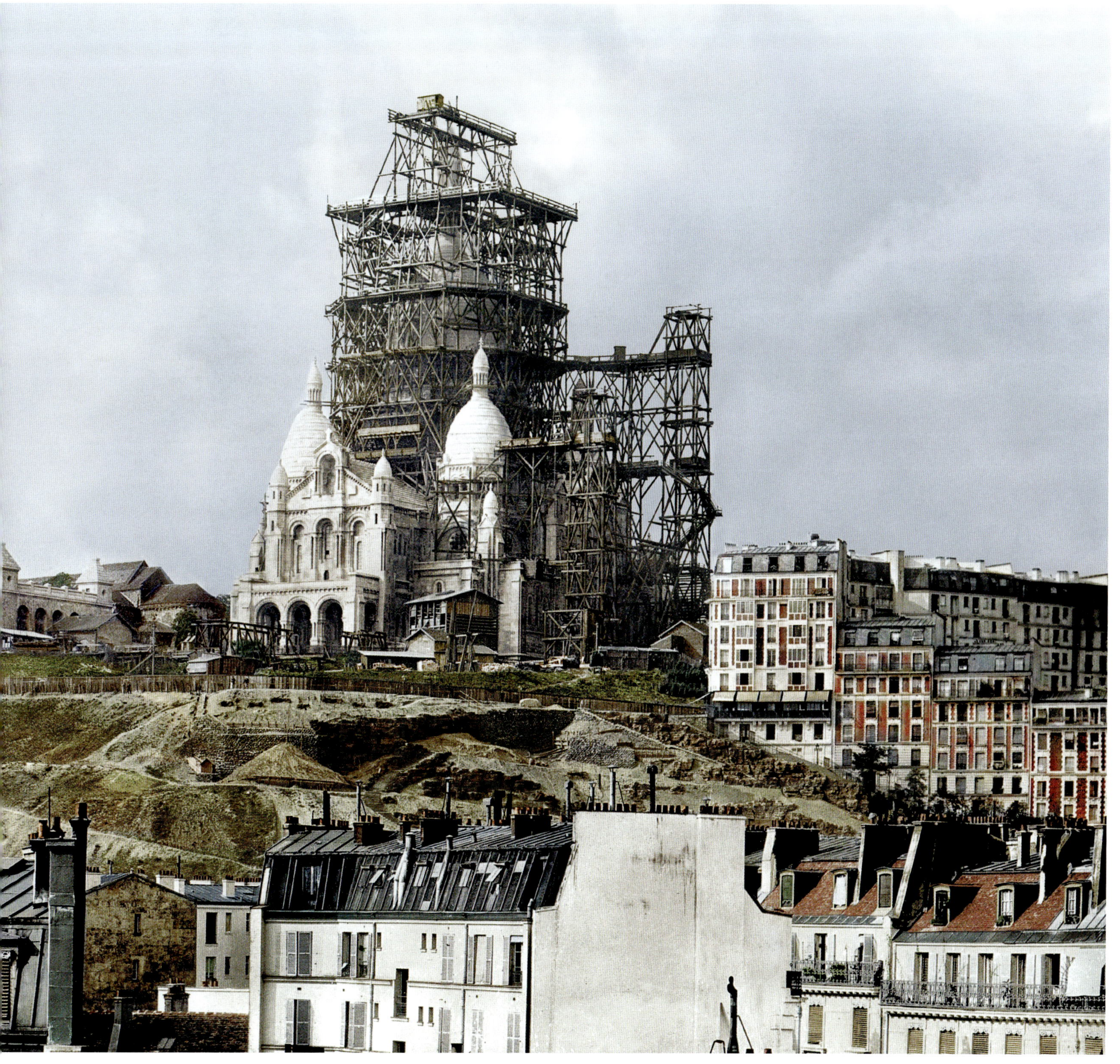

1880s

c. 1880s: Guides help a visitor to climb the Great Pyramid, Egypt

Giza, Egypt
(Félix Bonfils / Library of Congress)

Tourism to Egypt, and specifically to Cairo and the pyramids, had become a robust and thriving business by the late nineteenth century. The Levant, and Egypt in particular, allowed American and European visitors to experience a sense of the exotic while remaining within the known environment of the Mediterranean.

In 1869, Thomas Cook announced a tour of the Nile, and by the middle of the following decade, the company ran a timetabled steamboat facility for passengers on the river.

A key souvenir regularly obtained was a photograph of oneself and one's party being assisted to climb the Great Pyramid, such as this one. Almost always, the picture was taken at the North East corner, which came to be known as 'Tourist's Corner'.

What Bonfils' photograph doesn't show is that it was likely to have been taken at the very base of the pyramid. Tourists posed with local guides as though being helped to ascend the pyramid, without actually having to do so.

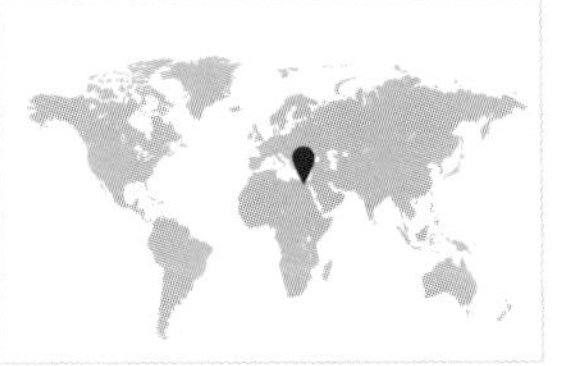

'To ascend the Great Pyramid a payment of three shillings from each tourist has to be made to the Sheikh of the Pyramids, and in addition to this a further fee must be paid for the assistance of some strong muscular Arabs. The usual plan is to have an Arab on each side; if the exigencies of the case require, an extra Arab or two pull in front and push behind. Some travellers make a point of getting up without aid, but the consequent exhaustion is scarcely worth the glory of having accomplished the task.'

Cook's Tourists' Handbook for Egypt, the Nile, and the Desert, 1876

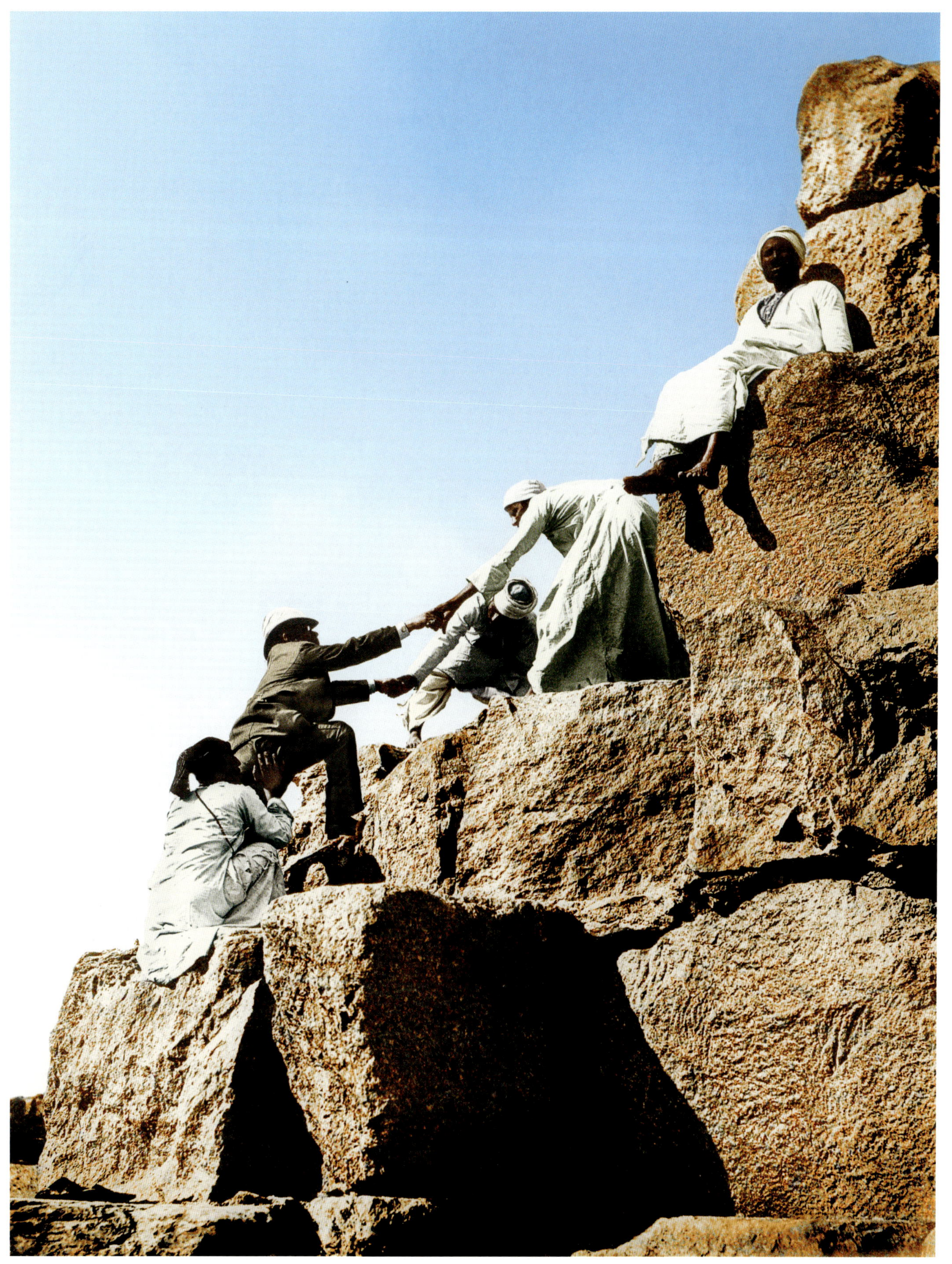

c. 1880: Mugshots of inmates at Wormwood Scrubs prison, London

Wormwood Scrubs, London, UK

(Science & Society Picture Library / Getty)

London's Wormwood Scrubs prison, opened in 1874, had originally been a number of wooden sheds. The sheds were replaced gradually using the labour of the prisoners, with bricks made on-site. The invention of photography was of enormous benefit to those charged with maintaining law and order, including in the identification of prisoners, and suspects, by their face, or, in slang, 'mug'.

This set of Wormwood Scrubs mugshots, of both men and women, date from the 1880s and 1890s. As well as the prisoners' faces, the images also use mirrors to capture their profiles. Their hands are also recorded: prisoners might have distinctive marks, tattoos or even missing digits.

The prisoners and their numbers shown here are: George Malone #3615, Oliver Hill #5496, Edward Smith #5497, Benjamin Morris #4706, Mary Pullbrook #4318, William Jenkins #965, James Jones #980, Tobias A. Teller #1026 and Thomas Springbolt #4488.

1880s

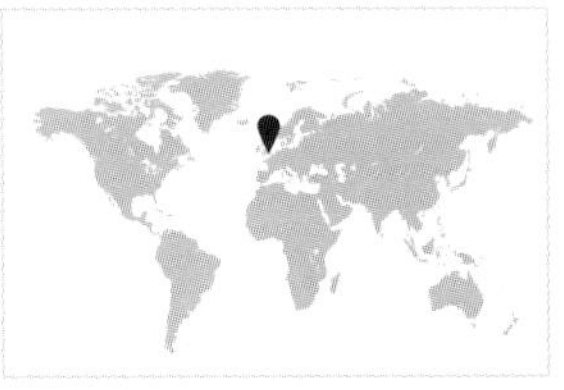

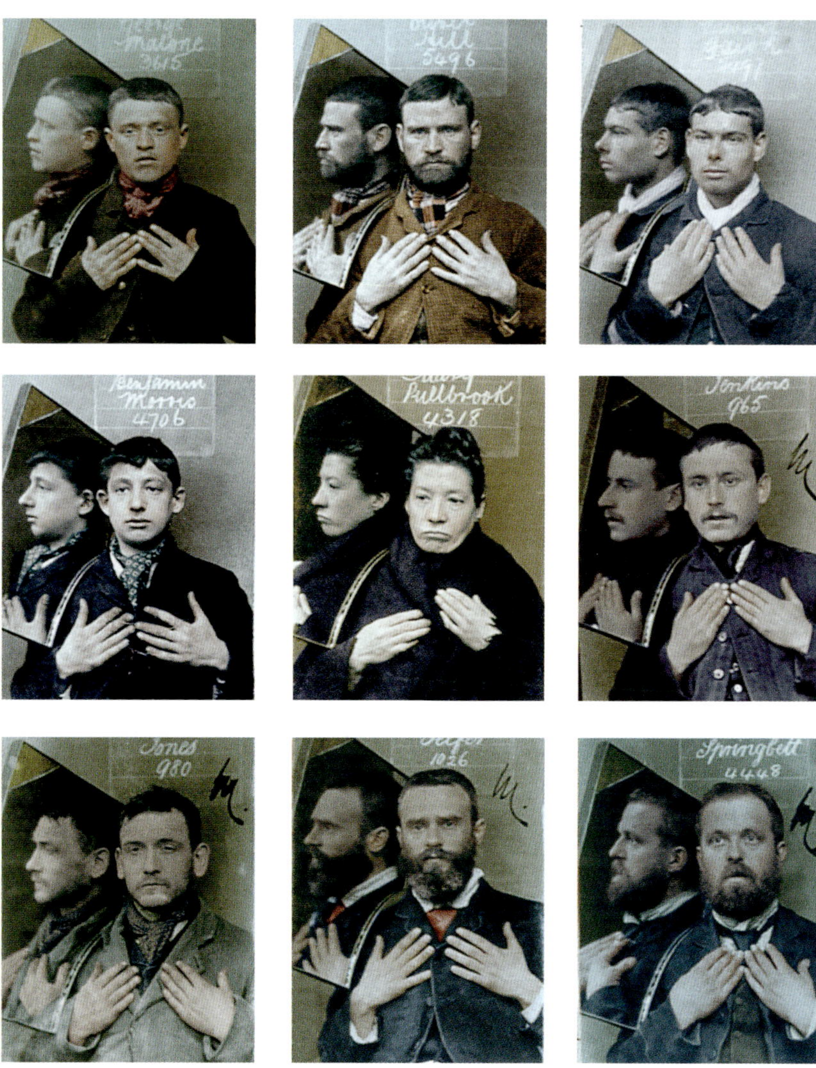

'After all the formalities had been complied with, I was placed in an empty cell and locked up for the night. So after the turmoil of the day, all my hopes had been crushed, my worst fears had been realised, and I was again alone in a prison cell with a long prison sentence before me, alone with my thoughts, alone with my grief, afraid of the future.'

Arthur Hardin, Wormwood Scrubs prison, 1902

1877: **British recruiting sergeants at Westminster, London**

Westminster, London, UK
(John Thomson / Science & Society Picture Library / Getty)

The British recruiting sergeant was a soldier tasked with inducing volunteers to enlist into the army. Such sergeants become notorious for using underhand and deceptive methods to secure a new recruit. In this picture, the sergeants stand on the corner of King Street and Great George Street in London, now part of Parliament Square, across the road from the sixteenth-century edifice of Saint Margaret's church.

The photograph is by John Thomson and taken from his *Street Life in London* with words by Adolphe Smith. Thomson worked in partnership with journalist Smith between 1873 to 1877 to portray the daily lives of Londoners, and in particular the poorest in the city. *Street Life in London* was published as a monthly subscription, before being released as a single volume.

1870s

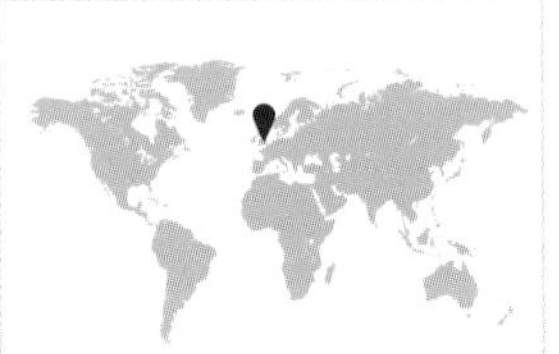

'Our system of recruiting, the soldier's long term of service, and the restrictions upon his marriage, act as a direct encouragement to drunkenness and debauchery in a great national establishment, which might, under different arrangements, be converted into a popular training school of the highest intellectual and moral value.'

The British Army in 1868,
Sir Charles E. Trevelyan

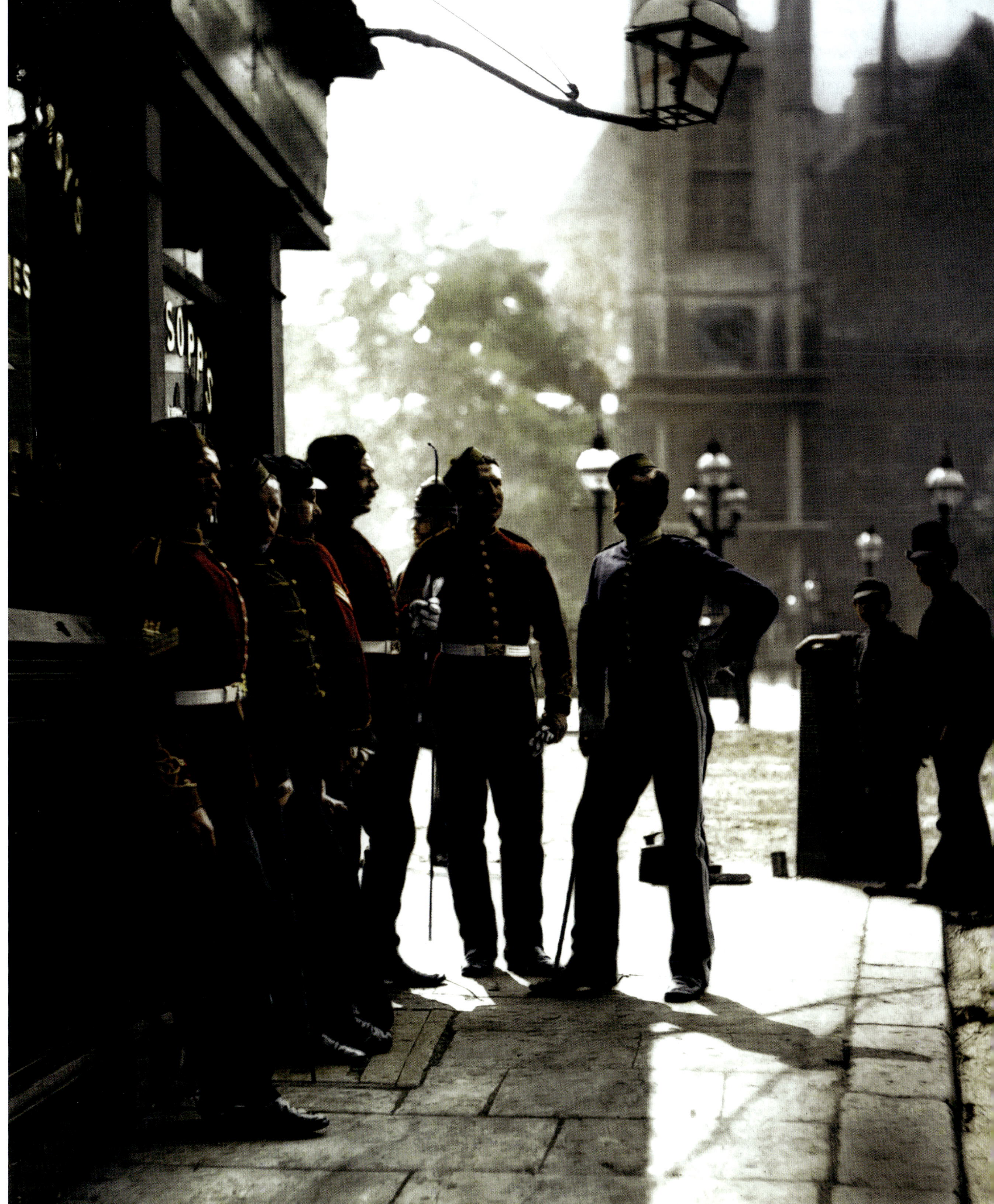
SOPP'S

1870s

1875: A man sells mummies and other grave goods, Egypt

Egypt
(Felix Bonfils)

French photographer Félix Bonfils worked largely in the Levant. First voyaging to the Eastern Mediterranean in 1860, he later moved permanently to the region with his wife and young son, Adrien, after Adrien developed respiratory problems. A dry climate was regarded as beneficial to Adrien's condition.

In 1867, Bonfils opened a studio – Maison Bonfils – in Beirut, capturing and selling images of local scenes and figures, such as this one of a street vendor, largely to tourists. The business thrived and branches of Maison Bonfils were established in France, Alexandria and Cairo.

Bonfils' uncle was Joseph Nicéphore Niépce, credited as the inventor of photography, and whose 'View from the Window' at Le Gras is the oldest known surviving camera photograph.

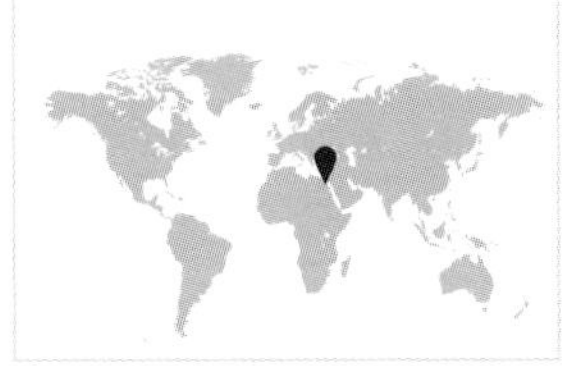

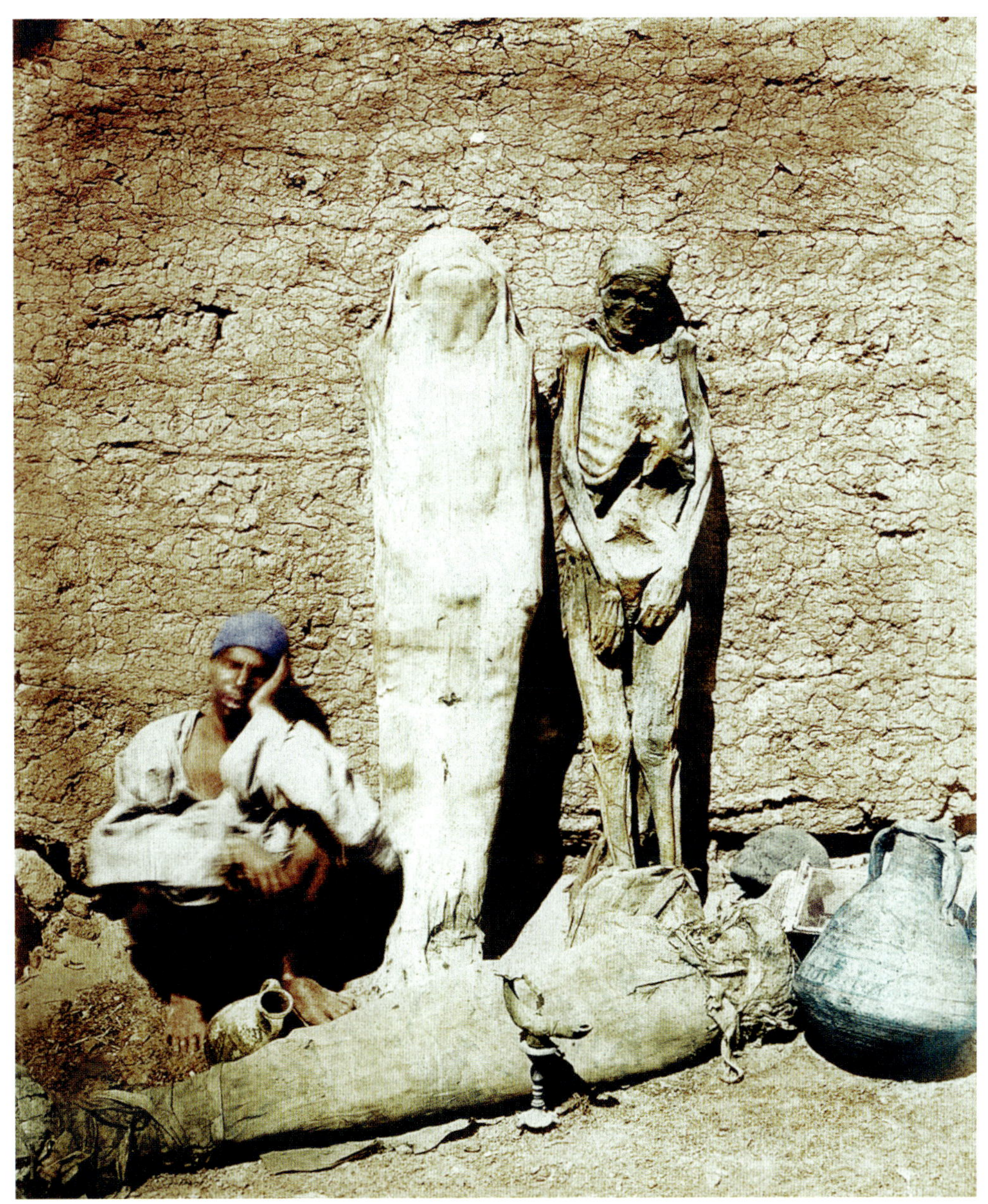

'Modern perfumers find means of preparing the perfumes and spices found inside the bodies of mummies to be exceedingly attractive to ladies.'

The Ohio Democrat, 13 August 1887

1870s

_c._ 1870: A 'female samurai' or *Onna-bugeisha* (女武芸者, 'female martial artist')

Possibly Yokohama, Japan
(Universal History Archive / Getty)

This woman, likely to be a model, is portraying an *Onna-bugeisha*, which can be translated as 'female martial artist'. The *Onna-bugeisha* was a samurai, serving the nobility of feudal Japan. Where a male samurai fought with a *katana* sword, the *onna-bugeisha* typically fought with the *naginata*, a polearm with a curved blade at the tip, and with bows and arrows.

Japanese women samurai are known from the first century BC and yet, during the Edo period (1603-1868), an *Onna-bugeisha* was not permitted to travel unless accompanied by a man.

'Mononofu no
Tateki kokoro ni kurabureba
kazu nimo iranu
wagami nagaramo.'

'When compared to the ranks
of warriors' stalwart hearts;
I cannot enter into their number,
despite this body of mine.'

Death poem of Nakano Takeko, female warrior, 1868

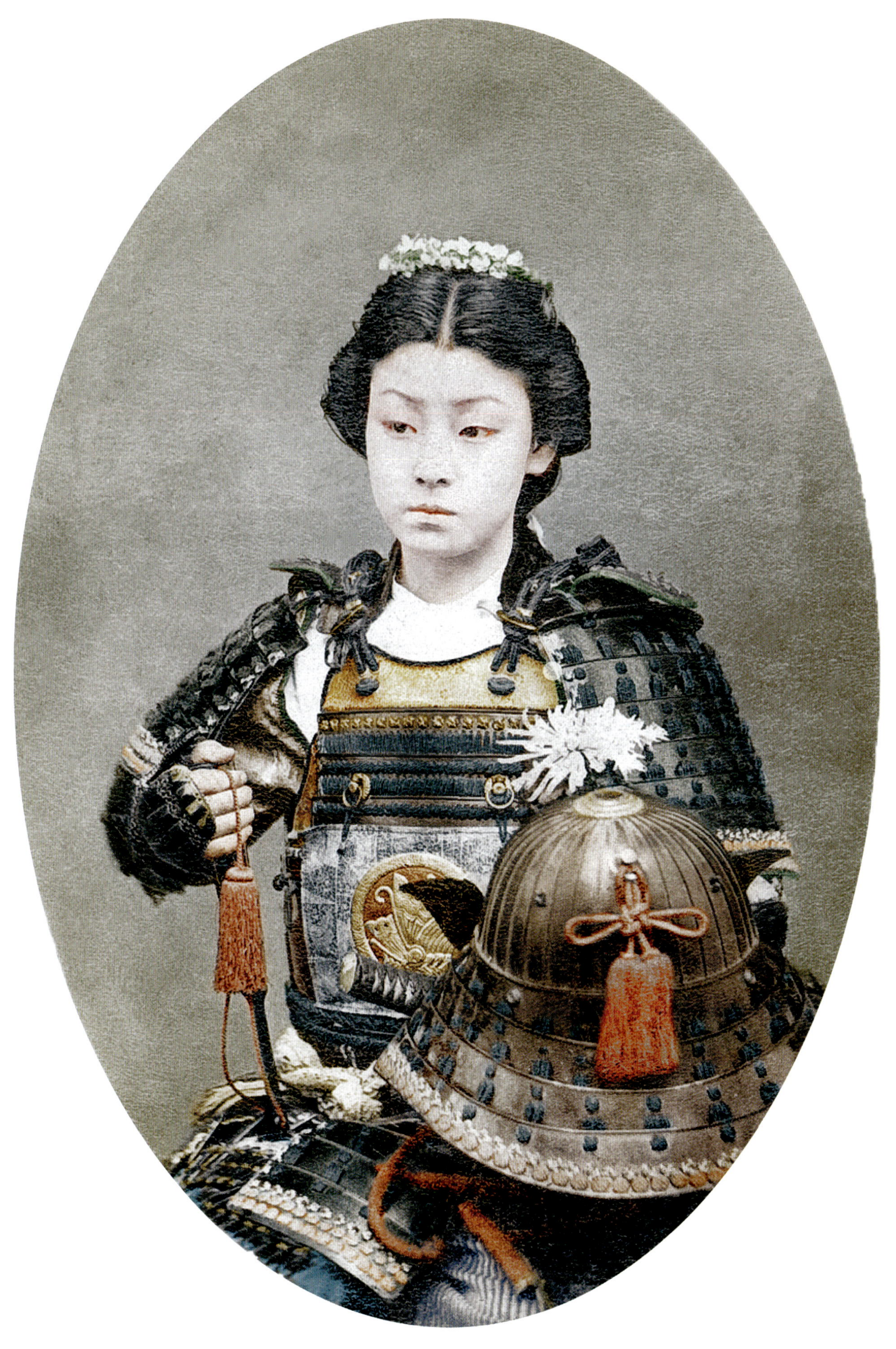

1860s

7 July 1865: The hanging of the conspirators in the assassination of Lincoln, at Fort McNair, Washington DC

Fort McNair, Washington DC, USA (Alexander Gardner / Library of Congress)

The assassination of Lincoln in April 1865 by William Booth was part of a conspiracy to bring down the Union government. The plot would have seen the simultaneous killing by conspirators of the President, Vice President Andrew Johnson and Secretary of State William Seward. Only Booth succeeded.

While Booth was killed before he could stand trial, other conspirators were taken and imprisoned. Three months after the assassination, on 7 July, four of them – Lewis Powell, David Herold, George Atzerodt and Mary Surratt – were hung at Fort McNair. The scene was captured by Scottish photographer Alexander Gardner.

The gallows was constructed specifically. Mary Surratt, whose Washington boarding house was a primary location in the conspiracy, became the first woman to be executed by the US federal government.

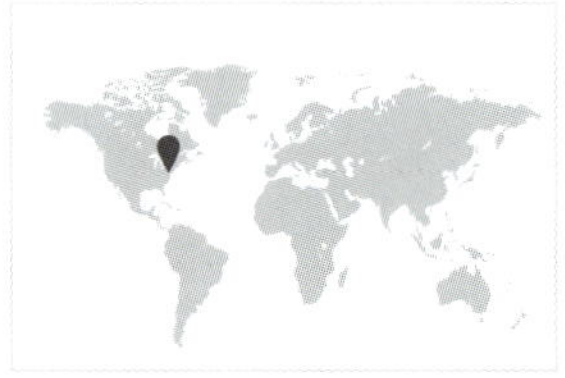

'Atzerodt, who seemed to grow excited as his moments approached, just before the white cap was placed over his head, attempted, in a gasping manner, to address the spectators. His parched lips would not obey, and it was distressing to see him convulsively endeavouring to make himself intelligible. At last he managed to get out the words "Gentlemen, take warnen".'

The Louisiana Democrat, 26 July 1865

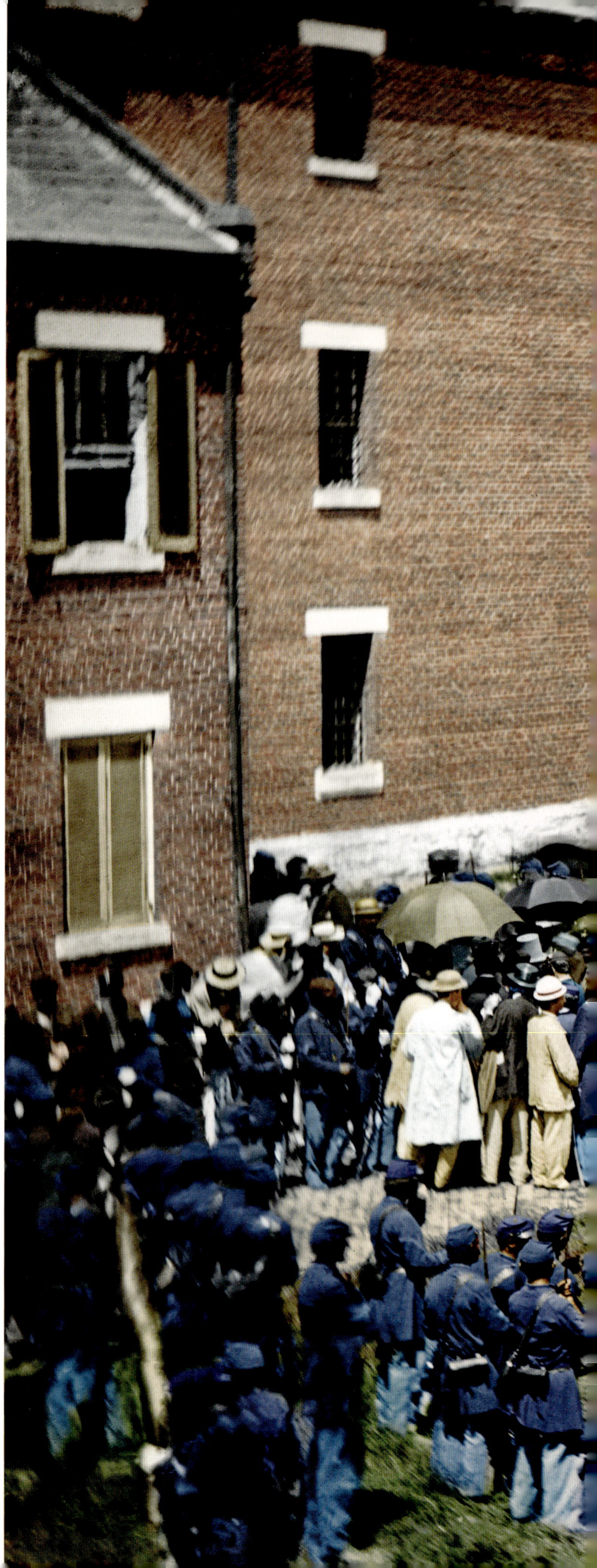

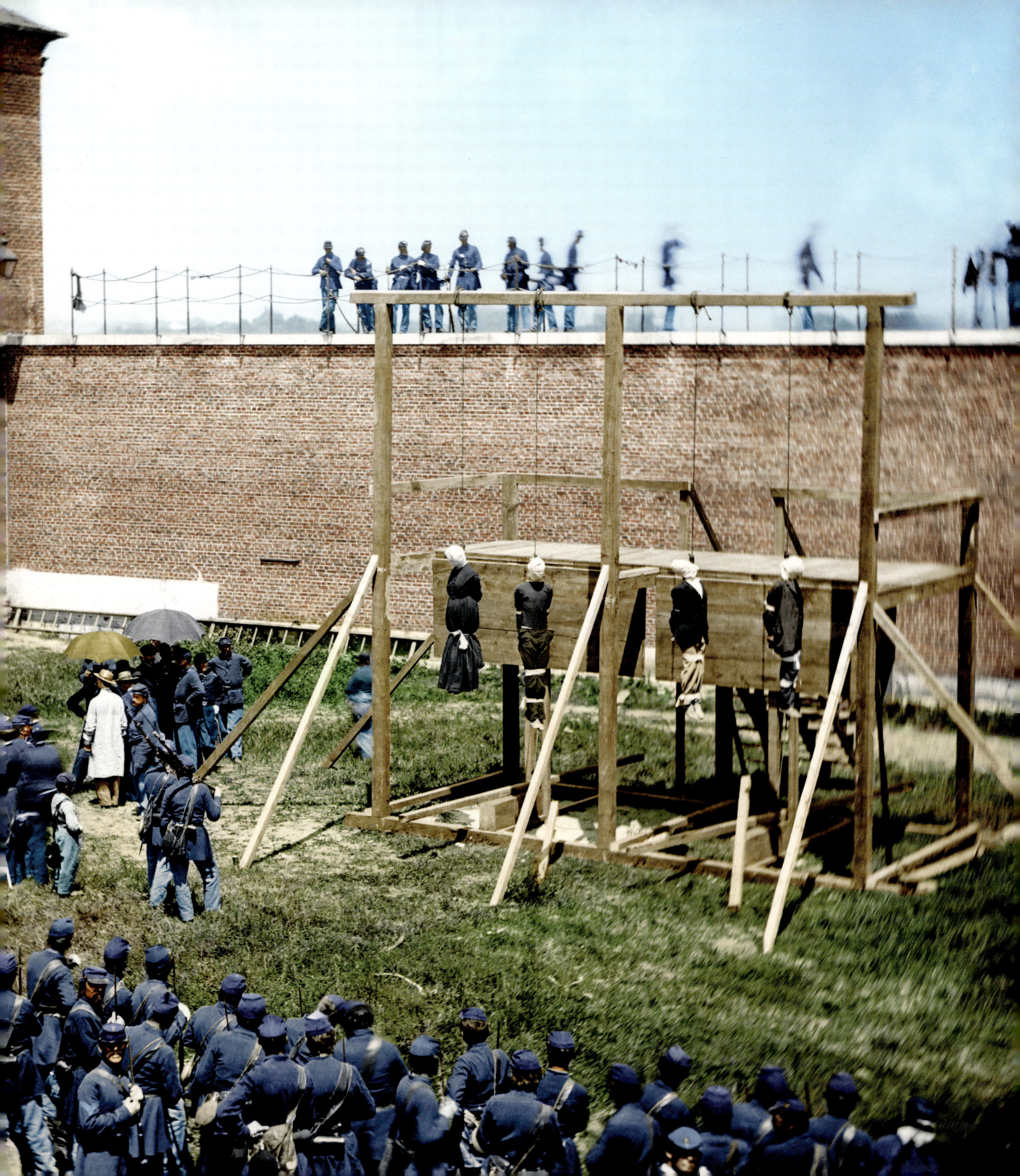

1860s

1865: A Turkestan Krai Jew

Turkestan, Russia
(Unknown / Library of Congress)

One of the 491 ethnographic photographs from a total of 1,200 in *The Turkestan Album*. Imperial Russia had taken control of this region of Central Asia in the 1860s, and *The Turkestan Album* was commissioned by Russian Turkestan's first governor-general, as a visual survey of the locale.

The Turkestan Krai – the area of Turkestan governed by Russia, as a Governor Generalship – stretched from the Caspian Sea to the Gobi Desert and included Kazakhstan, Kirghizia, Tadzhikistan, Turkmenistan, Uzbekistan, parts of Afghanistan and China. Many Jews came into the Turkestan region following the establishment of the Krai.

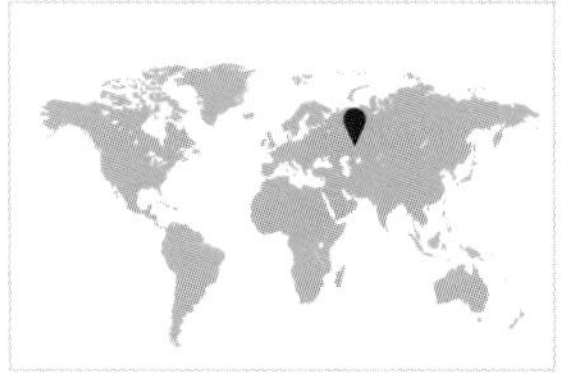

'In light of satisfying the common interest and for the rapid familiarisation of the reading public to our newly occupied land, by order of the Turkestan Governor-General, Adjutant-General K. P. von Kaufman 1st compiled the photograph album to introduce the world of enterprising administrations to the region.'

Foreword to *The Turkestan Album*, 1871–2

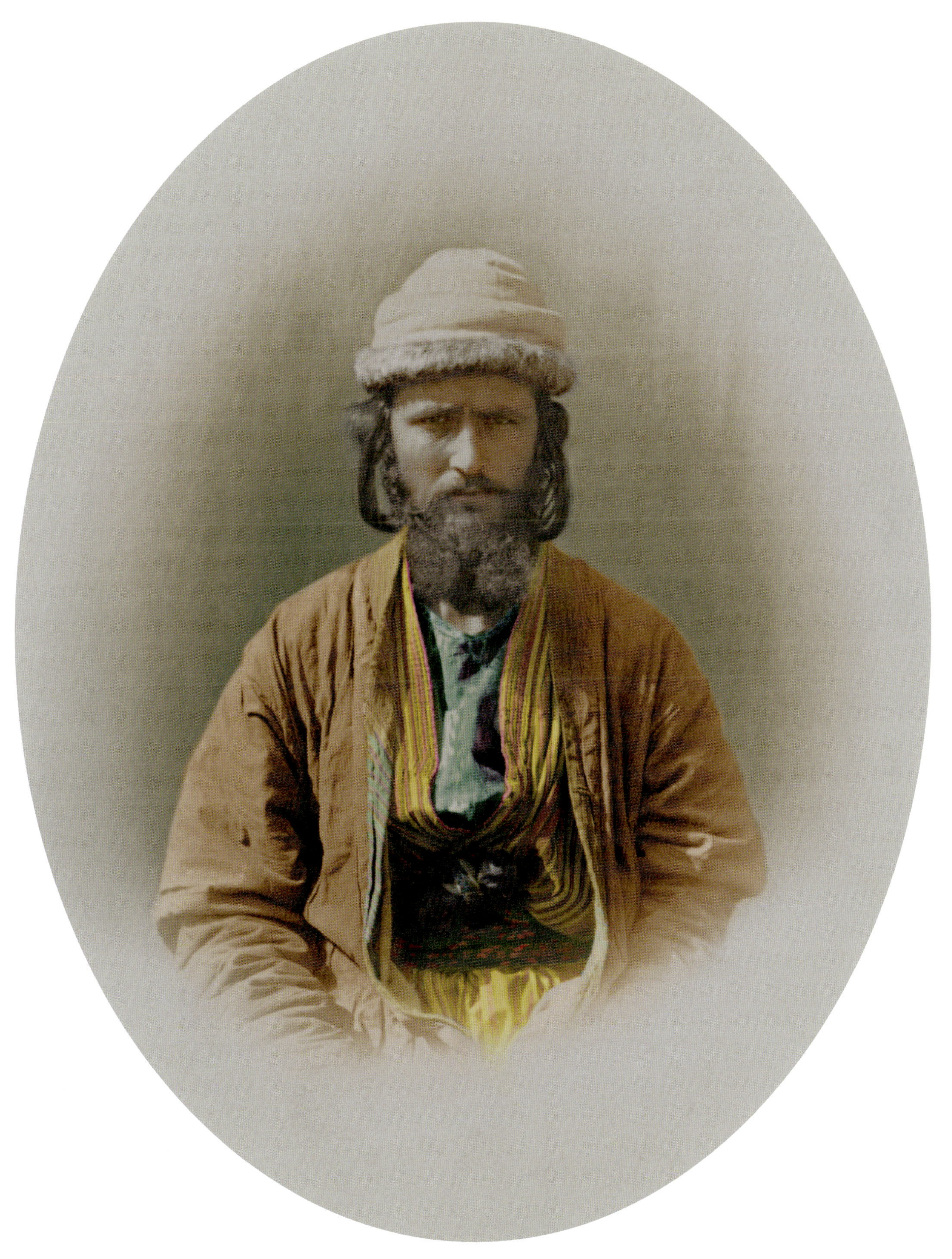

1860s

c. 1865: A portrait of Virginia Oldoïni, Countess of Castiglione
Paris, France
(Pierre-Louis Pierson / Getty)

Of an Italian aristocratic background, Virginia Elisabetta Luisa Carlotta Antonietta Teresa Maria Oldoïni, Countess of Castiglione, became known simply as La Castiglione. Born in 1837, she had married the Count of Castiglione at the age of seventeen. Voyaging to Paris with the Count the following year, she attained for herself the position of Napoleon III's mistress. As a result, she was elevated to the highest levels of European society, and acquired equally high levels of notoriety.

La Castiglione's true passion was her own appearance. Working with photographer Pierre-Louis Pierson, she created around 700 portraits across four decades. Pierson's role was often merely the camera's operator – all other elements, including lighting, staging and camera angles were executed by the Countess. The cost of the enterprise depleted her fortune and sent her into debt.

She died in November 1899 at the age of sixty-two. The years approaching her death were lived out in an apartment in central Paris, decorated in black, dark blinds drawn all day, and all mirrors removed. She remained in the apartment during daylight hours, only venturing outside under cover of darkness.

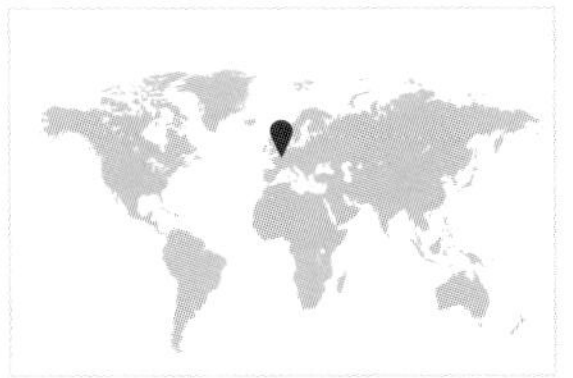

'In Parisian society the gay season has always its queen. The sovereign of last winter was the lovely Italian Countess of Castiglione. What elbowing in the seasons to obtain a glimpse of this new majesty, who so coquettishly endeavored to escape the admiring gaze of the crowd! Alas! For the consistency of Parisian worship, it is said that the countess is dethroned, and that the queen of the next few months will be Madame Serrano, wife of the Spanish Ambassador.'

Daily Dispatch, Richmond, Virginia, 31 December 1856

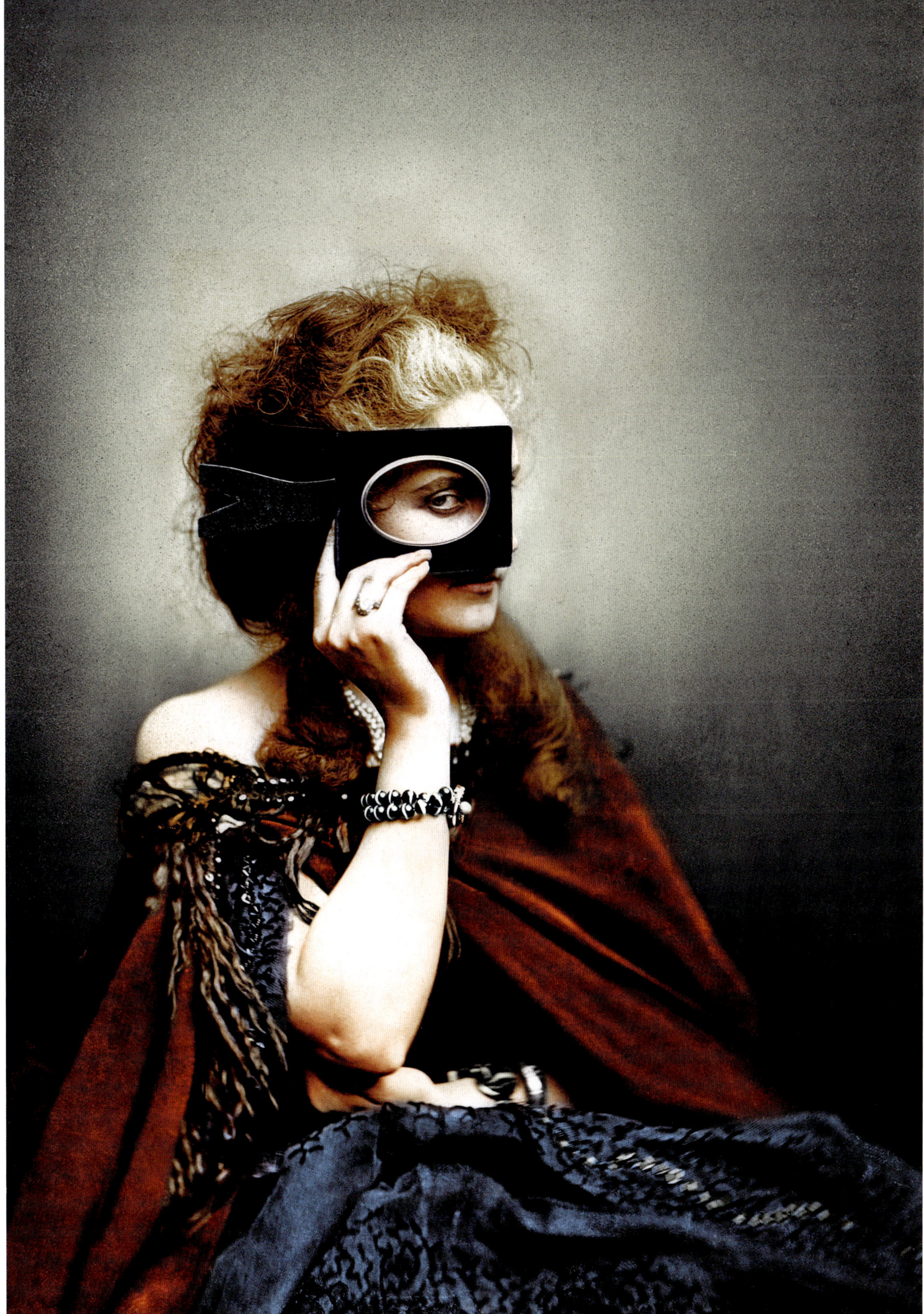

1865: A group of top-hatted men in front of the construction of the British ship *Tanjore*

Blackwall, London, UK
(Unknown/ Hulton Archive)

The *Tanjore* was an iron screw steam brig, built for the Peninsular and Oriental Steam Navigation Company (P&O). Launched on 13 April 1865 by a 'Miss Ford', the niece of the Thames Iron Works' Managing Director, the *Tanjore* ended her life sold to ship breakers in Bombay in 1894.

Ships such as the *Tanjore* were among the first post-Industrial Revolution vessels to be constructed with iron rather than wood, and to be propelled by steam rather than sail.

1860s

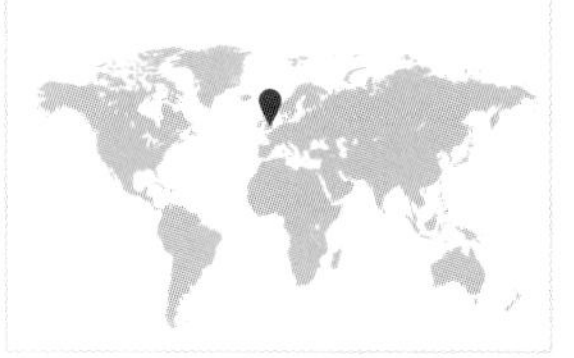

'ARRIVAL AT MELBOURNE, OF THE *TANJORE* SS, WITH THE MAILS FOR JUNE.

The *Tanjore*, not the *Nubia* as expected, which this month brought the mails to Australia, was sighted off Cape Otway on Friday night. She arrived in Hobson's Bay on Saturday, at 10:30 a.m., and immediately thereafter the Tasmanian portion of the mails was transferred on board the Derwent.'

The Mercury, 27 August 1872

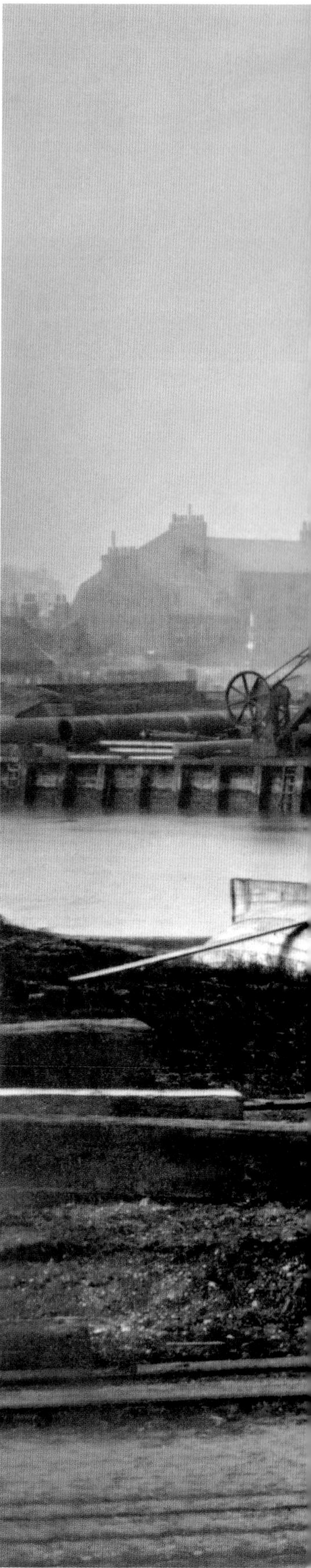

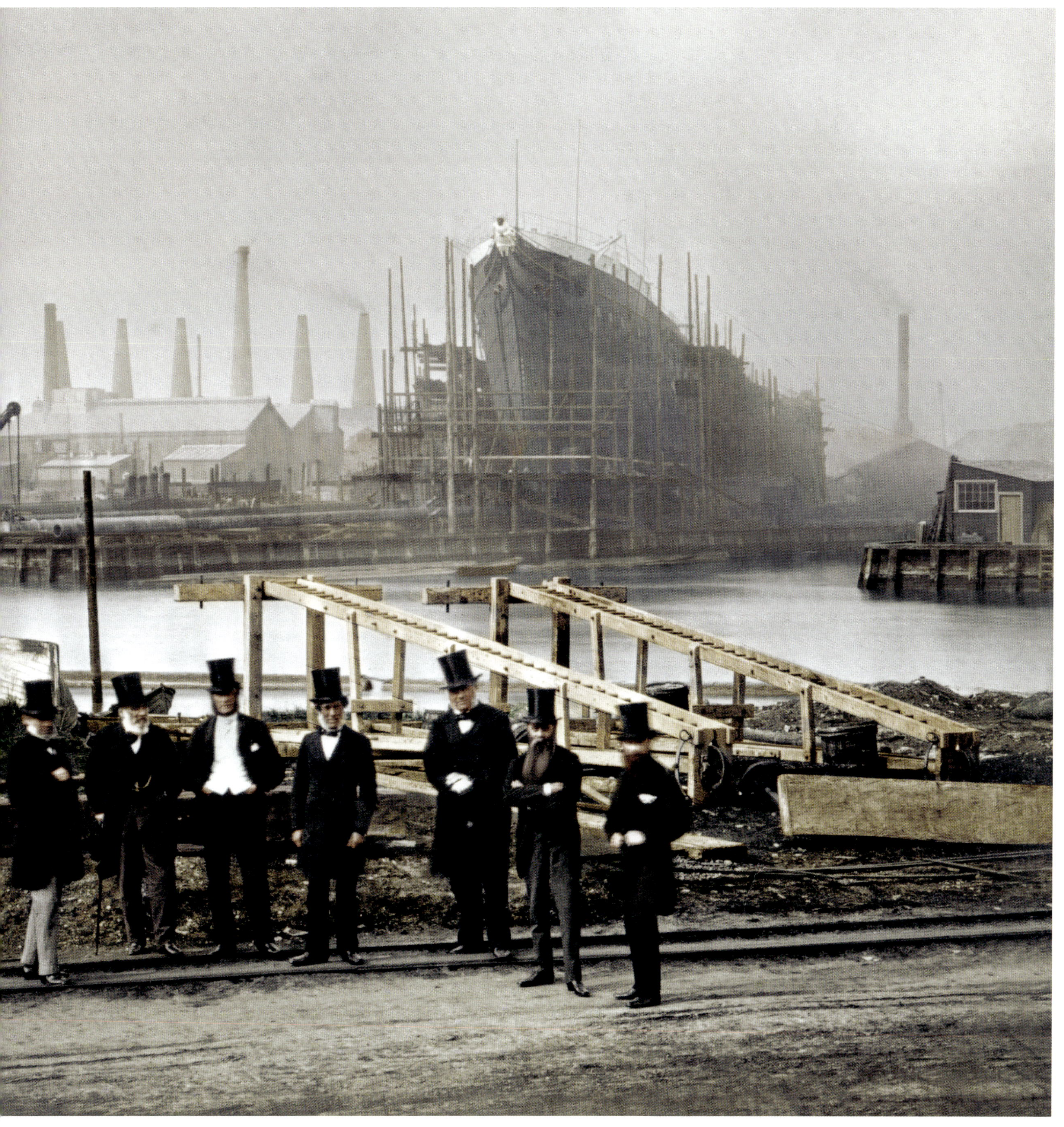

1860s

1864: Jesse James

USA
(St Louis Taylor Copying Co. / Library of Congress)

Outlaw Jesse James was around seventeen when this portrait was taken towards the latter part of the American Civil War. At this time, Jesse and his brother Frank had joined the confederate guerrilla outfit led by 'Bloody Bill' Anderson. All three were participants in the Centralia Massacre, during which their group killed or wounded more than twenty Union troops, all unarmed.

After the war, James gained fame and notoriety as a bank, train and coach robber in the James-Younger gang. Killed by Robert Ford, a member of his own gang, in 1882, Jesse and his gang became popular heroes in 'Dime' novels, published even when he was alive.

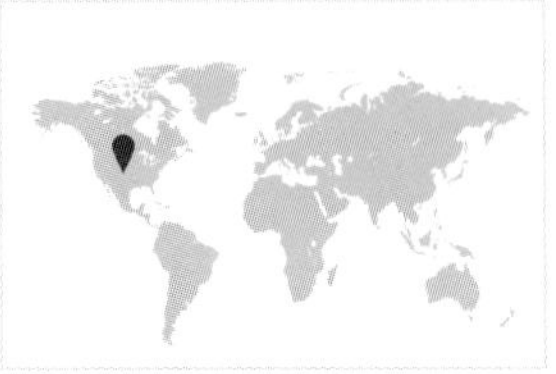

'Dear Sir: I and my brother Frank are charged with the crime of killing the cashier and robbing the bank at Gallatin, Mo., Dec. 7th, 1869. When I think I can get a fair trial, I will surrender myself to the civil authorities of Missouri. But I never will surrender to be mobbed by a set of bloodthirsty poltroons. It is true that during the war I was a Confederate soldier, and fought under the black flag, but since then I have lived a peaceable citizen, and obeyed the laws of the United States to the best of my knowledge.

Respectfully,
Jesse W. James'

Letter to the *Liberty Tribune* from Jesse James, 24 June 1870

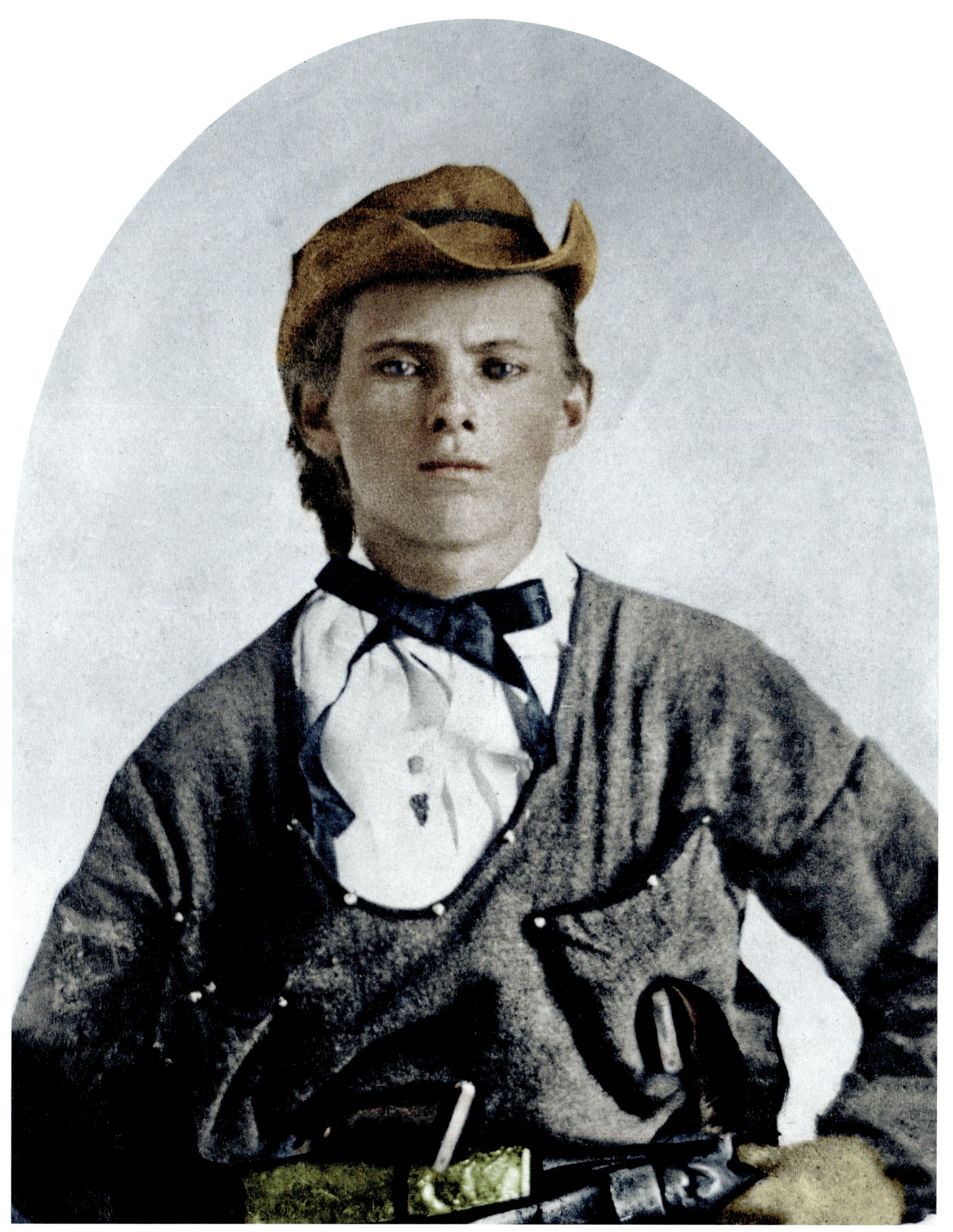

c. 1864: **An unidentified African-American soldier in Union uniform with wife and two daughters, Maryland**
Maryland, USA
(Library of Congress)

This soldier is believed to be Sergeant Samuel Smith, together with his wife Molle, and daughters Mary and Maggie. Smith served as a soldier in the 119th US Colored Infantry, enlisting at Camp Nelson, Kentucky.

Formed during the American Civil War, after Lincoln's Emancipation Proclamation came into effect on 1 January 1863, the 175 regiments of the United States Colored Troops (USCT) were largely but not exclusively formed of African-American soldiers. In total, around 180,000 free African Americans together with Native Americans, Asian Americans and Pacific Island Americans were enrolled in the USCT – around one-tenth of the Union force.

Almost 2,700 were killed in combat, but that is a figure dwarfed by a total of 68,000 killed chiefly by disease – the largest cause of death in the war. The regiments were led by white officers.

1860s

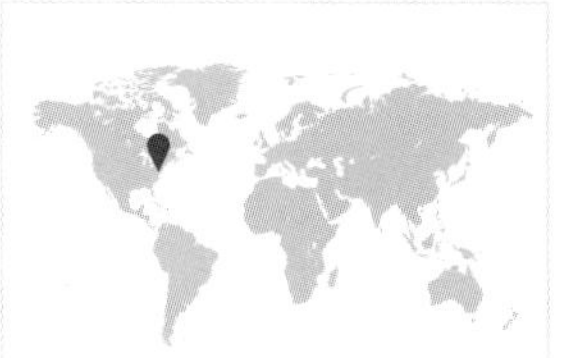

'THE NEGRO TROOPS ENTER CHARLESTON.

The first national soldiers that landed in Charleston in the capacity of masters of the rebel city were the South Carolina Negroes (thank God!) of the Twenty-first United States Colored Troops. There was also a detachment of gallant Massachusetts troops to demonstrate on Southern soil the splendid fighting qualities of the colored race.'

Daily Dispatch, Richmond, Virginia, 7 March 1865

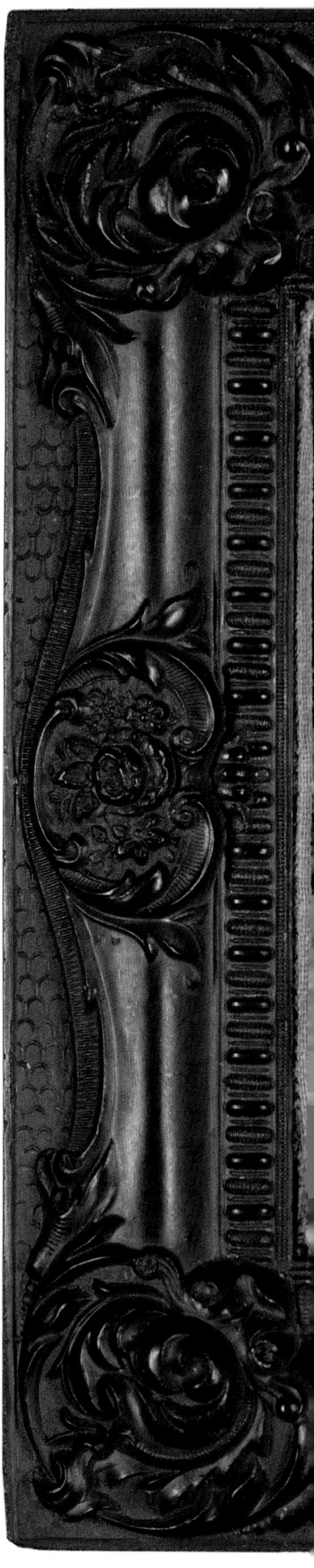

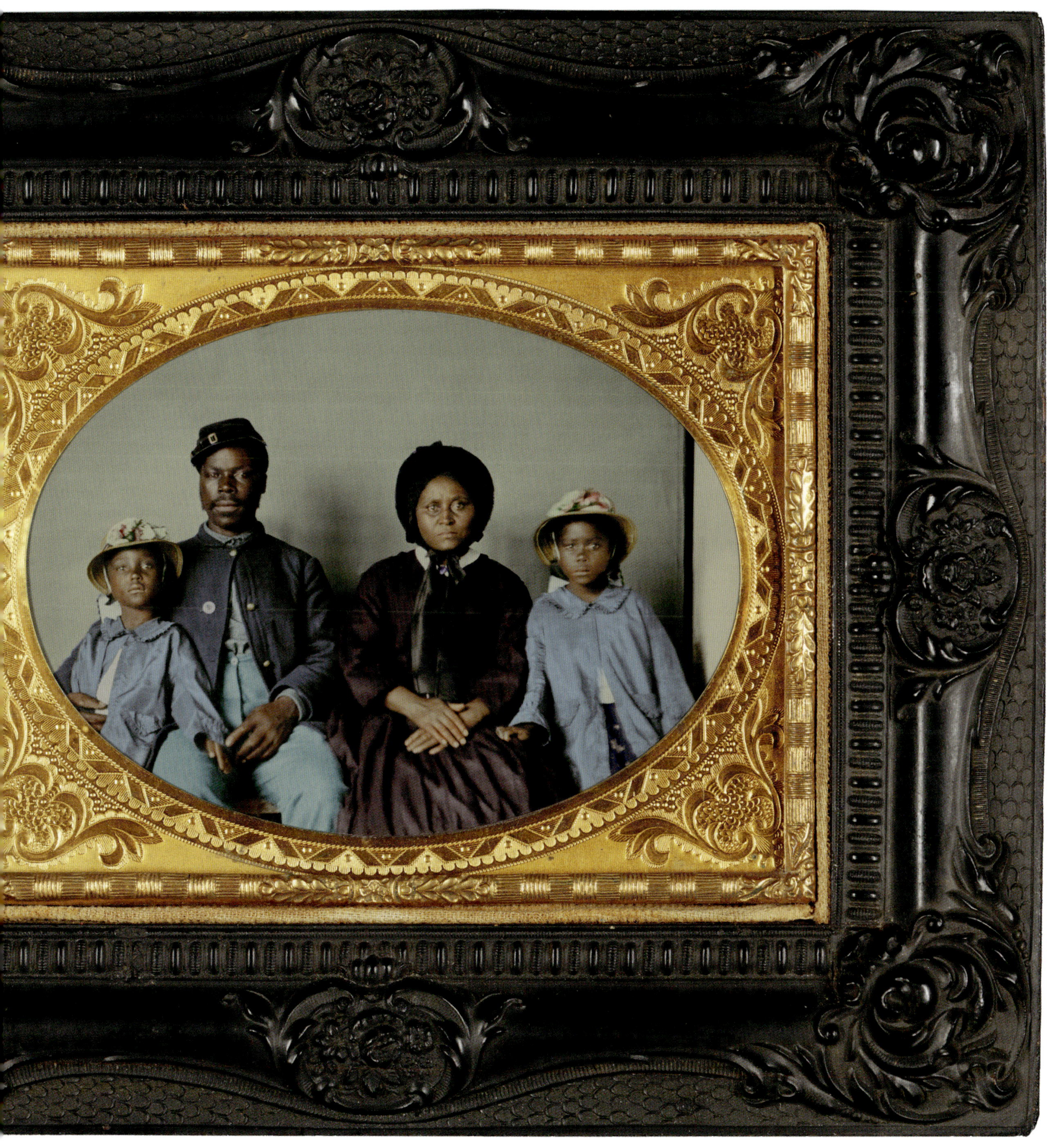

1864: **A Union soldier guards a slave auction house on Whitehall Street, Atlanta**

Atlanta, Georgia, USA
(George N. Barnard / Library of Congress)

It is likely that this photograph of an African-American soldier guarding Thomas Frazer and Company slave auction house at 8 Whitehall Street, Atlanta is both staged and an overt political expression on the part of George N. Barnard, official army photographer for General William Tecumseh Sherman during the American Civil War.

General Sherman believed African Americans were not suitable to fight as troops. But not only has Barnard placed an African American on guard as a soldier, he has also depicted the soldier reading.

Atlanta, the 'Gate City of the South', was a significant transport and supplies city during the American Civil War, and the fall of Atlanta to Sherman's Union forces in 1864 was a pivotal moment in the war.

In 1859, Frank Geutebruck had graduated as a surgeon from Marburg University in his native Germany. The following year, Geutebruck travelled to America to set up his practice in Atlanta – only for war to be declared in 1861. His surgery failed, and Geutebruck turned to selling tobacco.

1860s

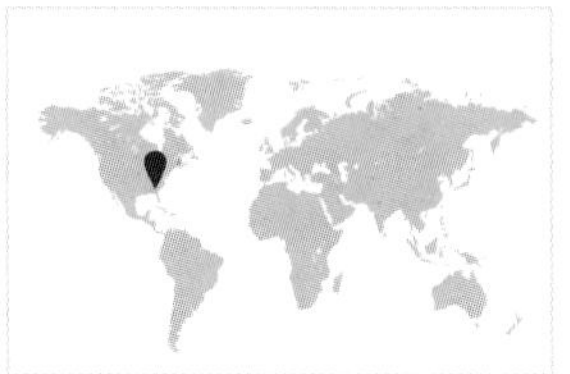

'The expression on the faces of all who stepped on the block was always the same, and told of more anguish than it is in the power of words to express. Blighted homes, crushed hopes and broken hearts, was the sad story to be read in all the anxious faces. Some of them regarded the sale with perfect indifference, never making a motion, save to turn from one side to the other at the word of the dapper Mr. Bryan, that all the crowd might have a fair view of their proportions, and then, when the sale was accomplished, stepped down from the block without caring to cast even a look at the buyer, who now held all their happiness in his hands.'

Journalist Q. K. Philander Doesticks, recounting a slave auction, 3 March 1859

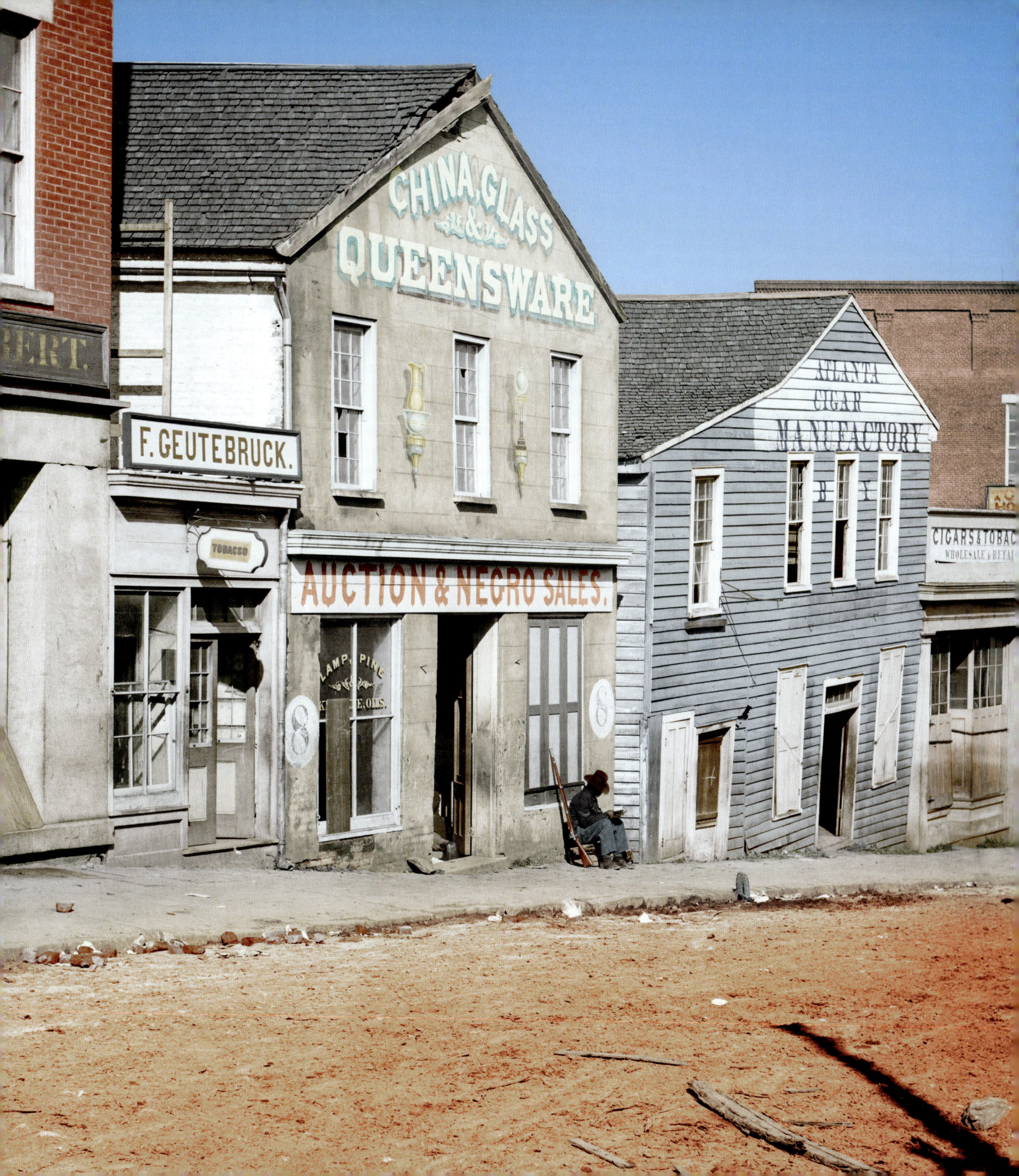

CHINA, GLASS & QUEENSWARE
F. GEUTEBRUCK.
TOBACCO
AUCTION & NEGRO SALES.
ATLANTA CIGAR MANUFACTORY

1860s

1863: Confederate prisoners at Seminary Ridge during the Battle of Gettysburg, Pennsylvania

Gettysburg, Pennyslvania
(Unknown / Library of Congress)

Until 1863, both sides in the American Civil War of 1861–1865 used a parole system for prisoners. A captured soldier vowed not to fight until he had been exchanged for a soldier fighting for the opposition. But in 1863, when this picture was taken, the parole system proved untenable, because Confederate authorities would not recognise a black prisoner as equal to a white prisoner. The direct result was that the number of troops being held in prisons increased massively, on both sides.

Just over 400,000 soldiers were captured and placed in prison camps during the American Civil War. One in ten of all deaths during the war occurred in a prison camp – a total of more than 55,000 men lost their lives incarcerated.

'For many weeks past, and long before the battle of Gettysburg, there were from four to five thousand Confederate prisoners confined in Fort Delaware. That fort is now crowded to its utmost capacity with a weltering mass of human beings, our own gallant Confederate soldiers, the sons and the brothers of our people, the stay and the pride of thousands of Southern families. Fort Delaware is the most unwholesome of their many dungeons.'

Richmond Enquirer, Virginia, 28 July 1863

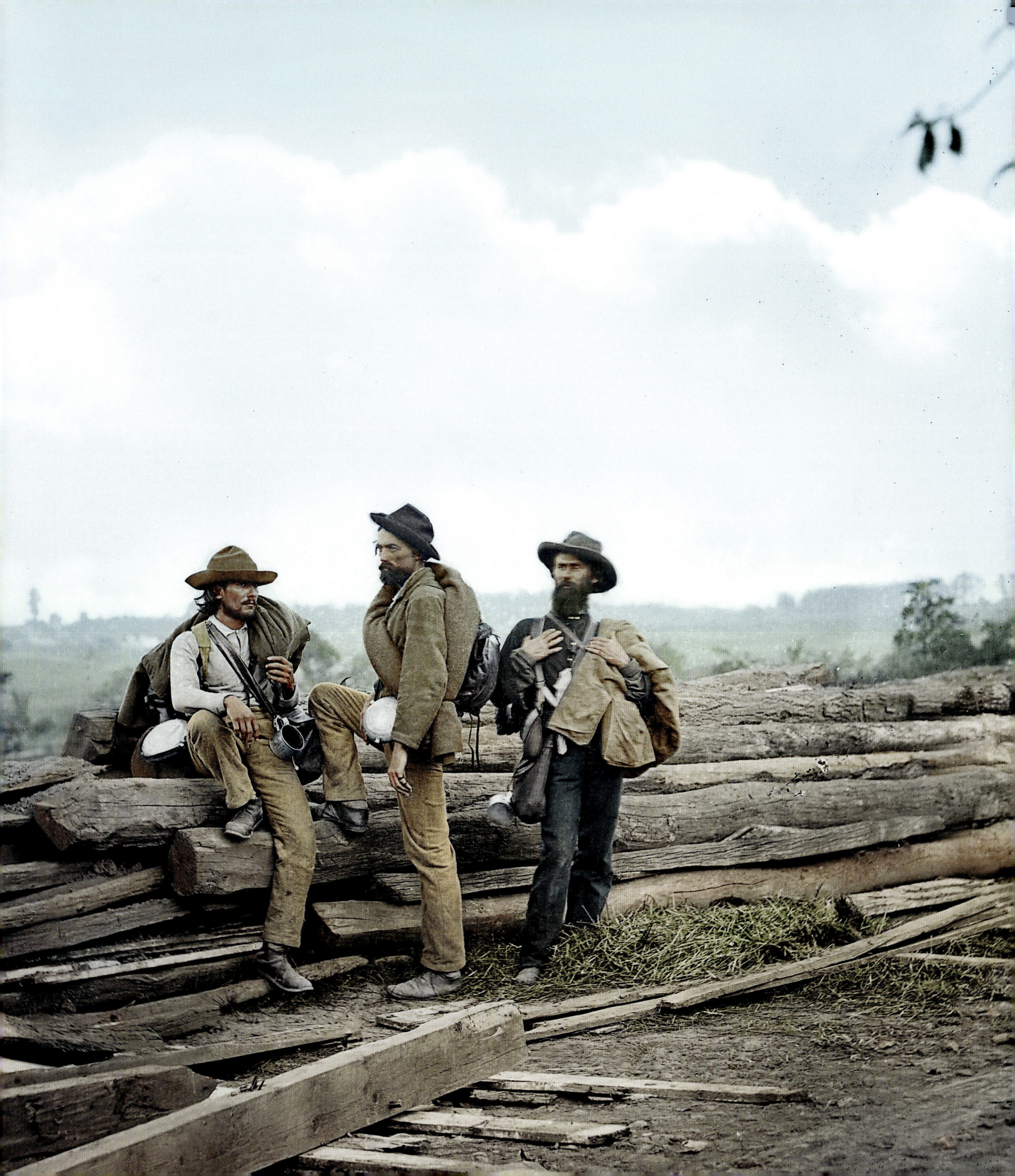

1850s

c. **1858:** Veterans of the Napoleonic Wars

Paris, France
(Anne S. K. Brown Military Collection, Brown University Library)

Napoléon Bonaparte died on 5 May 1821, but the regard in which he was held by men who had fought in his Grand Armée lived on. To commemorate their leader, surviving soldiers – known as the 'débris de la Grande Armée' – marched each 5 May to Paris's Vendôme column, erected in 1810 in honour of Napoléon's victory at Austerlitz.

In August 1857, every surviving veteran was issued with the Saint Helena medal at the command of Napoléon III. These photographs (*right* and *overleaf*), taken at the reunion the following year, show two of the men who had fought alongside Napoléon. Both wear the Saint Helena medal, and both are in their original uniforms and insignia – the only occasion on which Napoleonic soldiers are known to have been photographed in their original regalia.

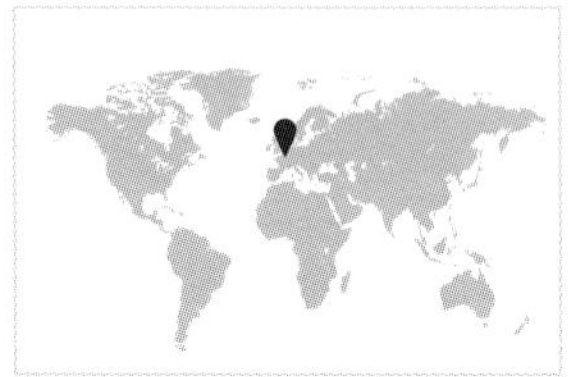

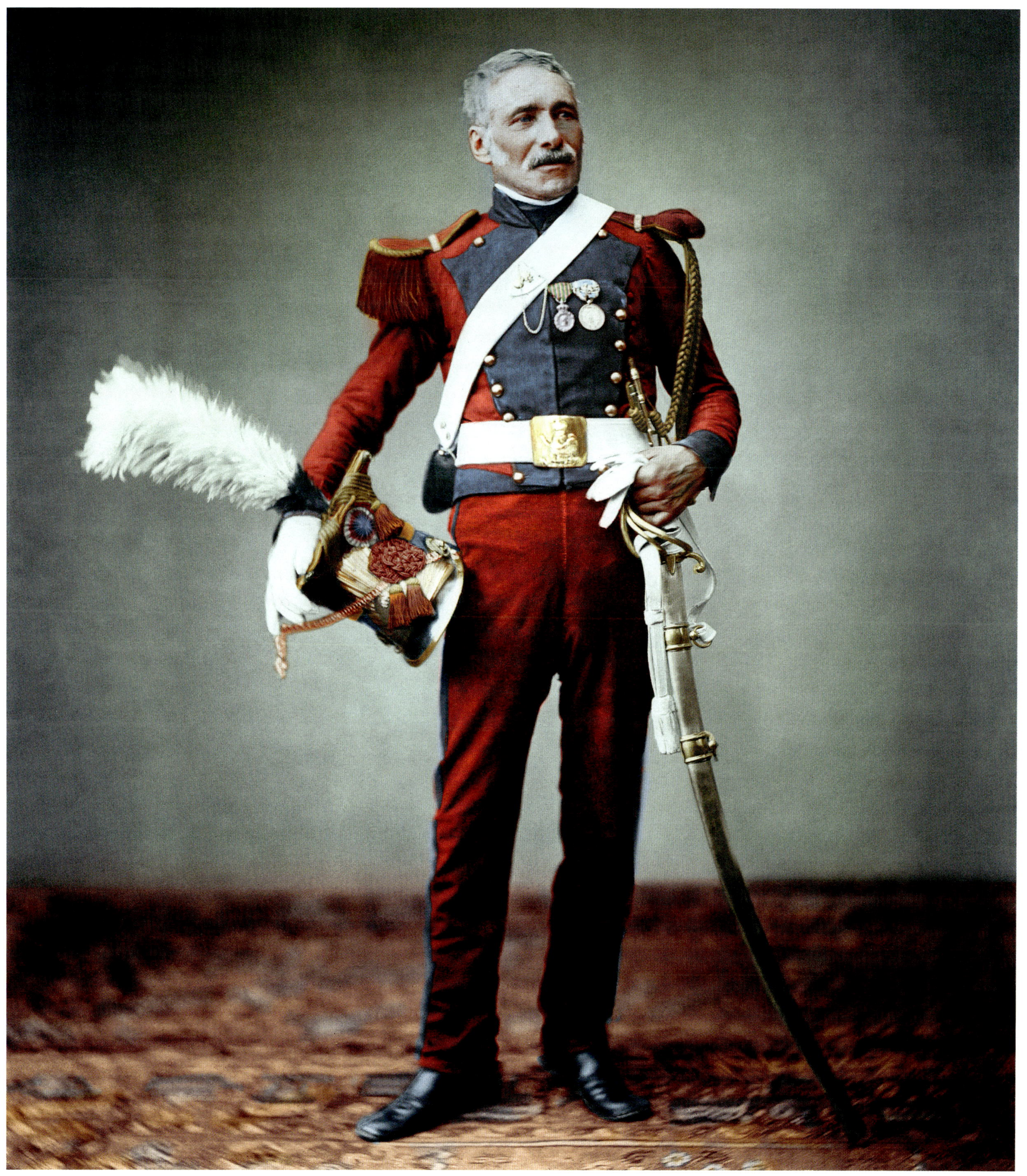

1850s

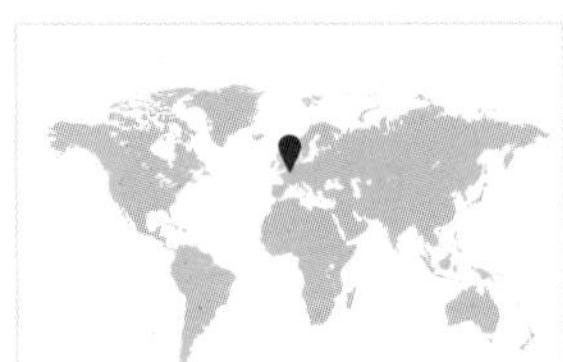

'I do not pretend to be an historical character; but I was long near a man who has been the object of base misrepresentation, and I commanded brave troops whose services have been disowned. The former overwhelmed me with favours; the latter would have laid down their lives for me: these things I cannot forget.'

Memoirs of General Rapp,
First Aide-de-Camp to Napoléon, 1823

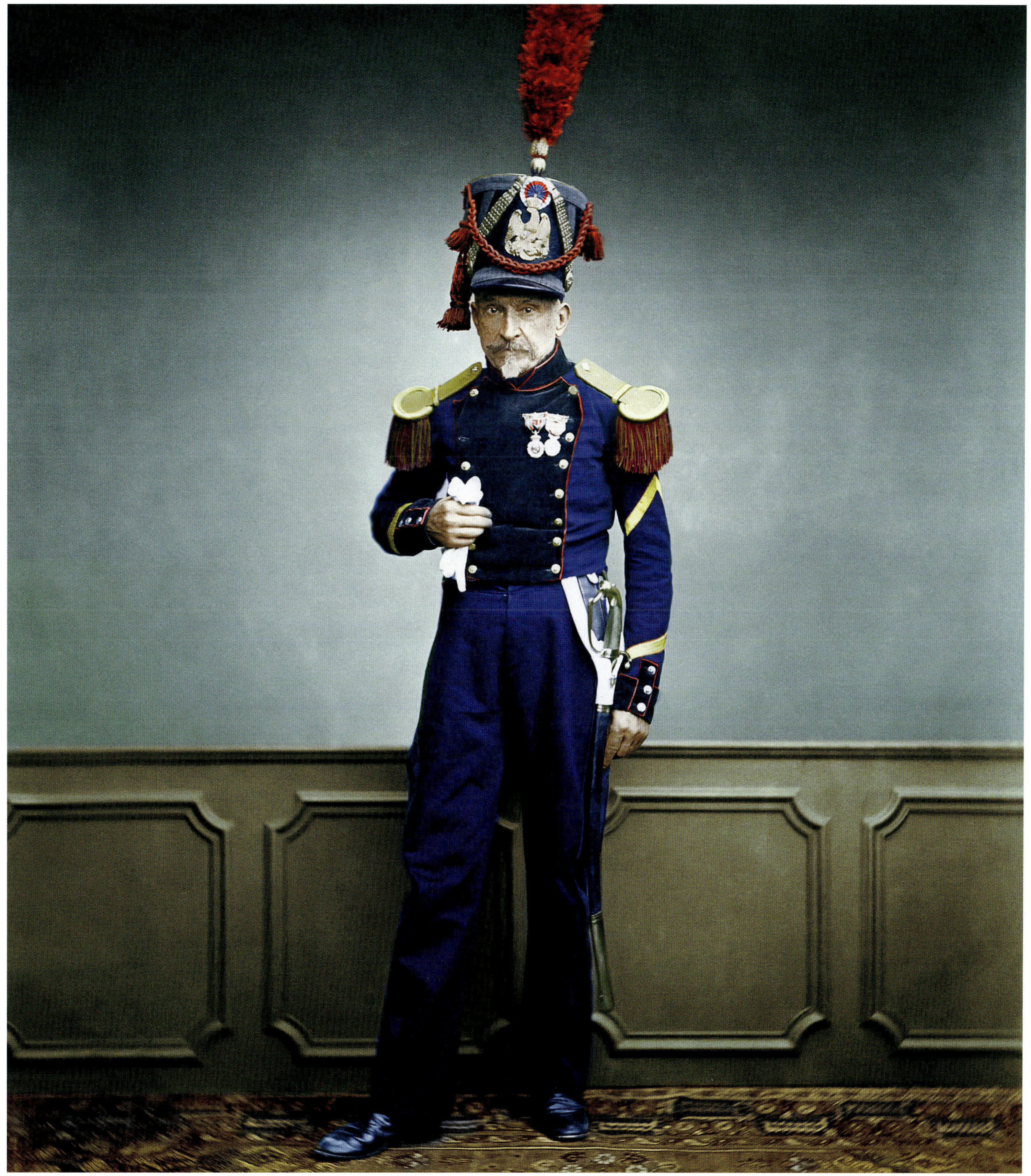

1850s

1858: Alice Lidell, the 'real' Alice in Wonderland, aged six

Christ Church College, Oxford, UK
(Charles Dodgson / National Media Museum / Science & Society Picture Library / Getty)

Six-year-old Alice Liddell is photographed here by Charles Dodgson, aka Lewis Carroll. Around four years later, on 4 July, 1862, Dodgson made up a story to entertain Alice and two of her sisters while boating from Oxford to nearby Godstow. Dodgson developed the story, and in 1865 it was published as *Alice's Adventures in Wonderland*.

Dodgson, a lecturer in mathematics at Christ Church College, Oxford, had befriended Alice and her family when her father, Henry Liddell, became Dean of Christ Church. Many of Dodgson's photographs, like this one, were taken in the grounds of Christ Church.

Alice Liddell married a wealthy cricketer and became a member of high society. She had three sons, two of whom were killed in the First World War. Alice died, aged eighty, in 1932.

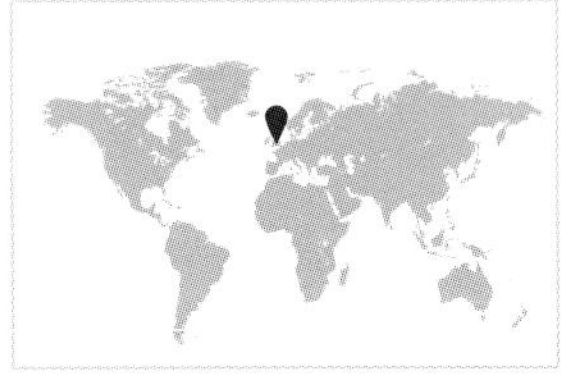

'The beginning of Alice was told one summer afternoon when the sun was so burning that we had landed in the meadows down the river, deserting the boat to take refuge in the only bit of shade to be found, which was under a new-made hayrick. Sometimes to tease us – and perhaps being really tired – Mr Dodgson would stop suddenly and say, "And that's all till next time," and pretend to go to sleep, to our great dismay.'

Alice Lidell

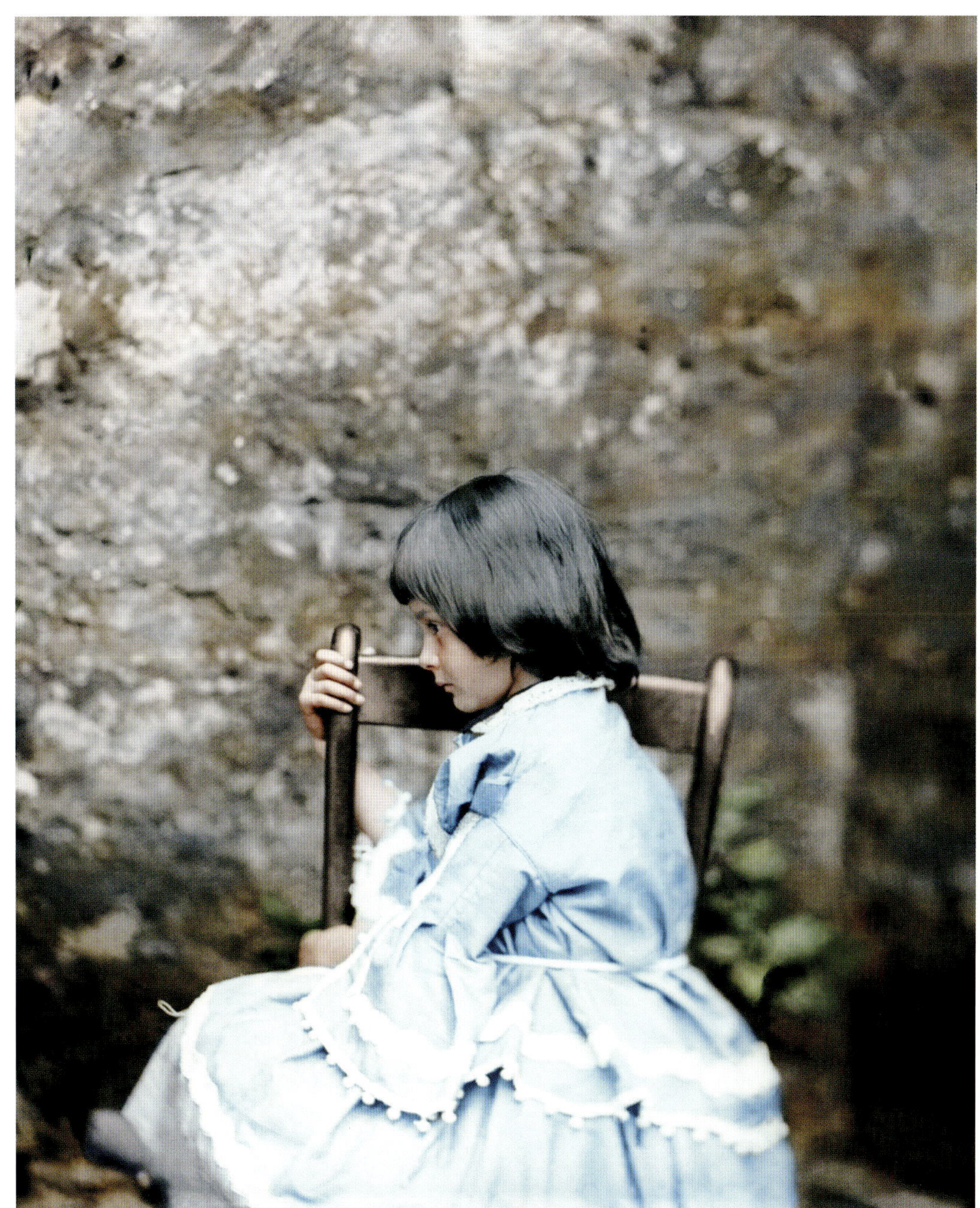

1850s

1855: General Sir George de Lacy Evans, Commander of the British Army 2nd Division during the Crimean War

Crimea, Russia
(Roger Fenton / Library of Congress)

The Crimean War – a conflict from 1853 to 1856 between the Russian Empire, and an alliance of Britain, France and Sardinia – was the first major war to be documented on camera. Roger Fenton, funded by the British government, spent three and a half months photographing participants in the conflict during 1855.

British Army General Sir George de Lacy Evans GCB (1787–1870) fought in four of the United Kingdom's wars of the nineteenth century. Responsible for the burning of the US Senate and House of Representatives chambers in the Capitol Building during the Burning of Washington, he was, aged twenty-eight, present at the Battle of Waterloo.

Evans' distinctive red-and-gold jacket is a British Army Lieutenant-General's coat. His three ribboned medals are (*left to right*): the Military General Service Medal; a Naval General Service Medal for his part in the War of 1812; a Naval General Service Medal for his service at Waterloo. The two larger medals are the Spanish Order of Saint Ferdinand (accompanied by the red) and the Spanish Order of Charles III, which Evans received for commanding the British Legion during the First Carlist War of the 1830s, and for which he was also knighted.

Evans is photographed in his late sixties by Fenton during the Crimean War. Evans had come out of public office to lead the 2nd Division of the British Army.

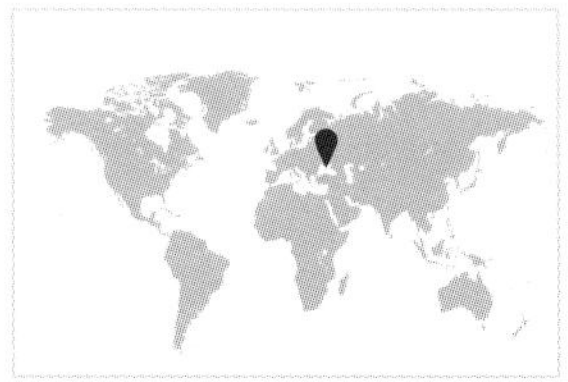

'Tall and thin, with very sallow complexion, and jet black hair and whiskers, one might almost have mistaken him for an Italian assassin. His speech was dull and but ill adapted to his audience.'

Le Marchant, of de Lacy Evans, 1830s

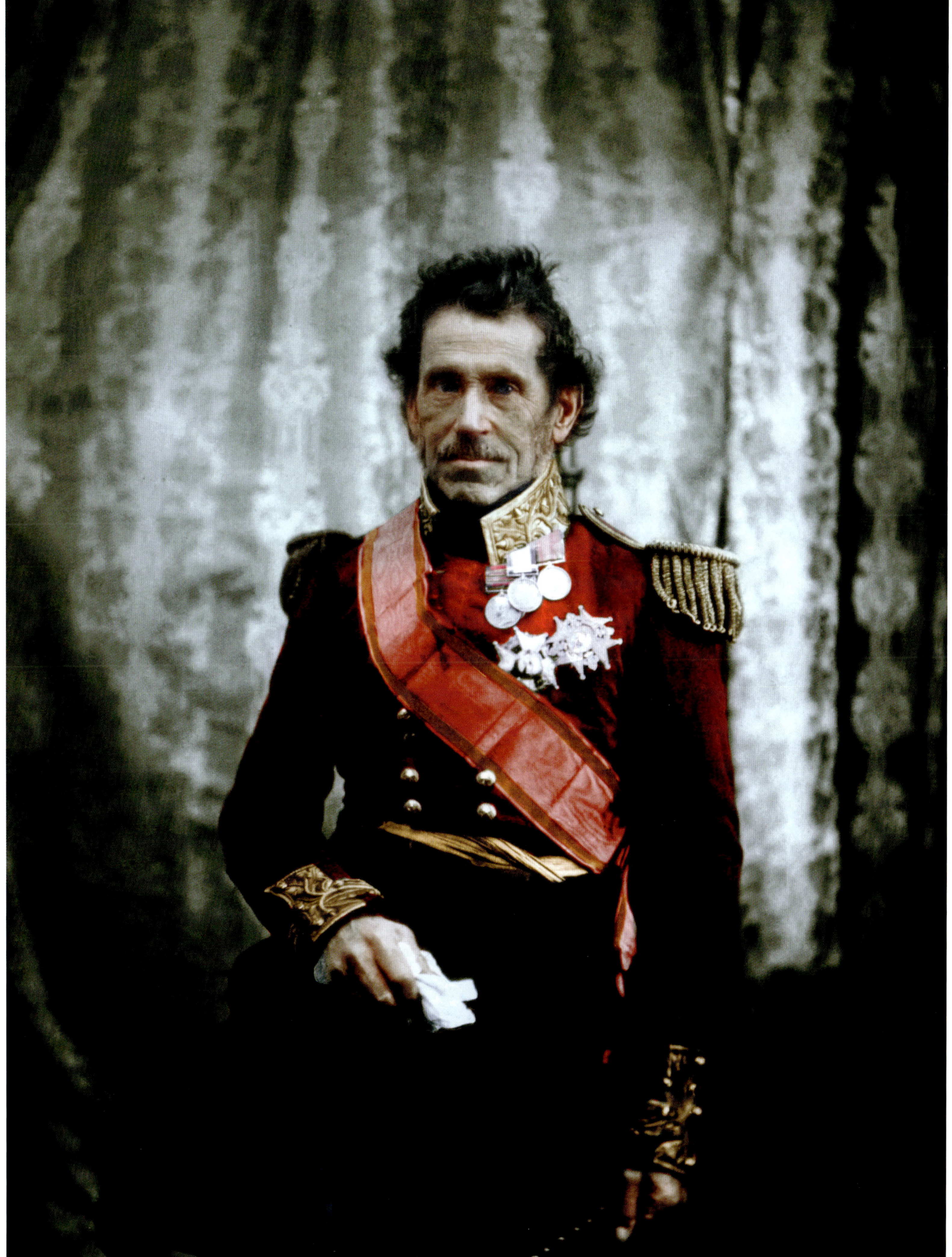

1850s

c. 1850s: Californian miners have a group portrait

California, USA
(California Historical Society)

In January 1848, James W. Marshall, a foreman building a mill for one James Sutter of Coloma, California, found shiny metal in part of the mill stream. With that discovery, Marshall triggered a gold rush, bringing some 300,000 people from across the globe to California between late 1848 and into 1849 and beyond – the 'Forty-Niners'.

One direct result of the Rush was the growth of San Francisco. In 1846, it was a very small enclave of 200 people. By 1852, its population was around 36,000. A total of 40,000 people came into San Francisco in 1849 alone, of which only 700 were women.

Taken around a year after the start of the California Gold Rush, this group portrait shows nine 'Forty-Niners'. One holds the handle of a shovel, another what is likely to be the handle of a pick, and another some kind of document. Judging by their smartly brushed hair, the good repair of their clothing and their confident expressions, it is possible they have yet to embark on their mining careers. Around half of all miners made a modest profit.

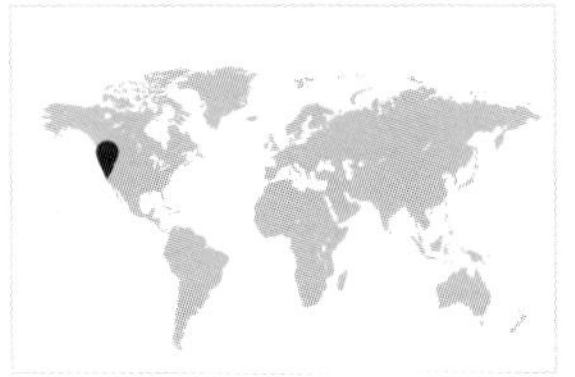

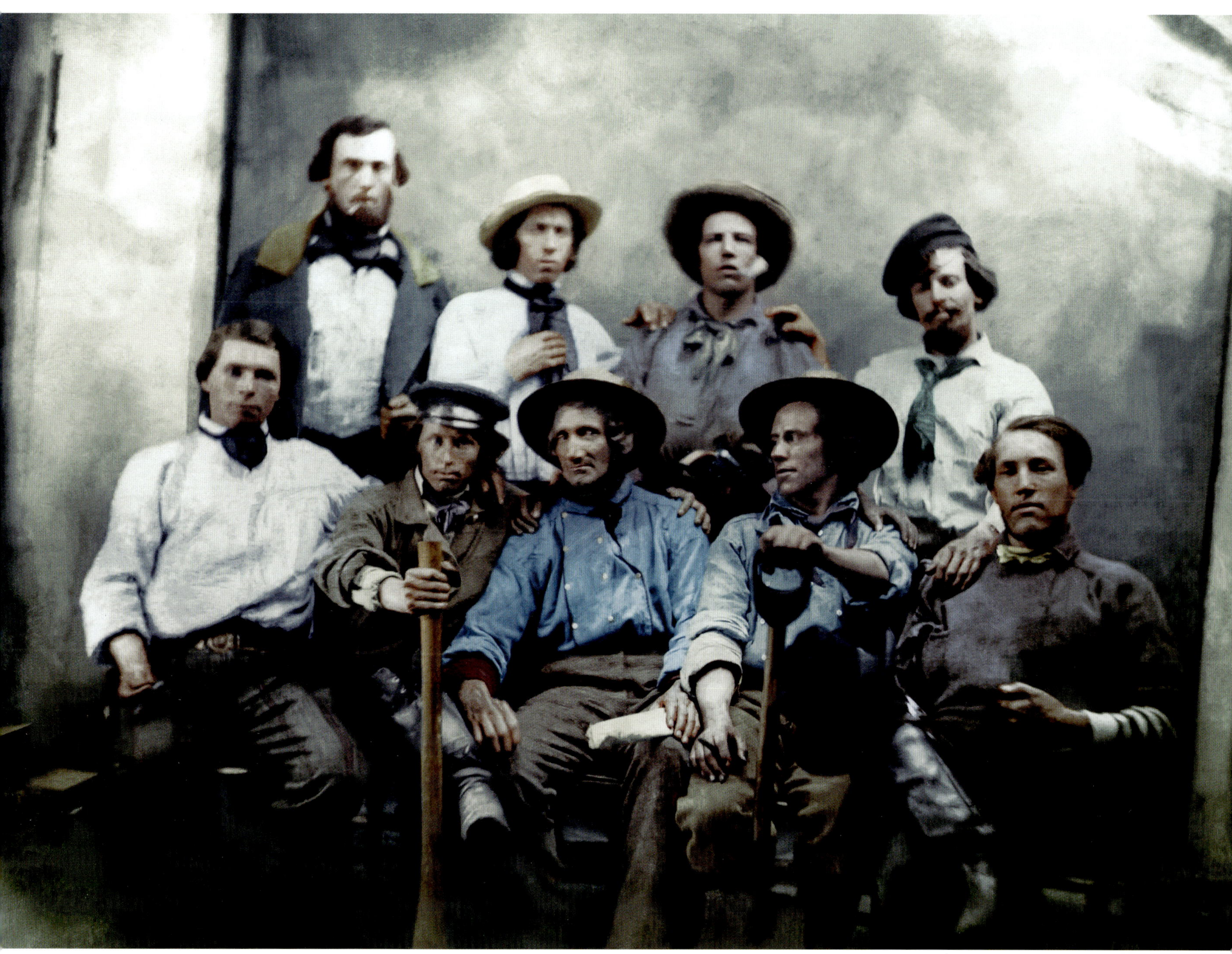

‘Many, very many, that come here meet with bad success & thousands will leave their bones here. Others will lose their health, contract diseases that they will carry to their graves with them. Some will have to beg their way home, & probably one half that come here will never make enough to carry them back. But this does not alter the fact about the gold being plenty here, but shows what a poor frail being man is, how liable to disappointments, disease & death.’

A letter from a gold miner, Placerville, California, March 1850

1846: **A portrait of Abraham Lincoln, without a beard, aged thirty-seven**

Springfield, Illinois, USA
(Nicholas Shepherd / Library of Congress)

It would be another fourteen years before Abraham Lincoln became the 16th President of the United States. Here, in an image by law student Nicholas Shepherd, Lincoln is photographed serving as a member of the US House of Representatives, just before he resumed his legal practice in Springfield, Illinois.

Notably, Lincoln is clean-shaven. He grew his whiskers in 1860 as a direct response to a letter from an eleven-year-old girl, Grace Bedell, who believed Lincoln's lack of beard was impeding his political career.

1840s

'You would look a great deal better for your face is so thin. All the ladies like whiskers and they would tease their husbands to vote for you and then you would be President.'

From Grace Bedell's letter to Abraham Lincoln, 15 October 1860

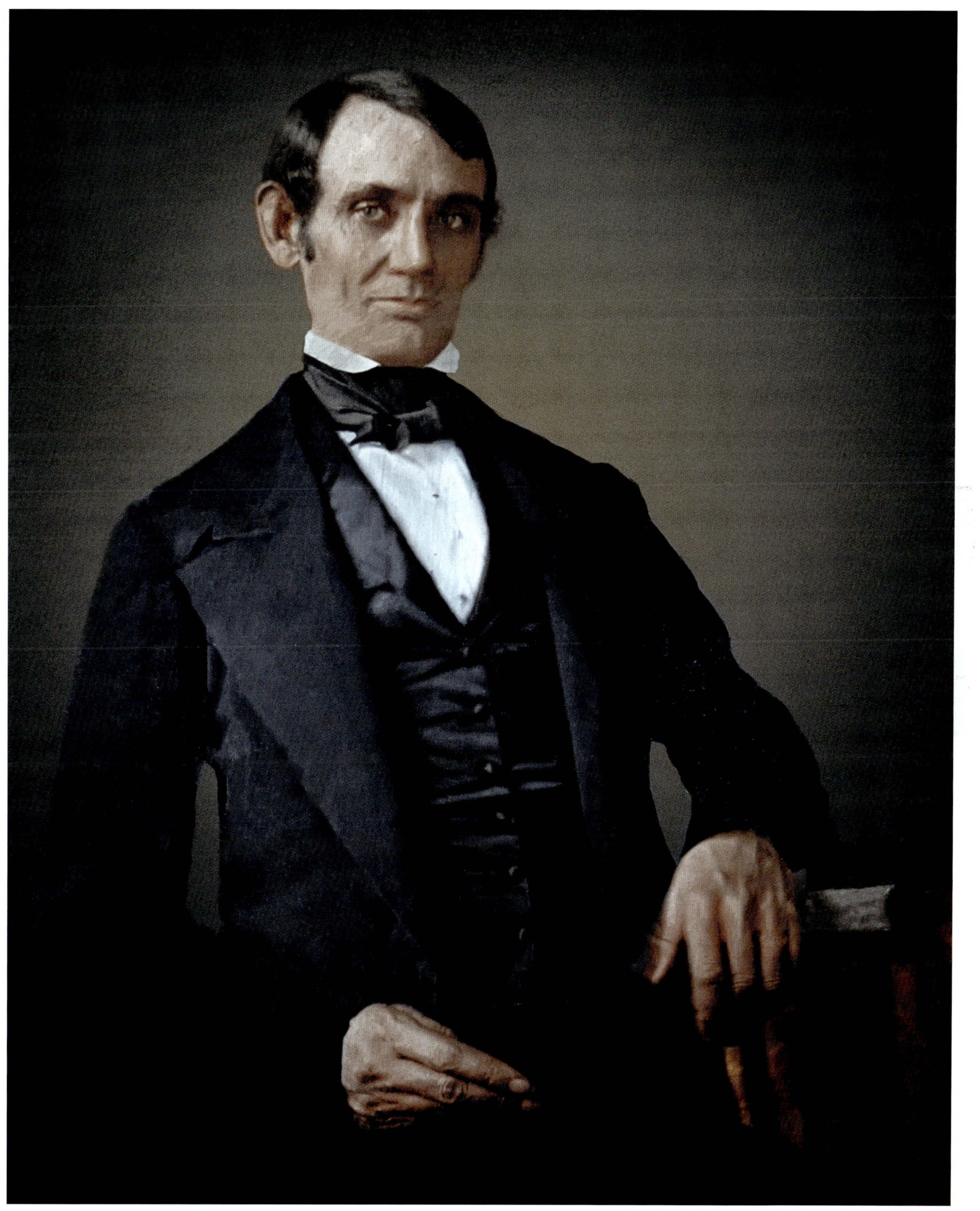

'After the statue of Nelson was raised, it appeared as if it would fall, having nothing to counter-balance the upper, rather overhanging appearance of the body on the left side, so that they were obliged to add another coil of carved cable to the statue.'

George Scharf senior, illustrator, 1843

1844: Construction of Nelson's Column, Trafalgar Square, London

Trafalgar Square, London, UK
(Henry Fox Talbot / Science & Society Picture Library / Getty)

Nelson's Column in London's Trafalgar Square was built to honour the British Admiral Horatio Nelson, killed in 1805 at the Battle of Trafalgar. The scene shown here seems to suggest industrious activity around the building works. However, when Talbot took this photograph, the building work had actually been halted while the government took over the project from the building committee, whose funds had run out.

Fox Talbot invented the Calotype process for making photographs, between 1835 and 1839. Using his revolutionary method, any number of prints could be made of a single image from the Calotype negative, unlike the Daguerreotype, which could not be reproduced at the time.

1840s

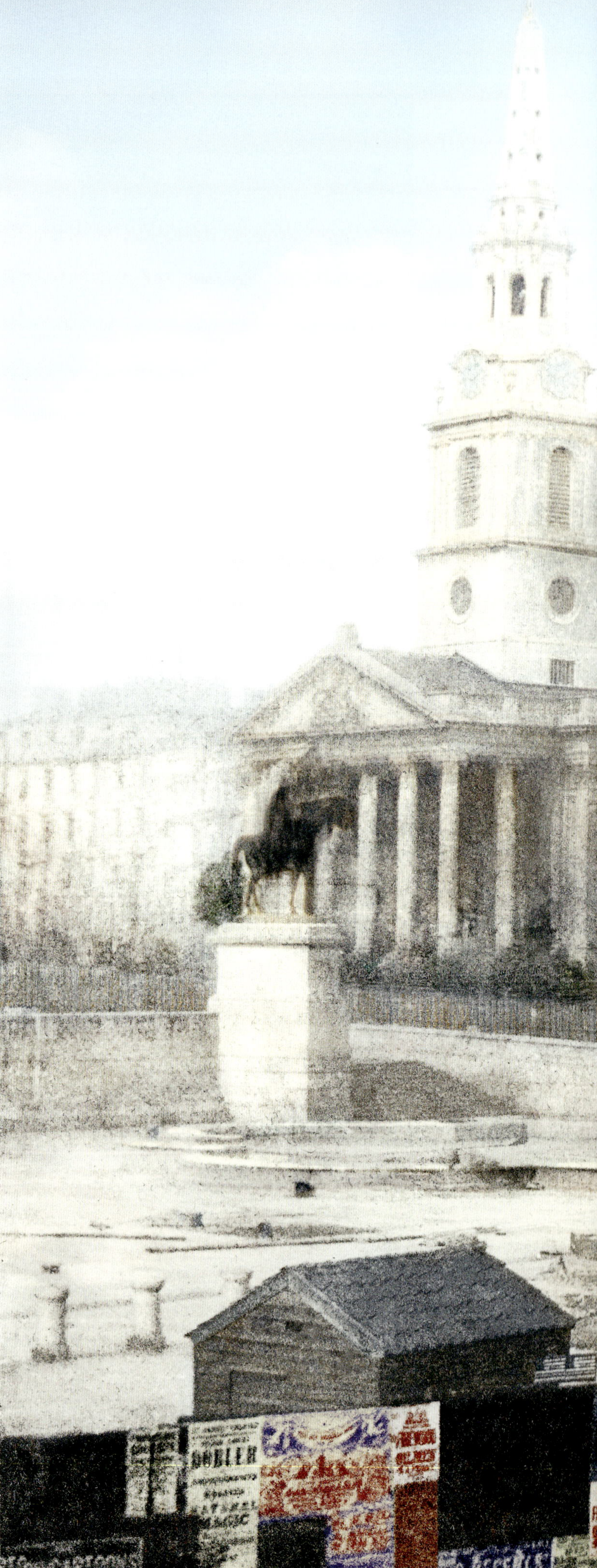

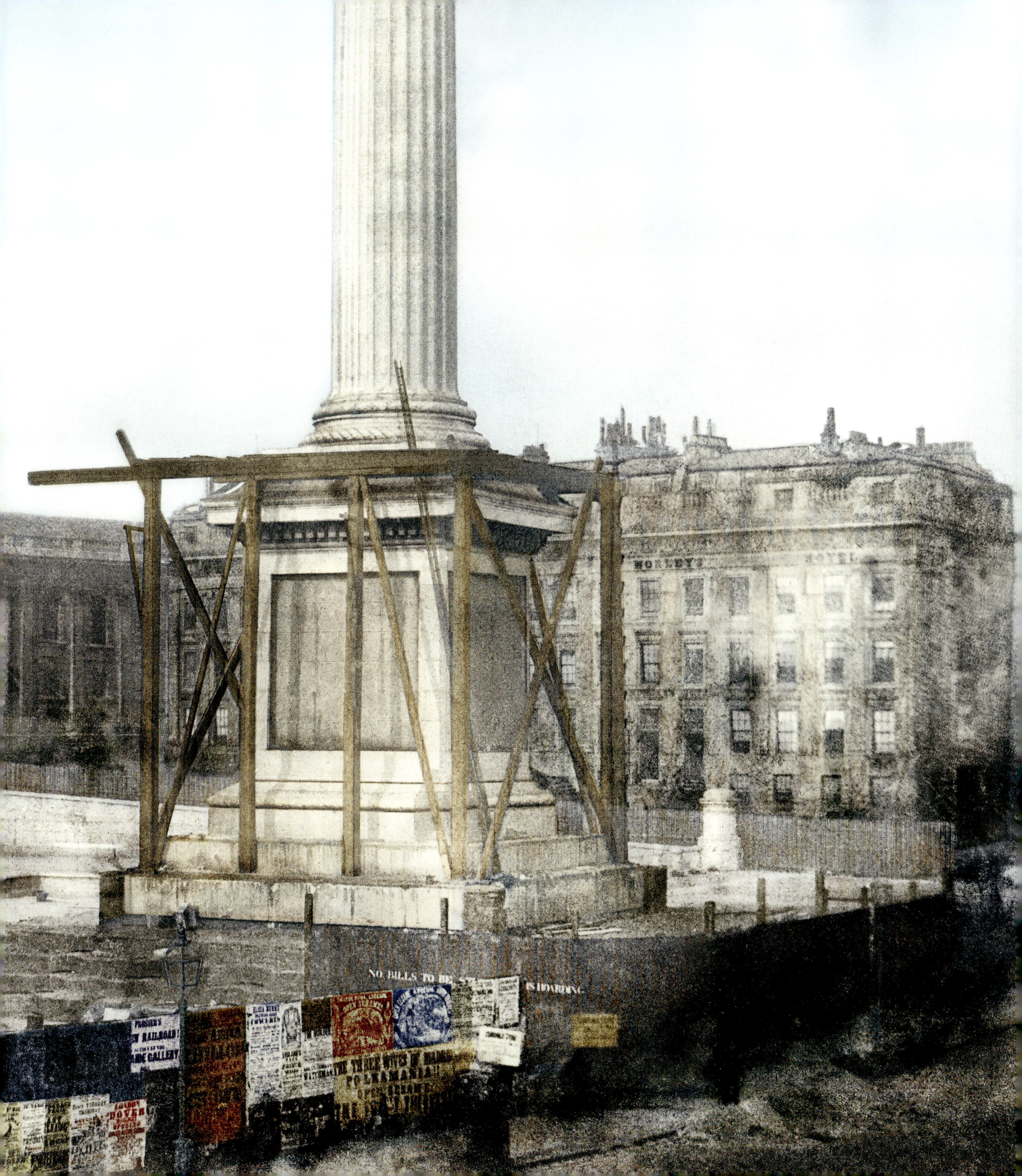
MORLEY'S
NO BILLS TO BE
IS HOARDING
RAILROAD!
GALLERY
DOVER

1839: The first photographic self-portrait

176 Chestnut Street, Philadelphia, USA (Robert Cornelius / Library of Congress)

Robert Cornelius was thirty when he took this striking Daguerreotype photograph in the rear of his father's shop at 176 Chestnut Street, Philadelphia. The exposure time meant Cornelius needed to remain static for around five minutes before replacing the lens cap. When he did so, he had created what is now widely believed to be the first photographic self-portrait.

At his retirement at the age of sixty-eight in 1877, Cornelius had created a thriving business. But not in photography – although he did create a portraiture business, he abandoned it after two years and returned to his father's lamp company, steering it to become America's biggest lighting business.

1830s

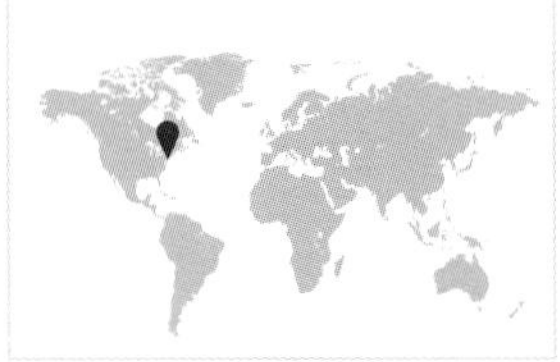

'You will notice the figure is not in the centre of the plate. The reason for it is, I was alone, and ran in front of the camera after preparing it for the picture, and I could not know until the picture was taken that I was not in the centre.

I am fully of the impression that I was the first to obtain a likeness of the human face.'

Robert Cornelius,
American Journal of Photography

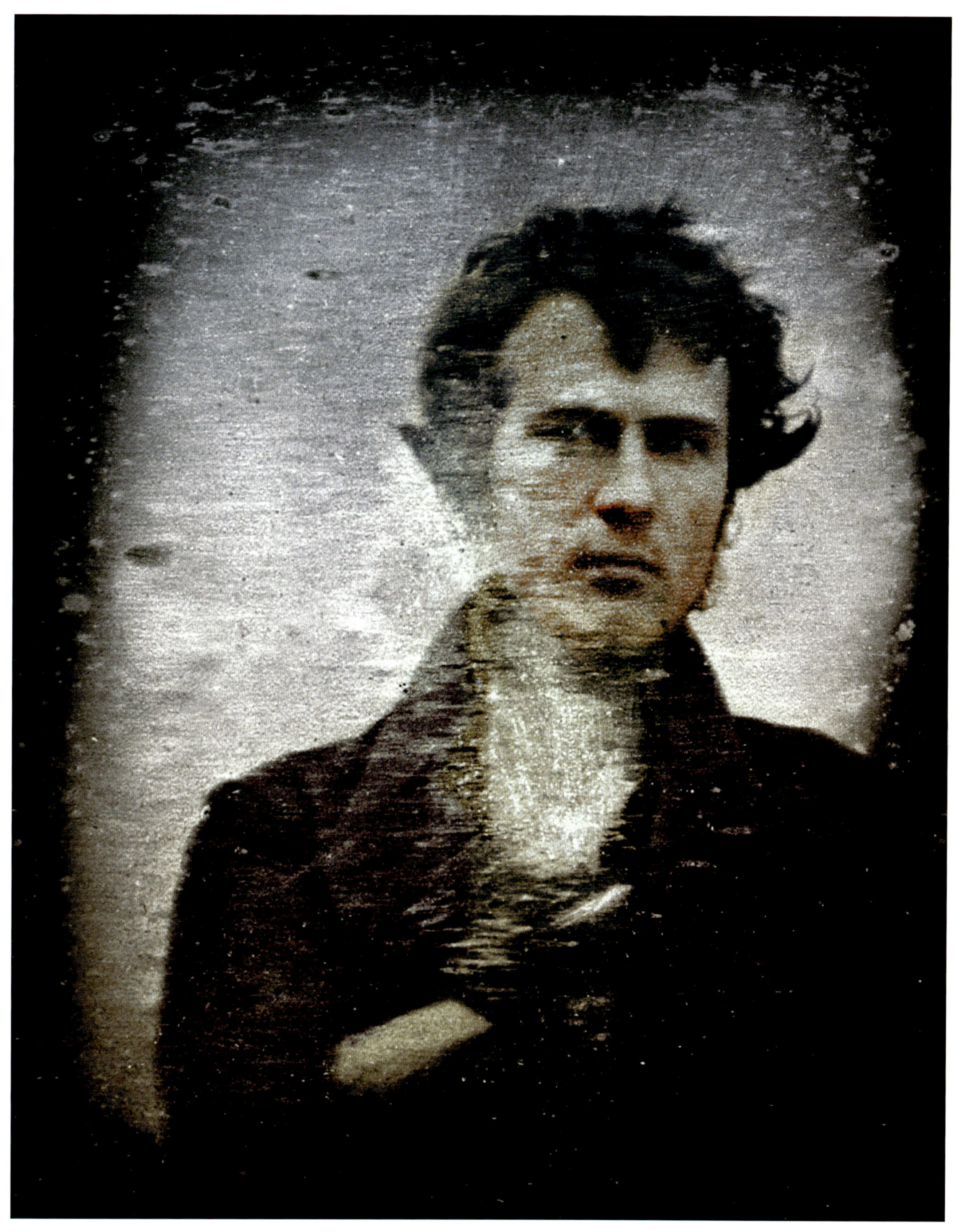

Building the time machine

I hope you enjoyed your trip.

Digital photo colourisation is a modern incarnation of a very old craft. The first hand-tinted photographs were created through the careful application of coloured powder, fixed in place by heat. Today, we use Adobe Photoshop.

Broadly speaking, the process I employed for each of the photographs in *The Paper Time Machine* followed the same set pathway. Stage one was to carry out a thorough appraisal of the level of damage that the photograph had sustained across time. This damage could be anything from a cracked glass plate, as was the case with the photograph of the hanging of the Lincoln conspirators (p. 178), to extensive destruction by mould, as seen on the photograph of daredevil Jammie Reynolds (p. 88).

Stage two was to implement an intensive digital clean and restoration, in order to ensure that the foundational black-and-white information underneath the later colour could be as close to its original state as possible.

Following this, stage three was to block-in the colour – a process that is simultaneously meditative and overwhelming in its detail. Blocking-in colour requires one to digitally 'paint' layers of colour onto the original photograph. How many layers? In some instances, thousands. I could expect a single face typically to have around fourteen or fifteen separate layers of colour, simply in order to reflect the complex tones of skin. You can imagine how quickly the number of layers grows exponentially.

Alongside the colour-blocking, my team and I carried out research. We catalogued all possible colour references, asking ourselves oblique questions about the photographs and eliminating guesswork as much as possible. We contacted all manner of experts in everything from obscure 1930s soda manufacturers to Napoleonic uniform livery. The results were dozens upon dozens of colour illustrations and pages upon pages of hyper-specific descriptions.

When that research had been collated and prepared, stage four was to use it all to transform, incrementally, the garishly coloured, blocked-in colour layers. Each layer of many thousands was adjusted to mirror the colour and lighting references – hundreds of decisions based on my working knowledge of lighting, perspective, atmosphere and particular photographic processes.

For me, this was the magical part of the work – witnessing the way colour seemed to emerge from the original photograph almost organically. It was at this point that details I had somehow completely overlooked before would suddenly leap out from the screen – like the chicken scratching about in front of the Gordonton country store (p. 18).

The goal of a colouriser should be to create work that is so authentic that the colour itself becomes unremarkable. For me, the images in this book are inherently extremely powerful, with or without colour, and this I attribute to the singular curatorial talents of Wolfgang Wild. Wolfgang also uses a rigorous yet unseen process, but, to the rest of us, he appears to be able to glance momentarily at a near-infinite stream of photographs and immediately pull out something unbelievable.

This is the process I went through on each of the photographs in *The Paper Time Machine*. As I worked, my hope was that when I had finished you might feel, if only just for a moment, as though you were standing next to the photographer when the shutter clicked.

Jordan J. Lloyd

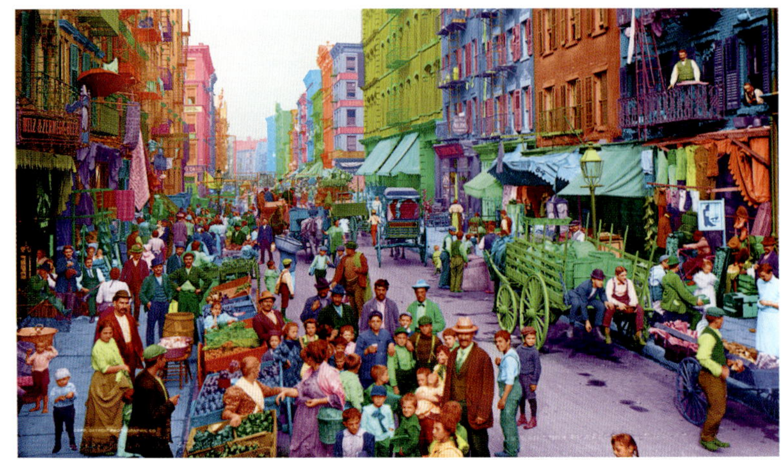

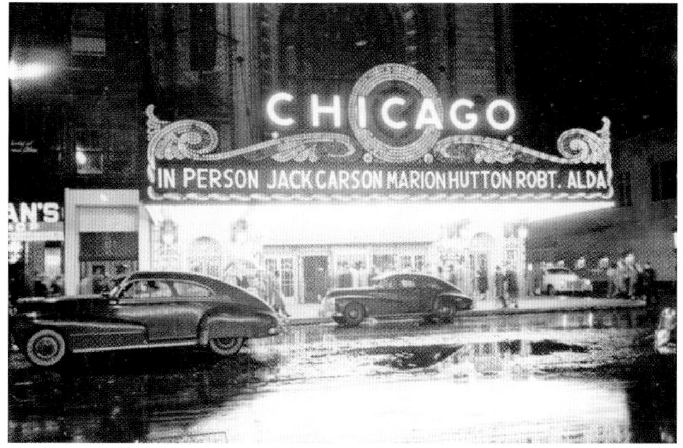

1949: **People arriving at the Chicago Theatre**
North State Street, Chicago, USA (Stanley Kubrick / Look Magazine / Library of Congress) pp. 4–5

This scene is flooded with colour and light, from the neon sign to the left of the theatre, to the huge number of bulbs on the underside of the theatre's portico – all reflected in the rain covering the street surface. The Chicago Theatre still retains its spectacular marquee of lights, although it had been replaced in the year this picture was taken. The left-hand car is a 1948 Pontiac Silver Streak Coupe, and the car under the 'Chicago' sign is a Chevy Fleetline 2-door Aero Sedan.

July 1947: **Portrait of Art Hodes, Kaiser Marshall, Henry (Clay) Goodwin, Sandy Williams and Cecil (Xavier) Scott**
Times Square, New York City, USA
(William Gottlieb / Library of Congress) pp. 6–7

We used around two dozen reference images for Times Square itself, as well as individual signage. The only internationally recognisable elements of this image that still exist today are the statue of Father Duffy and Pepsi-Cola. The whisky brand Kinsey went out of business in the mid-1980s, although Four Roses bourbon is still in operation, produced by Japanese beverage giant Kirin. Ruppert beer disappeared from the market at the end of 1965. The Warner Bros Strand Theatre was knocked down in 1987 and is now the site of the Morgan Stanley building.

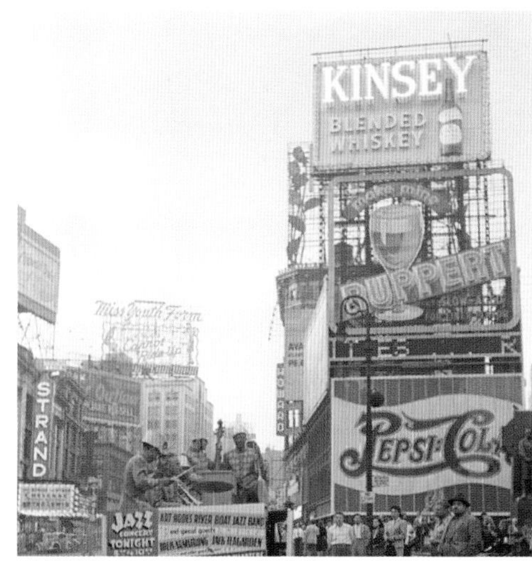

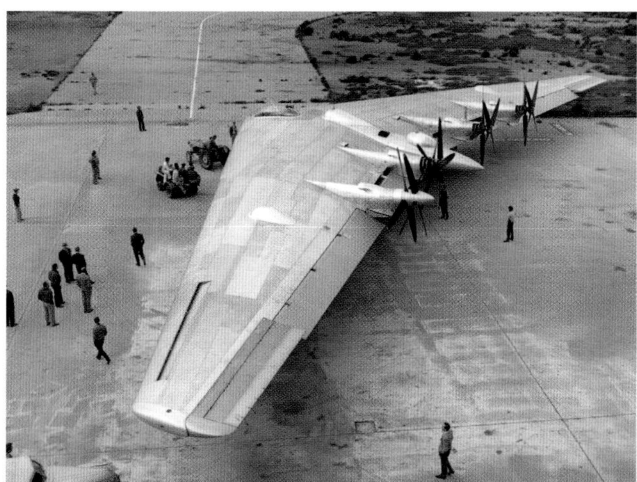

25 May 1946: **Northrop's XB-35 Flying Wing Bomber is wheeled onto the runway for its first taxi tests**
Hawthorne, California, USA
(Unknown / Underwood Archive / Getty) pp. 8–9

The market for model aircraft is huge and several modelling projects of the XB-35 exist. I cross-referenced these kits with a number of original colour photographs of the bomber. I then used contemporaneous examples of clothing and tractors for the surrounding details.

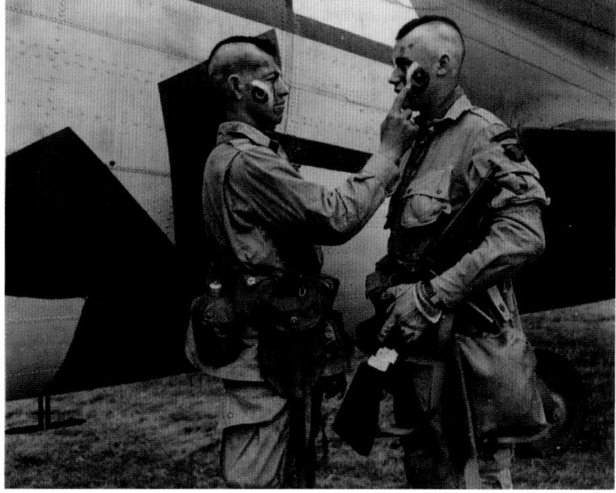

June 1944: **Private Ware applies last-second make-up to Private Plaudo**
Exeter Airfield, Devon, UK (US National Archives) pp. 10–11

In creating this image, I was able to draw on the expertise of the huge community of Second World War enthusiasts and re-enactors who collect original or replica uniform and detailing, such as the M7 carrier for the M5 gas mask. In the background is a Douglas C-47 Skytrain.

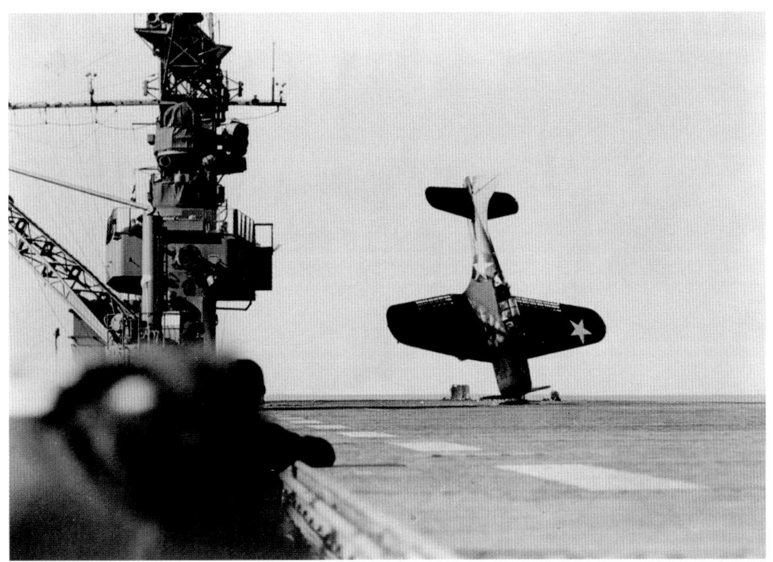

1943: **A Douglas SBD 'Dauntless' dive bomber balanced on its nose after crash-landing on a carrier flight deck**
Pacific Theatre of War (Library of Congress) pp. 12–13

The livery on the bomber is rendered in the Pacific variant rather than the Atlantic one, and, as with many things concerning the military, it was well documented. An aircraft-carrier's deck would exhibit signs of sea water, paint, fuel, oil, fire and rubber, so I incorporated this into the details.

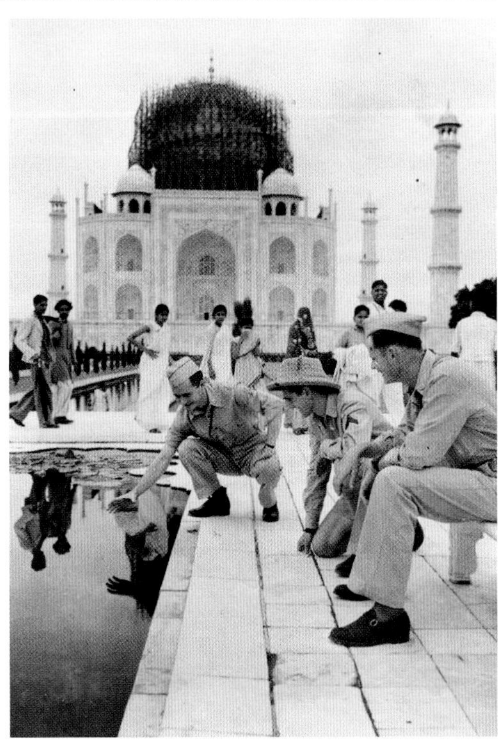

1942: **Members of the US Signal Corps at the Taj Mahal in protective bamboo scaffolding**
Agra, Uttar Pradesh, India (Uknown / Library of Congress) pp. 14–15

When this picture was taken, only the dome was covered. Later, the entire structure would sit within a bamboo framework. Uniforms and clothing were sourced from contemporaneous examples.

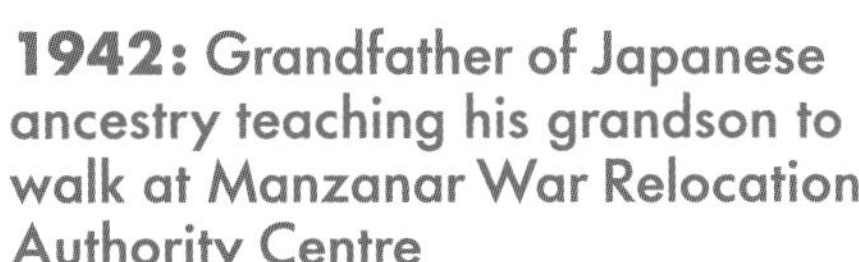

1942: **Grandfather of Japanese ancestry teaching his grandson to walk at Manzanar War Relocation Authority Centre**
Manzanar, California, USA (Dorothea Lange / Library of Congress) pp. 16–17

The barracks, some of which still stand today, are located within the Owens Valley. I believe the shot is taken looking east towards the mountains of Mount Keith and Mount Bradley in the Sierra crest, which indicates this shot was taken around late morning.

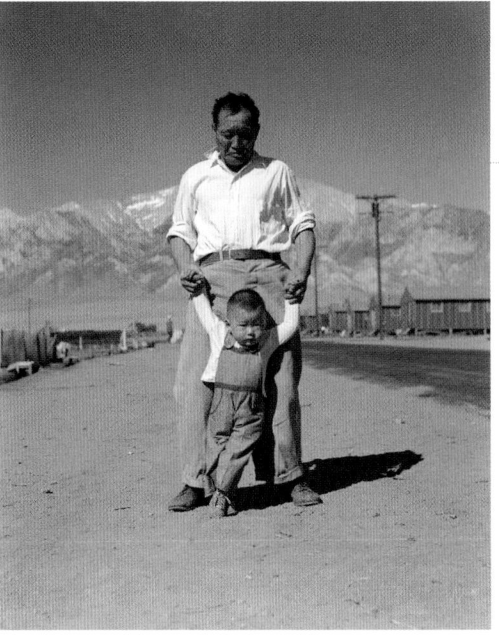

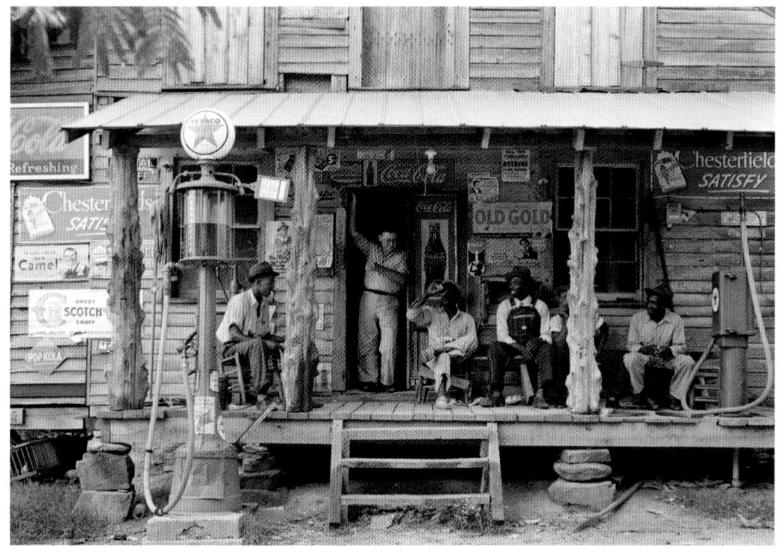

July 1939: Country store on dirt road, Sunday afternoon
Gordonton, North Carolina, USA
(Dorothea Lange / Library of Congress) pp. 18–19

We hunted down visual references to each original sign in the bewildering array on display here, using auction sites, collectibles and, in one case, a specialist soda pop retailer. We had to make sure we were referring to the right geographical source, as some signs even had regional variations. We also had access to a set of photographs that show the now-derelict building – though I needed to adjust the information to show that the building was around eighty years younger in Lange's photograph.

1938: Young boy in a Baltimore slum area, Maryland
Baltimore, Maryland, USA
(John Vachon / Library of Congress) pp. 20–21

This is a picture with a very narrow range of colour, and a very wide range of texture, from the pitted metal at the left, to the rough hewn pine boards on the right. I was able to look at a range of examples of utility and work-wear for reference, and also examples of painted timber in the background. Today, the boy's jeans would be worth an absolute fortune.

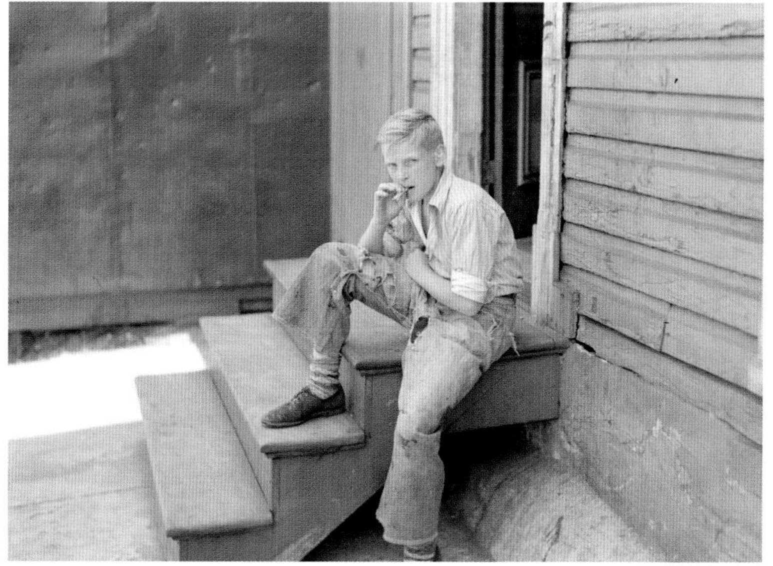

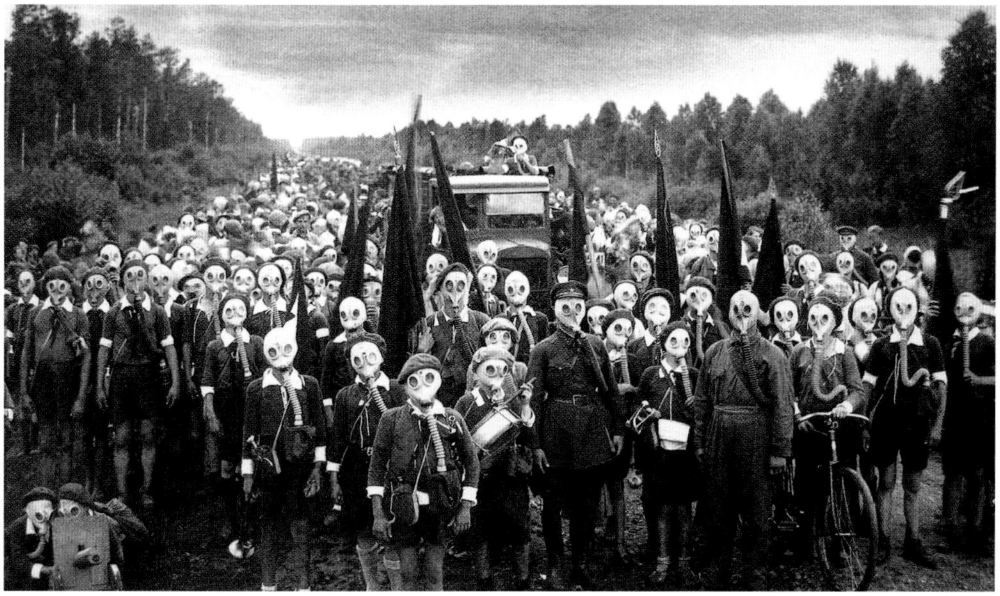

1937: Children's Pioneers defence drill, Leningrad
Leningrad, Soviet Union
(Viktor Bulla / Getty) pp. 22–23

The blue of a Young Pioneer uniform varied from navy to mid-blue, while the scarf was a standard tomato red. The truck is a Zis5. The forests outside St. Petersburg (the former Leningrad) are largely birch and pine – the pine needles have a particular yellow tonality.

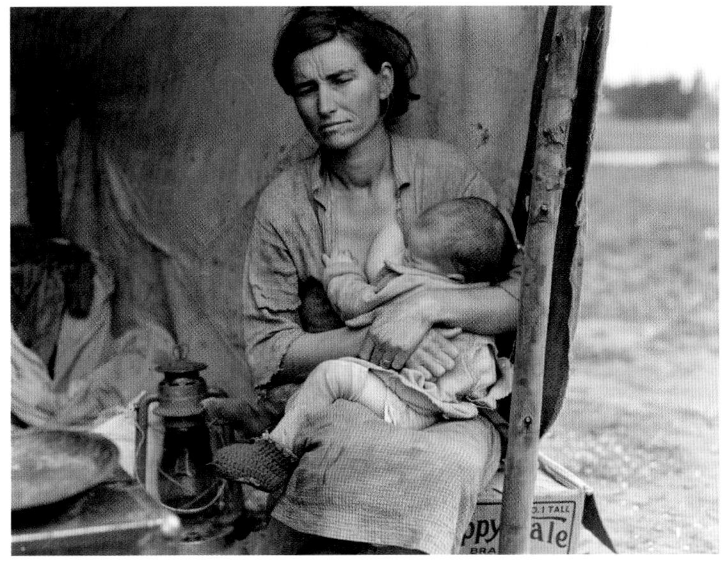

1936: Florence Thompson with one of her children as part of Dorothea Lange's 'Migrant Mother' series
Watsonville, California, USA
(Dorothea Lange / Library of Congress) pp. 24–25

Examples of working-class clothing of the period provided much of the references for our work on this image. While not remotely taking away from Lange's extraordinary original, the addition of colour seems to emphasise the sheer desperation and anguish of Mrs Thompson's situation.

1936: August Landmesser refuses to salute at a Nazi rally, Germany
Hamburg, Germany (Hulton Archive / Getty)
pp. 26–27

Crowd scenes such as this one may appear to be highly complex to carry out but can, in fact, be relatively straightforward in practice – if inordinately time-consuming. That was the case with this image. The crowd is composed of a mixture of both civilians and uniformed figures. We looked at similar crowd scenes in Nazi Germany, many of which do exist in colour. There is a very wide range of Nazi uniforms in this picture, all extensively documented today, in addition to the examples of 1930s civilian dress.

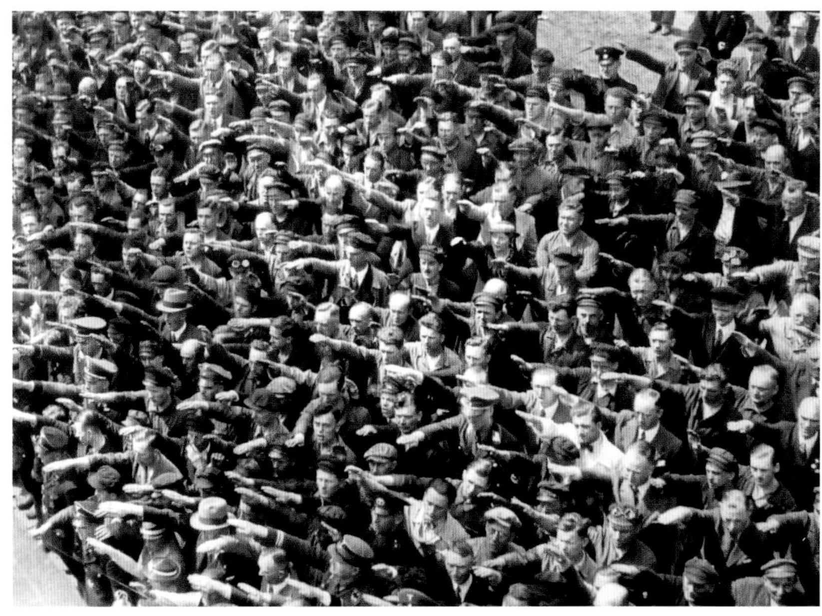

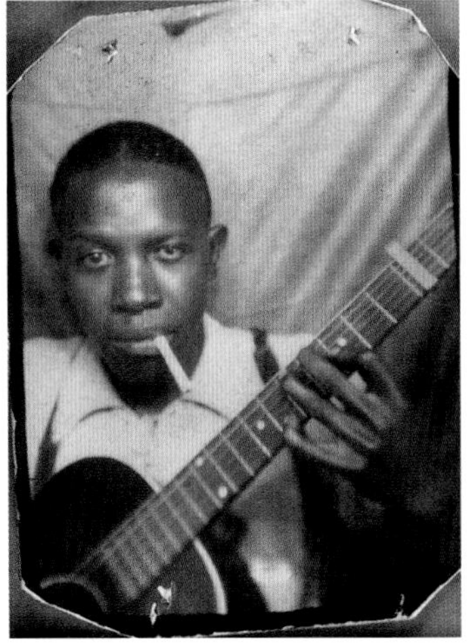

1935: Robert Johnson, blues singer and guitarist
USA (Unknown) pp. 28–29

Needless to say, I listened to Robert Johnson's seminal recordings on loop while working on this rare photograph. It was essential to ascertain the precise model of guitar that Johnson is holding, though there is little of it showing. Despite this, we believe it to be a 1936 Gibson L-00 featuring a black ebony-finished sunburst mahogany body and a rosewood fingerboard.

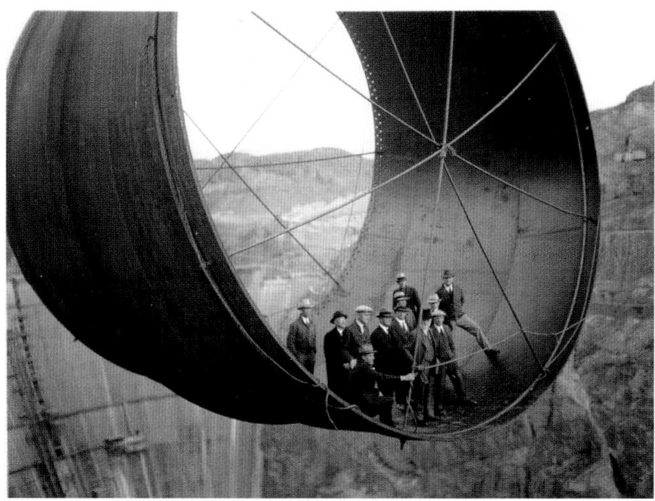

1935: **Officials ride in one of the penstock pipes of the soon-to-be-completed Hoover Dam**
Hoover Dam, Arizona, USA
(Unknown / Bureau of Reclamation) pp. 30–31

Much of Hoover Dam looks exactly the same today as it did back in 1935, so we were able to colour reference the surrounding geology using satellite and contemporary colour photographs.

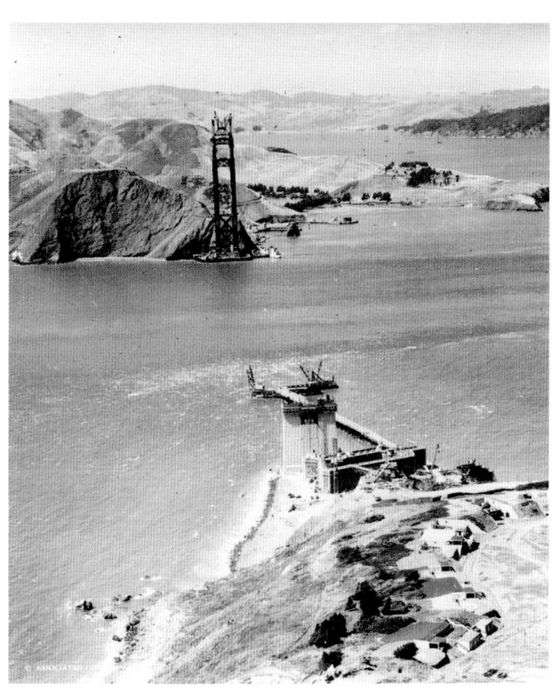

16 July 1934: **The Golden Gate Bridge under construction**
San Francisco, California, USA
(Chas Hiller / Library of Congress) pp. 32–33

International Orange is a very precise shade. The CMYK colours are: C = Cyan: 0%, M = Magenta: 69%, Y = Yellow: 100%, K = Black: 6%. On the bridge, the International Orange primer is continually repainted, completed every twenty years. The original paint was lead-based but from 1965 has been replaced by a zinc-based primer and acrylic topcoat. Although it is now illegal for pedestrians to venture under the bridge, historically original rivets have been found in the water, complete with their International Orange paint. We used aerial and satellite photography as reference points for the surrounding geology, and were fortunate to draw on a range of near and far side Kodachrome images taken across the next twenty years, including one from the family collection of *The Paper Time Machine* researcher Deborah Humphries. Taken together, these gave us a good range of variations for water and sky colour.

1933: **A 'Hooverville' shanty town in Central Park, New York**
Central Park, New York City, USA
(Unknown / Bettman / Getty) pp. 34–35

This site is now part of the Great Lawn at Central Park. We could draw on modern pictures of several elements of the scene, including the distinctive grey stone, Manhattan schist rock. The large building to the left is The Beresford apartment block, built in 1929 and still in place today. It has a limestone base, brick-clad upper floors and terracotta detailing. Indeed, the entire skyline to the right of The Beresford is essentially identical today.

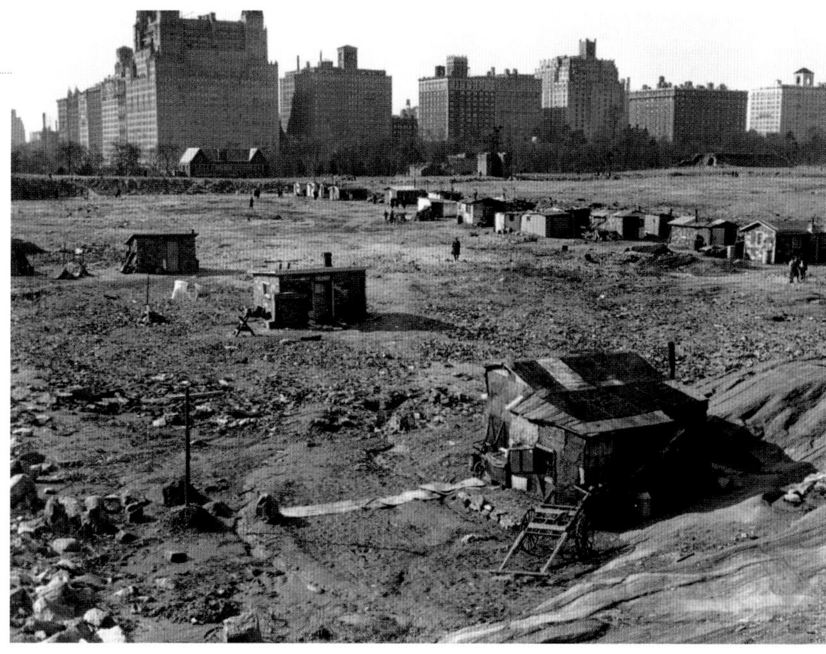

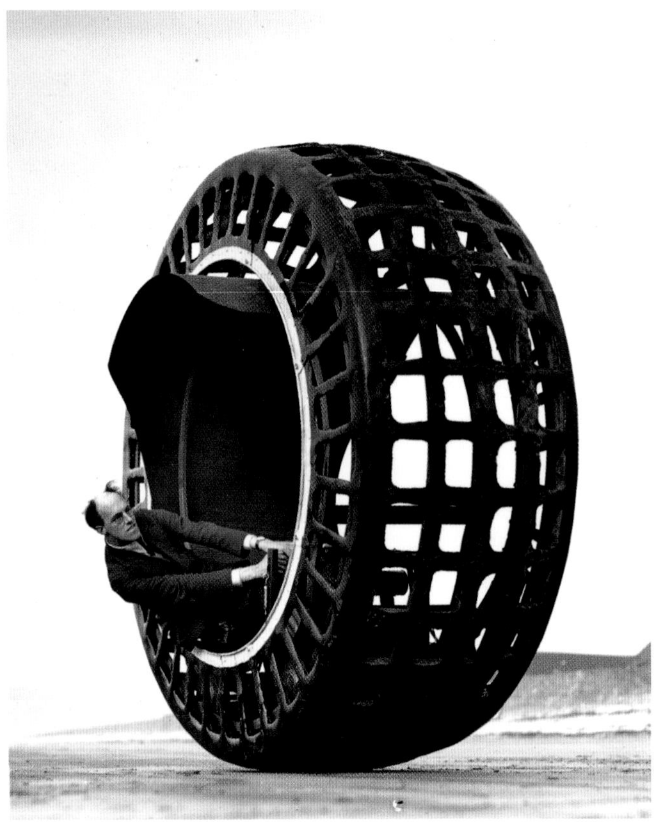

1932: **The Dynasphere being tested on the beach at Weston-super-Mare by Mr J. A. Purves of Taunton, who invented the machine with his son**
Weston-super-Mare, Somerset, UK
(Fox Photos / Getty) pp. 36–37

I found an article in the May 1932 issue of *Popular Science* on the Dynasphere 'unicycle'. The article locates this image specifically on Brean Sands, near Weston-super-Mare, from which I was able to generate modern-day colour references.

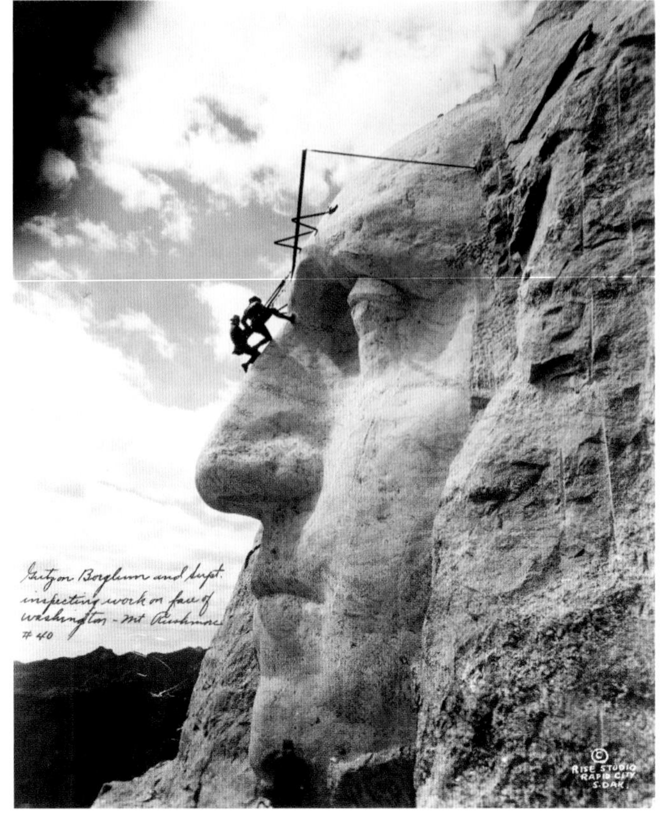

31 May 1932: **At Mount Rushmore, Gutzon Borglum and another sculptor hang from the forehead of George Washington**
Mount Rushmore, South Dakota, USA
(Unknown / Library of Congress) pp. 38–39

This is another very well-documented monument, so sourcing good quality colour references was fairly straightforward. My favourite detail in the image is the smudge on the top left, which I believe to be the finger of the photographer creeping into the shot.

c. 1930: **An overhead view of people on 36th Street between 8th and 9th Avenues, in the heart of the Garment District, New York**
Garment District, New York City, USA (Margaret Bourke-White / Time & Life Pictures / Getty) pp. 40–41

There are some interesting details in this picture: a barber pole, a Coca-Cola sign, litter in the gutter and, on the far right, a news stand with periodicals. There are over 600 people in this photograph, and no shortcuts were taken filling in the colour from dozens of examples of clothing at the time. The two cars shown are (*left*) a 1930 Ford Model A 4-Door Sedan and (*right*) a Ford Model A Sports Coupe. Examples of the cars were also found after we managed to identify them.

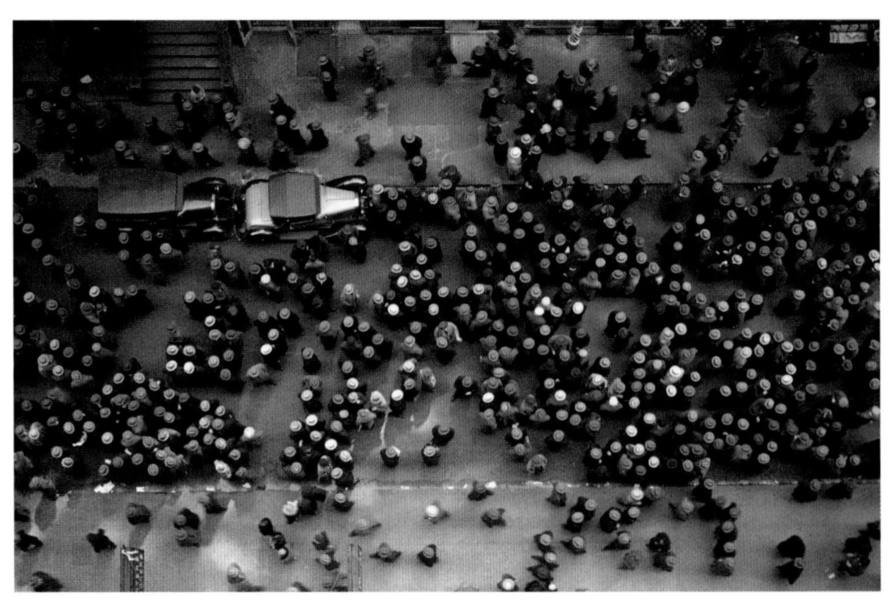

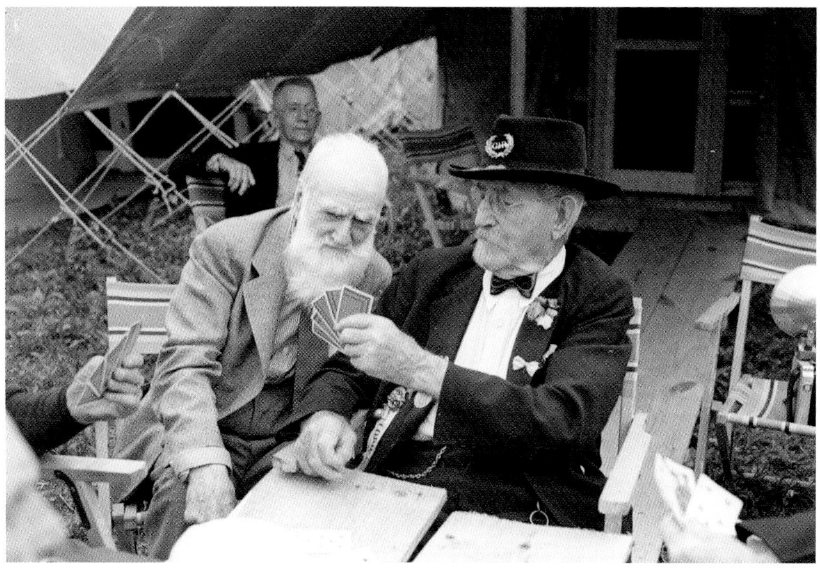

1930s: **A Confederate and a Union veteran play cards at a Civil War reunion**
Gettysburg Battlefield, Pennsylvania, USA
(Bettmann / Getty) pp. 42–43

The man on the right wears a Union 'GAR' (Grand Army of the Republic) hat pin on his Slouch hat. He also wears a Gettysburg 50th Reunion medal, dating from 1913. The long ribbon below his left hand appears to be a Florida State ribbon. Florida was a Confederate State – perhaps this man had moved to Florida after the war.

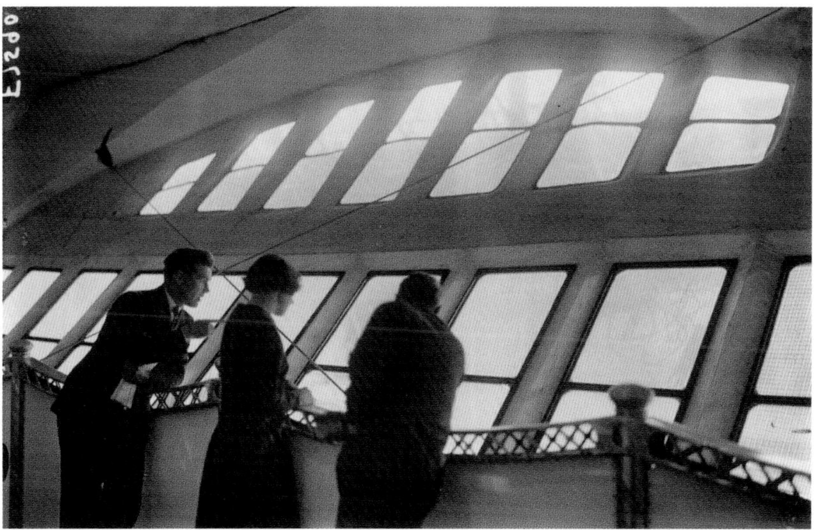

19 October 1929: **Passengers surveying the scene from the verandah deck of the British Airship R100**
Somewhere above the earth (A. R. Coster / Getty)
pp. 44–45

The lighting of this photograph is extraordinary and this remains one of my favourite photographs. My absolute favourite detail, as I pointed out to Wolfgang when he asked, are the doodles on the dust on one of the glass panes.

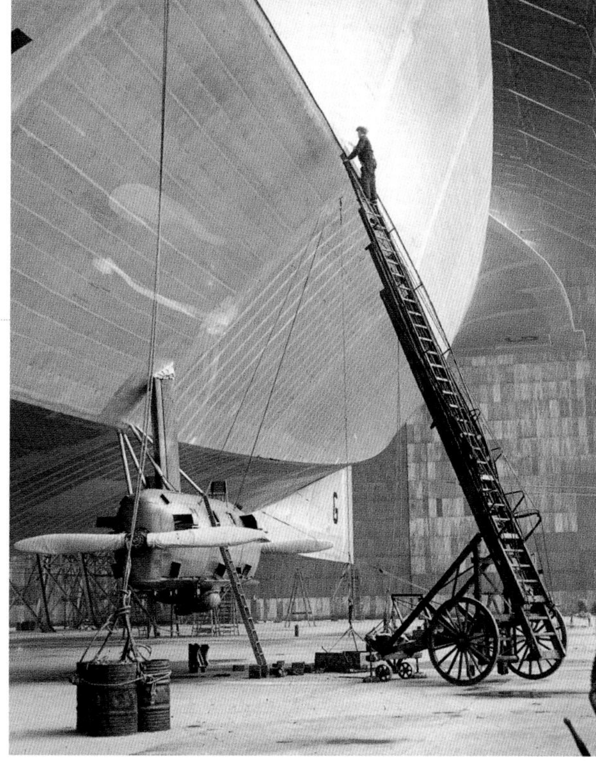

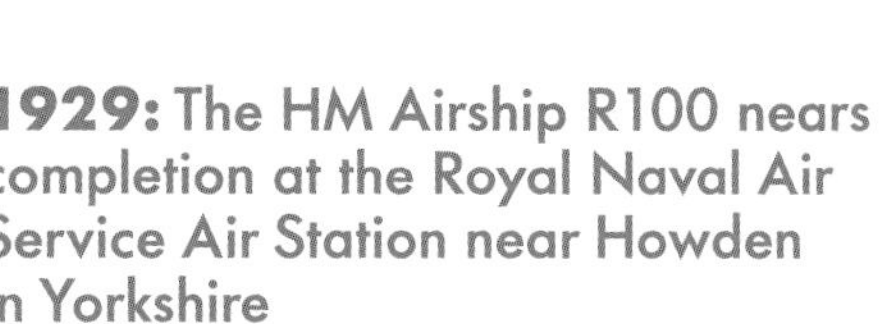

1929: **The HM Airship R100 nears completion at the Royal Naval Air Service Air Station near Howden in Yorkshire**
Howden, Yorkshire, UK
(Fox Photos / Hulton Archive) pp. 46–47

The rear walls of the No. 2 Double Rigid Shed are rusting corrugated iron sheets – the shed was known to have a leaky roof.

1928: **Looking down Glasshouse Street to the junction with Sherwood Street and towards the lights of Piccadilly Circus in London**
Piccadilly, London, England
(Topical Press / Getty) pp. 48–49

Eagle-eyed readers will note the damage in the top left-hand corner of the black-and-white photograph, which in the end I had to reconstruct digitally from a photograph I myself took at the exact angle and location. The livery of the London Midland and Scottish Railway is quite distinctive.

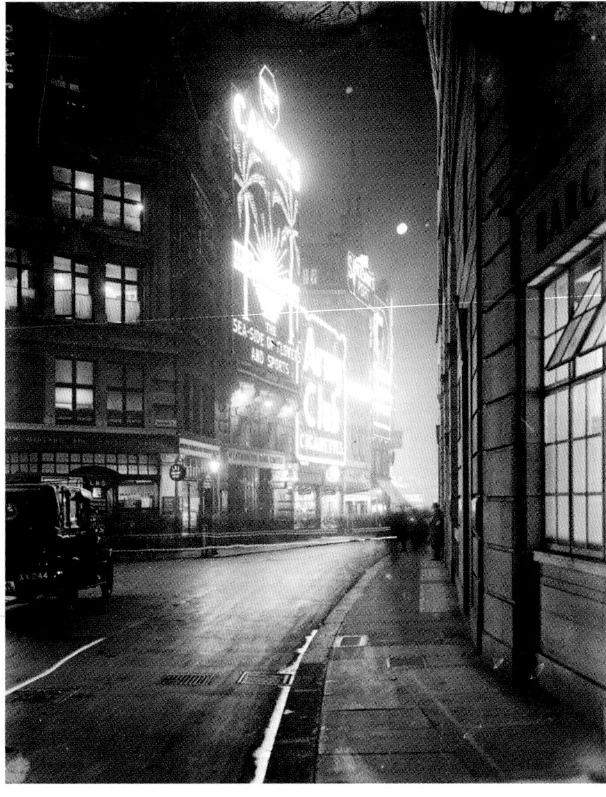

28 December 1928: **A cameraman and a sound technician record the roar of Leo the Lion for MGM's famous movie ident**
Hollywood, California, USA
(John Kobal Foundation / Getty) pp. 50–51

The camera is a Bell & Howell 2709 and is now very rare, with only around ten surviving examples. In 1928, the 2709 was the pinnacle of camera technology and the highest-priced device on the market. With a brass frame on its side, the body was machined from cast aluminium. The camera has wooden legs, with a steel geared head.

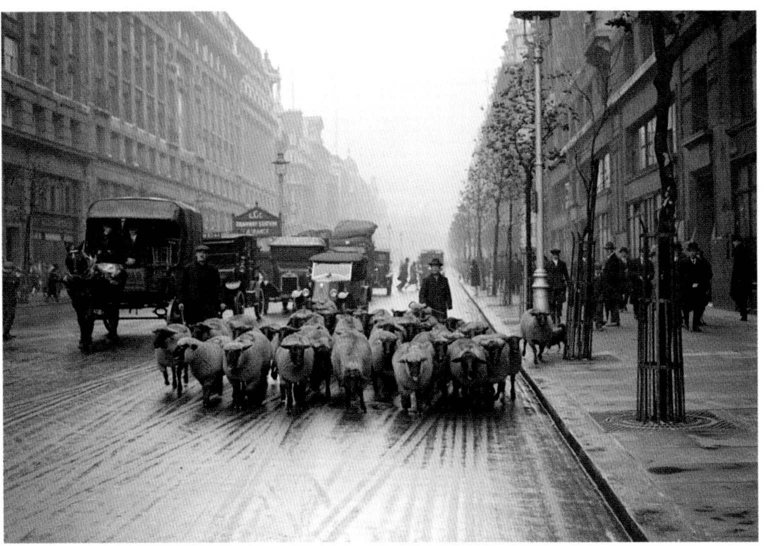

1926: **A flock of sheep walking along the Kingsway in London**
Kingsway, London, UK
(Unknown / Fox Photos / Getty) pp. 52–53

The London plane trees in this photograph, in their infancy during the 1920s, have now fully matured. Many of the stone-fronted neo-classical and neo-baroque buildings have been completely replaced. London County Council Tramways produced a poster during the 1920s, which included the Kingsway Tramway sign, providing me with the dark red tone. The car immediately behind the flock is a Renault.

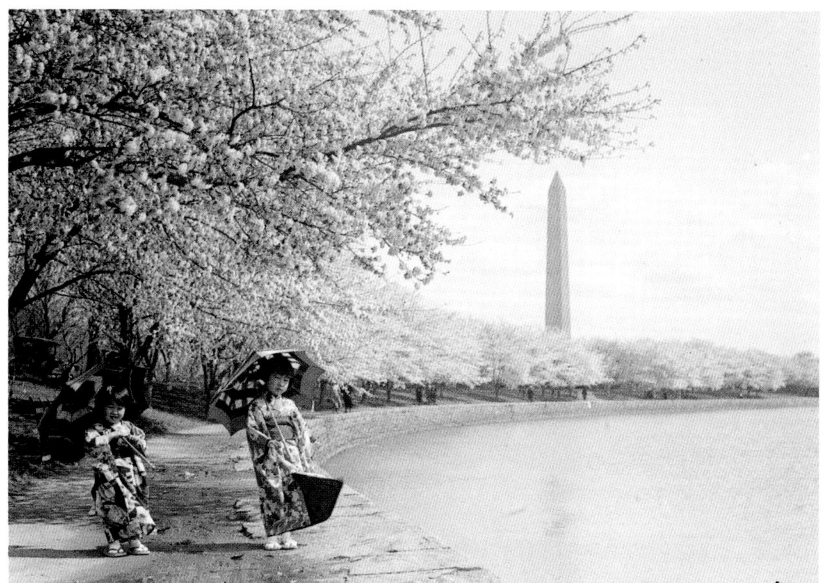

28 March 1925: Sakura cherry blossom, Potomac Park, Washington DC
East Potomac Park, Washington DC, USA
(Library of Congress) pp. 54–55

Working from a photomechanical colour postcard and cross-referencing satellite imagery, we could establish that this picture was taken on the morning of Saturday, 28 March 1925. I can only use hand-coloured or tinted images as general guidelines, as often the companies that created the postcards were not necessarily the people who took the image. In this case, much of the location remains the same, so I could use contemporary photographs as well as examples of children's kimonos of the period.

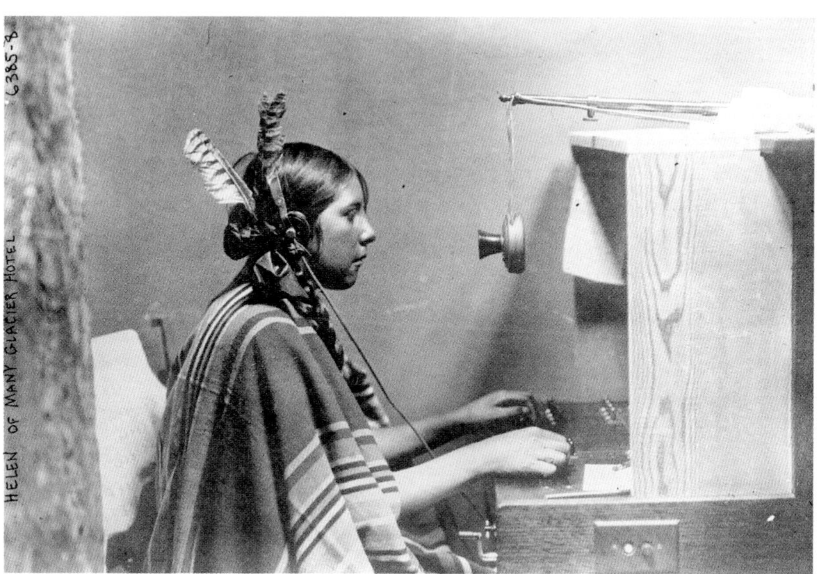

26 June 1925: A female Native American telephone switchboard operator
Glacier National Park, Montana
(Bain News Service / Library of Congress) pp. 56–57

Helen's feathers are likely to be from a turkey, and her ring may well be silver with turquoise. Being of the Blackfoot Nation, examples of the blanket's distinctive blue, red and ochre striping were sourced from numerous examples and paintings.

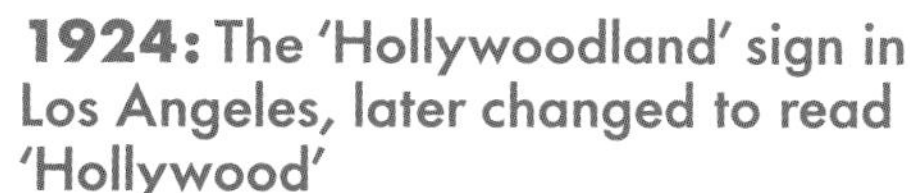

1924: The 'Hollywoodland' sign in Los Angeles, later changed to read 'Hollywood'
Hollywood, California, USA
(Underwood Archives / Getty) pp. 58–59

The Hollywoodland sign itself was built from sheet metal and wooden telephone poles. The traction engine is part of the Western Construction Company. Kanst's Art Gallery, with its red tile roof, was brand new in 1924 – it opened on April Fool's Day. The car is likely to be a Studebaker Special Six.

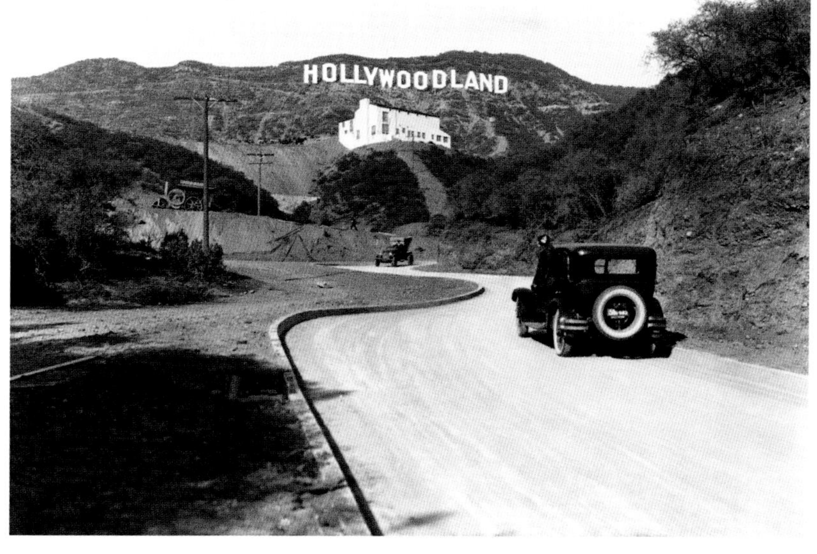

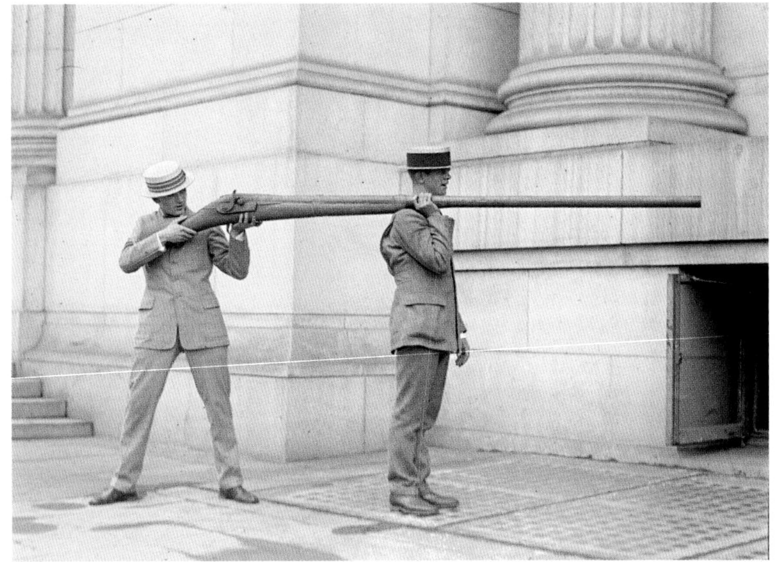

July 1923: A punt gun, used to shoot flocks of waterbirds from a punt
Washington DC, USA (Library of Congress) pp. 60–61

It's hard to be absolutely certain without visiting but the details suggest this is the Capitol Building, and so I took my references from there.

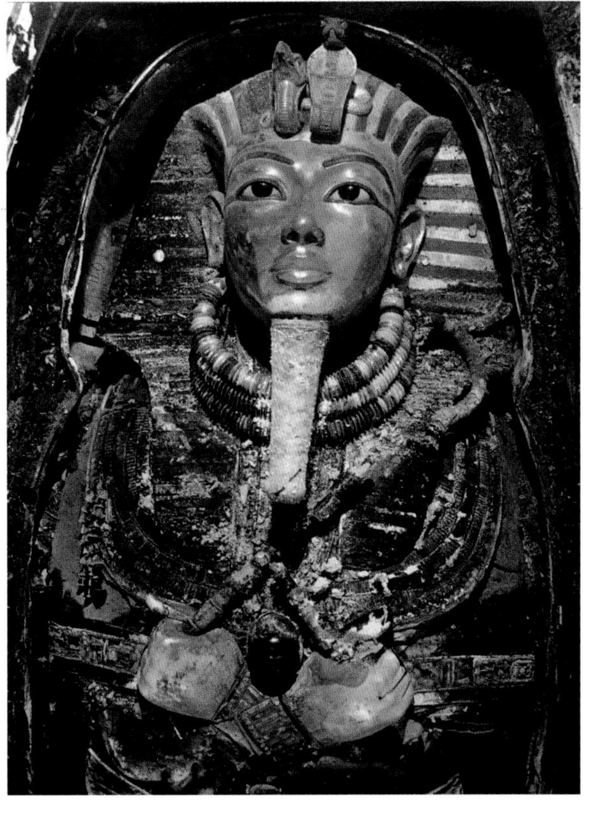

1922: The contents of the central coffin of Tutankhamun's tomb
East Valley of the Kings, Luxor, Egypt (Harry Burton / The Griffith Institute) pp. 62–63

Archaeologist and Egyptologist Howard Carter kept meticulous handwritten notes on flashcards describing in great detail the array of artefacts that were placed in the tomb. We cross-referenced all the elements in the photograph to the original notes with the restored artefact in the Museum of Egypt, and then dulled down the result to reflect over 3,000 years of dust and ageing.

7 September 1921: Margaret Gorman, the newly crowned Miss America, awaits the arrival of Neptune in her royal robes at the opening of the Atlantic City Beauty Pageant
Atlantic City, New Jersey, USA (Bettmann / Corbis / Getty) pp. 64–65

Miss America wore a sea-foam green and sequin dress on this occasion, in keeping with the overall maritime theme. After her time as Miss America, Margaret kept the dress, storing it in in the back of her cupboard. I didn't have access to Margaret's cupboard, so I used modern examples of a green chiffon dress instead.

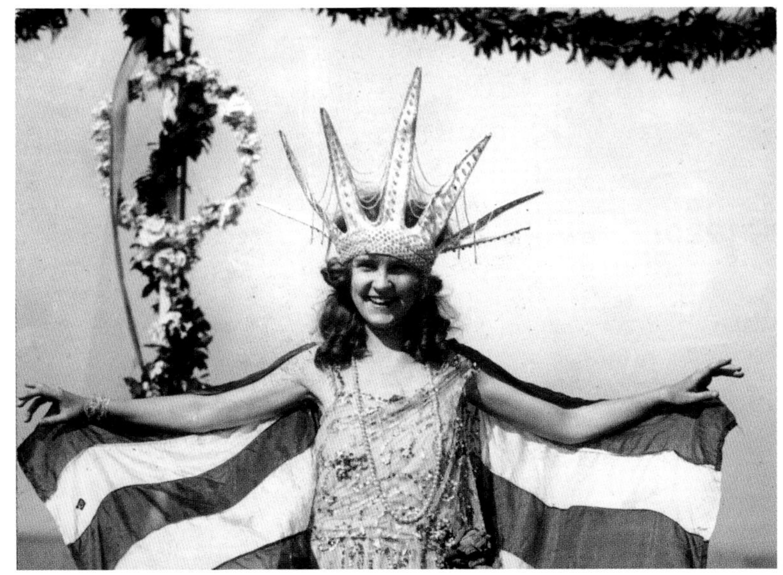

1921: Sound amplifiers at Bolling Field Air Force Base, Washington DC
Bolling Field Air Force Base, Washington DC, USA
(Unknown / Getty) pp. 66–67

Although there are no contemporary images taken of the location as it stands today, much of the fauna in the foreground and background is sourced from the surrounding area. The distinctive red brick and dressed stone of the Beaux Arts style National War College by McKim, Mead and White is still in use today by the National Defense University.

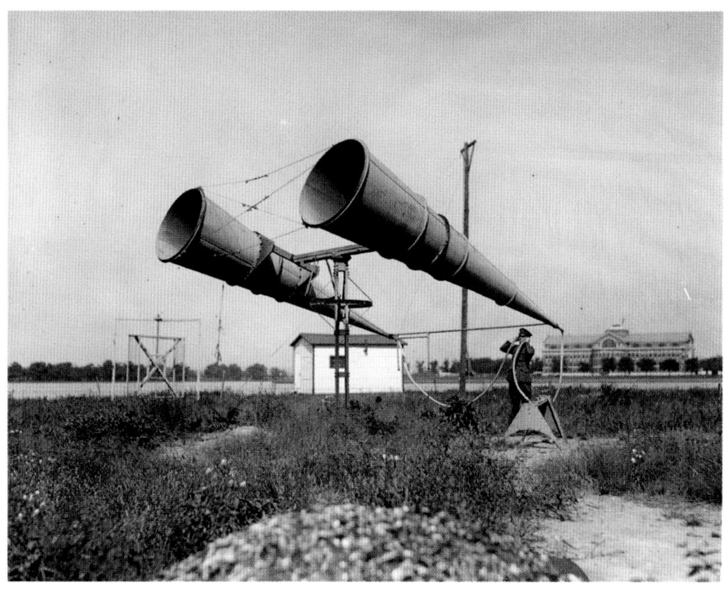

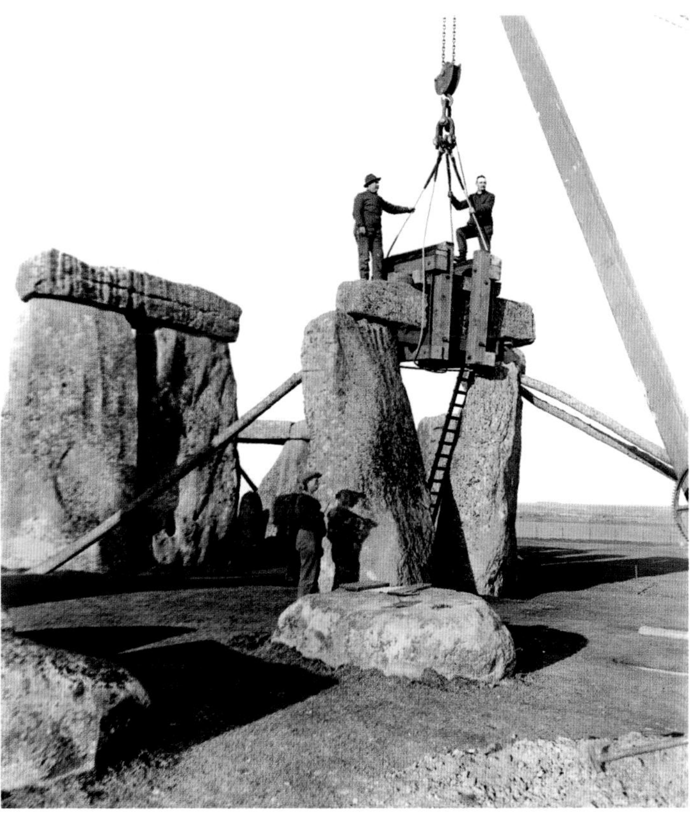

***c.* 1920:** A view of a trilithon being re-erected at Stonehenge
Near Amesbury, Wiltshire, UK
(English Heritage / Hulton Archive) pp. 68–69

Stonehenge is one of the world's most documented sites, so there were plenty of reference photographs of the trilithons for me to choose from, though determining the location from which the photograph was taken proved to be a more substantial challenge. In the end, satellite imagery in addition to inspecting a 3D model of the site allowed us to find a possible angle.

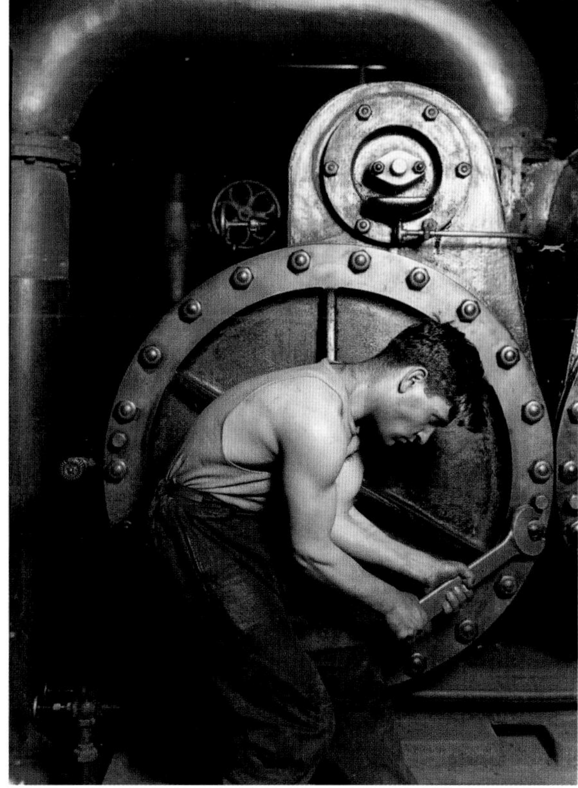

1920: Power house mechanic working on steam pump
Unknown, USA
(Lewis Hine / US National Archives) pp. 70–71

The machinery in this picture would not have been painted, because paint would not have survived the range of temperatures and conditions to which it was exposed.

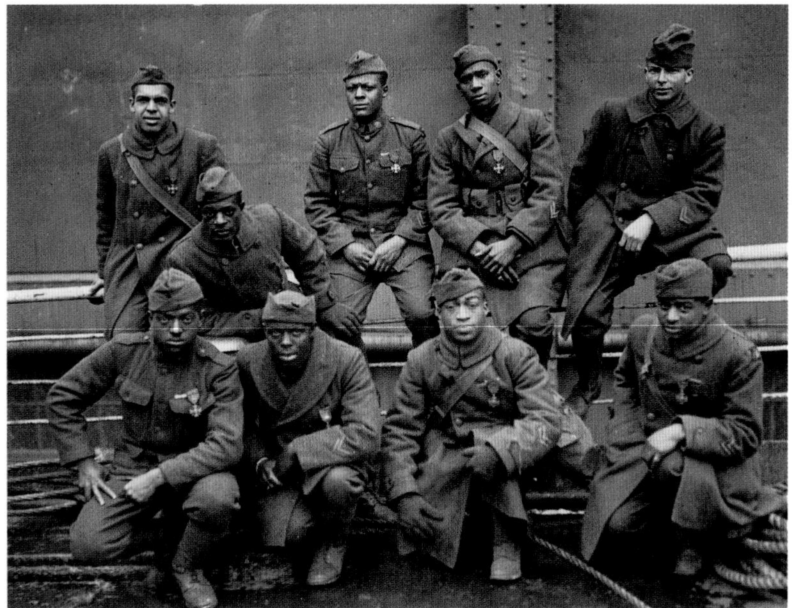

1919: **Soldiers of the 369th 'Harlem Hellfighters' wearing the Cross of War medal pose for a photo on their trip back to New York**
Unknown (US National Archives) pp. 72–73

You might be able to notice that the soldiers are all wearing the Croix de Guerre (1914–18), a French medal recognising courage or gallantry to a member of the French military or allied force. It is testament to the unit that by the end of the war, 171 members of the 369th were awarded either the Croix de Guerre or the Légion d'Honneur.

1918: **The control room of a U-boat looking aft, starboard side**
Wallsend, Tyne and Wear, UK
(Tyne and Wear Museums & Archives)
pp. 74–75

Given that the 110 U-boat had only been sunk for between three to four months, there is no real rust or other water damage to be seen in this shot. The black colouration is the result of the accumulation of grease, oil and soot, prior to the craft being rammed and depth-charged. The background wall colour is, in fact, ivory. As you can imagine, colour coding was vital to the operation of such a complex array of controls. Wheels and levers to be opened on 'rig for dive' conditions are red; wheels and levers to be closed on 'rig for dive' are green. Many controls, gauges and dials also used luminous paint.

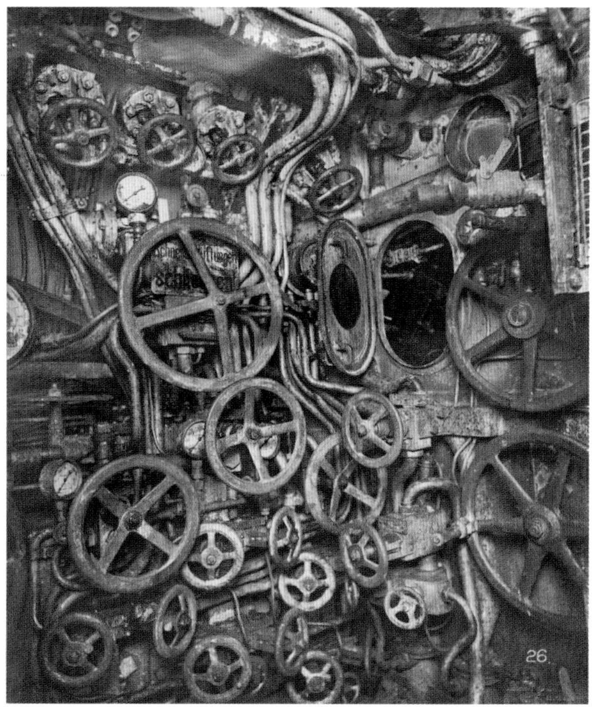

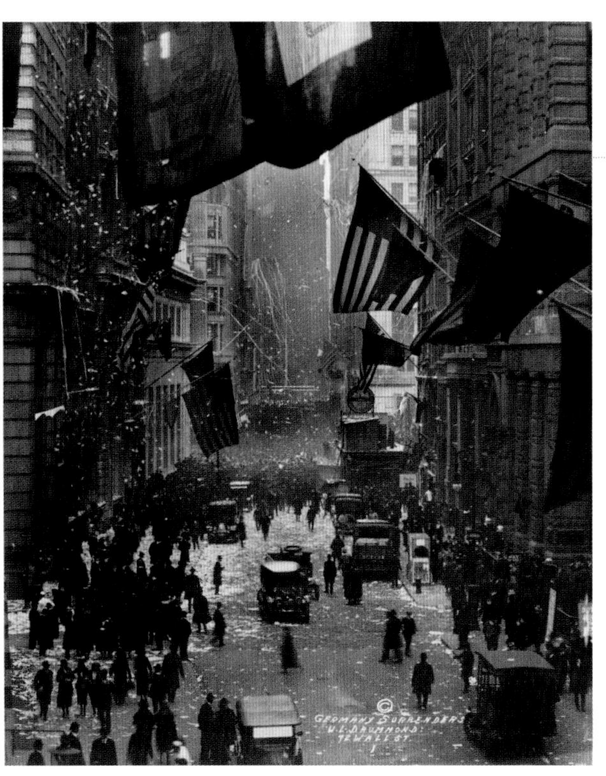

1918: **Celebrations on Wall Street, New York, following the surrender of Germany**
Wall Street, New York City, USA
(W. L. Drummond / Library of Congress) pp. 76–77

The street and sidewalks are littered with ticker tape: paper tape created by the machines used in stock brokerages to give up-to-date stock prices. Ticker is derived from the printing noise made by the machine. During the war, clothing became more and more subdued in colour, as more and more people were affected – often directly – by the deaths of people for whom they cared. Famously, a poster issued by the British National Savings Committee in 1916 stated, 'To Dress Extravagantly in War Time is Worse Than Bad Form; It is Unpatriotic.'

1918: **The interior of Amiens Cathedral with sandbag reinforcements against shell damage**
Amiens, France (Unknown) pp. 78–79

Thankfully, the anticipated destruction of the cathedral did not come to pass and therefore most of the detail could be sourced from contemporary colour photography. The carpets and ornaments in the foreground were sourced from other examples.

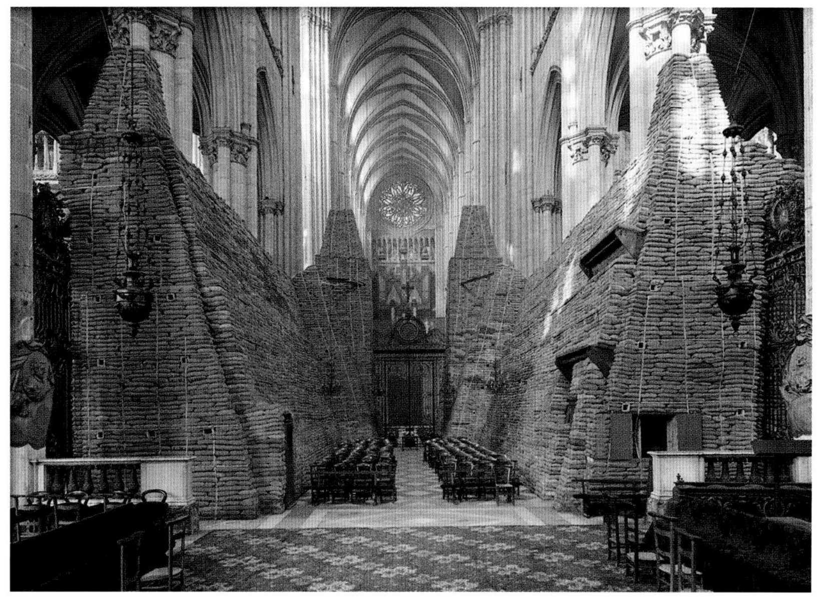

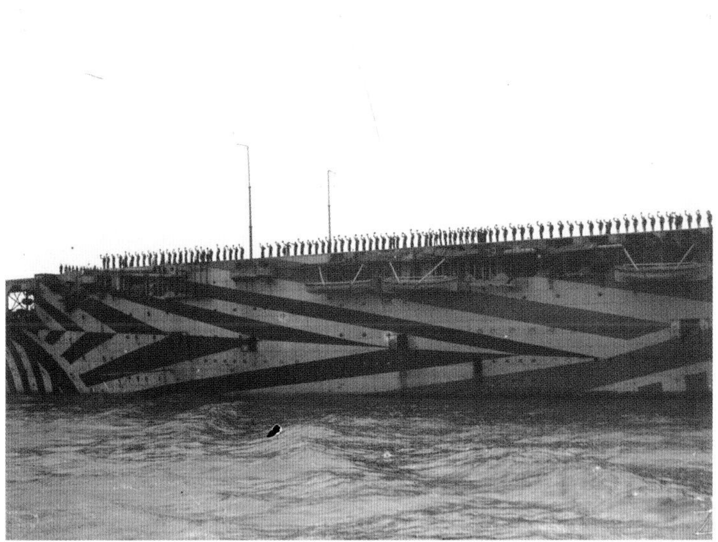

1918: **Airmen and sailors cheering the King from the aircraft carrier *Argus*, on his visit to the Fleet at Rosyth, Scotland. The carrier is painted in 'dazzle' camouflage**
Rosyth, UK (Topical Press / Getty)
pp. 80–81

The distinctive black-and-blue striping of the HMS *Argus* was actually referenced from a scale model of the ship at the Fleet Air Arm Museum in Somerset, UK – it was the most accurate colour reference I could find. Numerous other scale models and schematics exist, although, sadly, no colour photographs.

1918: **A pilot smiles for the camera, Kelly Field, San Antonio**
Kelly Field, San Antonio, USA
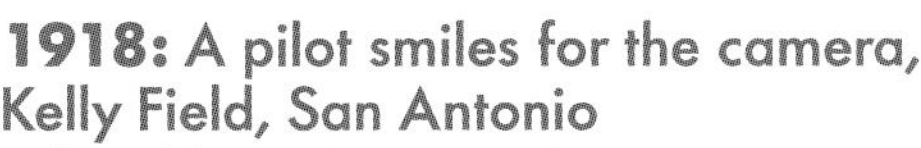
(Paul Aldin Smith Kelly Field Album / San Diego Air & Space Museum) pp. 82–83

There are two choices for the identity of this plane: it is either a Curtiss JN-4 Jenny biplane or De Havilland DH-4. Some of the De Havillands were painted in a khaki color, others in yellow, while all Jennys were yellow. So that's two against one in favour of yellow.

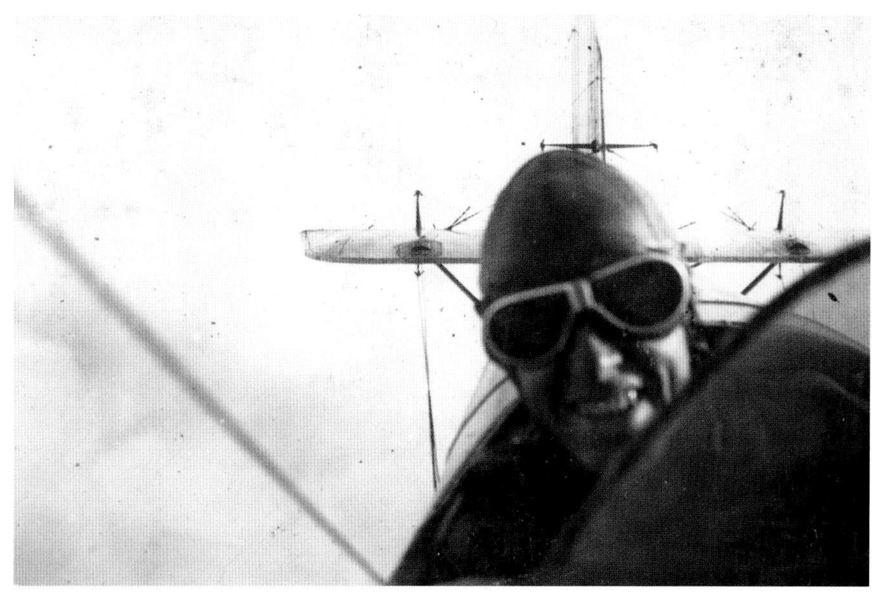

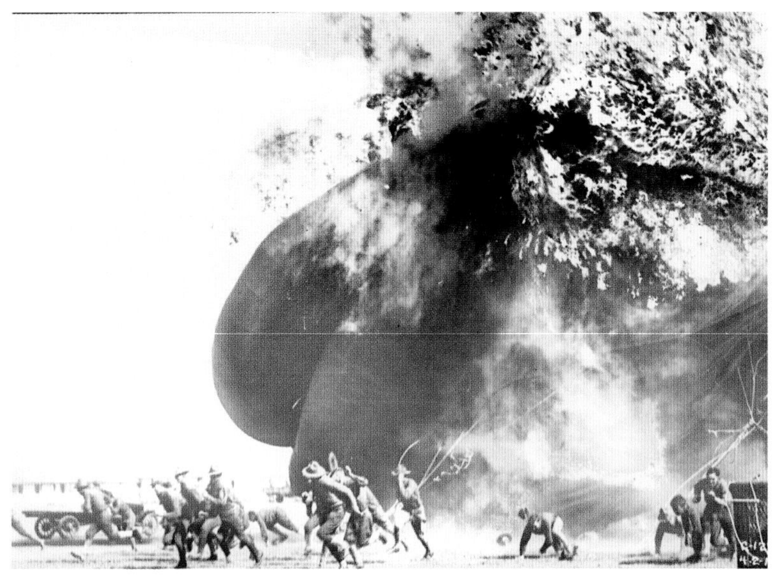

1918: **A dirigible catches fire at Fort Sill, Oklahoma**
Fort Sill, Oklahoma, USA
(Library of Congress) pp. 84–85

I honestly have no idea how the photographer captured the exact moment of the explosion, but the addition of colour does add a real sense of urgency to the servicemen scrambling around trying to get away from immediate danger.

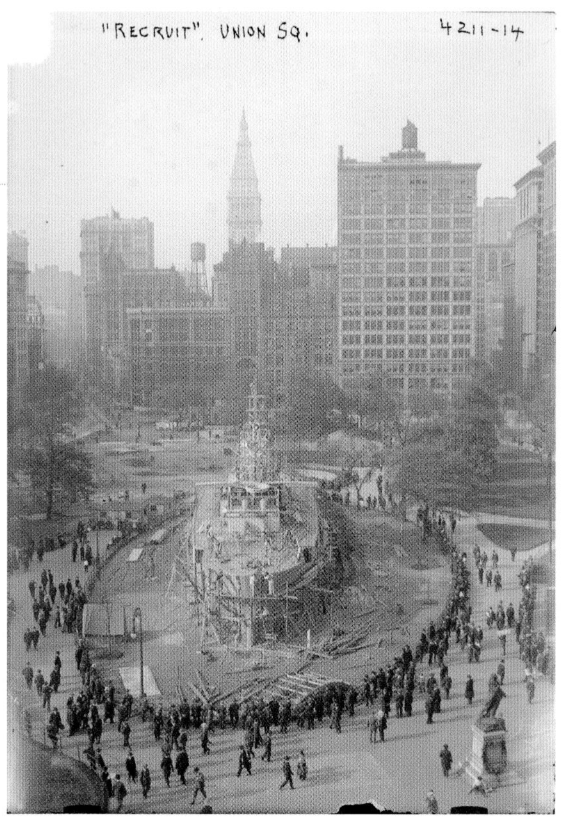

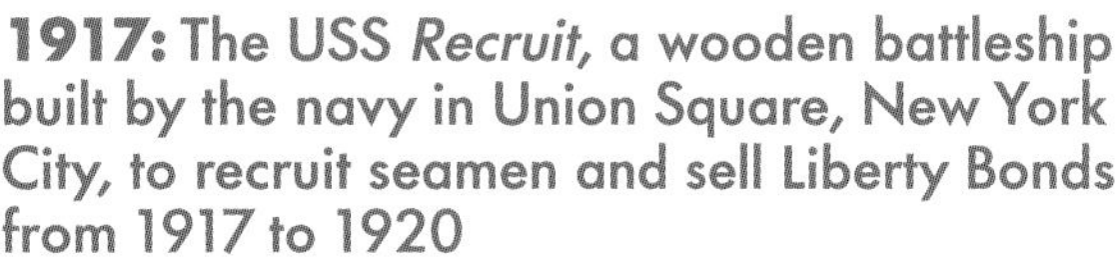

1917: **The USS *Recruit*, a wooden battleship built by the navy in Union Square, New York City, to recruit seamen and sell Liberty Bonds from 1917 to 1920**
Union Square, New York City, USA
(Bain News Service / Library of Congress) pp. 86–87

We know exactly where the USS *Recruit* was built and situated and many of the buildings in Union Square remain the same today, so it was fairly straightforward to obtain contemporary colour references.

1917: **'Jammie' Reynolds, daredevil**
Washington DC, USA
(Unknown / Library of Congress) pp. 88–89

As you can see, the glass plate negative shows extensive damage to the original coating, and the initial restoration work here took me several days. Often with restoration, my aim is to fix the blemish while retaining the overall shape and texture of the undamaged surroundings. We took colour references from modern images of buildings that have survived, and from hand-coloured postcards of the time. Based on maps and the angle of various landmarks, I could also figure out the exact location and angle of the photograph – and just in case you were wondering how high that drop is, it's a good six or seven storeys off the ground, as shown by another photographer's image of Reynolds, taken from the ground.

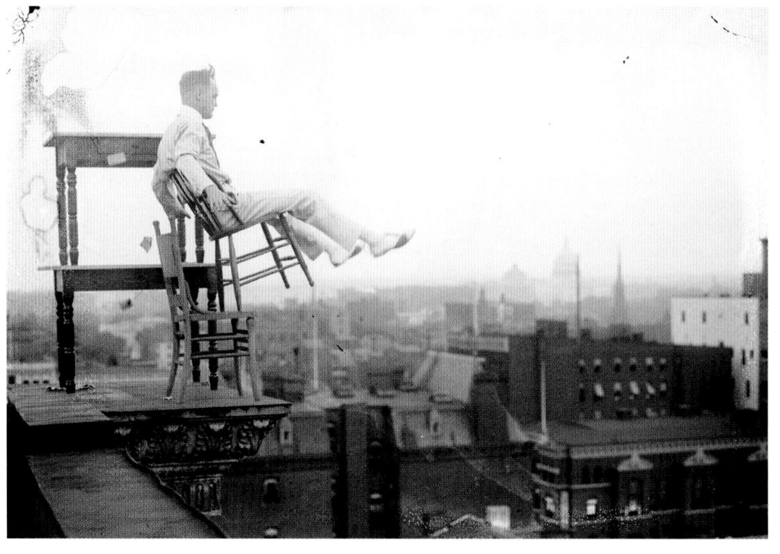

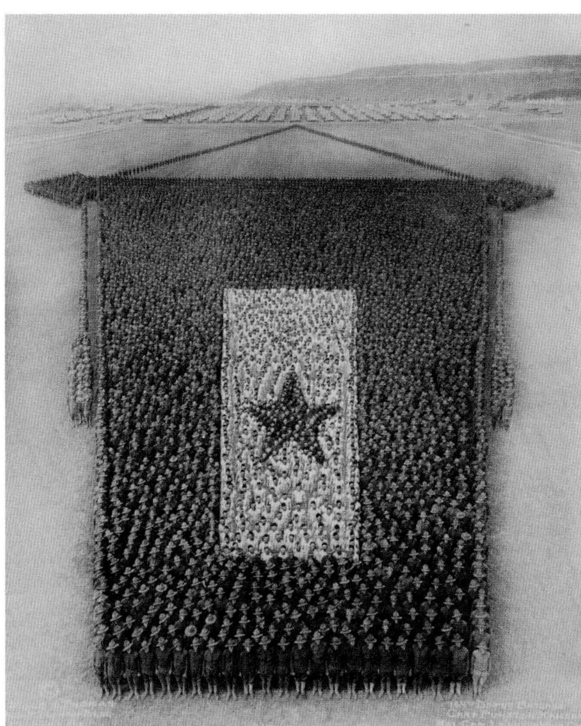

1917: Soldiers of the 164th Depot Brigade form a service flag at Fort Riley in Kansas.
Fort Riley, Kansas, USA
(Arthur Mole / Library of Congress) pp. 90–91

Arthur Mole would dress soldiers in a range of uniforms to enable him to show dark and light details in his photographs. He also had some figures hatted and others he left bare-headed, and he would also leave spaces between lines to create further shadows. For this colourisation, we looked at the summer and winter uniforms of the 164th. An actual service banner has a red border, a white interior, and a dark blue star.

1916: A wounded British soldier holding his steel helmet, which has been pierced by a piece of shrapnel, during the advance on the Somme front near Hamel
Beaumont-Hamel, Somme, France
(Lt. Ernest Brooks / IWM / Getty) pp. 92–93

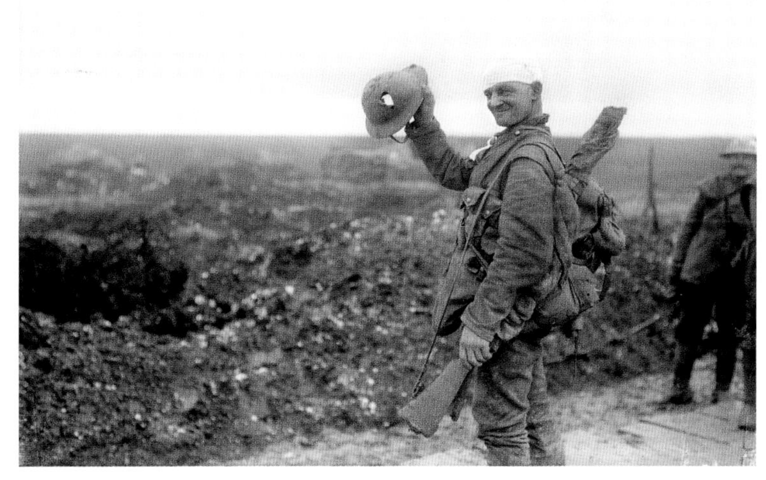

The 1916 Mark I model helmet of 1916 had a matte khaki paint finish. Cork, sand or sawdust was then used to further reduce shine. Surprisingly, Brodie's original suggested colour scheme was a camouflage of light green, blue and orange.

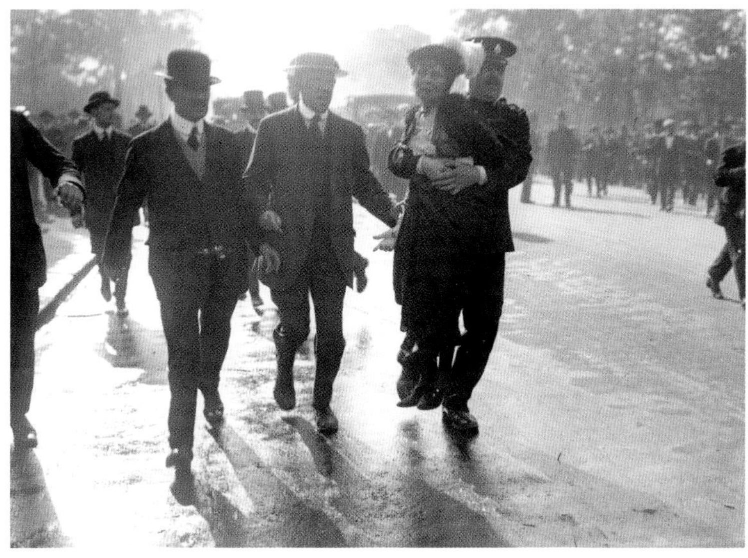

21 May 1914: Emmeline Pankhurst being removed from a suffragette protest by a policeman
Buckingham Palace, London, UK
(Topical Press / Getty) pp. 94–95

Contemporaneous examples of of civilian and police clothing were sourced for this photograph, though the sun coming in from behind adds an extra technical challenge. Often, the colour hues slightly change from a known sample to match the overall environment.

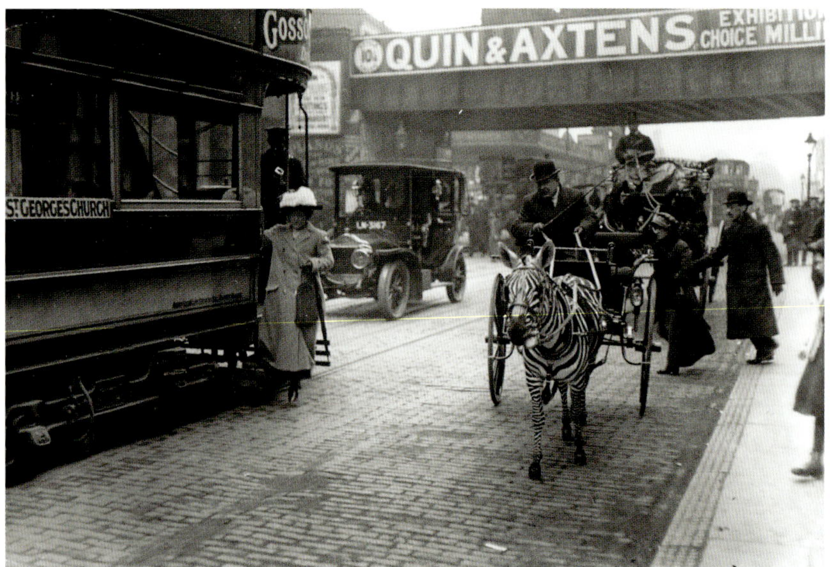

15 April 1913: A zebra and trap and a London tram vie for business in Brixton

Brixton, London, UK (Unknown / Hulton Archive / Getty) pp. 96–97

The buses advertise brands that still survive today, such as Colman's Mustard and Heinz soup. Gossages Soap as seen on the LCC tram is no longer sold. The building in the background next to the buses is a Woolworths branch, the sixth Woolworths store to open in Britain at the time. The railway bridge is still in place today. The 'Quin and Axtens' sign, an advert for Quin and Axtens's Brixton drapery department store, is likely to be constructed from wood, rather than painted. Note that the letters cast a shadow. The 'mill...' is the beginning of the word 'milliner's', or hat-maker's.

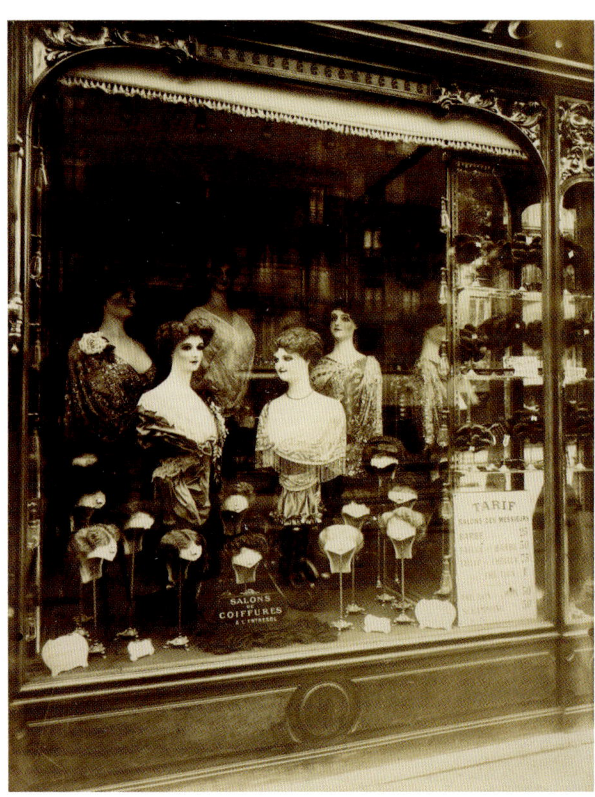

1912: Hairdresser's shop window, Boulevard de Strasbourg (Salon de Coiffures)

Boulevard de Strasbourg, Paris, France (Eugène Atget / George Eastman House) pp. 98–99

These French Mannequins are likely to be wax and are similar to those created by Pierre Imans – examples of which are, in real life, quite eerie. From a technical perspective, this was an extremely challenging image due to the sheer amount of reflective material present in the photograph, from the display mirrors to the reflection of the street.

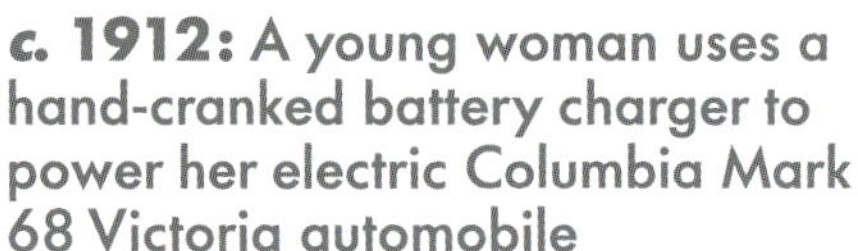

c. 1912: A young woman uses a hand-cranked battery charger to power her electric Columbia Mark 68 Victoria automobile

USA (Chenectady Museum; Hall of Electrical History Foundation / Getty) pp. 100–101

The young woman is standing next to a hand-cranked battery charger for a Columbia Mark 68 (LXVIII) Victoria automobile by the Pope Manufacturing Company of Hartford, Connecticut.

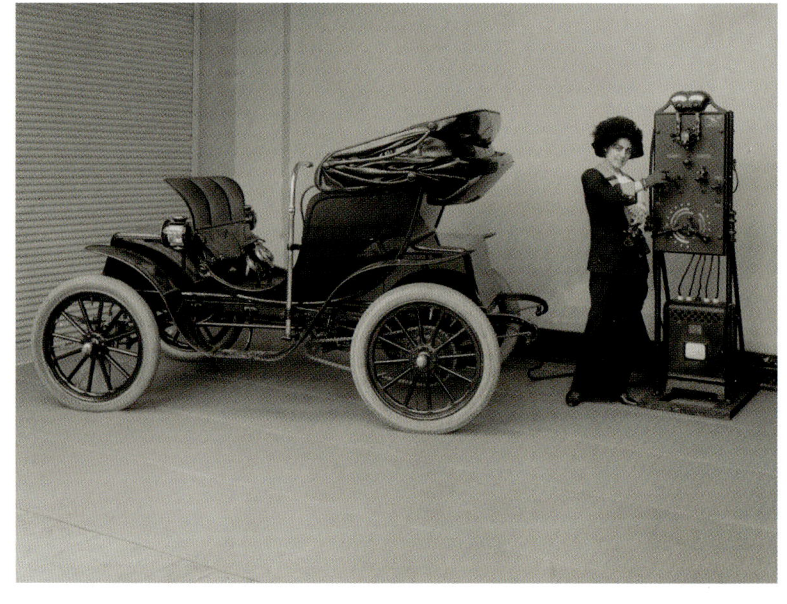

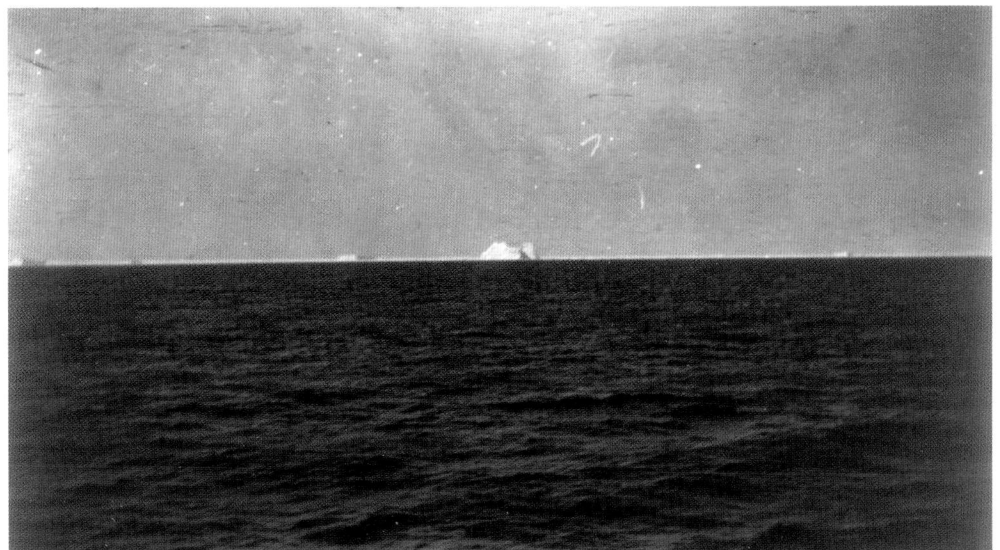

1912: The iceberg that sank the *Titanic*
North Atlantic (Universal Images Group / Getty)
pp. 102–103

Another truly astonishing photograph, I remember my mouth dropping open when I saw it for the first time – it had never even occurred to me that someone might have taken a picture of the iceberg shortly after the *Titanic* sank.

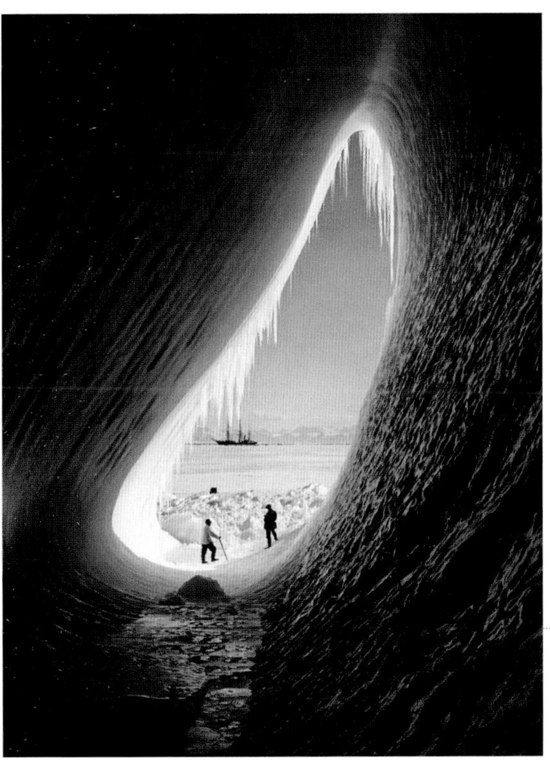

1911: Geologist Thomas Griffith Taylor and meteorologist Charles Wright in the entrance to an ice grotto during Captain Robert Falcon Scott's *Terra Nova* Expedition to the Antarctic. The *Terra Nova* is in the background.
Antarctica (Herbert G. Ponting / Getty) pp. 104–105

What strikes me about photography of the Antarctic region is the colour saturation, in a location where one might expect to find none. As such, many examples from magazines such as *National Geographic* provided excellent references: in this case, at least a dozen. What the reaction was to the original photograph at the time of publication is hard to say. Anything other than astonishment would be surprising – for me, the natural reaction to this bleak, alien landscape.

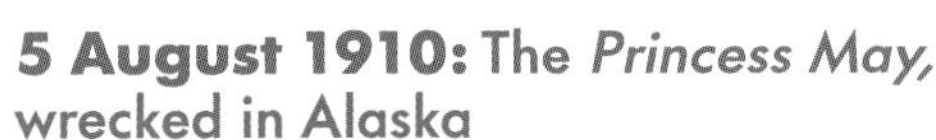

5 August 1910: The *Princess May,* wrecked in Alaska
Sentinel Island, Alaska, USA
(William Howard Case / Frank G. Carpenter / Library of Congress) pp. 106–107

Another extremely difficult image to work on, partly due to the sunlight coming in on the left of the photograph, as well as the overall quality of the image. Contemporary photographs of the area provided references for the water and rocks, and hand-tinted colour postcards for the ship.

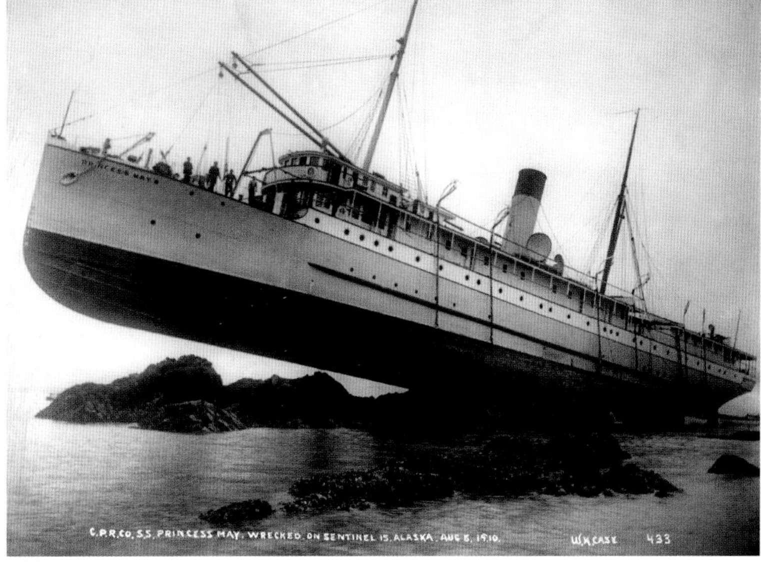

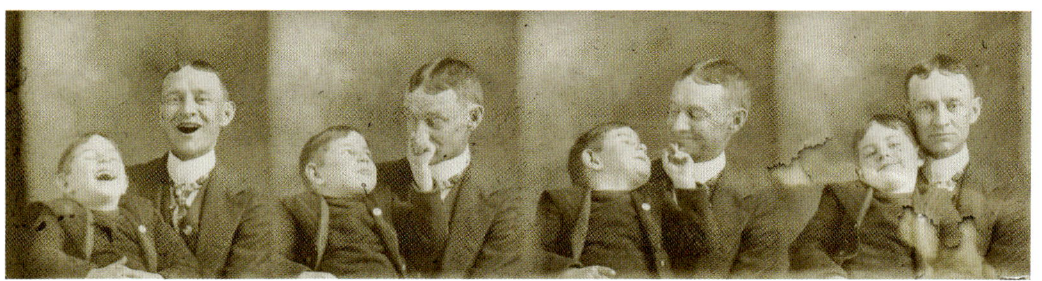

c. 1910: Father and son snapshots
Unknown (Unknown / Simple Insomnia)
pp. 108–109

There is a curious social phenomenon surrounding the expressions of subjects in early photographs – they are mainly serious. One reason might be that, in the very earliest days, the long exposure times meant that subjects couldn't move to prevent blurring, and it's difficult to smile for a long period of time. However, this particular reason became less of an issue as new camera technologies became available. A more likely cause was that having one's photograph taken was an expensive affair for ordinary people, and they typically wanted to give it the gravitas such an occasion deserved as they emulated old portraits of the wealthy rendered in paint, resulting in relatively few jovial and candid expressions.

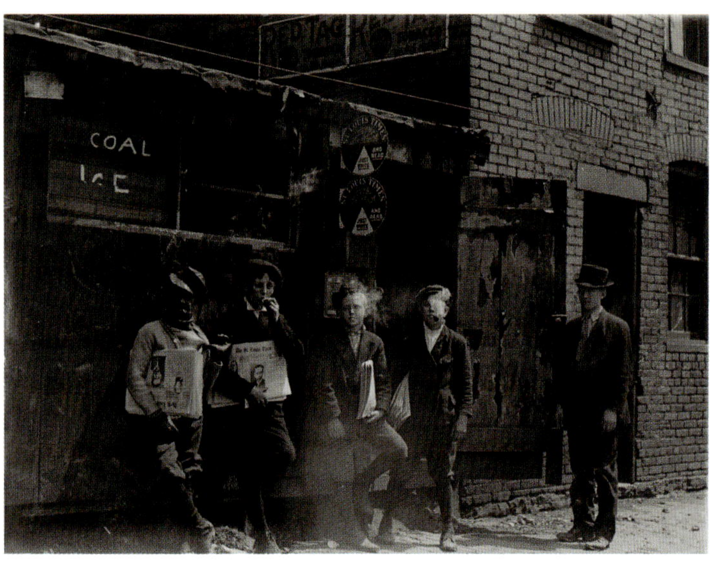

1910: 11 a.m. Newsies at Skeeter's Branch, Jefferson near Franklin. They were all smoking.
St. Louis, Missouri, USA (Lewis Hine / Library of Congress) pp. 110–111

Examples of older buildings in St. Louis provided clues as to the shade of brick, and the signs were pieced together from auction sites or brand colours. One of my favourite details is the newsprint pasted onto the inside of the door.

1909: Louis Blériot leaving Calais, France
Calais, France (Library of Congress)
pp. 112–113

We used contemporary images of the same stretch of coastline, in addition to sampling colours directly from the original Blériot XI plane.

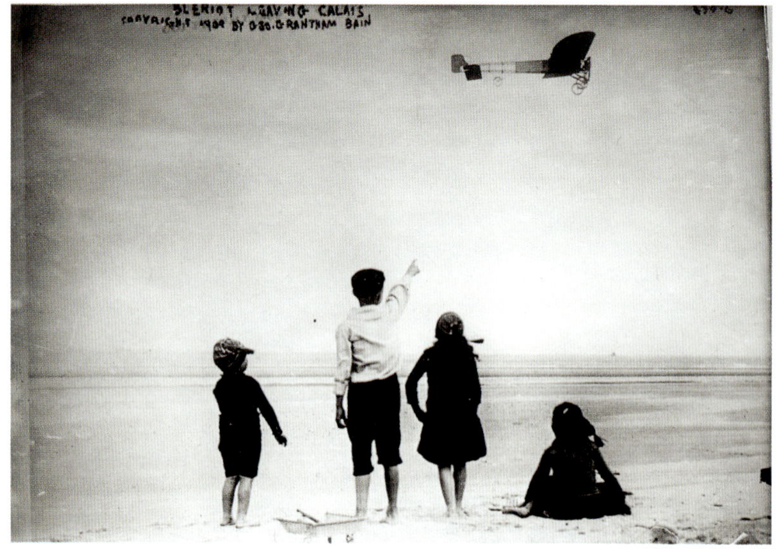

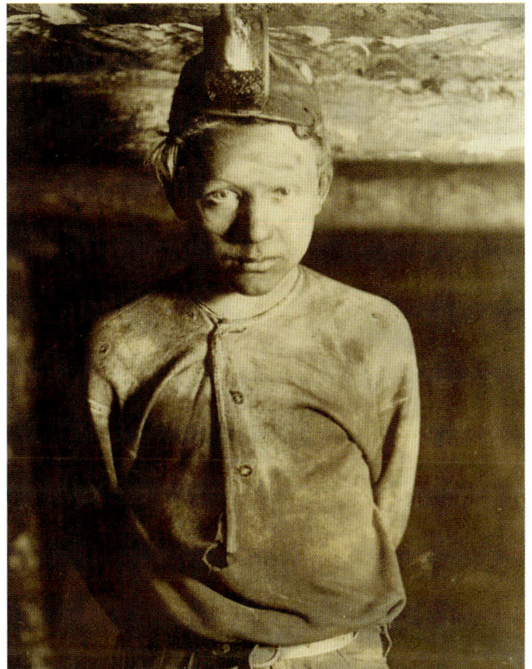

1908: Trapper boy, Turkey Knob Mine
Turkey Knob Mine, MacDonald, West Virginia, USA
(Lewis Hine / Library of Congress) Gatefold – p. 114

Breaking the darkness, the brief explosion of colour seen in the camera flash is sourced from contemporary examples of other mines within the region.

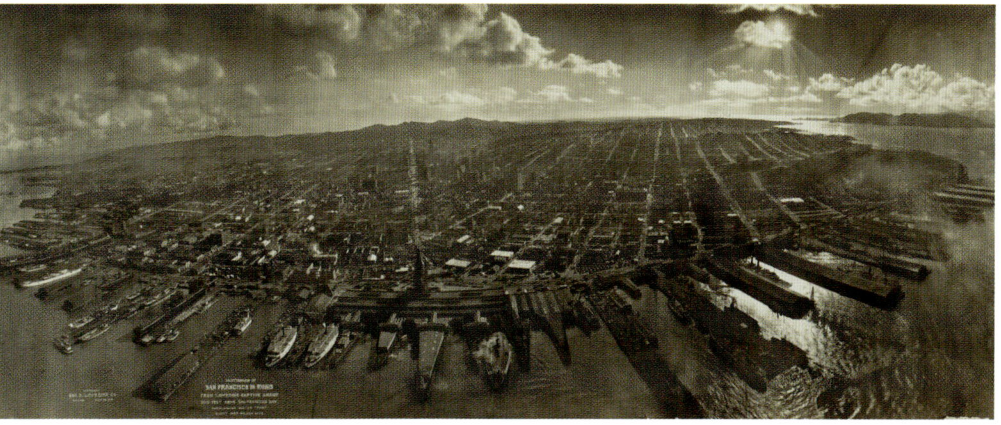

1906: San Francisco in ruins from Lawrence Captive Airship 2,000 feet (600 metres) above San Francisco Bay, overlooking waterfront. Sunset over Golden Gate.
San Francisco, California, USA
(George R. Lawrence / Library of Congress)
Gatefold

The research carried out for this image was, to say the least, extensive. We began by establishing, as far as possible, the exact location and angle of the camera. We also identified the names and locations of as many extant buildings as possible. Five actual colour photographs, taken of the scene in 1906, still exist. In addition to this set, we compiled around 120 other reference photographs, postcards, paintings and drawings. We also drew on insurance maps showing the damage, and in particular, the burn areas. As for shipping, documents tell us that craft present at this time included the USS *Boston*, the USS *Princeton*, the USS *Independence*, the US Training Ship *Pensacol*, the cutter *Golden Gate*, and the steam schooner *Chetco*.

1905: The Empire State Express (New York Central Railroad) passing through Washington Street, New York
Syracuse, New York State, USA (Detroit Publishing Company / Library of Congress) Gatefold – p. 115

We drew together modern colour photographs and hand-tinted postcards to source colours of the now demolished Yates Hotel in the foreground left of the photograph. The buildings in the background on E. Genesee Street are also intact. The engine number is 3837, originally built as 2897 and then renumbered in the mid-1920s.

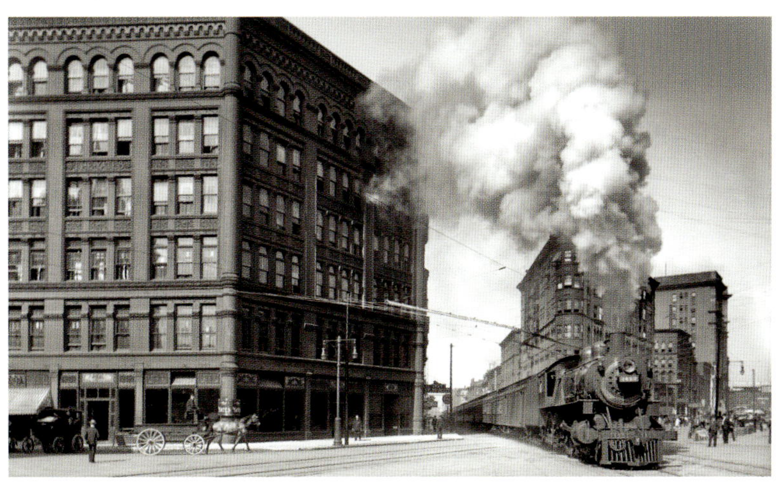

***c.* 1905:** Pulling out of the clearcut
Skagit County, Washington, USA (Darius Kinsey / Getty)
pp. 116–117

Painting and repainting engines in liveries was very much a non-essential expense for logging companies. Their locomotives were workhorses and dirty. Around 100 Shay engines survive today – this one was scrapped, so far as we can tell, in 1952. The men are in denim workwear.

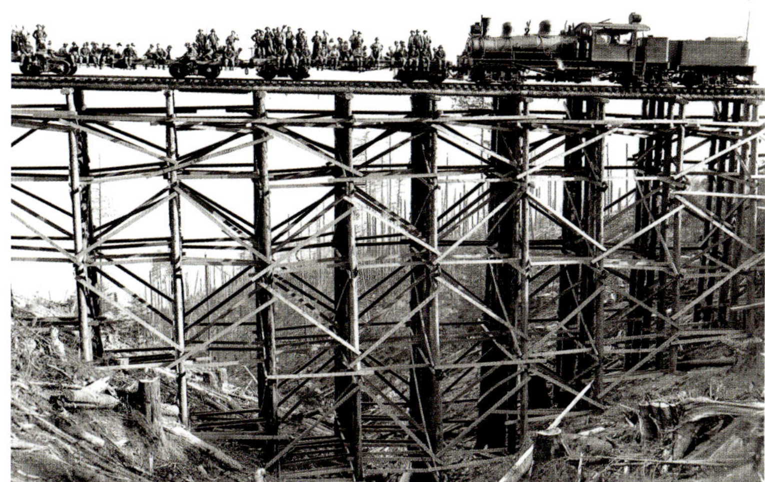

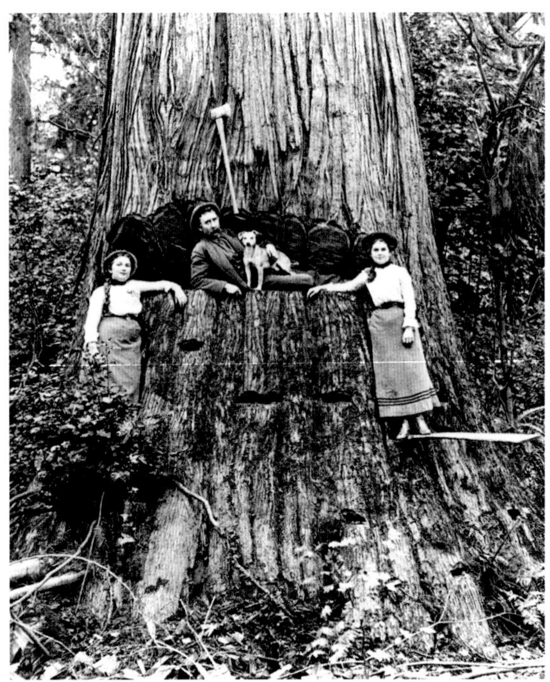

c. 1905: On the springboards and in the undercut: a Washington lumberjack and his daughters, in the Cascade Mountains near Seattle, Washington
Seattle, Washington, USA
(Darius Kinsey / Library of Congress) pp. 118–119

Contemporary images of the region were used for colour reference. When it comes to people, a trick I use often is to find a colour photograph of someone who looks very similar to the subject, perhaps someone I know, or a famous actor. In this case, the woman on the right looks quite similar to a friend of mine.

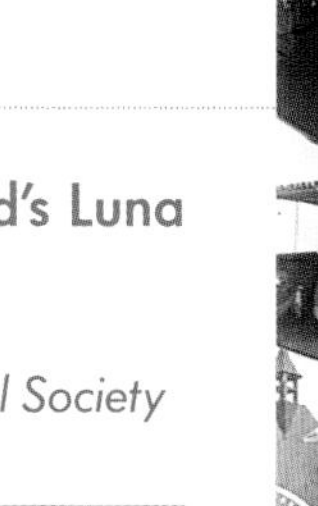

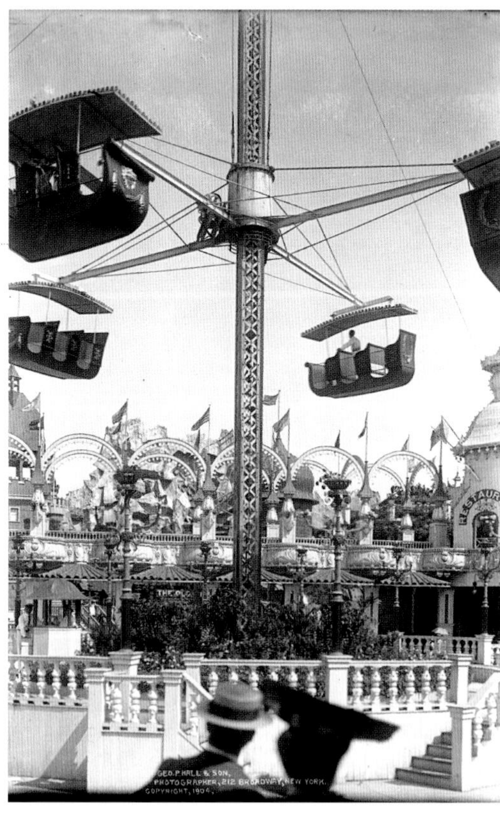

c. 1904: A ride at Coney Island's Luna Park
Coney Island, New York City, USA
(Geo. P. Hall & Son / New York Historical Society / Getty) pp. 120–121

I drew on half a dozen hand-tinted colour postcards for this image – although the colours displayed varied from one postcard to another, which illustrates the point that much of early colour was not about accuracy, but commercially driven vibrancy. In the end, I achieved a visual consensus by finding matching colours across several postcards and cross-referencing these results with the colours suggested by the black-and-white information on the original monochrome.

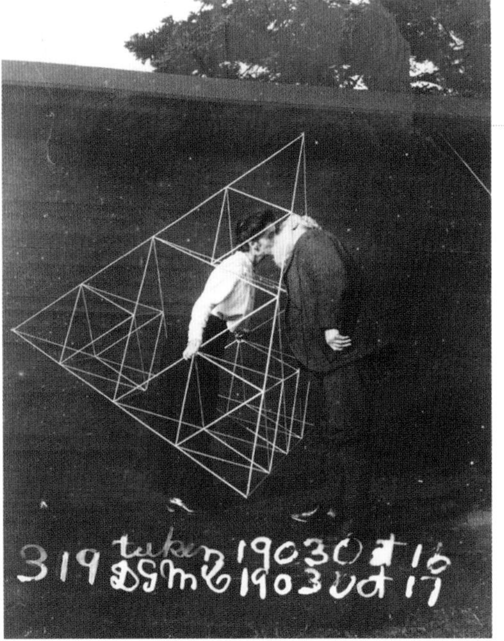

16 October 1903: **Alexander Graham Bell kissing his wife, Mabel Hubbard Gardiner Bell, who is standing in a tetrahedral kite**
Baddeck, Nova Scotia, Canada
(Library of Congress) pp. 122–123

Looking at maps and satellite imagery, I believe this photograph was taken outside one of Bell's laboratories on his private estate of Beinn Bhreagh in Nova Scotia. Contemporary photographs gave an indication of the background tree and wood of the cabin.

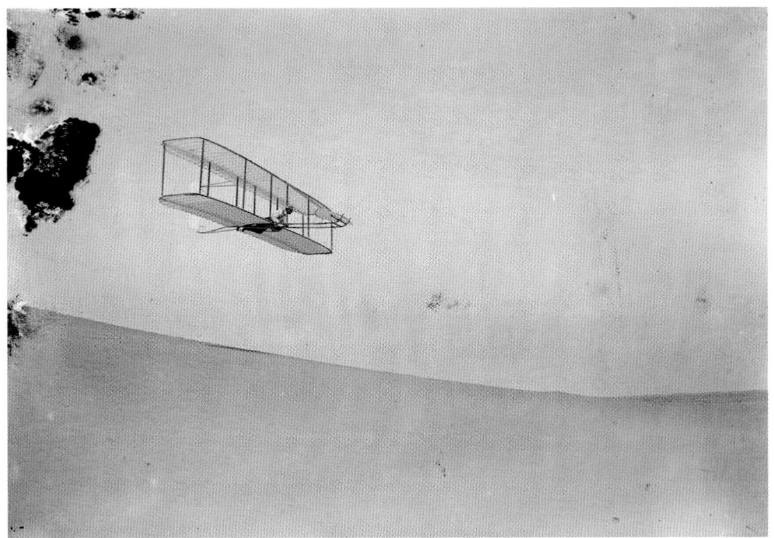

1902: **Wilbur Wright gliding down the steep slope of Big Kill Devil Hill**
Kitty Hawk, North Carolina, USA (Wright Brothers / Library of Congress)
pp. 124–125

Despite its seemingly simple composition, this image was in fact one of the hardest images to work on in the entire book. This is because much of the texture on the original plate is not, as it appears, detail of the sand dune, but rather damage to the substrate of the plate. Thankfully, the test runs at Kitty Hawk are well documented and I was able to digitally reconstruct the most heavily damaged parts of the photograph with other photographs of the same location on a different day, or at a slightly different angle on the same day. Numerous contemporary examples of models and colour images exist, though notably a full-size model of the flyer itself exists at the Wright Brothers National Memorial visitor centre in North Carolina.

1902: **The Cliff House Hotel, San Francisco**
San Francisco, California, USA (Unknown / Library of Congress)
pp. 126–127

There are some really great contemporary photographs of this exact location, which provided a solid foundation for getting an accurate overall atmosphere. As the original photograph is sensitive to blue light, the sky you see in the photograph is actually composited in and blended with photographs. Making sure the sky haze blends in with the detail is a very challenging part of the process. Other references, such as the house, are sourced from hand-tinted postcards, which surprisingly were all consistent in their renditions. The clothing of the hundreds of people on the beach were all sourced from real examples of the period.

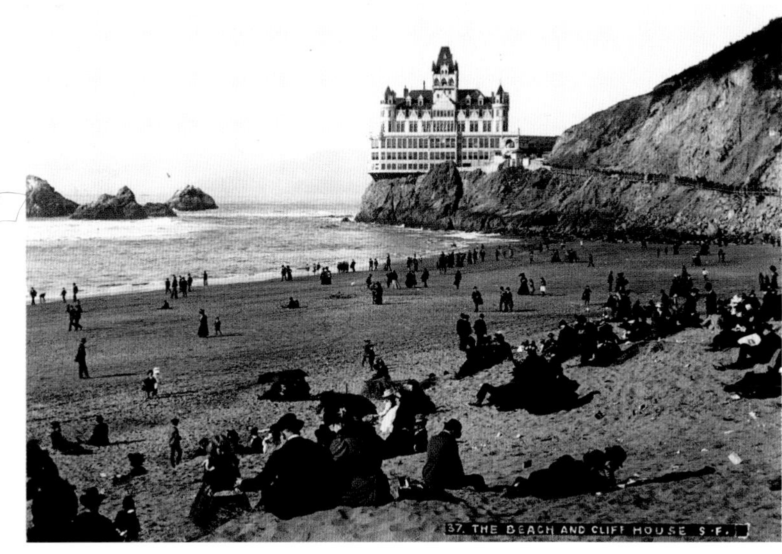

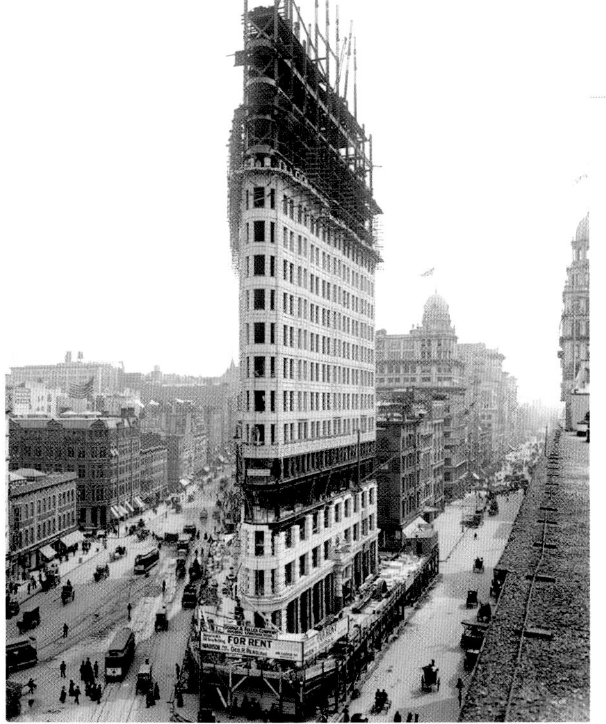

c. **1902:** **The Flatiron Building under construction, New York**
Broadway, New York City, USA (Detroit Publishing Company / Getty) pp. 128–129

New York Public Library holds a set of coloured-pencil elevations of the blocks on Broadway. The set was issued in 1899 so they provided an excellent colour reference, short of actual photographs. Fortunately for me, the elevations on 5th Avenue (*to the right*) haven't changed a great deal since this photograph was taken and – to my astonishment – some of the businesses are still located in the same address, such as the Brooks Brothers store on 670 Broadway, the red brick building seen to the left of the Flatiron.

Ellis Island immigrants

Ellis Island, New York City, USA (Augustus Francis Sherman / New York Public Library) pp. 130–135

The San Francisco panorama (gatefold) was the photograph that required the most detailed research. However, this set of images showing immigrants to Ellis Island, wearing their national dress, came a close second. Every single element, from thread to stitching to buttons, had a very specific and original colour – or, rather, colours, as the costumes are highly regional. Sometimes, even with our best efforts, we found we couldn't trace a particular material. I became paranoid about making an error and finding that I had inadvertently but understandably offended a large number of people. We released this set of images online around a year before the book was published, to generate publicity and support for the book's crowdfunding campaign through Unbound. This proved helpful to our research, as a number of online commenters pointed out detailed corrections for the series. Fortuitously, we were then also contacted by Jan T. Letowski, specialist in European ethnographic dress and founder of the Museum of Ethnic Dress and Adornment, whose help was invaluable. Some elements in these pictures, such as the *bunad* on the Norwegian woman and the Bavarian man, match the museum examples Jan showed us almost exactly.

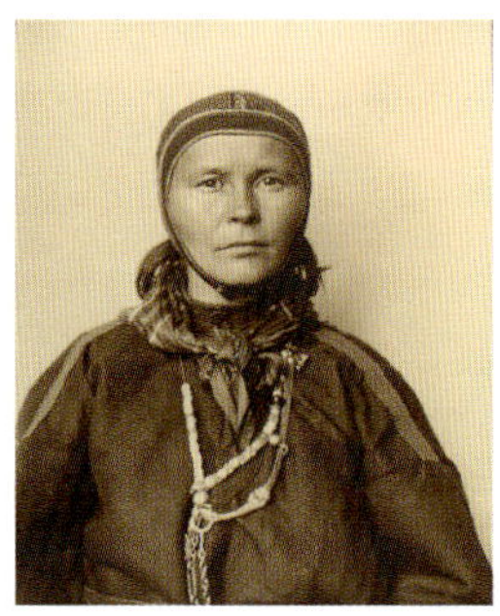

Gákti is the traditional costume of the Sámi people of the Arctic regions spanning from northern Norway to the Kola Peninsula in Russia. Traditionally made from reindeer leather and wool, velvet and silks are also used, with the (typically) blue pullover supplemented by contrasting coloured banding of plaits, brooches and jewellery. The decorations are region-specific.

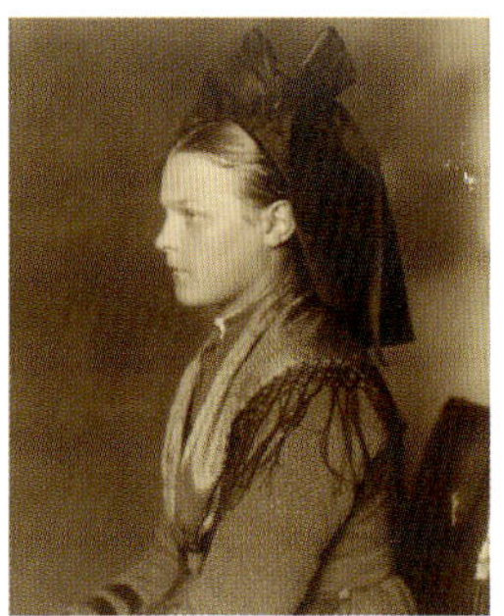

Hailing from the Germanic-speaking region of Alsace, now in modern-day France, the large bow in this regional dress is known as a *schlupfkàpp* and was worn by single women. The bows signified the bearer's religion – Protestants generally wore black, while Catholics favoured brightly coloured bows.

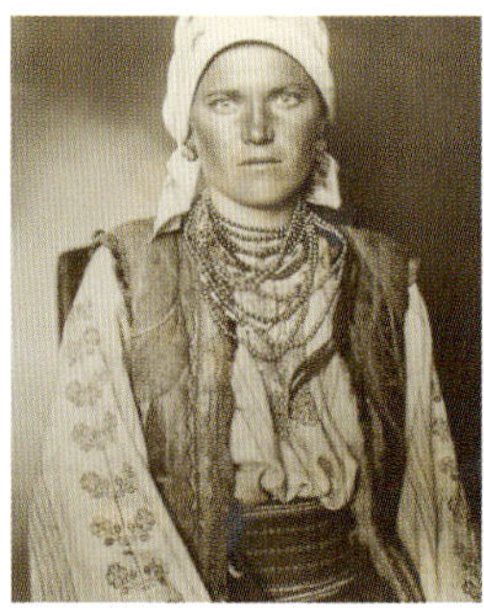

While there are clues in her garments, the exact home village of this Ruthenian woman – as she was originally titled – is uncertain. Her costume is characteristic of the Bukovina region, which is today divided between Ukraine and Romania. The embroidered motifs on her linen blouse suggest that she is likely from the Ukrainian side, but useful details are concealed by the lack of colour in the original image.

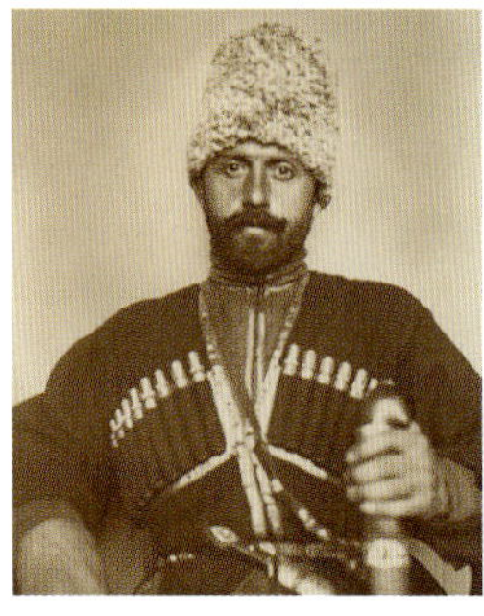

This man is wearing a traditional costume that enjoyed widespread popularity throughout the Caucasus, most notably among the population living in modern-day Georgia. The *choka* overcoat along with the traditional swords and daggers were seen both as elements of folk dress and military uniform. The rows of tubes across his chest are metal-capped wooden gunpowder containers.

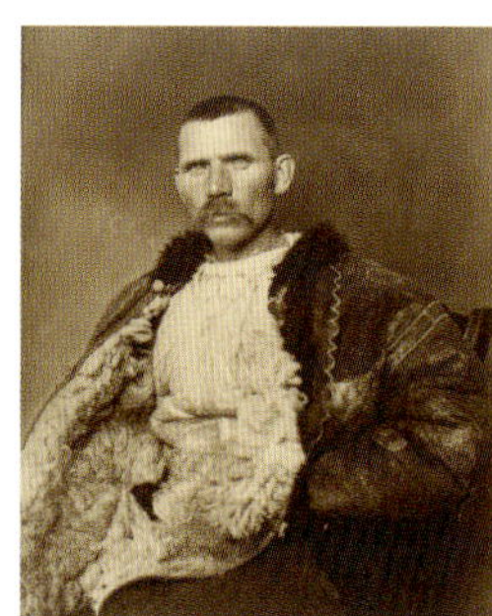

Dominating the photograph is a traditional shepherd's coat known as a *sarică*, made of three to four sheepskins sewn together. Depending on the region and style, a *sarică* could be worn either with the fleece facing inwards, as seen here, or outwards, resulting in an entirely different aesthetic. The size and softness of the garment also made it suitable for use as a pillow when sleeping outdoors.

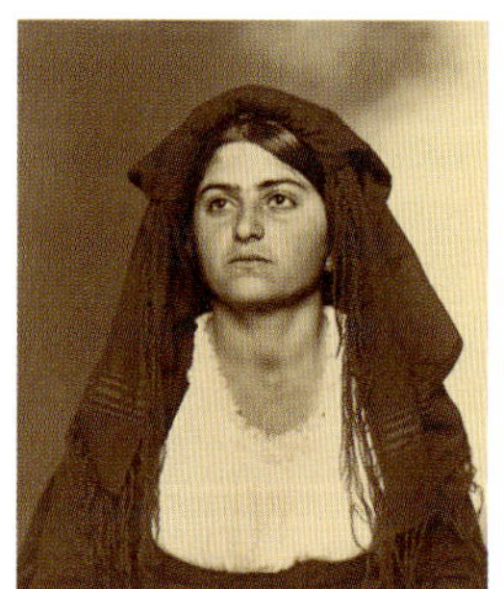

Elements of this dress may have been home-made, though the kerchief and earrings would have had to have been purchased – a considerable expense for many peasants. The colour and cut of garments were often region-specific, though manufactured elements such as shawls were a common feature throughout Italy. For special occasions, women often wore highly decorative aprons made of floral brocade.

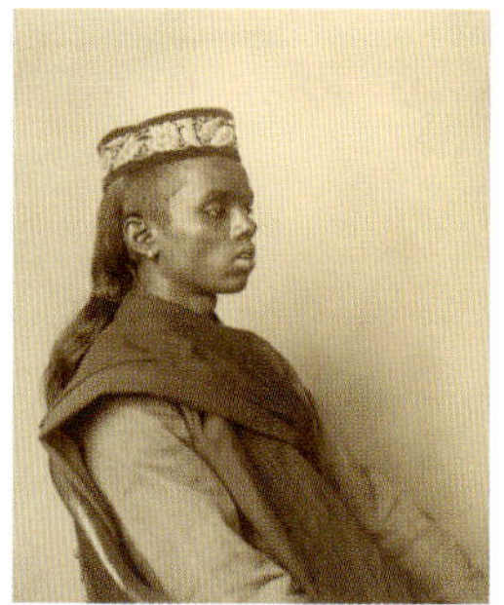

The *topi* (cap) is worn all over the Indian subcontinent with many regional variations. It is especially common in Muslim communities where it is known as a *taqiyah*. Both the cotton khadi and the prayer shawl are likely to have been hand-spun on a charkha, and were used all year round.

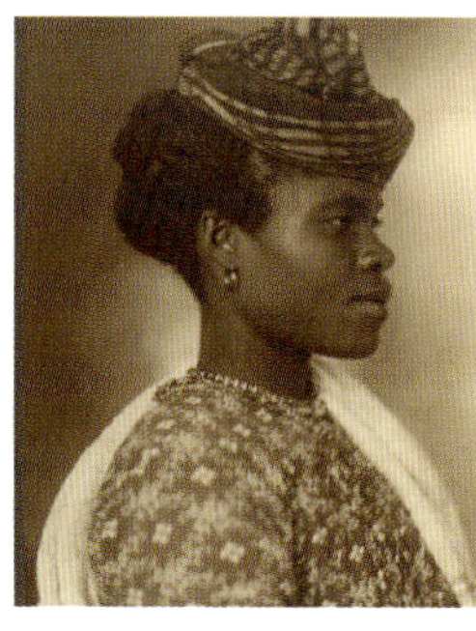

The elaborate tartan headpiece, symbolising marital status or mood, worn by Guadeloupean women can be traced back to the Middle Ages. First plain, then striped and in increasingly elaborate patterns, the Madras fabric exported from India and used as headwraps was eventually influenced by the Scottish in Colonial India, leading to a Madras-inspired tartan known as 'Madrasi checks'.

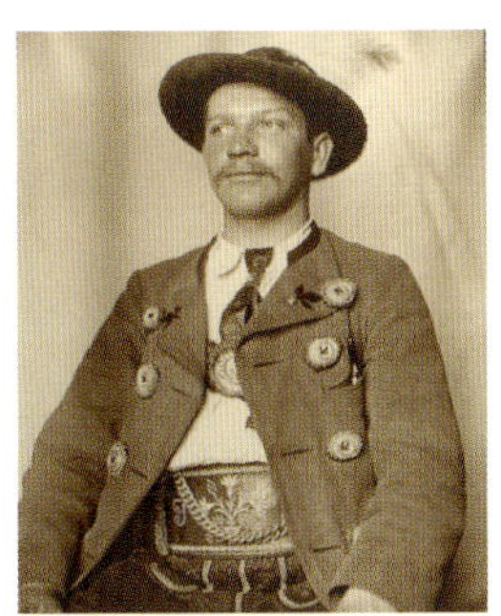

Traditional dress in Bavaria is known as *Trachten* and there are many regional variations. In the Alpine region, leather breeches known as *Lederhosen* were worn by men and became part of the typical Bavarian style known as *Miesbacher Tracht*. This standardised form is now typically associated with the annual Oktoberfest. The grey jacket is made from fulled wool and decorated with horn buttons.

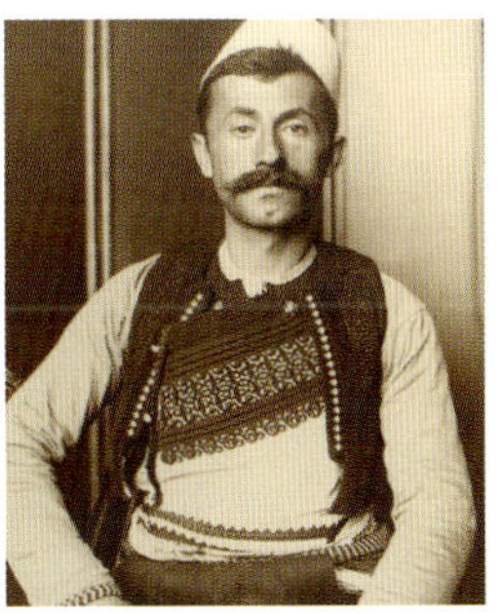

The truncated, brimless felt cap is known as a *qeleshe*. Its shape was largely determined by region and moulded to one's head. The vest, a *jelek* or *xhamadan*, was decorated with embroidered braids of silk or cotton. Colour and decoration denoted the regional home of the wearer and their social rank. This man is likely to come from the northern regions of Albania.

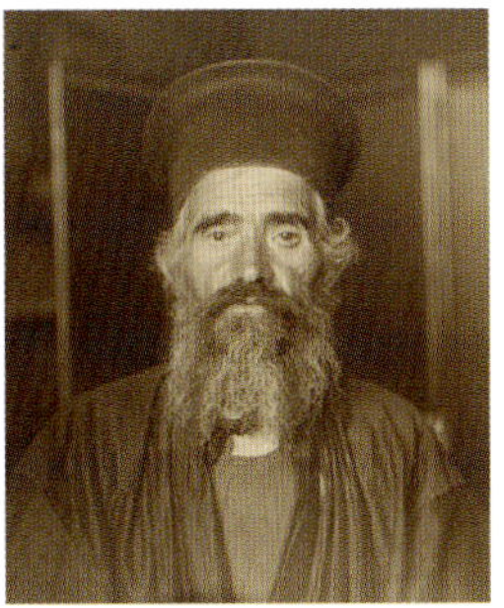

The vestments of the Greek Orthodox church have remained largely unchanged. In this photograph, the priest wears an *anteri*, an ankle-length cassock (from the Turkish *quzzak*, from which the term 'Cossack' also derives) worn by all clergymen over which an *amaniko*, a type of cassock vest, is sometimes worn. The stiff cylindrical hat is called a *kalimavkion* and worn during services.

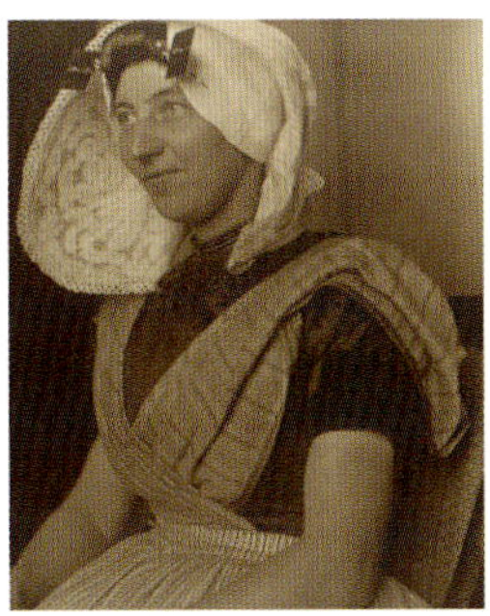

The Dutch bonnet was usually made of white cotton or lace. The shape of the headdress, in addition to the gold pins and square *stikken*, identifies where this woman is from (South Beveland), her religion (Protestant), and her marital status (married). Necklaces were often red coral, though black was common during mourning. Elements of the dress changed depending on the availability of fabrics.

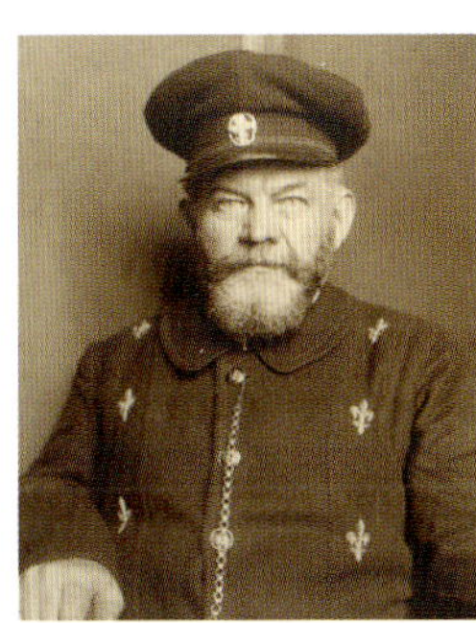

Evolving since the 1750s, the Danish dress was simple with more decorated attire saved for special occasions. As with many nations before mass industrialisation, much of the clothing was homespun. In contrast, this man is wearing items made of commercial cloth and a hat that suggests he is wearing a uniform rather than a strictly regional costume. His tailored jacket is decorated with metal buttons and a chain.

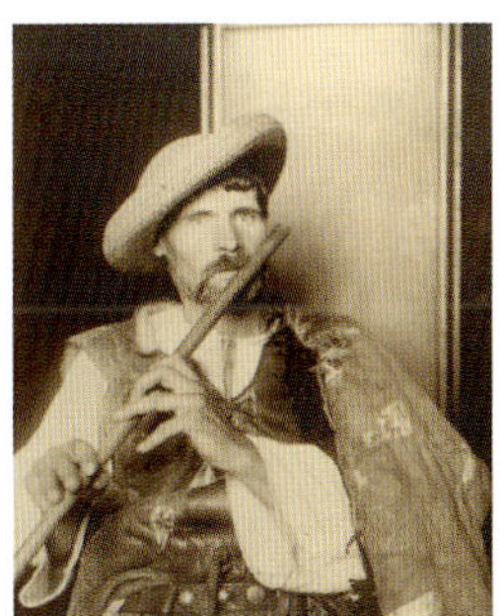

This man's sheepskin garments are noticeably plainer than the shepherd seen earlier, indicating his relative lack of wealth. He is likely a farm labourer, but the fact that he has posed with an instrument could suggest that his earnings were supplemented at least in part by playing music. The waistcoat, known as a *pieptar*, was worn by both men and women and came in a variety of shapes, sizes and ornamental styles.

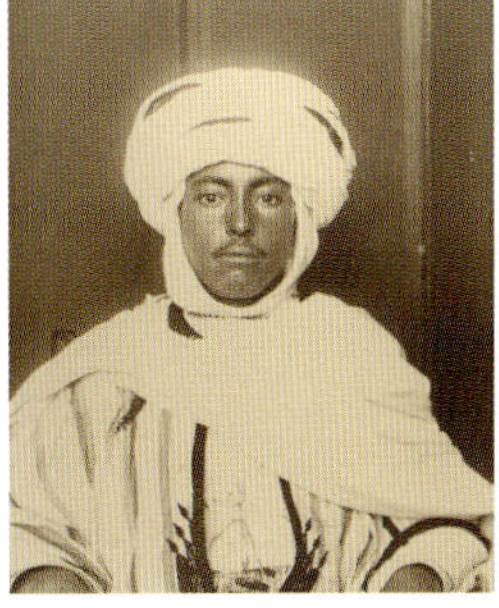

The large turban-style headdress is made up of a large square of fabric folded and wrapped around a *fez* hat and secured using a special cord. Visible beneath the *djellaba* robe is a multi-colored, striped silk belt that was common throughout the Ottoman Empire. These belts had different regional names, for example, *taraboulous*, revealing the city where they were made: Tripoli (Tarabulus in Arabic).

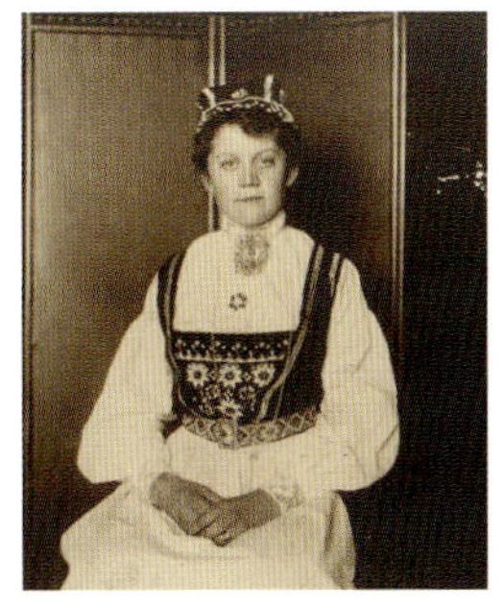

Bunad is the the Norwegian term for regional clothing that developed through traditional folk costumes. In some regions the *bunad* is a direct continuation of the local peasant style, while in others it was reconstructed based on historical information and personal tastes. This woman is wearing a *bunad* from the Hardanger region, one of the most famous in all of Norway. The main elements are decorated with beadwork.

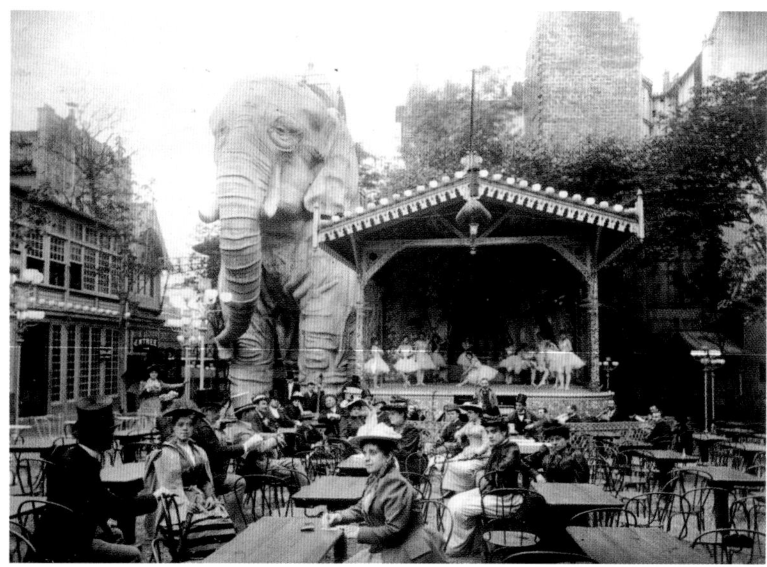

1900: Patrons enjoying a ballet at the outdoor theatre of the Moulin Rouge, Paris
Boulevard de Clichy, Paris, France
(Unknown / Hulton Archive / Getty) pp. 136–137

We drew on two rare 1920s Autochrome colour photographs of the Moulin Rouge, as well as early photochrom postcards and paintings. Clothing colours were sourced from a range of museum collections.

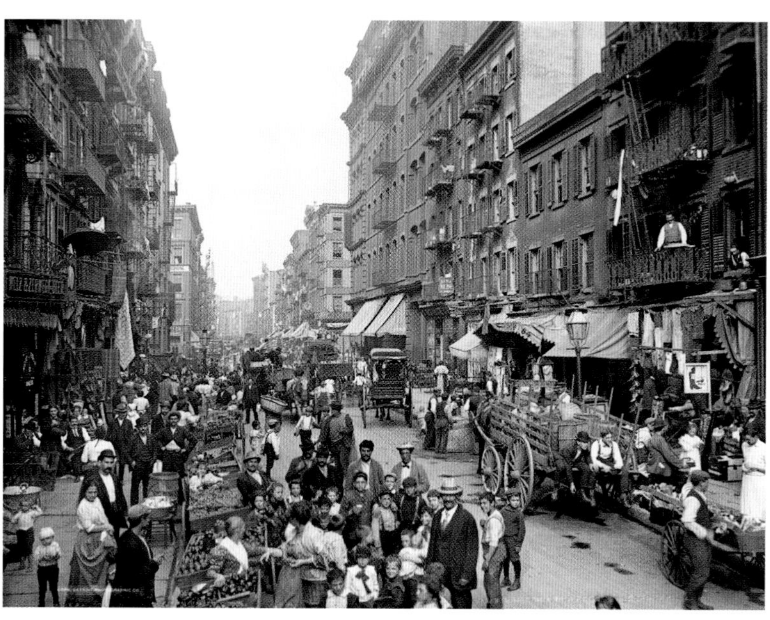

1900: Mulberry Street, Manhattan
Mulberry Street, New York City, USA
(Detroit Publishing Co. / Library of Congress) pp. 138–139

In 2016, New York was the first place in America I had the good fortune of visiting in my adult life. I was working with Wolfgang on an exhibition and I dragged *The Paper Time Machine* researcher Deborah through the rain to get a shot of the exact angle and location from which this photograph was taken. The original may have been taken on a ladder or horse cart; the best I could do on that cold, rainy day in New York was to balance one foot on top of some street railings.

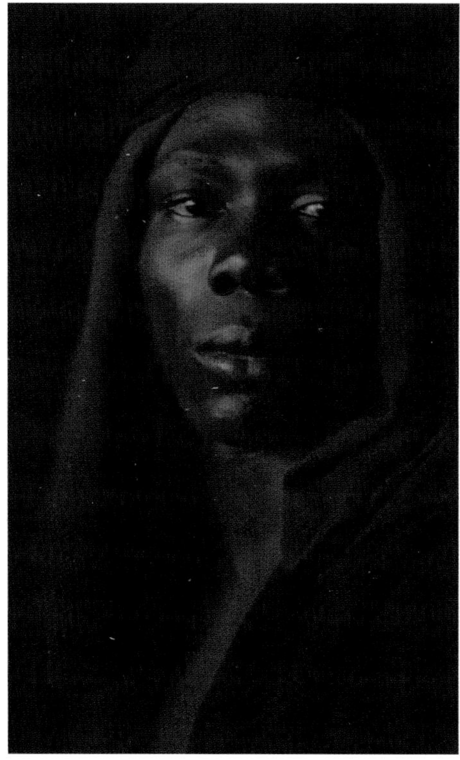

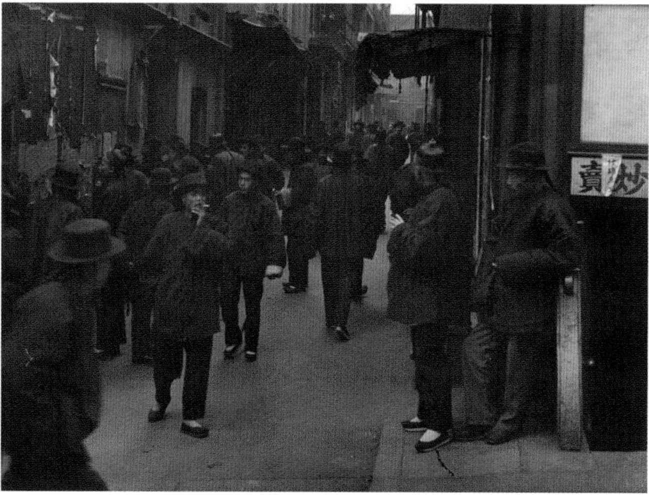

1896: The 'Street of Gamblers', Chinatown, San Francisco
Street of Gamblers, San Francisco, California, USA (Arnold Genthe / Library of Congress) pp. 142–143

Some of the buildings still exist today and we could use them as colour references, alongside photographs of markets in Hong Kong and China. Shots like this, featuring little colour variation, are technically difficult. Achieving fifty shades of black convincingly is a challenge.

***c.* 1897: Portrait of an unidentified man**
USA (Fred Holland Day / Science & Society Picture Library / Getty) pp. 140–141

The cropping and lighting of the photograph go beyond historical posterity and into fine art. I've sought to maintain the simplicity and allow the lighting to do the work.

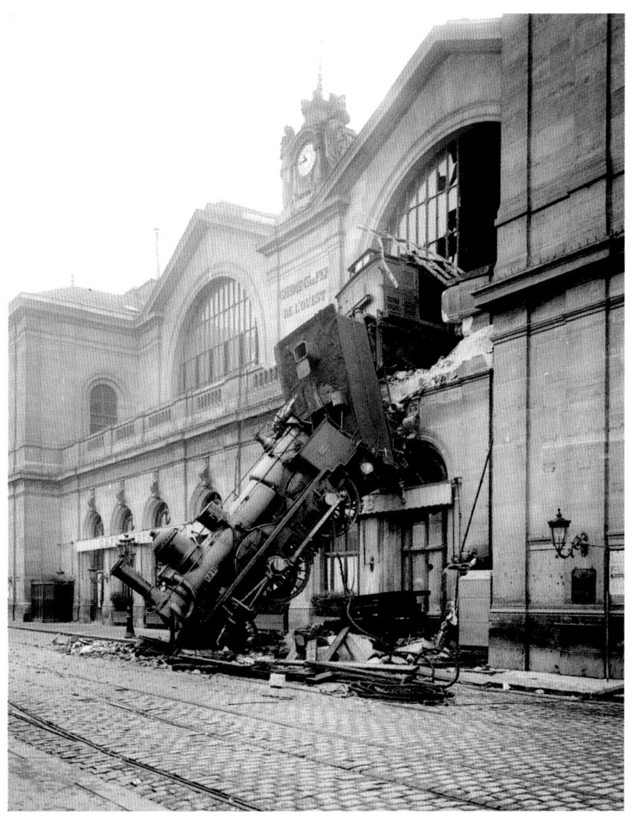

22 October 1895: Train wreck at Montparnasse, Paris
Montparnasse, Paris, France
(ND / Roger Viollet / Getty) pp. 144–145

The stone building seen in this photograph no longer exists; it was demolished and redeveloped in the late 1960s. The train itself is a steam locomotive No. 721 (a type 2-4-0, French notation 120) hauling three baggage vans, a post van and six passenger carriages, painted in the operating company's livery.

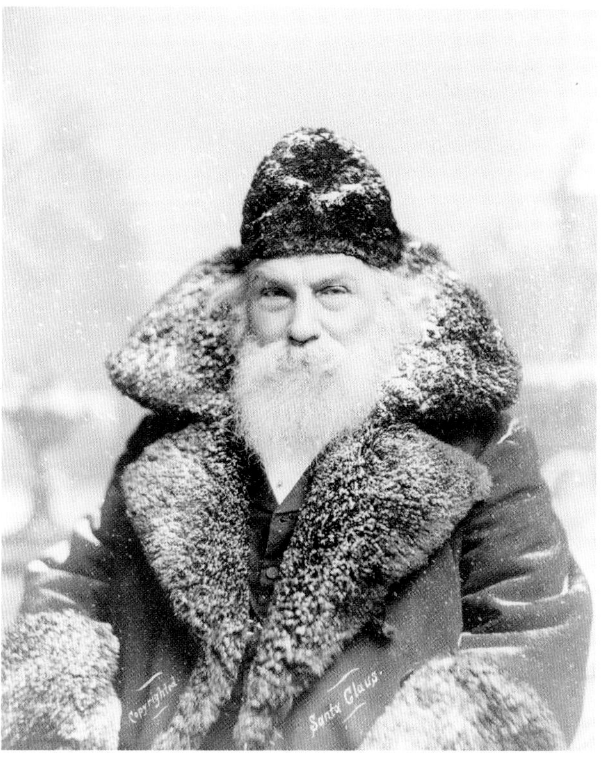

***c.* 1895:** Man portraying Santa Claus in snowy scene
USA (Unknown / Library of Congress)
pp. 146–147

The shot is characteristically over-exposed, like many of its era, to emphasise the caucasian skin tones. The 'snow' was most likely to have been white paint, flicked on with a brush.

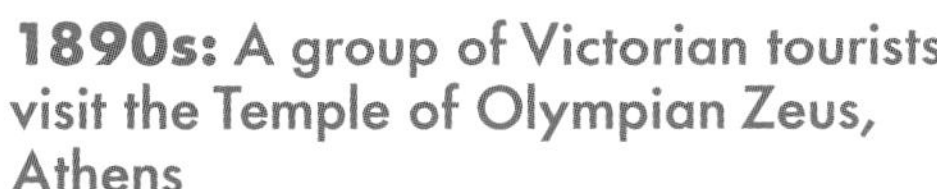

1890s: A group of Victorian tourists visit the Temple of Olympian Zeus, Athens
Athens, Greece (Unknown / School of Archaeology, University of Oxford) pp. 148–149

The expansive background is now unrecognisable in modern Athens. It is filled in with rows of apartment blocks and modern infrastructure, though the numerous tourist photographs of the site indicate the colour of the ground and, indeed, of the columns themselves.

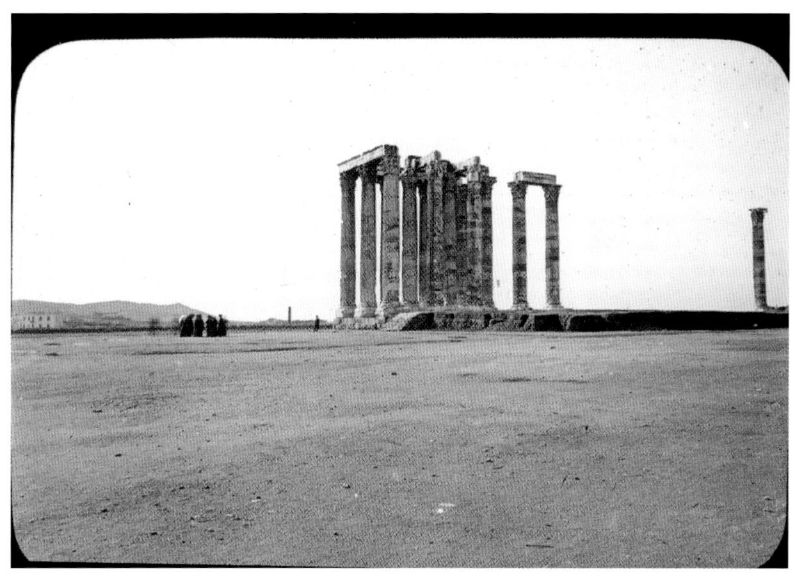

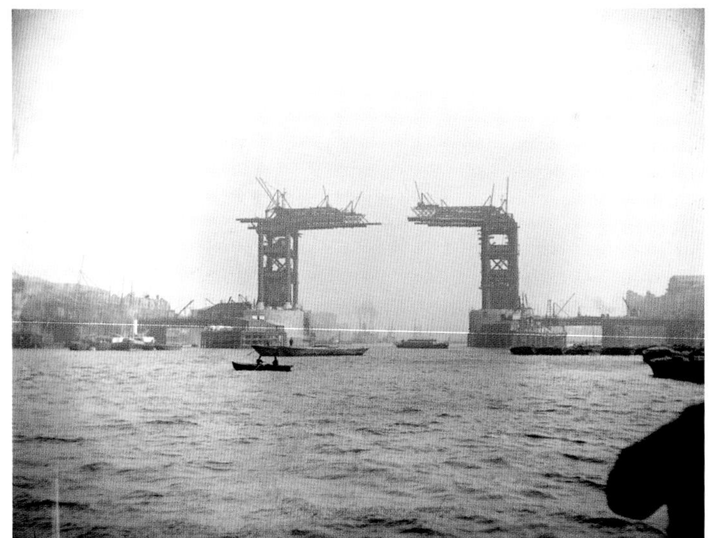

1889: Construction of Tower Bridge, London
Southwark, London, UK
(Unknown / English Heritage / Getty) pp. 150–151

We sourced the numerous ships and skiffs lurking in the background from contemporaneous paintings of the 1880s.

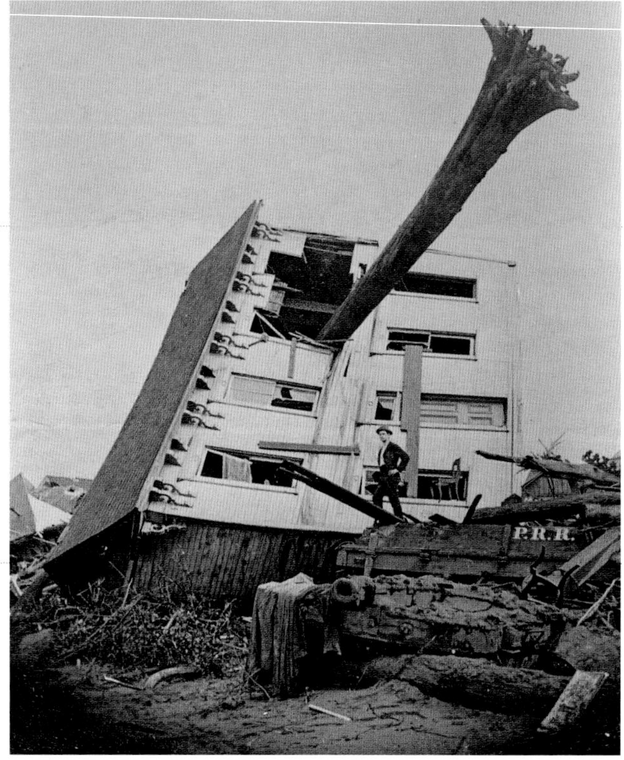

June 1889: A tree pierces a house in the Johnstown flood calamity, Pennsylvania
Johnstown, Pennsylvania, USA
(George Barker / Library of Congress) pp. 152–153

The photograph seems so improbable that it resembles a movie set. We used examples of painted houses of the period. The lack of sharp shadows indicated that the photograph was taken on an overcast day, adding to the dystopian landscape.

July 1888: The Eiffel Tower under construction, Paris
Champs de Mars, Paris, France (Roger Viollet / Getty) pp. 154–155

Due to the increased blue sensitivity of the photographic emulsion used in the image, the sky appears very washed-out, but the lack of cast shadows in the photograph suggest an overcast day. We used several paintings and picture postcards of the Exposition site as reference for the background buildings and could sample the stonework of Port de la Bourdonnais on the Seine riverbank, under construction in the middle of the photograph, from contemporary photographs.

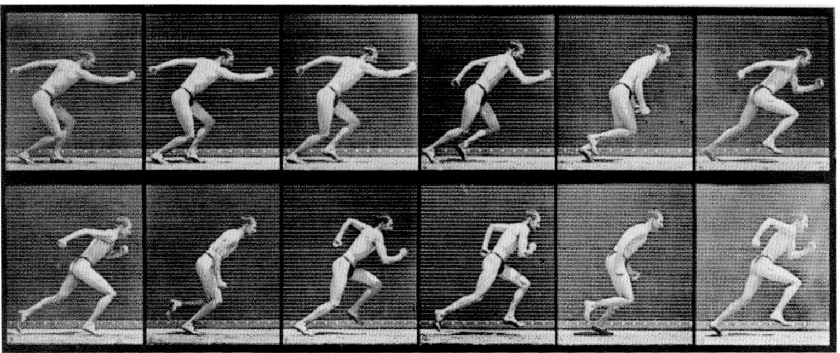

1887: A study in human locomotion
University of Pennsylvania, Pennsylvania, USA (Eadweard Muybridge / Library of Congress) pp. 156–157

There are a few more photographs showing Muybridge's elaborate rig at the University of Pennsylvania, from which these photographs were derived for the locomotion series. The human subjects were generally almost nude.

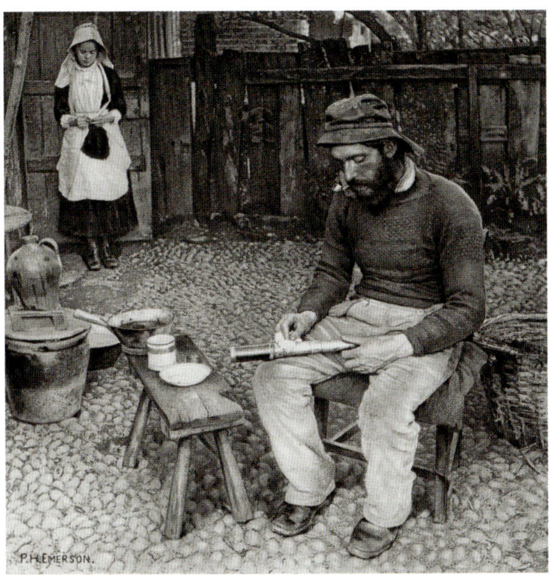

1887: A fisherman at home, Norfolk
Norfolk, UK (Peter Henry Emerson / Royal Photographic Society / SSPL / Getty)
pp. 158–159

The posing, composition and relief detail on this photograph suggest a Dutch painting rendered in oils, rather than a photograph. My favourite detail is the small, white clay pipe the subject is using whilst he goes about his work.

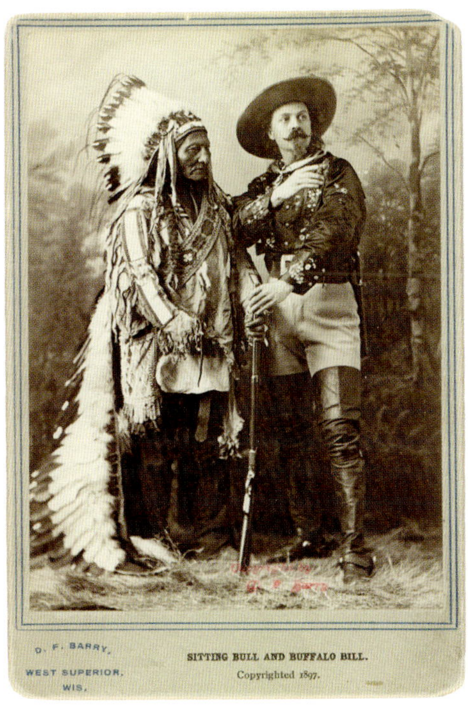

1885: Sitting Bull and Buffalo Bill
Montreal, Quebec, Canada (William Notman / David Francis Barry / Library of Congress) pp. 160–161

Sitting Bull's braids are wrapped, possibly in fur. Many of the clothes in this photograph still exist in museums. Cody wears beige wool riding pants, with seven mother-of-pearl buttons on the lower leg. Strange as it may seem to our eyes, many of the backdrops used in Victorian photographic studios were black and white. Prior to the turn of the century, colour photography was the preserve of only a handful of scientific pioneers. Colouring a backdrop for a monochrome photograph was a waste of time and money – though, for postcards issued using the image, the scene would be hand-tinted.

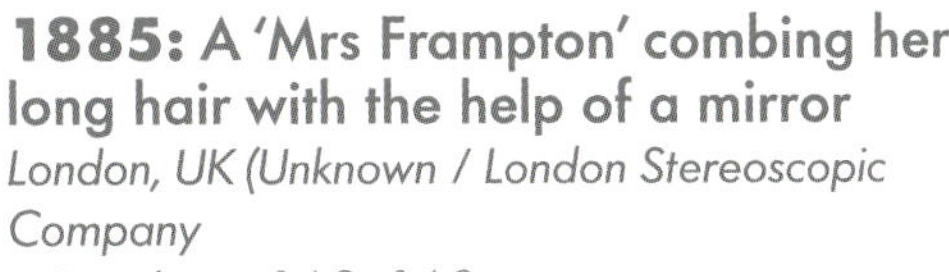

1885: A 'Mrs Frampton' combing her long hair with the help of a mirror
London, UK (Unknown / London Stereoscopic Company / Getty) pp. 162–163

The original plate of Mrs Frampton has extensive fracturing and flecking, all of which it was possible to repair. Her clothes and her hair appear to be competing with each other for opulence and lustre. The colouration of the carpet, and indeed her clothes, were inspired by comparable museum objects – though my research has yet to surface who Mrs Frampton was, or Mr Frampton for that matter. The light on the surface of the mirror edge is particularly striking.

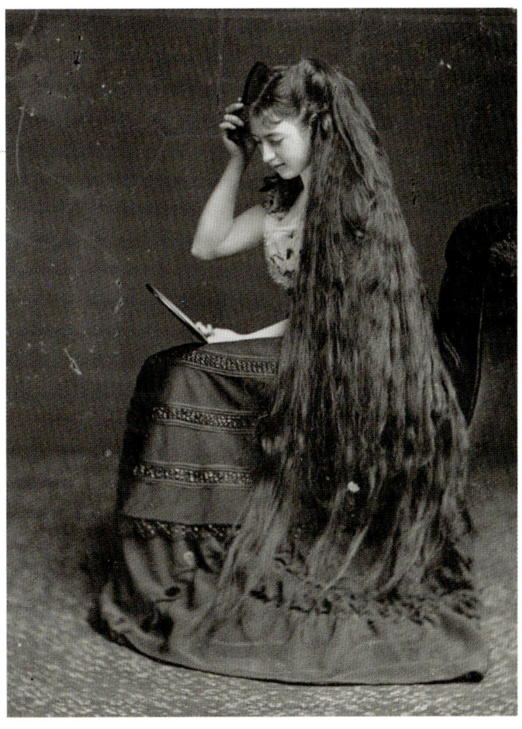

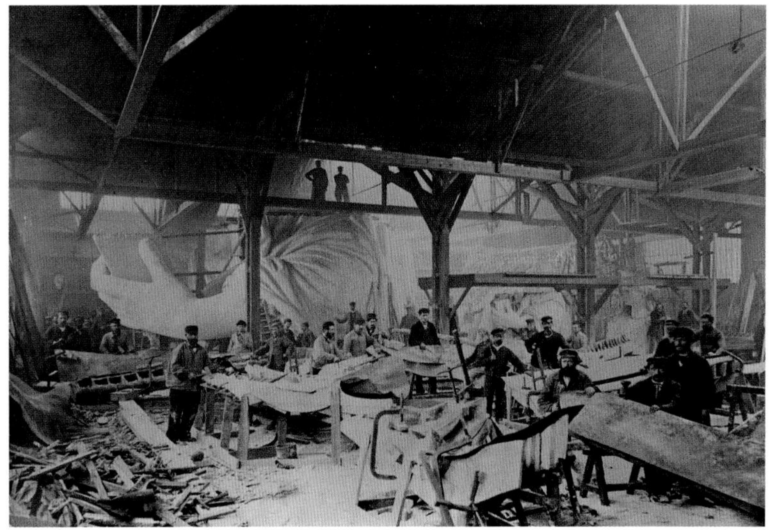

1882: Workers build the Statue of Liberty inside French sculptor Frédéric Auguste Bartholdi's workshop, Paris
Paris, France (Albert Fernique / Library of Congress) pp. 164–165

This was a complex scene to do. The interplay between the darkness of the workshop and the natural light (in an era before electric lighting) made this a particularly challenging photograph, compounded by the lack of mid-tone detail. The recognisable elements of the statue in the background are plaster cast references. The wooden moulds are visible in the foreground over which the copper was beaten to form the shape.

1880s: The bell tower of the Sacré-Cœur Basilica under construction on the Montmartre Hill, Paris
Montmartre, Paris, France (Unknown / Keystone France / Getty) pp. 166–167

There are several contemporary colour photographs taken from the same vista, although not the same location, which provided a good overall reference. As many of the buildings in the foreground and background exist, everything from tourist photographs to Google Street View was used as a reference for specific examples.

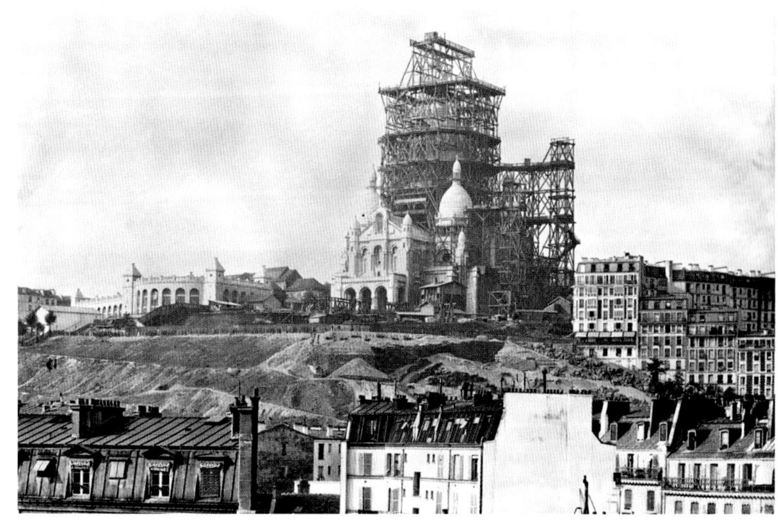

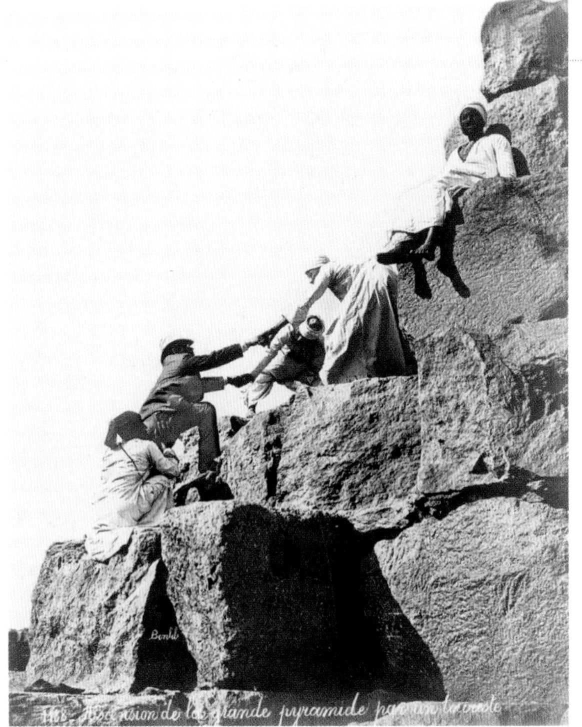

c. 1880s: Guides help a visitor to climb the Great Pyramid, Egypt
Giza, Egypt (Félix Bonfils / Library of Congress) pp. 168–169

The pyramids at Giza still remain one of the world's most documented monuments, so finding accurate colour references was a rather straightforward affair.

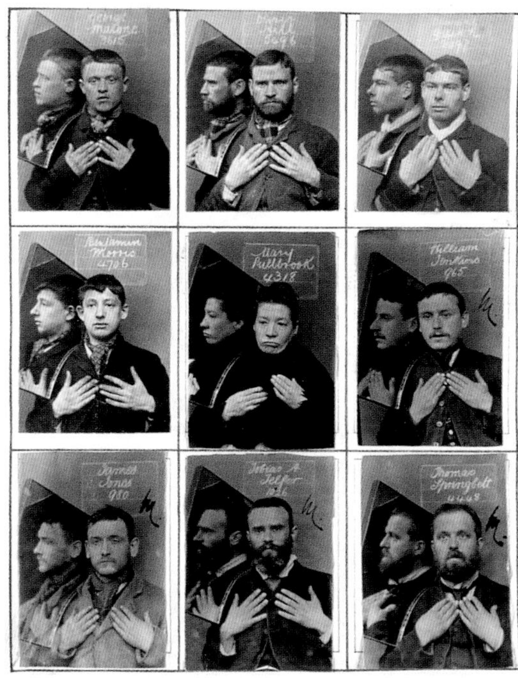

c. 1880: Mugshots of inmates at Wormwood Scrubs prison, London
Wormwood Scrubs, London, UK (Science & Society Picture Library / Getty) pp. 170–171

Examples of clothing of the time were used for reference. One of my favourite details, which you can see if you look closely, is the shape of the mirror – curved to arch over the subject's shoulder when the photograph is being taken.

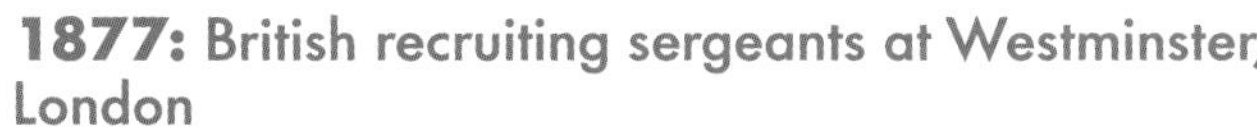

1877: British recruiting sergeants at Westminster, London
Westminster, London, UK (John Thomson / Science & Society Picture Library / Getty) pp. 172–173

Like many of the military units of the time, the dress uniforms of the British Army were very colourful and were distinct to differentiate between units. From left to right, the soldiers are: 6th Inniskilling Dragoons, a 4th Hussar, a recruiting sergeant on the staff, the Royal Scots Greys, a Dragoon Guard and a member of the 6th Dragoon Guard in stable dress.

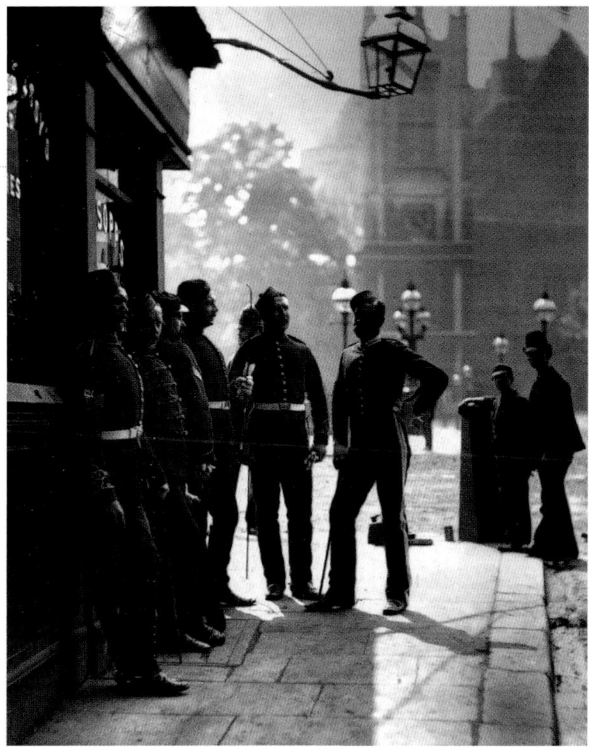

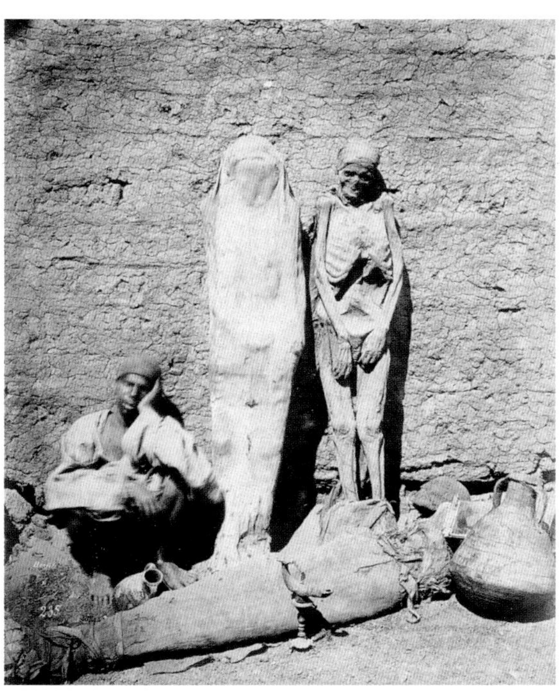

1875: A man sells mummies and other grave goods, Egypt
Egypt (Felix Bonfils) pp. 174–175

This is by far one of the most extraordinary images in the entire book for me, mainly due to the apparent indifference the dozing seller has towards his product – he could just as easily be selling fruit and veg. After working on the artefacts from the tomb of Tutankhamun, I had a great deal many more examples of colour references, and the large blue Faience vase to the right made sense in the context of the photograph.

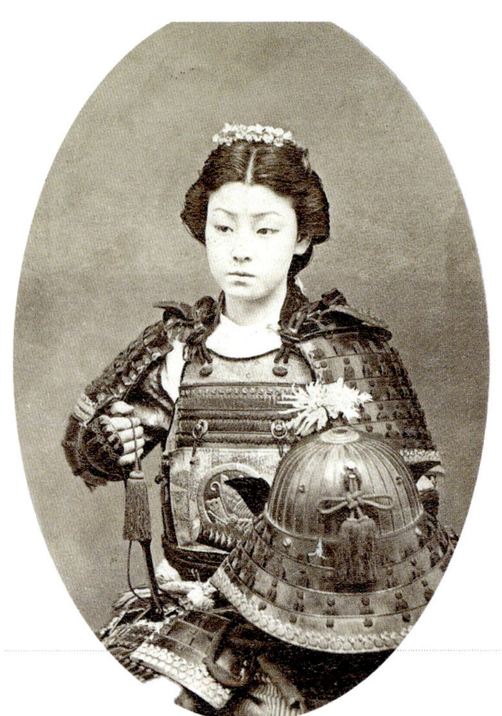

c. 1870: A 'female samurai' or *Onna-bugeisha* (女武芸者, 'female martial artist')
Japan (Universal History Archive / Getty) pp. 176–177

The abolition of Japan's isolationist *Sakoku* foreign policy during this period allowed the Port of Yokohama to flourish as a hub of foreign trade, thus introducing new Western technologies such as the camera. A number of Western-owned photographic studios operated in Yokohama, notably Beato & Wirgman, and the Japan Photographic Association (Stillfried & Andersen), whose commercial portraits and views of the country were in high demand both within Japan and beyond.

7 July 1865: The hanging of the conspirators in the assassination of Lincoln, at Fort McNair, Washington DC
Fort McNair, Washington DC, USA
(Alexander Gardner / Library of Congress) pp. 178–179

Bricks can be made in an almost-infinite number of shades, but what colour were these bricks? Remarkably, a lone brick from the Old Capitol prison survives in a commemorative wooden box. The soldiers are wearing the uniform of the Union Invalid Corps, which existed from 1863 to 1869. A description of the execution tells us that the soldiers present were of Company F of the 14th Veteran Reserves. Improbably, the site of the hanging at Fort McNair is now a tennis court.

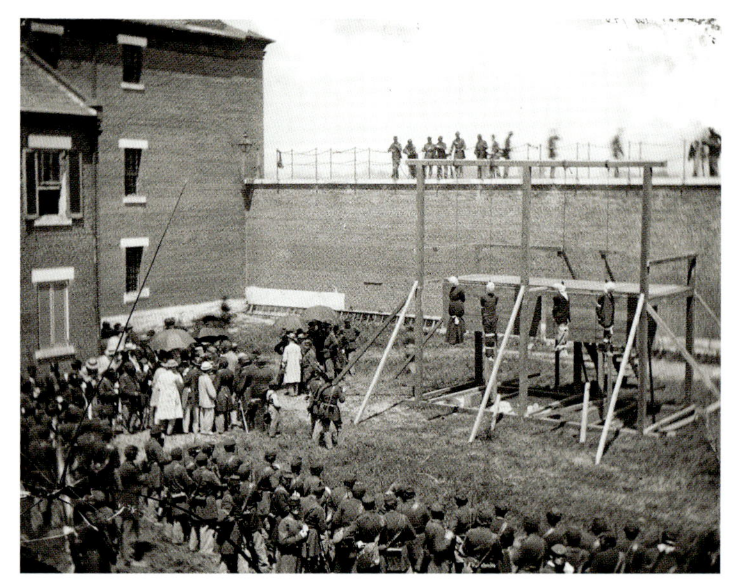

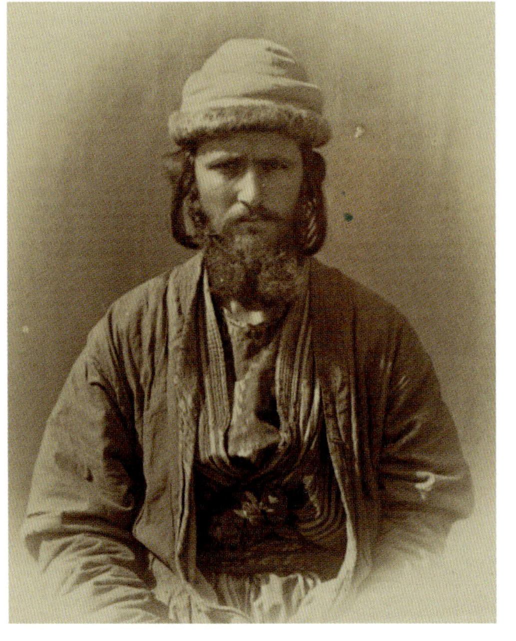

1865: A Turkestan Krai Jew
Turkestan, Russia (Unknown / Library of Congress)
pp. 180–181

I am continually amazed by the vibrancy of the dyes and patterns used in clothing from different cultures. This man is likely to be wearing work garb despite the riot of colour and patterning, which haven't changed all that much over the last century.

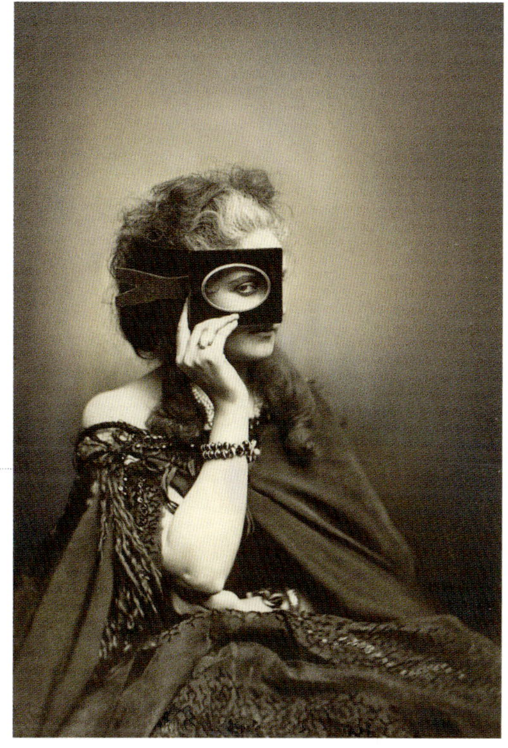

c. 1865: A portrait of Virginia Oldoïni, Countess of Castiglione
Paris, France (Pierre-Louis Pierson / Getty)
pp. 182–183

You would be forgiven for thinking that the Countess is affecting an elaborate face-mask, but in fact, if you look closely, you'll see that she is peering through a picture frame.

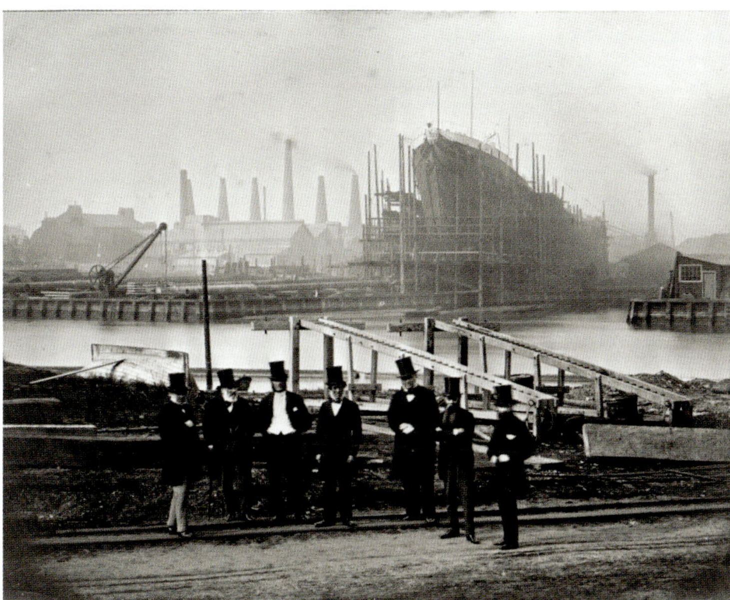

1865: A group of top-hatted men in front of the construction of the British ship *Tanjore*
Blackwall, London, UK (Unknown / Hulton Archive)
pp. 184–185

We could reasonably assume the numerous work buildings in the background of the image supplied iron for the dry docks, as all timber ship construction had been phased out by the time this photograph was taken.

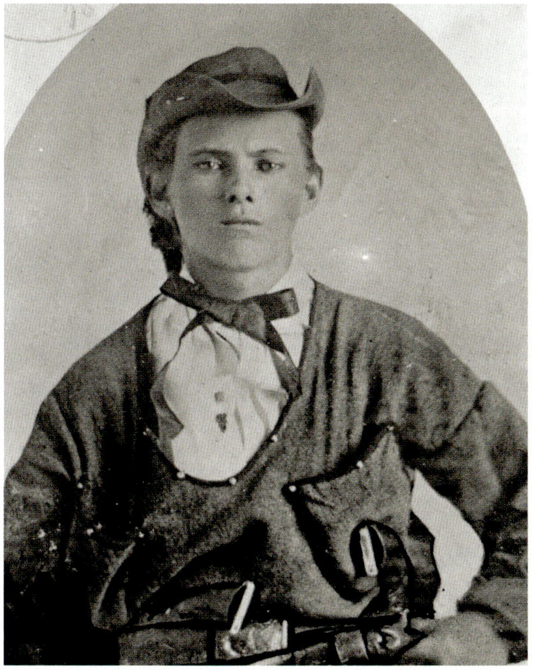

1864: Jesse James
USA (St. Louis Taylor Copying Co. / Library of Congress) pp. 186–187

Remarkably, one of the Colt .45 revolver pistols still exists, and the colour reference was supplied by a newspaper article about the gun going to auction.

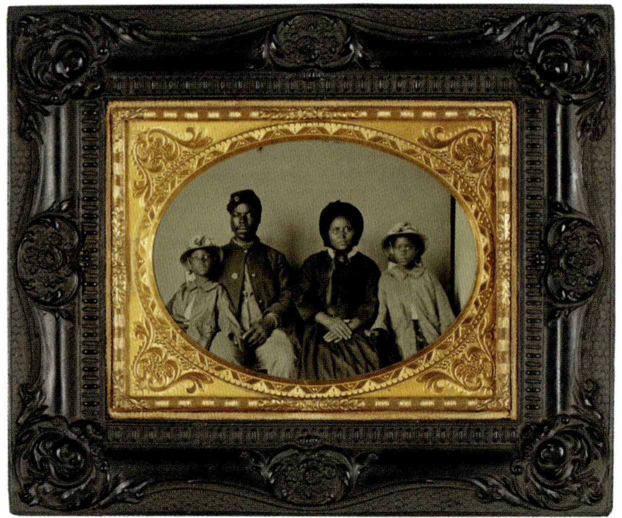

c. 1864: An unidentified African-American soldier in Union uniform with wife and two daughters, Maryland
Maryland, USA (Library of Congress) pp. 188–189

Sergeant Smith and his family lived most of their post-war lives in Mount Vernon, Rockcastle County, Kentucky. In the 1870 census, two other children are in the household as well. Although they look like twins, his daughters Mary and Maggie were, according to census records, a few years apart.

1864: A union soldier guards a slave auction house on Whitehall Street, Atlanta
Atlanta, Georgia, USA (George N. Barnard / Library of Congress) pp. 190–191

Any paint on these buildings would have been applied before the Civil War began in 1861, and by 1864 would be faded. The buildings also show evidence of water damage, which can indicate mould. The building to the far right is the brick-built concert hall. Situated next to the railroad tracks, it was stained with the pine soot and smoke from the locomotives. While it can vary according to weather and season, Georgia earth is indeed an orangey-red in hue.

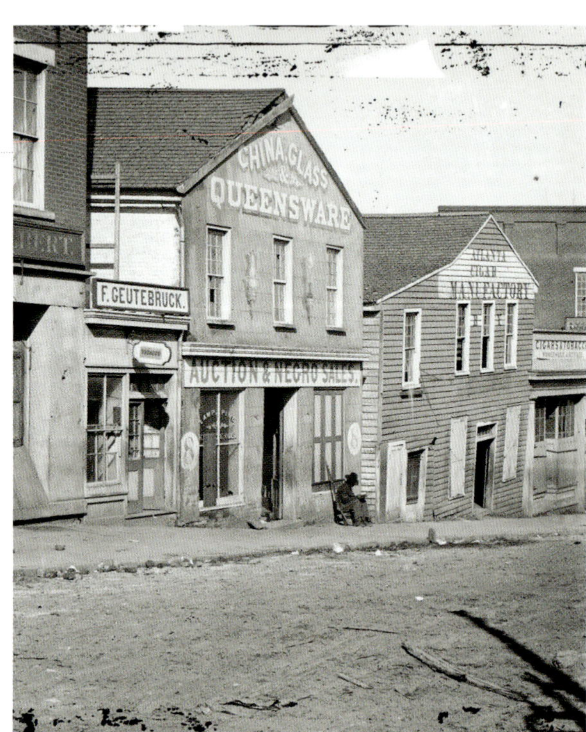

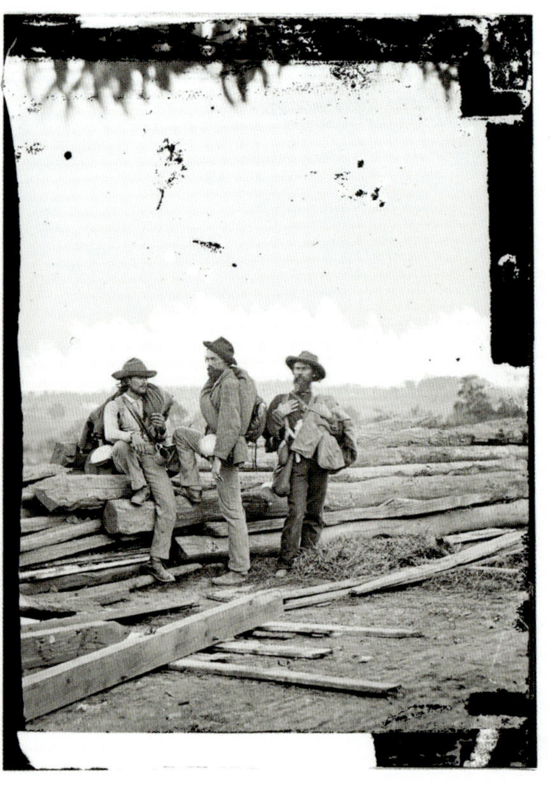

1863: Confederate prisoners at Seminary Ridge during the Battle of Gettysburg, Pennsylvania
Gettysburg, Pennyslvania (Unknown / Library of Congress) pp. 192–193

This image entailed a full restoration from a damaged glass plate. Due to the plate being shot in orthochromatic, I needed to adjust the blue and red channels to compensate for the washed out sky of the original image. The clouds, I composited.

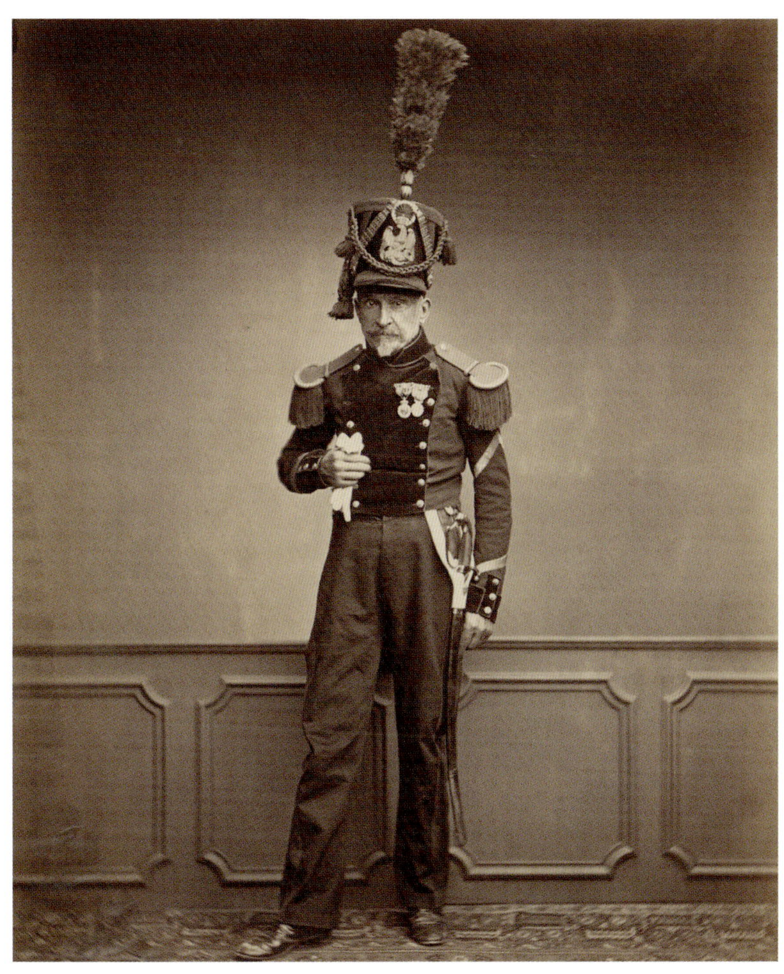

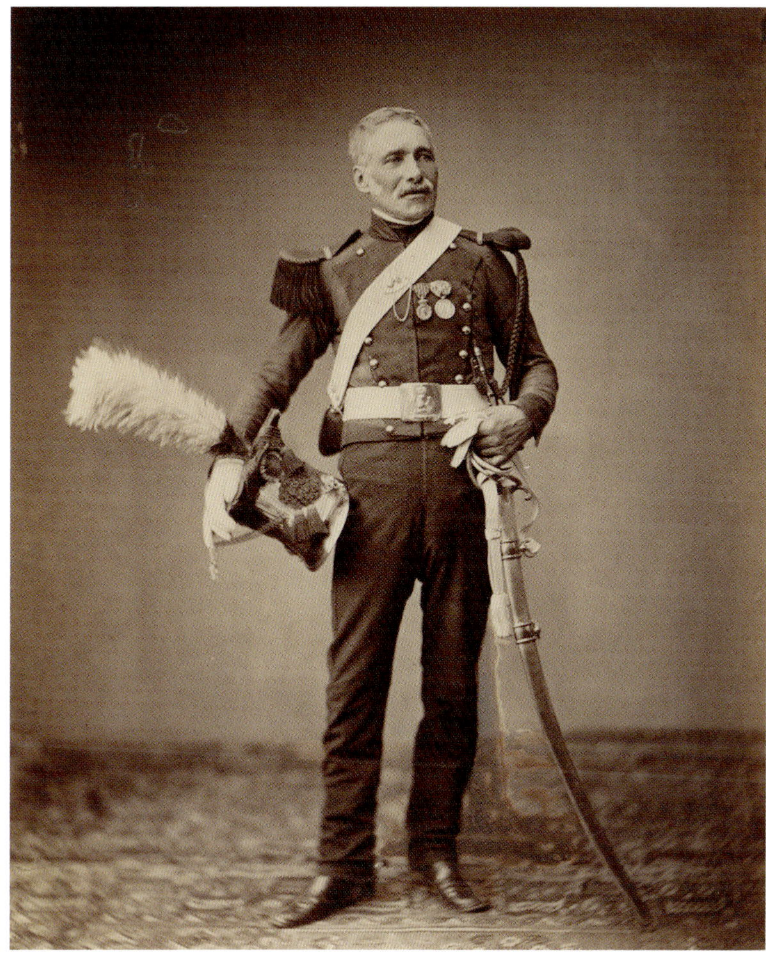

***c.* 1858: Veterans of the Napoleonic Wars**
Paris, France (Anne S. K. Brown Military Collection, Brown University Library) pp. 194–197

The engineer sappers of Napoléon's Imperial Guard (Sapeurs de la Garde) were established by 1810. Sergeant Lefebvre's (*right*) rank is denoted by the gold striping on the sleeve and epaulette loops of gold braid. In place of a helmet, the engineers wore a black felt hat called a *shako*, with brass chin-scales and scarlet plumes and cord. In addition to the Médaille de Sainte Hélène, Lefebvre also wears an insigne de La Société Philanthropique des Débris de l'Armée Impériale.

Officially known as the '2e régiment de chevau-légers lanciers de la Garde Impériale', a light cavalry regiment in Napoéon's Imperial Guard, the Dutch Lancers wore a distinct red uniform. It is possible that Monsieur Dreuse (*left*) was a Maréchal-des-logis, featuring red-and-yellow epaulettes rather than the standard blue-and-yellow.

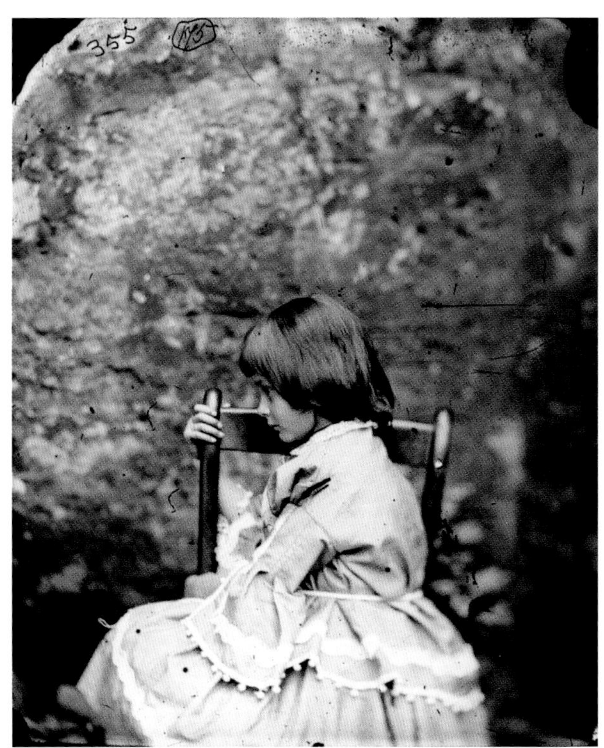

1858: **Alice Lidell, the 'real' Alice in Wonderland, aged six**
Christ Church College, Oxford, England (Charles Dodgson / National Media Museum / Science & Society Picture Library / Getty)
pp. 198–199

The background stonework and foliage suggest this wet-collodion portrait of Lidell was almost certainly taken in the Deanery Garden at Christ Church, where Alice and her two sisters would often play.

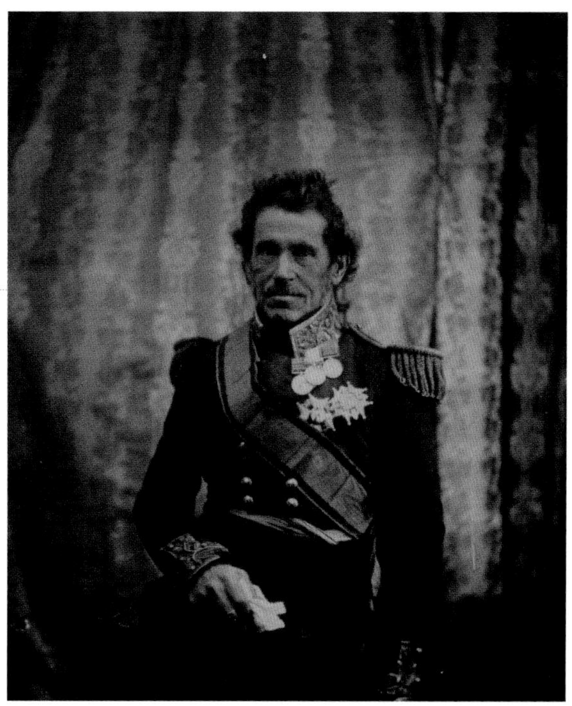

1855: **General Sir George de Lacy Evans, Commander of the British Army 2nd Division during the Crimean War**
Crimea, Russia (Roger Fenton / Library of Congress) pp. 200–201

George de Lacy's medals are housed at The Queen's Own Hussars Museum within the fourteenth-century Lord Leycester Hospital in Warwickshire, England. The curator, Julian Spilsbury, was on hand to relate Lacy's involvement in Washington DC, and expand on the histories of the different medals.

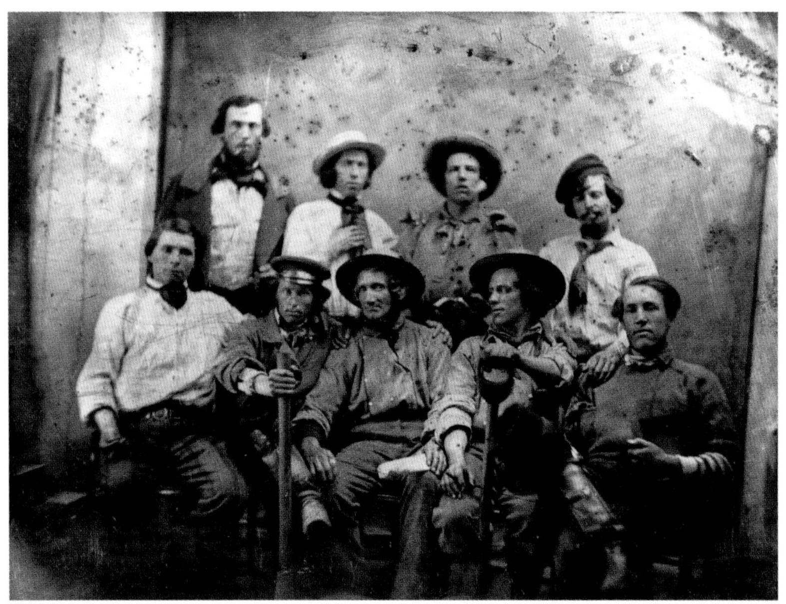

c. 1850s: **Californian miners have a group portrait**
California, USA (California Historical Society) pp. 203–204

Wolfgang and I spent a considerable amount of time poring over real examples of clothing from the time – as well as replicas and other sources such as advertising – and debating likely colours for the outfits. It was tricky, especially given the orthochromatic effect of the photograph. The result, we hope, is an authentic expression of these pioneers in the photographic studio.

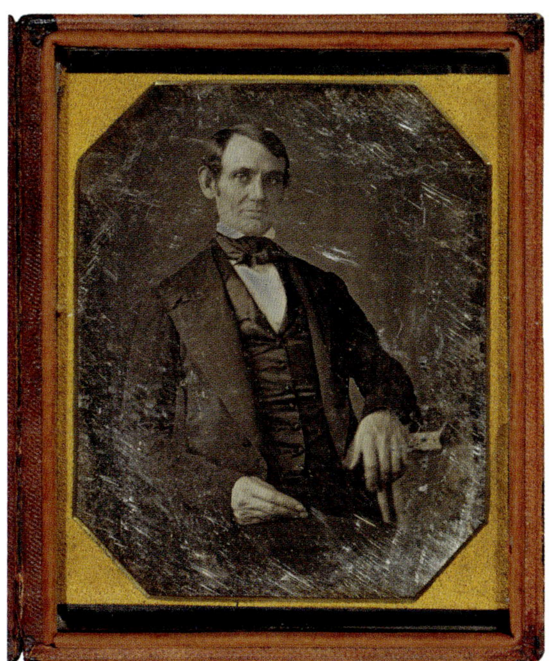

1846: **A portrait of Abraham Lincoln, without beard, aged thirty-seven**
Springfield, Illinois, USA (Nicholas Shepherd / Library of Congress) pp. 204–205

There are extensive markings across the original plate, all of which I needed to eliminate. I made a very precise background swap around Lincoln, matching the lighting, and I also composited the heavily damaged parts of Lincoln's right sleeve, and leg – Lincoln often sat in this pose – and the tablecloth.

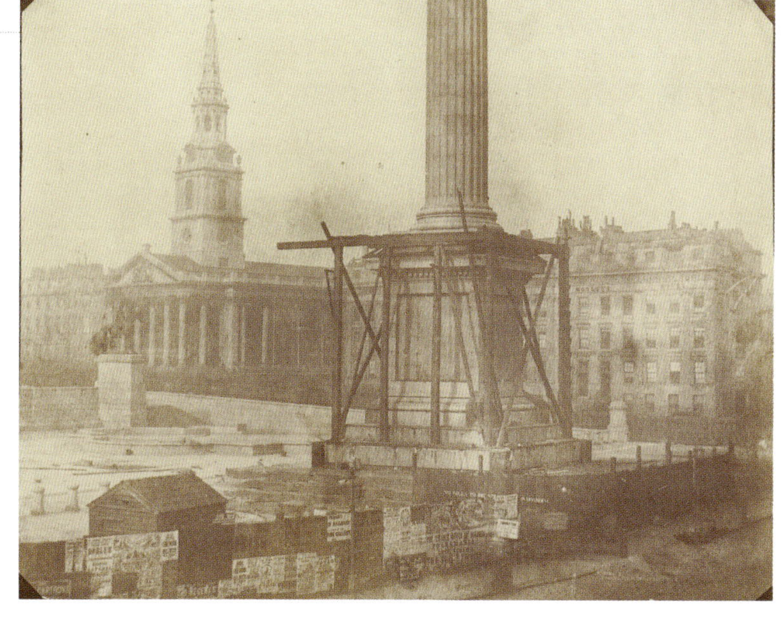

1844: **Construction of Nelson's Column, Trafalgar Square, London**
Trafalgar Square, London, UK (Henry Fox Talbot / Science & Society Picture Library / Getty) pp. 206–207

Having the good fortune to live in London, I spent an afternoon trying to figure out the exact spot where this the photograph was taken, which I believe to be the second floor of 64 Trafalgar Square (presently occupied by a franchised sandwich shop). I couldn't get access to the building so I settled with climbing on top of a kiosk located fifteen feet away and took some reference shots looking towards St Martin-in-the-Fields. Technically, this was an extremely difficult image to do, due to the overall lack of definition. I was taken aback to find advertising even as far back as the 1840s was as vibrant as this, after discovering the painting *A London Street Scene* (1835) by James Orlando Parry.

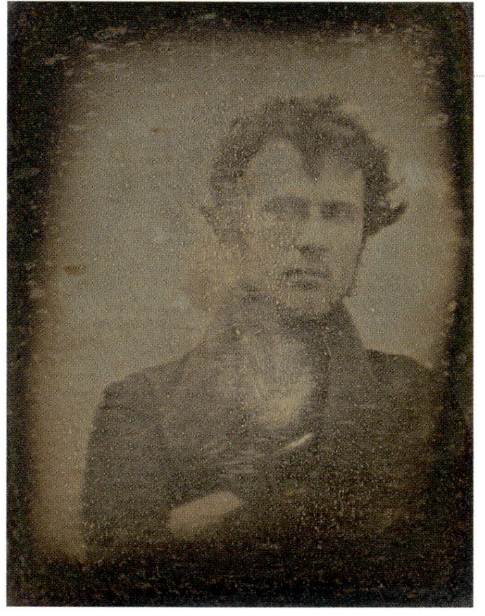

1839: **The first photographic self-portrait**
176 Chestnut Street, Philadelphia, USA (Robert Cornelius / Library of Congress)
pp. 208–209

Robert Cornelius's original plate is now heavily, and fundamentally, damaged. Often, digitally restoring an image to repair damage such as this can yield spectacular results. However, in this case, Wolfgang and I chose to take a different approach. We left the damage intact, and endeavoured to place the colour behind the damage. For us, the result has a special emotional resonance, which we could describe in the following way: Wolfgang and I are imprisoned within the camera – within our perspectives, filters and our assumptions about the past. Cornelius, seen in the past, appears grainy, damaged, indistinct. Yet in 1839, Cornelius was none of those things – he was sharp, clear, distinct. We peer through to his present, seeking to remove the damage from our own eyes.

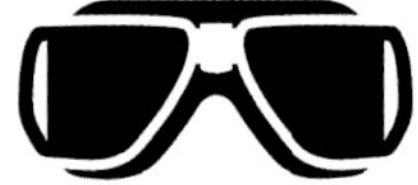

RETRONAUT | THE PAST LIKE YOU WOULDN'T BELIEVE

'Frozen fragment of times. This is the fascination of "Retronauting".'

Jonathon Jones, *Guardian*

We take your map of time and we tear tiny holes in it.

We scour the world's archives and museums, physical and digital, looking for material that just doesn't fit. We're dedicated to hunting down pictures, film, sound, stories and songs that are not on our maps.

What we find has the power to change the way you think of the past. And it also has the power to make the past go viral.

We partner with museums, archives and brands to make their collections go viral too.

retronaut.com

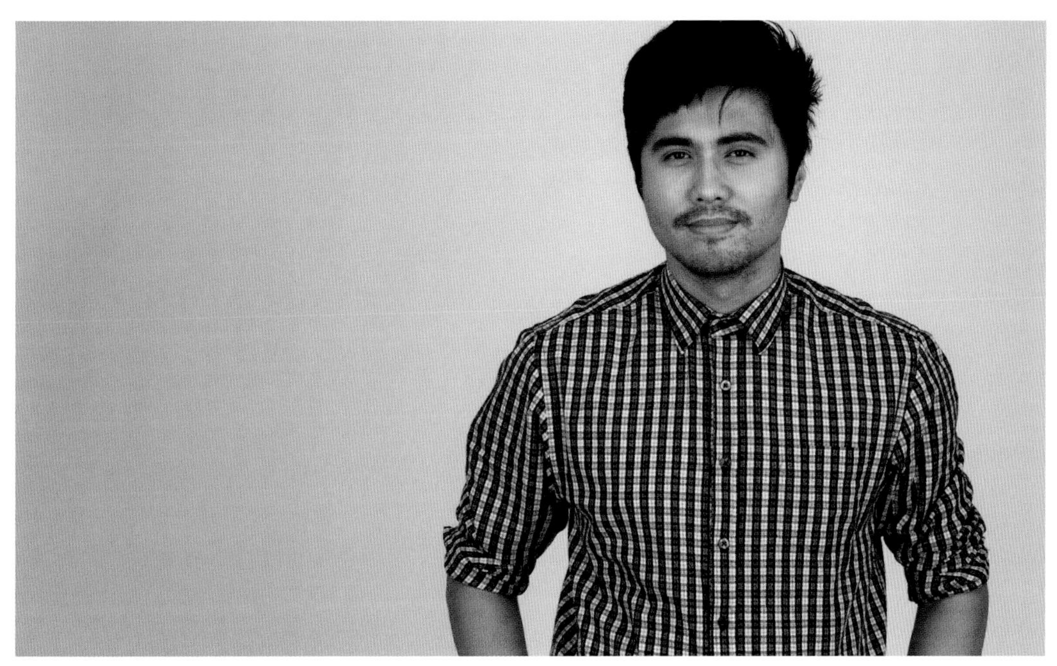

Jordan J. Lloyd

I'd been playing around with Photoshop for years when I started to notice colourisations online. I thought to myself, 'I could do that.'

I had a go and the first ten images I did were absolutely rubbish – but the eleventh blew up online, and people started offering me money to do more. I resolved at that point to get much, much better, and all of a sudden I was hitting the news. At that point I knew I wanted to make it into a business. And here I am.

jordanjlloyd.com

Acknowledgements

Wolfgang Wild:

Jordan J. Lloyd is not only, IMHO, The Best Colouriser In The World™, he is also The Easiest Person to Work With in the World™.

Jo Keeling and Tina Smith transform book concepts into beautiful artefacts seemingly without effort. Working with Jo and Tina, nothing is ever remotely a problem – or, at least, that's how they make it feel. They also create *Ernest Journal*, a publication almost painfully gorgeous. You would be well advised to purchase it immediately.

Amanda Uren carried out the research for the newspaper and document quotes in this book. She appears to have a magic magnet, which she waves over the haystack of historical documentation and suddenly all the shiniest and most interesting needles jump out. Amanda's work is also faster than should be possible in a universe governed by scientific laws.

Alex Q. Arbuckle, who writes and curates Retronaut's posts, is a magnificent writer. If he is still available, I would like him to craft the words for my tombstone.

Toby Hopkins at Getty Images has shown unfailing enthusiasm for this book from the very first moment we met, and has routinely gone out of his way to provide us with exactly the right image. Matt Butson's support has meant we have had the privilege of drawing on the wonders of Getty's vast archives.

The US Library of Congress is an almost unbelievable array of riches. Thank you to everyone who works to let people like me and Jordan explore these treasures.

The frustrating thing about making a book with John Mitchinson is that you then don't really ever want to make a book with anyone else. To see myself through John's eyes has been to see my favourite version of myself.

Unbound have enabled Jordan and I to make exactly the book we imagined, only even better-er. Thank you to Alex Bugden, Kate Burton, Xander Cansell, Mathew Clayton, Phil Connor, Jason Cooper, Mark Ecob, Isobel Frankish, Lauren Fulbright, Charlie Gleason, Caitlin Harvey, Rachael Kerr, Dan Kieran, Jimmy Leach, DeAndra Lupu, Georgia Odd, Kwaku Osei-Afrifa, Cyril Picardi, Justin Pollard, Christoph Sander, Anna Simpson, Kieran Topping, Hannah Whelan and Amy Winchester.

Even more than Unbound, thank you to every single person whose name appears at the back of this book. This is your book – thank you for giving us the chance to create it for you.

There is also a whole list of people who have provided exactly the right piece of information at exactly the right moment: 'Atlanta' Rob, Jack Betts, The Cody Archive, Dinah Dunn, Scott K. Fish, Dr Sally Crawford, Historic Shipping, *Kentucky Explorer* magazine, Dr Janice Kinory, Anna Krentz and 'The Passion of Former Days', Lincoln heights LA, Mary Murray, Niente de Nada, Seattle's Museum of History and Industry, Alan Skerrett and Jubilo!, Heather S. Sonntag, Dr Katharina Ulmschneider, The USCT Chronicle, Urban75 and Angela Y. Walton-Raji.

Also, a shout-out to the following inspiration transmission vehicles: Sacha Baker, Alan Capel, Gemma Cottingham, Ava Finnis, Kirsty Etheridge, Jane Finnis, Luci Gosling, Andrew Gordon, Greg Lockwood, Simon Mallindine, Steven Riley, Elizabeth Robinson, Sarah Saunders, Christoph Scholz, Jayne Smith, Bruce Woolley and Nick Wright.

Finally, the point of it all – Ruby, Zeb and Annie. Walled garden?

Jordan J. Lloyd

First and foremost, any undertaking of this size requires the assistance and talents of a group of extraordinary people: Deborah Humphries (deborahhumphries.com), whose amazing eye for finding even the smallest details has yielded the most impressive range of colour references. I have spent many hours collaborating with Deborah, poring over and debating even the most minute of details that accompanies her splendid research – a cornucopia of images and essays that could be a book in its own right. Whilst the work we do cannot guarantee historical accuracy, Deborah's fantastic information for many of the photographs you see is as close to it as I can imagine.

Marina Amaral (marinamaral.com), whose raw talent and persistence has been indispensable in preparing many of the photographs for *The Paper Time Machine*. She is responsible for the unenviable task of blocking in the colour for many of the mind-melting images in the book – most notably the photograph of over 600 people milling around in the garment district in New York (p. 40).

Emily and Robert Kern are possibly two of my favourite people in existence – they are not just good friends but also great collaborators. Emily's research is dotted throughout the book. Robert, despite being colour-blind, continues to fascinate me with his demonstrations of auto-colourisation algorithms and pixel sampling using code; it truly is a wonder, even if it may one day make me professionally obsolete.

Jaana Seppälä, textile conservator and researcher at Satakunnan Museo, continues to correct and inform me of the most obscure details regarding period clothing – thank you.

Jan T. Letowski: independent researcher, consultant and specialist in European ethnographic dress. Founder of the Museum of Ethnic Dress & Adornment, Pittsburg, PA, whose incredible subject knowledge regarding the immigrant clothing you see in the portraits at Ellis Island are also books in their own right – thank you.

I would be at a loss for many of the dizzying array of military-related details but for the specialist knowledge of Bruce Bassett-Powell at Uniformology, John and Kristina Barrick, Julian Spilsbury and Bro. Bill Bradford at The Queen's Own Hussars Museum, Lord Leycester Hospital in Warwick, UK.

Hugh Llewelyn, author, photographer; formerly of the Railways Directorate Great Britain, Vern Tyler, Transportation Manager Emeritus, Maryland, USA, and Norm Anderson, Railfan.net member; lifelong train enthusiast, for their considerable knowledge of the liveries and makes of US and European railways.

James Buttles, owner/CEO of Oceanic Evergreen Technologies, Virginia, USA, for his comments regarding Lewis Hines' Power house mechanic.

Jessie Quichocho, US Navy veteran, based in Virginia, USA, for his working knowledge of the truly mind-bending image of the U-boat and making sense of it all.

To my friends in New York: Limor Garfinkle, Jose Fresh and Madison Salters – I look forward to roaming around the locations in which many of the photographs in this book were taken.

Back across the Atlantic, my friends in Spain: Carles Marsal and the team at Adobe Spain, Natalia Lopez Beswick, Ana Mesas and María José González for their continued professional support. Without Adobe's amazing technology I'd be out of a job!

And to those who have lent a helping hand or provided better information when we needed it: Stuart Scheinman, Christoph Scholz, Richard de Pesando, Ayako Takahashi-Evans, Gareth Evans, Colin Eaton, Luci Jones, Mads Madsen, Sanna Dullaway, Doug Banks, Tony Koorlander, Sari de Groot, Ardi Arjela Kule, Clarice Ecanvil, Peter Searle, Andy Pritchard – thank you.

To Shane Killen, whose enthusiasm for the book has never wavered. I am sorry you can't be here to see it.

To my fellow colourisers around the world and online, your support has always been most welcome. Particular thanks to the talented folks and subscribers at reddit.com/r/ColorizedHistory – who knew where the rabbit hole would lead to?

To Tina Smith and Jo Keeling at *Ernest Journal*: I couldn't have asked for better people to craft the time machine.

Huge thanks to not only the fantastic team at Unbound, who have made this happen, but also Unbound's community: it goes without saying I am incredibly grateful for every pledge from friends, colleagues and family, but also to all the pledges from people I don't know – you helped kick-start the time machine. I would love to hear what you think and I am humbled by your generosity.

I am grateful to John Mitchinson and Rachael Kerr, whose hospitality and faith in my abilities at a medieval cottage in the Cotswolds, what seemed like an age ago, was hugely galvanising.

Last but not least, my partner in crime, a lifelong collaborator and, most importantly, a good friend – Wolfgang Wild, whose curatorial skills are beyond reproach. Being a fan of Retronaut long before I met him in person, I never could have envisaged the things we would do together. He is the Doc Brown to my Marty McFly, the Rufus to my Bill and Ted, and the Doctor to my Sarah Jane Smith. Wolfgang is the outrageous character who appears in your life almost at random, irrevocably changing it forever by handing you the keys to the time machine and asking simply, 'When to?'

Supporters

Unbound is a new kind of publishing house. Our books are funded directly by readers. This was a very popular idea during the late eighteenth and early nineteenth centuries. Now we have revived it for the internet age. It allows authors to write the books they really want to write and readers to support the books they would most like to see published.

The names listed below are of readers who have pledged their support and made this book happen. If you'd like to join them, visit **www.unbound.com**.

@arthostess
Andrea Abbott
Marie Abbott
Mark Abbott
Gloria Acosta
Robert Addison
Tammy Albright
Bruce Alcorn
Glen Alldredge
Charlotte Allen
Dan Allsobrook
Liz Ambra
Tobias Ander
Jimmy Anderson
Colin Anderton
Luke Anklesaria
archeiobooks.gr
Sandra Armor
Andrew Arsenault
Gary Arthurs
Stephen & Regina Ash
Marnie Aulabaugh
Sandra Austin
Aimee Aver
Charlotte Dalgarno Bacci
Joris Bak
Mike Baker
Hynek Bakstein
Christopher Ball
Jason Ballinger
Michał Banach
Saurabh Banerjee
Adrian & Annie Banham and
Jack Pudding
Greg Barber
Pascal Bardoux
Tanya Barlow
Emma Barraclough
David Barrett
Mary Barrett
Lyndon Barrois Jr.
Laura Bärthel
Chris Bartlett
Kenn Begley
Adrian Belcher
Stephen Bell
Luciano Belli
Mats Bengtsson
Chad Benner
Jon Bennett
Steve Bennington
Francisco Bernasconi
Janine Berriedale-Johnson
James Best
Adam Bethlehem
Matt, Terri, Joseph &
Clara Betts
Vicky Biancolo
Richard Biggs
Andrew Binding
Dorothy Birtalan
Stefan Blaser
Jackalie Blue
Stephen Bodger
Kristof Boeckx
Diane Boettcher
Andrea Bonvicini
Frank Boosman
Charles Boot
Airi Palm Borden
Marco Borraccino
Richard Boulter
Doug Bowers
Jules Bowes
James Boyce
Emma Brackenbury
Louise Brady
Laurence Branigan
Sebastien Brasseur
Richard W H Bray
Paul Breach
Mayer Brenner
Grant Bright
Trowby Brockman
Sandie Brosnan
Alan "Blinovitch Limitation
Effect" Brown
Guy Brown
Gwen Brown
Luke Brown
Pauline Brown
Paul Browne
Lori Brunson
A BS
Veronica Buffoni
Kate Bulpitt
Christian Bussmann
Gary Butcher
Stuart Butler
Clare Buxton

Basil Byrne
Pazit Cahlon
Christian Calcatelli
Suzannah Caldicott
Georgie Callé
David V. Caloia
Monique Campbell
Xander Cansell
Fay Capstick
James V. Carmichael, Jr.
Tony Carnell
Pascal Casper
Germain Cauvy
Ashley Cavers
Jesper Cederholm
Rick Challener
Ian Challis
Maria Chalupa
Richard Chambury
Fanny Chan
Lindsay Chancellor
Mark Chaney
Sarah Chard
Monique Charlesworth
Brian Cheney
Peter Chernyshov
Amy Cheung
Cristy Chory
Kathryn Christensen
Meagan Cihlar
Ryan Clark
Wendy Clark
Jeroen Claus
Julian Clayton
Lee Clements
Barbara Clusky
cmekb
Garrett Coakley
Kevin Cochrane
Adrienne Cohen
Stevyn Colgan
Larry Collins
Terry Collins
Eric Sean Conner
Nikolaos Contomichalos
Karl Conway
Ben Cooper
Claire Cooper
Jess Cooper
Matt Cooper
Allan Corbett
Carol Cosenza
Jo Cosgriff
Tanya Cotter
Denise Cowie
Gordon Cowley and all at GCAMS
John Crawford
William Cress
Daisy Cresswell
Tayler Cresswell
Ulf Cronsell
Jeanne Crown
Patrick Crowther
Robert Crump
Stephy Cue
John Cullen
Patrick Cusic
Steve Daldry
Talia Dardis
Ian Davey-Wilson
Maugis David
Nia Davies
Charlotte Day
Emily de Groot
Henry De Labouchere
Philip de Lacy White
Reinier de Vlaam
Imar de Vries
Robert de Waal
Frank Decaire
Stu Decay
Patrick Defort
Julie Degasperi
Jürgen Deinlein
Emma Dermott
Magdalena Derwojedowa
Jay Dhillon
Emily Diamand
A Dickson
Tom Digweed
Jeffrey Dinardo
Petra Disse
Lauretta Dives
Paul Dobson
Linda Dodd
Michael Dodd
Andy Doddington
Albert Doherty
James Dolby-Glover
Stephen Dollin
David Dollman
PK Donson
Gabriella Doran
Justin Doran
Anna Dowuona-Kludze
Robert Doyle
Benjamin Dunn
Vivienne Dunstan
Catherine Dupont
Matthew Dvorin & Kiki Smith-Archiapatti
Marvin Eaglecock
Nettie Edwards
Paul Edwards
Rosie Edwards
David Egan
Karen Eils
Birgit Einhoff
Loretta Ekoniak
Gary Eldredge
Bob Eldridge
Nicole Emmenegger
Jörn Engström
Tim Entwistle
Anette Lundskov Eriksen
Rosemary Ervin
Gareth Evans
Jonathan Evans
Lissa Evans
Scott Evans
Marianne Everett
Michelle Everitt
Charlie Evett
Heike Fademrecht
Adam Falkowitz
Giulia Farias
Reto Fausch
Jessica Fellowes
Charles Fernyhough
Joe Ferraro
Gemma Ferrier
Brandon Filoramo
Kimberly Fisher
Lindsey Fitzharris
Michael Fitzharris
Kim Fitzpatrick
Julia Flauaus
Frank Fleming
Karen Fletcher
Laurens Floyd Jr.
Paul Forster
William Forsyth
Deanne Fowke
Mike Foxall
Jacques Francis
Peter Franks
Laura Freeman
Barbara Frey
Brigid Gaffikin
Neil Gaiman
Jim Galbraith
Andres A. Galvez
Mark Gamble
Lucinda Ganderton
Macarena Garcia
Limor Garfinkle
Peter Garrod
Andre Gauthier
Carolina Georgatou
Kristina Georges
Mark Gethings
Warren Getty
Daniele Gianola
Paul Gibbinson
Dona Gibbs
Jeanne Gibson
Katherine J Gil
William Gill
Hilary Gindi
Keith A Gish
Giacomo Giudici
Lynne Glazer
Adam Glover
Matt Gochnour
Alexander Golev
Carole Linda Gonzalez
Laia Gonzalez
George Goodfellow
Dave Goody
Andrew Gordon
Stephen Gow

David Graham
Evan Grant
Dominic Gregory
Karen Gregory
Denise Gribbin
David Grievson
James Griffin
Judith Griffith
Sylvie Griffiths
Laurens Groenendijk
Elisabeth Gstarz
Karl Guder
Cédric Guillod
Clément Guimet
Martin Gygax
Geoff Haederle
Anthony Hajos
Nic Halley
Michael Halls
Cary Hammond
Mark Hammond
Lara Hancock
Tim Hanford
Melissa Hansen
Theodora Hansen
Julia Hare
Scott Hargrave
Estelle Hargraves
Jordan Harper
Paul Harrington
Ant Harris
Pete Harris
Sarah Grace Harris
Sylvia Harrison
Caitlin Harvey
Jennifer Harvey
Kenna Hawes
Tom Hay
Arlen Heginbotham
Elyse Heise
Jane Henderson
Rachel Herman
David Herron
Linda Hewett
Jazzmine Hill
Nick Hines
Birla Hood
Gareth J. Hope
Toby Hopkins
George Hornby
Jeff Horne
Tom Hostler
Eric Houze
Catherine Howard-Dobson
Jack Hughes
Peter Hughes
Deborah Humphries
Christopher Hunt
Scott Huntley
Syahril Hussin
Fiona & Chris Hutchings
Stefan Hüttenmoser
Andrew Hutton
Brigitte Hyde
Michael Imber
Anton Ingham
Cat Ingrams
Richard Innes
Richard Ireland
Reece Irons
George Stanley Irving
Lee Jackson
Jenny Jacoby
Edward James
Lee Jaschok
Benjamin Jeffs
Phil Jenkins
Will Jenkins
Martin Jennings
Meg Jobe
Heinrich John
Kevan Johnson
Rosalyn Krieger Johnson
James Robert Patrick Johnston
Andy Jones
Henry Jones
Niki Jones
Thomas Jones
Robert Jonsson
Aleksandar Jovanovic
Caroline Joyce
Kai Kampmann
Constance Kane
Jon Kane
Pius Karlinger
Mary Kay & Tom Beattie
Matthew Kearney
Jo Keeling
Liz Keenan
Damon Kendrick
John Kenner
Michal Khan
Dan Kieran
Amanda & Shane Killen
Haram Kim
John Kirk
Gareth Kitching
Tommy Klein
David Klotz
Hannah Knowles
Krista Knutson
Martin Koddenberg
Laura Koehn
Frank Köhntopp
Marcel Kooijman
Ramon Kool
Mitchel Kotula
Angela Kramer
Cameron Krost
Daniel Kuehn
Denise Kujawa
Paul Kummer
Andreas Laass
Andrew Ladd
Mit Lahiri
Peter Lake
Kerry Lamb
James Lambert
Charlie Langridge
Sam Larsson
Charles Laszyca
Andrew Lauren
Antonis Lazaridis
Jimmy Leach
Charlotte Lee
John Leonard
Lap Gong Leong
Mikki Levi
Margo L. Levine
David Levisohn
Matthew Libatique
The Licudi Family
Scott Liddell
Susie Liddle
Markus Liebler
Bonnie Lilienfeld
Doc List
Tamasin Little
Victoria Lloyd-Hughes
Giuseppe Lo Presti
Matt Lockett
K. M. Lockwood
Gertrude Lok
Clare Long
Edward F. Lough
Steve Lowe
Roger Luethy
Fernan Luna
Niklas Lundborg
Angela Maria Lungu
Elizabeth Lutz
José Machado
Alan Machin
Alexander Mackay
Lynn Mackay-Thomas
Patrice Mackey
Jeanene MacLean
Katie Maddock
Joan Maffei
Ben Maher
Steven Maher
Mark Malone
Hedy Manders
Patrick Marber
Rune Mareliussen
Mary Markland
Jonathan Marks
Ellen Marsh
Gulliver Martin
Colm Marum
Robert Maskell
Gregory Massat
William Henry Massey & Elliott Robert Massey
Matti Mattila
Han Shu May
John Mayberry
Cynthia McArthur
Anne McCarthy
Sam McCarthy
Sarah McCartney

Finn McCleave
Leonie Blatchford McDonald
Meg McGhee
Heather McGill
Beatrix McIntyre
Mary McKenney
Faye McLennan
Niamh McManus
Roy McMillan
Wendell McMurrain
Calvin Mcphaul
Blake Meadows
James Medd
David Megins-Nicholas
Lynne Mendoza
Charles Meyer
Joanne Mildenhall
Debbie Miller
Kirsten Miller
Michael Miller
Tracy Miller
Paul John Millichip
Jennifer Millimet
Rich Mills
John Mitchinson
Marcel Molenaar
Eduardo Basterrechea Molina
Kate Moody
Donna Moore
Leslee Moore
Jade Moores
Helen Morris
Jessica Morris
Angela Mortenson
Richard Moseley
Jon Moslet
K. Lothrop Mueller
Kit Muffett
Jelle Mulder
Mark Mullen
Matthias Müller
Hana Müllerová
Jeffrey Mulvey
Philippe Munn
Paul Murphy
Szilvia Nagy
Ajit Nair
Carolina Nakiri
Dan Nascimbeni
Linda Nathan
Stu Nathan
Adam Nathanson
Carlo Navato
Benjamin Nelson
New York Stereoscopic Association
Amy Newkirk
Gary Nicol
John Nicoll
Chris Nielsen
Sara Sainz Nieto
D. Nihot
Edward Noble
Mikey Noon
Paul Nordland
Molly Nye
Dominic O'Reilly
Richard Ogle
Natalie Openshaw
Emily Oram
Marcus Östman
Sophie Overment
Keith Painter
Judy Palmaers
Bruno Palombo
Wiebke Pandikow
Frank Papenbroock
Martin Parker
Chris Parkington
Henry Parsley
Vipul Patel
Luke Paterson
Sarah Patmore
Matthew Paton
Joe Patten
Amy Pattenden
Cecil Patterson
Carol Peachee
Bryan Peacock
Hilthart Pedersen
Viggo Pedersen
Richard Pederson
Nicholas Perkins
Michael Perry
Joan Peterdi
Jon Petrie
Kristin Petrone
Giuseppe Peveri
Caroline Phély
Derek Phillips
Stephanie Phillips
Thea Piegdon
Phil Pierce
Ruth Pietroni
Justin Pinner
Sacha Platteeuw
Angela Pledge
Matt Plummer
Justin Pollard
John Pollock
Felix Pool
Nicholas Poole
Thomas Power
Gaurav Prasad
Janet Pretty
Rhian Heulwen Price
John Priddy
Tommi Principe
Andy Pritchard
Matthew Proudfoot
Helena Pulkkinen and Jarno Lehtinen
Martin Pyper
David Quantrell
Andy Quin
Cristina Quiñones-Betancourt
Claudia Raffman
Victor Raggio
Helen Randle
JP Rangaswami
Jesper Rye Rasmussen
Katherine Rasmussen
Philip Rawlins
Georgia Raysman
Dolly Reaves
Victoria Redclift
David Rees
William Renninger
Ekaterina Riabinkina
Simon Richards
David Riker
Steven Riley
Carlo Ritchie
Matthew Riva
Jennifer L Roberson
Colin Roberts
Wyn Roberts
Alexis Rollin
Daniel Rosenbloom
Marc Rosenthal
Gianna Rosica
Yannick Roux
Tara Royston
Michael Ruffing
Daniel & Rachel Ruiz
Conrad & JoAnn Ruppert
Stephanie Russin
DJ Ryan
David Salariya
Madison Salters
Jesse Sampson
Jeremy Sams
Christoph Sander
Steven Santos
Shannon Sarver
Michael Satterwhite
Nigel Saunders
Sarah Saunderson
Arda Savcı
Lara Scaiola
Sarah Scanlan
Ionathan Schaeff
Michele Schaffer
Jean Scheltjens
Blair Schertenleib
Arthur Schiller
Joan Schulze
Adam Schuster
Joe Schwan
Alexandra Schweitzer
William Seaburg
Diane Seaver
Peter Seedholm
Antje Seemann
Sebastian Sehinson
Navroop Sehmi
Oscar Selling
Stuart Senior
Laura Sewell
Laurence Shapiro

Yvonne Shapiro
Jeremy Shatan & Karen Capucilli
David Shepherd
Sondra Sherman
Keith Sherratt
Linda Shoare
Philippa Sigler
Jason Signora
Julie Silverman
Amanda Simons
Mark Simonson
Hazel Simpson
Kevin Sinclair-Noble
Gary Singer
Thomas Singlehurst
Rebecca Smart
Alice Smith
Duncan Smith
Jane Smith
Nigel Smith
Richard Smith
Ron Smith
Scott Smith
Thomas Smits
Colin Smythe
Lisa Snider
Hanne Sørensen
Jette Sørensen
Ramzi Souki
Peter Spriggs
Teresa Squires
Edlef Stabenau
Lawrence Staden
Tess Stahl
Janice Staines
Susannah Stapleton
Michael Start
Anthony Harry Stead
Drew Stean
Markus Steck
David Stelling
Jeremy Stephens
Andrew Stocker
Christian Stoll
Katherine Stone
Toby Stone
Alexander Stricker, SQUADRAT Architects, Zurich
Mirko Strugar
Nina Stutler
SUK
Annie Sutherland
Lindsay Swann
Petra Sweiss
Andy Syed
Kornelia Szwarc
Kathleen Talenco
Jacob Tan
Claudia Tansini
Roberto Taurino
Alan D Taylor
Maisie Taylor
Howard Tee
Steve Teso
Torsten Thieme
David Thomas
Gemma Thomas
Ian Thompson
Jem Thorpe-Woods
Adam Tinworth
Deana Tollerton
Darren Tome
Ani Toncheva
Henry Tovey
Sarah Towle
Gene Toye
Steve Travis
Sakhile Tshuma
Nico Tuin
Andrew Turner
Pavel Tvaroh
Annie Underwood
Simon Unwin
Sam Urquhart
Marina Valner
Michelle Van Ellis
Tom van Heel
Angela Van Liew
Elizabeth Van Pelt
Esther van Wijck
Jason Vanderhill
William Vanderweken, MD
David Vanstone
Santiago Fernandez Vega
Matthew Vella
Mark Vent
David Verey
Ingeborg Verheul
James Vernier
Harry Verwayen
Pietro Viecelli
Thomas Vincent-Townend
Henry Vines
Matthew Vittitow
Gustavo von Bischoffshausen
Marsha Vonduerckheim
Artem Voss
Sukhi Wahiwala
Jonathan Wakeham
Olivia Walder & Nikita Sorokin
Dan Walker
Björn Wallgren
Simon Walsh
Lisa Walters
Christopher Walton
Gill Walton
Sarah Warburton
Cynthia Carbone Ward
Debbie Ward
Lee Ward
Mike Ward
Berry Wardana
Stuart Warren
John Wates
Jim Watkins
Eric Weaver
Kelly Webster
Thomas Webster
Andreas Weinberger
Steve Weintraub
Erin Welther
Sasha Wertheim
Samuel West
Leslie Whaley
Kristin Wheeler
Charles T Wheeler III
Paul Whelan
Richard Whitaker
Graham White
Luke White
Pete White
Dr Nick Whitehead
Mark Whitfield
Louise Whittle
Mark Whyte
Clare Wigfall & Troy Giunipero
Thomas Wigley
Suzie Wilde
David Williams
John Williams
Mark Williams
Matthew Williams
David Williamson
John Wilton
Robert S Winter
Jason Wolf
Stephen Wonfor
Elaine Wong
Gratiano Wong
Andie Wood
David Wood
Jonathan Wooddin
Stacey Woods
Steve Woodward
Bruce Woolley
Colin and Rachel Wright
Andy Würsch
www.andrewcatlin.com
Francesca Peggy Wynne
Alan Yaxley
Einav Yifrach
Elliott Young
Richard Young
Seth Young
Katie Younger
Sandra Zeevenhooven
Judy Zehr
William Zeigler
Daan Zeijdner
Yifan Zhang
Tonja Züllig
Heather Jean Zylstra

Index